The Book of

Unsolved Mysteries

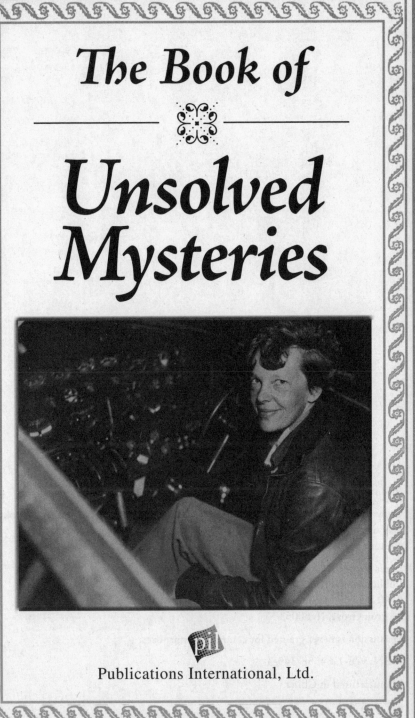

Publications International, Ltd.

ISBN: 978-1-64558-349-3

Manufactured in China.

8 7 6 5 4 3 2 1

Contents

✳ ✳ ✳ ✳

CHAPTER 1

GRUESOME, UNSOLVED, AND UNUSUAL DEATHS

Ghosts of a Murdered Dynasty

The fate of Russia's imperial family remained shrouded in mystery for nearly a century.

✳ ✳ ✳ ✳

The End of a Dynasty

IN THE WAKE of Russia's 1917 uprisings, Tsar Nicholas II abdicated his shaky throne. He was succeeded by a provisional government, which included Nicholas and his family—his wife, Tsarina Alexandra; his four daughters, Grand Duchesses Olga, Tatiana, Maria, and Anastasia; and his 13-year-old son, Tsarevich Alexei—under house arrest.

When the radical Bolshevik party took power in October 1917, its soldiers seized the royal family and eventually moved them to the Ural Mountain town of Yekaterinburg, where they were held prisoner in the home of a wealthy metallurgist. As civil war waged between the "White" and "Red" factions in Russia, the Bolsheviks worried that the White Army might try to free the royal family and use its members as a rallying point. When White troops neared Yekaterinburg in July 1918, the local executive committee decided to kill Nicholas II and his family.

The bedraggled imperial family was rudely awakened by their captors in the middle of the night. The sounds of battle echoed not far from the spacious home that had become their make-shift prison, and the prisoners were ordered to take shelter in the basement. Outside the basement, a waiting truck revved its engine.

After a long wait, the head jailer reappeared, brandishing a pistol and backed by ten men armed with rifles and pistols. He declared, "Because your relatives in Europe carry on their war against Soviet Russia, the Executive Committee of the Ural has decided to execute you." Raising his revolver, he fired into Tsar Nicholas II's chest as his family watched in horror.

With that shot, the militia opened fire. Bullets ricocheted around the room as family members dove for cover, trying to escape the deadly fusillade. None made it. The wounded chil-dren who clung to life after the firing stopped were dragged into the open and set upon with rifle butts and bayonets until all lay quiet in the blood-splattered room. Tsar Nicholas II, the last of the Romanov emperors, died alongside his beloved family.

A Bungled Body Disposal

After the murders, the bodies were taken by truck into nearby woods, stripped, and thrown into an abandoned mine pit. The corpses were visible above the pit's shallow waterline. Fearing that the bodies would be discovered, the communist officials tried to burn them the following day. When that did not work, they decided to move the bodies to a deeper mine pit farther down the road. The truck got stuck in deep mud on the way to the mines, so the men dug a shallow grave in the mud, buried the bodies, and covered them with acid, lime, and wooden planks, where they remained untouched until 1979.

In his official report, the lead executioner, Yakov Yurovsky, stated that two of the bodies were buried and burned separately, giving rise to speculation that one or two of the Romanov children escaped the massacre. Several pretenders came forth claiming to be Tsarevich Alexei, heir to the Russian throne, and his sister Grand Duchess Maria. But the most famous of the "undead Romanovs" was young Anastasia.

Did Anastasia Survive?

Anastasia, the fourth daughter of Nicholas and Alexandra, was 17 at the time of the executions. At least 10 women have stepped forward claiming to be the lost grand duchess. The most famous of these was the strange case of Anna Tchaikovsky.

In Berlin, two years after the murders, a woman named Anna Tchaikovsky, hospitalized for an attempted suicide, claimed to be Anastasia. She explained that she had been wounded but survived the slaughter with the help of a compassionate Red Army soldier, who smuggled her out of Russia through Romania.

Anna bore a striking physical resemblance to the missing Anastasia, enough to convince several surviving relatives that she was indeed the last of the imperial family. She also revealed details that would be hard for an impostor to know—for instance, she knew of a secret meeting between Anastasia's uncle, the grand duke of Hesse, and Nicholas II in 1916, when the two men's countries were at war.

Other relatives, however, rejected Anna's claim, noting, among other things, that Anna Tchaikovsky refused to speak Russian (although she understood the language and would respond to Russian questions in other languages). A drawn-out German court case Anna commenced in 1938 to claim her inheritance ended in 1970 with no firm conclusions.

Anna, later named Anna Anderson, died in 1984. It was not until DNA evidence became available in the 1990s that her claim to imperial lineage could finally be disproved.

The Romanov Ghosts

But what of the hidden remains?

After the location of the royal resting place was made public in 1979, nine skeletons were exhumed from the muddy pit. The bodies of the royal couple and three of their children—Olga, Tatiana, and Anastasia—were identified by DNA tests as Romanov family members. Their remains, as well as those of four servants who died with them, were interred in 1998 near Nicholas's imperial predecessors in St. Petersburg.

By all accounts, 11 people met their deaths that terrible night in July 1918. In late August 2007, two more sets of remains were found in a separate grave near Yekaterinburg. Based on results of DNA analysis that was completed in 2009, experts agree that the sets of remains were those of Tsarevich Alexei and Maria.

Jack the Ripper

Between 1888 and 1891, he brutally murdered at least five women in London's East End. But was there really a connection between Jack the Ripper and the British royal family?

✳ ✳ ✳ ✳

THE SERIAL KILLER known as Jack the Ripper is one of history's most famous murderers. He breathed terror into the gas-lit streets and foggy back alleys of the Whitechapel area of London and became renowned the world over. Despite the countless books and movies detailing his story, however, his identity and motives remain shrouded in mystery. One of the most popular theories, espoused by the 2001 movie *From Hell* (starring Johnny Depp), links the killer to the British royal family.

The Crimes

Five murders are definitively attributed to Jack the Ripper, and he has variously been connected to at least six other unsolved slayings in the London area. The body of the first victim, 43-year-old Mary Ann Nichols, was discovered on the morning of August 31, 1888. Nichols's throat had been cut and her abdomen mutilated. The subsequent murders, which took place over a three-year period, grew in brutality. The killer removed the uterus of his second victim, Annie Chapman; part of the womb and left kidney of Catherine Eddowes; and the heart of Mary Kelly. All of his victims were prostitutes.

The Name

A man claiming to be the murderer sent a letter (dated September 25, 1888) to the Central News Agency, which passed it on to the Metropolitan Police. The letter included the line, "I am down on whores and I shant quit ripping them till I do get buckled." It was signed, "Yours truly, Jack the Ripper." A later postcard included the same sign-off. When police went public with details of the letters, the name "Jack the Ripper" stuck.

The Suspects

Officers from the Metropolitan Police and Scotland Yard had four main suspects: a poor Polish resident of Whitechapel by the name of Kosminski, a barrister who died by suicide in December 1888, a Russian-born thief, and an American doctor who fled to the States in November 1888 while on bail for gross indecency. Since there was little or no evidence against any of these men, the case spawned many conspiracy theories, the most popular of which links the killings to the royal family.

The Royal Conspiracy

The heir to the British throne was Prince Albert Victor, grandson of Queen Victoria and son of the man who would later become King Edward VII. The prince, popularly known as Eddy, had a penchant for hanging around in the East End, and rumors abounded that he had a daughter, Alice, out of wedlock with a shop girl named Annie Crook. To prevent major embarrassment to the Crown, Eddy sought assistance from Queen Victoria's physician, Dr. William Gull, who institutionalized Annie to keep her quiet. However, her friends, including Mary Kelly, also knew the identity of Alice's father, so Dr. Gull created the persona of Jack the Ripper and brutally silenced them one by one. A variation on this theory has Dr. Gull acting without the knowledge of the prince, instead driven by madness resulting from a stroke he suffered in 1887.

Royal involvement would certainly explain why the police were unable to uncover the identity of the Ripper or to even settle on a prime suspect. There *was* a shop girl named Annie Crook who had an illegitimate daughter named Alice, but there is nothing to connect her to either the prince or the murdered prostitutes. In fact, there is no evidence to suggest that the murdered women knew one another. Until the identity of Jack the Ripper is settled beyond doubt, these and other conspiracy theories will likely persist.

The Hollywood Sign Girl

Whatever happened to that young and promising movie star?

✳ ✳ ✳ ✳

IN THE 1930S, Millicent Lilian "Peg" Entwistle was a young, aspiring actress in New York when she was lured to Hollywood by two West Coast producers, Homer Curran and Edward Belasco, who asked Entwistle to costar in their play, *The Mad Hopes*. With dreams of finally hitting the big time, Entwistle moved to Hollywood. Although the play was a success, it closed on schedule on June 4, 1932, at which time Entwistle signed a one-movie deal with RKO Pictures and began working on the film *Thirteen Women* (1932). Several months later, test screenings for the film produced very negative comments, many of which were directed at Entwistle.

RKO held back the film from general release while the director heavily edited the picture, deleting many of Entwistle's scenes in the process. According to those close to her, Entwistle took this to mean that she was a failure and would never succeed in Hollywood.

On Friday, September 16, 1932, Entwistle said she was going to meet some friends, but instead, she made her way to the top of Mount Lee. After placing her personal belongings at the base of the Hollywood sign, she used a workman's ladder to climb to the top of the "H" and jumped to her death. She was only 24 years old. The suicide note found in her purse read simply:

"I am afraid I am a coward. I am sorry for everything. If I had done this a long time ago, it would have saved a lot of pain. P.E."

Thirteen Women officially opened after Entwistle's death, and while it did not get good reviews, her name was never mentioned. Her uncle speculated to the press after her death that she was disappointed by not being able to impress the movie industry, and the rumors spiraled from there. The real cause of her decision to end her life remains a mystery, but to this day, Entwistle's suicide symbolizes Hollywood's ability to smash the dreams of so many aspiring actors and actresses.

Thomas Ince: A Boating Excursion Turns Deadly

Film mogul Thomas Ince joins other Hollywood notables for a weekend celebration in 1924 and ends up dead. Was it natural causes or one of the biggest cover-ups in Hollywood history?

✳   ✳   ✳   ✳

THE MOVIE INDUSTRY has been rocked by scandal throughout its history, but few incidents have matched the controversy and secrecy surrounding the death of Thomas Ince, a high-profile producer and director of many successful silent films. During the 1910s, he set up his own studio in California where he built a sprawling complex of small homes, sweeping mansions, and other buildings that were used as sets for his movies. Known as Inceville, the studio covered several thousand acres, and it was there that Ince perfected the idea of the studio system—a factory-style setup that used a division of labor amongst large teams of costumers, carpenters, electricians, and other film professionals who moved from project to project as needed. This system, which allowed for the mass production of movies with the producer in creative and financial control, would later be adopted by all major Hollywood film companies.

Down on his luck by the 1920s, Ince still had many influential friends and associates. In November 1924, newspaper magnate William Randolph Hearst offered to host a weekend birthday celebration for the struggling producer aboard his luxury yacht the *Oneida*. Several Hollywood luminaries attended, including Charlie Chaplin and Marion Davies, as well Louella Parsons, then a junior writer for one of Hearst's East Coast newspapers. But at the end of the cruise, Ince was carried off the ship on a medical gurney and rushed home, where he died two days later. A hastily scribbled death certificate blamed heart failure.

The Rumors Fly

Almost immediately, the rumor mill churned out shocking and sordid versions of the incident, which were very different from the official line. A Chaplin employee, who was waiting at the docks when the boat returned, reportedly claimed that Ince was suffering from a gunshot wound to the head when he was taken off the *Oneida*. Could he have been the victim of a careless accident at the hands of a partying Hollywood celeb? Perhaps, but film industry insiders knew of complex and passionate relationships among those on board, and a convoluted and bizarre scenario soon emerged and has persisted to this day. As it turns out, Davies was Hearst's longtime mistress, despite being almost 34 years his junior. She was also a close friend of the notorious womanizer Chaplin. Many speculate that Hearst, enraged over the attention that Chaplin was paying to the young ingenue, set out to kill him but shot the hapless Ince by mistake.

Certain events after Ince's death helped the rumors gain traction. Ince's body was cremated, so no autopsy could be performed. And his grieving widow was whisked off to Europe for several months courtesy of Hearst—conveniently away from the reach of the American press. Louella Parsons was also elevated within the Hearst organization, gaining a lifetime contract and the plum assignment as his number-one celebrity gossip columnist, which she parlayed into a notoriously self-serving enterprise. Conspiracy theorists believe that she wrangled the deal with Hearst to buy her silence about the true cause of Ince's death.

Lingering Mystery

Was Ince the victim of an errant gunshot and subsequent cover-up? If anyone in 1920s California had the power to hush witnesses and bend officials to his will in order to get away with murder, it was the super rich and powerful Hearst. But no clear evidence of foul play has emerged after all these decades. Still, the story has persisted and even served as the subject for *The Cat's Meow*, a 2002 film directed by Peter Bogdanovich, which starred Kirsten Dunst as Davies and Cary Elwes as the doomed Ince.

Thelma Todd: Suicide or Murder?

During her nine-year film career, Thelma Todd costarred in dozens of comedies with the likes of Harry Langdon, Laurel and Hardy, and the Marx Brothers. Today, however, the "Ice Cream Blonde," as she was known, is best remembered for her bizarre death, which remains one of Hollywood's most enduring mysteries. Let's explore what could have happened.

✳ ✳ ✳ ✳

Sins Indulged

Todd was born in Lawrence, Massachusetts, in 1906 and arrived in Hollywood at age 20 via the beauty pageant circuit. Pretty and vivacious, she quickly became a hot commodity and fell headlong into Tinseltown's anything-goes party scene. In 1932, she married Pasquale "Pat" DiCicco, an agent of sorts who was also associated with gangster Charles "Lucky" Luciano. Their marriage was plagued by drunken fights, and they divorced two years later.

For solace, Todd turned to director Roland West, who didn't approve of her drinking and drug use, but he could not stop her. With his help, Todd opened a roadhouse called Thelma Todd's Sidewalk Café, located on the Pacific Coast Highway, and the actress moved into a spacious apartment above the restaurant. Shortly after, Todd began a relationship with gangster "Lucky" Luciano, who tried to get her to let him use a room at the Sidewalk Café for illegal gambling. Todd refused.

On the morning of December 16, 1935, Todd was found dead in the front seat of her 1934 Lincoln Phaeton convertible, which was parked in the two-car garage she shared with West. The apparent cause of death was carbon monoxide poisoning, though whether Todd was the victim of an accident, suicide, or murder remains a mystery.

Little evidence supports the suicide theory, outside the mode of death and the fact that Todd led a fast-paced lifestyle that sometimes got the better of her. Indeed, her career was going remarkably well, and she had purchased Christmas presents and was looking forward to a New Year's Eve party. So suicide does not seem a viable cause, though it is still mentioned as a probable one in many accounts.

The Accident Theory

However, an accidental death is also a possibility. The key to her car was in the "on" position, and the motor was dead when Todd was discovered by her maid. West suggested to investigators that the actress turned on the car to get warm, passed out because she was drunk, and then succumbed to carbon monoxide poisoning. Todd also had a heart condition, according to West, and this may have contributed to her death.

Nonetheless, the notion of foul play is suggested by several incongruities found at the scene. Spots of blood were discovered on and in Todd's car and on her mouth, and her nose was broken, leading some to believe she was knocked out and then placed in the car to make it look like a suicide. (Police attributed the injuries to Todd falling unconscious and striking her head on the steering wheel.) In addition, Todd's blood-alcohol level was extremely high—high enough to stupefy her so that someone could carry her without her fighting back—and her high-heeled shoes were clean and unscuffed, even though she would have had to ascend a flight of outdoor, concrete stairs to reach the garage, which was a 271-step climb behind the restaurant. Investigators also found an unidentified smudged handprint on the left side of the vehicle.

Two with Motive

If Todd was murdered, as some have suggested, who had motive? Because of her wild lifestyle, there are several potential suspects, most notably Pasquale DiCicco, who was known to have a temper, and "Lucky" Luciano, who was angry at Todd for refusing to let him use her restaurant for illegal activities.

Despite the many questions raised by the evidence found at the scene, a grand jury ruled Todd's death accidental. The investigation had been hampered by altered and destroyed evidence, threats to witnesses, and cover-ups, making it impossible to ever learn what really happened. An open-casket service was held at Forest Lawn Memorial Park, where the public viewed the actress bedecked in yellow roses. After the service, Todd was cremated, eliminating the possibility of a second autopsy. Later, when her mother, Alice Todd, died, the actress's ashes were placed in her mother's casket so they could be buried together in Massachusetts.

William Desmond Taylor

The murder of actor/director William Desmond Taylor was like something out of an Agatha Christie novel, complete with a handsome, debonair victim and multiple suspects, each with a motive. But unlike Christie's novels, in which the murderer was always unmasked, Taylor's death remains unsolved nearly 100 years later.

✳ ✳ ✳ ✳

O N THE EVENING of February 1, 1922, Taylor was shot in the back by an unknown assailant; his body was discovered the next morning by a servant, Henry Peavey. News of Taylor's demise spread quickly, and several individuals, including officials from Paramount Studios, where Taylor was employed, raced to the dead man's home to clear it of anything incriminating, such as illegal liquor, evidence of drug use, illicit correspondence, and signs of sexual indiscretion. However, no one called the police until later in the morning.

Numerous Suspects

Soon an eclectic array of potential suspects came to light, including Taylor's former butler, Edward F. Sands, who had gone missing before the murder; popular movie comedienne

Mabel Normand, whom Taylor had entertained the evening of his death; actress Mary Miles Minter, who had a passionate crush on the handsome director who was 28 years her senior; and Charlotte Shelby, Minter's mother, who often wielded a gun to protect her daughter's tarnished honor.

Taylor's murder was the last thing Hollywood needed at the time, coming as it did on the heels of rape allegations against popular film comedian Fatty Arbuckle. Scandals brought undue attention on Hollywood, and the Arbuckle story had taken its toll. Officials at Paramount tried to keep a lid on the Taylor story, but the tabloid press had a field day. A variety of personal foibles were made public in the weeks that followed, and both Normand and Minter saw their careers come to a screeching halt as a result.

Little Evidence

Police interviewed many of Taylor's friends and colleagues, including all potential suspects. However, there was no evidence to incriminate anyone specifically, and no one was formally charged.

Investigators and amateur sleuths pursued the case for years. Sands was long a prime suspect, based on his criminal past and his estrangement from the victim. But it was later revealed that on the day of the murder, Sands had signed in for work at a lumberyard in Oakland, California—some 400 miles away— and thus could not have committed the crime. Coming in second was Shelby, whose temper and threats were legendary. Shelby's own acting career had fizzled out early, and all of her hopes for stardom were pinned on her daughter. She threatened many men who tried to woo Mary.

In the mid-1990s, another possible suspect surfaced—a long-forgotten silent-film actress named Margaret Gibson. According to Bruce Long, author of *William Desmond Taylor: A Dossier*, Gibson confessed to a friend on her deathbed in

1964 that years before she had killed a man named William Desmond Taylor. However, the woman to whom Gibson cleared her conscience didn't know who Taylor was and thought nothing more about it.

The Mystery Continues

Could Margaret Gibson (aka Pat Lewis) be Taylor's murderer? She had acted with Taylor in Hollywood in the early 1910s, and she may even have been one of his many sexual conquests. She also had a criminal past, including charges of blackmail, drug use, and prostitution, so it's entirely conceivable that she was a member of a group trying to extort money from the director, a popular theory among investigators. But according to an earlier book, *A Cast of Killers* by Sidney D. Kirkpatrick, veteran Hollywood director King Vidor had investigated the murder as material for a film script and through his research believed Shelby was the murderer. But out of respect for Minter, he never did anything about it.

Ultimately, however, we may never know for certain who killed William Desmond Taylor, or why. The case has long grown cold, and anyone with specific knowledge of the murder is likely dead. Unlike a Hollywood thriller, in which the killer is revealed at the end, Taylor's death is a macabre puzzle that likely will never be solved.

Death from on High

When a troubled man exacted revenge from a lofty perch, a stunned nation watched in horror and disbelief. What could cause a man to kill indiscriminately? Why hadn't anyone seen it coming? Could such a thing happen again? Decades later the mystery continues.

✳   ✳   ✳   ✳

IN AN AMERICA strained by an escalating war in Vietnam, the 1966 headline still managed to shock the senses. The "Texas Tower Sniper" had killed his mother and wife before snuffing out the lives of 13 innocents on the University of Texas (UT) campus at Austin. At least the Vietnam conflict offered up motives. Like most wars, battle lines had been drawn, and a steady buildup of threats and tensions had preceded the violence. But here, no such declarations were issued. Bullets came blazing out of the sky for no apparent reason. After the victims breathed their last and the nightmare drew to a close, a stunned populace was left with one burning question: Why?

Undercurrents

Charles Whitman appeared to have enjoyed many of life's advantages. Hailing from a prominent family in Lake Worth, Florida, the future was Whitman's to make or break. But friction with his abusive father found Whitman seeking escape. After a brutal incident in which he returned home from a party drunk only to be beaten—and nearly drowned in a swimming pool—by his father, the 18-year-old Whitman enlisted in the U.S. Marines. He served for five years, distinguishing himself with a Sharpshooters Badge. After that he attended college at UT. During that period, he also married his girlfriend, Kathy Leissner.

Whitman's life plan appeared to be straightforward. After obtaining a scholarship, he would seek an engineering degree, hoping to follow it up with acceptance at officer's candidate school. But things didn't go as planned.

Opportunity Lost

After leaving the military, Whitman worked toward a variety of goals in and out of school. Unfortunately, the ex-Marine was fraught with failure, and his frustrations multiplied. In the spring of 1966, Whitman sought the help of UT psychiatrist Dr. Maurice Dean Heatly. In a moment of ominous foretelling, Whitman remarked that he fantasized "going up on the [campus] tower with a deer rifle and shooting people." The doctor, having heard similar threats in the past, was mostly unimpressed. Since Whitman hadn't previously exhibited violent behavior, Heatly took his statement as nothing more than an idle threat.

Surprise Assault

During the wee hours of August 1, 1966, Whitman's demons finally won out, and his killing spree began. For reasons still uncertain, the murderer kicked off his blood quest by first stabbing his mother in her apartment and his wife while she slept. Both died from the injuries.

Whitman then made his way to the UT campus and ascended the soon-to-be infamous tower. At his side he had enough provisions, weapons, and ammo to hole up indefinitely. Just before noon, he lifted a high-powered rifle and began shooting. He picked off victims one by one from the observation deck of the 307-foot-tall tower. Whitman's sharpshooting prowess (he once scored 215 points out of a possible 250 in target practice) added to the danger. When people finally realized what was happening, quite a few had already been cut down.

Lives Cut Short

As the attacks progressed, Austin police hatched a plan. Officers Ramiro Martinez and Houston McCoy snuck into the tower, surprising Whitman. Both sides exchanged fire. The 96-minute attack ended with two fatal shots to Whitman's head, compliments of McCoy's 12-gauge shotgun. The horror was over. In its ultimate wake lay 16 dead and 31 wounded. An autopsy performed on Whitman revealed a brain tumor that may have caused him to snap.

The authorities later found a note at his home. Its matter-of-fact tone is chilling to this day: "I imagine it appears that I brutaly [sic] kill [sic] both of my loved ones. I was only trying to do a quick thorough job. If my life insurance policy is valid . . . please pay off all my debts . . . Donate the rest anonymously to a mental health foundation. Maybe research can prevent further tragedies of this type."

The Dyatlov Pass Incident

Nine experienced hikers and skiers trek into the Russian wilderness and promptly disappear. Weeks later, their mangled bodies are found among the ruins of the campsite, with no trace of evidence as to how they died. Read on for a closer look at one of the greatest (and creepiest) unsolved mysteries of modern times.

✳ ✳ ✳ ✳

Off to the Otorten Mountain

IN EARLY 1959, a group of outdoor enthusiasts formed a skiing and hiking expedition to Otorten Mountain, which is part of the northern Ural Mountain range in Russia. The group, led by Igor Dyatlov, consisted of seven other men and two women: Yury Doroshenko, Georgy Krivonischenko, Alexander Kolevatov, Rustem Slobodin, Nicolas Thibeaux-Brignolle, Yuri Yudin, Alexander Zolotaryov, Lyudmila Dubinina, and Zinaida Kolmogorova.

The group's journey began on January 27. The following day, Yudin became ill and had to return home. It would be the last time he would see his friends alive. Using personal photographs and journals belonging to the members of the ski trip to piece together the chain of events, it appeared as though on February 1, the group got disoriented making their way to Otorten Mountain and ended up heading too far to the west. Once they realized they were heading in the wrong direction, the decision was made to simply set up camp for the night. What happened next is a mystery to this day.

Mountain of the Dead

When no word had been heard from the group by February 20, eight days after their planned return, a group of volunteers organized a search. On February 26, they found the group's abandoned campsite on the east side of the mountain Kholat Syakhl. (As if the story were written by a horror novelist, *Kholat Syakhl* happens to mean "Mountain of the Dead" in the Mansi language.) The search team found a badly damaged tent that appeared to have been ripped open from the inside. They also found several sets of footprints. Following the trail of footprints, searchers discovered the bodies of Krivonischenko and Doroshenko, shoeless and dressed only in their underwear. Three more bodies—those belonging to Dyatlov, Kolmogorova and Slobodin—were found nearby. It was later determined that all five had died from hypothermia.

On May 4, the bodies of the four other hikers were recovered in the woods near where the bodies of Krivonischenko and Doroshenko had been found. The discovery of these four raised even more questions. To begin with, Thibeaux-Brignolle's skull had been crushed and both Dubunina and Zolotaryov had major chest fractures. The force needed to cause these wounds was compared to that of a high-speed car crash. Oddly, Dubinina's tongue appeared to have been ripped out.

Looking at the evidence, it appeared as though all nine members had bedded down for the night, only to be woken up by something so frightening that they all quickly left the tent and ran into the freezing cold night. One by one, they either froze to death or else succumbed to their injuries, the cause of which was never determined.

Remains a Mystery

Things got even stranger at the funerals for the nine individuals. Family members would later remark that some of the deceased's skin had become orange and their hair had turned grey. Medical tests and a Geiger counter brought to the site showed some of the bodies had high levels of radiation.

So what happened to the hikers? Authorities eventually concluded that "an unknown compelling force" caused the deaths. The case would be officially closed in the spring of 1959 due to the "absence of a guilty party." Stories and theories still abound, pointing to everything from the Russian government covering up secret military exercises in the area to violent UFO encounters. Today, the area where the nine hikers met their untimely demise is known as Dyatlov Pass, after the leader of the ill-fated group.

The Deaths of Tupac and The Notorious B.I.G.

Tupac Shakur—known as Tupac—and Christopher Wallace—known as The Notorious B.I.G.—were two of the biggest rappers in the 1990s and arguably in history. Onetime friends, the young rappers later become rivals. Sadly, both would end up dead following drive-by shootings just six months apart. And more than 20 years after the slayings, both murders remain unsolved.

✻ ✻ ✻ ✻

Difficult Upbringings, Big Successes

BORN IN 1971, Tupac Shakur came from a family of Black Panthers and radical politics. He grew up in challenging homes and homeless shelters, but his creative chops landed him at the Baltimore School for the Arts, where he studied ballet, poetry, and acting. His family later moved from Baltimore to the San Francisco Bay Area; there, Shakur joined a rap group and signed a record deal. In 1991, Shakur released his debut solo album, *2Pacalypse Now*, which caused controversy with its biting social commentaries.

One year younger than his contemporary, Christopher Wallace grew up in Brooklyn. He was an accomplished student who, by age 15, was selling drugs. Wallace also began rapping as a teenager, at that time for fun. An editor at a rap scene national magazine got hold of one of Wallace's rap tapes, and the young rapper subsequently appeared in the magazine.

Shakur and Wallace would later meet in the early 1990s. When they met, Shakur was already an accomplished artist, while Wallace was working on his first album, *Ready to Die*, which would go on to sell millions of copies. The two struck up a friendship, and Wallace even asked Shakur to become his manager, an offer Shakur declined. But a feud ultimately developed between their dueling record labels, and this feud turned personal in 1994 when Shakur was shot five times during a robbery at a New York City recording studio. Shakur—who somehow survived—believed Wallace was behind the shooting.

Unsolved Mysteries

On September 7, 1996, Shakur attended a Mike Tyson boxing match in Las Vegas. After leaving the event with Suge Knight, the then-CEO of Death Row Records, Shakur got into a brawl with Orlando Anderson, a Crips gang member, in the MGM Grand casino's lobby. Shortly after the fight, a white Cadillac pulled up beside Shakur's vehicle at a traffic light, and an occupant in the Cadillac fired into Shakur's vehicle, striking him four times. Six days later, Shakur died at a Las Vegas hospital.

A 2002 investigation by *Los Angeles Times* suggested that the gang Southside Crips carried out Shakur's killing in retaliation for the brawl in the MGM Grand lobby hours before the attack on Shakur's vehicle. The story also said that Wallace supplied the weapon for Shakur's murder, and he agreed to pay the gang $1 million for Shakur's killing. Orlando Anderson—a suspect involved in the MGM Grand brawl—later died in a drug-related shooting.

Meanwhile, Wallace was shot dead on March 9, 1997 in Los Angeles, after leaving a music industry party. A dark-colored Chevrolet Impala pulled up next to his vehicle and an occupant fired into Wallace's side of his vehicle. An unsealed autopsy later revealed that a single bullet that pierced several vital organs killed Wallace.

Though speculation swirled about the role of corrupt police officers in Wallace's killing, the FBI ended its inquiry in 2005 after prosecutors concluded that there was scant evidence to pursue a case. That year, a federal judge concluded that a Los Angeles police detective intentionally withheld evidence in a wrongful death lawsuit filed against the city by Wallace's family; the lawsuit, however, was dismissed in 2010. Kevin McClure, a former LAPD captain who oversaw the investigation into Wallace's murder, told the *Los Angeles Times* in 2017 that the shooter is likely dead.

H. H. Holmes: Serial Killer at the World's Fair

H. H. Holmes has secured a place in history as one of the cruelest, most horrifyingly prolific killers the world has ever seen. From his headquarters at a Chicago hotel, Holmes slaughtered at least 27 people starting in the early 1890s.

Many filmmakers, scholars, and authors have tried to understand the mind of the madman Holmes. Here is an overview of the twisted, convoluted details of the real-life "Doctor Death."

✳ ✳ ✳ ✳

Troubled Child

BORN IN MAY 1860, Herman Webster Mudgett was a highly intelligent child and did well in school, but he was constantly in trouble. As a teen, he became abusive to animals and small children—a classic characteristic of serial killers.

Fascinated with bones, skeletons, and the human body, Mudgett decided to pursue a degree in medicine. He changed his name to H. H. Holmes, married Clara Lovering, and with her inheritance, enrolled in medical school in Burlington, Vermont.

Swindler, Liar, Cheat

In medical school, Holmes was able to be around skeletons, cadavers, and fresh corpses all the time, which suited him just fine. Very soon, however, it was obvious that Holmes wasn't in the medical field for humanitarian reasons. Ever the swindler, Holmes came up with a scheme whereby he'd take insurance policies out on family members he didn't actually have. He would steal cadavers from the school, make them look as if they'd had an accident, then identify the bodies as those of his family members to collect the insurance money. Some of these frauds brought in $10,000 or more per body.

When authorities became suspicious of all these dead "family members," Holmes abandoned Clara and their newborn baby. Where he went after that is a little murky, as the next six or so years of Holmes's life are not well documented. But by the mid-1880s, Holmes was back on the radar as a charming, intelligent, bold-faced liar and thief with murderous intentions. This time, his mark was Chicago. The city would become the site of Holmes's biggest, deadliest swindle of all.

The Roots of a Murderous Plan

If you lived in Chicago in the late 1800s, you were likely consumed with thoughts of the World's Fair. Officially known as the World's Columbian Exposition of 1893, the colossal event had most of the Midwest working for its success. It was to be the event that would make America a superstar country and make Chicago one of the country's A-list cities. The Great Fire of 1871 had demolished the town; the World's Fair vowed to bring it back in a big way.

It was during the years of preparation for the big fair that Holmes began his path of murder. With so many people flooding the city every day looking to nab one of the thousands of new jobs in the area, Chicago was experiencing a population boom that made it very easy to lose track of people. Holmes recognized this as an opportunity to lure women into his clutches while most people had their focus elsewhere.

He married his second wife, Myrtle, in 1885, even though he had never actually divorced Clara. While Myrtle lived in suburban Wilmette, Holmes took a place in Chicago, and the couple lived apart for most of their marriage. Holmes needed to be in the city because he was working at a drugstore in Chicago's Englewood neighborhood. He worked for the elderly Mrs. Holdens, a kind woman who was happy to have such an attractive young doctor help out at her busy store. When Mrs. Holden disappeared without a trace in 1887 and Holmes purchased the store, no one suspected a thing.

Holmes (who now had full access to a well-stocked drugstore with countless medical tools, chemicals, and medicines) purchased a vacant lot across the street from the drugstore and began construction on a house with a strange floor plan he'd designed himself. The three-story house would have 60 rooms, more than 50 doors placed in an odd fashion throughout the structure, trap doors, secret passageways, windowless rooms, and chutes that led down to a deep basement. Holmes hired and fired construction crews on a regular basis, and it was said that his swindler's streak got him out of paying for most (or perhaps all) of the materials and labor used to create what would later be known as the "Murder Castle."

Death: Up & Running

As construction of the "castle" wrapped up, Holmes made plans for several of his employees. The bookkeeper Holmes had at the store around 1890 was Ned Connor, a man who had come to Chicago with his lovely wife, Julia, and their baby daughter, Pearl. Holmes found Julia irresistible and quickly put the make on her, firing Ned so his wife could take his place. It is believed that as his new bookkeeper, Julia was possibly an accomplice in the fraudulent actions at the drugstore, which eased Holmes's mind and allowed him to concentrate on his new building.

Advertised as a lodging for World's Fair tourists, the building opened in 1892. Holmes placed ads in the newspaper to rent rooms, but also listed fake classifieds, calling for females interested in working for a start-up company. He also placed ads for marriage, posing as a successful businessman in need of a wife. Any woman who answered these fake ads was interviewed by Holmes, was told to keep everything a secret, and was instructed to withdraw all funds from her bank account in order to start a new life with him as his worker, wife, or whatever role he had offered. Holmes was a brilliant liar and quite the charmer, and naive 19th-century women fell for it. Once they passed Holmes's tests, these women became his prisoners, doomed to meet their grisly ends.

Gas pipes were secretly installed throughout the house with nozzles that piped noxious fumes into the rooms. Holmes would turn on the gas so that the victim du jour would drop to the floor unconscious. While she was out cold, Holmes would usually rape her, then send the girl down to the basement via the chute. Once there, he would perform experiments on her at his dissection table or torture her with various equipment. He reportedly listened to the screams of the victims from an adjacent room.

Once he had brutalized the unfortunate soul, he would dump her body into a vat of lime acid to completely destroy the evidence. Other times, he sold bones and organs to contacts in the medical field. Holmes murdered at least 22 people in his home, mostly women, though every once in awhile a worried male neighbor or a concerned relative looking for a missing young woman would get too suspicious for Holmes's liking and go missing themselves.

While the "Murder Castle" was in operation, Holmes continued to marry various women and carry out insurance fraud and other deviant acts. After the World's Fair ended, creditors put pressure on him again, and Holmes knew it was time to flee. He traveled across the United States and Canada, scamming and murdering along the way. Strange as it seems, when Holmes was finally caught and brought to justice, it wasn't initially for homicide; a horse-swindling scheme he attempted to pull off with longtime partner in fraud Ben Pietzel was what gave authorities enough evidence to arrest Holmes. When they searched Holmes's Chicago dwelling, their investigation turned up a lot more than they anticipated.

The End of "Doctor Death"

Over the years, one detective had been hot on Holmes's trail. Detective Frank Geyer, a veteran Pinkerton detective, had done his best to follow this creepy man whose identity changed with the weather. Geyer had traced many of the missing World's Fair women back to Holmes's lodging house and had discovered trails that pointed to his fraudulent activities. In 1895, Holmes entered a guilty plea for the horse-fraud case, and Geyer took that opportunity to expand the investigation. He was particularly interested in the whereabouts of three children—Howard, Nellie, and Alice Pietzel, children of Holmes's now murdered accomplice, Ben Pietzel.

Geyer traced the children—and then Holmes—by following his mail. When his search took him to Canada, Geyer knocked on doors all over Toronto to track down Holmes. Finally, he found a house where Holmes had allegedly stayed with several children in tow. Buried in a shallow grave in the backyard were the bodies of the two Pietzel girls. The boy was found several months later in an oven in an Indianapolis home.

When the evidence was brought back to court, Geyer got full clearance to investigate every dark nook and cranny of Holmes's house and business, and one of America's most chilling stories of murder and crime officially broke. As detectives and police officers uncovered layer after layer of hideous evidence, the public became more and more frightened—and fascinated. The *Chicago Tribune* published the floor plan of the "Murder Castle," tourists flocked to ogle the building, and tabloids ran horrifying descriptions of what had happened to the victims inside, events both real and embellished. Then, in August 1895, Holmes's house of horrors burnt to the ground.

While all that took place, inside his heavily guarded cell, Herman Webster Mudgett confessed to his crimes. He officially confessed to 27 murders, six attempted murders, and a whole lot of fraud. What he didn't confess to, however, were any feelings of remorse. Holmes claimed at times to be possessed by the devil, though depending on the day, he'd also claim to be innocent of any wrongdoing whatsoever. All told, estimates of his victims may have hit the 200 mark. Just because he confessed to 27 murders doesn't mean that's what his final tally was—indeed, with the kind of liar Holmes was, it's pretty certain that the number isn't accurate at all.

Holmes was executed by hanging in 1896. He was buried in a coffin lined with cement, topped with more cement, and buried in a double grave—instructions he gave in his last will and testament so that "no one could dig him back up." Was he ready to rest eternally after a life of such monstrosity? Or was he afraid that someone would conduct experiments on him as he had done to so many hapless victims?

The Black Dahlia Murder Mystery

One of the most baffling murder mysteries in U.S. history began innocently enough on the morning of January 15, 1947. Betty Bersinger was walking with her young daughter in the Leimert Park area of Los Angeles, when she spotted something lying in a vacant lot that caused her blood to run cold. She ran to a nearby house and called the police. Officers Wayne Fitzgerald and Frank Perkins arrived on the scene shortly after 11:00 A.M.

✳ ✳ ✳ ✳

A Grisly Discovery

LYING ONLY SEVERAL feet from the road, in plain sight, was the naked body of a young woman. Her body had numerous cuts and abrasions, including a knife wound from ear to ear that resembled a ghoulish grin. Even more horrific was that her body had been completely severed at the midsection, and the two halves had been placed as if they were part of some morbid display. The killer appeared to have carefully posed the victim close to the street because he wanted people to find his grotesque handiwork.

Something else that troubled the officers was that even though the body had been brutally violated and desecrated, there was very little blood found at the scene. The only blood evidence recovered was a possible bloody footprint and an empty cement package with a spot of blood on it. In fact, the body was so clean that it appeared to have just been washed.

Shortly before removing the body, officers scoured the area for a possible murder weapon, but none was recovered. A coroner later determined that the cause of death was from hemorrhage and shock due to a concussion of the brain and lacerations of the face, probably from a very large knife.

Positive Identification

After a brief investigation, police were able to identify the deceased as Elizabeth Short, who was born in Hyde Park, Massachusetts, on July 29, 1924. At age 19, Short had moved to California to live with her father, but she moved out and spent the next few years moving back and forth between California, Florida, and Massachusetts. In July 1946, Short returned to California to see Lt. Gordon Fickling, a former boyfriend, who was stationed in Long Beach. For the last six months of her life, Short lived in an assortment of hotels, rooming houses, and private homes. She was last seen a week before her body was found, which made police very interested in finding out where and with whom she spent her final days.

The Black Dahlia Is Born

As police continued their investigation, reporters jumped all over the story and began referring to the unknown killer by names such as "sex-crazed maniac" and even "werewolf." Short herself was also given a nickname: the Black Dahlia. Reporters said it was a name friends had called her as a play on the movie *The Blue Dahlia*, which had recently been released. However, others contend Short was never called the Black Dahlia while she was alive; it was just something reporters made up for a better story. Either way, it wasn't long before newspapers around the globe were splashing front-page headlines about the horrific murder of the Black Dahlia.

The Killer Is Still Out There

As time wore on, hundreds of police officers were assigned to the Black Dahlia investigation. They combed the streets, interviewing people and following leads. Although police interviewed thousands of potential suspects—and dozens even confessed to the murder—to this day, no one has ever officially been charged with the crime. More than 60 years and several books and movies after the crime, the Elizabeth Short murder case is still listed as "open." We are no closer to knowing who killed Short or why than when her body was first discovered.

There is one bright note to this story. In February 1947, perhaps as a result of the Black Dahlia case, the state of California became the first state to pass a law requiring all convicted sex offenders to register themselves.

The Lizzie Borden Murder Mystery

Most people know the rhyme that begins, "Lizzie Borden took an axe and gave her mother 40 whacks . . . " In reality, approximately 20 hatchet chops cut down Abby Borden, but no matter the number, Lizzie's stepmother was very much dead on that sultry August morning in 1892. Lizzie's father, Andrew, was killed about an hour later. His life was cut short by about a dozen hatchet chops to the head.

No one knows who was guilty of these murders, but Lizzie has always carried the burden of suspicion.

✳ ✳ ✳ ✳

Andrew Borden, an American "Scrooge"

ANDREW JACKSON BORDEN had been one of the richest men in Fall River, Massachusetts, with a net worth of nearly half a million dollars. In 1892, that was enormous wealth. Andrew was a shrewd businessman: At the time of his death, he was the president of the Union Savings Bank and director of another bank plus several profitable cotton mills.

Despite his wealth, Andrew was miserly. Though some of his neighbors' homes had running hot water, the three-story Borden home had just two cold water taps, and there was no water available above the first floor. The Bordens' only latrine was in the cellar, so they generally used chamber pots that were either dumped onto the lawn behind the house or emptied into the cellar toilet. And, although most wealthy people used gas lighting, the Bordens lit their house with kerosene lamps.

Worst of all, for many years, Andrew was an undertaker who offered some of the lowest prices in town. He worked on the bodies in the basement of the Borden home, and allegedly, he bent the knees of the deceased—and in some cases, cut off their feet—to fit the bodies into smaller, less expensive coffins in order to increase his business.

So, despite the brutality of Andrew's murder, it seems few people mourned his loss. The question wasn't why he was killed, but who did it.

Lizzie vs. William

In 1997, when psychic Jane Doherty visited the murder site, she uncovered several clues about the Lizzie Borden case. Doherty felt that the real murderer was someone named "Willie." There is no real evidence to support this claim, but some say Andrew had an illegitimate son named William, who may have spent time as an inmate in an insane asylum. His constant companion was reportedly his hatchet, which he talked to as though it were a friend. Also, at least one witness reportedly saw William at the Borden house on the day of the murders. William was supposedly there to challenge Andrew about his new will.

Was William the killer? A few years after the murders, William took poison and then hung himself in the woods. Near his swinging body, he'd reportedly left his hatchet on the ground. So with William dead and Lizzie already acquitted, the Borden murder case was put to rest.

Lizzie's Forbidden Romance

One of the most curious explanations for the murder involves the Bordens' servant Bridget Sullivan. Her participation has always raised questions. Like the other members of the Borden household, Bridget had suffered from apparent food poisoning the night before the murders. She claimed to have been ill in the backyard of the Borden home.

During the time Abby was being murdered, Bridget was apparently washing windows in the back of the house. Later, when Andrew was killed, Bridget was resting in her room upstairs. Why didn't she hear two people being butchered?

According to some theories, Lizzie and Bridget had been romantically involved. In this version of the story, their relationship was discovered shortly before the murders. Around this same time, Andrew was reportedly rewriting his will. His wife was now "Mrs. Borden," to Lizzie, not "Mother," as Lizzie had called her stepmother for many years. The reason for the estrangement was never clear.

Lizzie also had a strange relationship with her father and had given him her high school ring, as though he were her sweetheart. He wore the ring on his pinky finger and was buried with it.

Just a day before the murders, Lizzie had been attempting to purchase prussic acid—a deadly poison—and the family came down with "food poisoning" that night. Some speculate that Bridget was Lizzie's accomplice in the murders and helped clean up the blood afterward.

This theory was bolstered when, a few years after the murders, Lizzie became involved with actress Nance O'Neil. For two years, Lizzie and the actress were inseparable. This prompted Emma Borden, Lizzie's sister, to move out of their home.

At the time, the rift between the sisters sparked rumors that either Lizzie or Emma might reveal more about the other's role in the 1892 murders. However, neither of them said anything new about the killings.

Whodunit?

Most people believe that Lizzie was the killer. She was the only one accused of the crime, with good reason. Lizzie appeared to be the only one in the house at the time, other than Bridget. She showed no signs of grief when the murders were discovered. During questioning, Lizzie changed her story several times. The evidence was entirely circumstantial, but it was compelling enough to go to trial.

Ultimately, the jury accepted her attorney's closing argument, that the murders were "morally and physically impossible for this young woman defendant." In other words, Lizzie had to be innocent because she was petite and well bred. In 19th-century New England, that seemed like a logical and persuasive defense. Lizzie went free, and no one else was charged with the crimes.

But Lizzie wasn't the only one with motive, means, and opportunity. The most likely suspects were family members, working alone or with other relatives. Only a few had solid alibis, and—like Lizzie—many changed their stories during police questioning. But there was never enough evidence to officially accuse anyone other than Lizzie.

So whether or not Lizzie Borden "took an ax" and killed her parents, she's the one best remembered for the crime.

Lizzie Borden Bed & Breakfast

The Borden house has been sold several times over the years, but today it is a bed-and-breakfast—the main draw, of course, being the building's macabre history. The Victorian residence has been restored to reflect the details of the Borden home at the time of the murders, including the couch on which Andrew lay, his skull hideously smashed.

As a guest, you can stay in one of six rooms, even the one in which Abby was murdered. Then, after a good night's sleep, you'll be treated to a breakfast reminiscent of the one the Bordens had on their final morning in 1892. That is, if you got to sleep at all. (They say the place is haunted.)

As with all good morbid attractions, the proprietors at the Lizzie Borden B&B don't take themselves too seriously. Before you leave, you can stop by the gift shop and pick up a pair of hatchet earrings, an "I Survived the Night at the Lizzie Borden Bed & Breakfast" T-shirt, or an ax-wielding Lizzie Borden bobblehead doll.

A Voice from Beyond the Grave

After the murder of Teresita Basa in the late 1970s, another woman began to speak in Basa's voice—saying things that only Teresita could have known—to help solve the mystery of her murder.

❋　❋　❋　❋

IN FEBRUARY 1977, firemen broke into a burning apartment on North Pine Grove Avenue in Chicago. Beneath a pile of burning clothes, they found the naked body of 47-year-old Teresita Basa, a hospital worker who was said to be a member of the Filipino aristocracy. There were bruises on her neck and a knife was embedded in her chest. Her body was in a position that caused the police to suspect that she had been raped.

However, an autopsy revealed that she hadn't been raped; in fact, she was a virgin. Police were left without a single lead: They had no suspects and no apparent motive for the brutal murder. The solution would come from the strangest of all possible sources—a voice from beyond the grave.

"I Am Teresita Basa"

In the nearby suburb of Evanston, shortly after Teresita's death, Remibios Chua started going into trances during which she spoke in Tagalog in a slow, clear voice that said, "I am Teresita Basa." Although Remibios had worked at the same hospital as Teresita, they worked different shifts, and the only time they are known to have even crossed paths was during a new-employee orientation. Remibios's husband, Dr. Jose Chua, had never heard of Basa.

While speaking in Teresita's voice, Remibios's accent changed, and when she awoke from the trances, she remembered very little, if anything, about what she had said. However, while speaking in the mysterious voice, she claimed that Teresita's killer was Allan Showery, an employee at the hospital where both women had worked. She also stated that he had killed her while stealing jewelry for rent money.

Through Remibios's lips, the voice pleaded for them to contact the police. The frightened couple initially resisted, fearing that the authorities would think that *they* should be locked away. But when the voice returned and continued pleading for an investigation, the Chuas finally contacted the Evanston police, who put them in touch with Joe Stachula, a criminal investigator for the Chicago Police Department.

Lacking any other clues, Stachula interviewed the Chuas. During their conversation, Remibios not only named the killer, but she also told Stachula exactly where to find the jewelry that Showery had allegedly stolen from Teresita. Prior to that, the police were not even aware that anything had been taken from the apartment.

Remarkably, when police began investigating Showery, they found his girlfriend in possession of Teresita's jewelry. Although the authorities declined to list the voice from beyond the grave as evidence, Showery was arrested, and he initially confessed to the crime. When his lawyers learned that information leading to his arrest had come from supernatural sources, they advised him to recant his confession.

The Surprise Confession

Not surprisingly, the voice became a focal point of the case when it went to trial in January 1979. The defense called the Chuas to the witness stand in an effort to prove that the entire case against Showery was based on remarks made by a woman who claimed to be possessed—hardly the sort of evidence that would hold up in court.

But the prosecution argued that no matter the origin of the voice, it had turned out to be correct. In his closing remarks, prosecuting attorney Thomas Organ said, "Did Teresita Basa come back from the dead and name Showery? I don't know. I'm a skeptic, but it doesn't matter as to guilt or innocence. What does matter is that the information furnished to police checked out. The jewelry was found where the voice said it would be found, and Showery confessed."

Detective Stachula was asked if he believed the Chuas: "I would not call anyone a liar," he said. " . . . Dr. and Mrs. Chua are educated, intelligent people . . . I listened and acted on what they told me . . . [and] the case was wrapped up within three hours."

Showery told the jury that he was "just kidding" when he confessed to the crime; he also claimed that the police had coerced him into an admission of guilt. Nevertheless, after 13 hours of deliberation, the jury reported that they were hopelessly deadlocked and a mistrial was declared.

A few weeks later, in a shocking development, Allan Showery changed his plea to "guilty" and was eventually sentenced to 14 years in prison. Some say that Teresita's ghost had visited him and frightened him into confessing.

Obviously shaken by the experience, the Chuas avoided the press as much as possible. In 1980, in her only interview with the press, Remibios noted that during the trial, people were afraid to ride in cars with her, but she said that she was never afraid because the voice said that God would protect her family. Still, she hoped that she would never have to go through such an experience again. "I've done my job," she said. "I don't think I will ever want to go through this same ordeal."

Having attracted national attention, the case quickly became the subject of a best-selling book and countless magazine articles, a TV movie, and a 1990 episode of *Unsolved Mysteries*. The case is often cited as "proof" of psychic phenomena, possession, and ghosts, but it's simply another mystery of the paranormal world. Exactly what it proves is impossible to say; after all, the ghost of Teresita Basa is no longer talking.

Ohio's Greatest Unsolved Mystery

From 1935 until 1938, a brutal madman roamed the Flats of Cleveland. The killer—known as the Mad Butcher of Kingsbury Run—is believed to have murdered 12 men and women. Despite a massive manhunt, the murderer was never apprehended.

✳ ✳ ✳ ✳

IN 1935, THE Depression had hit Cleveland hard, leaving large numbers of people homeless. Shantytowns sprang up on the eastern side of the city in Kingsbury Run—a popular place for transients—near the Erie and Nickel Plate railroads.

It is unclear who the Butcher's first victim was. Recent research suggests it may have been an unidentified woman found floating in Lake Erie—in pieces—on September 5, 1934; she would be known as Jane Doe I but dubbed by some as the "Lady of the Lake." The first official victim was found in the Jackass Hill area of Kingsbury Run on September 23, 1935. The unidentified body, labeled John Doe, had been dead for almost a month. A mere 30 feet away from the body was another victim, Edward Andrassy. Unlike John Doe, Andrassy had only been dead for days, indicating that the spot was a dumping ground. Police began staking out the area.

After a few months passed without another body, police thought the worst was over. Then on January 26, 1936, the partial remains of a new victim, a woman, were found in downtown Cleveland. On February 7, more remains were found at a separate location, and the deceased was identified as Florence Genevieve Polillo. Despite similarities among the three murders, authorities had yet to connect them—serial killers were highly uncommon at the time.

Tattoo Man, Eliot Ness, and More Victims

On June 5, two young boys passing through Kingsbury Run discovered a severed head. The rest of the body was found near the Nickel Plate railroad police station. Despite six distinctive tattoos on the man's body (thus the nickname "Tattoo Man"), he was never identified and became John Doe II.

At this point, Cleveland's newly appointed director of public safety, Eliot Ness, was officially briefed on the case. While Ness and his men hunted down leads, the headless body of another unidentified male was found west of Cleveland on July 22, 1936. It appeared that the man, John Doe III, had been murdered months earlier. On September 10, the headless body of a sixth victim, John Doe IV, was found in Kingsbury Run.

Ness officially started spearheading the investigation. Determined to bring the killer to justice, Ness's staff fanned out across the city, even going undercover in the Kingsbury Run area. As 1936 drew to a close, no suspects had been named nor new victims discovered. City residents believed that Ness's team had run the killer off. But future events would prove that the killer was back . . . with a vengeance.

The Body Count Climbs

A woman's mutilated torso washed up on the beach at 156th Street on February 23, 1937. The rest would wash ashore two months later. (Strangely, the body washed up in the same location as the "Lady of the Lake" had three years earlier.)

On June 6, 1937, teenager Russell Lauyer found the decomposed body of a woman inside of a burlap sack under the Lorain-Carnegie Bridge in Cleveland. With the body was a newspaper from June of the previous year, suggesting a timeline for the murder. An investigation indicated the body might belong to one Rose Wallace; this was never confirmed, and the victim is sometimes referred to as Jane Doe II. Pieces of another man's body (the ninth victim) began washing ashore on July 6, just below Kingsbury Run. Cleveland newspapers were having a field day with the case that the "great" Eliot Ness couldn't solve. This fueled Ness, and he promised justice.

Burning of Kingsbury Run

The next nine months were quiet, and the public began to relax. When a woman's severed leg was found in the Cuyahoga River on April 8, 1938, however, people debated its connection to the Butcher. But the rest of Jane Doe III was soon found inside two burlap sacks floating in the river (*sans* head, of course).

On August 16, 1938, the last two confirmed victims of the Butcher were found together at the East 9th Street Lakeshore Dump. Jane Doe IV had apparently been dead for four to six months prior to discovery, while John Doe VI may have been dead for almost nine months.

Something snapped inside Eliot Ness. On the night of August 18, Ness and dozens of police officials raided the shantytowns in the Flats, ending up in Kingsbury Run. Along the way, they interrogated or arrested anyone they came across, and Ness ordered the shanties burned to the ground. There would be no more confirmed victims of the Mad Butcher of Kingsbury Run.

Who Was the Mad Butcher?

There were two prime suspects in the case, though no one was ever charged. The first was Dr. Francis Sweeney, a surgeon with the knowledge many believed necessary to mutilate the victims the way the killer did. (He was also a cousin of Congressman Martin L. Sweeney, a known political opponent of Ness.)

In August 1938, Dr. Sweeney was interrogated by Ness, two other men, and the inventor of the polygraph machine, Dr. Royal Grossman. By all accounts, Sweeney failed the polygraph test (several times), and Ness believed he had his man, but he was released due to lack of evidence. Two days after the interrogation, on August 25, 1938, Sweeney checked himself into the Sandusky Veterans Hospital. He remained institutionalized at various facilities until his death in 1965. Because Sweeney checked himself in, he could have left whenever he desired.

The other suspect was Frank Dolezal, who was arrested by private investigators on July 5, 1939, as a suspect in the murder of Florence Polillo, with whom he had lived for a time. While in custody, Dolezal confessed to killing Polillo, although some believe the confession was forced. Either way, Dolezal died under mysterious circumstances while incarcerated at the Cuyahoga County Jail before he could be charged.

As for Eliot Ness, some believe his inability to bring the Butcher to trial weighed on him for the rest of his life. Ness went to his grave without getting a conviction. To this day, the case remains open.

Lana Turner and the Death of a Gangster

On the evening of April 4, 1958, Beverly Hills police arrived at the home of actress Lana Turner to discover the dead body of her one-time boyfriend Johnny Stompanato, a violent gangster with underworld ties. He had been stabbed to death, but the exact circumstances of his demise were muddied by the sensational reporting of the tabloid press.

✳ ✳ ✳ ✳

Sweater Girl

LANA TURNER'S FIRST credited film role came in 1937 with *They Won't Forget*, which earned her the moniker "Sweater Girl," thanks to the tight-fitting sweater her character wore. Turner went on to star in hits such as *Honky Tonk* (1941), *The Postman Always Rings Twice* (1946), and *Peyton Place* (1957).

Hanging with the Wrong Crowd

Offscreen, Turner was renowned for her many love affairs. During her lifetime, she amassed eight marriages to seven different husbands. It was shortly after the breakup of her fifth marriage to actor Lex Barker in 1957 that Turner met Johnny Stompanato. When she discovered that his name was not John Steele (as he had told her) and that he had ties to underworld figures such as Mickey Cohen, she realized the negative publicity that those ties could bring to her career, so she tried to end the relationship. But Stompanato incessantly pursued her, and the pair engaged in a number of violent incidents, which came to a head on the night of April 4.

Turner's 14-year-old daughter, Cheryl Crane, rushed to her mother's defense after hearing Stompanato threaten to "cut" Turner. Fearing for her mother's life, the girl grabbed a kitchen knife, then ran upstairs to Turner's bedroom. According to Crane's account, Turner opened the door and Cheryl saw Stompanato with his arms raised in the air in a fury. Cheryl then rushed past Turner and stabbed Stompanato, killing him. Turner called her mother, who brought their personal physician to the house, but it was too late. By the time the police were called, much time had passed and evidence had been moved around. According to the Beverly Hills police chief, who was the first officer to arrive, Turner immediately asked if she could take the rap for her daughter.

At the crime scene, the body appeared to have been moved and the fingerprints on the murder weapon were so smudged that they could not be identified. The case sparked a media sensation, especially among the tabloid press, which turned against Turner, essentially accusing her of killing Stompanato and asking her daughter to cover for her. Mickey Cohen, who paid for Stompanato's funeral, publicly called for the arrests of Turner and Crane. For years, rumors surrounding the case persisted.

"The Performance of a Lifetime"?

During the inquest, the press described Turner's testimony as "the performance of a lifetime." But police and authorities knew from the beginning that Turner did not do it. At the inquest, it took just 20 minutes for the jury to return a verdict of justifiable homicide, so the D.A. decided not to bring the case to trial. However, Turner was convicted of being an unfit mother, and Crane was remanded to her grandmother's care until she turned 18, further tainting Turner's image. There was an aura of "guilt" around Turner for years, though she was never seriously considered a suspect in the actual murder.

As fate would have it, Turner's film *Peyton Place*, which features a courtroom scene about a murder committed by a teenager, was still in theaters at the time of the inquest. Ticket sales skyrocketed as a result of the sensational publicity, and Turner parlayed the success of the film into better screen roles, including her part in a remake of *Imitation of Life* (1959), which would become one of her most successful films. She appeared in romantic melodramas until the mid-1960s, when age began to affect her career. In the '70s and '80s, she made the transition to television, appearing on shows such as *The Survivors, The Love Boat*, and *Falcon Crest*.

Anything but Splendor: Natalie Wood

The official account of Natalie Wood's tragic death is riddled with holes. For this reason, cover-up theorists continue to run hog-wild with conjecture. Here's a sampling of the questions, facts, and assertions surrounding the case.

A Life in Pictures

THERE ARE THOSE who will forever recall Natalie Wood as the adorable child actress from *Miracle on 34th Street* (1947) and those who remember her as the sexy but wholesome grown-up star of movies such as *West Side Story* (1961), *Splendor in the Grass* (1961), and *Bob & Carol & Ted & Alice* (1969). Both groups generally agree that Wood had uncommon beauty and talent.

Wood appeared in her first film, *Happy Land* (1943), in a bit part alongside other people from her hometown of Santa Rosa, California, where the film was shot. She stood out to the director, who remembered her later when he needed to cast a child in another film. Wood was uncommonly mature and professional for a child actress, which helped her make a relatively smooth transition to ingenue roles.

Although Wood befriended James Dean and Sal Mineo—her troubled young costars from *Rebel Without a Cause* (1955)—and she briefly dated Elvis Presley, she preferred to move in established Hollywood circles. By the time she was 20, she was married to Robert Wagner and was costarring with Frank Sinatra in *Kings Go Forth* (1958), which firmly ensconced her in the Hollywood establishment. The early 1960s represent the high point of Wood's career, and she specialized in playing high-spirited characters with determination and spunk. She added two more Oscar nominations to the one she received for *Rebel* and racked up five Golden Globe nominations for Best Actress. This period also proved to be personally turbulent for Wood, as she suffered through a failed marriage to Wagner and another to Richard Gregson. After taking time off to raise children, she remarried Wagner and returned to her acting career.

Shocking News

And so, on November 29, 1981, the headline hit the news-wires much like an out-of-control car hits a brick wall. Natalie Wood, the beautiful, vivacious 43-year-old star of stage and screen, had drowned after falling from her yacht the *Splendour*, which was anchored off California's Santa Catalina Island. Wood had been on the boat during a break from her latest film, *Brainstorm*, and was accompanied by Wagner and *Brainstorm* costar Christopher Walken. Skipper Dennis Davern was at the helm. Foul play was not suspected.

In My Esteemed Opinion

After a short investigation, Chief Medical Examiner Dr. Thomas Noguchi listed Wood's death as an accidental drowning. Tests revealed that she had consumed "seven or eight" glasses of wine, and the coroner contended that in her intoxicated state Wood had probably stumbled and fallen overboard while attempting to untie the yacht's rubber dinghy. He also stated that cuts and bruises on her body could have occurred when she fell from the boat.

Doubting Thomases

To this day, many question Wood's mysterious demise and believe that the accidental drowning theory sounds a bit too convenient. Pointed questions have led to many rumors: Does someone know more about Wood's final moments than they're letting on? Was her drowning really an accident, or did someone intentionally or accidentally *help* her overboard? Could this be why she sustained substantial bruising on her face and the back of her legs? Why was Wagner so reluctant to publicly discuss the incident? Were Christopher Walken and Wood an item as had been rumored? With this possibility in mind, could a booze-fueled fight have erupted between the two men? Could Wood have then tried to intervene, only to be knocked overboard for her efforts? And why did authorities declare Wood's death accidental so quickly? Would such a ruling have been issued had the principals not been famous and influential?

Ripples

At the time of Wood's death, she and Wagner were seven years into their second marriage to each other. Whether Wood was carrying on an affair with Walken, as was alleged, may be immaterial, even if it made for interesting tabloid fodder. But Wagner's perception of their relationship could certainly be a factor. If nothing else, it might better explain the argument that ensued between Wagner and Walken that fateful night.

Case Closed?

Further information about Wood's death is sparse because no eyewitnesses have come forward. However, a businesswoman whose boat was anchored nearby testified that she heard a woman shouting for help, and then a voice responding, "We'll be over to get you," so the woman went back to bed. Just after dawn, Wood's body was found floating a mile away from the *Splendour*, approximately 200 yards offshore. The dinghy was found nearby; its only cargo was a stack of lifejackets.

CASE CLOSED

In 2008, after 27 years of silence, Robert Wagner recalled in his autobiography, *Pieces of My Heart: A Life*, that he and Walken had engaged in a heated argument during supper after Walken had suggested that Wood star in more films, effectively keeping her away from their children. Wagner and Walken then headed topside to cool down. Sometime around midnight, Wagner said he returned to his cabin and discovered that his wife was missing. He soon realized that the yacht's dinghy was gone as well. In his book, he surmised that Wood may have gone to secure the dinghy that had been noisily slapping against the boat. Then, tipsy from the wine, she probably fell into the ocean and drowned. Walken notified the authorities.

Was Natalie Wood's demise the result of a deadly mix of wine and saltwater as the coroner's report suggests? This certainly could be the case. But why would she leave her warm cabin to tend to a loose rubber dinghy in the dark of night? Could an errant rubber boat really make such a commotion?

Perhaps we'll never know what happened that fateful night, but an interview conducted shortly before Wood's death proved prophetic: "I'm frightened to death of the water," said Wood about a long-held fear. "I can swim a little bit, but I'm afraid of water that is dark."

The Mysterious Death of Christopher Marlowe

Who exactly was responsible for the death of Christopher Marlowe?

✳ ✳ ✳ ✳

IN 1593, CHRISTOPHER Marlowe, the most famous playwright in London, was killed when he accidentally stabbed himself during a tavern brawl. His premature death is one of the greatest tragedies in English literature, snuffing out a career that may have still been in its infancy—Shakespeare, who was Marlowe's same age, was just coming into his own as a writer at the time. But some people continue to doubt the official story (i.e., that Marlowe accidentally stabbed himself while fighting over the bill). After all, Marlowe and some of the others in the room with him had ties to the Elizabethan underworld. Was his really an accidental death—or could it have been murder?

Rise of a Shoemaker's Son

Born to a shoemaker the same year that Shakespeare was born to a glove maker, Marlowe attended Cambridge University, where he posed for a portrait that showed him in a black velvet shirt, smirking beside his Latin motto, *Quod met nutrit me destruit* ("What nourishes me destroys me.") He was a distinguished enough scholar that he seems to have been recruited, as many Cambridge scholars of the day were, to work as an undercover agent. Letters from the government excusing him from missing classes seem to back up the widely held theory that he went on spy missions in Spain. When he returned to London, he found fame as a playwright, churning out "blood and thunder" shockers such as *Doctor Faustus* that helped pioneer the use of blank verse, and were some of the first great pieces of secular theatrical entertainment produced in the English language.

But to say that Marlowe had a wild side is to put things mildly. He was imprisoned twice, once for his role in a fight that left a tavern keeper dead (he was acquitted when a jury determined that he'd acted in self-defense), and ran with an underground group of atheists who called themselves "The School of Night." They hung around in graveyards, reading poetry and having the sort of blasphemous debates that were illegal in Elizabethan England, where everyone was required to be a member of the Church of England. Breaking somewhat from her predecessors, Queen Elizabeth generally didn't care too much if people doubted religion in their minds, as long as they kept their mouths shut and kept attending church services. But for someone as famous as Marlowe to be a heretic was dangerous.

Richard Baines, a professional snitch, wrote a letter to the government containing a bunch of blasphemous things that he claimed to have heard Marlowe say, such as that Moses was really just a juggler, that people in the New World had stories and histories dating back 10,000 years (which went against the "official" view that the Adam and Eve had lived "within six thousand years,"), and that the Virgin Mary was "dishonest." Around the same time, the government arrested Thomas Kyd, Marlowe's former roommate, for possessing atheist literature, and Kyd said under torture that it was Marlowe who had turned him on to atheism in the first place.

And so, at the height of his fame, Marlowe was arrested for blasphemy. He was released on parole and ordered to check in every day until he was brought to trial, at which he faced a possible sentence of death. If lucky, he would just get his nose chopped off.

Marlowe never once checked in with authorities, so far as is known, and he was killed in Deptford only a couple of weeks later, while awaiting trial.

An Accident?

The exact circumstances of his death are still not quite agreed upon, though a detailed coroner's report exists. Documents state that Marlowe and a few other men had spent the day in an establishment owned by "The Widow Bull," but what sort of business this was is a matter of some mystery—it's been variously described as a tavern, a brothel, or a sort of bed and breakfast. The fact that the investigations into what happened that day mention a "reckoning" (bill) is about the only evidence we have that it was any sort of business at all, not just a house owned by Ms. Eleanor Bull.

However, according to official reports, a bill was presented to Marlowe and his friends. A fight broke out over who should pay it, and in the scuffle, Marlowe accidentally stabbed himself below the eye and "then and there instantly died."

Now, most fights over bills ("I shouldn't have to pay an equal share, because I just had water and appetizers, not steak and beer....") don't end in knife fights, but this explanation seems sensible enough on the surface: The theatres were closed at the time due to a plague outbreak, and Marlowe was probably hard up for money. Perhaps he had taken up an offer of going to dinner thinking that his meal was being paid for, and when he was asked to kick in for the bill, his hot temper got the best of him. He reached for the dagger of one of the other men present— one Ingram Frizer—and stabbed himself while the other men tried to stop him from attacking.

The death was officially determined to be the result of an accidental, self-inflicted wound, but more and more scholars now believe that Marlowe was murdered to make sure he didn't reveal sensitive information at his upcoming trial. It does seem that a lot of people may have had a reason to want Marlowe to be killed before he could go to trial. Frizer, for example, had been working for Thomas Walsingham, a relative of Queen Elizabeth's secretary of state, and had Marlowe been convicted of atheism, Walsingham himself would have been disgraced, and financially ruined, for having once been Marlowe's patron. Perhaps Frizer was acting on his boss's orders and killed Marlowe to ensure his own future.

But others believe that the "political murder" theory doesn't go far enough, and that the body on the coroner's slab wasn't Marlowe at all, but the body of a man named John Penry who had been hastily hanged. According to this theory, Marlowe wasn't killed at all, but instead escaped to the continent, where he kept on writing. Some of the wildest theories in this vein hold that he was the true author of Shakespeare's plays.

It seems far-fetched, but if anyone could have pulled off faking his own death, it was Christopher Marlowe. And while conspiracies have tried to claim several people as the "true" author of Shakespeare's works, Marlowe is the only one who was a good enough author that he could have rivaled Shakespeare for the title of greatest dramatist of the English language.

The Sad Saga of Sonny Liston

Climbing up from utter poverty, this world heavyweight champ found controversial success in the boxing ring but couldn't maintain his balance on the outside.

✳ ✳ ✳ ✳

CHARLES "SONNY" LISTON was born the son of an impoverished sharecropper in rural Arkansas, probably on May 8, but the year of his birth is unknown. This is the first of many mysteries in the life of a complicated, impenetrable man. Though many who knew him said he was born in 1927, Liston himself claimed he was born in 1932, and contemporary documents seem to back him up. Emotionally and physically abused, young Liston was not unhappy when his miserable parents split up and his mother moved to St. Louis—in fact, he followed her there as soon as he could.

The Hard Time

Liston was only in his early teens when he made his way north, and like everyone else in his family, he was illiterate. He had his imposing build going for him, however, and this led local organized crime to recruit him as a debt collector. As long as Liston stuck to breaking kneecaps, he was to some degree under the mob's protection from law enforcement. But when he struck out on his own, robbing two gas stations and a restaurant with other youths in 1950, the police caught up to him, and he was busted. Liston pleaded guilty to two counts of robbery and two counts of larceny—he was lucky to be sentenced to concurrent prison terms that ran only five years.

In the penitentiary, a Roman Catholic priest noticed Liston's remarkable physique and urged him to take up boxing. Liston followed that advice, and after serving only two years of his time, he was paroled to a team of "handlers" who worked for St. Louis mobster John Vitale. Vitale set Liston up in the boxing world and controlled his contract for six years before selling it to Frankie Carbo and Blinky Palermo, underworld figures on the East Coast. Eventually, Liston's criminal ties would lead him all the way to the U.S. Senate, where in 1960 he testified before a sub-committee investigating orga-nized crime's control of boxing.

The Big Time

Liston's first professional fight lasted only 33 seconds—he took out Don Smith with only one punch. His first five fights were in St. Louis, but his sixth was in Detroit. In that nationally televised bout, he won an eight-round decision against John Summerlin. The odds had been long, so the fight garnered the young upstart a lot of attention. He suffered his first profes-sional defeat from his next opponent, when Marty Marshall broke his jaw. Nevertheless, Liston moved steadily up the ranks, and finally, at Chicago's Comiskey Park in 1962, he became the heavyweight champion of the world by knocking out Floyd Patterson in the first round.

Fighting success did not keep him out of trouble with the law, however. A total of 19 arrests and a second jail sentence made Liston an unpopular figure on the American sports scene. Many of his fights were thought to be fixed, and some considered him a puppet of the mob. Unfortunately for him, Liston's most famous moment was one of defeat: his knockout by Muhammad Ali on May 25, 1965. In one of the most famous sports photos ever taken, *Sports Illustrated* photographer Neil Leifer shot Liston sprawled on the mat with a menacing, screaming Ali towering over him. Some claim that Ali's punch was a "phantom punch" that never connected and that Liston had taken a dive because he feared the Nation of Islam.

Strange Death

On January 5, 1971, he was found dead in his Las Vegas home by his wife, Geraldine, who had been out of town. Though the coroner ruled that he had died from heart failure and lung congestion, Liston's body was in a state of decomposition, and there was much speculation that Liston had been murdered by unsavory associates.

The man who came into the world so anonymously that his birth year was not really known left it in fame, but with just as many unanswered questions.

Sister Aimee Dies for Love

Did a well-known early 20th century evangelist stage her own death?

✳   ✳   ✳   ✳

S ISTER AIMEE SEMPLE McPherson (1890–1944) was a woman far ahead of her time. In a male-driven society, McPherson founded a religious movement known as the Foursquare Church. Using her natural flamboyance and utilizing modern technologies such as radio, McPherson reached thousands with her Pentecostal message of hope, deliverance, and salvation. But turbulent waters awaited McPherson. Before the evangelist could grow her church to its fullest potential, she'd first have to survive her own "death."

The Seed Is Planted

It was said that McPherson was something of a firebrand right from the get-go. Born Aimee Elizabeth Kennedy in Salford, Ontario, the future evangelist was daughter to James Kennedy, a farmer, and Mildred "Minnie" Kennedy, a Salvation Army worker. As a teenager, the inquisitive Aimee often came to loggerheads with pastors over such weighty issues as faith and science—even as she openly questioned the teaching of evolution in public schools.

In 1908, Aimee married Robert James Semple, a Pentecostal missionary from Ireland. The marriage was short-lived. Semple died from Malaria in 1910, but their union produced a daughter, Roberta Star Semple, born that same year.

Working as a Salvation Army employee alongside her mother, Aimee married accountant Harold Stewart McPherson in 1912. One year later they had a son, Rolf Potter Kennedy McPherson. But this marriage would also dissolve. Citing desertion as the cause for their rift, Harold McPherson divorced his wife in 1921.

By this point McPherson was well on her way as an evangelist. In 1924 she began to broadcast her sermons over the radio. This new electronic "reach"—coupled with McPherson's flair for drama—drew hordes into her fold. From an evangelistic standpoint, it was the best of times. But as Dickens demonstrated in the immortal opening line of *A Tale of Two Cities*, such heady times rarely come without strings attached. McPherson would soon experience this directly—ostensibly from the afterworld.

Gone with the Tide?

On May 18, 1926, the shocking news broke like a wave crashing against a beach: Nationally famous evangelist Aimee Semple McPherson had gone missing while swimming in the Pacific Ocean near Venice Beach, California. She was presumed drowned. Adding to the tragedy, two of her congregants perished while searching for her in the ocean. Despite continued efforts, no trace of McPherson—or her body—could be found.

From Death Comes Life

Oddly, police received hundreds of tips and leads that suggested that McPherson hadn't drowned at all. One letter—signed "The Avengers"—said that Aimee had been kidnapped and demanded $500,000 for her safe return. One month later, a very alive McPherson emerged near Douglas, Arizona. She claimed she had been kidnapped and held in a shack in Mexico. No such shack, however, could be found.

Even stranger, radio operator and church employee Kenneth G. Ormiston vanished at precisely the same time as McPherson. Gossip spread like wildfire that the married Ormiston and McPherson had in fact shacked up for a month of tawdry, un-Christianlike romance. Charges of perjury and manufacturing evidence were brought against Mcpherson and Ormiston but were inexplicably dropped months later.

Scandal Sells

Despite the scandal, McPherson's church continued to grow by leaps and bounds. McPherson married a third time in 1931, but was divorced once again by 1934. In 1944, Aimee Semple McPherson died from an overdose of sedatives. Her death was ruled accidental, but many believed that McPherson had in fact committed suicide. Whatever the cause of her death, the woman of faith who faltered at love left behind a strong legacy. By the end of the 20th century, the church she founded boasted more than two million members worldwide.

Marilyn Monroe

Marilyn Monroe was—and still is—one of the sexiest women ever to grace the silver screen. But, like so many of her fellow movie stars, Monroe's deeply troubled personal life often overshadowed her professional achievements. This was especially true when the world learned of her tragic death on August 5, 1962, at age 36.

✳ ✳ ✳ ✳

Troubled Beginnings

MARILYN MONROE WAS born Norma Jean Baker on June 1, 1926. Her life was troubled almost from the start; her mother was institutionalized with mental problems, and the man she was told was her father, Edward Mortensen, was killed in a motorcycle accident when she was three. As a result, Norma Jean spent most of her childhood in foster care.

Norma Jean married at 16, then found success as a model, which eventually led to a name change and a brief contract with 20th Century Fox. Her first credited role came in *Dangerous Years* (1947). It was a critical flop, and studio head Darryl F. Zanuck didn't know what to do with this breathy starlet, so her contract was not renewed. However, she later returned and made most of her films for Fox.

Monroe's chaotic personal life made constant news. She married baseball legend Joe DiMaggio in 1954, but their union was tumultuous, and they divorced nine months later. In 1956, she married playwright Arthur Miller, who was nearly 11 years her senior; the marriage lasted until 1961. There are rumors that Monroe was also involved with President John F. Kennedy and his brother Robert as well.

A Hollywood Starlet's Tragic End

In her final months, Monroe was living in a house in the Brentwood section of Los Angeles. On the evening of August 4, she was visited by her psychiatrist, Dr. Ralph Greenson, then she made several phone calls from her bedroom, including one to actor Peter Lawford, a Kennedy family confidante.

Late that night, Monroe's housekeeper, Eunice Murray, noticed a light coming from under the actress's bedroom door, which she thought was odd. When Monroe didn't respond to her knocks, Murray went around to the side of the house and peered through the bedroom window. Monroe looked peculiar, Murray later told police, so she called Greenson, who broke into Monroe's bedroom and found her on the bed unconscious. Greenson then called Monroe's personal physician, Dr. Hyman Engelberg, who pronounced the actress dead. It was then that the police were notified.

Los Angeles Police Sgt. Jack Clemmons was the first on the scene. He said he found Monroe naked and facedown on her bed with an empty bottle of sleeping pills nearby. A variety of other pill bottles littered the nightstand.

Monroe's body was taken to Westwood Village Mortuary then transferred to the county morgue, and her house was sealed and placed under guard. Los Angeles Deputy Medical Examiner Dr. Thomas T. Noguchi performed Monroe's autopsy and concluded in his official report that the actress had died from an overdose of Nembutol (a sleeping pill) and chloral hydrate (a mild sedative) and ruled that it was a "probable suicide."

Suicide, Murder, or Accidental Overdose?

Over the years, conspiracy theorists have had a field day with Monroe's death because of numerous inconsistencies between Noguchi's autopsy report and the evidence at the scene, as well as in the stories of those who were at the scene. Some conspiracy theorists believe that Monroe was murdered and that her death was made to look like a suicide. By whom remains a mystery, though the most prevalent theory—unproved by anyone—is that the Kennedy family had her killed to avoid a scandal. However, given Monroe's habit of taking more medication than doctors prescribed, because she thought she had a high tolerance for it, accidental overdose cannot be ruled out.

Today, Marilyn Monroe remains as popular as ever. Her image graces a wide variety of products worldwide, and the resulting royalties generate nearly a million dollars per year. Even in death, Hollywood's most famous blonde goddess continues to bask in the bright spotlight of fame.

Curse of the (Polish) Mummy

In 1973, a group of research scientists entered the tomb of King Casimir IV, a member of the Jagiellon dynasty that once ruled throughout central Europe. Within weeks of entering the tomb, only two scientists remained alive.

✳   ✳   ✳   ✳

The Jagiellon Curse

INDIANA JONES DIDN'T have it easy, but as archaeologist work hazards go, there are worse fates than snake pits and big rolling boulders. For example, there are strains of mold fungi that eat your body from the inside out. This was the inauspicious fate of several scientists who opened a tomb that had been shut for centuries, thereby unleashing a powerful mummy's curse—or, more realistically and less fantastically—powerful microorganisms.

The tomb of King Casimir IV of Poland and his wife, Elizabeth of Habsburg, is located in the chapel of Wawel Castle in Krakow, Poland. Casimir served as king for more than 40 years in the 13th century. He left behind 13 children, many of whom went on to positions of great power. In 1973, Cardinal Wojtyla (who later went on to become Pope John Paul II) gave a group of scientists permission to open King Casimir's tomb and examine its contents. Within the tomb, the unlucky group found a heavily rotted wooden coffin— not so surprising, given the box had been decaying for nearly

500 years. However, within a few days, four of the 12 research-ers were dead; six more died soon after.

Killer Fungi

While sensationalists blamed the tragedy on a mummy's curse, the scientific-minded questioned whether the sudden deaths were related to the icky molds, fungi, and parasites that would linger in a room that had been sealed off for centuries. This was precisely the suspicion of Dr. Boleslaw Smyk, one of the two surviving scientists. He set out to discover what exactly had killed his colleagues, and he came up with three species of fungi mold that had lingered in King Casimir's tomb: *Aspergillus flavus*, *Penicillim rubrum*, and *Penicillim rugulosum*.

Not a Mummy, But No Less Scary

These are not the kindest of specimens. *Aspergillus flavus* is toxic to the liver, while *Penicillim rubrum* causes, among a host of other afflictions, pulmonary emphysema. These toxins grow on decaying wood and lime mortar, both of which were in Casimir's tomb. The toxins remained in the tomb in the form of mold spores, which can survive for thousands of years in closed environments. It is likely the researchers breathed in the spores immediately upon entering the coffin, since the sud-den flow of fresh air into a closed tomb would blow the spores about. Toxic spores that are inhaled in this fashion can lead to organ failure and death in a very short time.

It's therefore unsurprising that whisperings of a "mummy's curse" abound. The more famous legend came from the 1922 Egyptian excavation of Pharaoh Tutankhamun's tomb. Lord Carnarvon, one of the main financiers of the King Tut excavation, died a few months after he entered the fungi-laden tomb—the same fungi spores that were identified in King Casimir's tomb were also present in King Tut's. Stories of a mummy's curse followed, although it's unclear whether Carnarvon's death actually was related to his archaeologi-cal pursuits: Carnarvon had a cut on his cheek that became infected weeks after the excavation. He fell ill and eventually died of pneumonia and septicemia from the cut.

Whether or not Carnarvon died of natural causes, rumors of the supernatural took on a life of their own. After news of his death spread, fantastical stories grew regarding the grisly deaths of anyone who had entered King Tut's tomb. Today, even modern archaeologists are warned of their potential exposure to the dreaded Mummy's Curse.

Lying in Wait

There are those who are famous in life, and there are those who are more famous in death—and "Eugene" is certainly the latter. An unclaimed body in the town of Sabina turned a funeral home into a tourist attraction and drew visitors from far and wide.

✳   ✳   ✳   ✳

WHEN MOST PEOPLE die, their remains are quickly taken care of. Not so for the mystery man known as Eugene. After being embalmed, he hung around for nearly 35 years before finally being laid to rest.

Eugene's decades-long saga began and ended in the tiny town of Sabina, about ten miles outside of Wilmington, where he died along the 3C highway on June 6, 1929. Several people reported seeing him walk listlessly through town, as if he were ill, but he didn't stop or ask for help.

A Man Without a Name

No identification was found on his body except for a slip of paper containing an address in Cincinnati. But when the Cincinnati police went to investigate, they found only a vacant lot. Police talked to a man living next door named Eugene Johnson, and thus did the unknown dead man get the moniker Eugene.

All that is known about Eugene is that he was African American, was thought to be between 50 and 80 years old, and died of natural causes. Authorities took him to the Littleton Funeral Home, where he was embalmed. But rather than bury Eugene in a pauper's grave, the funeral home's owners decided to wait on the off chance that his survivors might be located.

On Display

Eugene spent the next three and a half decades at the Littleton Funeral Home, lying in state in a small house in the side yard. As his legend grew, curiosity seekers started dropping by to see the man that no one knew—so many, in fact, that the owners erected a screen across the room to protect him from grabby souvenir seekers. Out of respect, the funeral home provided Eugene with a brand-new suit every year.

Before long, Eugene had become a bona fide tourist attraction. Buses passing through town would stop by the funeral home so travelers could stretch their legs and take a peek at the "Sabina mummy." On holidays and summer weekends, a line of people waiting to pass by Eugene's resting place would form, which only proves how hungry the citizens of Sabina were for entertainment on a Saturday night.

During the 35 years that Eugene lay in state, an estimated one and a half million people paid their respects—while a million of them, including several celebrities, signed his voluminous guest books. None of the visitors claimed to recognize him.

Eugene sometimes became the victim of pranksters during his years at the Littleton Funeral Home. On a number of occasions he was kidnapped but quickly recovered. Once, members of a fraternity drove him all the way to the Ohio State campus.

Resting in Peace

In 1964, Eugene was finally put to rest. It was evident that no one was going to claim him, and many found the pranks being played on him demeaning and harmful to business. Rather than bury Eugene in Potter's Field, the owners of the funeral home purchased a plot in Sabina Cemetery and paid for his burial expenses, including another brand-new suit.

Only a handful of people attended the service for Eugene on October 21, and employees of the Sabina Cemetery, Spurgeon Vault Company, and Littleton Funeral Home acted as pall-bearers. A local Methodist minister offered a few words and a prayer, and Eugene was—finally—able to rest in peace.

The Mystery of the Missing Comma

Legend implies that a punctuation error sparked one of history's greatest unsolved mysteries: Did Queen Isabella give the order for her husband's death, or was it a misunderstanding?

* * * *

KING EDWARD II of England is primarily remembered for his weakness for certain men and the way he died. He spent most of his life in submission to his alleged lovers, Piers Gaveston and, later, Hugh le Despenser, granting their every wish. When Edward married 12-year-old Princess Isabella of France in 1308, he politely greeted her upon her arrival in England—and then gave her wedding jewelry to Gaveston.

Isabella grew up as a queen accustomed to being pushed aside in favor of her husband's preferred companions. Even after Gaveston was murdered for being a bad influence on the king, Edward did not change, turning his affections to the greedy Despenser, whom the queen loathed and feared. When the opportunity arose for her to negotiate a treaty with her brother, the King of France, she took it, traveling to Paris and refusing to return.

The Queen's Revenge

After nearly 20 years in an unhappy marriage, Isabella had had enough. Along with her lover, Roger Mortimer, she raised an army and led it into England in order to depose her husband. Once the king was in custody, the queen forced him to abdicate the throne to their 14-year-old son, Edward III, and proceeded to send a letter giving orders on how the deposed Edward should be treated in captivity.

Conspiracy or Miscommunication?

Something very important was missing from Isabella's orders. In the letter, she wrote, "Edwardum occidere nolite timere bonum est." Many historians think she intended this to mean, "Do not kill Edward, it is good to fear." However, she neglected to write in a necessary comma. If the comma is inserted in a different place, the letter means "Do not be afraid to kill Edward; it is good." It's clear how Edward's jailers construed the message: Shortly after it was received, several men allegedly murdered Edward in his cell. Who knew that forgetting something as small as a comma could result in the murder of a king?

Back from the Dead

Nothing is certain but death and taxes ... yet sometimes that's not so true. History is riddled with strange tales of people who just weren't content staying dead.

✳ ✳ ✳ ✳

✳ After a major automobile accident in 2007, Venezuelan Carlos Camejo was declared dead. The coroner had just begun the autopsy by cutting into Camejo's face when the man began to bleed. Immediately realizing that the crash victim was still alive, the doctor became even more stunned when Camejo regained consciousness as he was stitching up the incision. "I woke up because the pain was unbearable," Camejo told reporters after his ordeal.

✳ Ann Greene, a young servant in Oxford, England, was convicted of killing her illegitimate newborn child after the baby was stillborn in 1650. After she was hanged, Greene's body was cut down and transported to Oxford University where it was to be used for anatomy classes. As the lesson progressed, Greene began to moan and regained consciousness. The students helped revive her and treated her injuries. Eventually she was given a pardon, gained a level of celebrity, married, and had several children.

* In 1674, Marjorie Erskine died in Chirnside, Scotland, and was buried in a shallow grave by a sexton with less than honorable intentions. Erskine was sent to her eternal rest with some valuable jewelry the sexton was intent on adding to his own collection. After digging up her body, the sexton was trying to cut off her finger to steal her ring when, much to his surprise, she awoke.

* After being found unconscious and sprawled on the floor of her Albany, New York, apartment by paramedics in 1996, Mildred Clarke, 86, was pronounced dead by a coroner. About 90 minutes later an attendant noticed that the body bag containing Clarke was, in fact, moving. Clarke recovered but unfortunately only lived for another week, giving into the stress of age and heart failure.

* When 19th-century Cardinal Somaglia took ill and passed out, he was thought to be dead. Being a high-ranking church official, embalming was begun immediately so he could lie in state, as was customary. As a surgeon began the process by cutting into the cardinal's chest, he noticed that the man's heart was still beating. Somaglia awoke and pushed the knife away. However, the damage was done, and he died from the embalming process.

* Oran was a devout sixth-century monk on Iona, a small island off the coast of Scotland. According to legend, he was buried alive by his own urging to sanctify the island but was dug up three days later and found alive. He told his fellow monks that he had seen heaven and hell and a host of other

sights. "There is no such great wonder in death, nor is hell what it has been described," he claimed as he was pulled from the ground. The head monk, Columba, ordered that he be reburied immediately as a heretic. To this day, when someone in the region broaches an uneasy subject, people will tell the person to "throw mud in the mouth of St. Oran."

* In 1740, 16-year-old William Duell was convicted of rape and murder and sentenced to death by hanging. After his lifeless body was removed from the gallows it was taken to the local college for dissection. His body was stripped and laid out in preparation for the process when a servant who was washing the corpse noticed it was still breathing. After a full recovery, he was returned to prison, but it was decided that instead of being hanged again he would be exiled to the then-prison state of Australia.

* A victim of the horrors of war, three-year-old Lebanese Hussein Belhas had his leg blown off in an Israeli attack in 1996. Declared dead, the boy's body was placed in a morgue freezer, but when attendants returned he was found alive. After he recovered from his injuries, Belhas took a stoic stance on his fate. "I am the boy who died, and then came back to life. This was my destiny," he said.

* In late 1995, Daphne Banks of Cambridgeshire, England, was declared dead. On New Year's Day, 1996, as she lay in the mortuary, an undertaker noticed a vein twitching in her leg. Examining closer, the attendant could hear snoring coming from the body. The 61-year-old Banks was quickly transferred to a local hospital where she made a full recovery.

* As mourners sadly paid their last respects to the Greek Orthodox bishop Nicephorus Glycas on the island of Lesbos in 1896, they were met with quite a shock. Glycas had been lying in state for two days as preparations for his burial were being made. Suddenly, he sat up and looked around at the stunned congregation. "What are you staring at?" he reportedly asked.

* During the 16th century, a young man named Matthew Wall died in the village of Braughing, England. As pallbearers were carrying him to his final resting place, they dropped his coffin after one of them stumbled on a stone. When the coffin crashed to the ground, Wall was revived and went on to live a full life. When he actually did pass away years later, the terms of his will stipulated that Old Man's Day be celebrated in the village every October 2, the anniversary of his return from the dead.

Murder, Inc.

A gun; an ice pick; a rope; these were some of the favorite tools of Albert Anastasia, notorious mob assassin. When he wasn't pulling the trigger himself, this head of Murder, Inc.—the enforcement arm of New York's Five Families Mafia—was giving the orders to kill, beat, extort, and rob on the mob-controlled waterfronts of Brooklyn and Manhattan.

✳   ✳   ✳   ✳

BORN IN ITALY in 1902 as Umberto Anastasio, Anastasia worked as a deck hand before jumping ship in New York, where he built a power base in the longshoremen's union. Murder was his tool to consolidate power. Arrested several times in the 1920s, his trials were often dismissed when witnesses would go missing. It wasn't long before he attracted the attention of mob "brain" Lucky Luciano and subsequently helped whack Joe "the Boss" Masseria in 1931, an act that opened the way for Luciano to achieve national prominence within the organization.

Luciano put Anastasia, Bugsy Siegel, and Meyer Lanksy in charge of what became known as Murder, Inc., the lethal button men of the Brooklyn Mafia. With his quick temper and brutal disposition, Anastasia earned the nickname "Lord High Executioner."

A psychopathic assassin named Abe "Kid Twist" Reles was a

key man of Murder, Inc., but turned prosecution witness when he was arrested in 1940. Reles fingered Anastasia, only to mysteriously "fall" from his hotel room while under police protective custody.

A History of Violence

Anastasia climbed the next rung in the mob ladder by ordering the violent 1951 deaths of the Mangano brothers and ultimately taking over the Mangano family. Eventually, however, he alienated two powerful rivals, Vito Genovese and Meyer Lansky. On October 25, 1957, as Albert Anastasia dozed in a barber's chair at New York's Park Sheraton Hotel, he was riddled by two masked gunmen (possibly Larry and Joe Gallo), who acted on orders from Genovese.

Anastasia had evaded justice for decades, but he couldn't escape the violence he himself cultivated in organized crime.

The Brief Death of Sherlock Holmes

"I am in the middle of the last Holmes story," wrote Sir Arthur Conan Doyle, author of the Sherlock Holmes series of mysteries, to his mother in April 1893, "after which the gentleman vanishes, never to reappear. I am weary of his name." Doyle was wrong—Sherlock Holmes did not die then. It would take several more months for the author to figure out a suitable demise for his world-famous and wildly popular detective. But why kill Holmes at all?

* * * *

It's a Mystery

EVER SINCE HE first burst onto the literary scene in 1887, Holmes had become one of the most popular literary characters of all time. His popularity enabled Doyle to achieve the financial and artistic freedom to pursue whatever creative avenue he chose. However, as the years went by, Doyle began to feel strangled by his own creation.

It seems as if more theories have been advanced about the decision to kill off Holmes, a fictional character, than have been put forward for the demise of an actual person. Some postulate that publishing deadlines were tight, and the pressure of always having to come up with intricate plots was wearing on Doyle and affecting his overall literary output. "The difficulty of the Holmes work," Doyle wrote, "was that every story really needed as clear-cut and original a plot as a longish book would do. One cannot without effort spin plots at such a rate."

Another theory is that he was so busy living the life of a writer and meeting deadlines for Holmes stories that he did not notice the beginnings of an illness in his wife that eventually became tuberculosis of the lungs. "As a doctor, [Doyle] should have recognized her condition long before it developed advanced symptoms," wrote biographer Martin Booth. The speculation is that Doyle felt guilty for overlooking his wife's symptoms and blamed Holmes. Perhaps killing the character was a form of revenge.

Whatever the reason, Doyle had been thinking about killing Holmes for quite some time. Toward the end of 1891, he mentioned to his mother his plans, and she frantically pleaded with him to change his mind. Doyle changed his mind, albeit briefly. "He still lives," he told his mother, "thanks to your entreaties."

Sherlock
Holmes

Fearful Falls

Doyle knew that his creation, the ultimate detective, needed a proper death. "A man like that mustn't die of a pin-prick or influenza," he said. "His end must be violent and intensely dramatic."

In the summer of 1893, Doyle visited Switzerland and told Silas K. Hocking, a cleric and novelist, of his plans to kill Holmes. "Why not bring him out to Switzerland and drop him down a crevasse?" Hocking said.

Doyle laughed, but the conversation stuck with him. During the trip, he visited the famous Reichenbach Falls, and he decided the foaming waters there would be a suitable end for his detective. Doyle then set about writing *The Final Problem*, in which he created the criminal mastermind Professor Moriarty. At the end of the story, the two adversaries, locked in combat, apparently plunge into Reichenbach Falls.

"Killed Holmes," Doyle noted in his diary.

Or so he thought.

A Cry Heard Around the World

The death of Sherlock Holmes unleashed worldwide protest. *The Strand* magazine, publisher of the Holmes stories, lost 20,000 subscriptions. Doyle received thousands of hostile letters. People wore black mourning armbands in London. Even the British royal family was upset.

For eight years, Doyle resisted the pressure to bring back Holmes. Finally, in 1901, he published *The Hound of the Baskervilles*, but set it before Holmes's death. However, the public still wasn't satisfied. In 1903, Doyle relented and published *The Adventure of the Empty House*, which brought Holmes back safe and sound (turns out he never went into the falls at all). Doyle's creation had a life of its own, and he went on to write Holmes stories for another two decades.

Bugsy Siegel's "Screen Test"

When mobster Bugsy Siegel acted out a scene at the behest of actor pal George Raft, the results proved eye-opening. Much to the surprise of all, the gangster could really act. Unfortunately, Siegel never pursued acting, choosing instead to remain on his murderous course. This begs the obvious question: "What if?"

✳ ✳ ✳ ✳

I N THE ANNALS of the underworld, there was perhaps no one more dapper, or more ruthless, than Benjamin "Bugsy" Siegel (1906–1947). Nearly six feet tall, with piercing blue eyes that melted the heart of many a woman, Siegel had movie-star looks and savoir faire that disguised a temperament that could easily be described as hair-triggered. During his hard-lived life, Siegel committed nearly every crime in the book and was implicated by the FBI for more than 30 murders.

Born Benjamin Hymen Siegelbaum, the up-and-coming mobster picked up the nickname "Bugsy" (the slang term *bugs* means "crazy") for his high level of viciousness. Siegel hated the tag, considering it a low-class connection to his hardscrabble youth, and threatened to kill anyone who used it in his presence. Still, the mobster was said to be a natural born charmer who never seemed at a loss for companionship, female or otherwise.

One of Siegel's closest friends was Hollywood actor George Raft, who was known for such memorable films as *Scarface* (1932), *I Stole a Million* (1939), and *They Drive by Night* (1940). The two had both grown up on the gritty streets of New York City's Lower East Side. Throughout their lives, the pair would engage in a form of mutual admiration. For example, Raft's movie career featured many mob-related roles. So, when he needed the proper tough-guy "inspiration," the actor would mimic mannerisms and inflections that he picked up from his real-life mobster pals. Siegel, on the other hand, made no secret of the fact that he was starstruck by Hollywood and sometimes wished that he too had become an actor. He viewed Raft as the Real McCoy in this arena and gave him due respect. Hoping to get ever closer to the Hollywood action, while at the same time expanding his "operations," Siegel moved to California in 1937.

A Natural Born . . . Actor?

In no time, Siegel was hobnobbing with major celebrities even as his deadly business dealings escalated. In 1941, Raft was shooting *Manpower* with the legendary Marlene Dietrich, when Siegel showed up on the set to observe. After watching Raft go through a few takes before heading off to his dressing room, Siegel told his buddy that he could do the scene better. An amused Raft told his friend to go ahead and give it a shot. Over the course of the next few minutes, the smirk would leave Raft's face.

Siegel reenacted Raft's scene perfectly. He had not only memorized the dialogue line for line, but he interpreted Raft's nuanced gestures as well. This was no small feat given the fact that Siegel had absolutely no training as an actor. Raft told Siegel that he just might have what it takes to be an actor.

A Dream Unfulfilled

But such Tinseltown dreams were not to be. Despite his demonstrated talent, moviemakers probably wouldn't have used him. And who could blame them? What if Siegel decided to go "Bugsy" on them for not awarding him a role, for critiquing his performance, or for changing his lines? Temperamental actors are one thing; homicidal ones, quite another.

History shows that Siegel played it fast and loose from that point forward, putting most of his energies into creating the Flamingo Hotel and, along with it, the gaming capital of the world—Las Vegas. Siegel's mob associates from the East Coast put him in charge of construction of the opulent hotel. Siegel envisioned an extravagent hotel and, at least for him, money was no object. But when costs soared to $6 million—four times the original budget—Siegel's associates became concerned.

On June 20, 1947, Siegel's dreams of a life on the silver screen came to an abrupt end when a number of well-placed rounds from an M-1 Carbine sent the Hollywood gangster into the afterworld at age 41. It is believed that Siegel was killed by his own mob associates who were convinced that he was pilfering money from the organization. Siegel's life and grisly end are grand pieces of mob drama that got their due on the silver screen in the 1991 flick *Bugsy*, which starred Warren Beatty as the doomed mobster.

Teresa Halbach's Justice

In 1985, Steven Allan Avery was wrongfully convicted of sexual assault and attempted murder. After 18 years in prison, DNA evidence exonerated him; but two years later he once again found himself in hot water, accused of a heinous murder. But was he the right man this time? Or was he once again facing prison for a crime he didn't commit?

✳ ✳ ✳ ✳

The Budding Photographer

TERESA HALBACH WAS born in 1980 and grew up on a dairy farm in Green Bay, Wisconsin. Described by friends as "outgoing," "brave," and "spontaneous," Halbach took the opportunity to see some of the world during her college years, traveling to Spain, Mexico, and Australia, where she learned to scuba dive. After graduating from the University of Wisconsin, Halbach moved back to Green Bay to be near her parents, and began working as a photographer.

According to one of Halbach's old boyfriends, "photography was her life." But getting started in the photography business meant taking some odd jobs to get a foot in the door. Halbach went to work for *Auto Trader* magazine, photographing cars to be listed for sale. On October 31, 2005, Halbach had three appointments booked for the magazine, the last being at Avery's Auto Salvage, where she met with Steven Avery.

A Troubled and Difficult Life

Steven Avery was born in 1962 in Manitowoc County, Wisconsin. His mother once said that he attended a school for "slower kids," and school records showed that his intelligence quotient was somewhere around 70. He began running into trouble at an early age, spending 10 months in prison when he was 18 for breaking into a bar. He was jailed again in 1982, after two friends came forward and said that Avery poured gasoline on his cat and threw it in a bonfire, something he later said he did because he was "young and stupid."

So perhaps it seemed only a matter of time before he was accused of something more serious, which is exactly what happened in 1985. On July 29 that year, a woman jogging alone on the shores of Lake Michigan in Two Rivers, Wisconsin, was attacked, sexually assaulted, and beaten. When the woman later described her attacker, police thought he sounded a lot like Steven Avery. And when shown a picture of Avery, the woman identified him as her attacker.

But Avery insisted that he'd been 40 miles away in Green Bay at the time of the attack, a claim that he backed up with a time-stamped store receipt and the testimony of 16 eyewitnesses. However, this was not enough evidence to convince a jury, and Avery was convicted and sentenced to 32 years in prison. After 18 years of claiming his innocence, DNA evidence, along with the confession of the real rapist, finally freed Avery in 2003. Ready to get on with his life, he moved to Gibson, Wisconsin, where his family has operated a salvage yard since 1965.

The Search for Teresa

It was the salvage yard where Halbach met up with Avery on Halloween, her last stop of the day. Avery was selling his sister's minivan, and wanted to list it on *Auto Trader*. The young photographer arrived in her dark-green Toyota RAV4, ready to snap pictures of Avery's car. But later that day, it became evident that something was wrong: Halbach never returned home.

Search parties were soon sent out, with one group searching the area that Halbach was last known to have visited: Avery's Auto Salvage. On November 5, her car was found on the property, covered with tree branches and plywood, the license plates removed. Inside, police discovered bloodstains, which prompted an immediate search of the salvage yard. By the next day, 200 officers were on the property, combing through the yard, garage, and the trailer where Avery lived.

Within days, investigators had found the missing license plates from Halbach's car hidden in an abandoned station wagon on the property. They also found a spare key to her RAV4 in Avery's bedroom. And most disturbing of all, charred human bones were discovered in a burn pit near his trailer. When the blood from Halbach's car was tested, the DNA matched Avery. It seemed clear that Avery had something to do with Halbach's disappearance, and on November 15, he was arrested for murder.

An Open and Shut Case?

In a January 17, 2006, hearing, Avery pled not guilty. Two days later, an FBI crime lab announced that the charred bone fragments, were, in fact, from Halbach, putting to rest any question that she might still be alive. And on March 3, Avery's nephew, Brendan Dassey, confessed to helping his uncle kill Halbach and dispose of her body. It seemed that prosecutors had an open and shut case.

But Avery's lawyers weren't so sure. First, Dassey recanted his confession, saying he'd been coerced. Then there was the matter of the blood in Halbach's car: Avery's lawyers discovered an unsealed evidence box which contained a vial of Avery's blood collected in 1996 which appeared to have a puncture hole in the stopper. Could Avery's blood have been planted in the RAV4? An FBI crime technician said the blood in the car lacked a specific acid that would've been used to preserve the blood in the vial, but an expert for the defense said the test could be inconclusive. And what about the key that was found in Avery's bedroom? Defense lawyers contended that it was planted by the two police officers who claimed to have found it.

But all of this raises the question: Why would investigators want to pin a murder on Avery if he wasn't guilty? After he was released from prison in 2003, Avery filed a $36 million wrongful conviction lawsuit against Manitowoc County. His lawyers allege that sheriff's officers were so angry about the lawsuit that they planted evidence to make Avery seem guilty.

One thing is certain: No matter who is guilty, Teresa Halbach was the victim of a terrible crime and deserves justice. If Steven Avery is not responsible, who is? Why were her bones found on Avery's property? Since many of Avery's family members also worked at the salvage yard, could one of his relatives be the culprit? Whatever the answer is, investigators owe it to Halbach to see her story through to the truthful end.

The Strange Case of the Somerton Man

Somerton Park Beach is just south of Adelaide, South Australia. Known for its clear water and white sand, the beach also features plenty of playgrounds and picnic areas for families to enjoy. It seems like the perfect place for some weekend relaxation; but the beach is also known for a more morbid—and very mysterious— event that occurred in 1948.

✳   ✳   ✳   ✳

The Body on the Beach

IN THE SOUTHERN Hemisphere, summer arrives in December, just as the north is bundling up in the cold and snow. The evening of November 30, 1948, was warm and balmy in Adelaide, perfect for a stroll on Somerton Beach.

Two couples who took walks on the beach that night noticed the same strange scenario: A well-dressed man, wearing a suit and newly polished shoes, lounging in the sand with his out-stretched legs crossed and his head propped against a seawall. One couple noticed the man moving an extended arm, and assumed he was smoking a cigarette. The other couple thought he was asleep, as he sat motionless, his face surrounded by buzzing mosquitoes.

It was not until the next morning that the man was found to be dead. He was still in the same position the witnesses had seen him in the previous night, propped against the seawall with his legs outstretched and crossed. There was also a half-smoked cigarette lying on his collar, as if it had fallen out of his mouth as he sat there.

The man's body was transported to the Royal Adelaide Hospital, where his time of death was determined to be no earlier than 2 A.M. In his pockets, the man was carrying several odds and ends, but noticeably absent was a wallet or any form of identification. Even the labels on the man's clothes had been snipped away, and one previously torn pocket had been neatly repaired with an unusual orange thread.

Strange Clues . . . Yet No Answers

An autopsy revealed some strange findings. The man's spleen was three times the normal size, and his liver was congested with blood. His stomach also contained blood, along with the remnants of his last meal. These clues led pathologists to believe that the man had been poisoned, but tests showed zero traces of any poison in the food, the man's blood, or in his organs. Although pathologists agreed that the man's death could not have been natural, there was no conclusive evidence of the actual cause. It was not even clear if the death had been a murder, or a suicide.

As the investigation wore on, it became evident that identifying the man would not be simple. Police circulated a set of the man's fingerprints, not only throughout Australia, but throughout the English-speaking world, with no results. The man's mortuary photo was published in the paper, and scores of people who thought he looked familiar were brought to the mortuary to view the body. But not one person could name the man they saw there. Families of missing persons were brought in, but still the man remained unidentified.

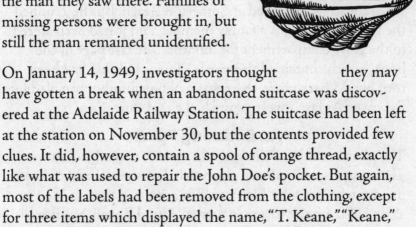

On January 14, 1949, investigators thought they may have gotten a break when an abandoned suitcase was discovered at the Adelaide Railway Station. The suitcase had been left at the station on November 30, but the contents provided few clues. It did, however, contain a spool of orange thread, exactly like what was used to repair the John Doe's pocket. But again, most of the labels had been removed from the clothing, except for three items which displayed the name, "T. Keane," "Keane," and "Kean." But a search for the name concluded that no one named "T. Keane" had been reported missing. As it seemed like meticulous care had been taken to conceal the man's identity, police theorized that the name was left on the items because it was not, in fact, the name of the man.

The Hidden Pocket

Then, just when investigators thought that things couldn't get more mysterious, the case got stranger. Four months after the discovery of the body, police brought in an expert, a professor of pathology at the University of Adelaide named John Cleland. Cleland made a bizarre discovery. In a small pocket in the trousers of the man's waistband that had been overlooked by previous investigators, he found a tiny piece of rolled up paper. The scrap of paper contained two words in an elaborate script: Tamam Shud.

The phrase, Persian for "it is ended," were the last words from a book of poetry—the Rubaiyat of Omar Khayyam. The 12th-century book had become quite popular in Australia during World War II, and the police launched a search for the specific book that the scrap of paper came from. On July 23, after seeing a newspaper article about the book search, a man showed up at the police station with a copy of the book. He said that it had mysteriously shown up in his car the previous December when the car was parked at Somerton Beach. But he assumed the book belonged to a family member, and it had been stored in the glove compartment for months. The last page of the book, which contained the words "Tamam Shud," had been torn out. What's more, there was a phone number penciled into the cover. At last, investigators had a real clue.

An Enduring Puzzle

The phone number belonged to a woman named Jessica Thompson who lived near the beach, but she claimed to have no idea who the John Doe was. She admitted that she'd given a copy of the book to a man named Alfred Boxall, but Boxall was alive and well and still owned his copy. Things took an even more bizarre turn when police discovered a faint impression of letters written on the rear cover of the book. Under ultra-violet light, they could make out five lines of jumbled letters, presumed to be a code of some sort. But no one, even the Australian Naval Intelligence, was able to crack the strange cypher. The police soon ran out of leads, and the case grew cold.

Today, amateur sleuths continue to look into the strange case of the Somerton Man. Many believe he was a spy who was murdered for what he knew. Some people, including Jessica Thompson's daughter, are convinced that Thompson knew his identity, and that she and Boxall knew far more than they ever admitted. While the discovery of the paper bearing "Tamam Shud"—"it is ended"—hint at suicide, the final coroner's report concluded that the man's cause of death, and his identity, were a mystery.

What Happened to Jimmy Hoffa?

James Riddle Hoffa was born on February 14, 1913, in Brazil, Indiana, but his family moved to Detroit in 1924. It was here that a teenaged Hoffa became active in unions, after working for a grocery chain that paid poorly and offered substandard conditions for its employees. Hoffa eventually became a powerful figure in the Teamsters union, and he spent the rest of his life working with unions in Detroit. At least, that's the assumption. In truth, no one knows where Hoffa spent the end of his life, because in 1975, he simply disappeared.

✳ ✳ ✳ ✳

A Poor Career Choice

IN A 2004 EPISODE of the popular Discovery Channel show *MythBusters*, the show's hosts, Adam Savage and Jamie Hyneman, traveled to Giants Stadium in East Rutherford, New Jersey, for a reason that had nothing to do with football. The curious television hosts were exploring an oft-told urban legend claiming that the body of Jimmy Hoffa had been encased in concrete and buried in the end zone of the stadium. Using ground-penetrating radar, Savage and Hyneman searched the field for anything unusual beneath the surface, but ultimately found nothing. Their findings were later confirmed when Giants Stadium was demolished to make way for a new sports complex in 2010.

The *MythBusters* search was just one of many investigations into Hoffa's disappearance, which is rife with unknowns. But here's what we do know: Hoffa began to rise to power in the International Brotherhood of

Teamsters (IBT) union in the 1940s, eventually becoming president of the IBT in 1957. While it seems like a respectable career path, the union was heavily influenced by organized crime, and Hoffa spent much of his time with the IBT making deals and arrangements with gangsters to strengthen and expand its power in the region.

By the 1960s, Hoffa's corrupt dealings began to catch up with him, and in 1967, he was sentenced to 13 years in prison for bribery and fraud.

A Struggle to Regain Power

Hoffa's sentence was commuted by President Richard Nixon in 1971, under the condition that he not seek "direct or indirect management of any labor organization" until 1980. But, with newfound freedom and a thirst for the power he once had, Hoffa ignored this term. Within two years, he was once again vying for presidency of the IBT.

But if Hoffa thought he'd be welcomed back with open arms, he was wrong. His attempts to regain power were met with strong resistance, not only by IBT members, but also many of the gangsters he had once worked with. On July 30, 1975, Hoffa was invited to attend a "peace meeting" between him and two of his organized crime contacts, Anthony Provenzano and Anthony Giacalone, presumably to smooth out tensions between the groups.

The Meeting, the Mob, and the Mystery

Several witnesses saw Hoffa at the location of the meeting, which was set for 2:00 P.M. in the afternoon. At 2:15 P.M., he called his wife from a pay phone to impatiently say that Provenzano and Giacalone hadn't shown up yet. What happened next has been the subject of countless speculation. Hoffa simply vanished, leaving behind his unlocked car and very few other clues. Provenzano and Giacalone denied ever setting up a meeting, and both had alibis that placed them away from the meeting location that afternoon.

Many theories have circulated about Hoffa's fate, but he was officially declared legally dead in 1982. Over the years, various Teamsters and mobsters have alleged to "know the truth" about what happened to him, but none of these claims have panned out. The FBI has investigated scores of tips, searching for traces of Hoffa in the homes of gangsters, backyard sheds, horse farms, landfills, and even the Florida Everglades. A particularly creative theory posits that Hoffa's body was dismembered and the pieces were added to steel in a Detroit auto factory, which were then exported to Japan. The real story is probably much more mundane. But until we know for sure, the mysterious fate of Jimmy Hoffa will no doubt continue to inspire macabre tales.

Honoring the Nameless

Occupying land that once belonged to the adopted grandson of George Washington, Arlington National Cemetery spans 624 acres of hillside on the Potomac River. The cemetery is the final resting place for hundreds of thousands of veterans and military personnel, as well as presidents, Supreme Court justices, and other public servants. But no grave in this hallowed location is more frequently visited than one that marks the location of those who are unknown.

✳   ✳   ✳   ✳

A Place for Remembrance

IN 1920, THE Memorial Amphitheater at Arlington National Cemetery was dedicated, giving the public a place to honor fallen service members. The next year, on March 4, Congress gave the go-ahead for the burial of an unidentified American soldier at the location. U.S. Army Sgt. Edward F. Younger, who was wounded in combat during World War I and awarded the Distinguished Service Medal, was tasked with selecting a soldier to receive the honor. In order for the selection to be truly random and unbiased, four different unknown service members were exhumed from four different WWI American

cemeteries in France. Their four identical caskets were then lined up in front of Younger, and he placed a bouquet of white roses on the casket third from the left, signifying his choice.

The unknown soldier was transported back to the United States, where the body lay in state in the Capitol rotunda until November 10, 1921. On Armistice Day—now known as Veteran's Day—the unknown soldier was escorted to the cemetery by President Warren G. Harding, Vice President Calvin Coolidge, members of Congress and the Supreme Court, and military personnel. The soldier was awarded the Medal of Honor and the Distinguished Service Cross at a ceremony, and then interred into the crypt.

The Old Guard

The location of the tomb—which is now commonly known as the Tomb of the Unknown Soldier but has no official name—quickly became a place of respect and reflection for many people, who considered the site a symbol of the sacrifices made for our country. But it also attracted curious tourists and hawkers hoping to cash in on the influx of visitors, leading some to worry that the sacred site could succumb to vandals. So in 1926, Congress appointed military guards to protect the tomb during daylight hours, and on July 2, 1937, the Army began a 24-hour watch over the tomb. On April 6, 1948, this duty was taken over by soldiers from the 3rd U.S. Infantry Regiment, known as "The Old Guard," and are now referred to as Tomb Guards or Sentinels. The Sentinels keep watch over the tomb, 24 hours a day, seven days a week, 365 days a year, in every kind of weather.

Three More Brought Home, and One Mystery Solved

After the Korean War, the process began to inter unknown soldiers from that war as well as World War II. Eighteen unidentified soldiers were exhumed from North Africa, Europe, the Philippines, and Hawaii to represent those who died during World War II, with the final choice made by Medal of Honor recipient Navy Hospitalman 1st Class William R. Charette. The candidates for the Korean War were exhumed from the National Cemetery of the Pacific in Honolulu, and one solider was chosen by Army Master Sgt. Ned Lyle. The soldiers chosen by Charette and Lyle were transported to Washington, D.C., and on May 30, 1958—the official date of Memorial Day that year—the two were laid to rest beside their World War I counterpart.

Interestingly, when the process was repeated after the Vietnam War, the unknown soldier, chosen by U.S. Marine Corps Sgt. Maj. Allan Jay Kellogg, Jr., did not remain unknown for long. Thanks to DNA testing, in 1998 the remains were discovered to be those of Air Force 1st Lt. Michael Joseph Blassie, whose family requested he be reinterred at Jefferson Barracks National Cemetery in St. Louis, Missouri. The crypt for a Vietnam unknown has remained empty, inscribed with the words, "Honoring and Keeping Faith with America's Missing Servicemen, 1958–1975."

The Death of the Prime Minister

As August 14 rolled into August 15 in 1947, India and Pakistan became two separate countries, while simultaneously gaining independence from the British Empire. Since that day, the two countries have been tense neighbors, facing off in four wars and numerous other conflicts. But in 1966, the day after signing a peace treaty, India would be faced with a mysterious—and possibly sinister—circumstance that is still in question today.

✳ ✳ ✳ ✳

Gandhi's Protégé

THE FAMOUS MAHATMA Gandhi, whose nonviolent resistance movement helped lead India to independence, was born on October 2, 1869. Thirty-five years later, on the same date, Lal Bahadur Shastri was born in Ramnagar, in the United Provinces of Agra and Oudh (now known as Uttar Pradesh). As a teenager, Srivastava became interested in the independence movement and was so drawn to Gandhi's teachings that he dropped out of school and began to volunteer with the Indian National Congress party, which was the first nationalist movement to arise in the British Empire.

Leaders within the Congress party recognized that young people were leaving school to join the cause, so, to emphasize the importance of continuing education, they established the Kashi Vidyapith, an institute of higher learning that emphasized Indian heritage and nationalism. Srivastava graduated from the school in 1925 with a degree in philosophy and ethics, which awarded him the title of "Shastri," or "scholar." For the rest of his life, the title would be a part of his name.

The Rallying Cry

Shastri spent years working toward the goal of an independent India. After this goal was finally realized in 1947, Shastri began climbing the political ranks in his newly independent country, first as a parliamentary secretary, then as a cabinet minister under Prime Minister Jawaharlal Nehru, and lastly, after Nehru's death in 1964, prime minister.

Shastri became a popular leader, maintaining many of the policies put in place by his predecessor. But his greatest accomplishment would be leading India during the Indo-Pakistani War of 1965. On October 19 of that year, he gave a stirring speech in which he coined the slogan "Jai Jawan, Jai Kisan" (hail the soldier, hail the farmer), which became a rallying cry for the country.

Although there had been a United Nations-mandated ceasefire on September 23, 1965, the war did not officially end until early the following year. On January 10, 1966, Shastri traveled to Tashkent in the former USSR (now Uzbekistan) to meet with Pakistani president Ayub Khan and sign a peace agreement, known as the Tashkent Declaration.

Questions and Conspiracies

What happened next has been the subject of conspiracy theories for decades. After signing the peace treaty, Shastri retired to the room provided to him by his Russian hosts, had dinner and a glass of milk, then retired to bed. At around 1:25 A.M., he woke up in a coughing fit and stumbled to another room to ask his staff to find his personal physician. But by the time Dr. R.N. Chugh arrived, it was already too late. Seemingly suffering from a massive heart attack, there was nothing that could be done for the prime minister, and he died within minutes.

Almost immediately, the official cause of death—heart attack—was questioned. Shastri's wife, Lalita, was convinced that he was poisoned, and she and Shastri's mother both questioned "blue patches" and "cuts" they claimed to see on his body. Lalita later published a book of poetry in which she described the version of events as she believed they happened.

Making the situation even more mysterious was the fact that no autopsy was performed on the body, the Indian government released no information about the prime minister's death, and the media was kept silent. There's also the matter of the decided lack of records and documentation concerning Shastri's death. The Prime Minister's Office is in possession of one classified document, which it has repeatedly refused to declassify, claiming its release would "harm national interest."

After so many decades, it would be reasonable to assume that the Indian government could release any information it had on Shastri's death. The fact that they won't leads many to assume they have something to hide. Until there is indisputable evidence that Shastri died of a heart attack, the conspiracy theories will continue.

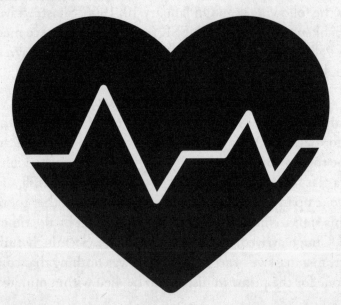

✳ CHAPTER 2

MYSTERIOUS DISAPPEARANCES

D. B. Cooper: Man of Mystery

D. B. Cooper is perhaps the most famous criminal alias since Jack the Ripper. Although the fate of the infamous hijacker remains a mystery, the origins of the nom de crime "D. B. Cooper" is a matter that's easier to solve.

✳ ✳ ✳ ✳

The Crime

AT PORTLAND (OREGON) International Airport the night before Thanksgiving in 1971, a man in a business suit, reportedly in his mid-40s, boarded Northwest Orient Airlines flight 305 bound for Seattle, Washington. He had booked his seat under the name Dan Cooper. Once the flight was airborne, Cooper informed a flight attendant that his briefcase contained an explosive device. In the days before thorough baggage inspection was standard procedure at airports, this was a viable threat. The flight attendant relayed the information to the pilots, who immediately put the plane into a holding pattern so that Cooper could communicate his demands to FBI agents on the ground.

When the Boeing 727 landed at Seattle-Tacoma Airport, the other passengers were released in exchange for $200,000 in unmarked $20 bills and two sets of parachutes. FBI agents photographed each bill before handing over the ransom and then scrambled a fighter plane to follow the passenger craft when Cooper demanded that it take off for Mexico City via Reno, Nevada. At 10,000 feet, Cooper lowered the aft stairs of the aircraft and, with the ransom money strapped to his chest, parachuted into the night, still dressed in his business suit. The pilot noted the area as being near the Lewis River, 25 miles north of Portland, somewhere over the Cascade Mountains.

The mysterious hijacker was never seen again. The FBI found a number of fingerprints on the plane that didn't match those of the other passengers or members of the crew, but the only real clue that Cooper left behind was his necktie. On February 10, 1980, an eight-year-old boy found $5,800 in decaying $20 bills along the Columbia River, just a few miles northwest of Vancouver, Washington. The serial numbers matched those included in the ransom. Other than that, not a single note of the ransom money has turned up in circulation.

Origins of the Name

The FBI launched a massive hunt for the man who had hijacked Flight 305. This included checking the rap sheets of every known felon with the name Dan Cooper, just in case the hijacker had been stupid enough to use his real name. When Portland agents interviewed a man by the name of D. B. Cooper, the story was picked up by a local reporter. This D. B. Cooper was cleared of any involvement in the case, but the alias stuck and was adopted by the national media.

Who Was Dan Cooper?

Countless books, TV shows, and even a movie have attempted to answer this question. The FBI has investigated some 10,000 people, dozens of whom had at some point confessed to family or friends that they were the real D. B. Cooper. In October 2007, the FBI announced that it had finally obtained a partial DNA profile of Cooper with evidence lifted from the tie he left on the plane. This has helped rule out many of those suspected of (or who have confessed to) the hijacking.

The author of one book about the case, a retired FBI agent, offered a $100,000 reward for just one of the bills from the ransom money. He's never had to pay out. Officially, the FBI does not believe that Cooper survived the jump. However, no evidence of his body or the bright yellow and red parachute he used to make the jump has ever been found. On December 31, 2007, more than 36 years after the man forever known as D. B. Cooper disappeared into the night sky, the FBI revived the case by publishing never-before-seen sketches of the hijacker and appealing for new witnesses.

Mysterious Disappearances in the Bermuda Triangle

The Bermuda Triangle is an infamous stretch of the Atlantic Ocean bordered by Florida, Bermuda, and Puerto Rico where strange disappearances have occurred throughout history. The Coast Guard doesn't recognize the Triangle or the supernatural explanations for the mysterious disappearances. There are some probable causes for the missing vessels—hurricanes, undersea earthquakes, and magnetic fields that interfere with compasses and other positioning devices. But it's much more interesting to think they were sucked into another dimension, abducted by aliens, or simply vanished into thin air.

✳   ✳   ✳   ✳

Flight 19

ON THE AFTERNOON of December 5, 1945, five Avenger torpedo bombers left the Naval Air Station at Fort Lauderdale, Florida, with Lt. Charles Taylor in command of a crew of 13 student pilots. About 90 minutes into the flight, Taylor radioed the base to say that his compasses weren't working, but he figured he was somewhere over the Florida Keys.

The lieutenant who received the signal told Taylor to fly north toward Miami, as long as he was sure he was actually over the Keys. Although he was an experienced pilot, Taylor got horribly turned around, and the more he tried to get out of the Keys, the further out to sea he and his crew traveled. As night fell, radio signals worsened, until, finally, there was nothing at all from Flight 19. A U.S. Navy investigation found that Taylor's confusion caused the disaster, but his mother convinced them to change the official report to read that the planes went down for "causes unknown." The planes have never been recovered.

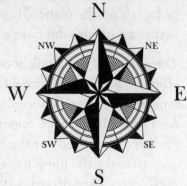

The *Spray*

Joshua Slocum, the first man to sail solo around the world, never should have been lost at sea, but it appears that's exactly what happened. In 1909, the *Spray* left the East Coast of the United States for Venezuela via the Caribbean Sea. Slocum was never heard from or seen again and was declared dead in 1924. The ship was solid, and Slocum was a pro, so nobody knows what happened. Perhaps he was felled by a larger ship or maybe he was taken down by pirates. No one knows for sure that Slocum disappeared within the Triangle's waters, but Bermuda buffs claim Slocum's story as part of the area's mysterious and supernatural legacy.

USS *Cyclops*

As World War I heated up, America went to battle. In 1918, the Cyclops, commanded by Lt. G. W. Worley, was sent to Brazil to refuel Allied ships. With 309 people onboard, the ship left Rio de Janeiro in February and reached Barbados in March. After that, the *Cyclops* was never seen or heard from again. The navy says in its official statement, "The disappearance of this ship has been one of the most baffling mysteries in the annals of the navy, all attempts to locate her having proved unsuccessful. There were no enemy submarines in the western Atlantic at that time, and in December 1918, every effort was made to obtain from German sources information regarding the disappearance of the vessel."

Star Tiger

The *Star Tiger*, commanded by Capt. B. W. McMillan, was flying from England to Bermuda in early 1948. On January 30, McMillan said he expected to arrive in Bermuda at 5:00 A.M., but neither he nor any of the 31 people onboard the *Star Tiger* were ever heard from again. When the Civil Air Ministry launched an investigation, they learned that the S.S. *Troubadour* had reported seeing a low-flying aircraft halfway between Bermuda and the entrance to Delaware Bay. If that aircraft was the *Star Tiger*, it was drastically off course. According to the Civil Air Ministry, the fate of the *Star Tiger* remains unknown.

Star Ariel

On January 17, 1949, a Tudor IV aircraft like the *Star Tiger* left Bermuda with seven crew members and 13 passengers en route to Jamaica. That morning, Capt. J. C. McPhee reported that the flight was going smoothly. Shortly afterward, another more cryptic message came from the captain, when he reported that he was changing his frequency, and then nothing more was heard—ever. More than 60 aircraft and 13,000 people were deployed to look for the *Star Ariel*, but no hint of debris or wreckage was ever found. After the *Star Ariel* disappeared, production of Tudor IVs ceased.

Flight 201

This Cessna left for Fort Lauderdale on March 31, 1984, en route for Bimini Island in the Bahamas, but it never made it. Not quite midway to its destination, the plane slowed its airspeed significantly, but no distress signals came from the plane. Suddenly, the plane dropped from the air into the water, completely vanishing from the radar. A woman on Bimini Island swore she saw a plane plunge into the sea about a mile offshore, but no wreckage has ever been found.

Teignmouth Electron

Who said that the Bermuda Triangle only swallows up ships and planes? Who's to say it can't also make a man go mad? Perhaps that's what happened on the *Teignmouth Electron* in 1969. The Sunday Times Golden Globe race of 1968 left England on October 31 and required each contestant to sail his ship solo. Donald Crowhurst was one of the entrants, but he never made it to the finish line. The *Electron* was found abandoned in the middle of the Bermuda Triangle in July 1969. Logbooks recovered from the ship reveal that Crowhurst was deceiving organizers about his position in the race and going a little bit nutty out there in the big blue ocean. The last entry of his log was dated June 29—it is believed that Crowhurst jumped overboard and drowned himself in the Triangle.

Vanished: The Lost Colony of Roanoke Island

Twenty years before England established its first successful colony in the New World, an entire village of English colonists disappeared in what would later be known as North Carolina. Did these pioneers all perish? Did Native Americans capture them? Did they join a friendly tribe? Could they have left descendants who live among us today?

✳   ✳   ✳   ✳

Timing Is Everything

TALK ABOUT BAD timing. As far as John White was concerned, England couldn't have picked a worse time to go to war. It was November 1587, and White had just arrived in England from the New World. He intended to gather relief supplies and immediately sail back to Roanoke Island, where he had left more than 100 colonists who were running short of food. Unfortunately, the English were gearing up to fight Spain. Every seaworthy ship, including White's, was pressed into naval service. Not a one could be spared for his return voyage to America.

Nobody Home

When John White finally returned to North America three years later, he was dismayed to discover that the colonists he had left behind were nowhere to be found. Instead, he stumbled upon a mystery—one that has never been solved.

The village that White and company had founded in 1587 on Roanoke Island lay completely deserted. Houses had been dismantled (as if someone planned to move them), but the pieces lay in the long grass along with iron tools and farming equipment. A stout stockade made of logs stood empty.

White found no sign of his daughter Eleanor, her husband Ananias, or their daughter Virginia Dare—the first English child born in America. None of the 87 men, 17 women, and 11 children remained. No bodies or obvious gravesites offered clues to their fate. The only clues—if they were clues—that White could find were the letters CRO carved into a tree trunk and the word CROATOAN carved into a log of the abandoned fort.

No Forwarding Address

All White could do was hope that the colonists had been taken in by friendly natives.

Croatoan—also spelled "Croatan"—was the name of a barrier island to the south and also the name of a tribe of Native Americans that lived on that island. Unlike other area tribes, the Croatoans had been friendly to English newcomers, and one of them, Manteo, had traveled to England with earlier explorers and returned to act as interpreter for the Roanoke colony. Had the colonists, with Manteo's help, moved to Croatoan? Were they safe among friends?

White tried to find out, but his timing was rotten once again. He had arrived on the Carolina coast as a hurricane bore down on the region. The storm hit before he could mount a search. His ship was blown past Croatoan Island and out to sea. Although the ship and crew survived the storm and made it back to England, White was stuck again. He tried repeatedly but failed to raise money for another search party.

No one has ever learned the fate of the Roanoke Island colonists, but there are no shortage of theories as to what happened to them. A small sailing vessel and other boats that White had left with them were gone when he returned. It's possible that the colonists used the vessels to travel to another island or to the mainland. White had talked with others before he left about possibly moving the settlement to a more secure location inland. It's even possible that the colonists tired of waiting for White's return and tried to sail back to England. If so, they would have perished at sea. Yet there are at least a few shreds of hearsay evidence that the colonists survived in America.

Rumors of Survivors

In 1607, Captain John Smith and company established the first successful English settlement in North America at Jamestown, Virginia. The colony's secretary, William Strachey, wrote four years later about hearing a report of four English men, two boys, and one young woman who had been sighted south of Jamestown at a settlement of the Eno tribe, where they were being used as slaves. If the report was true, who else could these English have been but Roanoke survivors?

For more than a century after the colonists' disappearance, stories emerged of gray-eyed Native Americans and English-speaking villages in North Carolina and Virginia. In 1709, an English surveyor said members of the Hatteras tribe living on North Carolina's Outer Banks—some of them with light-colored eyes—claimed to be descendants of white people. It's possible that the Hatteras were the same people that the 1587 colonists called Croatoan.

In the intervening centuries, many of the individual tribes of the region have disappeared. Some died out. Others were absorbed into larger groups such as the Tuscarora. One surviving group, the Lumbee, has also been called Croatoan. The Lumbee, who still live in North Carolina, often have Caucasian features. Could they be descendants of Roanoke colonists? Many among the Lumbee dismiss the notion as fanciful, but the tribe has long been thought to be of mixed heritage and has been speaking English so long that none among them know what language preceded it.

Aztalan: A Prehistoric Puzzle

A millennium ago, Wisconsin ruled the north.

✳ ✳ ✳ ✳

A Mysterious Site

AZTALAN IS A fortified settlement of mysterious outsiders who worshiped the sun. The Middle Mississippian culture erected stepped pyramids, may have practiced cannibalism, and enjoyed coast-to-coast trade. Some have linked the Mississippians to the Aztecs and even to the legendary city of Atlantis. All that is truly certain is that they lived at Aztalan for 150 years. Then they disappeared.

Aztalan, near present-day Lake Mills, is now a state park and, in fact, a National Historic Landmark. Still, what happened at Aztalan and the truth about the people who lived there are among the greatest archaeological puzzles in the world.

Aztalan is ancient. During the period when it was settled, sometime between A.D. 1050 and 1100, gunpowder was invented in China. Macbeth ruled Scotland. The Orthodox and Roman Catholic churches split. In America, across the Mississippi from St. Louis in what is now Illinois, there was a strange, 2,000-acre city of earthen pyramids later dubbed "Cahokia." Its population was roughly 20,000—more than London at that time.

Aztalan appears to be the northern outpost of the Cahokia peoples. Because of location, archaeologists call their civilization Middle Mississippian. They are distinct from the Woodland peoples, who were there first and remained afterward. The Mississippians were quite enamored with the sun, and at Cahokia, residents erected wooden solar observatories, similar to Britain's Stonehenge.

Like Cahokia, Aztalan was a truly weird place: 22 acres surrounded by a stockade with 32 watch towers, all made from heavy timbers and then covered with hard clay. Inside, pyramidal mounds stood as high as 16 feet. Outside the fortifications, crops were planted. According to Cahokia experts, the Mississippians are the ones who introduced corn to North America.

Today, Aztalan looks much different than it did at its peak. The mounds remain, and part of the stockade has been rebuilt. Also, the Friends of Aztalan group is trying to recreate antique agriculture with a small garden of gourds, squash, sunflowers, and an early type of corn, all planted just as the Mississippians would have.

In addition to vegetables, the Mississippian diet may have included some more interesting dishes—namely human flesh. At Cahokia there's evidence of human sacrifice, and since the time of Aztalan's discovery by whites in 1836, it has been thought that its residents practiced at least some sort of canni-balism. But science and interpretations change with time. There is speculation that the so-called "cannibalism" could have simply been a ceremonial or funerary practice that had nothing to do with eating human flesh.

Gone Without a Trace

Another puzzle is why the Mississippians suddenly vanished from the Midwest sometime between A.D. 1200 and 1300. Author Frank Joseph has taken the folklore of three continents and made a case linking Atlantis, Aztalan, and the Aztecs in his books, *The Lost Pyramids of Rock Lake* and *Atlantis in Wisconsin*. Joseph's theory is that the people of Atlantis founded Cahokia and Aztalan, mined copper, cast it into ingots, and shipped it back, fueling Europe's Bronze Age. After a cataclysm destroyed their Mediterranean island empire, lead-erless survivors in the Wisconsin settlement migrated south. They created a new Aztalan in Mexico and became the Aztecs.

The Aztecs themselves referred to their far-away, long-ago homeland—wherever it was—as "Aztlan." However, scholars deny that residents of Aztalan ever used that name. It was merely a fanciful label applied by European settlers.

Joseph's evidence is circumstantial but intriguing. One of the great mysteries of Europe's Bronze Age is where all the neces-sary copper came from (bronze is made of copper and tin). Known low-grade deposits in Great Britain and Spain would have been quickly exhausted. Yet Lake Superior's shores have, and had, the only known workable virgin, native copper depos-its in the world.

The Mississippians certainly knew that—they mined Michigan's Upper Peninsula. Meanwhile, according to legend, Atlantis was reigning supreme, enjoying great wealth derived from its trade throughout the known world of precious met-als, especially copper. The Lake Superior mines closed precisely when Europe's Bronze Age ended. Coincidentally, or perhaps not, it was at this time that Atlantis supposedly sank and disappeared forever.

Many more answers about the Mississippian culture are yet be found. According to the Cahokia Mounds Museum Society, archaeologists have explored only 1 percent of the site.

Could the decisive link to Atlantis or the Aztecs still be buried beneath the grounds of Cahokia or Aztalan? Only time will tell.

* As the name suggests, Mississippian culture spanned the length of the Mississippi River, including areas in what are now the states of Mississippi, Georgia, Alabama, Missouri, Arkansas, Illinois, Indiana, Kentucky, Ohio, Wisconsin, and Minnesota.

* It must have been desirable real estate! While Aztalan is usually considered to be a Mississippian settlement, there are many artifacts at the site from other groups of people that predate their arrival.

* For many years before it was studied and preserved, the area of Aztalan was plowed for farming; pottery and other artifacts were carted away by souvenir hunters.

* Aztalan became a National Historic Landmark in 1964 and was added to the National Register of Historic Places in 1966.

* There is speculation that some of the mounds at Aztalan could have been used for astronomical purposes.

* It is believed that Aztalan was a planned community with spaces for the general public, ceremonial locations, residential areas, and sections designated for elite individuals.

* Based on the artifacts unearthed at Aztalan, it appears that the people living there were skilled at farming, hunting, and fishing.

The Philadelphia Experiment

In 1943, the Navy destroyer USS Eldridge *reportedly vanished, teleported from a dock in Pennsylvania to one in Virginia, and then rematerialized—all as part of a top-secret military experiment. Is there any fact to this fiction?*

✳ ✳ ✳ ✳

The Genesis of a Myth

THE STORY OF the Philadelphia Experiment began with the scribbled annotations of a crazed genius, Carlos Allende, who in 1956 read *The Case for the UFO,* by science enthusiast Morris K. Jessup. Allende wrote chaotic annotations in his copy of the book, claiming, among other things, to know the answers to all the scientific and mathematical questions that Jessup's book touched upon. Jessup's interests included the possible military applications of electromagnetism, antigravity, and Einstein's Unified Field Theory.

Allende wrote two letters to Jessup, warning him that the government had already put Einstein's ideas to dangerous use. According to Allende, at some unspecified date in October 1943, he was serving aboard a merchant ship when he witnessed a disturbing naval experiment. The USS *Eldridge* disappeared, teleported from Philadelphia, Pennsylvania, to Norfolk, Virginia, and then reappeared in a matter of minutes. The men onboard the ship allegedly phased in and out of visibility or lost their minds and jumped overboard, and a few of them disappeared forever. This strange activity was part

of an apparently successful military experiment to render ships invisible.

The Navy Gets Involved

Allende could not provide Jessup with any evidence for these claims, so Jessup stopped the correspondence. But in 1956, Jessup was summoned to Washington, D.C., by the Office of Naval Research, which had received Allende's annotated copy of Jessup's book and wanted to know about Allende's claims and his written comments. Shortly thereafter, Varo Corporation, a private group that does research for the military, published the annotated book, along with the letters Allende had sent to Jessup. The Navy has consistently denied Allende's claims about teleporting ships, and the impetus for publishing Allende's annotations is unclear. Morris Jessup committed suicide in 1959, leading some conspiracy theorists to claim that the government had him murdered for knowing too much about the experiments.

The Fact Within the Fiction

It is not certain when Allende's story was deemed the "Philadelphia Experiment," but over time, sensationalist books and movies have touted it as such. The date of the ship's disappearance is usually cited as October 28, though Allende himself cannot verify the date nor identify other witnesses. However, the inspiration behind Allende's claims is not a complete mystery.

In 1943, the Navy was in fact conducting experiments, some of which were surely top secret, and sometimes they involved research into the applications of some of Einstein's theories. The Navy had no idea how to make ships invisible, but it *did* want to make ships "invisible"—i.e., undetectable—to enemy magnetic torpedoes. Experiments such as these involved wrapping large cables around Navy vessels and pumping them with electricity in order to descramble their magnetic signatures.

The Anasazi

Across the deserts and mesas of the region known as the Four Corners, where Arizona, New Mexico, Colorado, and Utah meet, backcountry hikers and motoring tourists can easily spot reminders of an ancient people.

✳   ✳   ✳   ✳

Living in Ancient Times

FROM THE TOWERING stone structures at Chaco Culture National Historical Park to cliff dwellings at Mesa Verde National Park to the ubiquitous scatters of broken pottery and stone tools, these remains tell the story of a culture that spread out across the arid Southwest during ancient times. The Anasazi are believed to have lived in the region from about A.D. 1 through A.D. 1300 (though the exact beginning of the culture is difficult to determine because there is no particular defining event). In their everyday lives, they created black-on-white pottery styles that distinguish subregions within the culture, traded with neighboring cultures (including those to the south in Central America), and built ceremonial structures called kivas, which were used for religious or communal purposes.

The Exodus Explained

Spanish conquistadors exploring the Southwest noted the abandoned cliff dwellings and ruined plazas, and archaeologists today still try to understand what might have caused the Anasazi to move from their homes and villages throughout the region. Over time, researchers have posed a number of theories, including the idea that the Anasazi were driven from their villages by hostile nomads, such as those from the Apache or Ute tribes. Others believe that the Anasazi fought among themselves, causing a drastic reduction in their populations, and a few extraterrestrial-minded theorists have suggested that the Anasazi civilization was destroyed by aliens. Today, the prevalent hypothesis among scientists is that a long-term drought affected the area, destroying agricultural fields and forcing people to abandon their largest villages. Scientists and archaeologists have worked together to reconstruct the region's climate data and compare it with material that has been excavated. Based on their findings, many agree that some combination of environmental and cultural factors caused the dispersal of the Anasazi from the large-scale ruins seen throughout the landscape today.

Their Journey

Although many writers—of fiction and nonfiction alike—romanticize the Anasazi as a people who mysteriously disappeared from the region, they did not actually disappear. Those living in large ancient villages and cultural centers did indeed disperse, but the people themselves did not simply disappear. Today, descendants of the Anasazi can be found living throughout New Mexico and Arizona. The Hopi tribe in northern Arizona, as well as those living in approximately 20 pueblos in New Mexico, are the modern-day descendants of the Anasazi. The Pueblos in New Mexico whose modern inhabitants consider the Anasazi their ancestors include: Acoma, Cochiti, Isleta, Jemez, Laguna, Nambe, Picuris, Pojoaque, San Felipe, San Ildefonso, Ohkay Owingeh (formerly referred to as San Juan), Sandia, Santa Ana, Santa Clara, Santo Domingo, Taos, Tesuque, Zia, and Zuni.

What Happened to Malaysia Airlines Flight 370?

On March 8, 2014, Malaysia Airlines Flight 370 (also known as MH370) from Kuala Lumpur, Malaysia, to Beijing, China, mysteriously disappeared along with its 227 passengers and 12 crew members. The Boeing 777 jetliner completely dropped off the radar.

✳ ✳ ✳ ✳

THE PLANE TOOK off at 12:41 A.M. and soon reached its cruising altitude of 35,000 feet. At 1:07 A.M. the plane's communications system issued what would be its last transmission. The Aircraft Communications Addressing and Reporting System (ACARS), which transmitted data about the aircraft's performance, showed nothing unusual and normal routing to Beijing. At 1:19 A.M. the last voice check-in was made as the plane was entering Vietnamese airspace. Two minutes later, the plane's transponder, which communicated with air-traffic controllers on the ground, was curiously turned off.

Although there was no communication by ACARS or transponder, at 2:15 A.M. Malaysian military radar tracked the plane passing over the Strait of Malacca. This would indicate that Flight 370 had turned around and flown southwest over the Malay Peninsula. At 2:22 A.M., the last primary radar contact was made by the Malaysian military determining Flight 370 had flown out across the Andaman Sea. A final "ping" was detected by a satellite at 8:11 A.M. The aircraft responded electronically, providing evidence that Flight 370 ended somewhere in the southern Indian Ocean.

No crash site has ever been discovered, nor have any bodies been recovered. The first piece of debris from MH370 was found in 2015 on the French island of Reunion, east of Madagascar. It was part of a wing called a flaperon. In total, more than 30 pieces of debris have turned up in Tanzania, Mauritius, South Africa, Mozambique, and Madagascar. However, only three wing fragments have been confirmed to be from MH370.

Due to the nature of the plane's complete disappearance there have been no shortage of conspiracy theories over the years. Investigations have ruled out the pilot's mental state, aircraft malfunction, and remote control of operation systems as possible factors in the disappearance.

In January 2017, the official search for MH370 by Malaysia, China, and Australia was called off. An American company, Ocean Infinity, continued the search sweeping 112,000 square kilometers of the ocean floor, but turned up nothing.

In what was billed as their "final" report on Flight 370 in July 2018, the Malaysian government declared they could not determine with any certainty why the Boeing 777 had disappeared. They did, however, concede that the critical turn made by the plane was done manually.

The Imposter

Imagine being told that a strange boy is your missing son, but when you adamantly insist the obvious imposter is not your child, you are committed to a psychiatric hospital. It sounds like a ridiculous work of fiction, but this is exactly what happened to one grief-stricken mother in a bizarre missing child case in 1928 Los Angeles.

✳   ✳   ✳   ✳

The Missing Boy

CHRISTINE IDA DUNNE was born on December 14, 1888, in Los Angeles, California. She married a man who went by the name of Walter Collins, but she later found out that her husband was a criminal named Walter Anson who had changed his name and attempted to hide from the law. Anson was soon caught and convicted of eight armed robberies, and sent to Folsom State Prison.

But before her husband's true identity was discovered, the couple had a son, named Walter Collins, Jr. And in a strange turn of fate, it would soon be Walter's identity that was in question.

On March 10, 1928, Christine gave nine-year-old Walter some money to go to the cinema. When he didn't return, his mother immediately reported him missing, and the Los Angeles Police Department began an investigation. The police suggested that the boy may have run away, but Christine was convinced he had been kidnapped, possibly as some sort of retribution for his father's crimes. The LAPD followed up on hundreds of leads, but without success.

Hope, Heartbreak, and a Hospital

That is, until five months later, when miraculously, a boy claiming to be Walter and matching his description turned up 2,000 miles away in DeKalb, Illinois. Christine, no doubt overjoyed by this news, paid to have the boy escorted to Los Angeles. But the hope that she felt was instantly replaced with heartbreak when she realized the boy, while bearing a striking resemblance to her son, was not Walter. The police captain in charge of the case, J.J. Jones, told Christine that perhaps Walter

simply seemed different because of his five-month absence, and she should take him home and "try the boy out."

Reluctantly, Christine took "Walter" home, but within three weeks she returned to the LAPD—this time with Walter's dental records—to prove that the boy was not her son. But instead of apologizing, Jones, who had faced negative publicity over the disappearance, had Christine committed to the psychiatric ward of the Los Angeles County General Hospital, calling her "difficult" and an "inconvenience."

For ten days, Christine was held against her will in the hospital. In the meantime, the boy admitted to Jones that he was not Walter, but rather a 12-year-old runaway from Iowa named Arthur Hutchins, Jr. When Arthur heard about Walter's disappearance and realized how similar they looked, he saw a chance to score a free trip to California.

Now that the truth was out, Jones could no longer justify Christine's commitment, and she was freed. She sued the city for false imprisonment and won, and Jones was ordered to pay her $10,800 (more than $160,000 in today's dollars), but he never paid.

A Question Left Unanswered

After her heart-wrenching ordeal, Christine was still left with the question: What happened to Walter? Many investigators believe that the boy was the victim of a local serial killer named Gordon Stewart Northcott, who was convicted in 1929 of abducting, molesting, and killing three boys on his chicken farm, in what became known as the Wineville Chicken Coop Murders. However, Walter's body was never found, and Northcott never admitted to abducting the boy.

Christine never accepted the theory that Walter was one of Northcott's victims, instead preferring to hold on to the hope that he was alive somewhere. She continued to search for her son until she passed away in 1964 at the age of 75.

Mystery at Flannan Isles

The Flannan Isles is a small group of islands located in the Outer Hebrides of Scotland. The islands are now devoid of human residents, but they are home to many species of seabird— including Atlantic puffins, northern fulmars, and black-legged kittiwakes—as well as the occasional rabbit. These islands, with their rocky cliffs and heather-covered moors, are also the setting of an enduring mystery.

✳   ✳   ✳   ✳

An Unlit Light

THE 75-FOOT-HIGH LIGHTHOUSE on the Flannan Isles, which has been automated since 1971, was built between 1895 and 1899, on the highest point of an island called Eilean Mor. For the time, it was quite a complicated construction project, as all the materials used had to be hoisted off supply boats and up 148-foot cliffs. To make work easier for the keepers who would be overseeing the lighthouse, a small railway track was built from the boat landing area to the lighthouse, for the purpose of hauling up supplies and the large amount of paraffin needed to keep the light aflame. On December 7, 1899, the lighthouse was lit up for the first time, providing approaching ships with a warning of the rocky conditions.

But on December 15, 1900, the captain of the steamer ship *Archtor*, nearing the end of its journey from Philadelphia, Pennsylvania, to Leith, Scotland, noticed something strange. The lighthouse on Eilean Mor was not lit, even though weather conditions were poor that evening. When the *Archtor* docked in Leith on December 18, the incident was reported to the Northern Lighthouse Board.

The Relief Keeper

Three men—James Ducat, Thomas Marshall, and Donald McArthur—were tasked with overseeing the lighthouse on Eilean Mor and were the only inhabitants of the island. A fourth man, Joseph Moore, was a relief keeper who had been spending time ashore, but at the end of December he readied himself to start his shift at the lighthouse. After a delay because of bad weather, Moore boarded the lighthouse relief vessel, the *Hesperus*, and the ship reached the island on December 26. As they neared the island, Moore and the crew felt an ominous sense of dismay, as they realized that none of the keepers were at the landing to welcome them.

Moore went ashore alone to see if he could find one of the keepers, but as he climbed toward the lighthouse, he felt overwhelmed with a sense of dread. The outer gate and the door to the lighthouse were both firmly closed. Inside, the lighthouse was neat and tidy, although the clock was stopped, and two of the lighthouse keepers' coats were missing. The only sign that anything was amiss was an overturned chair. But, ominously, the lighthouse—and, in fact, the entire island—was completely deserted.

Sea Monsters?

What had happened to Ducat, Marshall, and McArthur? The condition of the lighthouse raised more questions than it answered: Rules stated that at least one person should man the lighthouse at all times, so why did all three of the men leave? And why did one of them leave without a coat? Entries in the lighthouse's logbook provided even more confusing details. Marshall wrote that between December 12 and 15, the island was besieged by "severe winds the likes of which I've never seen before." Yet no storms were reported in the area until December 17. An investigation did find severe damage to one of the boat landings, however, lending credence to the idea that there may have been some kind of storm.

Because of the strange clues and the fact that no bodies were ever found, the public speculated on the fate of the men. Theories ranged from sea monsters to supernatural entities, but the official investigation concluded that the trio must've gone outside to secure supplies and were swept out to sea by a huge wave. The truth of what happened at the Flannan Isles lighthouse will likely remain a mystery, but Marshall's last words in the lighthouse's logbook are haunting: "Storm ended, sea calm. God is over all."

Who Was Annie McCarrick?

Approximately 33 million Americans—around 10 percent of the U.S. population—are said to have Irish ancestry. That's five times more than the population of Ireland itself, which is home to about 6.5 million people. Every year, millions of travelers visit the Emerald Isle, many of them Irish Americans curious about the country of their ancestors. But sadly, not everyone who travels the world returns home.

✳ ✳ ✳ ✳

A New Life in Ireland

ANNIE MCCARRICK DIDN'T want to simply visit Ireland. Born on March 21, 1966, in Long Island, New York, to parents of Irish heritage, the young graduate student wanted to make the country her new home. She'd already spent two years at the National University of Ireland in Maynooth, and after returning to the U.S. to earn a master's degree at the State University of New York at Stony Brook, McCarrick decided to move to Ireland to complete her education.

So in January of 1993, McCarrick settled into a flat with two roommates in Sandymount, a suburb of Dublin located right along the Irish Sea. She found a job at a café, and began her new life in her adopted country. She made friends, including her ex-boyfriend's brother, Hilary Brady, and his fiancée, Rita Fortune, and one day in late March she invited the couple over for dinner. Hilary and Rita accepted, planning to be at McCarrick's flat on Saturday, March 27.

The Last Known Details

March 26 was McCarrick's day off work. That morning, she bid farewell to her two roommates, who were each going out of town for the weekend, and then she ran a few errands. She first visited a bank, where a CCTV camera captured the smiling, friendly McCarrick on video. She then stopped into a market to pick up food for her dinner the next day. On her way home, McCarrick made two phone calls from a public kiosk—one to Hilary and Rita to confirm they'd be at dinner, and another to a hiking buddy named Anne, who she asked to accompany her on a walk in Enniskerry, a village just south of Dublin, that afternoon. Anne declined the offer, as she was recovering from an injury, so it is assumed that McCarrick planned to go to Enniskerry on her own.

Details of what happened next are fuzzy. Sometime before 3 P.M., McCarrick returned to her flat and placed the groceries on the counter, then was seen leaving the apartment around 3 P.M. At 3:40 P.M., an acquaintance reported seeing McCarrick waiting for the 44 bus in Ranelagh, just outside of Sandymount, which would've taken her to Enniskerry. And then, Annie McCarrick vanished.

An Unknown Fate

Her coworkers thought it was strange when she failed to show up for work the next day, but no one was truly alarmed until Hilary and Rita arrived for the 8 P.M. dinner that evening and McCarrick didn't answer the door. They continued trying to reach her the next day, until her flatmates retuned to the apartment and discovered her unpacked bag of groceries on the counter. At that point, Hilary and Rita knew something was amiss, and they contacted McCarrick's parents in America.

McCarrick's mother rushed to Ireland, and headed straight for the Irish police, known as An Garda Siochana, to report her daughter missing. Her father, a retired police officer, soon joined the search as well, but there were very few leads to go on. One witness swore he saw McCarrick at a crowded pub on Friday night, but it was later believed to be an American tourist. Another witness thinks that McCarrick bought stamps in a post office in Enniskerry, but this sighting was not confirmed, either.

The theories about what happened to Annie McCarrick are disturbing. An ex-Garda detective believes she may have crossed paths with an IRA hitman, who, after drinking with the friendly American at a pub and revealing too many secrets, killed her to keep her quiet. Another theory posits that she was murdered by a serial killer named Larry Murphy, who was responsible for the deaths of at least six women in Ireland's "Vanishing Triangle," the same area where McCarrick disappeared.

Sadly, McCarrick's father passed away without knowing what happened to his daughter. But her mother continues to search, hoping to one day bring Annie McCarrick home.

The Case of the "Missingest" Man

Back in the 1930s and 1940s, New Yorkers told a running joke: "Judge Crater, call your office." If an elevator operator responded to a call light and no one was waiting when the elevator arrived, the operator might stick his head out and ask, "Judge Crater?" to make the riders laugh. And Groucho Marx liked to end his comedy shows by walking off stage as he was saying, "I'm going out to look for Judge Crater." But the source of all these jokes wasn't funny at all.

* * * *

From Clerk to Justice

JOSEPH FORCE CRATER was born on January 5, 1889, in Easton, Pennsylvania. He attended Lafayette College in Easton before heading to Columbia University in New York City, where he earned a law degree in 1916. Crater worked his way up through the legal ranks, starting his career as a law clerk and eventually becoming a successful lawyer.

By April of 1930, Crater had so impressed New York Governor Franklin D. Roosevelt that the governor appointed him as a New York State Supreme Court Justice. At the time, an often-corrupt political organization known as Tammany Hall had great influence over New York politics. Tammany Hall had suggested their own candidate for the Supreme Court position, but when FDR bypassed their choice for Crater, rumors began circulating that Crater must have paid off the bosses of Tammany for his lucrative new job.

The Disappearance

A few months later, Crater and his wife, Stella Mance Wheeler, were vacationing at a summer cabin in Maine. On August 3, Crater left to attend to business in New York, but he promised his wife he'd return to Maine in time for her birthday the next week. According to his wife, Crater was in good spirits and acting normally when he departed for the city; but that would be the last time she ever saw her husband.

On August 6, Crater went to his office, where he destroyed a few documents and asked his law clerk to cash several checks for him, amounting to around $5,000 (the equivalent of about $79,000 today). He then moved two locked briefcases to his Fifth Avenue apartment. That evening, Crater bought a ticket to a Broadway show; he then went to dinner with fellow lawyer William Klein and a showgirl—reportedly also his mistress—named Sally Lou Ritz. After dinner, at about 9:30 P.M., Klein and Ritz said goodbye to Crater. Crater walked down the street, never to be seen or heard from again.

Plenty of Theories, but No Answers

Strangely, Crater's disappearance didn't spark an immediate manhunt. In fact, his wife didn't even begin asking questions until August 13, days after he'd promised to be back in Maine. His fellow justices didn't notice anything amiss until Crater failed to appear at the opening of the courts on August 25. And an official search wasn't launched until September 3, almost a month after he disappeared. But once his disappearance hit the front page of New York's newspapers, he was dubbed "The Missingest Man in New York."

Police thought they had some promising leads at first, as they discovered that Crater's safe deposit box had been emptied and the two locked briefcases he'd taken to his apartment were missing. But these clues never amounted to much. One theory was that the judge, an alleged womanizer, had fled the country with a mistress. Another notion was that Crater had been blackmailed by a showgirl with a gangster boyfriend, who later killed the judge. And others believed that corrupt Tammany Hall, still bitter about Crater's appointment, somehow played into the picture. Crater was declared legally dead in 1939.

In 2005, some surprising evidence surfaced. A woman who died that year left behind a handwritten note which claimed that her husband knew who had murdered Crater, and that his body was buried under the Coney Island Boardwalk. Unfortunately, that section of boardwalk had been excavated in the 1950s to construct the New York Aquarium, and there are no records of anyone discovering a body during the construction. So it seems that Judge Crater will continue to be the Missingest Man in New York.

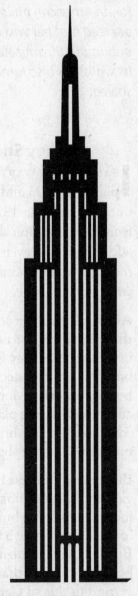

The Museum of Empty Frames

Located in Boston, Massachusetts, the Isabella Stewart Gardner Museum contains paintings, sculptures, tapestries, and other works from Europe, Asia, and America. The museum was named for an American philanthropist and art collector, whose will decreed that her vast collection be permanently displayed to the public. But the museum is not only known for the art that adorns its walls; it is also famous for a brazen heist that has never been solved.

❋　❋　❋　❋

They Should Have Seen It Coming

ISABELLA STEWART GARDNER opened her museum to the public in 1903 and continued to add to her vast collection until her death in 1924. Her will stipulated that no artwork from her collection should ever be sold, and none should be added, and that even the arrangement of the artwork in the museum should remain untouched. In a sense, the museum was frozen in time.

Although Gardner left the museum a $3.6 million endowment, the institution was financially struggling. In 1982, after the FBI uncovered a plot by Boston criminals to rob the museum, the board of trustees decided to use what little funds they had to beef up security. Motion detectors were added, and closed-circuit cameras were placed around the perimeter of the building. The museum also hired more security guards, although it could only afford to pay slightly above minimum wage.

But even with these improvements, there were still flaws and gaps in the museum's security. For one, there were no cameras located inside the building. Also, the police could only be summoned by pushing a button located at a single security desk. By 1988, independent security consultants had warned the board of trustees that their security measures needed improvement; but due to Gardner's insistence that the museum remain unchanged, no more improvements were made.

A Brazen Heist

In the early morning hours of March 18, 1990, two security officers—23-year-old Rick Abath and 25-year-old Randy Hestand—were on duty in the Gardner Museum. At 1:20 A.M., a buzzer for the outside door rang an intercom at Abath's desk. On the closed-circuit television, Abath could see two men dressed as police officers, who told the guard that they were investigating a disturbance and needed to come in.

Once the "police officers" were inside, they asked Abath to summon Hestand, then lured the pair away from the security desk (the location of the only button to call for help), handcuffed them, and wrapped duct tape around their eyes. The thieves took the two guards down to the basement and handcuffed them to a pipe and workbench, their intention to rob the museum now more than obvious.

In just over an hour, the thieves were able to pack thirteen works of art into their car, making two trips back and forth, pilfering works by Rembrandt, Vermeer, Flinck, Degas, and Manet. They also stole an ancient Chinese vase and a bronze eagle finial. At 2:45 A.M., they left the museum, Abath and Hestand still tied up in the basement. The two guards weren't able to get free until the morning guard shift arrived and called the police.

Empty Frames and a Huge Reward

Right off the bat, the heist puzzled art experts. The objects taken were seemingly random and unconnected. Some of the art was extremely valuable, but others had little worth. What's more, the thieves completely bypassed the third floor of the museum, which housed some of the most valuable paintings in the world. All of this would suggest that the thieves were not hired to execute a specific heist.

Regardless, the items the thieves stole still have an estimated value of between $500 and $600 million. One dealer at Sotheby's even puts the estimate at $1 billion. But to this day, no one knows who pulled off the heist or where they hid the art. Sotheby's, along with Christie's auction house, have posted a reward for the return of the art, which now stands at $10 million.

Because of Gardner's insistence that her museum remain unchanged, empty frames now hang where the stolen art was once displayed. Still frozen in time, the museum patiently awaits their return.

Amelia Earhart: An Open Secret

Was Amelia Earhart the victim of some kind of conspiracy? Her choice not to keep up with technological knowhow is more likely to blame for her disappearance.

✳ ✳ ✳ ✳

Opening the Books

AFTER ORVILLE AND Wilbur Wright made the first powered airplane flight in 1903, an ugly patent war began among inventors in the U.S. A huge number of researchers from all kinds of backgrounds—the Wrights themselves were bicycle mechanics, publishers, and journalists—had made incremental improvements on one another's work, brainstormed similar ideas, and generally squabbled over who was making the best progress. Think of it as a grade school classroom where all the students are grown men, and they've propped up folders and textbooks to hide their tests from their classmates.

These aviation pioneers were out-pettying today's worst startup companies in Silicon Valley. They went to court over fine details of one aircraft versus another, citing their own notes and evidence that had largely been kept secret. But after a decade of brutal lawsuits and public fighting over who was first, who invented what, and where credit was due, the United States entered World War I. Aviation companies were de facto forced to pour their proprietary research and patents into a large pool shared by all of America's aircraft industry.

Making their technology "open source" was part of the war effort, but as with software and other inventions today, the open industry led to better and more rapid developments. After World War I ended, pilots began to set records left and right using ingenious inventions like the artificial horizon—something pilots still use in cockpits today, in a modernized form. And some pilots made their livings in traveling airshows as airplanes became more and more familiar to the American people. Amelia Earhart was one of these pilots, traveling to build buzz for her own career.

The Morse the Merrier

Earhart was a gifted and remarkable pilot, the first woman to ride in a plane (as a passenger) across the Atlantic and then to fly across it as the pilot. She started a professional organization for women pilots and took a faculty position at Purdue University. She and fellow groundbreaking pilot Charles Lindbergh were like movie stars by the 1930s, and Earhart was witty and engaging when she spoke with the press or members of the public. Her career was at a perfect point for her to make an outsize gesture in the form of a trip around the world. She wasn't the first, but she was definitely the most famous.

Technology leapt ahead during her career, and Morse code was in wide use by the time Earhart began her trip around the world. The world's leading navigation instructor offered to teach Earhart radio operation, Morse code, and cutting-edge navigation, but she didn't have time before her trip, which had already been delayed by a failed first attempt. The navigator she chose didn't know Morse code. When they grew disoriented in poor weather over the Pacific Ocean, they could not call for help in Morse code, and their radio reception was too poor to send or receive verbal messages from the Navy ships assigned to support the open water sections of their flight.

The "what ifs" of Earhart's failed final journey stoke pop culture across the decades, and who can say what could have happened if she and her navigator were able to get help?

CHAPTER 3

GHOSTLY APPEARANCES

The Ghost of the Sausage Vat Murder

The story of Louisa Luetgert, the murdered wife of "Sausage King" Adolph Luetgert, is a gruesome tale of betrayal, death, and a lingering specter. It is also one of the greatest stories in Chicago lore. According to legend, each year on the anniversary of her death, Louisa appears on the corner of Hermitage Avenue where it once crossed Diversey Parkway. But her ghost not only haunts her old neighborhood; allegedly, she also coaxed her treacherous husband into an early grave.

✳ ✳ ✳ ✳

Land of Opportunity

ADOLPH LUETGERT WAS born in Germany and came to America after the Civil War. He arrived in Chicago around 1865 and worked in tanneries for several years before opening his first business—a liquor store—in 1872. Luetgert married his first wife, Caroline Roepke, that same year. She gave birth to two boys, only one of whom survived childhood. Just two months after Caroline died in November 1877, Luetgert quickly remarried a much younger woman, Louisa Bicknese, and moved to the northwest side of the city. As a gift, he gave her an unusual gold ring that had her initials inscribed inside the band. Little did Luetgert know that this ring would prove to be his downfall.

Trouble for the "Sausage King"

In 1892, Luetgert built a sausage factory at the southwest corner of Hermitage and Diversey. But just a year later, sausage sales declined due to an economic depression. Luetgert had put his life's savings into the factory, along with plenty of borrowed money, so when his business suffered, creditors started coming after him.

Instead of trying to reorganize his finances, however, Luetgert answered a newspaper ad posted by an English millionaire who made a deal with him to buy out the majority of the sausage business. The Englishman proved to be a con man, and Luetgert ended up losing even more money in the deal. Luetgert eventually laid off many of his workers, but a few remained as he attempted to keep the factory out of the hands of creditors for as long as possible.

Luetgert's business losses took a terrible toll on his marriage. Friends and neighbors frequently heard the Luetgerts arguing, and things became so bad that Luetgert eventually started sleeping in his office at the factory. He carried on with several mistresses and even became involved with a household servant who was related to his wife. When Louisa found out about his involvement with her relative, she became enraged.

Luetgert soon gave the neighbors even more to gossip about. One night, during another shouting match with Louisa, he allegedly took his wife by the throat and began choking her. After noticing alarmed neighbors watching him through the parlor window, Luetgert reportedly calmed down and released his wife before she collapsed. A few days later, Luetgert was seen chasing his wife down the street, shouting at her and waving a revolver.

Vanishing Louisa

Louisa disappeared on May 1, 1897. When questioned about it days later, Luetgert stated that Louisa had left him and was possibly staying with her sister or another man. When Louisa's brother, Dietrich Bicknese, asked Luetgert why he had not informed the police of Louisa's disappearance, the sausage maker told him that he'd hired a private investigator to find her because he didn't trust the police.

When Bicknese informed the police of his sister's disappearance, Captain Herman Schuettler and his men began to search for Louisa. They questioned neighbors and relatives, who detailed the couple's violent arguments. Schuettler summoned Luetgert to the precinct house on a couple of occasions and each time pressed him about his wife's disappearance. Luetgert stated that he did not report Louisa's disappearance because he could not afford the disgrace and scandal.

During the investigation, a young German girl named Emma Schimke told police that she had passed by the factory with her sister at about 10:30 P.M. on May 1 and remembered seeing Luetgert leading his wife down the alleyway behind the factory.

Police also questioned employees of the sausage factory. Frank Bialk, a night watchman at the plant, told police that when he arrived for work on May 1, he found a fire going in one of the boilers. He said Luetgert asked him to keep the fire going and then sent him on a couple of trivial errands while Luetgert stayed in the basement. When Bialk returned to the factory, he went back to the boiler fire and heard Luetgert finishing his work at around 3:00 A.M.

Later that morning, Bialk saw a sticky, gluelike substance on the floor near the vat. He noticed that it seemed to contain bits of bone, but he thought nothing of it. After all, Luetgert used all sorts of waste meats to make his sausage, so he assumed that's what it was.

On May 3, Luetgert asked another employee, Frank Odorofsky, to clean the basement and told him to keep quiet about it. Odorofsky put the slimy substance into a barrel, and scattered it near the railroad tracks as Luetgert had requested.

A Gruesome Discovery

On May 15, the police search was narrowed to the factory basement and a vat that was two-thirds full of a brownish, brackish liquid. Using gunnysacks as filters, officers drained the greasy paste from the vat and began poking through the residue with sticks. Officer Walter Dean found several bone fragments and two gold rings—one a heavy gold band engraved with the initials "L. L."

Luetgert, proclaiming his innocence, was questioned again shortly after the search and was subsequently arrested for the murder of his wife several days later. Despite the fact that Louisa's body was never found and there was no real evidence to link her husband to the crime, the police and prosecutors believed they had a solid case against Luetgert. He was indicted for Louisa's murder, and the details of the crime shocked the city. Even though he had been charged with boiling Louisa's body, rumors circulated that she had actually been ground up into sausage that was sold to local butcher shops and restaurants. Not surprisingly, sausage sales dropped dramatically in Chicago in 1897.

Hounded to the Grave?

Luetgert's trial ended in a hung jury on October 21. The judge threw out the case, and prosecutors had to try the whole thing over again. A second trial was held in 1898, and this time Luetgert was convicted and sentenced to a life term at Joliet Prison.

While in prison, Luetgert continued to maintain his innocence and was placed in charge of meats in the cold-storage warehouse. Officials described him as a model prisoner. But by 1899, Luetgert began to speak less and less and often quarreled with other convicts. He soon became a shadow of his former, blustering self, fighting for no reason and often babbling incoherently in his cell at night. But was he talking to himself or to someone else?

Legend has it that Luetgert claimed Louisa haunted him in his jail cell, intent on having revenge for her murder. Was she really haunting him, or was the ghost just a figment of his rapidly deteriorating mind? Based on the fact that neighbors also reported seeing Louisa's ghost, one has to wonder if she did indeed drive Luetgert insane.

Luetgert died in 1900, likely from heart trouble. The coroner who conducted the autopsy also reported that his liver was greatly enlarged and in such a condition of degeneration that "mental strain would have caused his death at any time."

Perhaps Louisa really did visit him after all.

The Ghost of Louisa Luetgert

Regardless of who killed Louisa, her spirit reportedly did not rest in peace. Soon after Luetgert was sent to prison, neighbors swore they saw Louisa's ghost inside her former home, wearing a white dress and leaning against the fireplace mantel.

The sausage factory stood empty for years, looming over the neighborhood as a grim reminder of the horrors that had taken place there. Eventually, the Library Bureau Company purchased the factory for a workshop and storehouse for library furniture and office supplies. During renovations, they discarded the infamous vats in the basement.

On June 26, 1904, the old factory caught on fire. Despite the damage done to the building's interior, the Library Bureau reopened its facilities in the former sausage factory. In 1907, a contracting mason purchased the old Luetgert house and moved it from behind the factory to another lot in the neighborhood, hoping to dispel the grim memories—and ghost—attached to it.

Hermitage Avenue no longer intersects with Diversey, and by the 1990s, the crumbling factory stood empty. But in the late '90s, around the 100th anniversary of Louisa's death, the former sausage factory was converted into condominiums and a brand-new neighborhood sprang up to replace the aging homes that remained from the days of the Luetgerts. Fashionable brick homes and apartments appeared around the old factory, and rundown taverns were replaced with coffee shops.

But one thing has not changed. Legend has it that each year on May 1, the anniversary of her death, the ghost of Louisa can still be spotted walking down Hermitage Avenue near the old sausage factory, reliving her final moments on this earth.

The Greenbrier Ghost: Testimony from the Other Side

The strange tale of the Greenbrier Ghost stands out in the annals of ghost lore. Not only is it part of supernatural history, it is also part of the history of the U.S. judicial system. To this day, it is the only case in which a crime was solved and a murderer convicted based on the testimony of a ghost.

✳   ✳   ✳   ✳

A Doomed Marriage

LITTLE IS KNOWN about her life, but it is believed that Zona Heaster was born in Greenbrier County, West Virginia, around 1873. In October 1896, she met Erasmus "Edward" Stribbling Trout Shue, a drifter who had recently moved to the area to work as a blacksmith. A short time later, the two were married, despite the animosity felt toward Shue by Zona's mother, Mary Jane Heaster, who had instantly disliked him.

Unfortunately, the marriage was short-lived. In January 1897, Zona's body was discovered at home by a young neighbor boy who had come to the house on an errand. After he found Zona lying on the floor at the bottom of the stairs, he ran to get the local doctor and coroner, Dr. George W. Knapp. By the time Dr. Knapp arrived, Shue had come home, found his wife, and carried her body upstairs where he laid her on the bed and dressed her in her best clothing—a high-necked, stiff-collared dress with a big scarf tied around her neck and a veil placed over her face.

While Dr. Knapp was examining Zona's body in an attempt to determine the cause of death, Shue allegedly stayed by his wife's side, cradling her head, sobbing, and clearly distressed over anyone touching her body. As a result, Knapp did not do a thorough examination. Although he did notice some bruising on Zona's neck, he initially listed her cause of death as "everlasting faint" and then as "childbirth." Whether or not Zona was pregnant is unknown, but Dr. Knapp had been treating her for some time prior to her death.

When Mary Jane Heaster was informed of her daughter's death, her face grew dark as she uttered: "The devil has killed her!" Zona's body was taken to her parents' home where it was displayed for the wake.

Those who came to pay their respects whispered about Shue's erratic behavior—one minute he'd be expressing intense grief and sadness, then displaying frenetic outbursts the next. He would not allow anyone to get close to the coffin, especially when he placed a pillow and a rolled-up cloth around his wife's head to help her "rest easier." Still, when Zona's body was moved to the cemetery, several people noted a strange looseness to her head. Not surprisingly, people started to talk.

Ghostly Messages from the Other Side

Mary Jane Heaster did not have to be convinced that Shue was acting suspiciously about Zona's death. She had always hated him and wished her daughter had never married him. She had a sneaking suspicion that something wasn't right, but she didn't know how to prove it.

After the funeral, as Heaster was folding the sheet from inside the coffin, she noticed that it had an unusual odor. When she placed it into the basin to wash it, the water turned red.

Stranger still, the sheet turned pink and then the color in the water disappeared. Even after Heaster boiled the sheet, the stain remained. To her, the bizarre "bloodstains" were a sign that Zona had been murdered.

For the next four weeks, Heaster prayed fervently every night that Zona would come to her and explain the details of her death. Soon after, her prayers were answered. For four nights, Zona's spirit appeared at her mother's bedside, first as a bright light, but then the air in the room got cold and her apparition took form. She told her mother that Shue had been an abusive and cruel husband, and in a fit of rage, he'd attacked her because he thought she had not cooked any meat for supper. He'd broken her neck, and as evidence, Zona's ghost spun her head around until it was facing backward.

Heaster's suspicions were correct: Shue had killed Zona and she'd come back from beyond the grave to prove it.

Opening the Grave

After Zona's ghostly visit, Heaster tried to convince the local prosecutor, John Alfred Preston, to reopen the investigation into her daughter's death. She pleaded that an injustice was taking place and, as evidence, she told him about her encounters with Zona's spirit. Although it seems unlikely that he would reexamine the case because of the statement of a ghost, the investigation was, in fact, reopened. Preston agreed to question Dr. Knapp and a few others involved in the case. The local newspaper reported that a number of citizens were suspicious of Zona's death, and rumors were circulating throughout the community.

Dr. Knapp admitted to Preston that his examination of Zona's body was cursory at best, so it was agreed that an autopsy would be done to settle any lingering questions. They could find out how Zona really died, and, if he was innocent, ease the suspicions surrounding Shue.

The local newspaper reported that Shue "vigorously complained" about the exhumation and autopsy of his wife's body, but he was required to attend. A jury of five men gathered together in the chilly building to watch the autopsy along with officers of the court, Shue, and other witnesses.

The autopsy findings were rather damning to Shue. When the doctors concluded that Zona's neck had been broken, Shue's head dropped, and a dark expression crossed his face. "They cannot prove that I did it," he said quietly.

A March 9 report stated: "The discovery was made that the neck was broken and the windpipe mashed. On the throat were the marks of fingers indicating that she had been choken [sic] . . . The neck was dislocated between the first and second vertebrae. The ligaments were torn and ruptured. The windpipe had been crushed at a point in front of the neck."

Despite the fact that—aside from Zona's ghost—the evidence against Shue was circumstantial at best, he was arrested, indicted, and formally arraigned for murder. All the while, he maintained his innocence and entered a plea of "not guilty." He repeatedly told reporters that his guilt in the matter could not be proven.

While awaiting trial, details about Shue's unsavory past came to light. Zona was actually his third wife. In 1889, while he was in prison for horse theft, he was divorced from his first wife, Allie Estelline Cutlip, who claimed that Shue had frequently beaten her during their marriage. In fact, at one point, Shue allegedly beat Cutlip so severely that a group of men had to pull him off of her and throw him into an icy river.

In 1894, Shue married his second wife, Lucy Ann Tritt, who died just eight months later under mysterious circumstances. Shue left the area in the autumn of 1896 and moved to Greenbrier. When word got out that Shue was suspected of murdering Zona, stories started circulating about the circumstances behind Tritt's death, but no wrongdoing was ever proven.

Despite the fact that he was in jail, Shue seemed in good spirits. Remarking that he was done grieving for Zona, he revealed that it was his life's dream to have seven wives. Because Zona was only wife number three and he was still fairly young, he felt confident that he could achieve his goal.

Testimony from a Ghost

When Shue's trial began in June 1897, numerous members of the community testified against him. Of course, Heaster's testimony was the highlight of the trial. She testified as both the mother of the victim and as the first person to notice the unusual circumstances of Zona's death. Preston wanted her to come across as sane and reliable, so he did not mention the spirit encounter, which would make Heaster look irrational and was also inadmissible as evidence. Zona's testimony obviously could not be cross-examined by the defense and, therefore, was hearsay under the law.

But unfortunately for Shue, his attorney did ask Heaster about her ghostly visit. Certainly, he was trying to destroy her credibility with the jury, characterizing her "visions" as the overactive imagination of a grieving mother. He was tenacious in trying to get her to admit that she was mistaken about what she'd seen, but Heaster zealously stuck to her story. When Shue's attorney realized that she was not going to budge from her story, he dismissed her.

But by then, the damage was done. Because the defense—not the prosecution—had brought up Zona's otherworldly testimony, the judge had a difficult time ordering the jury to ignore it. Clearly, most of the townspeople believed that Heaster really had been visited by her daughter's ghost. Shue testified in his own defense, but the jury quickly found him guilty. Ten of the jury members voted for Shue to be hanged, but because they could not reach a unanimous decision, he was sentenced to life in prison.

Shue didn't carry out his sentence for long—he died in March 1900 at the West Virginia State Penitentiary in Moundsville. Until her death in 1916, Heaster told her tale to anyone who would listen.

It seems that after visiting her mother to offer details of her murder, Zona was finally able to rest in peace. Although her ghost was never seen again, she did leave a historical mark on Greenbrier County, where a roadside marker still commemorates the case today. It reads:

"Interred in nearby cemetery is Zona Heaster Shue. Her death in 1897 was presumed natural until her spirit appeared to her mother to describe how she was killed by her husband Edward. Autopsy on the exhumed body verified the apparition's account. Edward, found guilty of murder, was sentenced to the state prison. Only known case in which testimony from ghost helped convict a murderer."

Ghosts in the Witch City

One of the darkest chapters in American history, the Salem Witch Trials have haunted our country for more than 300 years. Numerous plays and movies have recounted the tale of two young girls from Massachusetts who, in 1692, wrongfully accused people in their town of witchcraft. This sparked a mass hysteria that led to charges against hundreds and the executions of 20 innocent people. The lessons learned from this miscarriage of justice have stuck with the people of the United States, but so have the restless spirits of the victims of this tragedy.

✳ ✳ ✳ ✳

The Last House

TODAY, THE PEOPLE of Salem, Massachusetts, acknowledge the crimes of the past, and the town recognizes its history in many ways, from witch logos on its police cars to a number of kitschy attractions erected solely to attract tourists. Among the gift shops and New Age bookstores, only one building with a connection to the trials remains: Known locally as "The Witch House," Judge Jonathan Corwin's former home still hosts visitors on Essex Street. Some of those visiting the historic site are overcome with feelings of anxiety, fear, and anger—all emotions likely experienced by those Corwin sentenced to death. Some have seen the apparition of a woman lingering in the bedrooms on the second floor, and others have witnessed a couple that vanishes into thin air while walking the grounds. Some employees report strange noises after hours, including what sounds like the shuffling of feet on the floorboards and the dragging of furniture from one room to another. The spirits of The Witch House have even been captured on film, although most appear to be little more than manifestations of light or swirling mists.

The Gallows

Judge Corwin's former home is not the only place in Salem where the spirits of those he condemned make their presence known. Photographs of orbs and mists that are similar to those snapped at The Witch House have been taken in the area once known as Gallows Hill. Though precise records of where the accused were hanged no longer exist, many believe that a playground and basketball court now reside where the town's gallows once stood. This would explain the eerie photographs of apparitions, as well as other strange phenomena that occur at the site. Electronics frequently malfunction there, and it isn't uncommon for people to hear otherworldly crying at the location at night. Some visitors have reported feeling an invisible presence brush up against them, while others have had their hair pulled by an unseen force.

Harbinger at Howard Street

Of course, a town as old as Salem inevitably has several cemeteries, and one of the most haunted is Howard Street Cemetery, which sits across from where the old jail once stood. Photographers at the graveyard have captured images of the same unexplainable mists, orbs, and lights that are found at other locations, and reports of physical contact with an invisible entity abound as well. For more than a hundred years now, passersby have witnessed apparitions wandering among the old tombstones. Although most of the graves at the Howard Street Cemetery don't date back further than the 1800s, the site itself is inextricably tied to the witch trials: The graveyard was built on the location where Sheriff George Corwin tried to crush a confession out of Giles Corey—and when Corey's ghost is seen, the entire town of Salem trembles.

More Weight . . .

When Anne Putnam accused Giles Corey of appearing to her as a spirit and trying to entice her with his satanic ways, Corey—who was over 80 years old at the time—didn't give the charge much credence. He even briefly supported accusations against his wife until he realized how seriously the charges were being taken. Sheriff Corwin, the son of Judge Jonathan Corwin, was getting rather wealthy off the prosecution of so-called witches in Salem because anyone found guilty of witchcraft was subject to having his or her property seized and redistributed. That placed Giles Corey in a tough situation: If he pleaded guilty to the accusations against him, he would lose everything; at the same time, no one who had pleaded not guilty had been found to be innocent. Either outcome would mean that Corey's sons would not inherit his estate; instead, it would fall into the hands of the sheriff and the other town leaders. Corey did the only thing he could do: He refused to play their game.

Corey's Curse

Sheriff Corwin attempted to press a plea out of the old man— literally—by placing more and more weight on his chest every time he refused to confess, instead demanding, "More weight!" The act preserved his sons' inheritance but cost Giles Corey his life. Before he died, however, Corey spat at Corwin and sneered, "Damn you, Sheriff! I curse you and Salem!" Since then, sightings of Corey's ghost have meant disaster for the town. The last time he was spotted was in 1914, just before a fire that nearly wiped Salem off the map. The curse doesn't only target the town itself, though: The very position that George Corwin once held is said to be cursed as well. Every sheriff of Salem since Corwin has either died in office or retired due to heart problems. Between the curse of Giles Corey and all the other restless spirits, one wonders why Salem hasn't changed its nickname from "The Witch City" to "The Haunted City."

The Cave of the Murderous Witch

While there have been reports of ghostly encounters in virtually every small town in the world, Adams, Tennessee, stands alone in that it is perhaps the only place where a ghost is said to have been directly responsible for the death of a human being.

✳ ✳ ✳ ✳

Meet the Bell Family

THIS ODD STORY begins in 1817, when John Bell Sr. was inspecting a field on his farm in Robertson County, Tennessee. He encountered a strange beast that he described as doglike with a rabbitlike head. John allegedly shot at the creature, and it fled into the woods.

Shortly afterward, the Bell family began to experience odd phenomena in their home. What began as soft knocks quickly turned into what sounded like an animal biting or gnawing on the structure of the house. The Bell family scoured the building for rodents, but they found nothing. The activity didn't stop there. What sounded like rocks hitting the house could be heard at all hours of the day and night. Soon, it began to sound like rocks were being thrown from *inside* the house. Once again, the family's searches turned up nothing.

From there, the activity escalated to personal attacks, most of which were centered on John Bell and his youngest daughter, Betsy, who was frequently pushed, grabbed, and slapped by an unseen force.

With nowhere else to turn, John Bell asked his neighbors—Mr. and Mrs. James Johnston—if they had any ideas about what was occurring. After spending some time in the Bell home and witnessing the unusual activity themselves, the Johnstons convinced the Bells that an investigation should be conducted. Reluctantly, John Bell agreed, and several family friends were invited over.

The Investigations Begin

Incredibly, thumping sounds were heard throughout the house when the investigation began. Soon the thumps and groans began to sound like someone growling or clearing his or her throat. And then it happened: The entity began to speak. It said that it wanted to prevent Betsy Bell from marrying a local boy named Joshua Gardner. It also said that it wanted to kill John Bell.

When asked why it wanted to break up Betsy and Joshua and kill John, the voice remained silent. However, one night, the voice said that it was the spirit of Kate Batts, an eccentric neighbor who had disliked John Bell because of some contentious business dealings between them in the past. Whether or not it was actually the spirit of Kate Batts is unknown, but people began to refer to the entity as "Kate."

Kate would engage in long-winded discussions with those present, and would often quote from Scripture—a rather odd thing for a malevolent spirit to do. She also seemed to know exactly what people were doing at any given time, even if they were miles away. Reports also suggest that Kate sometimes seemed to be drunk, as she would slur her speech and sing bawdy songs.

Soon, word of the "Bell Witch" spread throughout the region and people came from all over to hear her speak. One legend states that when General Andrew Jackson and his men passed through the area, the future president decided that he wanted to hear her for himself. But the witch apparently had other ideas, as she reportedly caused Jackson's wagons to stop right at the Bell property line; more than 30 minutes passed before the entity allowed them to continue. Upon arriving at the Bell residence, the witch cried out that there were two frauds in Jackson's entourage and that she would expose them. However, Jackson and his men left quickly the following morning without Kate ever naming the frauds. Regarding his experience with the entity, Jackson supposedly declared, "I'd rather fight the entire British Army than deal with the Bell Witch."

The Torment Continues

The activity occurred at the Bell house for almost three full years. And while Betsy was certainly under constant attack, John Bell bore the brunt of the witch's anger. From time to time, he would fall deathly ill, his tongue swelling to the point where he could barely speak or swallow, and no medications helped. After some time, John would simply recover and seem fine...until the next time that he would be stricken with a mysterious malady. All the while, the witch would laugh and taunt John, claiming that one day, he would be dead.

On December 20, 1820, John Bell was found dead in his bed. After hearing Kate's maniacal laughter and shouts that she had finally "done it," the Bell family found a new medicine bottle containing a mysterious substance. John's son placed his finger in the bottle and then got a family cat to lick the substance off. Almost immediately, the cat went into convulsions and died. At that moment, it became clear to everyone that the witch had poisoned John Bell.

When Bell was laid to rest in the family cemetery, some people reported hearing the Bell Witch laugh out loud at the fact that she had succeeded in her mission to kill him.

Unfinished Business

But Kate's work wasn't done. She continued to focus on breaking up Betsy and Joshua Gardner, until finally, in the spring of 1821, Betsy broke off the relationship. After that, the Bell Witch left, but she promised to return in seven years to check up on the family.

According to legend, Kate did return in 1828, this time visiting the home of John Bell Jr. She apparently stayed for several weeks and had many casual conversations with John Jr., but she refused to explain why she needed to kill John Sr. or break up Betsy and Joshua. Before she left again, she promised to return in 107 years. However, 1935 came and went without the Bell Witch making an appearance. Or maybe she never really left the area.

Down into the Cave

Located on the former property of John Bell is a large cave. Many people believe that the Bell Witch fled to this cave when she was not actively haunting the Bell family. Others believe that the cave represents some sort of portal through which she would travel. The cave, which is open for tours, is still a hotbed of paranormal activity, such as strange sounds, moving shadows, and eerie mists that appear in photographs. So if you're looking for a chance to encounter a murderous entity, stop by the Bell Witch Cave . . . but beware if your last name is Bell.

King's Tavern

A love triangle and murder produce a spirit that resides at King's Tavern in Natchez, Mississippi? It seems likely. But the ghost of Madeline isn't the only disembodied soul flitting about at this historic pub.

✳　✳　✳　✳

From Fort to Tavern

THE OLD NATCHEZ Trace—a 500-mile trail stretching from Natchez, Mississippi, to about 17 miles southwest of Nashville, Tennessee—was cut by Native Americans centuries before Europeans arrived and was used as a crude highway to transport goods and people. It also attracted miscreants in the form of highwaymen, and during Colonial times, robberies and murders were common on the trail. Nevertheless, the path remained popular, and businesses catering to travelers sprouted up along it out of necessity. One such enterprise was King's Tavern. Originally built as a blockhouse for a fort, the building was acquired in 1799 by wealthy New Yorker Richard King, who turned it into a bar and inn. It was a great success, but it would also bring drama into King's life.

Cheating Ways

Despite having a loving wife, King succumbed to the oldest of temptations when he hired a young woman named Madeline as a server and subsequently seduced her. Attractive and industrious, Madeline was only too happy to become the rich man's mistress. Their tryst didn't last long, however: When King's irate wife learned of the affair, she took steps to end it. What occurred next is open to debate: Some believe that Mrs. King hired highwaymen to murder Madeline, while others say that she performed the deed herself. Either way, Madeline vanished without a trace. But without a body, there was officially no murder, so nothing further came of King's wife's permanent solution to her husband's tawdry affair.

Mystery Solved

In 1932, King's Tavern underwent significant renovations. While workers were repairing the fireplace in the pub's main room, they were horrified to find three human skeletons—two male and one female—hidden behind the bricks. The identities of the men were anyone's guess, but many believed that the female was Madeline, the young temptress who'd been done in by the jealous Mrs. King more than a century prior. When a Spanish dagger—a weapon that was quite popular during Colonial times—was discovered nearby, the theory became even more plausible. The bodies were buried in a local cemetery and the remodeling job was completed. A mysterious chapter in the tavern's history had been put to rest . . . or had it?

Manifestations

After the renovation, apparitions and other unexplained phenomena arrived like waves on a beach. Shadowy figures were often spotted walking up the staircases or passing directly through them. A spectral man wearing a top hat moved freely about the tavern; sporting a black jacket and tie string, his garb was consistent with that of the era in which the murders occurred. Members of the waitstaff who witnessed the apparition felt that he embodied evil, and many believed that he was involved in the murders—either as a perpetrator or a victim.

But ghosts of grown men aren't the only spirits lingering at the tavern: The unsettling sound of a crying baby has also been reported, and small footprints—presumably left by a woman—appear from out of nowhere on freshly mopped floors. Many believe that Madeline is responsible for the footprints, which usually move across the room directly toward startled employees. Madeline's ghost has also been blamed for spilling pitchers onto the floor, knocking jars from shelves, turning faucets and lights on and off, and opening doors. When her name is called out in protest, she has been known to slam doors.

Someone (or something) more sinister likes to forcefully throw dishes through the air and apply pressure around the necks or on the chests of visitors. And the fireplace where the bodies were discovered occasionally emits heat as if it is burning wood, even though no fire is lit and no firewood is present. Could this be a final plea for justice from a trio cheated out of life?

The Philip Phenomenon: Creating a Ghost Out of Thin Air

Which came first: the ghost or the séance? That's the million-dollar question regarding the Philip Phenomenon—an astonishing experiment that successfully conjured up a spirit. The only problem is that this ghost never really lived . . . Or did it?

✳   ✳   ✳   ✳

I T ALL BEGAN in 1972, when members of the Toronto Society for Psychical Research (TSPR) conducted an experiment to determine if they could "create" a ghost and study how the power of suggestion affected the results. They wanted to know if they could work with a totally fictitious character—a man they invented from scratch—and somehow make contact with its spirit. And they did.

Dr. A.R.G. Owen, the organization's chief parapsychology researcher, gathered a group of eight people who were interested in the paranormal but had no psychic abilities of their own. The Owen Group, as it was called, was made up of people from all walks of life, including Owen's wife, an accountant, an industrial designer, a former MENSA chairwoman, a housewife, a student, and a bookkeeper. Dr. Joel Whitton, a psychologist, was also present at many of the meetings as an observer.

The Making of a Ghost

The first order of business was to create the ghost, giving it physical characteristics and a complete background story. According to Dr. Owen, it was important to the study that the spirit be totally made-up, with no strong ties to any historical figure.

The group named the ghost Philip and proceeded to bring him to life—on paper, that is. A sketch artist even drew a picture of Philip as the group imagined him. Here is his story:

Philip Aylesford was an aristocratic Englishman who was born in 1624. As a supporter of the King, he was knighted at age 16 and went on to make a name for himself in the military. He married Dorothea, the beautiful daughter of a nobleman who lived nearby. Unfortunately, Dorothea's appearance was deceiving, as her personality was cold and unyielding. As a Catholic, Philip wouldn't divorce his wife, so he found escape by riding around the grounds of his estate. One day, he came across a gypsy camp. There, he found true love in the arms of the raven-haired Margo, whose dark eyes seemed to look into his soul. He brought her to Diddington Manor, his family home, and hid her in the gatehouse near the stable. But it wasn't meant to be: Dorothea soon discovered her husband's secret affair and retaliated by accusing the gypsy woman of stealing and practicing witchcraft. Afraid of damaging his own reputation, Philip did not step forward in Margo's defense, and she was burned at the stake. After the death of his beloved, Philip was tormented with guilt and loneliness; he killed himself in 1654 at age 30.

Focus, Focus, Focus

In September 1972, after the tale was written, the group began meeting regularly. Reports of these meetings vary. Some accounts describe them as mere gatherings in which group members would discuss Philip and meditate on the details of his life. With no results after about a year, the group moved on to a more traditional method of communing with ghosts: holding séances in a darkened room, sitting around a table with appropriate music and objects that might have been used by Philip or his family. Another version has the group beginning with séances and switching to the more casual setting later.

The setting itself is ultimately secondary to the results: Through the focus and concentration of the group, Philip soon began to make his presence known. He answered questions by tapping on the table for "yes" or "no." Just to be sure, a "yes" tap confirmed that he was, indeed, Philip.

A Physical Presence

After communication was established, the Philip Phenomenon took on a life of its own. Through the tapping, Philip was able to answer questions about the details of his life. He was also able to correctly answer questions about people and places of that historical time period, although these were all facts that were familiar to at least one member of the group. Philip even seemed to develop a personality, exuding emotions that changed the atmosphere of the entire room. But most amazingly, he was able to exhibit some remarkable physical manifestations, such as making objects move, turning lights on and off at the group's request, and performing incredible feats with the table: It shifted, it danced on one leg, and it even moved across the room.

In order to demonstrate the results of this experiment, the group held a séance in front of an audience of 50 people; the session was also videotaped. Philip rose to the occasion—and so did the table. In addition to tapping on the table and manipulating the lights, Philip made the entire table levitate half an inch off the ground!

The experiment was deemed a success, as there was little doubt that something paranormal was occurring during the sessions. However, the Owen Group never actually realized its original goal of getting the ghost of Philip to materialize. But the TSPR did go on to re-create the experiment successfully on several other occasions with a new group and a new fictional "ghost."

Real, Random, or Re-creation?

So what can be concluded from all this? No one knows for sure, but several schools of thought have developed regarding the matter. Some believe that Philip was a real ghost and that he had once been a living, breathing person. Perhaps he had a few of the characteristics of the fictional Philip and simply responded to the group's summons. Some who believe in the ghost theory say that it may have been a playful spirit (or a demonic one) that just pretended to be Philip as a prank.

A less-popular theory suggests that someone close to the group was aware of the background information as well as the times and places of the meetings. He or she might have planned an elaborate hoax to make it appear as though the ghost was real.

But it is also possible that after creating Philip, the Owen Group put forth enough energy, focus, and concentration to bring him to life, in a manner of speaking. Ghosts may be products of our imaginations, existing only in our minds, but this study does prove one thing: When people put minds together, anything is possible—even a visit from the Other Side.

Ghosts of Glensheen

In 1905, self-made millionaire Chester Congdon was one of Minnesota's richest men. When the banking and iron-mining magnate and his wife, Clara, moved into their stupendous mansion on the shore of Lake Superior in 1908, they never dreamed that their elegant home would someday be famous for murder ... and ghosts.

✳   ✳   ✳   ✳

THE CONGDONS NAMED their sprawling estate "Glensheen." The brick lakefront house features multiple gables and chimneys and 39 richly furnished rooms. The Congdons spared no expense on their state-of-the-art abode, equipping it with electricity, running water, and a humidification system and covering the grounds with lush gardens where they entertained Minnesota's elite with impressive parties.

Chester only lived in his dream home for eight years: He died in 1916 at age 63. The estate passed to Clara and then to the couple's youngest daughter, Elisabeth. To this day, the house retains most of the family's original furnishings, which makes the area where a grisly double murder took place seem even eerier to visitors.

Family Ties, Lies, and Sighs

In 1977, Elisabeth was 83 years old and was partially paralyzed. She had never married, although she had adopted two girls: Jennifer—who married a businessman and led a quiet life in Racine, Wisconsin—and Marjorie, the black sheep of the family. Elisabeth's life of luxury ended violently when an intruder smothered the helpless woman in her sleep with her own pink satin pillow; he also bludgeoned Elisabeth's protective night nurse, Velma Pietila, with a candlestick.

Suspicion immediately fell on Marjorie, but it was her husband, Roger Caldwell, who was charged with killing the elderly heiress to obtain Marjorie's $8 million share of the estate; Marjorie was charged with aiding and abetting him in the crime. Caldwell went to prison and later confessed to the crime, but Marjorie was acquitted. In fact, the trial's jurors felt so sorry for her that they threw her a posttrial party!

That was a nice gesture, but even being honored so highly was not enough to change Marjorie's basic nature. Although she did get her hands on a pile of her dead mother's money, her life deteriorated further thereafter. In 1981, she married Wallace Hagen (without divorcing Roger Caldwell), and in 1984, she was convicted of arson and insurance fraud in Minnesota. By 1992, Marjorie and Hagen, were living in Arizona, where she was again found guilty of arson. After her conviction but before she went to jail, Hagen died of a mysterious drug overdose. Marjorie was arrested and charged with his murder, but the charges were later dropped.

Marjorie was released from prison in 2004, but in 2007, she was arrested again—this time on charges of committing fraud and forgery. In 2010, she again made headlines when she tried to get her probation dropped so that she could move into an assisted-living facility in Arizona.

A Soft Sheen of Spirits

Meanwhile, Glensheen remains as grand as ever. Now owned by the University of Minnesota-Duluth, the mansion is used for art fairs and theatrical productions, including readings of the macabre stories of Edgar Allen Poe during Halloween season. The house and gardens are also open for public tours. And although its tour guides are reportedly tight-lipped about hauntings, it is believed that the spirits of Elisabeth and Velma have never left the place. People have seen misty figures floating about, heard unidentifiable noises, and felt cold chills when viewing the room in which Elisabeth died.

In one story that was recounted in *The Minnesota Road Guide to Haunted Locations*, an employee felt something pulling on his ankles while he was standing on a ladder. Thinking that a coworker had snuck up the ladder to play a prank, he turned to face the culprit, but no one was there—at least, no one that he could see.

Who could blame Elisabeth and Velma for lingering at the Glensheen Mansion? It's certainly a beautiful place to spend eternity.

Five years before Elisabeth Congdon was killed, Patty Duke starred in a dark thriller filmed at Glensheen. The movie's title? *You'll Like My Mother*.

"Lotz" of Ghosts Gather at Carter House

Franklin, Tennessee, which is located about 20 miles south of Nashville, has a population of 64,000—unless you count its ghosts. The site of what some historians consider the bloodiest one-day battle of the Civil War, Franklin is rich with history—and restless spirits. It seems that many of the soldiers who lost their lives in that famous battle are still hanging around the city.

✳ ✳ ✳ ✳

Before the Blood

IN 1830, FOUNTAIN Branch Carter built a beautiful home in the heart of Franklin. In 1858, Johann Lotz constructed his own house across the street on land that he'd purchased from Carter. Both were blissfully unaware of what would occur there just a few years later.

After the fall of Nashville in 1862, Franklin became a Union military post. In 1864, in an attempt to "take the bull by the horns," the Confederate army decided to attack the enemy head-on in Franklin, hoping to drive General Sherman's army north. It didn't quite work out that way; instead, during the Battle of Franklin on November 30, 1864, more than

4,000 lives were lost, and because the battlefield was small, the concentration of bloodshed was very high. And most of it took place right in front of the Lotz and Carter homes.

The Battle Begins

When the Confederate troops arrived in town, Union General Jacob Cox commandeered the Carter House as his base of operations. Fearing for their lives, the Carter family took refuge in the basement during the five long hours of the battle. In all, 23 people—including the Lotz family—crowded into the cellar. They all survived, and when the fighting was over, both houses were converted into field hospitals. Surgeries, amputations, and death filled the days and weeks that followed. Between the violence and the chaos, it's no wonder that some of the dead never found peace.

One of the men who was killed during the battle was Tod Carter, Fountain's son and a Confederate soldier who was thrilled to be heading home. He was wounded just 300 feet from his front door and was taken to his sister's bedroom, where he died. Some say that his spirit remains there today.

History Comes to Life

In 1953, the Carter House was opened to the public. Today, it's a museum and a National Historic Landmark; its eight acres stand as a tribute to the battle that took place there so long ago. If you look closely, more than a thousand bullet holes can be found on the property. The Lotz House—which was added to the National Historic Register in 1976 and opened to the public in 2008—bears its share of scars as well: Bloodstains are evident throughout, and a round indentation in the wood floor is a reminder of a cannonball that crashed through the roof and flew through a second-floor bedroom before landing in the parlor on the first floor, leaving a charred path in its wake.

In the Spirit of Things

Visitors to the Carter House have reported seeing the specter of Tod Carter sitting on a bed or standing in the hallway. His sister Annie has also been spotted in the hallways and on the stairs. She's blamed for playful pranks such as rolling a ball along the floor and causing objects to appear and disappear. But then again, the mischief-maker might be the spirit of one of the children who took refuge in the cellar during the battle. After all, staff members and visitors have reported feeling the sensation of a child tugging at their sleeves, and one worker even saw a spectral child walking down the staircase.

The ghosts of soldiers and other family members may be responsible for some of the other unusual phenomena experienced in the house, such as furniture moving on its own, doors slamming, and apparitions peering through the windows.

Not to be outdone, the ghosts at the Lotz House manifest as phantom voices and household items that move on their own or come up missing. While they haven't been identified, they seem to be civilian spirits rather than military ones. It's tough sharing space with so many ghosts, but the staff members are used to it, and they're happy to share the history—and the spirits—with visitors who stop by on the Franklin on Foot Ghost Tour. And don't worry: These lively spirits have never followed anyone home—at least not yet!

Can Dogs See Spirits?

It's late at night and you're lying in bed watching TV with your faithful pooch snoring softly at your feet. Suddenly and without warning, your dog bolts upright and looks into the darkened hallway, growling while the hair on the back of his or her neck stands up. Cautiously you investigate, but you find nothing, which leads you to wonder, "Did my dog just see a ghost?"

✳ ✳ ✳ ✳

What Are You Looking At?

IN ORDER TO ascertain if dogs can see spirits, we must first determine what a ghost looks like. By most accounts, spirits appear as dark shadows or white, misty shapes, often only briefly visible out of the corner of one's eye. Sometimes, people report ghosts as balls of glowing light that move or dart about. In most cases, they are reported in low-light conditions, which is why many ghost hunters use infrared extenders when they shoot video or take photographs. So to sum up, if dogs are able to see ghosts, they would need to be able to see:

* Dark shadows or white, misty shapes

* Moving balls of light

* In low light

How a Dog Sees

Just like a human's eye, a dog's eye is made up of rods and cones. Rods function well in low light and are also helpful in detecting movement. Cones help to define colors. Unlike a human eye, the center of a dog's eye is made up mainly of rods, so dogs can't see colors very well. But because apparitions are usually described as dark shadows or white shapes, dogs should be able to see them just fine.

The rods in dogs' eyes allow them not only to detect motion but also to see phenomena such as flickering lights better than humans can. So if ghosts appear as flitting lights that move quickly, dogs should be able to see them.

Finally, the additional rods in the centers of dogs' eyes make it possible for dogs to see much better than humans in low-light situations. So while humans scramble for flashlights and infrared extenders to try to see ghosts, dogs only have to use their eyes.

A Dog's-Eye View

Another factor to consider is from where dogs are seeing. Most adult humans spend the majority of their time viewing the world from a standing position—in general, more than five feet off the ground. Dogs, however, spend most of their lives looking up at things from two feet or so off the ground. That doesn't sound like a big difference, but it is. Just lie on the floor at night and look up at some objects; it really gives you a unique perspective. Perhaps that different vantage point is what's needed to see spirits.

Refusing to Conform

Finally, consider the idea that, despite what most ghost-hunting shows would like you to think, the majority of people do not believe that ghosts exist. Maybe that's exactly why dogs see them: Because modern society cannot force dogs to conform to its beliefs. In other words, dogs don't know that they're not supposed to see ghosts because they allegedly don't exist. Therefore, it would stand to reason that a dog, upon seeing an apparition, simply acknowledges it as being a living, breathing person, unlike many skeptical humans who would immediately try to convince themselves that they did not just have a paranormal encounter.

The Hoosac Tunnel

By the mid-1800s, the train was the preeminent form of transportation in America, and competition between railroad lines was fierce. If a means could be found to shorten a route, create a link, or speed up a journey, it was generally taken to help ensure a railroad's continued profitability.

✳   ✳   ✳   ✳

I N 1848, THE newly formed Troy and Greenfield Railroad proposed a direct route that would link Greenfield and Williamstown, Massachusetts. In Williamstown, it would connect to an existing route on which trains could travel to

Troy, New York, and points west. The time-saving measure seemed like a brilliant move, except for one not-so-small detail: Between Greenfield and Williamstown stood a forbidding promontory known as Hoosac Mountain. In order to tame it, the railroad would need to drill a tunnel—but not just any tunnel: At nearly five miles in length, it would have to be the world's *longest* tunnel.

The Great Bore

In 1851, the project was set in motion. Almost immediately, trouble arose when drillers learned that the soft rock stratum through which they were supposed to be boring was, in fact, harder than nails. In 1861, funding dried up, and by 1862—realizing that it had bitten off more than it could chew—the Troy and Greenfield Railroad defaulted on its loan. The state of Massachusetts stepped in to complete the tunnel.

With a steady infusion of cash and a government bent on completing the project, the Hoosac Tunnel was finally finished in 1873; in 1876, the "Great Bore" officially opened for business. The project had taken a quarter century to complete at a total cost of $21 million. Nearly 200 lives were lost while the tunnel was built, with 13 being the result of an incident that's legendary to this day.

Tragedy Strikes

It happened on October 17, 1867, inside the tunnel's central shaft—a vertical hole that was drilled from atop the mountain to intersect with the midpoint of the tunnel 1,028 feet below. The shaft would supply much-needed ventilation to the tunnel and allow drillers two more facings from which to attack, a measure that would greatly speed up operations.

On this particular day, the shaft reached into the mountain some 538 feet. While attempting to light a lamp, a workman accidentally ignited a gasoline tank. Within seconds, an inferno rocketed up to the surface, claiming the pumping station and hoist house located above, causing them to collapse into the deep pit. Unfortunately, 13 men were working in the shaft during the incident. As soon as was humanly possible, a miner was lowered into the smoldering cavity to search for survivors; he passed out during the long trip but managed to gasp "no hope" upon his return to the surface.

Without an operational pump, the cavity eventually filled to the brim with seepage and rainwater. It wasn't until a year later that the central shaft gave up its grisly contents. As it turns out, most of the victims hadn't died from the flames or from drowning: The stranded men had built a survival raft but were slowly asphyxiated by the poisonous gases and the oxygen-hungry flames raging above them.

Spirits Rise

In a 1985 article, Glenn Drohan—a reporter for the *North Adams Transcript*—told of strange phenomena at the tunnel, such as "vague shapes and muffled wails near the water-filled pit." Shortly after the accident occurred, workmen allegedly saw the spirits of the lost miners carrying picks and shovels. The workers called out to the missing men, but they did not answer, and their apparitions quickly vanished.

Other tragic goings-on at the Hoosac Tunnel include the strange death of Ringo Kelley. In 1865, when explosive nitroglycerin was first used for excavation, experts Kelley, Billy Nash, and Ned Brinkman attempted to set a charge of nitro before running for cover. Nash and Brinkman never made it: Kelley somehow set off the explosion prematurely, burying his coworkers in the process.

Shortly thereafter, Kelley vanished. He was not seen again until March 30, 1866, when his lifeless body was found two miles inside the tunnel. Bizarrely, he had been strangled to death at the precise spot where Nash and Brinkman had perished. Investigators never developed any leads, but workmen had an ominous feeling about Kelley's demise: They believed that the vengeful spirits of Nash and Brinkman had done him in.

Present-Day Poltergeists

If the preceding tales seem quaint due to the passage of time, it's worth noting that the tunnel still features its share of hauntings; standouts among these are railroad worker Joseph Impoco's trio of supernatural tales. In an article that appeared in *The Berkshire Sampler* on October 30, 1977, Impoco told reporter Eileen Kuperschmid that he was chipping ice from the tracks one day when he heard a voice say, "Run, Joe, run!" As Impoco tells it, "I turned, and sure enough, there was No. 60 coming at me. Boy, did I jump back fast! When I looked [back], there was no one there."

Six weeks later, Impoco was working with an iron crowbar, doing his best to free cars that were stuck to the icy tracks. Suddenly, he heard, "Joe! Joe! Drop it, Joe!" He instinctively dropped the crowbar just as 11,000 volts of electricity struck it from a short-circuited power line overhead.

In the final incident, Impoco was removing trees from the tunnel's entrance when, from out of nowhere, an enormous oak fell directly toward him. He managed to outrun the falling tree, but he heard a frightening, ethereal laugh as he ran; he was certain that it hadn't come from any of his coworkers.

Travel Tips

For the brave at heart, a visit to the Hoosac Tunnel can prove awe-inspiring and educational. The tunnel is still used, so walking inside it is strictly off-limits, but a well-worn path beside the tracks leads to the Hoosac's entrance. For those who are looking to avoid things that go bump in the night, a trip to the nearby North Adams' Hoosac Tunnel Museum in the Western Gateway Heritage State Park will reveal the incredible history of this five-mile-long portal into another dimension—and will do so far away from Ringo Kelley's haunts. All aboard.

The Rolling Hills Are Alive with Spirits

You can turn an asylum into a mall, but you can't take the spirits out of it. That seems to be the case in East Bethany, New York, a small town located between Rochester and Buffalo. The main attraction there is a building that used to be a poorhouse and has undergone many changes during the nearly two centuries since it was constructed. However, it seems that its former residents just don't understand that the Rolling Hills Asylum is no longer their home.

✳ ✳ ✳ ✳

The Poorhouse

OPENED IN 1827, the Genesee County Poorhouse was a residence for a wide array of people: Paupers, orphans, widows, and unwed mothers shared space with drunks, the mentally ill, the criminally insane, and the physically disabled. The massive structure served this eclectic group for 125 years before it was transformed into a nursing home in the 1950s.

Imagine the number of people who must have died there over the years. Some sources list the number of deaths at 1,750, but experts estimate that it was actually much higher. It's hard to say, because the dead were often dumped into unmarked graves.

In the early 1990s, the building was converted into a group of specialty shops known as Carriage Village. It wasn't long before store employees and shoppers began to notice some strange phenomena. When paranormal investigators were summoned, they observed mysterious shadows and doors that seemed to be held shut by an invisible force, as well as disembodied voices and screams. The property was officially declared "haunted." In 2003, the building was renamed Rolling Hills Country Mall, and the following year, it was opened to the public and became known as "Rolling Hills Asylum."

Bargain Hunters Give Way to Ghost Hunters

Rolling Hills Country Mall has since closed its doors to shoppers, but in 2009, Sharon and Jerry Coyle purchased the property; they keep the building open as a paranormal research center, which hosts ghost tours and other special events.

Former owner Lori Carlson said that shadows and electronic voice phenomena (EVPs) are common occurrences at Rolling Hills, especially on the first and second floors of the East Wing—an area that was added to the building in 1958. Perhaps trying to avoid modern-day visitors, the spirits there seem to be most active between 3 A.M. and 5 A.M. And if you walk around the second floor of this wing, you might hear footsteps above you; the trouble is, the building has no third floor.

The apparition of an older woman has been glimpsed heading into the ladies' room just outside the former cafeteria area; a man with a goatee has also been seen walking around the same area. And a former meat locker nearby is a good place to catch a few EVPs.

Another paranormal hot spot is the building's old solitary confinement cell, which was added in 1828 to house violent residents. These segregated souls frequently show themselves today.

See for Yourself

Rolling Hills Asylum attracts ghost hunters from all over the country, but working there isn't for the faint of heart. Staff member Suzie Yencer tells of one paranormal investigation during which the researcher wanted to try an experiment. The group gathered in a basement area known as the Christmas Room, where toys are often seen moving by themselves. No lights or detectors were used; the only illumination came from a pink glow stick that was set in the middle of the circle of people. Only Suzie was allowed to speak in the eerily quiet room: She was asked to try to make contact with the spirit world . . . and it worked. To her surprise, the glow stick moved back and forth, and a toy rocking horse in the room started to sway. Suzie and several others actually saw a phantom arm that appeared to reach for a ball; then, just as suddenly, it was gone.

In 2010, the *Ghost Adventures* team devoted an episode to the spirits of the old asylum. When Zak Bagans, Nick Groff, and Aaron Goodwin spent the night locked inside the old building, they heard disembodied voices and saw apparitions in their photos. Their experience, combined with the testimony of staff members and visitors, convinced them that Rolling Hills is a hotbed of paranormal activity.

Investigators from Central New York Ghost Hunters agreed. Members documented unexplained cold spots, phantom footsteps, hushed voices (which were captured on audio recorders), and actual physical contact, such as hair pulling and light taps or pokes.

The Naughty and the Nice

Visitors to Rolling Hills frequently report seeing the shadow of Roy, a former resident who suffered from gigantism, a disease that caused him to become unusually large. He grew to be over seven feet tall at a time when six feet tall was considered exceptionally large. Embarrassed by Roy's appearance, his parents left him at Rolling Hills in the late 1800s, when he was 12 years old; he lived there until he died at age 62. Roy was a gentle soul whose spirit emits friendly energy.

But not every entity at Rolling Hills is as benevolent as Roy. Nurse Emmie Altworth was known to abuse patients and was thought to practice the dark arts and black magic. Inmates and other staff members feared her. Modern visitors have reported a feeling of evil and unease in the building's infirmary—possibly due to Emmie's negative energy.

If you visit Rolling Hills Asylum, watch out for its many spirits—the friendly and the anguished alike. And when you get home, be prepared to sleep with the lights on.

"The death is not smooth. When there is trauma—an unacceptable accident or shock or surprise—this will, in some cases, cause the personality to go into a state of psychotic shock. In that state of shock, they are not aware that they've passed on. They are confused as to their real status because they can see everybody and nobody seems to be able to see them."

—HANS HOLZER, ON WHAT CAUSES SOME PEOPLE TO BECOME GHOSTS

Get Your Kicks—and Your Haunts—on Route 66

Route 66 was the historic two-lane highway that guided travelers from Chicago to Santa Monica, California, by way of small rural towns. Although it may no longer appear on maps, portions of the windy road that passed through eight states can still be traveled today. And as befits a ride through the past, plenty of ghosts can be found along the way.

✳ ✳ ✳ ✳

The Mill (Lincoln, Illinois)

DESIGNED TO LOOK like a Dutch windmill, The Mill originally opened in 1929 as a quaint restaurant known as The Blue Mill. Travelers on Route 66 could stop in at any time, day or night, to enjoy a tasty grilled sandwich served by a waitress dressed in a blue dress with a white apron. The restaurant was famous for its fried schnitzel, but rumors suggested that notorious Chicago gangster Al Capone had buried at least one body near the building.

Unfortunately, as interstate highways replaced Route 66, drivers bypassed small towns such as Lincoln, and The Mill fell on hard times. In the mid-1980s, the restaurant was replaced by a museum that displayed oddities such as a mechanical leg that emerged from the ceiling. The museum closed in 1996, but Illinois Route 66 enthusiasts launched a campaign to save The Mill. During a paranormal investigation at the building in 2009, no apparitions were seen, but the researchers sensed their presence. A few investigators felt as if their hair, shoulders, and arms were being touched, even though no one else was nearby. Others experienced cold sensations on their necks, and photos revealed orbs and inexplicable beams of light. Worst of all, several members of the team were overwhelmed by a sense of dread, the words "Help me," and symptoms of drunkenness, including dizziness and headaches.

Tri-County Truck Stop (Villa Ridge, Missouri)

Like The Mill, the Tri-County Truck Stop was a restaurant that Route 66's drivers appreciated for its grub. It is now closed, but former employees and customers shared many stories about strange things that occurred there. Several of these reports centered on the basement, where a misty figure was seen pacing back and forth and hot and cold spots would suddenly pop up despite a lack of ventilation. A paranormal research team investigating the basement had a lightbulb thrown at them from some 50 feet away, even though they were the only living beings there at the time. A former employee said that she'd also had objects thrown at her when she was the only person in the building.

All over the building, doors open and shut by themselves. At least two people witnessed a spectral man stab a ghostly woman on the stairs that used to lead to apartments and an office on the top floor; the next day, a red stain appeared on the wall. Another person saw chairs moving themselves into a circle on the top floor. One former patron said that he hated going there because he felt as though he was being watched all the time, even when he was in the bathroom.

Oklahoma's Spook Light

The Tri-State Spook Light (aka the Hornet Spook Light) is an orb that appears almost nightly near Quapaw, Oklahoma. While many claim that it's merely the headlights from cars on Route 66, the phenomenon was witnessed in the area long before cars were even invented; in fact, local Native American tribes knew of it centuries ago. The orb maintains a careful distance from those who gather to see it; it pulses and varies in intensity and then disappears when cars on the road approach it. Many theories speculate as to what (or who) the orb is: Some believe that it's the ghost of a miner carrying a lantern; others believe that it is two Native American lovers who killed themselves because their romance was forbidden; and still others speculate that it is a solitary Native American, or even a portal to another world.

The Nat (Amarillo, Texas)

The old Amarillo Natatorium—affectionately known as The Nat—has had a long life with many identities, and those who enjoyed it most are reluctant to leave. The structure was initially used as a natatorium—a building housing an indoor pool—but in 1926, when the pool was covered with a wood floor, it became a dance hall. During its heyday, The Nat played host to legendary acts such as Benny Goodman, Louis Armstrong, and Buddy Holly; oddly, a sign advertising "Monty McGee and His Orchestra" has reappeared through every coat of paint administered to the structure's exterior since 1942. In the 1990s, when the building housed an antique mall, several people commented on strange cold spots in some of the stores. Often, storeowners would arrive in the morning to find that the furniture in their shops had been rearranged overnight. People also witnessed a female ghost with red wine stains on her white dress, and a spectral couple was spotted dancing in the former ballroom. When a paranormal research team spent a night in the building in 1996, cameras mysteriously shut themselves off, but a tape recorder captured a woman singing and a phantom drummer playing a tune. The past was obviously too much fun for these playful spirits to let go.

KiMo Theatre (Albuquerque, New Mexico)

In 1951, Bobby Darnall was just six years old when the boiler at the KiMo Theatre exploded and killed him. The boiler was located in the lobby behind the concession stand in the

1927 Pueblo Deco-style building; Bobby had been watching a film with his friends but decided to get a snack. Just as he approached the concession stand, the boiler blew; the force of the explosion demolished part of the lobby. These days, employees appease Bobby's hungry spirit by leaving doughnuts on a pipe that runs along the back wall of the theater, behind the stage. If any doughnuts remain the next morning, they sometimes contain child-sized bite marks. Bobby has also been seen playing by the stairs wearing jeans and a striped T-shirt, but he is not the only ghost in the theater: A woman in a bonnet has also been seen roaming the building, but she generally keeps to herself. The KiMo Theatre closed in 1968, but it was restored and reopened in 2000, just in time for Route 66's 75th anniversary celebration.

Hotel Brunswick (Kingman, Arizona)

For the most part, the ghosts at the Hotel Brunswick seem to be friendly, and some are downright playful. A spectral young girl has been seen in the dining room, and elsewhere in the hotel, several guests have seen a small ghost-child, who seems to be seeking a playmate. Others have reported that something tugged on their legs or feet while they were sleeping. One family woke up in the morning to discover that their necks had yellow marks on them. (Fortunately, the marks washed off easily with soap and water.) Old coins were found in stacks lined up in hallways and near the bar, which a former owner interpreted as the spirits letting him know that prosperous times were ahead. Another owner saw a ghostly man walking up the stairs when he opened the cellar door; he got chills as the figure passed right through him. Guests have experienced similar shadow phenomena in the second-floor hallway. It is not known who most of these ghosts were in life, but some believe that one of the spirits is W. D. McKnight, a wealthy gentleman who died in his room at the Hotel Brunswick in 1915. Although it can be a bit unsettling to bunk with a ghost, no one has reported any harmful encounters with the hotel's resident spirits.

Colorado Street Bridge (Pasadena, California)

When the Colorado Street Bridge opened in Pasadena, California, in 1913, it was one of the many impressive bridges that Route 66 crossed before it terminated in Santa Monica. But these days, it is commonly referred to as "Suicide Bridge" because it is believed that 100 to 200 people have ended their lives by jumping off this high span; many of these deaths took place during the Great Depression. But the high suicide rate can't be blamed entirely on economic circumstances because the first one occurred there only six years after construction was finished. It is also believed that a construction worker died there six months before the bridge was complete, when he fell off the structure into a concrete pit supporting a pillar; his body was never recovered, but legend has it that his ghost lures people to follow him.

Many people have witnessed a spectral woman in a flowing robe throwing herself off the bridge. She may be the ghost of a mother who flung her baby and then herself from the span in 1937. (The baby actually landed on some treetops and survived.) People have also heard strange cries coming from the canyon 150 feet below the bridge.

Ghostly Guests Stay for Free at the Hotel del Coronado

If you're like most people, you love to get extras during a hotel stay: Complimentary breakfast, Wi-Fi, and fancy shampoo are all welcome. But how about an extra guest? At the Hotel del Coronado in Coronado, California, you get all the usual amenities plus the chance to share your room with resident ghost Kate Morgan.

✳   ✳   ✳   ✳

Guests and Ghosts

ANY BUILDING THAT dates back to 1888 is certainly rich with history, and the Hotel del Coronado is no exception.

For more than a century, travelers—many with stories and secrets of their own—have passed through its elegant doors. When it was built, this grandiose structure—which is perched right next to the Pacific Ocean—was the largest building outside of New York City to feature electric lighting. Today, Coronado is a rather affluent town, but in the late 1800s, it was filled with crime and debauchery. "The Del," as the hotel is affectionately known, offered its guests a peaceful escape where they could relax and forget their troubles. The building was named a National Historic Landmark in 1977, and it is still in operation today.

Over the years, the Del became a vacation hot spot for celebrities and politicians. Marilyn Monroe stayed there while filming *Some Like It Hot* (1959), and author L. Frank Baum is said to have written much of *The Wonderful Wizard of Oz* in his room at the famous hotel. In fact, it is believed that the Emerald City was inspired by the Del's architecture. But the hotel's most notable guest may be Kate Morgan—a young woman who checked into the Del in November 1892 . . . and never left.

Many stories have been told about Kate Morgan, but most accounts agree that the 24-year-old woman checked into Room 302 under the alias Lottie Bernard. Strikingly beautiful, she appeared to be either ill or upset, and she had no luggage. She said that she was planning to meet her "brother" for the Thanksgiving holiday, but several days later, she was found on the hotel steps . . . with a bullet in her head. Her death was ruled a suicide.

The Background
The story behind the story is that Kate and her husband, Tom, had been staging a bit of a con game. They traveled the rails setting up card games that Tom invariably won. While Kate pretended to be Tom's sister, she flirted shamelessly with men who tried to impress her with their card-playing skills. She was impressed all right—to the tune of hundreds of dollars.

Kate finally tired of the scheming and the traveling, and like other young women her age, she longed to settle down in a home and start a family. For a brief time, Tom and Kate lived in Los Angeles, but Tom grew restless and headed back out on the rails. Shortly thereafter, when Kate discovered that she was pregnant, she made the mistake of telling this joyous news to her husband while on a train to San Diego. They quarreled, and he went on to another city, while she continued to her final destination: the Hotel del Coronado.

Evidence suggests that Kate may have tried to abort her baby by drinking large amounts of quinine. When that didn't work, she traveled across the bay to San Diego, where she purchased a gun and some bullets. Those who saw her reported that she seemed pale and sickly; they weren't surprised when she was found dead.

The Spirited Kate

Guests and employees alike have felt Kate's presence in several places around the Del, including her guest room, the beach, and some of the hotel shops. One boutique, known as Established in 1888, has been the site of some particularly unusual activity. A display of Marilyn Monroe memorabilia was often targeted—items literally flew off the shelves. Staff members came to the conclusion that Kate was jealous of the famous starlet. When the Marilyn souvenirs were moved to a corner and replaced with mugs, both areas settled down and no more unusual activity was reported.

An apparition dressed in a long black dress has been seen around the shop and in the hallways. And a maintenance man at the hotel reports that there is one light on the property that will never stay lit: It's the one over the steps where Kate's lifeless body was found.

The most notable haunting, however, is in the room where Kate stayed in 1892. The room number has since changed from 302 to 3312, and recently to 3327. Possibly confused as to which room is hers, Kate also seems to make frequent visits to Room 3502, which is thought to be haunted as well. Strange, unexplained events have occurred in both of these rooms. Guests staying in these rooms have reported toilets flushing by themselves, lights flickering on and off, curtains blowing when the windows are closed, and a lingering floral scent. Ashtrays have been seen flying through the air, temperatures mysteriously dip and surge, and televisions blare one minute and are silent the next. Several visitors have also reported seeing a ghostly figure standing by the window of Kate's room, and a strange glow has been observed just inside that window from the outside. The screen on that same window has fallen off mysteriously more than once, and hotel guests have reported hearing soft murmurs inside the room. Is it the ocean . . . or the sound of a woman reliving her distress over and over again?

Room 3519 at the Del is also thought to be haunted, perhaps even more intensely than Kate's room. In 1983, a Secret Service agent stayed in Room 3519 while guarding then-Vice President George H.W. Bush. The agent bolted from the room in the middle of the night claiming that he'd heard unearthly gurgling noises and that the entire room seemed to glow.

Lincoln's Ghost Train

Abraham Lincoln's funeral train appears to have been much like the president himself: uncommonly determined and larger-than-life.

✳ ✳ ✳ ✳

Final Journey

WHEN PRESIDENT LINCOLN was assassinated in April 1865, the nation was understandably plunged into a state of mourning. Swept away was the "Great Emancipator," who had not only put an end to slavery but also preserved a fractured American union. For everything that he had done for the nation, it was decided that Lincoln's funeral procession should be as great as the man himself. In order to bring the president

close to the citizens who loved and mourned him, his funeral train would trace the same route—in reverse—that Lincoln had traveled when he went to Washington, D.C., four years earlier as president-elect. Covering a vast 1,654 miles, the procession left Washington on April 21, 1865, and finally pulled into Springfield, Illinois, on May 3. Officially, this was Lincoln's last ride—but unofficially, some say that Abe and his funeral train have never stopped chugging along.

First Phantom

In April 1866, one year after Lincoln's assassination, the first report of the ghost train surfaced. The sighting occurred along a stretch of railway in New York's Hudson Valley. Witnesses told a fantastic tale of a spectral train that whooshed by them without making a sound. They identified it as Lincoln's funeral train after they observed the president's flag-draped coffin on board. Surrounded by black crepe, the casket was identical to the original but with one notable difference: This time, a *skeletal* honor guard stood at attention beside it. Witnesses also recalled an equally skeletal band playing what must have been a dreary funeral dirge; that no sounds were emitted from their musical instruments also seemed bizarre. A strange bluish light surrounded the train as it chugged silently northward. Witnesses recalled that a blast of warm air could be felt and that clocks inexplicably stopped for six minutes as the train slowly passed by. Over time, this vision would be reported surprisingly often along much of the original train's route.

Mass Hysteria?

With a tragedy of such immensity seizing the national psyche, it was almost a given that sightings of Lincoln's ghost would occur. Psychologists attribute such phenomena to denial—the subconscious act of refusing to let go. Lincoln had saved the union and restored peace to a nation whose future had hung precariously in the balance. It seemed extremely unfair that he should be taken away in such a brutal fashion. Yet, he had been.

Still, what can be said of a phantom train that appears to numerous people along so vast a route? While shock and denial might account for individual sightings of a spectral president, it seems doubtful that an entire funeral train could be hallucinated by scores of people at precisely the same time. And how could the details of such sightings match so closely from person to person and region to region?

Just Passing Through

If witnesses are to be believed, Lincoln's ghost train still chugs along on its seemingly endless journey. Sightings of it generally occur in April (the month in which the original funeral train began its trek), and details of eyewitness accounts are surprisingly similar to each other. But a few differences in these sightings have been documented. Some people say that the spectral train contains several cars that are all draped in black; others say that it only consists of an engine and one flatbed car that holds the dead president's coffin. And every so often, someone claims to hear a shrieking whistle coming from the phantom locomotive.

Despite such detailed accounts, naysayers exist. In his book *The Lincoln Funeral Train*, author Scott Trostel discusses his belief that these accounts are simply the products of people's "vivid and fertile imaginations." Perhaps, but how is it that different people in different states have such similar vivid and fertile imaginations? Like Lincoln himself, the question belongs to the ages.

North Carolina's Train of Terror

North Carolina is rife with haunted houses. In fact, even the Governor's Mansion in Raleigh is said to contain a ghost or two. But one of the Tarheel State's most unusual paranormal events isn't housebound—it takes place on an isolated train trestle known as the Bostian Bridge near the town of Statesville.

✳ ✳ ✳ ✳

ON AUGUST 27, 1891, a passenger train jumped the tracks while crossing the Bostian Bridge, plunging seven railcars 60 to 75 feet to the ground below. Nearly 30 people perished in the tragic accident.

According to local legend, on the anniversary of the catastrophe, the sounds of screeching wheels, screaming passengers, and a thunderous crash can be heard near the Bostian Bridge. The ghostly specter of a uniformed man carrying a gold pocket watch has also been observed lingering nearby.

Another Victim Claimed

Sadly, on August 27, 2010, Christopher Kaiser, a Charlotte-based amateur ghost hunter, was struck and killed by a real-life train that surprised him on the Bostian Bridge.

According to police reports, Kaiser had brought a small group to the trestle in hopes of experiencing the eerie sounds that are said to occur on the anniversary of the 1891 crash. The group was standing on the span when a Norfolk-Southern train turned a corner and headed toward them. With the train rapidly approaching, Kaiser managed to push the woman in front of him off the tracks. His heroic action saved her life but cost him his own.

Other than witnessing this horrific accident, Kaiser's group saw nothing unusual that night. But many others claim to have seen strange phenomena on the Bostian Bridge. On the 50th anniversary of the 1891 tragedy, for example, one woman reportedly watched the wreck occur all over again. More than 150 people gathered near the trestle on the 100th anniversary of the crash in 1991, but nothing supernatural happened that night.

When the Gray Man Speaks, You'd Better Listen

One of the oldest summer resorts on the East Coast, Pawleys Island is a small barrier island located along the coast of South Carolina. Only a handful of people live there year-round, and one of the perennial residents is the Gray Man. Many say that this restless spirit has no face. However, that seems to be a minor inconvenience; after all, when it comes to warning the living of impending doom, a pretty face—or any face at all—is hardly necessary.

✳ ✳ ✳ ✳

Apparition Identity Crisis

ACCORDING TO LEGEND, before every major hurricane that has hit Pawleys Island since the early 1820s—including Hurricane Hugo in 1989—the Gray Man has appeared to certain folks on the island to warn them to leave before the approaching storm strikes. When they return after the storm, the people who encountered the Gray Man find their homes undamaged, while other buildings nearby have been destroyed.

The identity of the Gray Man is unknown, but there are several candidates. One theory suggests that it's Percival Pawley, the island's first owner and its namesake; others believe that the helpful spirit is Plowden Charles Jennett Weston, a man whose former home is now the island's Pelican Inn.

But the more romantic legends say that the Gray Man is the ghost of a young man who died for love. Stories about how he perished vary: One tale says that on his way to see his beloved, he fell into a bed of quicksand and died. Soon after, while the object of this deceased man's affection was walking along the beach, a figure in gray approached her and told her to leave the island. She did, and that night a hurricane slammed into the area, destroying just about every home—except hers.

Another story concerns a woman who married a man after she thought that her beloved had died at sea. Later, when she met a man who had survived a shipwreck off Pawleys Island, she realized that he was her lost love, waterlogged but still very much alive. However, he didn't take the news of her marriage too well; he slinked away and died shortly thereafter. But according to legend, ever since then, he's been warning folks to flee when they're in danger from an upcoming storm.

The Ghostly Lifesaver

No matter who this ghost was in life, he has supposedly appeared before hurricanes in 1822, 1893, 1916, 1954, 1955, and 1989. And for decades, local fishermen have told stories of the Gray Man appearing to them hours before a sudden storm roiled up that would have put their lives in jeopardy.

The Gray Man is credited with saving many lives before the advent of contemporary forecasting techniques. In 1954, a couple was spending their honeymoon on the island when they heard a knock on their door at around 5 A.M. When the husband opened the door, he saw a figure in gray whose clothes reeked of salty brine and whose features were obscured by a gray hat. The man in gray said that the Red Cross had sent him to warn people to evacuate because a huge storm was heading for the island. Before the honeymooning husband could question him further, the man in gray vanished. Realizing that this was no ordinary Red Cross worker, the man and his new bride left the island immediately.

Later that evening, ferocious Hurricane Hazel struck the island with the deadly force of a Category 4 storm, with winds gusting as high as 150 miles per hour. In her wake, Hazel left thousands of homes destroyed and 95 people dead. The newlywed couple, however, had been spared by the ghostly grace of the Gray Man.

A Ghost Who Keeps on Giving

The Gray Man apparently doesn't care much for modern technology—he was still on the job as recently as 1989. That year, just before Hurricane Hugo hit, a couple walking along the beach spotted the Gray Man. Although the phantom vanished before the couple could speak to him, his reputation preceded him, and the couple fled the island. When they returned, their home was the only one in the area that had not been devastated by the storm. This incident got the Gray Man a moment in the national spotlight: He was featured on an episode of *Unsolved Mysteries* in 1990.

The Weeping Woman in Gray

If you ever find yourself at Camp Chase Confederate Cemetery in Columbus, Ohio, find the grave of Benjamin F. Allen and listen very closely. If you hear the faint sound of a woman weeping, you're in the presence of the cemetery's Lady in Gray.

✳ ✳ ✳ ✳

ESTABLISHED IN MAY 1861, Camp Chase served as a prison for Confederate officers during the Civil War. However, as the number of Confederate POWs grew, the prison could not be quite so selective. As 1863 dawned, Camp Chase held approximately 8,000 men of every rank.

The sheer number of prisoners soon overwhelmed Camp Chase. Men were forced to share bunks, and shortages of food, clothing, medicine, and other necessities were common. Under those conditions, the prisoners were vulnerable to disease and malnutrition, which led to many deaths—500 in one particular month alone, due to an outbreak of smallpox. Eventually, a cemetery was established at the camp to handle the large number of bodies.

Although Camp Chase was closed shortly after the war, the cemetery remains. Today, it contains the graves of more than

2,100 Confederate soldiers. Although restless spirits are commonly found where miserable deaths occurred, just one ghost is known to call Camp Chase its "home haunt": the famous Lady in Gray. Dressed in a flowing gray dress with a veil hiding her face, she is often seen standing and sobbing over Allen's grave. At other times, she can be found weeping at the grave of an unidentified soldier. Occasionally, she leaves flowers on the tombstones.

The Lady in Gray has also been spotted walking among the many gravestones in the cemetery; she's even been observed passing right through the locked cemetery gates. No one knows who she was in life, but some speculate that she was Allen's wife. However, her attention to the grave of the unknown soldier baffles researchers. One thing seems certain, though: As long as the Camp Chase Confederate Cemetery exists, the Lady in Gray will watch over it.

The Ubiquitous Lady in White

"So there I was, sitting in the empty hallway, when all of a sudden I felt like a cold wind was blowing through me. I felt a chill down to my bones, and then I looked up and saw a woman in a long white dress walking down the staircase without touching the ground."

✳   ✳   ✳   ✳

NO ONE KNOWS why so many ghostly women wear white dresses (or, for that matter, exactly why ghosts wear clothes at all), but stories of ladies in white go back hundreds of years. In fact, tales of some of the spectral women in white that supposedly wander the forests of New England were among the very first American ghost stories.

Today, when paranormal investigators interview witnesses who talk about seeing women in white, they tend to be instantly skeptical. But these stories didn't just come from out of nowhere. Some say it's an image of ghosts that was created by Hollywood or by Victorian-era novelist Wilkie Collins (whose hit novel *The Woman in White* wasn't even about a ghost). However, such stories have actually been common in supernatural lore for centuries, and these spectral women are reported—often by reputable witnesses—more and more every year. Ladies in white were following children in dark woods, stalking the lonely hallways of old buildings, and wandering the streets of small rural towns long before movies could have created such images.

Forever Awaiting His Return

One of the more venerable ladies in white is the White Lady of the Bridgeport Inn, which was built in 1877 for Hiram Leavitt and his family in the mining town of Bridgeport, California. There, a woman in white has been seen in Room 19 so often that she's mentioned on the building's historical marker.

The most common story surrounding the origin of this ghost is that she was the fiancée of a young miner during the late 1800s. After a particularly good day of prospecting, the miner decided to walk from the room that he'd rented from Leavitt to the nearest bank—which was several miles away—to trade his gold for cash. His fiancée wanted to go with him, but they didn't call it "the Wild West" for nothing: The young miner knew that he risked being robbed while carrying so much gold, so he told her to wait in their room (Room 19) at the inn. And so she waited . . . and waited . . . and waited . . .

After several hours of listening for his footsteps and hearing nothing but the howling of the wind, she began to fear the worst. Finally, her fears were realized when she heard the news that her fiancé had been robbed and murdered by highwaymen.

In her grief, the poor woman hanged herself in Room 19, where her ghost has been seen ever since—often wearing a long white wedding gown.

Connecticut's Lady in White

In Easton, Connecticut—on the other side of the country from Bridgeport—is Union Cemetery, a burial ground that dates back to New England's earliest settlers, who arrived nearly 400 years ago. Dressed in a long white dress and a bonnet, Easton's Lady in White is sometimes seen at the graveyard or on the road outside of it, which stretches between Union Cemetery and the nearby Stepney Cemetery.

Countless witnesses—including police officers and firefighters—have reported hitting a woman in white with their vehicles on the road that connects the graveyards. They slam on their brakes when she mysteriously appears in front of their cars, but it's too late: The terrified drivers hear the dreadful thud of the impact and watch her limp body fly away from their vehicles to the side of the road. They pull over, rush to the side of the road, and find nothing. The woman has vanished, leaving nothing but an imprint in the snow where her body landed. In 1993, a collision with the ghostly woman even left a dent in a firefighter's car. Roadside phantoms that vanish after being hit are not uncommon, but for them to leave behind such physical evidence is quite unusual.

So common were sightings of Easton's Lady in White that paranormal experts Ed and Lorraine Warren—founders of the New England Society for Psychic Research and one of the first couples to turn ghost hunting into a profession—used Union Cemetery as the subject of their 1992 book *Graveyard*.

During their research, the Warrens spoke with a man whose late wife had been buried in Union Cemetery. One evening, while he was visiting his wife's grave, he heard something rustling the leaves behind him. When he turned, he saw the Lady in White looking down at him.

"I wish," she said, as he knelt frozen in place, "that my husband had loved me as much as you loved your wife." Before he could reply, she disappeared.

Others have seen the Lady in White surrounded by darker forms, with whom she appears to be engaged in a heated argument. When she vanishes, the dark shadows disappear along with her.

No one is sure who this Lady in White was in life, but sightings of her were not reported before the late 1940s, despite the fact that the cemetery dates back to the 1600s. Ed Warren speculated that it is the spirit of a woman who was murdered shortly after World War II.

Ed also claimed to have captured video evidence of the Lady in White, but in 2008, his widow, Lorraine, told reporters from NBC that she keeps it under lock and key "because it's so valuable." He's hardly the only person to photograph her, though—several ghost hunters have taken photographs that feature strange phenomena at the cemetery.

The Lady in White may not be the only ghost at Union Cemetery. Many paranormal investigators have encountered an entity there known as "Red Eyes," which is exactly that: a pair of glowing red eyes that keep watch over the cemetery.

The fame of Connecticut's Lady in White has spread throughout the ghost-hunting community, so much so that the town of Easton has had to take steps to protect the cemetery from vandals: It is closed after dark, and the police vigilantly keep trespassers from entering it after hours. But it's not unheard of for officers to see a pale, glowing form behind the gates in the middle of the night.

We Interrupt This Program . . .

Max Headroom was a popular television character introduced in 1985, portrayed by actor Matt Frewer. The fictional artificial intelligence personality was immediately recognizable with his slicked back blond hair, Wayfarer sunglasses, and dark suit. He even possessed a witty sense of humor and distinctive stutter. But on one autumn evening in Chicago, Max Headroom took on a whole new meaning.

✳ ✳ ✳ ✳

The First Hack

ON THE EVENING of November 22, 1987, viewers in Chicago, Illinois, sat down for *The Nine O'clock News* on WGN-TV. During the live broadcast, just as sports anchor Dan Roan began covering highlights of a Bears football game, something strange happened. For 15 seconds, screens on televisions across the city went black; then, suddenly, a masked figure appeared.

The figure was dressed in a Max Headroom mask and sunglasses. He was positioned in front of a rotating background that appeared to be corrugated metal, mimicking the television character's striped simulated background effect. The figure bobbed around on the screen while buzzing static played, in what can only be described as an unsettling display. The interruption lasted for 28 seconds, until engineers at WGN were able to switch their broadcast frequency. A clearly confused Roan popped back up on the screen, quipping, "Well, if you're wondering what's happened, so am I." Roan picked up the newscast where he left off, and the rest of the show continued without incident.

The Second Hack

But the Max Headroom hacker wasn't finished. Two hours later, local PBS station WTTW was broadcasting an episode of *Doctor Who*. At 11:15, without warning, the interloper in the Max Headroom mask reappeared, this time featuring some creepy, distorted audio. The figure made a strange reference to WGN sportscaster Chuck Swirsky, sung some lyrics from a Temptations song, and held up a can of Pepsi while reciting the Coca-Cola slogan "catch the wave," apparently a reference to the fact that Max Headroom was a spokesperson for Coke at that time. He also said he "made a giant masterpiece for all the greatest world newspaper nerds," a nod to WGN's call letters, which stand for World's Greatest Newspaper.

As if things weren't already weird enough, what happened next was even weirder. The image cut to a man with partially exposed buttocks, and a voice yelling, "they're coming to get me!" A woman off to the side of the screen began spanking the man with a fly swatter, while he continued to yell, mostly incoherently. Finally, after 90 seconds of the bizarre display, the screen went to static, and then *Doctor Who* returned.

Who Was Behind the Mask?

At the time of the hack, there were no engineers on duty at the Sears Tower, where WTTW maintained their transmitters. By the time anyone attempted to intervene, the disturbing transmission was over. While some Chicagoans were upset that their television show had been interrupted, most just found the incident amusing, albeit strange. But a spokesperson for the Federal Communications Commission, who spoke to a reporter the next day, reminded everyone that hacking the airwaves is a federal crime that can result in a fine of up to $100,000, a year in prison, or both.

Of course, in order to punish any offenders, their identities must be known. And in the case of the Max Headroom hack, the perpetrator has managed to elude identification for decades. At one point, authorities believed they found the location that the video was shot, discovering a warehouse with a corrugated metal door that matched the footage. They even managed to figure out how the hacker broke into the signal and transmitted his own video.

But although there have been tips and theories throughout the years, the identity of the hacker has remained a mystery. Whoever did it seems to have simply vanished from the radar, disappearing as quickly as he appeared all those years ago.

The Ghosts of Antietam

With nearly 23,000 total casualties, the Battle of Antietam was one of the bloodiest single-day skirmishes of the American Civil War. More than 3,600 of these men died suddenly and violently that day—ripped out of this world and sent reeling into the next. It's no wonder that the ghosts of some of these soldiers still haunt the Antietam battlefield in western Maryland. Perhaps they're still trying to understand what happened to them on that terrible day.

✳ ✳ ✳ ✳

Gaelic Ghosts

BLOODY LANE AT Antietam National Battlefield is a sunken road that's so named because of the incredible slaughter that took place there on September 17, 1862. One of the notable battalions that fought at Bloody Lane was the Union's Irish Brigade, which lost more than 60 percent of its soldiers that day. The brigade's Gaelic war cry was "faugh-a-ballaugh" (pronounced "fah-ah-bah-LAH"), which means "clear the way."

Many years ago, a group of schoolchildren took a class trip to Antietam. After touring the battlefield, several boys walked down Bloody Lane toward an observation tower that had been built where the Irish Brigade had charged into the battle. Later, back at the school, the boys wrote that they heard odd noises coming from a nearby field. Some said that it sounded like a chant; others, however, likened the sounds to the "fa-la-la-la-la" portion of the Christmas carol "Deck the Halls." Did the boys hear the ghostly battle cry of the Irish Brigade?

On another occasion, some battle reenactors were lying on the ground near the sunken road when they suddenly began hearing a noise that they were very familiar with—the sound of a regiment marching in full battle gear. Their experience as reenactors allowed them to pick out specific sounds, such as knapsacks, canteens, and cartridge boxes rattling and scraping. However, no matter how hard they looked, the men could see no marching soldiers. They concluded that the sounds were made by an otherworldly regiment.

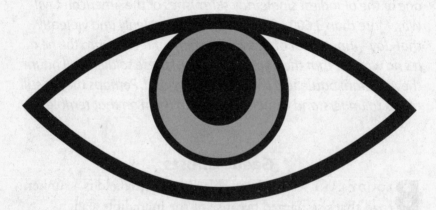

Prying Eyes

Because of its strategic location on the battlefield, the Phillip Pry House was pressed into service as a makeshift hospital during the battle. Much misery took place there, including the death of Union General Israel B. Richardson, despite the loving care of his wife Frances. In 1976, the house was damaged by fire, and one day during the restoration, the wife of a park ranger met a woman dressed in Civil War-era attire coming down the stairs. She asked her husband who the woman was, but he had no knowledge of a woman at the park.

Later, a woman was seen staring out an upstairs window in the room where General Richardson died. Nothing was particularly unusual about this . . . except that the room was being renovated at the time and didn't have a floor. Was it the ghost of Frances Richardson, still trying to take care of her dying husband?

Members of the construction crew that was working at the house decided that this was not the project for them and abandoned it immediately after sighting this female phantom. Disembodied footsteps have also been reported going up and down the home's stairs.

Screaming Specters

The spirits of Antietam are not just confined to the battlefield. Injured Confederate soldiers were brought to St. Paul Episcopal Church in Sharpsburg, and sometimes, the sounds of the wounded screaming in agony can still be heard there. Mysterious lights have also been seen in the church tower.

A Bridge Between Two Worlds

Burnside Bridge was another scene of massive slaughter at Antietam, as Union troops repeatedly tried to take the tiny stone span only to be driven back by intense Confederate fire. Many of the soldiers who died there were quickly buried in unmarked graves near the bridge, and now it seems as if that arrangement wasn't to their liking. Many credible witnesses, including park rangers, have reported seeing blue balls of light floating near the bridge at night. The faint sound of a phantom drumbeat has also been heard in the vicinity.

Although the Battle of Antietam took place around 150 years ago, it seems that in some places, the battle rages on—and for some, it always will.

Bobby Mackey's: Ghosts That Like Country Music

Just over the Ohio River from downtown Cincinnati is the town of Wilder, Kentucky, home of Bobby Mackey's—a country-music nightclub and allegedly one of the most haunted locations in the United States. Over the years, the property is said to have seen such atrocities as a beheading, a poisoning, a suicide, numerous unsolved murders, and even a case of possession. On top of all that, some say there's an entrance to hell in the basement.

✳ ✳ ✳ ✳

Hell's Gate

THE FIRST BUILDING that is believed to have stood on the property now occupied by Bobby Mackey's was a slaughterhouse, which operated from the 1850s until the late 1880s. During that time, it was said to have been so busy that the ground floor was often literally coated with blood. To alleviate that, a well was dug in the basement, which allowed the blood to be washed off the floor and carried out to the nearby river. Needless to say, gallons upon gallons of blood and other assorted matter were dumped into that well. Perhaps that's why legend has it that after the slaughterhouse closed, a satanic cult used the well as part of its rituals. Some even claim that these rituals opened a portal to the Other Side, a portal that—to this day—has yet to be closed.

An Unspeakable Crime

On February 1, 1896, the headless body of Pearl Bryan was found less than two miles from the site of the former slaughterhouse. It was later discovered that Bryan's boyfriend, Scott Jackson, and his friend, Alonzo Walling, had murdered her after a botched abortion attempt. The two men were arrested, but they refused to reveal the location of Bryan's head. Both men were hanged for the crime in March 1897, without ever disclosing the location of Bryan's head. The consensus was that the head was probably thrown into the old slaughterhouse well. Perhaps that's why Pearl Bryan's ghost is seen wandering around inside Bobby Mackey's, both with and without her head. And although Jackson and Walling did not take their last breaths on the property, it is believed that their ghosts are stuck there too; they have both been seen throughout the building, but Jackson's ghost seems to be more active . . . and angry. Those who have encountered his ghost—usually around the well in the basement—say that it is a dark and unhappy spirit.

Gangsters and Unsolved Murders

Shortly after the executions of Jackson and Walling, the former slaughterhouse was torn down, leaving only the well. In the 1920s, the building now known as Bobby Mackey's was built on the property directly over the well. During Prohibition, it functioned as a ruthless speakeasy and gambling den where several people lost their lives. Eventually, the building was shut down and cleared out—presumably of everything except the restless spirits.

In 1933, after Prohibition was lifted, E. A. "Buck" Brady purchased the building and renamed it The Primrose. Brady was competing with powerful gangsters who began showing up at The Primrose trying to scare him into giving them a cut of the profits. But Brady refused to be intimidated and continually turned them down. All this came to a head on August 5, 1946, when Brady and gangster Albert "Red" Masterson were involved in a shootout. After that, Brady decided that he was done. After many years of having to continually (and often forcibly) reject advances by Cincinnati-area gangsters, Brady sold the building. But if the stories are to be believed, as he handed over the keys, he cursed the building, saying that because he couldn't run a successful business there, no one should.

Today, the ghosts of both Buck Brady and Red Masterson are seen inside Bobby Mackey's. Brady's ghost has been identified from photographs taken of him when he was alive. And even though he cursed the building, his ghost seems harmless enough. Masterson's ghost, on the other hand, has been described as "not friendly" and has been blamed for some of the alleged attacks on bar patrons.

Johanna

After Brady sold the building, it reopened as The Latin Quarter. According to legend, Johanna, the daughter of The Latin Quarter's owner, fell in love with (and became pregnant by) Robert Randall, one of the singers at the nightclub. After Johanna's father found out about the pregnancy, he ordered Randall killed. When Johanna learned of her father's involvement in her boyfriend's death, she first unsuccessfully tried to poison him and then committed suicide in the basement of the building.

Johanna's ghost is seen throughout the building, but it is most often reported on the top floor and in the stairwells, where she will either push or hug people. She is also said to hang out in the Spotlight Room, a secret place in the attic where she allegedly wrote a poem on the wall before committing suicide. Even those who cannot see her apparition can always tell that Johanna is around by the scent of roses.

One of the strangest phenomena attributed to Johanna's ghost is that the turned-off (and unplugged) jukebox sometimes springs to life by playing "The Anniversary Waltz"—despite the fact that the song is not even a selection on the device's menu and the record is not even in the machine.

Bobby Mackey's Music World

In the spring of 1978, musician Bobby Mackey purchased the building, and it has been in operation ever since. Besides operating as a bar, Bobby Mackey's has a stage and a dance floor and has featured performances by many popular country music acts over the years.

Shortly after her husband purchased the building, Janet Mackey was working in the upstairs apartment when she was shoved out of the room toward the stairs while being told to "Get out" by a spirit that she later identified as Alonzo Walling. After that, Janet refused to set foot in the room. So Bobby hired Carl Lawson as a caretaker and allowed him to stay in the apartment. Upon moving in, Lawson reportedly heard strange noises and saw shadowy figures moving around the bar late at night. Believing that the spirits were coming in through the well in the basement, Lawson threw holy water down the hole. As a result, Lawson claimed that he became possessed and was only able to break free from the demon's grasp after an exorcism was performed on him.

In 1993, a man sued Bobby Mackey's alleging that while he was in the bar's men's room, he was punched and kicked by a "dark-haired apparition" wearing a cowboy hat. The victim stated that he might have angered the ghost because he dared it to appear shortly before being attacked. While the suit was thrown out, it did result in the now-famous sign that hangs above the front doors of Bobby Mackey's, which alerts guests to the possibility that the building may be haunted and that they are entering at their own risk.

CHAPTER 4

CONSPIRACIES ... OR COINCIDENCES?

The Death of John Dillinger ... Or Someone Who Looked Like Him

On July 22, 1934, outside the Biograph Theater on Chicago's north side, John Dillinger, America's first Public Enemy Number One, passed from this world into the next in a hail of bullets. Or did he? Conspiracy theorists believe that FBI agents shot and killed the wrong man and covered it all up when they realized their mistake. So what really happened that night? Let's first take a look at the main players in this gangland soap opera.

✳ ✳ ✳ ✳

Hoover Wants His Man

BORN JUNE 22, 1903, John Dillinger was in his early thirties when he first caught the FBI's eye. They thought they were through with him in January 1934, when he was arrested after shooting a police officer during a bank robbery in East Chicago, Indiana. However, Dillinger managed to stage a daring escape from his Indiana jail cell using a wooden gun painted with black shoe polish.

Once Dillinger left Indiana in a stolen vehicle and crossed into Illinois, he was officially a federal fugitive. J. Edgar Hoover, then director of the FBI, promised a quick apprehension, but Dillinger had other plans. He seemed to enjoy the fact that the FBI was tracking him—rather than go into hiding, he continued robbing banks. Annoyed, Hoover assigned FBI Agent Melvin Purvis to ambush Dillinger. Purvis's plan backfired, though, and Dillinger escaped, shooting and killing two innocent men in the process. After the botched trap, the public was in an uproar and the FBI was under close scrutiny. To everyone at the FBI, the message was clear: Hoover wanted Dillinger, and he wanted him ASAP.

The Woman in Red

The FBI's big break came in July 1934 with a phone call from a woman named Anna Sage. Sage was a Romanian immigrant who ran a Chicago-area brothel. Fearing that she might be deported, Sage wanted to strike a bargain with the feds. Her proposal was simple: In exchange for not being deported, Sage was willing to give the FBI John Dillinger. According to Sage, Dillinger was dating Polly Hamilton, one of her former employees. Melvin Purvis personally met with Sage and told her he couldn't make any promises but he would do what he could about her pending deportation.

Several days later, on July 22, Sage called the FBI office in Chicago and said that she was going to the movies that night with Dillinger and Hamilton. Sage quickly hung up but not before saying she would wear something bright so that agents could pick out the threesome in a crowd. Not knowing which movie theater they were planning to go to, Purvis dispatched several agents to the Marbro Theater, while he and another group of agents went to the Biograph. At approximately 8:30 P.M., Purvis believed he saw Dillinger, Sage, and Hamilton enter the Biograph. As she had promised, Sage indeed wore something bright—an orange blouse. However, under the marquee lights, the blouse's color appeared to be red, which is why Sage was forever dubbed "The Woman in Red."

Purvis tried to apprehend Dillinger right after he purchased tickets, but he slipped past Purvis and into the darkened theater. Purvis went into the theater but was unable to locate Dillinger in the dark. At that point, Purvis left the theater, gathered his men, and made the decision to apprehend Dillinger as he was exiting the theater. Purvis positioned himself in the theater's vestibule, instructed his men to hide outside, and told them that he would signal them by lighting a cigar when he spotted Dillinger. That was their cue to move in and arrest Dillinger.

"Stick 'em up, Johnny!"

At approximately 10:30 P.M., the doors to the Biograph opened and people started to exit. All of the agents' eyes were on Purvis. When a man wearing a straw hat, accompanied by two women, walked past Purvis, the agent quickly placed a cigar in his mouth and lit a match. Perhaps sensing something was wrong, the man turned and looked at Purvis, at which point Purvis drew his pistol and said, "Stick 'em up, Johnny!" In response, the man turned as if he was going to run away, while at the same time reaching for what appeared to be a gun. Seeing the movement, the other agents opened fire. As the man ran away, attempting to flee down the alleyway alongside the theater, he was shot four times on his left side and once in the back of the neck before crumpling on the pavement. When Purvis reached him and checked for vitals, there were none. Minutes later, after being driven to a local hospital, John Dillinger was pronounced DOA. But as soon as it was announced that Dillinger was dead, the controversy began.

Dillinger Disputed

Much of the basis for the conspiracy stems from the fact that Hoover, both publicly and privately, made it clear that no matter what, he wanted Dillinger caught. On top of that, Agent Purvis was under a lot of pressure to capture Dillinger, especially since he'd failed with a previous attempt. Keeping that in mind, it would be easy to conclude that Purvis, in his haste to capture Dillinger, might have overlooked a few things. First, it was Purvis alone who pointed out the man he thought to be Dillinger to the waiting agents. Conspiracy theorists contend that Purvis fingered the wrong man that night, and an innocent man ended up getting killed as a result. As evidence, they point to Purvis's own statement: While they were standing at close range, the man tried to pull a gun, which is why the agents had to open fire. But even though agents stated they recovered a .38-caliber Colt automatic from the victim's body (and even had it on display for many years), author Jay Robert Nash discovered that that particular model was not even available until a good five months after Dillinger's alleged death! Theorists believe that when agents realized they had not only shot the wrong man, but an unarmed one at that, they planted the gun as part of a cover-up.

Another interesting fact that could have resulted in Purvis's misidentification was that Dillinger had recently undergone plastic surgery in an attempt to disguise himself. In addition to work on his face, Dillinger had attempted to obliterate his fingerprints by dipping his fingers into an acid solution. On top of that, the man who Purvis said was Dillinger was wearing a straw hat the entire time Purvis saw him. It is certainly possible that Purvis did not actually recognize Dillinger but instead picked out someone who merely looked like him. If you remember, the only tip Purvis had was Sage telling him that she was going to the movies with Dillinger and his girlfriend. Did Purvis see Sage leaving the theater in her orange blouse and finger the wrong man simply because he was standing next to Sage and resembled Dillinger? Or was the whole thing a setup orchestrated by Sage and Dillinger to trick the FBI into executing an innocent man?

So Who Was It?

If the man shot and killed outside the theater wasn't John Dillinger, who was it? There are conflicting accounts, but one speculation is that it was a man named Jimmy Lawrence, who was dating Polly Hamilton. If you believe in the conspiracy, Lawrence was simply in the wrong place at the wrong time. Or possibly, Dillinger purposely sent Lawrence to the theater hoping FBI agents would shoot him, allowing Dillinger to fade into obscurity. Of course, those who don't believe in the conspiracy say the reason Lawrence looked so much like Dillinger is because he was Dillinger using an alias. Further, Dillinger's sister, Audrey Hancock, identified his body. Finally, they say it all boils down to the FBI losing or misplacing the gun Dillinger had the night he was killed and inadvertently replacing it with the wrong one. Case closed.

Not really, though. It seems that whenever someone comes up with a piece of evidence to fuel the conspiracy theory, some-one else has something to refute it. Some have asked that Dillinger's body be exhumed and DNA tests be performed, but nothing has come of it yet. Until that happens, we'll probably never know for sure what really happened on that hot July night back in 1934. But that's okay, because real or imagined, everyone loves a good mystery.

The Maligned Mrs. Lincoln

Mary Todd Lincoln was a lot of things: first lady, extravagant spender, generous hostess. And though a Southerner by birth, she was not, as is widely suspected, a Confederate spy.

※　※　※　※

Flawed First Lady

BEING THE PRESIDENT'S wife is a grueling job—the hours are long and the demands are wearisome. Most first ladies manage to get through it relatively well, but for Mary Todd Lincoln, wife of Abraham, it was an agonizing experience fraught with relentless criticism, borderline mental illness, and personal tragedy.

Mary deeply loved her husband, whom she married despite the disapproval of her family and social peers. She saw in Lincoln a good, honest, talented man and was delighted when he won the presidency in 1860. But because Mary was a native of Kentucky and thus a Southerner by birth, rumors swirled throughout the course of the Civil War that the first lady was, in fact, a Confederate spy.

Guilt by Relation

It's easy to see how such rumors got started. According to historians and biographers, Mary devotedly agreed with and supported her husband's political beliefs and, like him, wanted only that the nation become whole again.

But one of Mary's brothers, three half-brothers, and three brothers-in-law all served in the Confederate army during the Civil War. How then, people wondered, could she truly support the Union? Not surprisingly, certain individuals—including many of Lincoln's political enemies—started a whisper campaign that perhaps Mary wasn't the Unionist she said she was.

The entire issue, however, was just scandalous hearsay without a shred of proof. Even today, with nearly 150 years of hindsight, there is absolutely no evidence that Mary Todd Lincoln passed government secrets to the South, or even had the opportunity to do so. Indeed, Mary's interests as first lady were generally more social than political.

Can't Win for Losing

The whispered allegation that Mary Lincoln was a Confederate spy was just one of many things that made her time in the White House miserable. The belles of Washington society considered her silly and uncouth and took every opportunity to denigrate her. For example, when she hosted a large party in the White House as the war raged, she was condemned for her extravagance. And because two of her sons were ill at the time, she was castigated as being unmotherly and cold.

All of this was made worse by Mary's many emotional and physical problems. She suffered from excruciating headaches that sometimes left her bedridden for days, and she also experienced violent mood swings that caused more than one White House aide to describe her as unpredictable and difficult to get along with.

Mary Todd Lincoln was a flawed woman who did her best under dire circumstances. It's unfair and inaccurate for her character to be impugned by untrue rumors regarding her patriotism.

Who Shot JFK?
Conspiracy Theories

Conspiracy theories are a favorite American pastime, right up there with alien abductions and Elvis sightings. Perhaps no conspiracy theories are more popular than the ones involving that afternoon in Dallas—November 22, 1963—when the United States lost a president. John F. Kennedy's life and death have reached out to encompass everyone from Marilyn Monroe to Fidel Castro, Sam Giancana to J. Edgar Hoover.

✳   ✳   ✳   ✳

✳ **The single-shooter theory:** This is the one the Warren Commission settled on—that Lee Harvey Oswald (and only Lee Harvey Oswald), firing his Mannlicher-Carcano rifle from the window of the Texas Book Depository, killed the president in Dealey Plaza. But this is the official finding, and where's the excitement in that?

✳ **The two-shooter theory:** A second shooter on the nearby grassy knoll fired at the same time as Oswald. His bullets hit Texas Governor John Connally and struck President Kennedy from the front. This theory arose after U.S. Marine sharpshooters at Quantico tried to duplicate the single-shooter theory but found it was impossible for all the shots to have come from the Book Depository.

* **The LBJ theory:** Lyndon Johnson's mistress, Madeleine Brown, said that the vice president met with powerful Texans the night before the killing. She claimed he told her, "After tomorrow those goddamn Kennedys will never embarrass me again—that's no threat—that's a promise." Jack Ruby also implicated LBJ, as did E. Howard Hunt, just before his death.

* **The CIA theory:** After Kennedy forced Allen Dulles to resign as head of the CIA following the Bay of Pigs fiasco, the CIA, resenting Kennedy's interference, took its revenge on the president. They'd had plenty of practice helping plotters take out Patrice Lumumba of the Congo, Rafael Trujillo of the Dominican Republic, and President Ngo Dinh Diem of Vietnam.

* **The Cuban exiles theory:** Reflecting more bitterness over the Bay of Pigs, the powerful Cuban exile community in the United States was eager to see Kennedy dead and said so. However, this probably played no part in the assassination.

* **The J. Edgar Hoover and the Mafia theory:** The Mafia was said to have been blackmailing Hoover about his homosexuality for ages. The theory goes that when Attorney General Robert Kennedy began to legally pursue Jimmy Hoffa and Mafia bosses in Chicago, Tampa, and New Orleans, they sent Hoover after JFK as payback.

* **The organized crime theory:** Chicago Mafia boss Sam Giancana, who supposedly shared the affections of Marilyn Monroe with both JFK and RFK—using Frank Sinatra as a go-between—felt betrayed when RFK went after the mob. After all, hadn't they fixed JFK's 1960 election? This theory is a tabloid favorite.

* **The Soviet theory:** High-ranking Soviet defector Ion Pacepa said that Soviet intelligence chiefs believed that the KGB had orchestrated the Dallas killing. But they were probably just bragging.

* **The Roscoe White theory:** According to White's son, this Dallas police officer was part of a three-man assassination team. The junior White, however, gives no indication of the reasons behind the plot.

* **The Saul theory:** A professional hit man was paid $50,000 to kill Kennedy by a group of very powerful, unknown men. He was also supposed to kill Oswald. Clearly, this theory isn't thick with details.

* **The Castro theory:** Supposedly the Cuban government contracted Oswald to kill Kennedy, telling him that there was an escape plan. There wasn't.

* **The Israeli theory:** Angry with JFK for pressuring them not to develop nuclear weapons and/or for employing ex-Nazis in the space program, the Israelis supposedly conspired in his assassination.

* **The Federal Reserve theory:** Kennedy issued Executive Order 11110, enabling the U.S. Treasury to print silver certificates in an attempt to drain the silver reserves. It is theorized that such a development would severely limit the economic power of the Federal Reserve. Could this have played into his assassination?

People will probably still be spinning these theories in a hundred years. But then, everyone needs a hobby.

Who Betrayed Anne Frank?

Anne Frank and her family thwarted Nazis for two years, hiding in Amsterdam. They might have remained hidden and waited out the war, but someone blew their cover.

✳ ✳ ✳ ✳

ANNELIES MARIE FRANK was born in Frankfurt am Main, Germany, on June 12, 1929. Perhaps the most well-known victim of the Holocaust, she was one of approximately 1.5 million Jewish children killed by the Nazis. Her diary chronicling her experience in Amsterdam was discovered in the Franks' secret hiding place by friends of the family and first published in 1947. Translated into more than 60 languages, *Anne Frank: The Diary of a Young Girl* has sold 30 million copies and is one of the most read books in the world.

The diary was given to Anne on her 13th birthday, just weeks before she went into hiding. Her father, Otto Frank, moved his family and four friends into a secret annex of rooms above his office at 263 Prinsengracht, near a canal in central Amsterdam, on July 6, 1942. They relied on trustworthy business associates, employees, and friends, who risked their own lives to help them. Anne poignantly wrote her thoughts, yearnings, and descriptions of life in the secret annex in her diary, revealing a vibrant, intelligent young woman struggling to retain her ideals in the most dire of circumstances.

On August 4, 1944, four or five Dutch Nazi collaborators under the command of an Austrian Nazi police investigator entered the building and arrested the Franks and their friends. The family was deported to Auschwitz, where they were separated and sent to different camps. Anne and her sister, Margot,

were sent to Bergen—Belsen, where they both died of typhus a few weeks before liberation. Anne was 15 years old. Otto Frank was the only member of the group to survive the war.

Dutch police, Nazi hunters, and historians have attempted to identify the person who betrayed the Franks. Searching for clues, the Netherlands Institute for War Documentation (NIWD) has examined records on Dutch collaboration with the Nazis, the letters of Otto Frank, and police transcripts dating from the 1940s. The arresting Nazi officer was also questioned after the war by Nazi hunter Simon Wiesenthal, but he could not identify who informed on the Franks. For decades suspicion centered on Willem Van Maaren, who worked in the warehouse attached to the Franks' hiding place, but two police investigations found no evidence against him.

Two recent theories have been offered about who betrayed the Franks. British author Carol Anne Lee believes it was Anton Ahlers, a business associate of Otto's who was a petty thief and member of the Dutch Nazi movement. Lee argues that Ahlers informed the Nazis to collect the bounty paid to Dutch civilians who exposed Jews. She suggests he may have split the reward with Maarten Kuiper, a friend of Ahlers who was one of the Dutch Nazi collaborators who raided the secret annex. Ahlers was jailed for collaboration with the Nazis after the war, and members of his own family, including his son, have said they believe he was guilty of informing on the Franks.

Austrian writer Melissa Müller believes that a cleaning lady, Lena Hartog, who also worked in the warehouse, reported the Franks because she feared that if they were discovered, her husband, an employee of Otto Frank, would be deported for aiding Jews.

The NIWD has studied the arguments of both writers and examined the evidence supporting their theories. Noting that all the principals involved in the case are no longer living, it concluded that neither theory could be proved.

An Underground Mystery: The Hollow Earth Theory

For centuries, people have believed that Earth is hollow. They claim that civilizations may live inside Earth's core or that it might be a landing base for alien spaceships. This sounds like fantasy, but believers point to startling evidence, including explorers' reports and modern photos taken from space.

✳   ✳   ✳   ✳

A Prize Inside?

HOLLOW EARTH BELIEVERS agree that our planet is a shell between 500 and 800 miles thick, and inside that shell is another world. It may be a gaseous realm, an alien outpost, or home to a utopian society.

Some believers add a spiritual spin. Calling the interior world Agartha or Shambhala, they use concepts from Eastern religions and point to ancient legends supporting these ideas.

Many Hollow Earth enthusiasts are certain that people from the outer and inner worlds can visit each other by traveling through openings in the outer shell. One such entrance is a hole in the ocean near the North Pole. A November 1968 photo by the ESSA-7 satellite showed a dark, circular area at the North Pole that was surrounded by ice fields.

Another hole supposedly exists in Antarctica. Some Hollow Earth enthusiasts say Hitler believed that Antarctica held the true opening to Earth's core. Leading Hollow Earth researchers such as Dennis Crenshaw suggest that President Roosevelt ordered the 1939 South Pole expedition to find the entrance before the Germans did.

The poles may not hold the only entrances to a world hidden deep beneath our feet. Jules Verne's famous novel *Journey to the Center of the Earth* supported yet another theory about passage between the worlds. In his story, there were many access points, including waterfalls and inactive volcanoes. Edgar Allan Poe and Edgar Rice Burroughs also wrote about worlds inside Earth. Their ideas were based on science as well as fantasy.

Scientists Take Note

Many scientists have taken the Hollow Earth theory seriously. One of the most noted was English astronomer Edmund Halley, of Halley's Comet fame. In 1692, he declared that our planet is hollow, and as evidence, he pointed to global shifts in Earth's magnetic fields, which frequently cause compass anomalies. According to Halley, those shifts could be explained by the movement of rotating worlds inside Earth. In addition, he claimed that the source of gravity—still debated in the 21st century—could be an interior world.

In Halley's opinion, Earth is made of three separate layers or shells, each rotating independently around a solid core. We live on the outer shell, but the inner worlds might be inhabited, too.

Halley also suggested that Earth's interior atmospheres are luminous. We supposedly see them as gas leaking out of Earth's fissures. At the poles, that gas creates the *aurora borealis*.

Scientists Look Deeper

Hollow Earth researchers claim that the groundwork for their theories was laid by some of the most notable scientific minds of the 17th and 18th centuries. Although their beliefs remain controversial and largely unsubstantiated, they are still widely discussed and have a network of enthusiasts.

Some researchers claim that Leonhard Euler (1707–1783), one of the greatest mathematicians of all time, believed that Earth's interior includes a glowing core that illuminates life for a well-developed civilization, much like the sun lights our world. Another mathematician, Sir John Leslie (1766–1832), suggested that Earth has a thin crust and also believed the interior cavity was filled with light.

In 1818, a popular lecturer named John Cleves Symmes, Jr., proposed an expedition to prove the Hollow Earth theory. He believed that he could sail to the North Pole, and upon reaching the opening to Earth's core, he could steer his ship over the lip of the entrance, which he believed resembled a waterfall. Then he would continue sailing on waters inside the planet. In 1822 and 1823, Symmes petitioned Congress to fund the expedition, but he was turned down. He died in 1829, and his gravestone in Hamilton, Ohio, is decorated with his model of the Hollow Earth.

Proof Gets Woolly and Weird

In 1846, a remarkably well-preserved—and long extinct—woolly mammoth was found frozen in Siberia. Most woolly mammoths died out about 12,000 years ago, so researchers were baffled by its pristine condition.

Hollow Earth enthusiasts say there is only one explanation: The mammoth lived inside Earth, where those beasts are not extinct. The beast had probably become lost, emerged into our world, and froze to death shortly before the 1846 discovery.

Eyewitnesses at the North Pole

Several respected scientists and explorers have visited the poles and returned with stories that suggest a hollow Earth.

At the start of the 20th century, Arctic explorers Dr. Frederick A. Cook and Rear Admiral Robert E. Peary sighted land—not just an icy wasteland—at the North Pole. Peary first described it as "the white summits of a distant land." A 1913 Arctic expedition also reported seeing "hills, valleys, and snow-capped peaks." All of these claims were dismissed as mirages but would later be echoed by the research of Admiral Richard E. Byrd, the first man to fly over the North Pole. Hollow Earth believers suggest that Byrd actually flew into the interior world and then out again, without realizing it. They cite Byrd's notes as evidence, as he describes his navigational instruments and compasses spinning out of control.

Unidentified Submerged Objects

Support for the Hollow Earth theory has also come from UFO enthusiasts. People who study UFOs have also been documenting USOs, or unidentified submerged objects. These mysterious vehicles have been spotted—mostly at sea—since the 19th century.

USOs look like "flying saucers," but instead of vanishing into the skies, they plunge beneath the surface of the ocean. Some are luminous and fly upward from the sea at a great speed . . . and without making a sound.

UFO enthusiasts believe that these spaceships are visiting worlds beneath the sea. Some are certain that these are actually underwater alien bases. Other UFO researchers think that the ocean conceals entries to a hollow Earth, where the aliens maintain outposts.

The Search Continues

Scientists have determined that the most likely location for a northern opening to Earth's interior is at 84.4 N Latitude, 141 E Longitude. It's a spot near Siberia, about 600 miles from the North Pole. Photos taken by *Apollo 8* in 1968 and *Apollo 16* in 1972 show dark, circular areas confirming the location.

Some scientists are studying seismic tomography, which uses natural and human-made explosions as well as earthquakes and other seismic waves to chart Earth's interior masses. So far, scientists confirm that Earth is comprised of three separate layers. And late 20th-century images may suggest a mountain range at Earth's core.

What may seem like fantasy from a Jules Verne novel could turn out to be an astonishing reality. Hollow Earth societies around the world continue to look for proof of this centuries-old legend ... and who knows what they might find?

The Mysterious 27 Club

If you're a rock star approaching your 27th birthday, perhaps you should take a year-long hiatus. The curse known as the 27 Club is a relatively new one, but that doesn't make it any less freaky. For those about to blow out 27 candles, good luck.

✳   ✳   ✳   ✳

Founding Members

KEITH RICHARDS AND Eric Clapton both cite guitarist Robert Johnson as a major musical influence. Born on May 8, 1911, Johnson played guitar so well at such a young age that some said he must have made a deal with the devil. Those spooky speculations have survived in part due to Johnson's untimely death. The blues guitar legend died on August 16, 1938, at age 27, after the husband of a woman Johnson was involved with allegedly poisoned him.

After Johnson, the next rocker to join the 27 Club was Brian Jones, one of the founding members of the Rolling Stones. Jones was a lifelong asthma sufferer, so his descent into drug and alcohol addiction was probably not the wisest choice. Still, the sex and drugs inherent in the music biz proved to be too much for Jones to pass up. Some believe he committed suicide because his time with the Stones had recently come to an end. Due to his enlarged liver, autopsy reports led others to believe he overdosed. Either way, when Jones's body was found lifeless in a swimming pool in 1969, the British Invasion rocker was dead at age 27. Jones, another person who cited Johnson as a musical influence, was unfortunately following in his idol's footsteps—and he would soon have company.

A Trio of Inductees

About a year later, the 27 Club would claim its biggest star yet. The counterculture of the late 1960s had embraced the incredibly talented Jimi Hendrix. Legions of fans worshipped the man and his music and sang along to "Purple Haze" at Woodstock. On September 18, 1970, the rock star—who, like so many before him and since, had an affinity for drugs and alcohol—died in London at age 27. Hendrix aspirated on his own vomit after taking too many sleeping pills.

Texas-born singer-songwriter Janis Joplin was another mega-star at the time and a friend of Jimi. Largely regarded as one of the most influential artists in American history, Joplin's gravelly voice and vocal stylings were unique and incredibly popular. She screeched, growled, and strutted through numbers like "Me and Bobby McGee" and "Piece of My Heart." She also tended to play as hard as she worked, typically with the aid of drugs (including psychedelics and methamphetamines) and her signature drink, Southern Comfort whiskey.

On October 4, 1970, when Joplin failed to show up for a recording session for her upcoming album *Pearl*, one of her managers got worried and went to her motel room to check on her. He found the singer dead—at age 27—from a heroin overdose. After Joplin's death, rumors about this strange and tragic "club" began to take hold in the superstitious minds of the general public.

Florida-born Jim Morrison was yet another hard-living, super famous, devil-may-care rock star. He skyrocketed to fame as the front man for the 1960s band The Doors. The young musician was known for his roguish good looks, his dark, curly hair, and his charismatic and mysterious attitude. But his fans didn't have much time to love him. The Doors hit their peak in the late 1960s, and Morrison died (at age 27) from an overdose on July 3, 1971.

Another Inductee

If you were a fan of rock 'n' roll music in 1994 (especially if you were younger than 30), you probably remember where you were when you heard that Kurt Cobain had died. The tormented lead singer of the incredibly popular alternative rock band Nirvana had committed suicide after a lifelong battle with drug addiction, chronic pain, and debilitating depression.

At the tender age of (you guessed it) 27, Cobain had ended his life and had become the most recent member of the 27 Club. Cobain seemed to have known about the "elite" group of young, dead rock musicians: His mother told reporters, "Now he's gone and joined that stupid club. I told him not to join that stupid club."

Rock Steady? Probably Not

It is odd that these incredibly influential, iconic figures in music would all die before their time and all at age 27. However, when you think about all of the other rock stars who *didn't* die—Keith Richards, Paul McCartney, and Ozzy Osbourne, to name a few—the odds don't seem so bad. Plus, when you consider how hard these individuals lived while they were alive, it seems extraordinary that they lived as long as they did.

Rock musicians are shrouded in speculation and the all-powerful effects of idol worship, so it's no wonder that fans have elevated what's probably just a strange coincidence into the stuff of legend. Whether you believe in the 27 Club or not, you can still rock out to the music these tragic stars left behind.

27 Club

Creepy Coincidences

From a prophetic book written decades before a tragic event took place to a man struck repeatedly by lightning, life's great coincidences are often truly mind-boggling.

✳ ✳ ✳ ✳

The Numbers Don't Lie

THE TERROR ATTACKS of September 11, 2001, brought with them much speculation. Was this heinous act perpetrated by a group of rogue extremists or part of a larger conspiracy? Did everything happen precisely as reported, or was the public being misled? While these questions and others were being pondered, a curious and underreported event took place.

On September 11, 2002, the one-year anniversary of the attacks, the New York State Lottery conducted one of two standard daily drawings. In the three-number contest, the balls drawn were 9–1–1. Statisticians point out that this isn't particularly astounding, given the less than astronomical odds in a three-ball draw. Even so, that's one creepy coincidence.

Womb for One More

As if one womb were no longer good enough to get the job done, Hannah Kersey of Great Britain was born with two. Then, in 2006, to confound the medical world even more, the 23-year-old woman gave birth to triplets—identical twins Ruby and Tilly were delivered from one of Kersey's wombs, while baby Gracie was extracted from the other. All three girls came into the world seven weeks premature via cesarean section and were quite healthy upon arrival. For the record, there have been about 70 known pregnancies in separate wombs in the past 100 years, but the case of triplets is the first of its kind and doctors estimate the likelihood is about one in 25 million.

He's Awl That

Most people recognize the name Louis Braille, the world-renowned inventor of the Braille system of reading and writing for the blind. But what many people don't know is how Braille himself became blind and how it led to his invention.

When he was only three years old, Braille accidentally poked himself in the eye with a stitching awl owned by his father, a saddle maker. At first his injury didn't seem serious, but when an autoimmune disease known as sympathetic ophthalmia set in, he went blind in both eyes.

Over the years, Braille adapted well to his disability. Then, in 1824, at age 15, he invented a system of raised dots that enabled the blind to read and write through use of their finger-tips. To form each dot on a page, Braille employed a common hand tool found at most saddle maker's shops—a stitching awl, the same tool that had injured him as a child.

Lotsa Luck

Evelyn Adams had a couple of bucks and a dream. In 1985, she purchased a New Jersey lottery ticket and crossed her fingers. When the winning numbers were called, she realized she had hit the jackpot. The following year, Adams amazingly hit the jackpot once more. Her combined take for both wins totaled a cool $5.4 million. It was enough money to easily live out her days in comfort. But it wasn't to be.

Due to Adams's innate generosity and love of gambling, she eventually went broke. "I wish I had the chance to do it all over again," she later said. "I'd be much smarter about it now."

Think of Laura

On a whim, ten-year-old Laura Buxton of Burton, Staffordshire, England, jotted her name and address on a lug-gage label in 2001. She then attached it to a helium balloon and released it into the sky. Supported by air currents for 140 miles, the balloon eventually touched down in a garden in Pewsey, Wiltshire, England. Bizarrely, another ten-year-old girl named Laura Buxton read the note, got in touch with its sender, and the girls became fast friends. In addition to their identical

names and ages, each child had fair hair and owned a black
Labrador retriever, a guinea pig, and a rabbit.

Attractive Gent

Do some people attract lightning the way a movie star attracts
fans? In the case of Major Walter Summerford, an officer in
the British Army, the evidence nods toward the affirmative. In
1918, Summerford received his first jolt when he was knocked
from his horse by a flash of lightning. Injuries to his lower
body forced him to retire from the military, so he moved to
Vancouver, British Columbia.

In 1924, Summerford spent a day fishing beside a river.
Suddenly, a bolt of lightning struck the tree he was sitting
beneath, and he was zapped again. But by 1926, Summerford
had recovered from his injuries to the degree that he was able
to take walks. He continued with this therapy until one tragic
summer's day in 1930 when, unbelievably, lightning found him
yet again. This time it paralyzed him for good. He died two
years after the incident.

The story should end there, but it doesn't. In 1936, a lightning
bolt took aim at a cemetery and unleashed its 100,000-volt
charge. Luckily, no living soul was nearby at the time, and the
bolt passed its energy harmlessly into the ground, as do the vast
majority of lightning strikes. Still, before hitting the ground,
the lightning bolt injected its fearsome energy into Major
Summerford's headstone.

Four's a Crowd

In 1838, Edgar Allan Poe, famous author of the macabre,
penned a novel entitled *The Narrative of Arthur Gordon Pym
of Nantucket.* His fictitious account centers
around four survivors of a shipwreck who
find themselves adrift in an open lifeboat.
After many days of hunger and torment,
they decide the only way for any of them to
survive is if one is sacrificed for food. They

draw straws, and cabin boy Richard Parker comes up short. He is subsequently killed, and the three remaining seamen partake of his flesh.

In 1884, some 46 years after the tale was first told, the yacht *Mignonette* broke apart during a hurricane in the South Atlantic. Its four survivors drifted in a lifeboat for 19 days before turning desperate from hunger and thirst. One sailor, a cabin boy, became delirious after guzzling copious quantities of seawater. Upon seeing this, the other three determined that the man was at death's door and decided to kill him. They then devoured his remains. His name: Richard Parker.

Downed Damsels

Mary Ashford was born in 1797, and Barbara Forrest in 1954, yet circumstances surrounding their eventual murders are eerily similar. On May 27, 1817, Ashford was raped and killed in Erdington, England. On May 27, 1974, Forrest was also raped and murdered in Erdington, just 400 yards away from the site of Ashford's murder. The day preceding both of the murders was Whit Monday, a floating religious holiday on the Christian calendar celebrated mostly in Europe. The murders occurred at approximately the same time of day, and attempts had been made to conceal both bodies.

That's not all. Each woman had visited a friend on the night before Whit Monday, changed into a new dress during the evening, and attended a dance. Curiously, suspects in both cases shared the surname "Thornton." Both were subsequently tried and acquitted of murder. Paintings and photos show that the two women also shared very similar facial features.

Naughty but Nice

Whenever Brownsville, Texas, waitress Melina Salazar saw cantankerous customer Walter "Buck" Swords walking into her café, she felt an urge to walk out. Nevertheless, Salazar persevered through a fusillade of demands and curses heaped upon her by her most demanding, albeit loyal, customer.

When 89-year-old Swords passed away, no one was more shocked than Salazar to learn that he'd bequeathed her $50,000 and his car. Describing Swords as, "kind of mean," the waitress told a television news crew, "I still can't believe it."

Shhh! It's A Secret Society

Though documentation proves this secret organization to preserve the Southern cause did indeed exist, many mysteries remain about the Knights of the Golden Circle.

* * * *

THE KNIGHTS OF the Golden Circle was a pro-South organization that operated out of the Deep South, the border states, the Midwest, and even parts of the North both before and during the Civil War. Much of its history is unknown due to its underground nature, but it is known that this secret society, bound by passwords, rituals, and handshakes, intended to preserve Southern culture and states' rights. Its precise origin, membership, and purpose are documented in a handful of primary sources, including the club's handbook, an exposé published in 1861, and a wartime government report that revealed the K.G.C. to be a serious threat to the federal government and its effort to quash the rebellion and maintain the Union.

Some historians trace the organization of the Knights of the Golden Circle back to the 1830s, though the name did not surface publicly until 1855. According to a report by the U.S. government in 1864, the organization included as many as 500,000 members in the North alone and had "castles," or local chapters, spread across the country. Members included everyone from notable politicians to the rank and file, all prepared to rise up against federal coercion as they saw their rights to slavery slipping away.

What's in a Name?

The group's name referred to a geographic "Golden Circle" that surrounded the Deep South. Its boundaries were the border states on the north, America's western territories, Mexico, Central Amer-ica, and even Cuba. Southern leaders and organization members hoped to gain control of these lands to create a strong, agrarian economy dependent on slavery and plantations. This would either balance the numbers of slave states to free states in the federal government or provide a distinct nation that could separate from the Union. The proslavery leader John C. Calhoun of South Carolina was the group's intellectual mentor, although the K.G.C. didn't likely achieve great numbers before his death in 1850. The 1864 government report cited that members initially used nuohlac, Calhoun spelled backward, as a password.

Adding Fuel to the Fire

Once the Civil War began, the K.G.C. became a concern for both state and federal governments. The most obvious public figure associated with the K.G.C. was Dr. George Bickley, an eccentric pamphleteer of questionable character. He is credited with organizing the first castle of the Knights of the Golden Circle in his hometown of Cincinnati. He also sent an open letter to the Kentucky legislature declaring that his organization had 8,000 members in the state, with representatives in every county. The legislature called for a committee to investigate the organization, which had begun to menace that state's effort to remain neutral by importing arms and ammunition for the secession cause. Federal officers arrested Bickley in New Albany, Indiana, in 1863 with a copy of the society's Rules, Regulations, and Principles of the K.G.C. and other regalia on his person. He was held in the Ohio state prison until late 1865. Bickley died two years later, never having been formally charged with a crime.

Methods and Tactics

The underground group used subversive tactics to thwart the Lincoln administration's effort once the war began. A telegram between a Union colonel and Secretary of War Edwin Stanton states how the "Holy Brotherhood" sought to encourage Union soldiers to desert and to paint the conflict as a war in favor of abolition. Some of the government's more questionable wartime tactics, such as the suspension of habeas corpus and the quelling of some aspects of a free press, were rallying points in the Midwest, and they were issues that surely connected northern dissidents such as Copperheads with the Knights in spirit if not in reality. When antiwar sentiment and Peace Democrats influenced populations in Indiana, a U.S. court subpoenaed witnesses for a grand jury to learn more about the organization. The grand jury claimed the secret organization had recruited 15,000 members in Indiana alone and indicted 60 people in August 1862. The Union army attempted to infiltrate the organization and expose its subversive operations by sending new recruits back home to join the K.G.C.

Political Ties

Nationally known political leaders were also allegedly tied to the group. The 1861 exposé referred to a certain "Mr. V—of Ohio" as one of the few reliable members among prominent Northern politicians. It would likely have been assumed that this referred to leading Copperhead and Ohio Representative Clement Vallandigham, who decried abolition before the war and criticized Republicans in Congress and the administration. Union officers arrested Vallandigham, and a military court exiled him to the South. Another possible member was John C. Breckenridge, vice president under James Buchanan and a presidential candidate in 1860. Even former President Franklin Pierce was accused of having an affiliation with the organization.

Assassination Conspiracy

Some also believe that the K.G.C. had a hand in the assassination of Abraham Lincoln. The contemporary exposé stated, "Some one of them is to distinguish himself for—if he can, that is—the assassination of the 'Abolition' President." According to a later anonymous account, Lincoln's assassin, John Wilkes Booth, took the oath of the society in a Baltimore castle in the fall of 1860.

The organization had several counterparts during the war, including the Knights of the Golden Square, the Union Relief Society, the Order of American Knights, and the Order of the Sons of Liberty, to name a few.

The Curse of the Boy King

The discovery of King Tut's tomb in 1922 is said to be the most important find ever in the field of Egyptology. But was there anything to the story of a curse that led to the death of the interlopers who dared disturb the resting place of the boy king? Or was that just an urban legend?

❋ ❋ ❋ ❋

IN NOVEMBER 1922, English archaeologist Howard Carter announced one of the world's greatest archaeological finds: the resting place of Tutankhamen, Egypt's fabled boy king. At nine years old, he was the youngest pharaoh ever to rule the ancient land of the Nile. The tomb, discovered in the Valley of the Kings, was amazingly intact; it was one of the few Egyptian tombs to have escaped grave robbers. The furnishings and treasures were dazzling. In fact, the golden death mask that adorned the sarcophagus is purported to be the most renowned example of Egyptian art.

The boy king, who reigned from 1355 to 1344 B.C., was only 19 years old when he died. Until recently, the cause of his death was a mystery to historians. Many believed Tut had been murdered, but a recent CT scan of the mummy conducted by a team of researchers dispelled that possibility. According to experts, his death may have been from an infection that occurred as the result of a broken leg.

The Curse That Won't Die

Another mystery surrounding the boy king is the alleged curse on anyone disturbing his resting place. That rumor can be traced back to the press. In 1923, shortly after the tomb was discovered, the man who endowed the expedition to locate Tut's tomb, Lord Carnarvon, was bitten on the cheek by a mosquito and died from a resulting infection. This was not an ominous event in itself, but when the lights of Cairo went out at the exact moment of his death, the press had a field day, and an urban legend was born. The legend continues to this day, especially each time Tut goes on tour.

The Mystery of Montauk

Montauk, a beach community at the eastern tip of Long Island in New York State, has been deigned the Miami Beach of the mid-Atlantic. Conspiracy theorists, however, tell another tale. Has the U.S. government been hiding a secret at the former Camp Hero military base there?

* * * *

IN THE LATE 1950s, Montauk was not the paradise-style resort it is today. It was an isolated seaside community boasting a lighthouse commissioned by George Washington in 1792, an abandoned military base called Camp Hero, and a huge radar tower. This tower, still standing, is the last semiautomatic ground environment radar tower still in existence and features an antenna called AN/FPS-35. During its time of air force use, the AN/FPS-35 was capable of detecting airborne objects at a distance of more than 200 miles. One of its uses was detecting potential Soviet long-distance bombers, as the Cold War was in full swing. According to conspiracy theorists, however, the antenna and Camp Hero itself had a few other tricks lurking around the premises, namely human mind control and electro-magnetic field manipulation.

Vanishing Act

On October 24, 1943, the USS *Eldridge* was allegedly made invisible to human sight for a brief moment as it sat in a naval shipyard in Philadelphia. The event, which has never been factually substantiated but has been sworn as true by eyewitnesses and other believers for decades, is said to have been part of a U.S. military endeavor called the Philadelphia Experiment, or Project Rainbow. Studies in electromagnetic radiation had evidenced that manipulating energy fields and bending light around objects in certain ways could render them invisible. Since the benefits to the armed forces would be incredible, the navy supposedly forged ahead with the first experiment.

There are many offshoots to the conspiracy theory surrounding the alleged event. The crew onboard the USS *Eldridge* at the time in question are said to have suffered various mental illnesses, physical ailments, and, most notably, schizophrenia, which has been medically linked to exposure to electromagnetic radiation. Some of them supposedly disappeared along with the ship and relocated through teleportation to the naval base in Norfolk, Virginia, for a moment. Despite severely conflicting eyewitness reports and the navy's assertion that the *Eldridge* wasn't even in Philadelphia that day, many Web sites, books, a video game, and a 1984 science fiction film detail the event.

What's in the Basement?

Camp Hero was closed as an official U.S. Army base in November 1957, although the air force continued to use the radar facilities. After the air force left in 1980, the surrounding grounds were ultimately turned into a state park, which opened to the public in September 2002. Yet the camp's vast underground facility remains under tight government jurisdiction, and the AN/FPS-35 radar tower still stands. Many say there is a government lab on-site that continues the alleged teleportation, magnetic field manipulation, and mind-control experiments that originated with Project Rainbow. One reason for this belief is that two of the sailors onboard the *Eldridge* on October 24, 1943—Al Bielek and Duncan Cameron—claimed to have jumped from the ship while it was in "hyperspace" between Philadelphia and Norfolk, and landed at Camp Hero, severely disoriented.

Though Project Rainbow was branded a hoax, an urban legend continues to surround its "legacy," which is commonly known as the Montauk Project. Theorists cite experiments in electromagnetic radiation designed to produce mass schizophrenia over time and reduce a populace's resistance to governmental control, which, they believe, would explain the continual presence of the antenna. According to these suspicions, a large number of orphans, loners, and homeless people are subjected to testing in Camp Hero's basement; most supposedly die as a result. Interestingly, some conspiracy theorists believe that one outcropping of the experiments is the emergence and rapid popularity of the cell phone, which uses and produces electromagnetic and radio waves. Who knew that easier communication was really an evil government plot to turn people into mindless robots?

The Mystery of the Lost Dauphin of France

History is rife with conspiracy theories. More than 200 years later, the fate of the Lost Dauphin of France still baffles historians.

✳ ✳ ✳ ✳

Little Boy Lost

BORN IN 1785, Louis XVII, son of King Louis XVI and Queen Marie Antoinette, was the heir apparent to the throne (giving him the title of *le Dauphin*). The young boy's destiny was unfortunately timed, however, coinciding with the French Revolution's anti-royalist frenzy that swept away the monarchy. His father met his end on the guillotine in January 1793; as next in the line of succession, little eight-year-old Louis XVII was a dead boy walking.

The family was imprisoned and stripped of their regalia. A few months later, on the night of July 3, 1793, guards came for Louis. Realizing that she would never see her son again, Marie

Antoinette clung to Louis, and for the next two hours she pleaded for his life. She finally relented after the commissioners threatened to kill both her son and daughter.

To keep the monarchy from reestablishing, Louis was imprisoned in solitary confinement in a windowless room. Some reports state that the young boy was horribly starved and abused by his jailers. Less than two years later, on June 8, 1795, the ten-year-old Dauphin of France died. The official cause of death was tuberculosis.

But instead of ending the matter, the mystery of the true fate of Louis XVII had just begun.

Pretenders to the Throne

Rumors grew like wildfire that the body of Louis XVII was actually someone else. Like any good mystery, there were plenty of stories to fuel the flames of conspiracy:

* Louis's jailers were a husband and wife. Later, the aged wife told the nuns who were nursing her that she and her husband had once smuggled out the Dauphin. "My little prince is not dead," she reportedly said.

* A doctor who had treated the Dauphin died "mysteriously" just before the boy did. The doctor's widow suggested he had refused to participate in some strange practices concerning his patient.

* The Dauphin's sister was never asked to identify his body.

* In 1814, the historian of the restored French monarchy claimed that Louis was alive.

* In 1846, the mass grave where the Dauphin had been buried was exhumed. Only one corpse, that of an older boy, showed evidence of tuberculosis.

Contenders (Or Pretenders?) to the Throne

With all of these doubts about what really happened to Louis, it's amazing that only about 100 people came forward throughout the years claiming to be the lost Dauphin and rightful heir to the throne. Among them were:

John James Audubon: Many people thought the famous naturalist Audubon was Louis because he was adopted, was the same age as the Dauphin would have been, and spoke with a French accent. Audubon liked a good story and sometimes implied that he was indeed the Dauphin. In 1828, while visiting France, he wrote a letter to his wife that said, " . . . dressed as a common man, I walk the streets! I . . . who should command all!"

Eleazer Williams: Although his father was a member of the Mohawk tribe, this missionary from Wisconsin somehow convinced people that he was the Lost Dauphin and became a minor celebrity for a few years.

Karl Wilhelm Naundorff: Perhaps the most successful of all, this German clockmaker convinced both the Dauphin's nurse and the minister of justice under Louis XVI that he was indeed the lost heir. He was even recognized as such by the government of the Netherlands. DNA tests in the 1950s disproved his claim. Finally, in 2000, DNA tests confirmed that the boy who died in prison was indeed Louis XVII. Even so, as with many conspiracy theories, many people dispute the test's finding.

CHAPTER 5

HAUNTED HOMES AND OTHER ENTITIES

Phantom of the Opera House

Gaston Leroux's The Phantom of the Opera *has scared generations of readers, as well as untold numbers of theatergoers who have watched the many adaptations of the novel on the stage and silver screen. Leroux's story is fiction, but it's said that real-life phantoms haunt the Grand Opera House in Oshkosh, Wisconsin.*

✳ ✳ ✳ ✳

Everyone Has a Story

A REGIONAL INSTITUTION SINCE 1883, the Grand Opera House has served numerous purposes through the years: It was a venue for vaudeville and stage productions and was later used as a movie house. During its heyday, the theater showcased many of the biggest names in show business, including Enrico Caruso, Harry Houdini, and the Marx Brothers. Today, however, it is best known for housing a number of playful poltergeists.

Indeed, almost everyone who has spent time at the Grand Opera House has a tale or two to tell. Once, an actor was rushing from his dressing room to the stage when he turned a corner and almost ran into a spectral man decked out in 19th-century garb. The ghost was holding a playbill, which the actor was able to identify as being for an 1895 production of *The Bohemian Girl*.

Many others who have worked at or visited the theater report equally unusual phenomena, including fire doors opening and closing on their own and unexplained footsteps.

Ironically, in the mid-1970s, a television movie about a haunted theater was filmed at the Grand Opera House. According to producer Bob Jacobs, a variety of inexplicable occurrences took place during the production, but it quickly became evident that whatever was haunting the theater was not trying to scare the cast and crew—it was trying to protect them.

In one especially chilling incident, a young assistant was hoisted above the stage and left hanging there for nearly an hour while a scene was shot. As soon as the assistant was lowered down and his feet touched the stage, the rope that had been holding him suddenly snapped. Jacobs, who witnessed the incident, became convinced that an unseen force had been acting as the young man's guardian angel, protecting him until he was safely returned to the ground.

Ghosts Aplenty

Others involved in the production of the film reported seeing ghostly figures pass by. Assistant producer Jan Turner witnessed a spectral figure in an underground passage; another time, something grabbed her ankle. Production assistants Dennis Payne and John Jansen reported seeing a man walk out of the orchestra pit and into a room that had no other access point; when the man didn't come out, they checked the room, but it was empty . . . or so they thought.

Staff members and visitors at the Grand Opera House have long wondered who haunts its halls. The man with the playbill may have been a former actor who performed there, or perhaps he was a deceased audience member. Many ghost hunters believe that another resident spirit is that of Percy R. Keene, who worked as a stage manager at the theater from 1895 until his death in the mid-1960s. Keene was well liked by everyone, and it was evident to all that he loved the Grand Opera House. It makes sense then that after his death, his spirit would return to keep an eye on the place.

An Appreciative Specter

Bob Jacobs had an interesting encounter with a spirit that he believed was Percy Keene. Two days before the premiere of his movie, Jacobs held a private screening at the Grand Opera House for six people who had worked on the film. After the movie ended, Jacobs glanced up at the balcony and saw a figure smiling down at him; it looked just like Keene.

In the 1980s, renowned paranormal investigators Ed and Lorraine Warren visited the Grand Opera House to see what they could uncover. Lorraine reported sensing a male presence and also a dog. Keene's family later confirmed that the much-loved stage manager had once kept a pet dog at the theater.

Ghosts tend to reside at locations that were important to them in life. For Percy Keene and perhaps a few others, the Grand Opera House was a home away from home—and a place that they just couldn't bear to leave.

The Haunting of the Holly Hotel

The Holly Hotel in Holly, Michigan, is more than just a historical landmark—it's allegedly a hotbed of paranormal activity. But are the stories surrounding the place fact or fiction?

✳   ✳   ✳   ✳

A Hotel with a Future

IN THE 1860s, America's railway systems were enjoying epic expansion. As tracks were laid, more people and more products than ever before were crisscrossing the nation. Major midwestern cities such as Detroit and Chicago were bustling, and the need for hotels near stations was growing because they served locals and travelers alike.

Built in 1863, the Holly Hotel (originally called the Hirst Hotel after its first proprietor, John Hirst) and the surrounding area certainly looked different in that era than they do today. Back then, the building was larger than it is now, and Martha Street—on which the Holly stands—was lined with taverns that hosted brawls so often that it was dubbed "Battle Alley" (a nickname that persists to this day). It might've been rough-and-tumble outside the hotel, but inside, the Holly boasted hot water, elegant rooms, fine dining, and a large staff, which set a tone for luxury that continues to this day, even though the establishment is only a restaurant now.

In 1912, Hirst sold the hotel to Joseph P. Allen, who renamed it "the Holly Inn." But in 1913, a massive fire completely destroyed the building's second and third floors. Hirst, once a cigar-smoking, boisterous host, was crushed by the loss of the beautiful hotel that he'd built; when he passed away seven years later, the townspeople said that he never overcame the grief that he suffered following the devastating fire. Enter the Holly Hotel's first ghost.

Employees have long said that John Hirst haunts the Holly. The smell of cigar smoke is often perceived at the bar, even when no one is smoking. And over the years, numerous visitors have spotted the figure of a man wearing a frock coat and a top hat, and disembodied laughter is frequently heard traveling from the stairs down to what was once the hotel's lower-level parlor.

A Fiery Déjà Vu and More Ghostly Figures
Even if you don't believe in spooks, it's hard not to be freaked out by the fact that in 1978—exactly 65 years to the day *and hour* of the first disastrous fire—the Holly Hotel burned again.

Although no one was killed, the fire caused more than a half million dollars of damage. The building was repaired, and once again, stories about ghosts roaming the halls came pouring in.

The spirit of Nora Kane—a frequent visitor to the hotel in her days among the living—still lingers at the Holly. When photographers are contracted to shoot weddings at the restaurant—a popular place for receptions due to its lush Victorian decor and fine food—they're warned that apparitions or strange shadows may obscure some of their photos. On the websites of paranormal investigators who have visited the Holly, wispy, cloudlike strands can be seen in images of the stairwell. Is it a trick of photography, or is Nora Kane walking into the shot? Guests and employees have also claimed to hear her singing near the piano when things get too quiet.

One of the most active spirits at the Holly Hotel is that of a fiery red-haired girl who likes to play with a meat cleaver in the kitchen. Disembodied giggles and footsteps have been reported there, and during a séance in the 1990s, the girl allegedly manifested. It is believed that, in life, she was either the daughter of Nora Kane or a young girl who died tragically after sustaining injuries at the livery stable that once stood adjacent to the hotel.

Other unexplainable phenomena at the hotel include sudden drops in temperature, floating orbs, phantom barking and the sound of a dog running down the halls, and appearances of a Native American figure that vanishes as quickly as it arrives.

Not Just a Ghost Motel

The legacy of the Holly Hotel is worth studying, regardless of potential spirit activity, and the proprietors tend to focus on promoting it as a historical landmark and fine-dining establishment. High tea is held there weekly, and the grounds are often used for private events.

But for those who believe in ghosts, it remains a popular destination. Often cited as one of the most haunted places in

America, the Holly Hotel may hold secrets that none of us can unlock—at least not on this plane of existence.

San Diego Ghosts Gather at the Whaley House

Even if you don't believe in ghosts, you've got to be intrigued by all the chatter surrounding the Whaley House in San Diego. According to late ghost hunter Hans Holzer, this old family homestead might be the most haunted house in America. The U.S. Department of Commerce lists the building as an authentic Haunted House (it is one of only two structures in the country—along with the Winchester Mystery House—to hold this distinction), and the television show America's Most Haunted *called it the Most Haunted House in the United States.*

✳ ✳ ✳ ✳

How It All Began

THE FIRST TWO-STORY building in San Diego and now the oldest on the West Coast, the Whaley House needs all of its space to house the many spirits that reside inside it. Built by prominent Californian Thomas Whaley in 1856, it began as a one-story granary with an adjacent two-story residence. By the next year, Whaley had opened a general store on the premises. Over the years, the building also served as a county courthouse, a ballroom, a billiards hall, and a theater, among other things. Now it's a California State Historic Landmark and a museum.

Squatter's Rights

Hindsight is always 20/20, but perhaps Thomas Whaley should have thought twice about buying the property on which "Yankee Jim" Robinson was publicly hanged in 1852. Accused of attempted grand larceny, Robinson was executed in a particularly unpleasant display. The gallows were situated on the back of a wagon that was set up at the site; however, being a tall man, Yankee Jim was able to reach the wagon with his feet, thus delaying his death for several minutes. According to newspaper reports, when his legs were finally pulled out from under him, he "swung back and forth like a pendulum" until he died. Although Whaley was actually present at Robinson's execution, he apparently didn't associate the property with the gruesome event that had taken place there. Nevertheless, soon after the house was completed, he and his family began to hear heavy disembodied footsteps, as if a large man was walking through the house. Remembering what had taken place there a few years earlier, the Whaleys believed that the spirit of Yankee Jim himself was sharing their new home. Apparently, Robinson was not a malevolent ghost because the Whaleys' youngest daughter, Lillian, remained in the house with the spirit until 1953. But to this day, visitors to the site still report hearing the heavy-footed phantom.

Family Spirits

After the house became a historic landmark and was opened to the public in 1960, staff, tourists, and ghost hunters alike began to experience paranormal phenomena such as apparitions, noises, and isolated cold spots. Some have even caught glimpses of a small spotted dog running by with its ears flapping, which just might be the spirit of the Whaleys' terrier, Dolly Varden.

Although Thomas and Anna Whaley lived in several different houses, the couple must have dearly loved their original San Diego home because they don't seem quite ready to leave it, even a century after their deaths. They have been seen—and heard—going about their daily business and doing chores in the house. Don't they know there's a cleaning service for that?

The couple has also been captured on film acting as though it was still the 19th century. Thomas was seen wandering through the house and smoking a pipe near an upstairs window, while Anna seems to have kept up her duties as the matron of the house: People have seen her rocking a baby, tucking a child into bed, and folding clothes. Sometimes, the family's rocking chair is seen teetering back and forth all by itself.

Children are especially likely to see the building's former occupants. Employees frequently notice youngsters smiling or waving at people who the adults are unable to see. And the sound of piano music that sometimes drifts through the air? Most say that it's Anna, still playing the tunes that she loved most in life.

Long before he became one of America's most beloved TV personalities, Regis Philbin worked at a television station in San Diego. In 1964, when he and a companion paid a visit to the Whaley House to investigate the ghostly tales, Philbin was startled to see the wispy figure of Anna Whaley moving along one of the walls. When he turned on a flashlight to get a look, she disappeared, leaving only her portrait to smile back at him.

Wilted Violet

Thomas and Anna's daughter Violet had a particularly sad life and is thought to haunt the old house where she once lived. In 1882, in a double wedding with her sister Anna Amelia, the beautiful Violet was married at the Whaley House to a man that her parents did not trust. Unfortunately, the marriage lasted only two weeks, after which Violet was granted a divorce. Divorce was highly uncommon in those days, and the scandal was humiliating for both Violet and her family. Violet became extremely depressed, and in 1885, she took her own life by shooting herself in the heart.

It is believed that Violet makes her presence known by turning on lights in the upstairs rooms and setting off the burglar alarm. Her spirit is also thought to be responsible for the phantom footsteps that emanate from the second floor and the sudden icy chills often felt by visitors—as though a spirit had just walked right through them.

Ghosts Galore

Most of the spirits at the Whaley House seem to be related to the family or the site. A young girl has been seen in several locations in and around the house. Dressed in 19th-century clothing, she plays with toys in the playroom, sniffs flowers in the garden, and darts in and out of the dining room very quickly. Some say that she was a playmate of the Whaley children and that she died on the property when she got tangled in a clothesline and either broke her neck or was strangled; however, there is no record of such a death occurring at the Whaley House. Others say that although her spirit is real, her story was made up somewhere along the way, which only adds to the intrigue of the place. As if there wasn't enough of that already.

Another female ghost seems to be attached to the part of the house that once served as a courtroom. One visitor said that as she walked into the room, she saw a woman dressed in a calico skirt typical of the 1800s. The spirit didn't seem evil, but it didn't seem to be particularly welcoming either. The visitor captured the spectral woman's shadowy figure in a photo. It seems likely that the ghost is somehow connected to an event that took place in the courtroom.

The ghost of a man dressed in a businesslike frock coat has also appeared in the former courtroom. However, his spirit may not be strongly attached to the building because it fades away more quickly than others that are seen there.

Haunted Happenings

In addition to these apparitions, visitors, volunteers, and employees have reported other odd phenomena inside the house. Unexplained singing, organ music, and whistling have been heard, as has a toddler crying in an upstairs nursery. (This is believed to be the spirit of Thomas and Anna's son, who was also named Thomas; he died of scarlet fever at age 17 months.) Some have witnessed levitating furniture, and others have noticed mysterious scents, such as perfume, cigar smoke, and the scent of holiday baking coming from an empty kitchen.

When visitors first enter the house, they can examine photos taken by previous visitors. These images all have one thing in common: They contain mysterious objects such as shadows, orbs, and misty figures. One visitor reported trying to take photos with an otherwise reliable camera; as soon as she tried to focus, the camera beeped, indicating that she was too close to her subject despite the fact that she was nowhere near the closest (visible) object. Once developed, the photos featured an orb or filmy shadow in nearly every shot.

At least the Whaley House spirits take some responsibility for the place. Once, after an especially long day at the museum, a staff member was getting ready to close up when all the doors and windows on both floors suddenly locked on their own, all at the same time. Sometimes spirits just need a little alone time.

The Feisty Fenton Wraiths

The Fenton Hotel Tavern & Grille in Fenton, Michigan, no longer operates as an inn, but certain spectral guests seem unaware of that. As a result, the fine restaurant on the main floor of this historic building may be one of Michigan's most haunted places.

✳   ✳   ✳   ✳

BUILT IN 1856 AND originally known as the Vermont House, the Fenton Hotel Tavern & Grille was bought and sold several times before it received its current name. Over the years, this remarkable building has been the subject of numerous paranormal investigations and séances, but the spooks that reside there seem determined to avoid checking out.

The tin ceilings and original woodwork in the foyer and dining area of the Fenton add to the illusion of a place that's stuck in time. Maybe that's why Emery, the old hotel's legendary janitor, still treads the creaky floorboards of what used to be his room on the building's decrepit and unused second floor. In life,

Emery was a kindly gent who was a bit of a workaholic. When the last customer leaves in the evening, it is not uncommon for the staff to hear Emery banging on the floor of his room as if to say, "Get this place cleaned up!"

The hotel bar is another hot spot for unexplained phenomena. Bartenders have seen wine glasses scoot right off the stemware racks and fly across the room. Phantom voices call the staff members by name, and unseen entities brush up against them. Patrons once saw a mysterious shadow figure hug a bartender—while the bartender remained completely unaware of the affectionate display.

The Fenton's most unusual phenomenon—the thirsty ghost—occurs from time to time at Table 32: It is there that a man sits down and orders a shot of Jack Daniel's on the rocks, but before the wait staff can get the drink to the table, the man vanishes.

Table 32 is not the only haunted dining spot at the Fenton. A waitress and a manager have both seen a top-hat-clad shadow figure lounging at Table 63; this entity has even been captured in photos. The dining room is also rumored to house one overly frisky ghost that some waitresses claim has pinched their backsides.

The Fenton's Femme Fatales

Not all of the ghosts at the Fenton Hotel Tavern & Grille are male; supposedly, the spirits of some "working girls" who once lived on the third floor also remain. According to one legend, a young prostitute hung herself in the downstairs restroom and still makes her presence known there by opening and closing stall doors; another version says that the ghostly girl was an unwed, pregnant traveler. Regardless of who she was in life, strange things do happen in the ladies room. Once, a customer seated in a stall watched in disbelief as an unseen force lifted a strand of her long hair and then dropped it back into place. Another time, a workman, who had been sent in to complete some repairs, was unable to open an unlocked stall. After he felt a vaporous mist float through him, he was finally able to open the door. Perhaps this spirit was a modest ghost that just needed some privacy.

The Seal of Disapproval

The second-floor hotel rooms are off-limits to customers, but in the mid-2000s, *Weird Michigan* author Linda Godfrey was given an evening tour of the area. That night, she heard loud, unintelligible whispering directly in her ear while she, a hostess, and another researcher stood quietly in the hallway. Later in the investigation, Godfrey discovered that the viewfinder on her camera was covered with fresh candle wax—however, she had not been near a lit candle all evening. Godfrey felt as though some unseen entity was literally attempting to block her view of that section of the hotel. Perhaps, like all hotel guests, the ghosts of the Fenton simply value their privacy.

In February 1904, the Fenton Hotel's second- and third-story front porches were dragged away by a team of frightened horses. When something at the railroad depot spooked the equines, they took off galloping through town and thundered past the hotel, pulling down support posts as they went. Amazingly, no one was hurt, but the porches were never rebuilt.

Ghosts Live On at the Clovis Sanitarium

Picture this scene at the emergency call center in Clovis, California: "Hello. 911. What's your emergency?" Dead silence. "Hello? Is anyone there?" More silence. So the dispatcher checks to see where the call is coming from and finds that it's 2604 Clovis Avenue: the former home of the Clovis Sanitarium—a building that has no electricity and no working phone. It's probably not a life-or-death situation, since whatever is making the call is already dead.

O DDLY, THIS TYPE of phone call is not uncommon in Clovis—a city of 95,000 that is located just northeast of Fresno. Nicknamed "the Gateway to the Sierras," Clovis was the home of Anthony Andriotti, who built a magnificent mansion for his family in 1922. Unfortunately, he miscalculated the cost of the building's upkeep, and he went bankrupt, turned to alcohol and opium, and died in 1929 at age 36.

The estate sat empty until it was reopened in 1935 as the Hazelwood Sanitarium for tuberculosis patients. In 1942, it became the Clovis Avenue Sanitarium, which was dedicated to serving the area's physically and mentally ill.

A Place to Die

Families whose loved ones suffered from dementia or schizophrenia brought these unfortunate souls to the Clovis Sanitarium to die. It is said that at one point, the death rate at the facility reached an average of one person per day. Still, the building soon became overcrowded, with ten beds to a room and one nurse overseeing two or more rooms. Former employees told sad tales of patients who were abused and neglected.

When patients died, their bodies were stored in the relatively cool basement until they could be removed. Locals started talking about strange happenings at the sanitarium, and rumors began to suggest that the place was haunted. But it wasn't all idle gossip: It seems that there *were* some pretty strange things going on at 2604 Clovis Avenue.

A Call for Help

In 1992, the Clovis Sanitarium closed; that's when the mysterious phone calls began. Sometimes neighbors or passersby would call the police regarding trespassers or vandals. But then there were the other calls—the ones that came directly from the vacant building that had no working phone line.

Unfazed by these odd stories, Todd Wolfe bought the property in 1997 with hopes of creating a haunted-house-type Halloween attraction. Initially a skeptic, Wolfe was surprised when his employees complained about spirits interfering with their work. They saw apparitions and reported being touched and grabbed by unseen hands. It wasn't until he had his own encounter in "Mary's Room"—where he actually saw a shadowy apparition—that Wolfe began to believe. Today, Mary's Room is furnished with only original furniture because it seems that "Mary" gets quite upset when changes are made. And a disturbed Mary leads to increased paranormal activity, including phantom breathing, shoving by an invisible force, and objects that move seemingly on their own.

Many paranormal groups have visited the Clovis Sanitarium, and all agree that it is indeed haunted. They've heard shuffling footsteps and strange voices, and many have reported feelings of being watched.

Energetic Spirits

When the *Ghost Adventures* team visited the Clovis Sanitarium in a 2010 episode, they were greeted by a laughing spirit and a spike in electromagnetic energy (in a building with no electricity). Later, in the basement, the crew used a state-of-the-art ultraviolet camera to record a mysterious purple form; the shape even appeared to sit on a couch for a while. The team also captured some amazing EVPs (electronic voice phenomena), including one that told the group to "Get out" and another that said it wanted their energy.

Investigator Zak Bagans observed that the ghosts of Clovis Sanitarium are an unusual bunch. The original owners were a family with young children who lived a lavish lifestyle, full of happiness and laughter. But combine those feelings with those of the mentally ill who were neglected and abused after being brought there to die, and the mix becomes volatile. As Bagans concluded, "That contrasting energy has to do something weird to the atmosphere."

Canada's Most Haunted Resort

The Fairmont Banff Springs Hotel looks like an elegant castle fit for a fairy tale. Truly one of the most luxurious resorts in the world, it is also one of the most haunted.

✳ ✳ ✳ ✳

Wandering Spirits

THE STORY BEGINS in 1883, when three off-duty Canadian Pacific Railway workers were hiking around Banff and discovered the now-famous hot springs. Construction of a hotel was started about four years later, and in 1888, the Banff Springs Hotel opened. It was a large, partly wooden structure nestled in spectacular mountains about two hours from Calgary. For years, the only way to visit the hotel was by rail, making it an ideal, scenic getaway for tourists . . . and for ghosts.

From the hotel's earliest days, security staff noticed dark, shadowy figures floating in the hallways. The apparitions seemed to linger in one area before vanishing into a nearby wall where no hotel room existed. Banff's staff and owners were baffled, and guests were a little frightened.

Then in 1926, a fire destroyed part of the hotel. During the cleanup, workers uncovered a builder's mistake. At the exact location where ghosts had been sighted, the cleanup crew found an interior room with no windows or doors. People speculated that the secluded room had been the ghosts' home, or a portal to "the other side." The hotel was rebuilt without the odd, hidden room, so when it reopened in 1928, most people thought the phantom figures were gone for good, but they were wrong.

The Ghostly Bride

According to legend, during the 1920s, a woman left the hotel's bridal suite wearing her wedding gown. As she walked down the candlelit staircase, a gust of wind lifted the train of her gown and caught it on fire. Struggling to put out the flames, the bride lost her balance and fell, which caused her to break her neck and killed her instantly. Scorch marks on the marble stairs still indicate where she fell.

Since then, staff and guests have seen the ghostly bride on the stairs. Witnesses say she appears as a translucent figure before bursting into flames and vanishing. People have also noticed unexplained gusts of wind around the haunted staircase. Others have seen the ghostly bride dancing alone in the ballroom or seemingly waiting for someone at the hotel's Rob Roy Lounge. She fades away slowly if you continue to watch her. She may also haunt the bridal suite, where guests have reported recurring "cold spots." But the bridal suite isn't nearly as haunted as another room at the hotel.

Ghosts on the Eighth Floor

If you're looking for a murder mystery, visit the eighth floor of the Banff Springs Hotel. Staff members won't talk about it, but Room 873 has been sealed and its number removed. Nearby doors are numbered 871 and 872, followed by 874 and 875.

According to rumors, a family was murdered in Room 873. Afterward, the hotel cleaned the room and prepared it for new guests. However, each time the staff cleaned the large mirror in Room 873, a child's fingerprints reappeared. Eventually, the hotel closed the room and sealed it. Some guests say the outline of the door is still visible. Others have taken photos outside the sealed room, and vivid, unexplained orbs have reportedly appeared in the pictures.

Those orbs are dramatic, but there's an even more intense, ghostly manifestation at Banff. The ghost of a former hotel bellman, Sam McCauley, appears so real that guests often think he's a regular hotel employee.

Some Scots Never Leave

McCauley arrived from Scotland in the 1930s and worked as a porter at the Banff Springs Hotel for nearly 40 years. Before he died, he promised to return to the hotel as a ghost. It seems he kept his word: McCauley has been seen in the hallways and sometimes helps guests with their luggage. When they turn to tip the elderly man, he vanishes. McCauley is popular with staff and guests alike and is spotted regularly in the lobby and on the ninth floor, where he used to store his tips.

Another Scotsman haunts the Banff Springs Hotel, too. Very late at night, a Scottish piper appears around the Rob Roy Lounge. Some people apparently see him in full Scottish garb, but because this ghost is headless, his real identity is unknown.

In addition, a portrait hanging in the MacKenzie Room appears to be haunted. According to legend, a ghost comes out of the portrait's eyes. First, the eyes seem to light up slightly, then something with jagged edges appears to swirl out of the eyes. The apparition is so scary that no one has remained in the room long enough to see what happens next. Some say this ghost was partly responsible for a fire in the hotel in 1946.

The Helpful Housekeeper and the Singing Men

One of the hotel's newest ghosts is a former housekeeper. She allegedly visits rooms and straightens the covers on the beds—sometimes while guests are still sleeping! She's harmless, but it can be unsettling to wake up in the morning and find the bed more tidy than when you went to sleep.

For your listening pleasure, it has been reported that around 3:00 A.M., a male voice sings loudly in the downstairs ladies' washroom. He's never seen, nor is the male chorus that sings in the men's washroom near the ballrooms.

Other Figures and Phantom Lights

Though most people believe the hotel's earliest shadowy ghosts left when the resort was rebuilt in the 1920s, some have reported seeing those fleeting forms again. They're dark and move silently through the halls, like something out of a movie, then they vanish, passing through walls and locked doors. Other guests describe eerie, unexplained lights hovering outside their hotel room windows. These guests say that the lights aren't frightening, merely odd.

One thing is certain: Banff Springs Hotel is popular with everyone who visits it . . . including ghosts.

The Haunted Bunk Beds of Horicon

Haunted houses are supposed to sport broken windows, gothic architecture, and perhaps looming towers. However, a modest, well-kept ranch house in Wisconsin shattered that stereotype when it became one of the most famously haunted homes in America.

✳ ✳ ✳ ✳

THE SMALL TOWN of Horicon, Wisconsin, is best known for its proximity to a large marsh where thousands of Canada geese stop on their migratory route. But in the late 1980s, a small home on Larrabee Street stole the spotlight from the marsh when the young family living there claimed that it was sharing its home with a horrific entity.

Nightmare in the Nursery

In June 1987, Deborah and Allen (whose names have been

changed to protect their privacy) and their children (Kenny, Maryann, and Sarah) began to experience frightening and inexplicable events after purchasing a secondhand set of bunk beds for Kenny.

The unusual activity began in Kenny's room. First, a radio would change stations by itself. Then, a babysitter reported that an unoccupied chair teetered back and forth, and a suitcase that was stored under the bottom bunk shot out as if someone under the bed had shoved it. Kenny also told his parents that he often saw a glowing old lady with long black hair standing in his doorway.

Fog, Flames, and Fear

As events escalated during the fall and winter, Allen tried to verbally confront the spirit that he and Deborah were sure had somehow moved in with them. When he told the unseen presence to leave his children alone, he was shocked to receive a response from a loud voice that told him to "Come here." This was followed by the appearance of a glowing flamelike specter in the garage. The fiery entity glared at Allen with two large green eyes.

In early January 1988, Allen saw a "foggy" spirit with large green eyes rise out of the floor, and he again heard the loud voice. This time, the voice told Allen that he was dead, and then the apparition vanished in a streak of faux flames. Allen and Deborah asked their minister to try to bless the spirit away, but that didn't help. Rumors about the house being haunted quickly spread around town, and on January 11, the family moved out and trashed the bunk beds at a distant landfill.

By January 21, an onslaught of people who hoped to see some paranormal action had besieged Larrabee Street; in fact, the Horicon police had to patrol the area because of greatly increased traffic and trespassers. At the same time, the gossip grew wilder: Area newspapers reported that people were claiming that the house had blood dripping from the ceiling, strange graffiti had materialized on the walls, the family's snowblower was seen racing around the yard by itself, and the home's basement had a large hole in the floor that served as a gateway to hell. In short, the reaction from the populace was almost scarier than the family's actual experience.

Fame but No Fortune

Milwaukee Sentinel reporter James Nelson, who tracked down the family at a relative's house, wrote an extended series of articles based on exclusive interviews with Allen and Deborah, who agreed to participate on the condition that he withhold their identities. The Associated Press then spread the story far and wide. The *National Enquirer* offered the couple $5,000 for their story, but they declined, even though they had lost about $3,000 by returning the house's deed to their mortgage lender.

Later in 1988, the TV show *Unsolved Mysteries* filmed an episode about the haunted ranch house in Horicon, even though new owners had moved in and had reported nothing unusual. Actors played the roles of Allen and his son, whose chilling encounters ceased after the family moved and the bunk beds were discarded.

Skeptics claim that the family made up the story, but because the couple shunned publicity and offers of money—and even suffered considerable financial loss—that seems unlikely. The Horicon chief of police, the family's minister, and the *Sentinel* reporter all stated their belief in Allen and Deborah's sincerity.

Hopefully, the couple buried those bunk beds very deep in that landfill.

Stalked by an Invisible Entity

In November 1988, when Jackie Hernandez moved into a small bungalow on 11th Street in San Pedro, California, she was looking to make a fresh start. But her hopefulness quickly turned into what she described as the "nightmare of all nightmares."

From the time that Jackie moved in to her new place, she felt a presence in the house. At first, it made her feel safe—as if someone was looking out for her. But Jackie soon realized that the presence was less than friendly. Shortly after their arrival, Jackie and her young children heard a high-pitched screeching noise throughout the house. Then, in February 1989, Jackie's unseen houseguests manifested in the form of two separate apparitions: One was an old man that Jackie's friend also witnessed while she was babysitting in the home; the other was a disembodied head that Jackie saw in the attic.

❊ ❊ ❊ ❊

Call in the Cavalry

IN AUGUST 1989, Jackie asked a group of paranormal researchers to investigate the phenomena; parapsychologist Dr. Barry Taff, cameraman Barry Conrad, and photographer Jeff Wheatcraft had no idea how the case would impact their lives. On August 8, during their first visit to the Hernandez home, the group noted a foul odor in the house, heard noises in the attic, and captured glowing orbs of light in photographs. Skeptical of Jackie's claim of seeing a phantom head in the attic, Wheatcraft took several photos in the darkened space. But he left the room in terror after an unseen force yanked the camera from his hands. When he summoned the courage to go back into the attic (this time with a flashlight), he found the body of the camera on one side of the room and the lens on the other, inside a box.

Later that same evening, while Wheatcraft and Conrad were in the attic, Wheatcraft was violently pushed by an invisible hand.

After they returned to the main level of the house, loud banging noises were heard coming from the attic, as if someone (or something) was stomping above them.

When the researchers returned to the house later that month, they observed a liquid oozing from the walls and dripping from the cabinets. Samples that were analyzed at a lab determined that the substance was blood plasma from a human male. Why it would be oozing from the walls was anyone's guess.

Get Out and Don't Look Back

The phenomena that Jackie and the investigators experienced on the night of September 4, 1989, shook them to their very cores. During the day, the poltergeist ramped up its attention-seeking behavior. After watching objects fly through the air and hearing mysterious moaning and breathing noises, Jackie called the researchers for help.

Wheatcraft and Conrad's friend Gary Boehm were inspecting the pitch-black attic and were just about to leave when Wheatcraft screamed. Boehm took a photo hoping that the flash would illuminate the room so he could see Wheatcraft and help him. Boehm's photo captured the spirit's latest attack on Wheatcraft, who was hanging from the rafters with a clothesline wrapped around his neck; the cord was tied with a seaman's knot. Boehm was able to rescue Wheatcraft, who was understandably shaken by his encounter with the evil entity that seemed to have a personal vendetta against him.

After observing several other paranormal phenomena that night, Jackie and the researchers left the San Pedro house, never to return.

You Can Run but You Can't Hide

Frightened for the safety of her young children, Jackie moved her family nearly 200 miles away to Weldon, California. But it didn't take long for the poltergeist to find her. The haunting started with unusual scratching noises that came from a backyard shed; then, a black, shapeless form was spotted in the hallway of the home. As had been the case in San Pedro, others witnessed the phenomena as well: While moving an old television set out of the storage shed, Jackie's neighbors saw the ghostly image of an old man on the screen.

In April 1990, when the researchers heard that the paranormal activity had followed Jackie to her new home, they drove to Weldon to continue their work on the case. Besides, Wheatcraft had a personal interest in the matter: He wanted to know why the entity was focusing its physical attacks on him.

Hoping to provoke the spirit, Jackie, her friend, and the researchers decided to use a Ouija board. During the session, the table that they used shook violently, candles flickered, and the temperature in the room dropped dramatically. But the group may have received the answers it was seeking: Through the Ouija board, the spirit told them that he was a sailor who had been murdered in 1930 when his killer drowned him in San Pedro Bay. He also said that his killer had lived in Jackie's former home in San Pedro. When Wheatcraft asked the spirit why he was being targeted, the entity said that Wheatcraft resembled his killer. It then picked up Wheatcraft and threw him against the wall. He was naturally frightened, but he was not injured.

After that, Conrad searched old newspaper records to see if the information that they'd received from the spirit could be verified; it was. In 1930, sailor Herman Hendrickson was found drowned in San Pedro Bay. Although he'd also suffered a fractured skull, his death was ruled accidental. Perhaps Hendrickson's spirit was trying to make it known that his death was not accidental but that he was murdered.

Spirit Stalker

In June 1990, Jackie moved back to San Pedro and rented an apartment on Seventh Street. This time, she had a priest bless the place before she moved in. Nevertheless, the glowing orbs of light returned.

Later that year, Conrad's home was also infested with poltergeist activity, which he witnessed along with Boehm and Wheatcraft. Objects were mysteriously moved to new locations, burners on the gas stove turned on by themselves, scissors flew across the kitchen, a broom was left standing on top of the stove, and scissors were found underneath pillows in the bedroom. Also, Wheatcraft was again pushed by the invisible force, which left red scratch marks on his back.

The phenomena greatly diminished after that, although subsequent residents of the house on 11th Street in San Pedro also claimed to witness poltergeist activity; since then, it is said that no one has lived in the house for more than six months.

Although Jackie was terribly frightened by the mysterious activity at the time, she later said that she was grateful to have had a firsthand encounter with the Other Side, which not many people get to experience. Although some folks might welcome a visit from a ghost, few would want it to be as distressing as what Jackie went through.

The Ghosts of Bradford College

What came to be known as Bradford College started as a preparatory school in 1803 in Haverhill, Massachusetts. In 1932, it became a junior college for women, and in 1971, it became a four-year coed institution. When the school closed its doors for good in 2000, it left behind a host of ghosts. Two scandalous stories of romance resulted in less-than-fairytale endings for two young women who are said to haunt the campus to this day. And they're not alone: Ghost hunters have detected several other spirits on this old campus.

✳ ✳ ✳ ✳

A Holy Ghost

ONE RUMOR THAT has circulated around the campus for several years suggests that a young female student named

Amy had an affair with a priest. She became pregnant, and soon after, she died. Whether she took her own life or was killed by the priest is not known, but her ghost is said to haunt the Academy Building, which has served as both a dormitory and the home of the school's administrative offices.

When a team of ghost hunters investigated the college in 2000, they found that the Academy Building did indeed give off negative energy. They experienced cold spots and caught glimpses of two spirits that fit the descriptions of Amy and the priest. Inside, they saw a young blonde woman dressed in a school uniform; she appeared to be frightened. And in the alley just outside the building, they spotted an angry man dressed entirely in black.

Room 457

Students and investigators alike have experienced unusual phenomena in many of the former dorm rooms in the Academy Building, but Room 457 has proven to be especially disturbing. Some people felt like the room was closing in on them, and others sensed that very bad things had occurred there. Some reported feeling a sensation of falling, and one of the investigators said that she felt the room had once been full of children and had been used for discipline.

Some ghost hunters use pendulums to measure paranormal activity. While one group was in this eerie room, their pendulum suddenly broke; no one could fix it until it was off the property. Oddly, a camera also malfunctioned at the same time, in the same place.

The Denworth Ghost

In a tale that's similar to the one that allegedly took place in the Academy Building, a female student had an affair with a professor. When she found out that she was pregnant, she told her lover that she was going to tell administrators what had occurred. But she never got the chance: He killed her, and her ghost reportedly still haunts the Denworth Hall Theatre. Some people have heard her singing "Hush Little Baby," and others have been the subjects of her pranks.

This makes for a good story, but some paranormal investigators were skeptical. Many theaters have ghosts, and let's face it, actors can be dramatic. So they didn't have high hopes of finding any ghosts in the theater—until they came face-to-face with one.

While some of the researchers were waiting in a stairwell, the shadow of a girl with long hair appeared on the wall for everyone to see, yet no human body was there to create such a shadow. As the onlookers watched intently, the shape began to take form. It floated down the stairs singing "Hush Little Baby" to a doll in a clear, melodic female voice. The team sensed that the spirit had been through a terrible tragedy; it seemed to long for company and began to cry softly. As the group left the building, the specter could be heard imploring them, "Wait! Wait! Don't leave!"

Other stories of the Denworth ghost say that she's usually much more playful. But she's also rumored to be highly sensitive to gossip: She doesn't like to be discussed around campus, so her distress may have manifested itself in the sad, negative cloud of energy that surrounded her. Apparently, you need to mind your manners, even when dealing with a ghost.

Yuma Territorial Prison Holds Inmates for Life— and Some Even in Death

What could be worse than being locked in a prison cell for life? How about being locked in a prison that you were forced to help build? That's what happened to the first seven inmates at the Yuma Territorial Prison back in 1876. Is it any wonder that the place is considered one of the most haunted locations in Arizona?

✳ ✳ ✳ ✳

THERE WERE NO minimum- or maximum-security prisons in the 1800s, so inmates at the Yuma Prison ranged from petty thieves to murderers. By the time the prison closed in 1909, more than 3,000 convicts had been held within its walls. Compared to today's standards, prison life back then was hard. Each cell measured only nine feet by nine feet, and it was not uncommon for the indoor temperature to reach 110 degrees in the summer. A punishment known as the "Dark Cell" was similar to what we now call solitary confinement. And a ball and chain were used to punish prisoners who tried to escape. It must have worked because plenty of souls never left this place.

The Good, the Bad, and the Ghostly

Despite the brutal conditions, a library and educational programs were available to inmates, and a prison clinic even gave them access to medical care. But the jail soon became overcrowded, and in such close quarters, tuberculosis ran rampant. During its 33-year history, 111 prisoners died there, many from TB; eight were gunned down in unsuccessful escape attempts.

From 1910 to 1914, the former prison building housed Yuma High School. Considering the restless souls that were left over from the structure's days as a prison, it probably did not make for the best educational experience. During the Great

Depression, homeless families sought shelter within its walls. And later, local residents who wanted to have a little piece of Arizona history "borrowed" stones from the building's walls for their personal construction projects.

Solitary Spirits

Today, all that remains of the former Yuma Territorial Prison are some cells, the main gate, a guard tower, the prison cemetery—and the ghosts. A museum is located on the site, and visitors and employees report that spirits have settled there as well. Lights turn on and off randomly; objects are moved from one place to another; and once, the coins from the gift shop's cash register leaped into the air and then fell back into place.

The Dark Cell is also a focal point for ghostly activity: The restless spirits of prisoners who were sent there for disobeying rules are thought to linger. At least two inmates were transferred directly from that cell to an insane asylum, but whether anyone actually died there is unknown. It makes for a few unsettled spirits, though, doesn't it?

Linda Offeney, an employee at the prison site, once reported feeling an unseen presence in the Dark Cell. And a tourist who visited the prison in the 1930s had her photo taken near the Dark Cell; the picture looked perfectly normal—except for the ghostly figure of a man standing behind her within the cell.

Offeney also tells the story of a writer for *Arizona Highways* magazine who witnessed the hauntings: The journalist wanted to spend two days and two nights in the cell just as prisoners would have—in the dark, with only bread and water. She only made it a few hours before she called for assistance, explaining that she couldn't shake the feeling that something was in the cell with her.

In June 2005, Arizona Desert Ghost Hunters spent the night at the Yuma Territorial Prison and gathered enough evidence to convince them that the place is indeed haunted. Photos taken of the guard tower and in Cell 14 both show suspicious activity: An orb can be seen near the tower and a misty figure is clearly visible in Cell 14, where inmate John Ryan hung himself in 1903. The investigators also captured EVPs (electronic voice phenomena) in Cell 14, where a voice said, "Get away," and in the Dark Cell, where a male spirit told the group to "Get out of here."

Although the Yuma Territorial Prison only operated for 33 years, it certainly spawned its fair share of paranormal activity. This begs the questions: Was the prison built so soundly that for many, there was no escape, even in death? Or did the inmates just give up and choose to stay there forever?

The Residents of Lourdes Hall

In 1990, Lourdes Hall opened its doors on the campus of Winona State University in southeastern Minnesota. Since then, students have learned that they are not the dorm's only residents.

✳ ✳ ✳ ✳

LOURDES HALL WAS originally part of the College of St. Teresa, an all-women's Catholic school that was known for its nursing program. When St. Teresa's closed in 1989, the building was sold to Winona State; after all, with its heated swimming pool and large cafeteria, Lourdes Hall made for an attractive addition to the university—even if it was rumored to be haunted.

Priestly Indiscretions

Many of the stories about the building center on the tragic tale of a young woman named Ruth, who lived and died in Lourdes Hall during the 1920s. According to legend, Ruth was a nursing student at St. Teresa's, who became pregnant by a young Franciscan priest named Father William. For the duration of her pregnancy, Ruth hid herself in the infirmary on the fourth floor of Lourdes Hall. After giving birth, she tried to keep her baby, but fearing that his indiscretion would be exposed, Father William threw the infant down an elevator shaft. Unable to deal with the shame and heartbreak of this experience, Ruth committed suicide by throwing herself down the third-floor stairwell. Then, likely realizing that he had made every wrong choice that a person in his situation could make, Father William hanged himself in the vicinity of where the swimming pool is now located. Because the school was located in a mostly Catholic small town, the deaths were covered up, and most people hoped that the controversy would fade with time. But you can't forget something that refuses to be forgotten.

Shared Housing

Most students at WSU don't know about Ruth or Father William when they move into Lourdes Hall, but they soon learn their sad story. On the first floor, students wandering the halls toward the building's only elevator hear footsteps behind them, but when they turn around, they find that they are alone. The elevator leads to the laundry facilities in the basement, and more than one student has decided to wait out the spin cycle in his or her dorm room after the elevator doors open multiple times for no reason. At night, students wonder if the high-pitched noises that they hear are coming from a squeaky dryer—or if they're the unanswered cries of Ruth and William's murdered baby. It might seem that there's a reasonable explanation for these phenomena, but how do you explain Ruth's continued presence in her old room?

Room 4450

As is the case at many universities, on-campus housing is a valuable commodity at Winona State, and very few can afford to turn down a room—even if it's haunted. For years, residents on the fourth floor of Lourdes Hall have reported hearing strange sounds at night. A knock at the door may turn out to be no one at all, and footsteps heard echoing through the hall at night might come from an unseen source. But the students residing in Room 4450—Ruth's old room—always leave with stories. Oftentimes, posters and other decorations will fall off the walls; beds will be overturned when residents are away; and, no matter how many blankets Mom sends from home, it's impossible to stay warm in Room 4450. Ruth makes her presence known in her room and perhaps elsewhere in the building, but there is one place that she seems to avoid.

Night Swimming

It would seem that a pool in a college dorm would be very busy, but at Lourdes Hall, swimmers report feeling as if they're being watched, and rumor has it that if a student dares go for a nighttime swim alone, he or she is guaranteed to see the specter of Father William hanging from the rafters. The disgraced priest—condemned by his own actions—hates being alone, and many students have felt clammy hands tugging on their ankles while they swim at night.

Living with the ghosts of Lourdes Hall may not be easy, but the students who reside there know that one day they move out. For Ruth and Father William, however, Lourdes Hall is their eternal home.

These Lighthouses Harbor Spirits

There's something beautiful about the simplicity of lighthouses: They stand high above the water and shine their beacons to guide weary sailors home. But there's also something about lighthouses that seems to attract spirits. Ghosts of sailors and lighthouse keepers alike seem to find it hard to leave this earthly plane. Here are a few lighthouses that harbor phenomena that are a bit otherworldly.

✳   ✳   ✳   ✳

St. Augustine Light (St. Augustine, Florida)

VISITORS TO THE St. Augustine Light—one of the most haunted places in a very haunted city—have heard phantom footsteps on the tower stairs and observed a tall man who haunts the basement. Some have reportedly heard the laughter of two girls who drowned in 1873 while their father was working on the property. There's also a prankster ghost that likes to play tricks on staff members by relocating merchandise in the gift shop. And several times a week, someone reports the smell of cigar smoke wafting from the tower—even though no one else is around.

Gibraltar Point Lighthouse (Toronto, Ontario)

Toronto's Gibraltar Point Lighthouse doesn't hide its ghostly secrets—it announces them outright: A plaque on the property warns visitors that the site is thought to be haunted. According to legend, in the early 1800s, two drunken soldiers killed the lighthouse's first caretaker, John Paul Rademuller, but his body was never found. (In the late 19th century, another caretaker unearthed some human bones, which gave credibility to the tale.) Today, unexplained lights appear in the windows, bloodstains have reportedly been found on the stairway, moaning can be heard, and the ghostly figure of a man is seen walking on the beach nearby.

White River Light Station (Whitehall, Michigan)

Listen for the tap-tap-tapping of Captain William Robinson's cane as he continues to tend to his former home—the White River Light Station—even though he died in 1919, just two weeks after he was forced to retire at age 87. No scandal or tragedy occurred at this lighthouse; Robinson and his wife simply loved their home of 47 years so much that they've apparently found it impossible to leave. Mrs. Robinson has been known to help out by doing some light housekeeping, leaving display cases cleaner than they were without the help of human hands.

St. Simons Lighthouse (St. Simons, Georgia)

In 1880, an argument between lighthouse keeper Frederick Osborne and his assistant John Stevens ended with a fatal gunshot that killed Osborne. Stevens was arrested, but he was acquitted of the murder, and he subsequently took over tending the lighthouse. He later said that he could hear strange footfalls on the spiral staircase to the tower. Subsequent caretakers, their families, and visitors have also heard the same slow tread on the tower's 129 steps.

Boston Light (Boston, Massachusetts)

The ghost that resides at the Boston Light is thought to be that of a sailor who was once guided by the beacon. Cold spots, phantom footsteps, empty rocking chairs that move back and forth on their own, and something eerie that makes cats hiss are all hallmarks of this haunted lighthouse. These are all typical behaviors for a ghost, but this one does have its quirks: Coast Guard members on the premises report that whenever they turn on a rock-and-roll radio station, the receiver suddenly switches to a classical music channel further down the dial.

Heceta Head Lighthouse (Yachats, Oregon)

Home of Rue (aka "the Gray Lady"), this former lighthouse is now a bed-and-breakfast. It is believed that Rue was the mother of a baby who was found buried on the grounds. Perhaps she feels the need to stay and protect her child, but if that's the case, she finds plenty of other ways to stay busy: Objects are moved, cupboard doors open and close by themselves, and a fire alarm was once mysteriously set off. Although Rue doesn't seem to mean any harm, she once frightened a workman so terribly that he accidentally broke a window and fled, leaving broken glass all over the floor. That night, workers heard a scraping noise coming from upstairs; in the morning, they found that the broken glass had been swept into a nice, neat pile.

Barnegat Lighthouse (Barnegat, New Jersey)

If you travel with children, you may draw the attention of the ghosts at the Barnegat Lighthouse. According to legend, a couple was on a ship off the New Jersey coast when a severe storm struck. Feeling that the ship was safe, the man decided to stay aboard, and his wife stayed by his side. They did, however, send their baby ashore with one of the ship's mates. Although the ship survived the storm, the couple was not so lucky: They froze to death that winter night. Now, on cold, clear nights in January and February, their spirits approach other parents who are out for a stroll with their own infants. The friendly ghosts typically compliment the parents on their beautiful baby, and then they quickly disappear.

Seguin Island Lighthouse (Seguin Island, Maine)

Lighthouses can often be lonely places; this was the case for the wife of one of the Seguin Island Lighthouse's early caretakers. At great expense, her husband had a piano brought to the light-house for her. But she had only one piece of music, which she played over and over, until one day, her husband went insane. He took an ax to the piano and then to his wife and then killed himself. Death may not be the escape he hoped for, however: People still report hearing faint strains of the tune that his wife played incessantly.

Fairport Harbor Light (Fairport Harbor, Ohio)

Lake Erie's Fairport Harbor Light is home to an unusual spirit: a ghost cat. This old lighthouse was abandoned in 1925 and later became a museum; its curator was the first person to see the spectral kitty with golden eyes and gray fur. They became friendly, and the curator even threw socks for the cat to chase. In life, the animal most likely belonged to the last family who tended the lighthouse; when the caretaker's wife became ill, she was comforted by a small kitten that loved to chase a ball down the hall. In 2001, workers found a mummified cat in a crawl space; the little guy must have gotten trapped and was unable to get out.

Old Montana Prison Inmates Serve Life Sentences

In 1871, the Old Montana Prison opened its gates in Deer Lodge after citizens of the territory realized that laws needed to be enforced and the wilder elements of the region needed to be punished. Like many other prisons of the day, this facility soon became overcrowded, which led to sickness, poor living conditions, prisoner unrest, and the taut emotions that lead to restless spirits and residual hauntings.

✳   ✳   ✳   ✳

No Escape

THE YEAR 1890 MARKED the beginning of the Conley era—a time when prison warden Frank Conley ruled with an iron fist and put his prisoners to work. But Conley also made significant improvements to both the prison itself and the lives of the inmates. He even established camps that sent the prisoners outside to work in the community.

However, this outside work was a privilege, and in 1908, two prisoners who were not allowed this freedom decided to take matters into their own hands. Their attempted escape resulted in the murder of the deputy prison warden and 103 stitches in the back and neck of Warden Conley. The two would-be escapees were hanged in the prison yard for their crime.

After that, the prison underwent many changes, including the end of prisoners working outside the facility, the addition of a women's prison, and the creation of a license plate manufacturing plant.

In 1959, the Old Montana Prison experienced a riot that lasted for three days and nights. Several inmates attempted to escape by holding the warden hostage and killing the deputy warden on the spot. After the National Guard was called in to end the melee, the two ringleaders died in a murder/suicide.

The Main Attraction

The Old Montana Prison closed for good in 1979, and a year later, the building opened its doors to the public as a museum. In addition to offering historical tours, the museum also offers tours for those who are interested in things that go bump in the night. In fact, so much paranormal activity has been experienced at the Old Montana Prison that several ghost-hunting television shows have traveled there to investigate and film episodes.

A *Ghost Lab* episode titled "No Escape" depicted Brad and Barry Klinge's (founders of Everyday Paranormal) visit to the prison. A wealth of high-tech ghost-hunting equipment helped the investigators uncover supernatural phenomena ranging from mysterious whispers and the sound of footsteps in empty rooms and hallways to objects flying through the air. The investigators also experienced a general feeling of dread and the unshakeable sensation that they were being watched.

See for Yourself

While touring the old prison, one can almost imagine the place as it was in the old days. Many people report hearing the shuffling of cards in the cellblocks, as well as mumbled voices and footsteps. Arguments have even been known to break out between people who aren't visible.

Shadows and ghostly figures are common sights at the museum, and some visitors have reported seeing objects flying through the air in violent, threatening ways. People have also experienced a myriad of emotions and sensations: Some have reported feeling deep sadness or dread overtake them. And even more frightening, others have perceived that someone or something is choking or attacking them.

Living with the Ghosts

Museum Director Julia Brewer is rather matter-of-fact about the hauntings in the old prison. After all, she has smelled burning flesh in her office for the better part of a decade, so you could say that she's a believer.

Brewer leads many of the groups that tour the facility, so she knows most of the prison lore. She also knows how to treat the spirits, and cautions visitors to treat the dead with respect ... or else face the consequences.

A place known as the Death Tower produces a high level of otherworldly energy—it's where inmates Jerry Myles and Lee Smart died in a murder/suicide during the 1959 riot. A place called the Steam Hole carries some heavy energy of its own. Prisoners who were deemed unruly were often sent there; at least one prisoner died in the Steam Hole under suspicious circumstances, and another inmate took his own life there by hanging himself from a pipe.

Several ghosts are known to haunt the prison grounds, and many visitors—especially psychics and ghost hunters who are sensitive to the spirit world—have experienced odd and sinister sensations. Some have even reported feeling physically ill.

Playful Spirits

A couple of ghosts are even known to hang around the museum's gift shop. One is the spirit of an inmate named Calvin, who was beaten to death in a corner of the room when it was an industrial area of the prison. Now the site houses a shelf of dolls, perhaps to neutralize the violence. A spirit that the staff refers to as "Stinker" also frequents the gift shop. The jokester of the pair, he likes to play pranks, such as moving merchandise around.

You'd think that ghosts would stick to their old haunts within the prison, but another place on the grounds that definitely seems haunted is the Montana Auto Museum, which is located just outside the gift shop. Staffers and visitors have seen ghostly figures there, and people have heard car doors slam when no one else is around.

And then there's the spirit of a young girl that has been observed by visitors at the auto museum. When a group reached the building on one ghost tour, the leader invited any spirits to show themselves by turning on a flashlight; the playful ghost did. The group also asked her to move a chain that was cordoning off the cars; she did that too.

In a place that's harbored more than its share of violence and despair, the ghost of a little girl seems pretty benign. But as tour guides warn groups about the spirits of the Old Montana Prison: Be careful . . . they might just follow you home.

Restless Spirits at the Winchester Mystery House

Every night, in a room at the center of a mansion that was still under construction, an elegant woman with her face covered by a dark veil consulted a planchette board. She summoned good spirits, requesting their assistance with building her house. Only with their help could she continue to design a home that would allow her to outwit evil spirits bent on revenge. Each morning, she passed on new plans to the foreman, whose crews carried out her wishes—seven days a week, 24 hours a day. The woman was Sarah L. Winchester, and her deceased husband had left her a cursed family fortune earned through the invention of the Winchester rifle.

✳ ✳ ✳ ✳

I N 1884, CONSTRUCTION began on a spacious Victorian mansion in San Jose, California, after Sarah Winchester moved to the West Coast from New Haven, Connecticut, following two personal tragedies. Her infant daughter had died suddenly from a mysterious ailment in 1866, after which Sarah lapsed into a deep depression that plagued her for the rest of her life. Then, 15 years after the death of her daughter, Sarah's husband William died of tuberculosis at age 43.

The loss of her husband was a debilitating blow to the already distraught Sarah. Fearing that she might take her own life, one of her close friends suggested that she should visit a psychic to see if she could contact her husband, her daughter, or both; after all, this was at the height of the Spiritualism movement. The medium told Sarah that William was trying to contact her with a dire message: The Winchester family was cursed as a result of the invention of the repeating rifle. Native Americans, settlers, and soldiers all over the world were dead due to the weapon; those angry spirits were bent on revenge, and Sarah was their next target. The medium told Sarah that the only way to prolong her life was to move out west and build a large house. But here's the kicker: Sarah was told that the key to appeasing the spirits was that construction could never end; otherwise, the spirits would kill her.

Designed by Spirits

Sarah decided that it was not enough to maintain a never-ending construction project: She also needed to *confuse* the spirits that were out to get her. As a result, the house features strange design elements. Doors open into walls (or sheer drops outside). Some stairs end at ceilings or have odd proportions; for example, the steps on the "Switchback Staircase" are each two inches high, allowing a staircase with seven full flights to rise only nine feet. (Odd as this may seem, it may have been necessary for the arthritic Sarah.) Hallways twist and turn, and secret passageways end in bizarre nooks. One stairway goes down 7 steps and then up 11, and one particular linen closet is larger than most three-bedroom apartments. Many of the mansion's architectural elements incorporate the number 13, which was believed to keep unwelcome spirits at bay. Thirteen stairs lead to the 13th bathroom, which has a window with 13 panes.

Another benefit of living in such a large house was that Sarah did not have to sleep in the same bedroom for more than two nights in a row, which she believed made it difficult for ill-intentioned spirits to find her. Unfortunately, this also made it difficult for her staff to find her after a 7.9-magnitude earthquake rocked the Bay Area in 1906. Sarah was trapped in the

Daisy Bedroom (one of her favorite rooms) in the front of the house for hours, which led her to conclude that the spirits were sending her a message: She had spent too much money on the front of the building. As a result, the front 30 rooms—including an unused ballroom that cost more than $9,000 to build (when an average house could be built for less than $1,000)—were sealed off.

While Sarah worked desperately to appease the evil spirits, she also tried to make the good ones feel comfortable. She built a special Séance Room that she used nightly to contact friendly spirits and receive their input on how the construction of the house should proceed. Sarah also liked to play her pump organ late at night to entertain her spectral guests (and perhaps exercise her arthritic hands).

Every Good Project Has an End . . . Or Does It?

By the time Sarah Winchester died in 1922, construction had been under way for 38 years. The house sprawled over six acres and boasted 160 rooms, 2,000 doors, 10,000 windows, 47 stairways, 47 fireplaces, 13 bathrooms, and 6 kitchens, but it is estimated that more than 500 rooms were actually built and then sealed over or torn down and refashioned into new spaces.

Over the years, investigators have recorded various paranormal occurrences at the Winchester Mystery House. One group recorded faint sounds of an organ and saw not only moving balls of light but also two apparitions dressed in clothing that was popular in Sarah Winchester's time. Other visitors have felt icy chills in draft-free rooms and observed locked doorknobs turning, and when one guest developed photos that he took in the peculiar mansion, he discovered that he'd captured the ghostly image of a man in coveralls. A caretaker heard footsteps and breathing in otherwise empty rooms. And in 1975, during a midnight séance on Halloween, renowned medium Jeanne Borgen seemed to transform into an elderly Sarah, aging rapidly before the other attendees and falling over in pain.

Many say that the ghost of Sarah Winchester still roams her unusual home, and psychics firmly believe that the house is haunted. This can't be proven, of course, but that doesn't stop the claims—and it didn't stop the lady of the house from undertaking one of the world's most incredible construction projects.

When Sarah Winchester's husband passed away, she inherited a fortune—literally. In the late 1880s, the average family income hovered at around $500 per year; Sarah was pulling in about $1,000 per day!

The Tormented Souls of the LaLaurie Mansion

Marie Delphine LaLaurie was the crème de la crème of the high society of early 19th-century New Orleans. Rich, pretty, and intelligent, she entranced nearly everyone she met. But LaLaurie held a dark and diabolical secret: She delighted in torturing her slaves in heinous and despicable ways. Later, the spirits of those who died at LaLaurie's hand would come back to haunt the socialite's stately manor.

✳ ✳ ✳ ✳

Social Butterflies

MARIE WAS BORN in Louisiana around 1775. She was widowed twice and bore five children before marrying Dr. Leonard Louis LaLaurie in 1825. In the early 1830s, Marie and her husband moved into the stunning three-story mansion at 1140 Royal Street in New Orleans. It was regarded as one of the finest houses in the city and one that befit their social status, as the family was noted for its wealth and prominence in the community.

As visible parts of New Orleans society, the LaLauries frequently hosted grand parties that were attended by the city's most influential citizens. Like many wealthy people of the time, the LaLauries owned several slaves who cooked, cleaned, and maintained the property. Many guests remembered the servants who catered to their every need. But other LaLaurie slaves—sometimes glimpsed in passing—were surprisingly thin and hollow-chested. Rumors began to circulate that Madame LaLaurie was far from kind to her servants.

One neighbor claimed that he watched in horror as Madame LaLaurie chased a terrified female slave with a whip. The girl eventually made it to the roof of the mansion, where she chose to jump to her death rather than face her enraged owner's maniacal abuse. What happened to the girl's body remains a mystery: Some accounts say that it was buried on the property, while others report that it was dumped in an abandoned well.

A Fire Reveals All

The true extent of Marie LaLaurie's revolting cruelty was finally revealed in April 1834, when a fire broke out in the mansion. As the story goes, a cook who simply couldn't handle any more torture at the hands of Madame LaLaurie set the blaze. As the fire swept through the house and smoke filled the rooms, a crowd of onlookers gathered outside. Soon, the volunteer fire department arrived with buckets of water and bystanders offered their assistance. LaLaurie remained calm and directed the volunteers to save expensive paintings and smaller pieces of furniture. But when neighbors tried to enter the slave quarters to ensure that everyone got out safely, Madame LaLaurie refused to give them the key. Enraged, they broke down the door and were horrified to find several slaves tortured and mutilated. Many of the victims said that they'd been held captive for months.

The atrocities committed against the slaves in the LaLaurie home were depraved in the extreme. Some were found chained to the walls, and others were suspended by their necks with their limbs stretched and torn. One female slave was wearing a spiked iron collar that forced her head into an upright position. Some slaves were nearly starved to death, flayed with whips, and bound in painfully restrictive positions. Cruel experiments had been performed on some victims: Eyes were poked out, mouths were sewn shut, limbs were removed, and skulls were left open while they were still alive. The men who found the slaves were overwhelmed by the stench of death and decaying flesh, which permeated the confined chamber. A local newspaper reported that the bodies of tortured slaves were found buried around the grounds of the mansion.

When word of Marie LaLaurie's sadistic and grotesque crimes got out, an angry mob descended upon the mansion, breaking furniture, shattering windows, looting fine china and imported food, and destroying everything that it could find until only the walls remained. But by then, the LaLauries had already fled to France, never to be seen in New Orleans again.

Ghosts Take Up Residence

After the authorities restored order at the LaLaurie Mansion, the property was closed and sealed, and it sat completely empty for years . . . or so it seemed.

The spirits of the dead quickly claimed the house. Passersby often heard agonizing cries coming from the abandoned structure, and several people said that they saw apparitions of the murdered slaves walking on the home's balconies, peering out of windows, and roaming through the property's overgrown gardens. According to legend, vagrants who entered the building were never seen again.

The LaLaurie Mansion was purchased in 1837, but the buyer put it back on the market after only three months, claiming to have been driven out by weird noises and anguished cries in the night.

Hauntings Continue

In the years that followed, the LaLaurie Mansion was converted into a school for girls, abandoned again, and then converted into inexpensive apartments for immigrant laborers. Time and time again, the restless spirits of the tortured slaves made their presence known, much to the horror of the people who lived there. Once, a terrified tenant claimed that the spirit of a naked black man in chains attacked him and then vanished as quickly as it had appeared. Even cheap rent was not enough to convince tenants to stay for very long, and soon the house was vacant again.

The LaLaurie Mansion still stands today. Over the years, it has changed hands several times and has served as a saloon, a furniture store, a refuge for poor and homeless men, and an apartment building. In April 2007, actor Nicolas Cage purchased the property, but two and a half years later, it was back on the market. There have been no reports of ghostly activity there in recent years, but that doesn't mean the spirits of Marie LaLaurie's victims are resting in peace.

During a remodeling of the LaLaurie Mansion some years ago, workers discovered several unmarked graves under the floorboards of the house. This may explain why many of Madame LaLauries slaves simply disappeared, never to be seen again.

Hot Springs and Cool Spirits Fill the Banff Springs Hotel

Surrounded by majestic mountains and the healing waters of natural hot springs, the Banff Springs Hotel in Alberta, Canada, attracts many visitors . . . but not everyone staying at the hotel is among the living.

✳   ✳   ✳   ✳

IN THE LATE 19th century, William Van Horne, general manager of the Canadian Pacific Railway, decided to take advantage of the railroads' westward expansion by building a 250-room luxury hotel tucked away in the dense forest of the Canadian Rockies. The inn was a success, but in 1926, it was partially destroyed by a devastating fire. When it was rebuilt, the hotel took on the look of a Scottish castle: The stone walls and grand towers added a touch of class and mystery that was missing from the first building. This time, the hotel became even more successful, and due to its isolated location, it attracted royalty and celebrities who often referred to it as the "Castle of the Rockies."

The Secret Room

During the renovation, construction workers were surprised to discover a secret room that did not appear on any map of the hotel. It resembled a regular guest room, except that it had no windows or doors. This mysterious room is thought to have been an architectural error that was sealed off—and removed from blueprints—to cover up the mistake. Although the room was empty when it was discovered, many people who had experienced unusual phenomena—such as strange noises and apparitions—along a nearby corridor suspected that perhaps something about this odd room could be the cause. Did something sinister happen inside the room? Were spirits using it as a portal to the Other Side?

Regardless of the secret room's purpose, many ghosts call the Banff Springs Hotel home. But that doesn't seem to keep guests away. The hotel now boasts 778 rooms, several restaurants, a spa, a gift shop, and a golf course. But even with all those amenities, some guests still come to hunt for ghosts.

Sam the Bell-Ghost

One of the Banff Springs Hotel's friendly spirits is that of Sam McCauley, a Scottish immigrant who, for many years, worked there as a bellhop. He so loved the hotel and his job there that he told coworkers he hoped to stay and haunt the place after he died. And it seems that he may have gotten his wish. When Sam was asked to retire in the late 1970s, he became so distraught that he died soon after.

Since then, Sam's spirit has been spotted all around the hotel. Shortly after his death, two female guests were locked out of their room. They asked someone to call the front desk for help, but by the time a hotel employee arrived, the women were already in their room; they said that a friendly bellhop with white hair unlocked their door. After that, "Sam" sightings became commonplace at the Banff Springs Hotel. Some guests have reported seeing him in the hallways, while others have said that he let them into their rooms or carried their luggage. And invariably, when guests reach into their wallets to give him a tip, the kindly bellhop simply vanishes.

The Ghost of Weddings Past

Sam is not the only spirit to inhabit this old hotel. Another ghost that is seen there quite often is that of a bride who was planning to get married at the hotel shortly after it was remodeled. Because it happened so long ago, records of what happened to the poor bride no longer exist, and sources vary regarding the details. Some say that she was descending the grand staircase when her feet became tangled in the long flowing train of her gown, causing her to trip and fall down the stairs to her death. Another says that the staircase was accented with lit candles and her dress caught on fire; in a panic, she tried to put out the fire and fell down the stairs in the process. Regardless, guests and staff members have heard strange noises coming from the bridal suite when it's empty. Many have glimpsed the bride dancing alone in the ballroom, and others have seen her descending the staircase; as they watch, her dress catches on fire, and then she suddenly disappears.

Room 873

Yet another spirit at the Banff Springs Hotel is associated with a slightly more terrifying tale. Rumors say that a family was murdered in Room 873. However, a story like this is not so good for business, so the room was eventually sealed up after guests reported seeing a child's fingerprints on the mirrors. What's so frightening about that? Well, after they are cleaned off, they mysteriously—and immediately—reappear. Visitors have also reported seeing apparitions of this poor family strolling through the halls.

If these ghosts aren't enough to pique your interest, you might want to watch out for several other spirits that have been reported on the property. One is a bagpiper that plays melancholy tunes for guests. You'll certainly know him when you see him because he has no head.

And then there's the helpful bartender in the Rob Roy Dining Room. Concerned about his customers' safety—and possibly their potential embarrassment—he's not afraid to tell them when they've had a bit too much to drink.

Unlike some other hotels that use their ghostly visitors to attract curious guests, the Banff Springs Hotel does not promote the possibility of paranormal activity within its walls. But judging by the tales told by former guests and staff members, it's hard to deny that something is going on there. You might just have to check it out for yourself.

Ghost Towns of the Ancients

It's hard to think of great cities like New York or London ever becoming the ghost towns of future centuries. But many New Yorks and Londons of the ancient world did just that—then kept archeologists and scientists busy for hundreds of years looking for them.

✳ ✳ ✳ ✳

A Wall, a Horse, and a Mystery

MOST PEOPLE HAVE heard of the siege of Troy, that epic battle over a stolen princess that the blind poet Homer immortalized in the Iliad. The image of a "Trojan Horse" has made its way into film, literature, and even computer lingo. But the city that gave us the famed wooden horse faded into legend around 700 B.C. For the next 25 centuries, the city of Troy was dismissed as a fable—an elusive ghost for archeologists and historians.

Details of the real Troy are fragmentary, handed down mostly through Greek myths and Homer's poetry. The city, on the

Aegean coast of modern-day Turkey, lay along major trade routes from the Mediterranean to the Black Sea, and it steadily prospered since its Bronze Age founding around 3000 B.C.

As Troy grew wealthy and powerful, its inhabitants protected themselves with massive stone walls. Homer's Troy boasted towers nearly 30 feet high and probably contained around 10,000 inhabitants at the time of the Trojan War. The city rose and fell several times (the last around the end of the 8th century B.C.), and it was rebuilt as a Roman outpost around the time of Christ. The "Roman Troy" remained an important trading center until Constantinople became the capital of the Eastern Roman Empire and traders began to bypass the ancient town.

Troy then began its final journey into decline and ruin. By the time Europe emerged from the Dark Ages, the city had been lost to the ages.

But in the 1870s, an eccentric German businessman named Heinrich Schliemann, who had been schooled on the Iliad as a boy, built a small fortune and began searching for the lost city. Over a 19-year period, Schliemann completed several amateur digs around a city that, in due course, yielded nine sites to bear the name "Troy." The seventh "Troy," a city (or succession of cities) from around 1200–1000 B.C., appears to have been destroyed by fire and is the most likely candidate for the Troy of Homer's epic.

Go Tell the Whom?

Today we think of the ancient Greek city of Sparta as the "Spartan" (austere, militant, and culturally empty) counterpart to the more enlightened, democratic Athenian society. But in ancient times, Sparta lay at the "cutting edge" of political and military arts.

Sparta, the capital of the Lacedaemon kingdom on Greece's Ionic coast, inaugurated many idealistic traditions for which the Greek world became famous. It established a democratic assembly years before the Athenians adopted the practice; it allowed women broad rights to own property and attend schools; and it took its religion and art seriously.

After the Greek city-states combined to defeat the Persian invasion of 480 B.C., a rivalry between Sparta and Athens led to the bitter Peloponnesian War (431–403 B.C.). The war ended in Spartan victory, but Sparta's defeat by Thebes 30 years later sent the city into a period of decline. It fell under Roman rule and succumbed to barbarian invasions, ultimately vanishing into ruin before A.D. 400.

In a passage from Thucydides's ancient work *The History of the Peloponnesian War*, the old chronicler muses: "Suppose the city of Sparta to be deserted, and nothing left but the temples and the ground-plan, distant ages would be very unwilling to believe that the power of the Lacodaemonians was at all equal to their fame."

Sure enough, the city left little of its original grandeur for later generations. It was not until some 1,500 years later that serious efforts were made to recover the home of the Spartans. In 1906, the British School at Athens did serious archeological work, discovering a theater, temples, and beautiful examples of early Spartan art, and opening the world's eyes to the cultural world that was Sparta.

Rome: Total War

One of the ancient world's greatest cities had the misfortune of bumping up against the most powerful military force of its time. Set on the North African coast near modern Tunisia's capital city, Tunis, the great city of Carthage was the hub of a Mediterranean trading empire that rivaled that of the later Italian upstarts. This rivalry with Rome produced three great wars of antiquity, called the Punic Wars.

By virtue of its location—south of Sicily on Africa's Mediterranean coast—Carthage, a trading empire founded by the seagoing Phoenician people around 814 B.C., held a dominant position in Mediterranean trade from the 3rd and 2nd centuries B.C. In 264 B.C., Rome and Carthage got dragged by their allies into a war over Sicily. Round One went to the Romans. Two decades later, the Carthaginian general Hannibal led his elephants over the Alps into Italy on a legendary campaign of destruction, but the Romans won that one, too.

A half century later, Rome goaded the Carthaginians into a third war. This time, the Roman general Scipio Africanus led a three-year siege of Carthage. After storming the walls and capturing the city, he burned the metropolis to the ground, destroyed Carthaginian ships in the harbor, and sold the populace into slavery. By 146 B.C., the destruction of Carthage was complete.

In the 1st century A.D., the Romans rebuilt the city as a shipping hub, and the "new" Carthage became a major food supplier for the Roman Empire. It remained a center of Roman Christianity until the end of the 7th century, when Arab invaders toppled the city and replicated Scipio's "complete destruction" formula. The city was supplanted by nearby Tunis, and today the ancient capital is a series of ruins in Tunis's suburbs, where archeologists are digging up statues, tombs, and other relics of one of the ancient world's lost empires.

Riddles of the Riddle House

While functioning as a cemetery caretaker's home, West Palm Beach's Riddle House was always close to death. Since then, it's been relocated and repurposed, and now it sees its fair share of life—life after death, that is.

✳ ✳ ✳ ✳

The "Painted Lady"

BUILT IN 1905 AS a gatekeeper's cottage, this pretty "Painted Lady" seemed incongruent with the cemetery it was constructed to oversee. Cloaked in grand Victorian finery, the house radiated the brightness of life. Perhaps that's what was intended: A cemetery caretaker's duties can be gloomy, so any bit of spirit lifting would likely be welcomed. Or so its builders thought. In the case of this particular house, however, "spirit lifting" took on a whole new meaning.

The first ghost sighted in the area was that of a former cemetery worker named Buck, who was killed during an argument with a townsperson. Shortly thereafter, Buck's ghost was seen doing chores around the cemetery and inside the cottage. Luckily, he seemed more interested in performing his duties than exacting revenge.

In the 1920s, the house received its current name when city manager Karl Riddle purchased it and took on the duty of overseeing the cemetery. During his tenure, a despondent employee named Joseph hung himself in the attic. This sparked a frenzy of paranormal phenomena inside the house, including the unexplained sounds of rattling chains and disembodied voices.

After Riddle moved out, the reports of paranormal activity slowed down—but such dormancy wouldn't last.

Traveling Spirits

By 1980, the Riddle House had fallen into disrepair and was

abandoned. The city planned to demolish the building but instead decided to give it to John Riddle (Karl's nephew). He, in turn, donated it for preservation. The entire structure was moved—lock, stock, and barrel—to Yesteryear Village, a museum devoted to Florida's early years. There, it was placed on permanent display as an attractive token of days long past. There, too, its dark side would return—with a vengeance.

When workers began to reassemble the Riddle House, freshly awakened spirits kicked their antics into high gear. Ladders were tipped over, windows were smashed, and tools were thrown to the ground from the building's third floor. Workers were shocked when an unseen force threw a wooden board across a room, striking a carpenter in the head. The attacks were blamed on the spirit of Joseph, and the situation became so dangerous that work on the structure was halted for six months. After that, however, the Riddle House was restored to its previous glory.

Ghostly Unveiling

During the dedication of the Riddle House in the early 1980s, two unexpected guests showed up for the ceremony. Resplendent in Victorian garb, the couple added authenticity to the time period being celebrated. Many assumed that they were actors who were hired for the occasion; they were not. In fact, no one knew *who* they were. A few weeks later, century-old photos from the Riddle House were put on display. There, in sepia tones, stood the very same couple that guests had encountered during the dedication!

When the *Ghost Adventures* team spent a night locked inside the Riddle House in 2008, a medium warned the investigators that the spirit of Joseph is an evil entity that did not want them there. But that didn't stop investigator Zak Bagans from provoking the spirit. Bagans left a board at the top of the stairs and asked the entity to move it if it didn't want them there. Later, after the team heard footsteps in the room above them, the board fell down several stairs on its own. Throughout the course of the night, the team experienced unexplained noises and objects moving and falling by themselves. In the end, the researchers concluded that the Riddle House is definitely haunted and that whatever resides in the attic does not like men in particular, just as the medium had cautioned.

Ethereal stirrings at the Riddle House continue to this day. Unexplained sightings of a torso hanging in the attic window represent only part of the horror. And if history is any indicator, more supernatural sightings and activity are certainly to come.

The Haunted Castle of Mansfield, Ohio

As you turn onto Reformatory Road in Mansfield, Ohio, you can't help but gasp as you gaze upon the immense castlelike structure that looms before you. As we all know, every good castle needs at least one resident ghost, and the Mansfield Reformatory doesn't disappoint in that regard.

✳ ✳ ✳ ✳

From Camp to Castle

DURING THE CIVIL War, the property on which the Mansfield Reformatory now stands was the site of Camp Mordecai Bartley. After the war, the decision was made to construct a reformatory there that would function as a sort of "middle ground" for first-time offenders, allowing only hardened criminals and repeat offenders to be sent to the Ohio Penitentiary in Columbus. But the Mansfield Reformatory would be no ordinary structure—it would be an imposing edifice designed to strike fear into the heart of any prisoner forced to enter its massive gates.

In the 1880s, architect Levi T. Scofield began designing the reformatory. The entire front portion would house the warden, his family, and the administrative offices; the rear portion would contain the massive six-tier cellblock, which would be the tallest freestanding cellblock in the world.

Incredibly, when the Mansfield Reformatory finally opened in September 1896, the 150 inmates transferred there entered a building that still wasn't complete. In fact, the prisoners themselves were responsible for finishing the construction, a task that included completing a giant wall surrounding the main building. The structure would not be fully finished until 1910.

Cramped Quarters and Violence

It doesn't seem possible that such a massive building could become overcrowded, but that's exactly what happened: By 1930, the reformatory was already well over capacity. In fact, inmates were often sleeping three or four to a cell that was designed to fit only two.

The cramped quarters may have been one reason why prisoners at the Mansfield Reformatory were so aggressive. Considering the fact that the facility did not house hardened criminals, the amount of violence that took place there is staggering. A riot in 1957 involved more than 100 inmates. There were also a few instances in which one inmate killed another. Several prisoners couldn't take the living conditions and committed suicide, including one man who set himself on fire. Eventually, word of the horrible conditions reached the public, and in the early 1980s, officials declared the Mansfield Reformatory unfit to continue functioning as a prison; it would be another ten years before the facility was actually shut down.

The building seemed destined for the wrecking ball until Hollywood came calling in the early 1990s, when the majority of *The Shawshank Redemption*

(1994) was filmed at the former prison. Not long after, the Mansfield Reformatory Preservation Society was formed. One of the first items on the group's agenda was to open the building for overnight ghost tours. After that, people from all walks of life started to come face-to-face with spirits from the Other Side.

Haunted by the Past

One of the most enduring ghost stories associated with the Mansfield Reformatory centers on Warden Arthur L. Glattke and his wife, Helen. In 1950, Helen was getting ready for Sunday mass when she went into a closet in the warden's quarters to retrieve a box from a high shelf. As she grabbed the box, she bumped a revolver that Arthur had hidden in the closet; the gun went off and wounded her. She was rushed to the hospital, but she died several days later of pneumonia while recovering from her injury.

On February 10, 1959, Arthur was working in his office when he suffered a fatal heart attack. Almost immediately, rumors began to suggest that Helen's death had not been an accident, but rather that Arthur had killed her and made it look like an accident. Further, it was said that Arthur's heart attack was the result of Helen's ghost exacting its revenge. It's a creepy story, but it can't be proven. In fact, by all accounts, the couple truly loved each other. Perhaps that's why when people see the ghosts of the couple, they appear happy as they walk up and down the hallways of the warden's quarters.

Investigating the Reformatory

While the Mansfield Reformatory had been featured on numerous television shows such as *Scariest Places on Earth*, it wasn't until The Atlantic Paranormal Society (TAPS) visited in 2005 for *Ghost Hunters* that people everywhere got a look at a paranormal investigation inside the prison's walls.

During that investigation, TAPS members heard strange footsteps echoing throughout the prison; they also managed to videotape unexplained lights at the far end of the hallway in solitary confinement. But the most intriguing part of the evening came when investigators Dustin Pari and Dave Tango were walking on the second floor of the East Cellblock. The duo heard strange noises coming from one of the cells, but when they were unable to find the source of the sounds, they marked an "X" outside the cell so they could find it later. About an hour later, investigators Jason Hawes and Grant Wilson were in the same area when Hawes thought that he saw something moving inside the cell marked with an "X," and Wilson believed he heard something there. However, upon investigating the cell, it appeared to be empty.

Doing Time with the Ghosts

You don't have to be on a reality TV show to experience the unknown at Mansfield Reformatory. Over the years, paranormal research group The Ghosts of Ohio has spent several nights locked inside the prison. Each time, group members have witnessed strange phenomena, including hearing disembodied footsteps in the hallways, seeing shadowy figures moving in the cellblocks, having equipment malfunction, and experiencing feelings of heaviness while in solitary confinement.

The Mansfield Reformatory offers tours, so you can see for yourself if anything supernatural is lurking there. But if you're not lucky enough to spot the Glattkes, fear not: Plenty of other ghosts are said to lurk inside the old prison. So if you dare, head to Solitary Confinement, where people report experiencing cold chills, feeling lightheaded, and being touched by unseen hands while sitting in the cells. Or walk either the East or West Cellblock, where you might just hear some ghostly footsteps behind you. Some people have even had small rocks thrown at them from atop the cellblocks. So no matter where you go inside Mansfield Reformatory, keep in mind that you're never more than a stone's throw away from a ghost.

Myrtles Plantation: A Blast from the Past

Listed on the National Register of Historic Places and boasting more than 200 years of history, the Myrtles Plantation is a beautiful and sprawling old home in St. Francisville, Louisiana. Now used as a bed-and-breakfast, the mansion has seen its share of drama, including romance, death, and even murder. What better setting for a good old Southern-style haunting?

✳ ✳ ✳ ✳

Tales to Tell

IN 1796, DAVID Bradford built what would eventually become the Myrtles Plantation on 650 acres of land about 30 miles outside of Baton Rouge. At the time, the house—which was originally known as Laurel Grove—was much smaller than it is today. In 1834, Ruffin Stirling purchased and remodeled the plantation, doubling its size and renaming it after the many myrtle trees on the property.

Over the years, many people lived and died at the Myrtles Plantation, so it's not surprising that the place is home to a few restless spirits. Whether it's strange noises, disembodied voices, apparitions, or reflections in a haunted mirror, plenty of paranormal activity can be found at Myrtles Plantation.

In 2005, investigators from the television show *Ghost Hunters* paid a visit to the mansion and documented several strange phenomena. Thermal-imaging video cameras recorded the torso of something not really present, as well as a shadow that appeared to be moving up and down. The team also caught the unexplained movement of a lamp across a table: Over the course of a few minutes, it moved several inches with no help from anyone in the room.

If you visit the Myrtles Plantation, be sure to check out the Myrtles mirror: It is said to reflect the spirit of someone who died in front of it. People have repeatedly seen handprints on the mirror and orbs or apparitions in photos of it. Although many stories say that the images belong to one of the plantation's early owners and her children—all of whom were poisoned—the mirror was actually brought to the house in the 1970s. If it is indeed haunted, the ghosts may not be from the home originally.

A Spirited Place

Several ghosts are commonly seen inside the house. One is thought to be a French woman who wanders from room to room. Another is a regular at the piano; unfortunately, this spirit only seems to know one chord, which is heard over and over, stopping suddenly when anyone walks into the room. A third is the ghost of a young girl, who only appears right before thunderstorms.

The spirits of two young girls have also been seen playing outside on the veranda, and guests have also felt their presence at night while lying in bed. Sometimes, visitors feel pressure on the bed, as though someone is jumping on it. Soon after, people report seeing the spirit of a maid, who appears to smooth the covers. Another young girl with long curly hair has been seen floating outside the window of the toy room; she appears to be cupping her hands as if she's trying to see inside.

Some visitors report seeing a Confederate soldier on the porch; others have seen the spirit of a man that warns them not to go inside. Many people have glimpsed apparitions of slaves doing their chores inside the mansion. And two other resident ghosts that are certainly entertaining but have little connection to the plantation's rich history are those of a ballet dancer clad in a tutu and a Native American woman who appears naked in the outdoor gazebo.

The ghost of William Winter is also said to haunt the mansion. Winter lived at the Myrtles Plantation from 1860 to 1868 and again from 1870 until his death in 1871, when an unknown assailant shot him as he answered the door. By some accounts, he staggered back inside and died on the 17th step of the staircase, where his slow dragging footsteps can be heard to this day.

Chloe

Perhaps the best-known ghost at the Myrtles Plantation is that of Chloe, a former slave. Her spirit is thought to walk between the main house and the old slave quarters. People describe her apparition as that of a slender woman wearing a green turban.

As the story goes, David Bradford's daughter Sara married Clark Woodruff, who—it is rumored—had an affair with a beautiful slave girl named Chloe. After enjoying her station in the main house, Chloe was upset when Woodruff ended the affair. When he later caught her eavesdropping, Woodruff became enraged and cut off her ear. (It is said that she wears the green turban to cover the scar.) Two versions of the next part of this story exist: One has Chloe seeking revenge on Woodruff by poisoning his family; the other says that she poisoned them to secure her position as a nursemaid and nanny, so that she would be needed inside to nurse the family back to health, and therefore, she wouldn't be sent to work in the fields.

In either case, Chloe allegedly crushed up oleander petals and added them to a cake she was baking for the oldest daughter's birthday. Clark Woodruff didn't eat any of it, but his wife and two daughters did, and they soon died from poisoning. The other slaves, fearing punishment, dragged Chloe to the yard, where she was hanged. Legend has it that her ghost can be seen in the yard and wandering through the house in her signature headwear.

It's a great story, and it's easy to see why it would be repeated—and possibly twisted a bit each time. But researchers who have dug through old court records have found no evidence that there ever was a Chloe: There is nothing to suggest that a slave by that name (or anything close to it) ever lived at Myrtles Plantation. And although death records show that Sara

Woodruff and two of the children did die young, all the deaths were attributed to yellow fever, not poison.

So there you have it. Myrtles Plantation is rife with ghosts, but we may never know exactly who they were in life or why they're still attached to the mansion. Chloe may or may not have existed in the real world, but you never know what you may encounter at one of the most haunted houses in America.

The Unhealthy Mansion

Violent, unexpected deaths are likely to produce ghosts, and shipwrecks are no exception. And when drowning deaths are combined with injustice, it's pretty much a given that a few restless spirits will remain earthbound. That was exactly the recipe for the haunting at the Mansion of Health.

* * * *

BUILT IN 1822, on New Jersey's Long Beach Island, the Mansion of Health was the largest hotel on the Jersey Shore upon its completion. This sprawling three-story structure featured a sweeping top-floor balcony that ran the length of the building and provided an unencumbered view of the glistening ocean, which was just a few hundred feet away. However, on April 18, 1854, the sea was anything but sparkling.

On that day, a violent storm turned the water into a foaming cauldron of death. Into this maelstrom came the *Powhattan*, a ship that was filled with more than 300 German immigrants who were bound for new lives in America. Unfortunately, the ship never had a chance. As it approached the coast of Long Beach Island, the storm tossed the boat onto the shoals and ripped a hole in its side. Passengers tumbled overboard, and later, dozens of bodies washed up on the shore.

Stealing from the Dead

Back in those days, a person known as a "wreck master" was responsible for salvaging cargo from shipwrecks and arranging the storage of those killed until the coroner took charge of their bodies. The wreck master for Long Beach Island was Edward Jennings, who was also the manager of the Mansion of Health. Accordingly, all of the bodies from the *Powhattan* that had come ashore were brought to the beach in front of the Mansion of Health.

When the coroner arrived hours later, he examined the bodies, although it didn't take a medical degree to determine that they had died from drowning. However, the coroner did find something peculiar: None of the dead had any money in their possession. It seemed unusual to him that immigrants who were coming to America to start new lives didn't carry any cash. Money belts were fashionable at the time, yet not a single victim was wearing one.

Suspicion immediately fell upon Jennings, who was the only person who'd had access to the bodies for many hours. However, no one had any proof of such a crime occurring, so the accusations died down.

The Long Arm of the Ghostly Law

Four months later, another storm revealed a hole near the stump of an old tree on the beach near the Mansion of Health. In the hole, dozens of money belts were found; they were all cut open and empty.

When word of this discovery got out, Jennings took one look at the writing on the wall and hightailed it out of town, narrowly evading the long arm of the law. But there are some things that you can't escape, as Jennings found out the hard way. Supposedly, he became a broken man and was haunted by nightmares that destroyed his sleep and ruined his life. He died several years later in a barroom brawl in San Francisco.

However, the spirits of the *Powhattan* victims were not content to simply haunt Edward Jennings. Shortly after the accident, strange things began to happen at the Mansion of Health.

Disembodied sobs were heard at night, and ghostly figures were seen walking across the hotel's expansive balcony. Guests also reported feeling uneasy, which is not exactly the best advertisement for a place that was supposed to be restful and encourage good health.

The Haunted Mansion

Eventually, the Mansion of Health became known as the "Haunted Mansion," and people avoided it like the plague. Soon, the building was abandoned; the brooding hulk of a structure that towered over the beach slowly began rotting away.

During the summer of 1861, five young men who had more bravado than brains decided to spend the night in the gloomy structure. After cavorting through the empty halls and dashing around the balcony without seeing a single spirit, the men decided to sleep on the allegedly haunted third floor. After most of the young men had drifted off to sleep, one who remained awake suddenly noticed the luminous figure of a woman bathed in moonlight standing on the balcony; she held a baby in her arms. The apparition was gazing sadly out to sea, as if mourning the life that had been taken away from her so abruptly.

The startled young man quietly shook each of his companions awake, and all five gazed in disbelief at the figure. Each of them observed that the moonlight passed right through the woman. Then, suddenly and without warning, the woman vanished.

The young men quickly gathered their belongings and fled the building, and from then on, not even vandals dared to enter the Haunted Mansion.

In 1874, fire destroyed the Mansion of Health. But the hotel's real end had come years earlier, when Edward Jennings made the unfortunate decision to tamper with the dead.

Downtown Houston, Texas, may be haunted by 19th-century madam Pamelia Mann. According to staff members and patrons at establishments such as La Carafe, the late Ms. Mann is a nightly visitor. Dressed in a white Victorian gown, she has reportedly been seen outside on Congress Avenue and inside some of the buildings. She also frequents the ladies' rooms on the block of Market Square where her brothel once stood.

The Historic (and Haunted) Roosevelt Hotel

Situated at 7000 Hollywood Boulevard, the 12-story Roosevelt Hotel is an integral part of Hollywood's history. For more than 80 years, this hotel has served as a temporary home away from home for some of the world's biggest celebrities, who love to soak in the atmosphere. In fact, many of the stars who visit the Roosevelt enjoy themselves so much that they frequently return, even in death.

✳   ✳   ✳   ✳

Now Open for Business

THE ROOSEVELT, NAMED after President Theodore Roosevelt, was the brainchild of a group that included actor Douglas Fairbanks and was designed to function as a haven for actors who lived on the East Coast but found themselves in Hollywood making movies. When the doors swung open for business on May 15, 1927, nearly $3 million had been spent building the 400-room hotel. The design captured the flavor of southern California with its Spanish colonial style.

It didn't take long for the who's who of Hollywood to start visiting the Roosevelt, using it for industry functions and doing business in its sunken lobby or elegant Library Bar. The era's biggest stars, including Mary Pickford, Gloria Swanson, Greta Garbo, Charlie Chaplin, and Will Rogers, were present at the hotel's inaugural ball. The Roosevelt was even the site of the very first Academy Awards ceremony, which was held in the hotel's Blossom Room on May 16, 1929. The ceremony included several activities, but the actual awards presentation was the shortest in Academy Awards history, lasting approximately five minutes with a grand total of 15 awards handed out.

Over the years, more and more stars made the Roosevelt their hotel of choice, including Clark Gable, Errol Flynn, Hugh Hefner, Frank Sinatra, Elizabeth Taylor, Judy Garland, and Al Jolson. In addition, a variety of lesser-known but important personnel, from musicians to voice instructors to writers, stayed for extended periods of time on the studios' tabs while working on various movies.

But the years began to take their toll on the Roosevelt, and by the 1980s, the building had fallen into such disrepair that it came close to being demolished. A major hotel chain saved it from the wrecking ball and began making extensive renovations. They worked hard to reflect the Roosevelt's original charm and color schemes, focusing a lot of attention on the sunken Spanish-style lobby adorned with rounded Moorish windows and a bubbling fountain. The renovators discovered the lobby's huge, original, wrought-iron chandelier in pieces in the basement and spent six months putting it back together. It has been said that all of the banging during the renovation was enough to wake the dead—literally.

You're Never Alone at the Roosevelt

The first documented encounter with a ghost at the Roosevelt came in December 1985. The hotel was scheduled to reopen a month later, so employees were frantically working to complete the renovation. Employee Alan Russell was working in the Blossom Room when he felt a cold spot. Alarmed, he called some of his coworkers over and they felt it too, although they couldn't find a rational explanation as to why that one area would be cold.

Since then, guests and employees alike have reported seeing a man in dark clothing standing in precisely the same spot where Russell felt the cold spot. Who this man is remains a mystery.

Shortly after the newly renovated Roosevelt opened for business, the front desk started getting calls from confused guests who reported hearing disembodied voices coming from empty hallways. At other times, guests would call to complain about a loud conversation coming from the room next door, only to be told that the room was empty and locked up tight.

The ghosts of the Roosevelt might have started out being heard rather than seen, but that was to change, too. Guests and employees have also reported seeing dark figures roaming the hallways late at night. In one instance, the ghost of a man dressed all in white was seen walking through the walls of the hotel.

Over time, the ninth floor of the hotel became a haven for much of the paranormal activity. Things were said to have gotten to the point that some Roosevelt employees refused to go up to the floor alone at night.

In 1992, in an attempt to find some answers, psychic Peter James was invited to the Roosevelt. As he wandered the halls of the hotel, James claimed to have encountered several famous ghosts. He felt Humphrey Bogart's spirit near the elevators and bumped into Carmen Miranda's specter while walking down the hallway on the third floor. James stated that when he ventured down to the Blossom Room, the ghosts of Edward Arnold and Betty Grable were present.

The Roosevelt's Most Famous Ghost

Peter James also encountered one of the Roosevelt's most famous spectral residents—Marilyn Monroe. In life, Monroe frequented the Roosevelt and even had one of her very first photo shoots in the hotel's pool area. So while it's not surprising that Monroe's ghost would choose to hang around the hotel, it chose an unusual place to haunt. Her ghost is sometimes seen reflected in a mirror that hung in the room where she often stayed.

Weary of the stories of ghostly images appearing in the mirror, hotel management removed the mirror from the room and placed it in the manager's office. Apparently, Monroe's ghost made the move, too. One day, employee Susan Leonard was cleaning in the office when she looked into the mirror and saw a blonde woman standing behind her. When Leonard turned around, the woman had vanished.

Today, the mirror resides on the first floor near the elevators. And yes, Marilyn's ghost still makes an occasional appearance.

A Ghost with a Thing for the Ladies

The other famous ghost said to haunt the Roosevelt is that of Montgomery Clift. Specifically, Clift's ghost hangs out in Room 928, the room he called home for several months during the filming of *From Here to Eternity* (1953).

While Clift's ghost is traditionally only heard or felt, every once in a while he decides to reach out and touch someone. One evening in the 1990s, a young wife was reading in bed. When she felt her husband touch her on the shoulder, she rolled over to ask him what he wanted but found him fast asleep. It proves that just when you think you've eluded the ghosts of the Roosevelt and made it safely up to your room, you still might be in for a spooky surprise.

* CHAPTER 6

THE ODDEST OBJECTS (AND TREASURES)

Are You Going to Eat That Jesus?

Images of religious icons, particularly Jesus and the Virgin Mary, sometimes show up in the oddest places. Some people believe they are divine. What's the story?

※　※　※　※

SIGHTINGS OF RELIGIOUS symbols or images, called religious simulacra, in unexpected places are common enough that they've become incorporated into pop culture. Many of the people who discover or are involved in these sightings consider them to be miraculous events. Some also claim that the objects in which the images appear have special properties, such as bringing good luck or being immune to the ravages of time.

Jesus and Mary

For Christians, Jesus and the Virgin Mary are among the most significant religious figures, and not coincidentally, they also seem to make the most common appearances—often in food. Perhaps the quintessential sighting of a Christian religious symbol in food occurred in 1978, when a New Mexico woman named Maria Rubio was making a burrito. She noticed that a burn on the tortilla appeared to be in the shape of Jesus' head. After receiving the blessing of a priest, she built a shrine to house the tortilla and even quit her job to tend to the shrine full-time.

Islamic Words

Not surprisingly, religious sightings do not always involve Christian figures or symbols. In the Islamic world, the perception of the Arabic word for Allah roughly parallels the sighting of Jesus, the Virgin Mary, or other religious figures by Christians. Similarly, the objects involved sometimes have mystical properties ascribed to them. In 2006, a Kazakh farmer discovered an egg that villagers claimed had the name of *Allah* on its shell. After the sighting was verified by the local mosque, Bites Amantayeva, the farmer who discovered the egg, decided to keep it, saying, "We don't think it'll go bad." The name of *Allah* has also been sighted on fish scales, on beans, and in tomato slices.

Selling Simulacra

Sightings of religious images can have commercial as well as spiritual implications. In 1996, someone at a coffee shop in Nashville, Tennessee, discovered a cinnamon bun that bore a striking resemblance to Mother Teresa. The coffee shop parlayed the discovery into a line of merchandise, including coffee mugs and T-shirts. The merchandise was marketed with a NunBun trademark after Mother Teresa asked the shop to stop using the phrase "Immaculate Confection."

The proliferation of Internet auction sites such as eBay has created a market for these "miraculous" objects. One of the widest-known auctions occurred in 2004, when a Florida woman named Diane Duyser auctioned part of a grilled cheese sandwich she claimed bore the image of the Virgin Mary on eBay. Duyser asserted that the sandwich, which she had been storing since it was made in 1994, had never grown moldy and had brought her good luck, allowing her to win $70,000 at a casino. The sandwich was eventually purchased by another casino for $28,000.

Religious sightings—especially if they have been contrived somehow—are not always viewed in a positive light. In 1997,

Nike produced several models of basketball shoes that unintentionally featured a logo that, when viewed from right to left, resembled the Arabic word for Allah. The Council on American-Islamic Relations (CAIR) quickly demanded an apology, and Nike had little choice but to recall the shoes. The settlement between Nike and CAIR also included Arabic training for Nike graphic designers and Nike-built playgrounds in Muslim communities.

A Scientific Explanation?

While the parties involved in sightings of religious symbols often consider them to be miraculous in nature, the prevailing scientific view is that, rather than miraculous, they are occurrences of pareidolia, a psychological phenomenon in which random stimuli are interpreted as being meaningful in some way. As part of its intellectual process, the mind tries to make sense of what may be unrelated images. This is the same phenomenon that psychologists credit with forming the likeness of a man in the moon or shapes in clouds. It's also what's involved when the brain creates pictures from the famous Rorschach inkblots.

The Undiscovered Continent

Ahmed Muhiddin Piri was an Ottoman explorer, geographer, and cartographer who was born sometime between 1465 and 1470. His more well-known name, Piri Reis, means "Captain Piri," as he served in many naval wars for the Ottoman Empire, eventually rising to the rank of admiral. But he is most well-known for compiling a very unusual world map.

✳ ✳ ✳ ✳

A Forgotten Map

IN 1929, A German theologian named Gustav Adolf Deissmann was commissioned by the Turkish Ministry of Education to catalogue items in the Topkapi Palace library in Istanbul. As he sorted through some discarded bundles of material, he discovered a strange map drawn on gazelle skin parchment. Deissmann showed the parchment to German Paul Kahle, who identified it as a map drawn by the Turkish cartographer Piri Reis in the year 1513.

Inscriptions on the map claimed that Piri used at least 20 different maps and charts as source material to compile his own map, including Portuguese maps, Arabic maps, a map from Christopher Columbus, and Ptolemaic maps, which were maps based on Ptolemy's book *Geography*, written in the 2nd century. The inclusion of the Christopher Columbus map caused a particular stir amongst geographers, as the Piri Reis map was the only known copy of a map drawn by Columbus. The map was also notable for its accurate renderings of the Iberian Peninsula, the northern part of South America, and Africa.

Before the Ice Age

But one detail puzzled the geographers who pored over the map. Below the portion of the map that depicted the South American coast, the map appeared to show a representation of Antarctica. While this would seem totally normal on a modern map, the Piri Reis map, created in 1513, was drawn at least 200 years before Antarctica was known to exist. And that wasn't even the strangest part: The land mass on the map seemed to be an accurate depiction of Antarctica *before* it was covered in ice. This would mean that the map displayed the continent as it appeared more than 6,000 years ago.

How could anyone have created a map of Antarctica—especially before it was covered in ice—in the 16th century? Researchers considered the dozens of source maps Piri Reis claimed to have used to compile his map; could one of them have had knowledge of this sort? In 1965, a college professor named Charles Hapgood published a book entitled *Maps of the Ancient Sea Kings*, in which he argued for the affirmative. Hapgood believed that it was possible that an ancient, but advanced, civilization knew of Antarctica long before modern humans discovered it, and they had mapped its location when it was free of ice.

Ancient Aliens, Ancient Peoples

Others have suggested that this ancient civilization may have been alien in origin, and Hapgood himself believed that whoever mapped the continent would have to be not only able to navigate the sea, but also the air. Were ancient aliens flying across the globe millennia before the Wright Brothers? Or did a technologically advanced human civilization exist thousands of years ago, only to be inexplicably wiped out?

Skeptics point out that even in the 16th century, most sailors and geographers did believe that a continent existed somewhere in the south, so it's possible Piri Reis simply added one to his map. But others believe the map is too accurate for the land mass to have been added as a placeholder for a yet-to-be-discovered southern continent. We may never know the truth of how Piri Reis compiled his mysterious map, but it does make us question our ideas about "ancient" peoples. They may have possessed much more knowledge than we can imagine.

The Vanishing Treasure Room

In the Age of Enlightenment, kings and emperors built immense palaces to outdo one another—each one bigger and more gilded and bejeweled than the last. But one of Russia's greatest 18th century treasures became one of the 20th century's greatest unsolved mysteries.

✳   ✳   ✳   ✳

THE STORIED HISTORY of the Amber Room begins in 1701, when it was commissioned by Frederick I of Prussia. Considered by admirers and artists alike to be the "Eighth Wonder of the World," the sparkling, honey-gold room consisted of wall panels inlaid with prehistoric amber, finely carved and illuminated by candles and mirrors. In 1716, Prussian

King Freidrich Wilhelm I gifted the panels to then-ally Russian Tsar Peter the Great to ornament the imperial palace at his new capital, St. Petersburg.

After sitting at the Winter Palace for four decades, the Amber Room was moved to Tsarskoye Selo, the Romanov palace just south of St. Petersburg. During the mid-18th century, Prussia's King Frederick the Great sent Russia's Empress Elizabeth more of the amber material from his Baltic holdings, and Elizabeth ordered her court's great Italian architect, Bartolomeo Rastrelli, to expand the Amber Room into an 11-foot-square masterpiece.

The golden room was not finished until 1770, under the reign of Catherine the Great. Incorporating more than six tons of amber and accented with semiprecious stones, the fabled room became not only a prized jewel of the Russian empire, but a symbol of the long-standing alliance between Prussia and Russia.

From Peace to War

Two centuries after the Amber Room was removed to the Catherine Palace, the world was a much darker place. Prussia and Russia, formerly faithful allies, were locked in a deadly struggle that would bring down both imperial houses. By 1941, the former dominions of Frederick and Peter were ruled by Adolf Hitler and Joseph Stalin.

In a surprise attack, Hitler's armies drove across the Soviet border in June 1941 to launch the most destructive war in history. German panzers drove from the Polish frontier to the gates of Moscow in an epic six-month campaign, devouring some of the most fertile, productive territory in Eastern Europe.

One of the unfortunate cities in the path of the Nazi onslaught was St. Petersburg, renamed Leningrad by its communist masters. Frantic palace curators desperately tried to remove the Amber Room's antique panels, but the brittle prehistoric resin began to crumble as the panels were detached. Faced with probable destruction of one of Russia's greatest treasures or its abandonment to the Nazis, the curators attempted to hide the room's precious panels by covering them with gauze and wallpaper.

Although Leningrad withstood a long, bloody siege, German troops swept through the city's suburbs, capturing Tsarskoye Selo intact in October 1941. Soldiers discovered the treasure hidden behind the wallpaper, and German troops disassembled the room's panels over a 36-hour period, packed them in 27 crates, and shipped them back to Königsberg, in East Prussia.

The fabled Amber Room panels were put on display in Königsberg's castle museum. They remained there for two years—until the Third Reich began to crumble before the weight of Soviet and Anglo-American military forces. Sometime in 1944, the room's valuable panels were allegedly dismantled and packed into crates, to prevent damage by British and Soviet bombers. In January 1945, Hitler permitted the westward movement of cultural treasures, including the Italo-Russo-German masterpiece.

And from there, the Amber Room was lost to history.

The Great Treasure Hunt

The world was left to speculate about the fate of the famous imperial room, and dozens of theories have been spawned about the room's whereabouts. Some claim the Amber Room was lost—sunk aboard a submarine, bombed to pieces, or perhaps burned in Königsberg. This last conclusion was accepted by Alexander Brusov, a Soviet investigator sent to find the Amber Room shortly after the war's end. Referring to the destruction of Königsberg Castle by Red Army forces on April 9, 1945, he concluded: "Summarizing all the facts, we can say that the Amber Room was destroyed between 9 and 11 April 1945." An in-depth hunt by two British investigative journalists pieced together the last days of the Amber Room and concluded that its fate was sealed when Soviet troops accidentally set fire to the castle compound during the last month of combat, destroying the brittle jewels and obscuring their location.

Other treasure hunters, however, claim the room still sits in an abandoned mine shaft or some long-forgotten Nazi bunker beneath the outskirts of Königsberg. A German investigator claimed former SS officers told him the room's panels were packed up and hidden in a silver mine near Berlin; a Lithuanian official claimed witnesses saw SS troops hiding the panels in a swamp. Neither has been able to prove his claims.

The Trail Goes Cold

The hunt for the Amber Room has been made more difficult because its last witnesses are gone—several under mysterious circumstances. The Nazi curator in charge of the room died of typhus the day before he was scheduled to be interviewed by the KGB, and a Soviet intelligence officer who spoke to a journalist about the room's whereabouts died the following day in a car crash. In 1987, Georg Stein, a former German soldier who had devoted his life to searching for the Amber Room, was found murdered in a forest, his stomach slit open by a scalpel.

In 1997, the world got a tantalizing glimpse of the long-lost treasure when German police raided the office of a Bremen lawyer who was attempting to sell an amber mosaic worth $2.5 million on behalf of one of his clients, the son of a former German lieutenant. The small mosaic—inlaid with jade and onyx as well as amber—had been stolen from the Amber Room by a German officer and was separated from the main panels. After its seizure, this last true remnant of the legendary tsarist treasure made its way back to Russia in April 2000.

Decades of searches by German and Soviet investigators have come up empty. The fate of the fabled room—worth an estimated $142 million to $250 million in today's currency—has remained an elusive ghost for treasure seekers, mystery writers, and investigators looking for the Holy Grail of Russian baroque artwork.

Picking Up the Pieces

In 1979, the Soviet government, with help from a donation made by a German gas firm in 1999, began amassing old photographs of the Amber Room and pieces of the rare amber to create a reconstructed room worthy of its predecessor. Carefully rebuilt at a cost exceeding $7 million, the reconstructed room was dedicated by the Russian president and German chancellor at a ceremony in 2003, marking the tricentennial of St. Petersburg's founding. The dazzling Amber Room is now on display for the thousands of tourists who come to Tsarskoye Selo to view the playground of one of Europe's great dynasties.

The Mysterious Orb

If Texas were a dartboard, the city of Brownwood would be at the center of the bull's-eye. Maybe that's how aliens saw it, too.

BROWNWOOD IS A peaceful little city with about 20,000 residents and a popular train museum. A frontier town at one time, it became the trade center of Texas when the railroad arrived in 1885. Since then, the city has maintained a peaceful lifestyle. Even the massive tornado that struck Brownwood in 1976 left no fatalities. The place just has that "small town" kind of feeling.

An Invader from the Sky

In July 2002, however, the city's peace was broken. Brownwood made international headlines when a strange metal orb fell from space, landed in the Colorado River, and washed up just south of town. The orb looked like a battered metal soccer ball—it was about a foot across, and it weighed just under ten pounds. Experts described it as a titanium sphere. When it was x-rayed, it revealed a second, inner sphere with tubes and wires wrapped inside.

That's all that anybody knows (or claims to know). No one is sure what the object is, and no one has claimed responsibility for it. The leading theory is that it's a cryogenic tank from some kind of spacecraft from Earth, used to store a small amount of liquid hydrogen or helium for cooling purposes. Others have speculated that it's a bomb, a spying device, or even a weapon used to combat UFOs.

It's Not Alone

The Brownwood sphere isn't unique. A similar object landed in Kingsbury, Texas, in 1997, and was quickly confiscated by the Air Force for "tests and analysis." So far, no further announcements have been made.

Of course, the Air Force probably has a lot to keep it busy. About 200 UFOs are reported each month, and Texas is among the top three states where UFOs are seen. But until anything is known for sure, those in Texas at night should keep an eye on the skies.

Who Wants to Be a Billionaire?

According to legend, more than $2 billion in gold may be hidden on Oak Island in Mahone Bay, about 45 minutes from Halifax, Nova Scotia. For more than 200 years, treasure hunters have scoured the island, looking for the bounty, but the pirates who buried the treasure hid it well . . . and left booby traps, too.

✳ ✳ ✳ ✳

Folklore Leads to Fact

SINCE 1720, PEOPLE have claimed that pirate treasure was buried on Oak Island. Then, in the fall of 1795, young Daniel McGinnis went hunting on the island and found evidence that those stories might be true. But he found something rather odd: An oak tree had been used with a hoist to lift something very heavy. When McGinnis dug at that spot, he found loose sand indicating a pit about 12 feet in diameter.

He returned the next day with two friends and some digging tools. When the boys had dug ten feet down, they encountered a wooden platform—beneath it was more dirt. Ten feet further down, they reached another wooden platform with more dirt beneath it. At that point, the boys had to give up. They needed better tools and engineering expertise to continue their search.

They didn't get the help they needed, but one thing was certain: Something important had been buried on Oak Island. Soon, more people visited the island hoping to strike it rich.

An Encouraging Message

In the early 1800s, a Nova Scotia company began excavating the pit. The slow process took many years, and every ten feet, they found another wooden platform and sometimes layers of charcoal, putty, or coconut fiber.

About 90 feet down, the treasure hunters found an oily stone about three feet wide. It bore a coded inscription that read, "Forty feet below, two million pounds lie buried." (Gold worth two million pounds in 1795 would be worth approximately $2 billion today.)

However, as they dug past that 90-foot level, water began rushing into the hole. A few days later, the pit was almost full of seawater. No matter how much the team bailed, the water maintained its new level, so the company dug a second shaft, parallel to the first and 110 feet deep. But when they dug across to the original tunnel, water quickly filled the new shaft as well. The team abandoned the project, but others were eager to try their luck.

More Digging, More Encouragement, More Water

Since then, several companies have excavated deeper in the original shaft. Most treasure hunters—including a team organized by Franklin D. Roosevelt—have found additional proof that something valuable is buried there. For example, at

126 feet—nearly "forty feet below" the 90-foot marker—engineers found oak and iron. Farther down, they also reached a large cement chamber, from which they brought up a tiny piece of parchment, which encouraged them to dig deeper.

A narrow shaft dug in 1971 allowed researchers to use special cameras to study the pit. The team thought they saw several chests, some tools, and a disembodied hand floating in the water, but the shaft collapsed before they could explore further.

Since then, flooding has continued to hamper research efforts, and at least six people have been killed in their quests to find buried treasure. Nevertheless, the digging continues.

As of late 2007, the 1971 shaft had been redug to a depth of 181 feet. It offers the greatest promise for success. But just in case, investors and engineers plan to continue digging.

A Vacation Worth a Fortune?

But the digging isn't limited to professionals. Oak Island has become a unique vacation spot for people who like adventure and the chance to go home with a fortune. Canadian law says any treasure hunter can keep 90 percent of his or her findings.

Some vacationers dig at nearby islands, believing that the Oak Island site may be an elaborate, 18th-century "red herring." There are more than 100 other lovely islands in Mahone Bay. Perhaps the treasure is actually buried on one of them?

One Heck of a Hoax? The Mysterious Voynich Manuscript

Dubbed the "World's Most Mysterious Book," the Voynich manuscript contains more than 200 vellum pages of vivid, colorful illustrations and handwritten prose. There's only one small problem: No one knows what any of it means. Or whether it means anything at all.

✳   ✳   ✳   ✳

IT WAS "DISCOVERED" in 1912 after being hidden from the world for almost 250 years. An American antique book dealer named Wilfried Voynich came across the medieval manuscript at an Italian Jesuit College. Approximately nine inches by six inches in size, the manuscript bore a soft, light-brown vellum cover, which was unmarked, untitled, and gave no indication as to when it had been written or by whom.

Bound inside were approximately 230 yellow parchment pages, most of which contained richly colored drawings of strange plants, celestial bodies, and other scientific matter. Many of the pages were adorned by naked nymphs bathing in odd-looking plumbing and personal-size washtubs. Handwritten text written in flowing script accompanied the illustrations.

Although Voynich was an expert antiquarian, he was baffled by the book's contents. And today—nearly a century later—the manuscript that came to bear his name remains a mystery.

Weird Science

The mystery surrounding the Voynich manuscript begins with its content, which reads (so to speak) like a work of weird science presented in six identifiable "sections":

✳ a botanical section, containing drawings of plants that no botanist has ever been able to identify

* an astronomical section, with illustrations of the sun, moon, stars, and zodiac symbols surrounded by naked nymphs bathing in individual washtubs

* a "biological" section, showing perplexing anatomical drawings of chambers or organs connected by tubes—and which also features more nymphs swimming in their inner liquids

* a cosmological section, consisting mostly of unexplained circular drawings

* a pharmaceutical section, depicting drawings of plant parts (leaves, roots) placed next to containers

* a recipe section, featuring short paragraphs "bulleted" by stars in the margin

Weirder still are the ubiquitous nymphs—a nice touch perhaps, but how they relate to the subject matter is anyone's guess.

Many Mysteries, Still No Answers

And then there's the manuscript's enigmatic text. The world's greatest cryptologists have failed to unravel its meaning. Even the American and British code breakers who cracked the Japanese and German codes in World War II were stumped. To this day, not a single word of the Voynich manuscript has been deciphered.

This, of course, has led to key unsolved questions, namely:

* Who wrote it? A letter found with the manuscript, dated 1666, credits Roger Bacon, a Franciscan friar who lived from 1214 to 1294. This has since been discredited because the manuscript's date of origin is generally considered to be between 1450 and 1500. There are as many theories about who wrote it as there are nymphs among its pages. In fact, some believe Voynich forged the whole thing.

* What is it? It was first thought to be a coded description of

Bacon's early scientific discoveries. Since then, other theories ranging from an ancient prayer book written in a pidgin Germanic language to one big, elaborate hoax (aside from that supposedly perpetrated by Voynich) have been posited.

✳ Is it real writing? Is the script composed in a variation of a known language, a lost language, an encrypted language, an artificial language? Or is it just plain gibberish?

What Do We Know?

Despite the aura of mystery surrounding the manuscript, it has been possible to trace its travels over the past 400 years. The earliest known owner was Holy Roman Emperor Rudolph II, who purchased it in 1586. By 1666, the manuscript had passed through a series of owners to Athanasius Kircher, a Jesuit scholar who hid it in the college where Voynich found it 250 years later.

After being passed down to various members of Voynich's estate, the manuscript was sold in 1961 to a rare-book collector who sought to resell it for a fortune. After failing to find a buyer, he donated it to Yale University, where it currently resides—still shrouded in mystery—in the Beinecke Rare Book and Manuscript Library.

The Search for Meaning Continues . . .

To this day, efforts to translate the Voynich manuscript continue. And still, the manuscript refuses to yield its secrets, leading experts to conclude that it's either an ingenious hoax or the ultimate unbreakable code. The hoax theory gained some ground in 2004 when Dr. Gordon Rugg, a computer-science lecturer at Keele University, announced that he had replicated the Voynich manuscript using a low-tech device called a Cardan grille. According to Rugg, this proved that the manuscript was likely a fraud—a volume of jibberish created, perhaps, in an attempt to con money out of Emperor Rudolph II. Mystery solved? Well, it's not quite as simple as that. Many researchers remain unconvinced. Sure, Rugg may have proven that the manuscript might be a hoax. But the possibility that it is not a hoax remains. And thus, the search for meaning continues . . .

Deadly Bling?: The Curse of the Hope Diamond

Diamonds are a girl's best friend, a jeweler's meal ticket, and serious status symbols for those who can afford them. But there's one famous diamond whose brilliant color comes with a cloudy history. The Hope Diamond is one of the world's most beautiful gemstones—and one that some say causes death and suffering to those who possess it. So is the Hope Diamond really cursed? There's a lot of evidence that says "no," but there have been some really strange coincidences.

✳   ✳   ✳   ✳

The Origin of Hope

IT'S BELIEVED THAT this shockingly large, blue-hued diamond came from India several centuries ago. At the time, the exceptional diamond was slightly more than 112 carats, which is enormous. (On average, a diamond in an engagement ring ranges from a quarter to a full carat.) According to legend, a thief stole the diamond from the eye of a Hindu statue, but scholars don't think the shape would have been right to sit in the face of a statue. Nevertheless, the story states that the young thief was torn apart by wild dogs soon after he sold the diamond, making this the first life claimed by the jewel.

Courts, Carats, and Carnage

In the mid-1600s, a French jeweler named Tavernier purchased the diamond in India and kept it for several years without incident before selling it to King Louis XIV in 1668, along with several other jewels. The king recut the diamond in 1673, taking it down to 67 carats. This new cut emphasized the jewel's clarity, and Louis liked to wear the "Blue Diamond of the

Crown" around his neck on special occasions. He, too, owned the gemstone without much trouble.

More than a hundred years later, France's King Louis XVI possessed the stone. In 1791, when the royal family tried to flee the country, the crown jewels were hidden for safekeeping, but they were stolen the following year. Some were eventually returned, but the blue diamond was not.

King Louis XVI and his wife Marie Antoinette died by guillotine in 1793. Those who believe in the curse are eager to include these two romantic figures in the list of cursed owners, but their deaths probably had more to do with the angry mobs of the French Revolution than a piece of jewelry.

Right this Way, Mr. Hope

It is unknown what happened to the big blue diamond from the time it was stolen in France until it appeared in England nearly 50 years later. When the diamond reappeared, it wasn't the same size as before—it was now only about 45 carats. Had it been cut again to disguise its identity? Or was this a new diamond altogether? Because the blue diamond was so unique in color and size, it was believed to be the diamond in question.

In the 1830s, wealthy banker Henry Philip Hope purchased the diamond, henceforth known as the Hope Diamond. When he died (of natural causes) in 1839, he bequeathed the gem to his oldest nephew, and it eventually ended up with the nephew's grandson, Francis Hope.

Francis Hope is the next person supposedly cursed by the diamond. Francis was a notorious gambler and was generally bad with money. Though he owned the diamond, he was not allowed to sell it without his family's permission, which he finally got in 1901 when he announced he was bankrupt. It's doubtful that the diamond had anything to do with Francis's bad luck, though that's what some believers suggest.

Coming to America

Joseph Frankel and Sons of New York purchased the diamond from Francis, and by 1909, after a few trades between the world's most notable jewelers, the Hope Diamond found itself in the hands of famous French jeweler Pierre Cartier. That's where rumors of a curse may have actually originated.

Allegedly, Cartier came up with the curse concept in order to sell the diamond to Evalyn Walsh McLean, a rich socialite who claimed that bad luck charms always turned into good luck charms in her hands. Cartier may have embellished the terrible things that had befallen previous owners of his special diamond so that McLean would purchase it—which she did. Cartier even inserted a clause in the sales contract, which stated that if any fatality occurred in the family within six months, the Hope Diamond could be exchanged for jewelry valued at the $180,000 McLean paid for the stone. Nevertheless, McLean wore the diamond on a chain around her neck constantly, and the spookiness surrounding the gem started picking up steam.

Whether or not anything can be blamed on the jewel, it certainly can't be denied that McLean had a pretty miserable life starting around the time she purchased the diamond. Her eldest son died at age nine in a fiery car crash. Years later, her 25-year-old daughter killed herself. Not long after that, her husband was declared insane and was committed to a mental institution for the rest of his life. With rumors swirling about the Hope Diamond's curse, everyone pointed to the necklace when these terrible events took place.

In 1947, when McLean died (while wearing the diamond) at age 60, the Hope Diamond and most of her other treasures were sold to pay off debts. American jeweler Harry Winston forked over the $1 million asking price for McLean's entire jewelry collection.

Hope on Display

If Harry Winston was scared of the alleged curse, he didn't show it. Winston had long wanted to start a collection of gemstones to display for the general public, so in 1958, when the Smithsonian Institute started one in Washington, D.C., he sent the Hope Diamond to them as a centerpiece. These days, it's kept under glass as a central figure for the National Gem Collection at the National Museum of Natural History. So far, no one's dropped dead from checking it out.

It's a Bird! It's a Plane! It's . . . Avrocar?!?

Not all UFOs are alien spaceships. One top-secret program was contracted out by the U.S. military to an aircraft company in Canada.

❋ ❋ ❋ ❋

OH, THE 1950S—A time of sock hops, drive-in movies, and the Cold War between America and the Soviet Union, when each superpower waged war against the other in the arenas of scientific technology, astronomy, and politics. It was also a time when discussion of life on other planets was rampant, fueled by the alleged crash of an alien spaceship near Roswell, New Mexico, in 1947.

Watch the Skies

Speculation abounded about the unidentified flying objects (UFOs) spotted nearly every week by everyone from farmers to airplane pilots. As time passed, government authorities began to wonder if the flying saucers were, in fact, part of a secret Russian program to create a new type of air force. Fearful that such a craft would upset the existing balance of power, the U.S. Air Force decided to produce its own saucer-shape ship.

In 1953, the military contacted Avro Aircraft Limited of Canada, an aircraft manufacturing company that operated in Malton, Ontario, between 1945 and 1962. Project Silverbug was initially proposed simply because the government wanted to find out if UFOs could be manufactured by humans. But before long, both the military and the scientific community were speculating about its potential. Intrigued by the idea, designers at Avro—led by British aeronautical engineer John Frost—began working on the VZ-9-AV Avrocar. The round craft would have been right at home in a scene from the classic science fiction film The Day the Earth Stood Still. Security for the project was so tight that it probably generated rumors that America was actually testing a captured alien spacecraft—speculation that remains alive and well even today.

Of This Earth

By 1958, the company had produced two prototypes, which were 18 feet in diameter and 3.5 feet tall. Constructed around a large triangle, the Avrocar was shaped like a disk, with a curved upper surface. It included an enclosed 124-blade turbo-rotor at the center of the triangle, which provided lifting power through an opening in the bottom of the craft. The turbo also powered the craft's controls. Although conceived as being able to carry two passengers, in reality a single pilot could barely fit inside the cramped space. The Avrocar was operated with a single control stick, which activated different panels around the ship. Airflow issued from a large center ring, which was controlled by the pilot to guide the craft either vertically or horizontally.

The military envisioned using the craft as "flying Jeeps" that would hover close to the ground and move at a maximum speed of 40 mph. But that, apparently, was only going to be the beginning. Avro had its own plans, which included not just commercial Avrocars, but also a family-size Avrowagon, an Avrotruck for larger loads, Avroangel to rush people to the hospital, and a military Avropelican, which, like a pelican hunting for fish, would conduct surveillance for submarines.

But Does It Fly?

The prototypes impressed the U.S. Army enough to award Avro a $2 million contract. Unfortunately, the Avrocar project was canceled when an economic downturn forced the company to temporarily close and restructure. When Avro Aircraft reopened, the original team of designers had dispersed. Further efforts to revive the project were unsuccessful, and repeated testing proved that the craft was inherently unstable. It soon became apparent that whatever UFOs were spotted overhead, it was unlikely that they came from this planet. Project Silverbug was abandoned when funding ran out in March 1961, but one of the two Avrocar prototypes is housed at the U.S. Army Transportation Museum in Fort Eustis, Virginia.

A Discovery of Biblical Proportions

While rounding up a stray animal near Qumran, Israel, in early 1947, Bedouin shepherd Mohammed el-Hamed stumbled across several pottery jars containing scrolls written in Hebrew. It turned out to be the find of a lifetime.

✳ ✳ ✳ ✳

NEWS OF THE exciting discovery of ancient artifacts spurred archaeologists to scour the area of the original find for additional material. Over a period of nine years, the remains of approximately 900 documents were recovered from 11 caves near the ruins of Qumran, a plateau community on the northwest shore of the Dead Sea. The documents have come to be known as the Dead Sea Scrolls.

Tests indicate that all but one of the documents were created between the middle of the 2nd century B.C. and the 1st century A.D. Nearly all were written in one of three Hebrew dialects. The majority of the documents were written on animal hide.

The scrolls represent the earliest surviving copies of Biblical documents. Approximately 30 percent of the material is from the Hebrew Bible. Every book of the Old Testament is represented with the exception of the Book of Esther and the Book of Nehemiah. Another 30 percent of the scrolls contain essays on subjects including blessings, war, community rule, and the membership requirements of a Jewish sect. About 25 percent of the material refers to Israelite religious texts not contained in the Hebrew Bible, while 15 percent of the data has yet to be identified.

Since their discovery, debate about the meaning of the scrolls has been intense. One widely held theory subscribes to the belief that the scrolls were created at the village of Qumran and then hidden by the inhabitants. According to this theory, a Jewish sect known as the Essenes wrote the scrolls. Those subscribing to this theory have concluded that the Essenes hid the scrolls in nearby caves during the Jewish Revolt in A.D. 66, shortly before they were massacred by Roman troops.

A second major theory, put forward by Norman Golb, Professor of Jewish History at the University of Chicago, speculates that the scrolls were originally housed in various Jerusalem-area libraries and were spirited out of the city when the Romans besieged the capital in A.D. 68–70. Golb believes that the treasures documented on the so-called Copper Scroll could only have been held in Jerusalem. Golb also alleges that the variety of conflicting ideas found in the scrolls indicates that the documents are facsimiles of literary texts.

The documents were catalogued according to which cave they were found in and have been categorized into Biblical and non-Biblical works. Of the eleven caves, numbers 1 and 11 yielded the most intact documents, while number 4 held the most material—an astounding 15,000 fragments representing 40 percent of the total material found. Multiple copies of the Hebrew Bible have been identified, including 19 copies of the Book of Isaiah, 30 copies of Psalms, and 25 copies of Deuteronomy. Also found were previously psalms attributed to King David, and stories about Abraham and Noah.

Most of the fragments appeared in print between 1950 and 1965, with the exception of the material from Cave 4. Publication of the manuscripts was entrusted to an international group led by Father Roland de Vaux of the Dominican Order in Jerusalem.

Access to the material was governed by a "secrecy rule"—only members of the international team were allowed to see them. In late 1971, 17 documents were published, followed by the release of a complete set of images of all the Cave 4 material. The secrecy rule was eventually lifted, and copies of all documents were in print by 1995.

Many of the documents are now housed in the Shrine of the Book, a wing of the Israel Museum located in Western Jerusalem. The scrolls on display are rotated every three to six months.

Unidentified Submerged Objects

Much like their flying brethren, unidentified submerged objects captivate and mystify. But instead of vanishing into the skies, USOs, such as the following, plunge underwater.

✳   ✳   ✳   ✳

Sighting at Puerto Rico Trench

IN 1963, WHILE conducting exercises off the coast of Puerto Rico, U.S. Navy submarines encountered something extraordinary. The incident began when a sonar operator aboard an accompanying destroyer reported a strange occurrence. According to the seaman, one of the subs traveling with the armada broke free from the pack to chase a USO. This quarry would be unlike anything the submariners had ever pursued.

Underwater technology in the early 1960s was advancing rapidly. Still, vessels had their limitations. The U.S.S. *Nautilus*, though faster than any submarine that preceded it, was still limited to about 20 knots (23 miles per hour). The bathyscaphe *Trieste*, a deep-sea submersible, could exceed 30,000 feet in depth, but the descent took as long as five hours. Once there, the vessel could not be maneuvered side to side.

Knowing this, the submariners were stunned by what they witnessed. The USO was moving at 150 knots (170 miles per hour) and hitting depths greater than 20,000 feet! No underwater vehicles on Earth were capable of such fantastic numbers. Even today, modern nuclear subs have top speeds of about 25 knots (29 miles per hour) and can operate at around 800-plus feet below the surface.

Thirteen separate crafts witnessed the USO as it criss-crossed the Atlantic Ocean over a four-day period. At its deepest, the mystery vehicle reached 27,000 feet. To this day, there's been no earthly explanation offered for the occurrence.

USO with a Bus Pass

In 1964, London bus driver Bob Fall witnessed one of the strangest USO sightings. While transporting a full contingent of passengers, the driver and his fares reported seeing a silver, cigar-shape object dive into the nearby waters of the River Lea. The police attributed the phenomenon to a flight of ducks, despite the obvious incongruence. Severed telephone lines and a large gouge on the river's embankment suggested something far different.

Shag Harbour Incident

The fishing village of Shag Harbour lies on Canada's East Coast. This unassuming hamlet is to USOs what Roswell, New Mexico, is to UFOs. Simply put, it played host to the most famous occurrence of a USO ever recorded.

On the evening of October 4, 1967, the Royal Canadian Mounted Police (RCMP) were barraged by reports of a UFO that had crashed into the bay at Shag Harbour. Laurie Wickens and four friends witnessed a large object (approximately 60 feet in diameter) falling into the water just after 11:00 P.M. Floating approximately 1,000 feet off the coast they could clearly detect a yellow light on top of the object.

The RCMP promptly contacted the Rescue Coordination

Center in Halifax to ask if any aircraft were missing. None were. Shortly thereafter, the object sank into the depths of the water and disappeared from view.

When local fishing boats went to the USO crash site, they encountered yellow foam on the water's surface and detected an odd sulfuric smell. No survivors or bodies were ever found. The Royal Canadian Air Force officially labeled the occurrence a UFO, but because the object was last seen under water, such events are now described as USOs.

Pascagoula Incident

On November 6, 1973, at approximately 8:00 P.M., a USO was sighted by at least nine fishermen anchored off the coast of Pascagoula, Mississippi. They witnessed an underwater object an estimated five feet in diameter that emitted a strange amber light.

First to spot the USO was Rayme Ryan. He repeatedly poked at the light-emitting object with an oar. Each time he made contact with the strange object, its light would dim and it would move a few feet away, then brighten once again.

Fascinated by the ethereal quality of this submerged question mark, Ryan summoned the others. For the next half hour, the cat-and-mouse game played out in front of the fishermen until Ryan struck the object with a particularly forceful blow. With this action, the USO disappeared from view.

The anglers moved about a half mile away and continued fishing. After about 30 minutes, they returned to their earlier location and were astounded to find that the USO had returned. At this point, they decided to alert the Coast Guard.

After interviewing the witnesses, investigators from the Naval Ship Research and Development Laboratory in Panama City, Florida, submitted their findings: At least nine persons had witnessed an undetermined light source whose characteristics and actions were inconsistent with those of known marine organisms or with an uncontrolled human-made object. Their final report was inconclusive, stating that the object could not be positively identified.

A Tale of Two Armors

Spider silk may not be as strong as steel, but it weighs a small fraction as much and works in much different applications. Could spider silk be used to make body armor? Unbelievably, could corn starch?!

✳　✳　✳　✳

IT'S HARD TO browse the cable guide or Netflix homepage without seeing a handful of crime shows, if not more. Americans can't get enough of watching actors pretend to be law-enforcement agents, detectives, prosecutors, or military versions of any of those jobs. Terms like "armor-piercing round" are floating around in the vernacular now, but what does it really take to pierce the armor worn by law enforcement or private security?

Arming and Armoring

Sorting out the language of the ballistic or "bulletproof" industry and its armor-piercing counterparts is a slippery task. The language isn't standardized, and marketing has affected how makers describe their products. Traditional armor-piercing rounds are meant for use against armored vehicles or ships. Bullets designed for use in rifles, and therefore to shoot individuals, must be manufactured with super rigid materials like tungsten carbide in order to be able to penetrate body armor.

The goal with armor on a ship or person is to slow down a projectile enough to drastically reduce how much harm it does. We might picture bullets bouncing off of armor, but the truth is that plated armor seeks to smash the front of a bullet into a flat "mushroom" shape that won't get any further. Kevlar slows the bullet with layers of densely woven, incredibly tough man-made fibers. The person wearing the armor feels the full force of the bullet's mass and speed but the force is distributed over and absorbed by a larger area.

Sounds great, right? And it is . . . but the wearer can also expect *some* injury, ranging from a severe bruise to internal organ damage. Someone who's shot while wearing a "bulletproof" vest can very easily need to go to the hospital afterward, especially if multiple shots were fired. Armor can warp after impact, even Kevlar, and that warping affects how the armor absorbs subsequent shots.

Bulletproof vests save countless lives with technology that seems like magic to the average person, and scientists spend entire careers experimenting with ways to improve and update this technology. Potential for warping is a great place to begin those experiments.

Mysteries of Oobleck

If you have, know, teach, or exist near one or more children, you almost definitely know what oobleck is, if not by name alone. Oobleck is the term for a mixture of corn starch and water that reacts as a solid sometimes and a liquid sometimes. You can "walk on water" across a kiddie pool of oobleck if you move quickly. It's more like a run on water—check it out on YouTube. But if you stand on the oobleck, you'll sink in, and the oobleck will try to hold you down.

These special qualities make oobleck one of very few known "non-Newtonian fluids," meaning it literally defies the classic laws of physics as touched off by the lifetime's work of Sir Isaac Newton. And in 2014, an Air Force Academy cadet (meaning student) made the connection between oobleck and the liquid binders or epoxies used in body armor. She wanted to replace traditional gluey fillers that dried into a solid with a fluid that stayed flexible and loose.

The cadet and her advisors worked together to make layers of oobleck sandwiched between layers of Kevlar. They tried different setups and numbers of layers until they found an arrangement that can, in fact, stop bullets. Kevlar is a trademarked product, but oobleck is as close by as an 80 cent box of cornstarch. It's flexible until an impact and then again immediately afterward. It could be lighter than traditional armor and cost a lot less. The possibilities are endless.

Arach-ing Our Brains

Spiders produce strong natural proteins in the form of silk strands. Maybe a scientist started to wonder about the tensile strength of spider silk after walking through a web and trying to remove all traces of it for the rest of an entire day. This strong, durable, biological product requires no unusual ingredients or energy sources. In strength, flexibility, and other attributes, it could rival Kevlar, without the hangups of patent law or petrochemicals.

The U.S. military loves the idea of spider silk as a part of the armor kit soldiers wear. Its flexibility compared to Kevlar means it could be used to build comfortable underlayers that still offer protection, the same way consumer "worm silk" makes superlative long underwear. Scientists are working with the military to genetically engineer stronger, more versatile, or simply more abundant spider silk. They've bred silkworms that can make spider silk, because worms are much faster at silk production than spiders are.

Scaling to a military application is still a huge problem, literally. The U.S. Department of Defense employs over 2 million active duty or reserve military personnel. Can there ever be enough spider silk to supply these soldiers with even their smallest piece of armor? Will spider silk be used as one component in a much larger application?

So far, the investment in spider silk research is tiny compared to almost any other Department of Defense project. And the military has a terrific track record with technologies that trickle down to the civilian level: GPS navigation, the jet engine, walkie talkies, duct tape, and the Internet were all originally invented for military use.

Rebel with a Curse: James Dean and "Little Bastard"

From the moment James Dean first walked onto a Hollywood set, countless people have emulated his cool style and attitude. When Dean died in a car crash in 1955 at age 24, his iconic status was immortalized. Perhaps this is partly due to the strange details that surrounded his death. Did a cursed car take the rising star away before his time?

✳   ✳   ✳   ✳

How Much Is That Porsche in the Window?

IN 1955, HEARTTHROB James Dean purchased a silver Porsche 550 Spyder, which he nicknamed "Little Bastard." Dean painted the number "130" on the hood and the car's saucy name on the back.

On the morning of September 30, Dean drove the Porsche to his mechanic for a quick tune-up before heading to a race he was planning to enter. The car checked out, and Dean left, making plans to meet up with a few friends and a *Life* magazine photographer later that day.

Everyone who knew Dean knew he liked to drive fast. The movie star set out on the highway, driving at top speeds in his beloved Porsche. He actually got stopped for speeding at one point but got back on the road after getting a ticket.

But when the sun got in his eyes and another car made a quick left turn, Dean couldn't stop in time. Screeching brakes, twisted metal, and an ambulance that couldn't make it to the hospital in time signaled the end of James Dean's short life.

You Need Brake Pads, a New Alternator, and a Priest

Within a year or so of Dean's fatal car crash, his Porsche was involved in a number of unusual—and sometimes deadly—incidents. Were they all coincidental, or was the car actually cursed? Consider the following:

Two doctors claimed several of Little Bastard's parts. One of the docs was killed and the other seriously injured in separate accidents. Someone else purchased the tires, which blew simultaneously, sending their new owner to the hospital.

The Fresno garage where the car was kept for a while after Dean's death was the site of a major fire. The California State Highway Patrol removed the car from Fresno, figuring they could show the charred remains of Dean's car to warn teenagers about the dangers of careless driving. When the vehicle transporting the remains of the car crashed en route to the site, the driver was thrown from his vehicle and died.

The display the Highway Patrol produced was incredibly popular, of course, but it also turned out to be dangerous. The legs of a young boy looking at the car were crushed when three of the cables holding the vehicle upright suddenly broke, bringing the heavy metal down onto the boy's body. When the car left the exhibit, it broke in half on the truck used to haul it away and killed a worker involved in the loading process.

In 1959, there was another attempt to display the car. Though it was welded together, legend has it that the car suddenly broke into 11 pieces. The following year, the owner had finally had enough and decided to have the Porsche shipped from Miami back to California. Little Bastard was loaded onto a sealed boxcar, but when the train arrived in L.A., the car was gone. Thieves may have taken the car, sure, but there were reports that the boxcar hadn't been disturbed. Whether or not the car was cursed, with all the trouble it caused, perhaps it was for the best that it finally disappeared.

From Poland and Iraq to a Car Near You: The Wheel's Origins

It's not difficult to see how important the wheel is to human civilization. The hard part is figuring out who got there first.

✳   ✳   ✳   ✳

THE WHEEL IS such a simple tool—and yet, determining when it was invented and who did it earliest is anything but simple. Many accounts assert that it was invented in Asia around 8000 B.C. but fail to elaborate. The Bronocice Pot, found in Polish digs from the Funnel/Beaker culture, dates to 3500 B.C. and seems to depict a wheeled wagon. If so, these ancient late Stone Age people may have beaten the Sumerians to the punch; after all, the fact that the Bronocice included the image on a pot suggests that they actually used the wheel.

One of Earth's most ancient civilizations was Sumer, in southern Iraq, stretching from about 5300 B.C. to just after 2000 B.C. (Its relevance died out, not its people.) Our most descriptive, solid, early evidence of the wheel comes from the excavations at Ur, dated to about 3500 B.C. By Mesopotamian standards, Ur was a great city, though it never reached 100,000 people. Some believe its famous ziggurat was the biblical Tower of Babel.

We have no idea who invented Sumer's wheel, but we know its function: pottery, not transportation. While transportation was valuable to ancient cultures, pottery was more so. One key to civilization is the production of agricultural excess that can be bartered for other goods and services. Without good storage for that excess, varmints will infest it. Whether the first wheel came about by accident or design, it was an industrial tool. The first Sumerian depictions of wheeled donkey carts show up about 300 years later.

Could the Funnel/Beaker people have gotten the wheel from Sumer or vice-versa? It's doubtful. As the bird flies, it's about

1,200 miles from South Poland to Mesopotamia. Each culture probably invented it independently for the inventor's own reasons.

The Fountain of Youth

It's been an obsession of explorers for centuries, but no one has been able to find the magic elixir.

✳   ✳   ✳   ✳

SPANISH EXPLORER JUAN Ponce de León was suppos-edly searching for the fabled fountain of youth when he discovered Florida. However, it wasn't until after his death in 1521 that he became linked with the fountain.

The first published reference associating Ponce de León with the fountain of youth was the *Historia General y Natural de las Indias,* by Gonzalo Fernandez de Oviedo in 1535. The author cited the explorer's search for a fountain of restorative water to cure his impotence, but the veracity of this account is ques-tionable since Ponce de León had children at the time of his 1513 voyage and didn't even mention the fountain in his travel notes.

Moreover, the fountain of youth legend predates Ponce de León. In Arabic versions of the *Alexander Romance,* a collec-tion of myths about Alexander the Great, the Macedonian king and his troops cross a desert and come to a fountain in which they bathe to regain strength and youth. This story was translated to French in the 13th century and was known among Europeans.

If a fountain of youth actually exists, no one has found it in it in any of its supposed locations, which are most typically cited as Florida, the Bahamas, or the Bay of Honduras. It may turn out, however, that a fountain of youth exists in science. David Sinclair, a Harvard University professor and the founder of Sirtris Pharmaceuticals, discovered in 2003 that the molecule resveratrol could extend the lifespan of worms and fruit flies. In 2006, Italian researchers prolonged the life of the fish *Nothobranchius furzeri* with resveratrol.

Drugs that are based on this research could be on shelves soon, though initially they will be designed only to aid diabetics. It's not quite eternal life—it's basically just extended fitness. But that's more than Ponce de León found.

If These Bones Could Talk

Early in the 20th century, archaeologists searched frantically for the "missing link"—a fossil that would bridge the gap between apes and man. What was found, however, made monkeys out of everyone involved.

✳   ✳   ✳   ✳

Fossil Facts or Fiction?

IN NOVEMBER 1912, a story appeared in the English newspaper *Manchester Guardian*: Skull fragments had been found that could be of the utmost significance. "There seems to be no doubt whatever of its genuineness," wrote the reporter, characterizing the bones as perhaps "the oldest remnant of a human frame yet discovered on this planet." The story generated feverish speculation. On the night of December 18, 1912, a crowd jammed into the meeting of the Geological Society of London to learn about this amazing discovery.

What they heard was that solicitor and an amateur archeologist Charles Dawson had discovered two skull fragments and a jawbone from a gravel bed near Piltdown Common in East

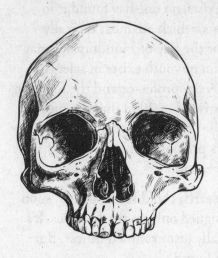

Sussex. He had been interested in this area ever since workmen, knowing of his archeological interest, had given him some interesting bone fragments from the pit several years before. Dawson had since been making his own excavations of the pit, aided by Arthur Smith Woodward, keeper of the Department of Geology at the British Museum.

The skull fragments were definitely human, but the jawbone was similar to an ape. If they came from the same creature, as Woodward and Dawson both hypothesized, then they had discovered the missing evolutionary link between ape and man. Woodward announced, "I therefore propose that the Piltdown specimen be regarded as a new type of genus of the family *Hominidae.*"

A Deep Divide

Almost immediately, two distinct camps were formed: doubters and supporters. In Woodward's favor were the facts that the remains were found close together, that they were similar in color and mineralization, and that the teeth were worn down in a flat, human way—unlike those of an ape. Doubters contended the jawbone and skull fragments were too dissimilar to be from the same creature. American and French scientists tended to be skeptical, while the British generally accepted the validity of the discovery.

Woodward's side scored valuable points when a canine tooth missing from the Piltdown jaw was discovered in 1913 close to where the jawbone originally had been found. Hard on the heels of that find came another—an elephant bone that had been rendered into some type of tool and supposed to have been used by Piltdown Man.

In 1915, there came perhaps the most conclusive evidence of all: Dawson found the remains of a similar creature a scant two miles away from the site of the first discovery.

Bone Betrayal

So Piltdown Man entered the archaeological record. After Dawson died on August 10, 1916, no significant new Piltdown discoveries were made, but no matter. Even when a few scientists identified the jaw as that from an ape, they were ignored.

However, as other fossil discoveries were made in subsequent years, it became evident that something wasn't quite right about Piltdown Man. Things really began unraveling in 1949, when a new dating technique called the fluorine absorption test was used on Piltdown Man. It revealed that the skull fragments were relatively modern and the jawbone was just a few decades old. Finally, in 1953 a group of scientists proved that Piltdown Man was a hoax. The jawbone had been stained to look old, the teeth filed down, and the bones placed at the site.

Although the identity of the Piltdown Man hoaxer has never been revealed—even Sir Arthur Conan Doyle, author of the Sherlock Holmes series of mysteries, is considered a suspect by some—most suspicion falls on Dawson, who was later found to have been involved in other archeological frauds. Ultimately, it seems that if seeing is believing, then Piltdown Man is proof that people will only see what they want to believe.

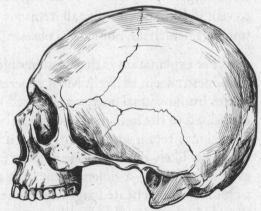

Haunted Objects: One Person's Treasure Is Another's Torment

Many people would be frightened to encounter a haunted object. The idea is just a little creepy, whether the object in question is a doll, a painting, or a hairbrush. But some people actually scour estate sales and surf the Web searching for haunted objects. To those people we say, "Let the buyer beware."

✳   ✳   ✳   ✳

What Is a Haunted Object?

A HAUNTED OBJECT IS an item that seems to give off a certain energy or vibe. Paranormal occurrences accompany the object itself and begin after the object is acquired. Sometimes, human characteristics—such as breathing or tapping sounds—are associated with the item. In other cases, a person can place a haunted object in one place only to find that it mysteriously moves while he or she is absent from the room, is sleeping, or is away from home.

Becoming Haunted

No one knows for sure what causes an object to become haunted. Some people think that the items are possessed. Renowned psychic Sylvia Browne says that oftentimes a spirit has a "lingering fondness" for an object and may just stop by to visit it. She stresses that all items are capable of holding imprints, which are not always pleasant.

Another explanation is that certain objects are cursed, but that doesn't seem as likely. Most experts feel that a "haunting" comes from residual energy associated with the people or places connected to the item. For example, a beloved doll or stuffed animal may retain some energy from its human owner. This is especially likely to be the case with an item that was near—or even involved in—a violent event such as a murder, the death of a child, or even a heated argument. The "haunting" occurs when the residual energy plays back or reenacts the traumatic event.

Like other residual phenomena, haunted objects can't communicate or interact with humans.

When people experience a paranormal event, they often assume that the building in which the incident occurs is haunted, but sometimes it's just one item. Here's a look at some objects that are reportedly haunted.

An Especially Evil Ouija Board

Many people avoid Ouija boards because they may connect us with the Other Side or evil entities. This certainly seemed to be the case with the board Abner Williams loaned to a group of El Paso "Goths." In mid-2000, after the board was returned to him, Williams complained of scratching noises coming from the board, along with a man's voice addressing him and the sound of children chanting nursery rhymes at his window. When Williams tried to throw the board away, it mysteriously reappeared in his house. A paranormal investigator borrowed the board, and a hooded figure appeared from out of nowhere and growled at his son.

When a paranormal research team investigated the Ouija board, they found spots of blood on the front of it and a coating of blood on the back. They measured several cold spots over areas of the board, and photos revealed a strange ectoplasm rising from it. The board was eventually sent to a new owner, who did not want it cleared of negative energy. That person has remained silent about more recent activity surrounding the board.

Although this is an unusually well-documented haunted Ouija board, it is not an uncommon tale. Many psychics warn that if you ask a spirit to communicate with you through a Ouija board, it's like opening a door between the worlds. You never know what kinds of spirits—good or evil—will use that Ouija board to visit you. Therefore, it's wise to be cautious with "spirit boards" of any kind.

Haunted Painting

Actor John Marley purchased a painting titled *The Hands Resist Him* after he saw it at a Los Angeles art show. Many years later, the piece of art—which Bill Stoneham painted in 1972—was found in a trash bin behind a brewery, and in strict accordance with "finder's keepers" rules, the person who found it took it home.

Unfortunately, it soon became clear why the artwork had been abandoned. The finder's four-year-old daughter claimed that she saw the children in the painting fighting. And sure enough, a webcam that recorded the painting for several nights confirmed that the figures were indeed moving. The artist didn't have any insight as to why this particular painting might be haunted, but he did remember that both the gallery owner and a Los Angeles art critic died soon after that show. Coincidence? Maybe. Nevertheless, the family listed the painting and its bizarre story on eBay and came away $1,025 richer.

Robert the Doll

When artist Robert Eugene "Gene" Otto was a young boy growing up in Florida in the early 1900s, he owned a doll, which he named Robert. He took this doll with him everywhere and liked to talk to it. The problem was that the doll talked back—and this was long before the days of Chatty Cathy and other "talking" dolls. It wasn't just the young boy's imagination either—servants and other family members also witnessed the phenomenon. Neighbors were surprised to see the doll moving by itself, and when Otto's parents found their son's bedroom trashed, Gene said that Robert the doll did it. Did it? Maybe so, at least according to the daughter of the family that bought the house in 1972: She was terrified when she discovered the doll in the attic. She said that it wanted to kill her. Her parents had no intention of finding out if this was true, so they gave the doll to a museum in Key West. Visitors to the museum are advised to ask permission before they snap a photo of the famous doll. A tilt of his head means yes, but if you don't get the OK, don't even think about taking a picture, or you'll be cursed.

Nathaniel Hawthorne and the Haunted Chair

You may have seen a creepy old chair or two, but when author Nathaniel Hawthorne encountered one that was actually haunted, he wrote a short story about it: "The Ghost of Dr. Harris."

According to Hawthorne, Dr. Harris sat and read the newspaper in the same chair at the Boston Athenaeum each morning. When Harris died, his ghost continued to visit, and Hawthorne, who was researching at the library, saw it daily. The author said that the spirit had a "melancholy look of helplessness" that lingered for several seconds, and then vanished. So if you visit the Boston Athenaeum, be careful where you sit: Dr. Harris may be in that "empty" chair.

Annabelle and the Haunted Doll

Raggedy Ann and Andy dolls have been popular for decades. But after a young woman named Donna received a Raggedy Ann doll in the 1970s, she didn't have such a warm and fuzzy experience. The doll would often change positions on its own: Once, it was found kneeling—a position that was impossible for Donna and her roommate Angie to create due to the soft and floppy nature of the doll's body. The girls also found mysterious notes that were written in a childish scrawl. Worried, Donna and Angie called in a medium, who told them that their apartment building was once the home of a young girl named Annabelle. But after the doll attacked Angie's boyfriend, the girls called in demonologists Ed and Lorraine Warren, who determined that "Annabelle" was not the friendly, playful spirit of a young girl, but instead was a demonic entity. The doll went to live with the Warrens, who knew how to handle its antics, and it now resides in a glass case at the Warren Occult Museum in Connecticut.

The Haunted Wedding Dress at the Baker Mansion

In the 19th century, the Baker Mansion in Altoona, Pennsylvania, was home to the Baker family. As the story goes, daughter Anna fell in love with and became secretly engaged to one of her father's employees. But when her father discovered the romance, he sent the suitor away. Poor Anna never got over her lost love, and she never married.

When the Blair County Historical Society took over the building in the 1920s, a beautiful wedding dress that belonged to Anna's rival, Elizabeth Bell, was put on display. Although the dress was showcased under glass in Anna's bedroom, it often moved and swayed of its own accord. Caretakers attributed the movement to a loose floorboard that jarred the case when visitors walked past. But security cameras recorded the dress moving when no one else was around. Eventually, like Anna's suitor, the wedding dress was removed.

Although the haunted dress is no longer displayed at the mansion, some Baker family spirits have apparently remained there. Apparitions have been seen in a mirror and on a staircase, and photos have also shown orbs and misty shadows.

The Relished Relic

Relics are an important element in several of the world's major religions. These ancient holy artifacts—thought to be pieces of a saint's or a significant leader's body or one of their personal belongings—are said to be imbued with spiritual power and are highly protected. But are they real or not? As some believers would say, you just have to have faith.

Many people dispute the authenticity of these holy objects. For example, it's impossible to be 100 percent sure that an old sword actually belonged to the real Saint Peter. Even so, people come from all over the world just to bask in the presence of these (often odd) artifacts.

✳ ✳ ✳ ✳

The Holy Prepuce

ACCORDING TO NEW Testament apocrypha (writings by early Christians about Jesus and his teachings that were not accepted into the holy canon), after baby Jesus was circumcised, an old Jewish woman saved his foreskin. But by the Middle Ages, several different foreskins were touted as the original and were worshipped as holy relics by various churches. Stories abound of various prepuces gifted to monks, stolen by thieves, dismissed by Popes, and marched in parades, all adding to the mystery of this particular (and particularly weird) relic.

The Tooth of Buddha

After the Buddha died (approximately 500 B.C.), it's said that his body was cremated. As the story goes, after the cremation, a follower retrieved the Buddha's left canine tooth from the funeral pyre. The tooth was given to the king and quickly became legendary: Whoever claimed the tooth would rule the land. Wars were fought over possession of the tooth for centuries, and now the tooth—or what's left of it 2,500 years later—rests in a temple in Sri Lanka.

The Sacred Relics

From the 16th to 19th centuries, sultans of the Ottoman Empire collected religious items of the Islamic faith. Most were said to be relics of various Islamic prophets, though many of the pieces are of questionable origin. Included in the collection, now held in Istanbul, are Moses's staff, a pot belonging to Abraham, and a piece of the prophet Muhammad's tooth. Perhaps the most important of the relics is the Blessed Mantle, the black wool shawl said to have been placed on a poet's shoulders by Muhammad himself.

Relics of Sainte-Chapelle

If you find yourself in Paris, visit Notre Dame to behold the collection of Sainte-Chapelle relics, including shards of the True Cross (believed to be actual wood from Christ's cross), relics of the Virgin Mary, the Mandylion (a piece of fabric similar to the Shroud of Turin on which Christ's face is said to appear), and something called the Holy Sponge, a blood-stained sponge that was said to be offered to Christ to drink from when he was languishing on the cross. The authenticity of these objects is as contested as any on this list, but the items are impressive if nothing else for surviving the French Revolution, when many relics were destroyed or lost.

Veronica's Veil

According to tradition, a woman named Veronica (she's not mentioned by name in the Bible) wiped the face of Jesus on his way toward Calvary. The fabric she used was said to have taken the imprint of Jesus' face. The veil can now be found in St. Peter's Basilica in Rome. Or maybe it's held in a friary outside of Rome—there's another version of the veil there. Regardless, plenty of people claim to have seen the bloodstained face of Jesus in the fabric of Veronica's veil and continue to make pilgrimages to worship it.

The Shroud of Turin

Of all the relics on this list, the Shroud of Turin is the one whose authenticity remains the most hotly debated, even more than 100 years after its discovery. Carbon dating originally proved the material, purportedly the shroud laid over Christ at the time of his burial, was produced in the Middle Ages, but it has since been proven incorrect—the garment is in fact older. Perhaps most fascinating about the Shroud is that the image itself is a negative; photographic methods were hardly known at the time of Christ's death, so how could anyone have faked such an image?

The Demise of Mohenjo-Daro

Located west of the Indus River in the Sindh province of Pakistan, the ancient city of Mohenjo-Daro is notable for its advanced infrastructure, which was unusually complex for its time. While the people who lived here seemed to possess greater knowledge and resources than their ancient counterparts, they abandoned their great city for unknown reasons, leaving behind some chilling clues.

An Amazing Find

AS EARLY AS the 1850s, British colonial officials discovered bricks belonging to the Mohenjo-Daro site, but they were unaware of their importance. It was not until 1920, when an Indian archaeologist by the name of R.D. Banerji visited the area, that the site was discovered. Banerji was excavating what he believed to be a Buddhist stupa—a mound-like structure used as a place of meditation—when he stumbled upon artifacts made of flint. Further excavation revealed an impressive Bronze-Age city. The city, thought to have been established around 2500 B.C., exhibited an impressive and advanced level of city planning, with a grid-like layout, a sewer system, and houses with bathrooms and toilets. Even the bricks used to build the city, once thought to be insignificant, were found to be more well-constructed than other bricks of the age.

Other finds included carved figures, copper and stone tools, metal bowls and pots, jewelry, and toys. Archaeologists also discovered tablets with writing in the Indus Script, but this language has never been fully deciphered, leaving researchers to glean what information they could about this civilization from the other discoveries at the site. Even so, it was clear that the inhabitants of this city were advanced for their time. Although its original name is unknown, archaeologists dubbed the city Mohenjo-Daro, which is often interpreted to mean "mound of the dead."

The Mystery of the 44

Much of Mohenjo-Daro had the appearance of a city abandoned. But in the uppermost levels of the city, researchers made a chilling discovery: 44 human skeletons, scattered throughout streets and houses, buried under layers of rubble, ash, and debris. The bodies were contorted into strange and unnatural positions. Some of the people appeared to have died while attempting to crawl to safety, which lead archaeologists to immediately assume that these 44 people had died a violent death. Had the city been attacked by an enemy? Some believed that an armed band of Indo-Aryans, a nomadic tribe from the northwest, ambushed the city as the 44 attempted to defend it. However, no weapons were found near the bodies, and none showed evidence of violent injuries.

Others believed that the bodies' contorted appearance was not due to violence, but rather illness. Cholera outbreaks were common at the time, and evidence seems to suggest that Mohenjo-Daro was prone to flooding. Even with their advanced sewer systems, a flood easily could have resulted in an outbreak in the city. But even this theory is not well-accepted, as modern scientific dating techniques have shown that these 44 people did not die at the same time. Some died years—and perhaps even centuries—earlier than others. Most scientists now conclude that the 44 probably died of natural causes.

The Mystery Deepens

Even if the 44 skeletons found at Mohenjo-Daro are the result of natural deaths, questions remain. Why, in a city so obviously advanced and orderly, were these people so unceremoniously and haphazardly buried? To archeologists, it appears as if the 44 were simply "dumped" into hastily-dug graves. Why have no other cemeteries or burial sites ever been found within the city? Estimates put the population of Mohenjo-Daro at around 40,000; surely these 44 were not the only people who died while the city existed.

But perhaps the most perplexing question is also the most basic: Why did the thousands of inhabitants of Mohenjo-Daro abandon their sophisticated city? With only an indecipherable language and few clues to go on, we may never know.

Antikythera's Mysterious Mechanism

In modern times, we've come to rely on computers for everything from daily correspondence to maintaining the temperature of our homes. Computers are used to fly planes, to calculate statistics, to inform, and to waste time. We think of this technology as a decidedly modern invention, created to keep pace with a progressing world. So it may be surprising to learn that the first computer was actually invented thousands of years ago.

✳ ✳ ✳ ✳

A Clock? Or Something More?

IN THE SPRING of 1900, a Greek ship captain named Dimitrios Kontos was leading a group of divers who were searching for sponges near the island of Antikythera. But they discovered something much more fascinating: a sunken Roman cargo ship. Archaeologists estimated the wreckage to be 2,000 years old, and over the next year, researchers with the

Hellenic Royal Navy retrieved artifacts from the site including vases, jewelry, and bronze statues.

The artifacts from the ancient ship were taken to the National Museum of Archaeology in Athens, where researchers began to comb through the items. This is when they came across an interesting find: in one of the recovered items, which first appeared to be nothing more than a lump of rock or wood, they noticed a gear wheel. The immediate assumption was that the artifact was some sort of clock or calendar, but after thousands of years at the bottom of the ocean, the corroded contraption was difficult to decipher. It was set aside, and, for decades, largely forgotten.

The First Computer

Then, in the 1950s, a Yale University professor by the name of Derek J. de Solla Price took an interest in the mechanism. He spent years studying the artifact, which was found to contain not just one gear but dozens of gears and other mechanisms. In a paper he wrote for *Scientific American*, Price concluded that the mechanism was an ancient version of "a modern analogue computer" which could predict the positions of planets and stars years in advance.

Price's research was limited by the technology of his time, but modern scientists have used X-rays, CT scans, and 3-D mapping technology to learn even more about the Antikythera mechanism. What they've discovered is amazing: This ancient device could perform complicated mathematical calculations in seconds. A user would input basic variables—like a date—then simply turn a knob or handle on the side of the device and the mechanism could display all kinds of astronomical information about that date.

Researchers have also recently discovered tiny inscriptions written in ancient Greek which provide even more information about the device. The machine could calculate the position of the sun and moon in relation to the 12 constellations of the zodiac; predict eclipses; contained a solar and lunar calendar; and possessed a dial that counted down the days to ancient sporting events.

Heed the Warning

The biggest mystery surrounding the Antikythera mechanism is how the ancient Greeks were capable of constructing such a complicated device. While it is thought to date to somewhere between 205 and 60 B.C., similar "calculating" technology was not seen again until the 17th century. It is astounding that whoever constructed the mechanism not only had modern-day knowledge of astronomy, but also mathematics and mechanics. Exactly who built the machine, and why, are also unknown. Perhaps it was used for research or a teaching tool. Some theorize that the sunken ship was traveling to a triumphal parade for Julius Caesar; was the mechanism created to impress the dictator?

Regardless of its origin or purpose, the Antikythera mechanism remains the earliest example of an analog computer ever discovered. Price seemed to believe that it could also serve as a warning to those of us in the modern age to never take our knowledge for granted. "It is a bit frightening," he once wrote, "to know that just before the fall of their great civilization the ancient Greeks had come so close to our age, not only in their thought, but also in their scientific technology."

Can You Crack the Code?

Located in Langley, Virginia, the Central Intelligence Agency is a service of the United States federal government that is focused on overseas intelligence gathering. The agency has a reputation for being secretive and covert, and most Americans know little about it. Which makes the bizarre sculpture that sits on the CIA's grounds even more mysterious.

✳ ✳ ✳ ✳

A Unique Commission

IN 1990, WORK began on a new building in which to house the headquarters of the CIA. Fittingly dubbed the New Headquarters Building (NHB), the agency decided that the courtyard of the building should be spruced up with a bit of artwork. Using a federal program called "Art in Architecture," which oversees the creation of artwork for federal buildings around the country, the agency evaluated potential artists in order to choose one for the project. They eventually gave the $250,000 commission for the NHB artwork to Washington, D.C., artist Jim Sanborn.

The CIA laid out several principles for the artwork to be displayed at the agency, including requirements that it to be "positive," and reflect "well-being" and "hope." But Sanborn's final piece was more than just an aesthetically pleasing statue in the middle of a courtyard. In fact, it went well beyond mere artwork, inspiring the imaginations of not just the employees at the CIA and visitors to the building, but curiosity seekers worldwide. So exactly what is it that is so unusual about Sanborn's art piece?

"Hidden" in Plain Sight

The sculpture, entitled "Kryptos" (the Greek word for "hidden"), is made up of several parts. Two red granite and copper plated constructions begin the piece, which are engraved with International Morse code and ancient cyphers. There is also a stone slab with an engraving of a navigational compass, which points to a lodestone, or a naturally magnetized rock.

While these pieces are certainly unique, it is the centerpiece of the installation that has been causing a stir for three decades. It consists of a large sheet of copper, shaped like a giant S, with exactly 1,735 alphabetic letters cut into it. At first glance, it seems to be random and nonsensical, the jumbled letters haphazardly carved into the metal like a giant sheet of gibberish. But nothing about Kryptos is random; Sanborn actually designed his sculpture to be a cryptographic message.

An Enigma Wrapped in a Puzzle

Kryptos contains four encoded messages, which, according to Sanborn, will reveal one final puzzle once they're decoded. But decoding the strange cypher has proven to be quite the challenge, even for the code experts at the CIA. It took nine years for anyone to come forward with a solution to part of the code, although computer experts at the NSA later proved to have solved the same sections in 1993 (presumably they kept quiet so as not to ruin the fun for anyone else).

While the first three sections of Kryptos have now been solved and can be found on many sites on the Internet, the fourth, while relatively short at only 97 characters, has confounded even the smartest people in the world and remains unsolved. Sanborn has offered help by releasing several clues: the words "NORTHEAST," "BERLIN," and "CLOCK," along with their positions within the code. But even with the clues, the message remains elusive.

It is fitting that an art piece at the CIA should honor the history of cryptography, which is the art of writing and solving codes. Sanborn's puzzle within a puzzle has provided cryptographers—both amateur and professional—a challenge worthy of the most gripping spy novel.

The Ten-Letter Mystery

In Staffordshire, England, there sits a country mansion full of ornately appointed rooms and opulent furniture. It once housed earls and duchesses (and even, for a time, Queen Victoria), but now it is owned by the National Trust, an organization dedicated to environmental and historical conservation, and is open to the public. But the house, known as Shugborough Hall, is not the only curiosity that draws visitors to this spot.

✳   ✳   ✳   ✳

An Idyllic, but Odd, Location

SHUGBOROUGH HALL WAS originally a monastery, until the mid-16th century when King Henry VIII decreed that all monasteries, convents, and friaries in England be disbanded. In 1624, the estate was purchased by a lawyer named William Anson. Over the next two centuries, members of the Anson family worked to make Shugborough Hall their vision of a "perfect paradise," extending the house, adding pavilions, and commissioning monuments for the grounds.

Some of the family's additions are a bit odd, such as a Chinese-style house and red iron footbridge that adorn the landscape. There are also monuments constructed in an ancient Greek style, including a Doric temple and an arch created in the style of the Arch of Hadrian in Athens. There's even a monument in honor of a cat—although it is unknown whose cat inspired its construction.

A Strange Carving

While the identity of the honored cat may be a mystery, it is a different monument on the grounds, tucked away in a stone arch, that has been a source of endless curiosity for hundreds of years. Known as the Shepherd's Monument, it was commissioned by the Anson family sometime between 1748 and 1763, and created by Flemish sculptor Peter Scheemakers. The main part of the sculpture consists of a mirrored, relief copy of Nicolas Poussin's painting *Et in Arcadia ego*, or *The Shepherds of*

Arcadia, which depicts a woman and three shepherds gathered around a tomb. Above the sculpture and over the stone arch, Scheemakers added stone heads—one a smiling bald-headed man, and the other the goat-like head of the Greek god Pan.

But below the relief carving is the strangest, yet simplest, part of the monument: ten letters, that seem to have no rhyme or reason. The letters "OUOSVAVV" are carved into the stone, flanked by a "D" and an "M." The meaning of these letters, and why they were added to the monument, has remained a mystery. It is not even known if Scheemakers added these letters himself, or if another craftsman carved the strange cypher into the stone.

A Search for the Holy Grail?

Regardless of who created them or why, these ten letters have completely confounded historians, investigators, and code-breakers, but theories abound. Many have interpreted the "D" and "M" to refer to the Latin phrase *Dis Manibus*, an inscription often found on Roman tombs that means "dedicated to the shades." Of course, the Shepherd's Monument is not a Roman tomb, so not everyone buys into this theory.

But the idea that each letter in the carving could correspond to the first letter of a word in a phrase is a strongly held hypothesis amongst investigators. One theory states that "OUOSVAVV" refers to *Orator Ut Omnia Sunt Vanitas Ait Vanitas Vanitatum*, a Latin interpretation of Ecclesiastes 12:8: "Vanity of vanities, saith the preacher; all is vanity." Another biblical theory posits that John 14:6, "I am the Way, the Truth, and the Life," is reflected in the letters, which may stand for *Oro Ut Omnes Sequantur Viam Ad Veram Vitam* ("I pray that all may follow the Way to True Life").

But some investigators believe the random letters are a code that refers to a name, a navigational direction, or, perhaps most fanciful of all, the location of the Holy Grail. This last theory was even mentioned in author Dan Brown's bestselling book *The Da Vinci Code*, inspiring a new generation of grail-seekers to visit the mysterious monument. None of the theories surrounding this bizarre inscription have ever been proven, making the Shepherd's Monument one of the most enduring uncracked codes in the world.

Who Was Robert C. Christian?

Elbert County, Georgia, is about 90 miles east of Atlanta. Its largest city, Elberton, has a population of only 4,653, and the entire county is home to just over 20,000 residents. But this rural county boasts many historical and cultural areas of interest, including several state parks, sites honoring Revolutionary War heroes, and, most famous of all, the Georgia Guidestones.

✳ ✳ ✳ ✳

Set in Stone

O N A STRETCH of barren land in rural Georgia, a collection of large stones—sometimes called "the American

Stonehenge"—has been fascinating and confusing visitors for decades. Arranged in a star pattern, the five gigantic slabs of granite support a 25,000-pound capstone. The stones are nearly twice as tall as the stones used at Stonehenge and are inscribed with 10 strange messages. These messages are written not only in English, but also in Swahili, Russian, Spanish, Sanskrit, Hebrew, Arabic, and Chinese.

The messages range from innocuous New Age ideology (prize truth, beauty, and love) to what sounds like a warning of overpopulation (maintain humanity in perpetual balance with nature). Since the population of the Earth far exceeds the 500 million directed by the stones, many have deduced that the bizarre structure is meant as a "guide" to the survivors of a cataclysmic apocalypse. But others worry that the stones are part of a "New World Order" and a plot to rid the planet of most of its population.

Even though visitors can see echoes of ancient Stonehenge in the Georgia Guidestones—like Stonehenge, the stones in Georgia have astronomical features—the monument was actually constructed in modern times, having been erected in 1980. So why can't we simply ask the architect of the monument about the purpose of the structure?

A Mysterious Visitor

The answer is that no one knows who designed this curious monument. As the story goes, a man using the pseudonym Robert C. Christian went to the offices of Elberton Granite Finishing in June 1979. Claiming to represent a "small group of loyal Americans," the man presented his concept of the structure to Joe Fendley, the president of Elberton Granite. Christian explained that the giant structure he had in mind would function as a compass, a calendar, and a clock, and would need to be strong enough to withstand even the most catastrophic events. This man and his "group of loyal

Americans" had been planning the monument for 20 years, he said, but they wished to remain completely anonymous.

At first, Fendley assumed that Christian was a bit off his rocker. To dissuade the mysterious man, Fendley quoted him a price several times higher than any previous project he'd worked on. But to his surprise, Christian quickly accepted the price and simply asked how long construction would take. Fendley next sent the man to Wyatt Martin, the president of Granite City Bank. Like Fendley, Martin was at first convinced that the enigmatic Christian was a "kook," but the more they spoke, the more Martin realized that the man was quite serious about constructing his strange monument.

Can You Keep a Secret?

But there was one problem: Martin needed to know the man's true identity so he could confirm that he would, in fact, be able to pay for the huge stone structure. So the two worked out a deal: Christian would reveal his identity to Martin, but Martin would have to sign a confidentiality agreement promising to never disclose his name. He also agreed to destroy all documents and records pertaining to the project once it was completed. To this day, Martin remains the only person who ever knew the identity of the architect of the Guidestones.

The theory that the stones are a guide for the survivors of an apocalypse is still the most common theory; however, many other notions exist. Some believe the stones are "Satanic," while others believe they were commissioned by a mystical spiritual group called the Rosicrucians. Some are even convinced that Christian was actually Ted Turner of CNN fame, who lived close by in Atlanta and could certainly afford to pay for such a structure.

While the identity of the mysterious Robert C. Christian and the reasoning behind his bizarre monument may never be known, the Georgia Guidestones will continue to fire the imaginations of visitors to this rural location.

The Easter Island Tablets

Rapa Nui, usually known by its more common name, Easter Island, lies in the southeastern Pacific Ocean and is famous for its moai, monolithic human figures carved by the island's inhabitants between 1250 and 1500. But this remote island is also the origin of a puzzling form of writing that has stumped scientists since its discovery.

✳ ✳ ✳ ✳

An Industrious People

CONSIDERED TO BE one of the most remote islands in the world, Easter Island is more than 1,200 miles away from its nearest inhabited neighbor. Polynesian explorers braved the open Pacific Ocean and somehow found their way to the island around the year 1200. Archaeologists believe that these people created a thriving community, evidenced most notably by the nearly 1,000 enormous stone moai on the island. These monolithic human figures, which all feature unusually large heads, are said to represent the ancestors of the Rapa Nui people.

The moai have fascinated archaeologists for centuries. It is remarkable that the inhabitants of this remote island were able to create such impressive sculptures using tools and methods that we would no doubt find "primitive" today. But studying these stone monoliths, and Easter Island itself, has provided researchers with valuable information about the Rapa Nui people and their culture.

There are other artifacts found on the island, however, that have proven to be much more mysterious than the famous moai figures.

Mysterious Symbols

In the 19th century, a Roman Catholic missionary named Eugene Eyraud visited Easter Island and kept a journal of his thoughts and impressions. He wrote of discovering dozens of "wooden tablets or sticks covered in several sorts of hieroglyphic characters." Ultimately, 26 objects were recovered from Easter Island that contained this peculiar script. The writing seems to mostly depict animals, plants, humans, and geometric forms.

The script was dubbed "rongorongo," which, in the Rapa Nui language, means "to recite, to declaim, to chant out." The writing on the tablets is neat and tidy, with many of the wooden objects "fluted" with grooves to provide a straight-lined guide. Expert scribes of rongorongo used small stones or shark teeth to carve the figures.

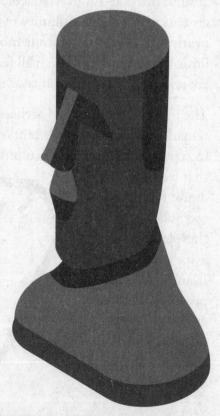

Lost in Translation

To this day, the rongorongo writing on these tablets has proved indecipherable. If it is true writing, that would mean that rongorongo is one of very few examples of a writing system that independently arose within a culture. But some researchers believe the script is not true writing but rather "proto-writing," which is a way to convey information without specific linguistic intent. Also unknown is the age of the tablets. Some of the writing is found on Pacific rosewood, a tree that was found throughout Polynesia and brought to Easter Island by the first settlers. But other rongorongo is found on oars that came from a Western boat. Since Europeans did not first arrive on Easter Island until the early 18th century, it is assumed that these tablets are much younger than the others.

Making translation of the tablets especially difficult are several factors. First is the fact that very few inhabitants of Easter Island were literate. The handful that were—the expert scribes, priests, and tribal leaders who inscribed the tablets—were wiped out, either due to epidemics of illness or during slave raids. Another problem is the very limited number of texts that have been found, giving researchers limited context to decipher the script. And finally, the Rapa Nui language spoken today is vastly different from what was spoken centuries ago, as influence from Tahiti and other Polynesian islands affected the language. In fact, today, as a territory of Chile, Spanish is most commonly spoken on Easter Island.

Although we don't know what the Rapa Nui people wanted to convey on these tablets, they believed it was important enough to painstakingly carve it into these artifacts. Perhaps one day, this linguistic mystery will be solved.

CHAPTER 7

UNEXPLAINED PHENOMENA

Odd Happenings

If a phenomenon can't be readily explained, does that make it any less true to those who witnessed it?

✳ ✳ ✳ ✳

The Philadelphia Experiment

THE PHILADELPHIA EXPERIMENT (aka Project Rainbow) is one for the "too strange not to be true" file. Allegedly, on October 28, 1943, a supersecret experiment was being conducted at the Philadelphia Naval Shipyard. Its objective? To make the USS *Eldridge* and all of its inhabitants disappear! That day, some reported that the *Eldridge* became almost entirely invisible amidst a flash of blue light. Inexplicably, it had not only vanished but also tele-transported—at the same instant, it was witnessed some 375 miles away at the U.S. Naval Base in Norfolk, Virginia. Legend has it that most sailors involved in the experiment became violently ill afterward. They were the lucky ones. Others were supposedly fused to the ship's deck or completely vaporized and were never seen again. Justifiably horrified by these results, the navy is said to have pulled the plug on future experiments and employed brainwashing techniques to help the affected seamen forget what happened.

Moodus Noises

The Moodus Noises are thunderlike sounds that emanate from caves near East Haddam, Connecticut, where the Salmon and Moodus Rivers meet. The name itself is derived from the Native American word *machemoodus*, which means "place of noises." When European settlers filtered into the area in the late 1600s, the Wangunk tribe warned them about the odd, supernatural sounds. Whether or not anything otherworldly exists there is open to debate. In 1979, seismologists showed that the noises were always accompanied by small earthquakes (some measuring as low as magnitude 2 on the Richter scale) spread over a small area some 5,000 feet deep by 800 feet wide. But this doesn't explain the fact that no known faultline exists at Moodus. Nor does it describe how small tremors—producing 100 times less ground motion than is detectable by human beings—can generate big, bellowing booms. The mystery and the booms continue.

Rock Concert

Visitors looking to entertain themselves at Pennsylvania's Ringing Rocks Park often show up toting hammers. Seems odd, but they're necessary for the proper tone. Ringing Rocks is a seven-acre boulder field that runs about ten feet deep. For reasons that are still unexplained, some of these rocks ring like bells when struck lightly by a hammer or other object. Because igneous diabase rocks don't usually do this, the boulder field has caused quite a stir through the years. In 1890, Dr. J. J. Ott held what may have been the world's first "rock concert" at the park. He assembled rocks of different pitches, enlisted the aid of a brass band for accompaniment, and went to town.

Cry Me a Red River

Tales of "crying" statues have become almost commonplace. Sometimes they're revealed as hoaxes, but other times they can truly confound the senses. The Mother Mary statue that cries "tears of blood" at the Vietnamese Catholic Martyrs Church in Sacramento apparently began crying in November 2005 when parishioners discovered a dark reddish substance flowing from her left eye. A priest wiped it away only to see it miraculously reappear a moment later. News of the incident spread like . . .

well, like news of a crying Mother Mary statue. Soon, hordes of the faithful made a pilgrimage to witness the miracle. Skeptics say that black paint used as eyeliner on the statue is the true culprit and that her "tears" are closer to this color than red. The faithful think the nonbelievers are blinded by anything but the light because the tears continually reappear even after the excess substance is wiped away.

The Kecksburg Incident

Did visitors from outer space once land in a western Pennsylvania thicket?

✳ ✳ ✳ ✳

Dropping in for a Visit

ON DECEMBER 9, 1965, an unidentified flying object (UFO) streaked through the late-afternoon sky and landed in Kecksburg—a rural Pennsylvania community about 40 miles southeast of Pittsburgh. This much is not disputed. However, specific accounts vary widely from person to person. Even after closely examining the facts, many people remain undecided about exactly what happened. "Roswell" type incidents—ultra-mysterious in nature and reeking of a governmental cover-up—have an uncanny way of causing confusion.

Trajectory-Interruptus

A meteor on a collision course with Earth will generally "bounce" as it enters the atmosphere. This occurs due to friction, which forcefully slows the average space rock from 6 to 45 miles per second to a few hundred miles per hour, the speed at which it strikes Earth and officially becomes a meteorite. According to the official explanation offered by the U.S. Air Force, it was a meteorite that landed in Kecksburg. However, witnesses reported that the object completed back and forth maneuvers before landing at a very low speed—moves that an un-powered chunk of earthbound rock simply cannot perform. Strike one against the meteor theory.

An Acorn-Shape Meteorite?

When a meteor manages to pierce Earth's atmosphere, it has the physical properties of exactly what it is: a space rock. That is to say, it will generally be unevenly shaped, rough, and darkish in color, much like rocks found on Earth. But at Kecksburg, eyewitnesses reported seeing something far, far different. The unusual object they described was bronze to golden in color, acorn-shape, and as large as a Volkswagen Beetle automobile. Unless the universe has started to produce uniformly shaped and colored meteorites, the official explanation seems highly unlikely. Strike two for the meteor theory.

Markedly Different

Then there's the baffling issue of markings. A meteorite can be chock-full of holes, cracks, and other such surface imperfections. It can also vary somewhat in color. But it should never, ever have markings that seem intelligently designed. Witnesses at Kecksburg describe intricate writings similar to Egyptian hieroglyphics located near the base of the object. A cursory examination of space rocks at any natural history museum reveals that such a thing doesn't occur naturally. Strike three for the meteor theory. Logically following such a trail, could an unnatural force have been responsible for the item witnessed at Kecksburg? At least one man thought so.

Reportis Rigor Mortis

Just after the Kecksburg UFO landed, reporter John Murphy arrived at the scene. Like any seasoned pro, the newsman immediately snapped photos and gathered eyewitness accounts of the event. Strangely, FBI agents arrived, cordoned off the area, and confiscated all but one roll of his film. Undaunted, Murphy assembled a radio documentary entitled *Object in the Woods* to describe his experience. Just before the special was to air, the reporter received an unexpected visit by two men. According to a fellow employee, a dark-suited pair identified themselves as government agents and subsequently confiscated a portion of Murphy's audiotapes. A week later, a clearly perturbed Murphy aired a watered-down version of his documentary. In it, he claimed that certain interviewees requested their accounts be removed for fear of retribution at the hands of police, military, and government officials. In 1969, John Murphy was struck dead by an unidentified car while crossing the street.

Resurrected by Robert Stack

In all likelihood the Kecksburg incident would have remained dormant and under-explored had it not been for the television show *Unsolved Mysteries*. In a 1990 segment, narrator Robert Stack took an in-depth look at what occurred in Kecksburg, feeding a firestorm of interest that eventually brought forth two new witnesses. The first, a U.S. Air Force officer stationed at Lockbourne AFB (near Columbus, Ohio), claimed to have seen a flatbed truck carrying a mysterious object as it arrived on base on December 10, 1965. The military man told of a tarpaulin-covered conical object that he couldn't identify and a "shoot to kill" order given to him for anyone who ventured too close. He was told that the truck was bound for Wright–Patterson AFB in Dayton, Ohio, an installation that's alleged to contain downed flying saucers. The other witness was a building contractor who claimed to have delivered 6,500 special bricks to a hanger inside Wright–Patterson AFB on December 12, 1965. Curious, he peeked inside the hanger and saw a "bell-shaped" device, 12-feet high, surrounded by several men wearing anti-radiation style suits. Upon leaving, he was told that he had just witnessed an object that would become "common knowledge" in the next 20 years.

Will We Ever Know the Truth?

Like Roswell before it, we will probably never know for certain what occurred in western Pennsylvania back in 1965. The more that's learned about the case, the more confusing and contradictory it becomes. For instance, the official 1965 meteorite explanation contains more holes than Bonnie and Clyde's death car, and other explanations, such as orbiting space debris (from past U.S. and Russian missions) reentering Earth's atmosphere, seem equally preposterous. In 2005, as the result of a new investigation launched by the Sci-Fi Television Network, NASA asserted that the object was a Russian satellite. According to a NASA spokesperson, documents of this investigation were somehow misplaced in the 1990s. Mysteriously, this finding directly contradicts the official Air Force version that nothing at all was found at the Kecksburg site. It also runs counter to a 2003 report made by NASA's own Nicholas L. Johnson, Chief Scientist for Orbital Debris. That document shows no missing satellites at the time of the incident. This includes a missing Russian Venus Probe (since accounted for)—the item that was once considered a prime crash candidate.

Brave New World

These days, visitors to Kecksburg will be hard-pressed to find any trace of the encounter—perhaps that's how it should be. Since speculation comes to an abrupt halt whenever a concrete answer is provided, Kecksburg's reputation as "Roswell of the East" looks secure, at least for the foreseeable future. But if one longs for proof that something mysterious occurred there, they need look no further than the backyard of the Kecksburg Volunteer Fire Department. There, in all of its acorn-shape glory, stands an full-scale mock-up of the spacecraft reportedly found in this peaceful town on December 9, 1965. There too rests the mystery, intrigue, and romance that have accompanied this alleged space traveler for more than 40 years.

The Watseka Wonder

The story of the "Watseka Wonder," a phenomenon that occurred in a small town in Illinois in the late 1800s, still stands as one of the most authentic cases of spirit possession in history. It has been investigated, dissected, and ridiculed, but to this day, no clear explanation has ever been offered.

✳   ✳   ✳   ✳

An Otherworldly Connection

BEGINNING ON JULY 11, 1877, 13-year-old Watseka resident Lurancy Vennum started falling into strange trances that sometimes lasted for hours. During these trances, she claimed to speak with spirits and visit heaven. But when she awoke, she could not recall what had occurred during the spell.

Doctors diagnosed Lurancy as mentally ill and recommended that she be sent to the state insane asylum. But in January 1878, a man named Asa Roff, who also lived in Watseka, visited the Vennums. He told them that his daughter Mary had displayed the same behavior as Lurancy nearly 13 years before, and he advised the family to keep Lurancy out of the asylum.

Roff explained that on July 5, 1865, his 19-year-old daughter Mary had died in the state insane asylum. In the beginning, strange voices filled her head. Then she fell into long trances where she spoke as though possessed by the spirits of the dead. She later developed an obsession with bloodletting, poking herself with pins, applying leeches to her body, and cutting herself with a razor. Finally, her parents took her to the asylum, where she died a short time later.

The Strange Case of Lurancy Vennum

At the time of Mary Roff's death, Lurancy Vennum was barely a year old. Born on April 16, 1864, Lurancy moved with her family to Watseka a few years after Mary Roff's death and knew nothing of the girl or her family. When Lurancy's attacks began in July 1877, her family had no idea that she was suffering from the same type of illness that Mary had.

On the morning of her first trance, Lurancy collapsed and fell into a deep sleep that lasted more than five hours. When she awoke, she seemed fine. But the spell returned again the next day, and this time, while Lurancy was unconscious, she spoke of seeing angels and walking in heaven. She told her family that she had talked to her brother, who had died three years before.

As rumors of Lurancy's affliction spread around town, Asa Roff realized how closely her symptoms mirrored those of his own daughter, and he was convinced that the illnesses were the same. Roff kept quiet, but when it was suggested that Lurancy be institutionalized, he knew he had to speak up.

When Roff contacted the Vennum family on January 31, 1878, they were skeptical, but they allowed him to bring Dr. E. Winchester Stevens to meet with Lurancy. Like Roff, Dr. Stevens was a spiritualist. They felt that Lurancy was not insane but was possessed by spirits of the dead.

When Dr. Stevens arrived, Lurancy began speaking in another voice, claiming that she was a woman named Katrina Hogan. A few moments later, her voice changed again, and she said that she was Willie Canning, a boy who had killed himself many years before. Willie spoke for more than an hour. Then, just as Dr. Stevens and Asa Roff prepared to leave, Lurancy threw her arms into the air and fell on the floor stiff as a board. After Dr. Stevens calmed her down, Lurancy claimed she was in heaven and that spirits, some good and some bad, were controlling her body. She said the good spirit who most wanted to control her was a young woman named Mary Roff.

The Return of Mary Roff

After about a week of being possessed by the spirit of Mary Roff, Lurancy insisted on leaving the Vennum house, which was unfamiliar to her, and going "home" to the Roff house.

When Mrs. Roff heard what was going on, she rushed over to the Vennum house with her daughter Minerva. As Lurancy watched the two women hurry up the sidewalk, she cried out, "There comes my ma and my sister Nervie!" "Nervie" had been Mary's pet name for her sister.

To those involved, it seemed evident that Mary's spirit had taken over Lurancy's body. She looked the same, but she knew nothing of the Vennum family or of her life as Lurancy. Instead, she had intimate knowledge of the Roffs and acted as though they were her family. Although Lurancy treated the Vennums politely, they were strangers to her.

On February 11, realizing that it was best for Lurancy, the Vennums allowed their daughter to go stay with the Roffs—although Lurancy told the Roffs that she would only be with them until "sometime in May."

On their way home, as the Roffs and Lurancy traveled past the house where they'd lived when Mary died, Lurancy wanted to know why they weren't stopping. The Roffs explained that they'd moved to a new home a few years back, which was something that Lurancy/Mary would not have known.

Within a short time, Lurancy began to exhibit signs that she knew more about the Roffs and their habits than she could have possibly known if she was only pretending to be Mary. She knew of incidents and experiences that were private and had taken place long before she was even born.

As promised, Lurancy stayed with the Roff family until early May. When it was time for Mary to leave Lurancy's body, she was saddened, but she seemed to understand that it was time to go. On May 21, Lurancy returned to the Vennums. She showed no signs of her earlier illness, and her parents and the Roffs believed that she had been cured of her affliction by the possession of Mary's spirit.

Lurancy grew into a happy young woman and exhibited no ill effects from the possession. She married and had 13 children.

An Unsolved Mystery

Although Lurancy had no memories of being possessed by Mary, she felt a closeness to the Roffs that she could never explain. She stayed in touch with the Roff family even after they moved away from Watseka in 1879. Each year, when they returned, Lurancy would allow Mary's spirit to possess her, and things were just as they were for a time in 1878.

A Fiery Debate: Spontaneous Human Combustion

Proponents contend that the phenomenon—in which a person suddenly bursts into flames—is very real. Skeptics, however, are quick to explain it away.

✳ ✳ ✳ ✳

The Curious Case of Helen Conway

A PHOTO DOCUMENTS THE gruesome death of Helen Conway. Visible in the black-and-white image—taken in 1964 in Delaware County, Pennsylvania—is an oily smear that was her torso and, behind, an ashen specter of the upholstered bedroom chair she occupied. The picture's most haunting feature might be her legs, thin and ghostly pale, clearly intact and seemingly unscathed by whatever it was that consumed the rest of her.

What consumed her, say proponents of a theory that people can catch fire without an external source of ignition, was spontaneous human combustion. It's a classic case, believers assert: Conway was immolated by an intense, precisely localized source of heat that damaged little else in the room. Adding to the mystery, the investigating fire marshal said that it took just 21 minutes for her to burn away and that he could not identify an outside accelerant.

If Conway's body ignited from within and burned so quickly she had no time to rise and seek help, hers wouldn't be the first or last death to fit the pattern of spontaneous human combustion.

The phenomenon was documented as early as 1763 by Frenchman Jonas Dupont in his collection of accounts, published as *De Incendis Corporis Humani Spontaneis*. Charles Dickens's 1852 novel *Bleak House* sensationalized the issue with the spontaneous-combustion death of a character named Krook. That humans have been reduced to ashes with little damage to their surroundings is not the stuff of fiction, however. Many documented cases exist. The question is, did these people combust spontaneously?

How It Happens

Theories advancing the concept abound. Early hypotheses held that victims, such as Dickens's Krook, were likely alcoholics so besotted that their very flesh became flammable. Later conjecture blamed the influence of geomagnetism. A 1996 book by John Heymer, *The Entrancing Flame*, maintained emotional distress could lead to explosions of defective mitochondria. These outbursts cause cellular releases of hydrogen and oxygen and trigger crematory reactions in the body. That same year, Larry E. Arnold—publicity material calls him a parascientist— published *Ablaze! The Mysterious Fires of Spontaneous Human Combustion*. Arnold claimed sufferers were struck by a subatomic particle he had discovered and named the "pyrotron."

Perhaps somewhat more credible reasoning came out of Brooklyn, New York, where the eponymous founder of Robin Beach Engineers Associated (described as a scientific detective agency) linked the theory of spontaneous human combustion with proven instances of individuals whose biology caused them to retain intense concentrations of static electricity.

A Controversy Is Sparked

Skeptics are legion. They suspect that accounts are often embellished or important facts are ignored. That the unfortunate Helen Conway was overweight and a heavy smoker, for instance, likely played a key role in her demise.

Indeed, Conway's case is considered by some to be evidence of the wick effect, which might be today's most forensically respected explanation for spontaneous human combustion. It holds that an external source, such as a dropped cigarette, ignites bedding, clothing, or furnishings. This material acts like an absorbing wick, while the body's fat takes on the fueling role of candle wax. The burning fat liquefies, saturating the bedding, clothing, or furnishings, and keeps the heat localized.

The result is a long, slow immolation that burns away fatty tissues, organs, and associated bone, leaving leaner areas, such as legs, untouched. Experiments on pig carcasses show it can take five or more hours, with the body's water boiling off ahead of the spreading fire.

Under the wick theory, victims are likely to already be unconscious when the fire starts. They're in closed spaces with little moving air, so the flames are allowed to smolder, doing their work without disrupting the surroundings or alerting passersby.

Nevertheless, even the wick effect theory, like all other explanations of spontaneous human combustion, has scientific weaknesses. The fact remains, according to the mainstream science community, that evidence of spontaneous human combustion is entirely circumstantial, and that not a single proven eyewitness account exists to substantiate anyone's claims of "Poof—the body just went up in flames!"

John Lennon Sees a UFO

Lucy in the sky with warp drive.

✳ ✳ ✳ ✳

I N MAY 1974, former Beatle John Lennon and his assistant/mistress May Pang returned to New York City after almost a year's stay in Los Angeles, a period to which Lennon would later refer as his "Lost Weekend." The pair moved into Penthouse Tower B at 434 East 52nd Street. As Lennon watched television on a hot summer night, he noticed flashing lights reflected in the glass of an open door that led onto a patio. At first dismissing it as a neon sign, Lennon suddenly realized that since the apartment was on the roof, the glass *couldn't* be reflecting light from the street. So—sans clothing— he ventured onto the terrace to investigate. What he witnessed has never been satisfactorily explained.

Speechless

As Pang recollected, Lennon excitedly called for her to come outside. Pang did so. "I looked up and stopped mid-sentence," she said later. "I couldn't even speak because I saw this thing up there . . . it was silvery, and it was flying very slowly. There was a white light shining around the rim and a red light on the top . . . [it] was silent. We started to watch it drift down, tilt slightly, and it was flying below rooftops. It was the most amazing sight." She quickly ran back into the apartment, grabbed her camera, and returned to the patio, clicking away.

Lennon friend and rock photography legend Bob Gruen picked up the story: "In those days, you didn't have answering machines, but a service [staffed by people], and I had received a call from 'Dr. Winston.'" (Lennon's original middle name was Winston, and he often used the alias "Dr. Winston O'Boogie.") When Gruen returned the call, Lennon explained his incredible sighting and insisted that the photographer come round to pick up and develop the film personally. "He was serious,"

Gruen said. "He wouldn't call me in the middle of the night to joke around." Gruen noted that although Lennon had been known to partake in mind-altering substances in the past, during this period he was totally straight. So was Pang, a non-drinker who never took drugs and whom Gruen characterized as "a clear-headed young woman."

The film in Pang's camera was a unique type supplied by Gruen, "four times as fast as the highest speed then [commercially] available." Gruen had been using this specialty film, usually employed for military reconnaissance, in low-light situations such as recording studios. The same roll already had photos of Lennon and former bandmate Ringo Starr, taken by Pang in Las Vegas during a recording session.

Gruen asked Lennon if he'd reported his sighting to the authorities. "Yeah, like I'm going to call the police and say I'm John Lennon and I've seen a flying saucer," the musician scoffed. Gruen picked up the couple's phone and contacted the police, *The Daily News*, and the *New York Times*. The photographer claims that the cops and the *News* admitted that they'd heard similar reports, while the *Times* just hung up on him.

It Would Have Been the Ultimate Trip

Gruen's most amusing recollection of Lennon, who had been hollering "UFO!" and "Take me with you!" was that none of his NYC neighbors either saw or heard the naked, ex-Beatle screaming from his penthouse terrace. Disappointingly, no one who might have piloted the craft responded to Lennon's pleas.

Gruen took the exposed film home to process, "sandwiching" it between two rolls of his own. Gruen's negatives came out perfectly, but the film Pang shot was "like a clear plastic strip," Gruen says. "We were all baffled . . . that it was completely blank."

Lennon remained convinced of what he'd seen. In several shots from a subsequent photo session with Gruen that produced the iconic shot of the musician wearing a New York City T-shirt (a gift from the photographer), John points to where he'd spotted the craft. And on his *Walls and Bridges* album, Lennon wrote in the liner notes: "On the 23rd Aug. 1974 at 9 o'clock I saw a U.F.O.—J.L."

Who's to say he and May Pang didn't? Certainly not Gruen, who still declares—more than 35 years after the fact—"I believed them."

And so the mystery remains.

The Magnetic Hill Phenomenon

It has taken researchers hundreds of years to finally solve the mystery of magnetic hills, or spook hills, as they're often called. This phenomenon, found all over the world, describes places where objects—including cars in neutral gear—move uphill on a slightly sloping road, seemingly defying gravity.

❋   ❋   ❋   ❋

MONCTON, IN NEW Brunswick, Canada, lays claim to one of the more famous magnetic hills, called, appropriately, Magnetic Hill. Over the years, it has also been called Fool's Hill and Magic Hill. Since the location made headlines in 1931, hundreds of thousands of tourists have flocked there to witness this phenomenon for themselves.

Go Figure

Much to the dismay of paranormal believers, people in science once assumed that a magnetic anomaly caused this event. But advanced physics has concluded this phenomenon is due "to the visual anchoring of the sloping surface to a gravity-relative eye level whose perceived direction is biased by sloping surroundings." In nonscientific jargon, all that says is that it's an optical illusion.

Papers published in the journal of the Association of

Psychological Science supported this conclusion based on a series of experiments done with models. They found that if the horizon cannot be seen or is not level then people may be fooled by objects that they expect to be vertical but aren't. False perspective is also a culprit; think, for example, of a line of poles on the horizon that seem to get larger or smaller depending on distance.

Engineers with plumb lines, one made of iron and one made of stone, demonstrated that a slope appearing to go uphill might in reality be going downhill. A good topographical map may also be sufficient to show which way the land is really sloping.

I Know a Place

Other notable magnetic hills can be found in Wisconsin, Pennsylvania, California, Florida, Barbados, Scotland, Australia, Italy, Greece, and South Korea.

Circle Marks the Spot: The Mystery of Crop Circles

The result of cyclonic winds? Attempted alien communication? Evidence of hungry cows with serious OCD? There are many theories as to how crop circles, or grain stalks flattened in recognizable patterns, have come to exist. Most people dismiss them as pranks, but there are more than a few who believe there's something otherworldly going on.

✳ ✳ ✳ ✳

Ye Ole Crop Circle

SOME EXPERTS BELIEVE the first crop circles date back to the late 1600s, but there isn't much evidence to support them. Other experts cite evidence of more than 400 simple circles 6 to 20 feet in diameter that appeared worldwide hundreds of years ago. The kinds of circles they refer to are still being found today, usually after huge, cyclonic thunderstorms pass over a large expanse of agricultural land. These circles are much smaller and not nearly as precise as the geometric, mathematically complex circles that started cropping up in the second half of the 20th century. Still, drawings and writings about these smaller circles lend weight to the claims of believers that the crop circle phenomenon isn't a new thing.

The International Crop Circle Database reports stories of "UFO nests" in British papers during the 1960s. About a decade or so later, crop circles fully captured the attention (and the imagination) of the masses.

No, Virginia, There Aren't Any Aliens

In 1991, two men from Southampton, England, came forward with a confession. Doug Bower and Dave Chorley admitted that they were responsible for the majority of the crop circles found in England during the preceding two decades.

Inspired by stories of "UFO nests" in the 1960s, the two decided to add a little excitement to their sleepy town. With boards, string, and a few simple navigational tools, the men worked through the night to create complex patterns in fields that could be seen from the road. It worked, and before long, much of the Western world was caught up in crop circle fever. Some claimed it was irrefutable proof that UFOs were landing on Earth. Others said God was trying to communicate with humans "through the language of mathematics." For believers, there was no doubt that supernatural or extraterrestrial forces were at work. But skeptics were thrilled to hear the confession from Bower and Chorley, since they never believed the circles to be anything but a prank in the first place.

Before the men came forward, more crop circles appeared throughout the 1980s and '90s, many of them not made by Bower and Chorley. Circles "mysteriously" occurred in Australia, Canada, the United States, Argentina, India, and even Afghanistan. In 1995, more than 200 cases of crop circles were reported worldwide. In 2001, a formation that appeared in Wiltshire, England, contained 409 circles and covered more than 12 acres.

Many were baffled that anyone could believe these large and admittedly rather intricate motifs were anything but human-made. Plus, the more media coverage crop circles garnered, the more new crop circles appeared. Other people came forward, admitting that they were the "strange and unexplained power" behind the circles. Even then, die-hard believers dismissed the hoaxers, vehemently suggesting that they were either players in a government cover-up, captives of aliens forced to throw everyone off track, or just average Joes looking for 15 minutes of fame by claiming to have made something that was clearly the work of nonhumans.

Scientists were deployed to ascertain the facts. In 1999, a well-funded team of experts was assembled to examine numerous crop circles in the UK. The verdict? At least 80 percent of the circles were, beyond a shadow of a doubt, created by humans. Footprints, abandoned tools, and video of a group of hoaxers caught in the act all debunked the theory that crop circles were created by aliens.

But Still . . .

So if crop circles are nothing more than hoaxers having fun or artists playing with a unique medium, why are we still so inter-ested? Movies such as *Signs* in 2002 capitalized on the public's fascination with the phenomenon, and crop circles still capture headlines. Skeptics will scoff, but from time to time, there is a circle that doesn't quite fit the profile of a human-made prank.

There have been claims that fully functional cell phones cease to work once the caller steps inside certain crop circles. Could it be caused by some funky ion-scramble emitted by an extra-terrestrial force? Some researchers have tried to re-create the circles and succeeded, but only with the use of high-tech tools and equipment that wouldn't be available to the average prank-ster. If all of these circles were made by humans, why are so few people busted for trespassing in the middle of the night? And where are all the footprints?

Eyewitness accounts of UFOs rising from fields can hardly be considered irrefutable evidence, but there are several reports from folks who swear they saw ships, lights, and movement in the sky just before crop circles were discovered.

To the Moon!

Television and film star Jackie Gleason was fascinated with the paranormal and UFOs. But he had no idea that an innocent game with an influential friend would lead him face-to-face with his obsession.

✳   ✳   ✳   ✳

JACKIE GLEASON WAS a star of the highest order. The rotund actor kept television audiences in stitches with his portrayal of hardheaded but ultimately lovable family man Ralph Kramden in the 1955 sitcom *The Honeymooners*. He made history with his regularly aimed, but never delivered, threats to TV wife Alice, played by Audrey Meadows: "One of these days Alice, one of these days, pow, right in the kisser," and "Bang, zoom! To the moon, Alice!"

But many fans didn't know that Gleason was obsessed with the supernatural, and he owned a massive collection of memorabilia on the subject. It was so large and impressive that the University of Miami, Florida, put it on permanent exhibit after his death in 1987. He even had a house built in the shape of a UFO, which he christened, "The Mothership." The obsession was legendary, and it climaxed in an unimaginable way.

A High Stakes Game

An avid golfer, Gleason also kept a home close to Inverrary Golf and Country Club in Lauderhill, Florida. A famous golfing buddy lived nearby—U.S. President Richard M. Nixon, who had a compound on nearby Biscayne Bay. The Hollywood star and the controversial politician shared a love of the links, politics, and much more.

The odyssey began when Gleason and Nixon met for a golf tournament at Inverrary in February 1973. Late in the day their conversation turned to a topic close to Gleason's heart—UFOs. To the funnyman's surprise, the president revealed his own fascination with the subject, touting a large collection of books that rivaled Gleason's. They talked shop through the rest of the game, but Gleason noticed reservation in Nixon's tone, as if the aides and security within earshot kept the president from speaking his mind. He would soon learn why.

Later that evening around midnight, an unexpected guest visited the Gleason home. It was Nixon, alone. The customary secret service detail assigned to him was nowhere to be seen. Confused, Gleason asked Nixon the reason for such a late call. He replied only that he had to show Gleason something. They climbed into Nixon's private car and sped off. The drive brought them to Homestead Air Force Base in South Miami-Dade County. Nixon took them to a large, heavily guarded building. Guards parted as the pair headed inside the structure, Gleason following Nixon past labs before arriving at a series of large cases. The cases held wreckage from a downed UFO, Nixon told his friend. Seeing all of this, Gleason had his doubts and imagined himself the target of a staged hoax.

Leaving the wreckage, the pair entered a chamber holding six (some reports say eight) freezers topped with thick glass. Peering into the hulls, Gleason later said he saw dead bodies—but not of the human variety. The remains were small, almost childlike in stature, but withered in appearance and possessing only three or four digits per hand. They were also severely mangled, as if they had been in a devastating accident.

Returning home, Gleason was giddy. His obsession had come full circle. The enthusiasm changed in the weeks that followed, however, shifting to intense fear and worry. A patriotic American, Gleason couldn't reconcile his government's secrecy about the UFO wreckage. Traumatized, he began drinking heavily and suffered from severe insomnia.

The "Truth" Comes Out

Gleason kept details of his wild night with Nixon under wraps. Unfortunately, his soon-to-be-ex-wife didn't follow his lead. Beverly Gleason spilled the beans in *Esquire* magazine and again in an unpublished memoir on her marriage to Gleason. Supermarket tabloids ate the story up.

Gleason only opened up about his night with Nixon in the last weeks of his life. Speaking to Larry Warren, a former Air Force pilot with his own UFO close encounter, a slightly boozy Gleason let his secret loose with a phrase reminiscent of his *Honeymooners* days: "We've got 'em . . . Aliens!"

The Nazca Lines—Pictures Aimed at an Eye in the Sky?

Ancient works of art etched into a desert floor in South America have inspired wild theories about who created them and why. Did space aliens leave them on long-ago visits? Decades of scientific research reject the popular notion, showing that the lines were the work of mere Earthlings.

❋   ❋   ❋   ❋

FLYING ABOVE THE rocky plains northwest of Nazca, Peru, in 1927, aviator Toribio Mejía Xesspe was surprised to see gigantic eyes looking up at him. Then the pilot noticed that the orbs stared out of a bulbous head upon a cartoonish line drawing of a man, etched over hundreds of square feet of the landscape below.

The huge drawing—later called "owl man" for its staring eyes— turned out to be just one of scores of huge, 2,000-year-old images scratched into the earth over almost 200 square miles of the parched Peruvian landscape.

There is a 360-foot-long monkey with a whimsically spiraled tail, along with a 150-foot-long spider, and a 935-foot pelican.

Other figures range from hummingbird to killer whale. Unless the viewer knows what to look for, they're almost invisible from ground level. There are also geometric shapes and straight lines that stretch for miles across the stony ground.

The Theory of Ancient Astronauts

The drawings have been dated to a period between 200 B.C. and A.D. 600. Obviously, there were no airplanes from which to view them back then. So why were they made? And for whose benefit?

In his 1968 book *Chariots of the Gods?*, Swiss author Erich Von Däniken popularized the idea that the drawings and lines were landing signals and runways for starships that visited southern Peru long before the modern era. In his interpretation, the owl man is instead an astronaut in a helmet. Von Däniken's theory caught on among UFO enthusiasts. Many science-fiction novels and films make reference to this desert in Peru's Pampa Colorado region as a site with special significance to space travelers.

Coming Down to Earth

Examined up close, the drawings consist of cleared paths— areas where someone removed reddish surface rocks to expose the soft soil beneath. In the stable desert climate—averaging less than an inch of rain per year—the paths have survived through many centuries largely intact.

Scientists believe the Nazca culture—a civilization that came before the Incas—drew the lines. The style of the artwork is similar to that featured on Nazca pottery. German-born researcher Maria Reiche (1903–1998) showed how the Nazca could have laid out the figures using simple surveying tools such as ropes and posts. In the 1980s, American researcher Joe Nickell duplicated one of the drawings, a condor, showing that the Nazca could have rendered parts of the figures "freehand"—that is, without special tools or even scale models. Nickell also demonstrated that despite their great size, the fig-

ures can be identified as drawings even from ground level. No
alien technology would have been required to make them.

Still Mysterious

As for why the Nazca drew giant doodles across the desert, no
one is sure. Reiche noted that some of the lines have astronomical relevance. For example, one points to where the sun sets at
the winter solstice. Some lines may also have pointed toward
underground water sources—crucially important to desert
people.

Most scholars think that the marks were part of the Nazca
religion. They may have been footpaths followed during ritual
processions. And although it's extremely unlikely that they were
intended for extraterrestrials, many experts think it likely that
the lines were oriented toward Nazca gods—perhaps a monkey
god, a spider god, and so on, who could be imagined gazing
down from the heavens upon likenesses of themselves.

Weird Weather

*We've all heard that neither rain, snow, sleet nor hail, will stop
our determined mail carriers, but how about a few rounds of ball
lightning or tiny frogs dropping from the sky? Apparently, Mother
Nature has a sense of humor. Here are some of the weirdest
weather phenomena encountered on Planet Earth.*

✳ ✳ ✳ ✳

Goodness, Gracious, Great Balls of Lightning!

PERHAPS IT WAS ball lightning, an unexplained spherical
mass of electrical energy, that Jerry Lee Lewis was singing
about in the popular tune "Great Balls of Fire." In 1976, the
strange phenomenon supposedly attacked a woman in the UK
as she ironed during an electrical storm. A ball of lightning
emerged from her iron, spun around the room, then threw her
across the room, ripping off half her clothes in the process. In
1962, a Long Island couple was astounded to see a fiery, basket-

ball-size orb roll into their living room through an open window. The fireball passed between the pair, continued through the room, and disappeared down an adjacent hallway. Exactly how lightning or any other electrical anomaly can form itself into a ball and zigzag at different speeds is not well understood.

Otherworldly Lights: St. Elmo's Fire

A weird haze of light glimmering around a church steeple during a storm, a rosy halo over someone's head, or a ghostly light swirling around the mast of a wave-tossed ship—these are all possible manifestations of the strange, bluish-white light known as St. Elmo's Fire, which may be a signal that a lightning strike to the glowing area is imminent. The light is a visible, electric discharge produced by heavy storms. It was named after St. Erasmus, aka St. Elmo, the patron saint of sailors.

When the Moon Gets the Blues

Everyone understands that the phrase "once in a blue moon" refers to a very unusual occurrence, since blue moons are rare. But a blue moon is not actually blue. In fact, a blue moon is determined by the calendar, not by its color. Typically, there is one full moon per month, but occasionally, a second full moon will sneak into a monthly cycle. When this happens, the second full moon is referred to as a "blue moon," which happens every two to three years. But at times, the moon has been known to appear blue, or even green, often after a volcanic eruption leaves tiny ash and dust particles in the earth's atmosphere.

Green Flash: When the Sun Goes Green

The term *green flash* may sound like a comic book superhero, but it is actually a strange flash of green light that appears just before the setting sun sinks into the horizon. Some have suggested that rare fluctuations in solar winds are responsible for green glows and flashes that sometimes appear in the atmosphere just before sunset. Some believe it's just a mirage. But others contend that a green flash occurs when layers of the earth's atmosphere act like a prism. Whatever causes the emerald hue, seeing a flash of green light along the horizon can be an eerie and unsettling experience.

Double the Rainbows, Double the Gold?

Rainbow stories abound; ancient Irish lore promises a pot of leprechaun's gold at the end of a rainbow, and Biblical tradition says God set a rainbow in the sky as a promise to Noah that Earth would never again be destroyed by water. Rainbows are formed when sunlight passes through water droplets, usually at the end of a rainstorm, and the droplets separate the light like tiny prisms into a spectrum from red to violet. A secondary rainbow, set outside the first one and in the reverse order of colors, is formed by a second set of light refractions to create the spectacular double rainbow. Conditions have to be just right to see the double rainbow because the secondary arch of colors is much paler than the primary rainbow and is not always visible.

Lava Lamps in the Sky: Aurora Borealis

Like a neon sign loosened from its tubing, the *aurora borealis* sends multicolored arches, bands, and streams of luminous beauty throughout the northern skies whenever solar flares are at their height. This occurs when electrons ejected from the sun's surface hit Earth's atmospheric particles and charge them until they glow. The electrons are attracted to Earth's magnetic poles, which is why they are seen mainly in the far northern or southern latitudes. In the southern hemisphere, they are called *aurora australis*. *Aurora polaris* refers to the lights of either pole.

It's Raining Frogs!

Startling as the thought of being pelted from above by buckets of hapless amphibians may be, reports of the sky raining frogs have occurred for so long that the problem was even addressed in the first century A.D., when a Roman scholar, Pliny the Elder, theorized that frog "seeds" were already present in the soil. But in 2005, residents of Serbia were shocked when masses of teensy toads tumbled out of a dark cloud that suddenly appeared in the clear blue sky. *Scientific American* reported a frog fall over Kansas City, Missouri, in July 1873, in numbers so thick they "darkened the air." And in Birmingham, England, the froglets that reportedly dropped from the heavens on June 30, 1892, were not green but a milky white. In 1987, pink frogs fell in Gloucestershire, England. No one knows for certain why this happens, but one theory is that the small animals—fish, birds, and lizards are also common—are carried from other locations by tornadoes or waterspouts.

Spouting Off

Ancient people feared waterspouts and understandably so. Waterspouts are actually tornadoes that form over a body of water, whirling at speeds as fast as 190 miles per hour. Waterspouts start with parent clouds that pull air near the surface into a vortex at an increasing rate, until water is pulled up toward the cloud. One of the world's top waterspout hot spots is the Florida Keys, which may see as many as 500 per year. They can also occur in relatively calm areas such as Lake Tahoe, on the California–Nevada border. There, a Native American legend said that waterspouts, which they called "waterbabies," appeared at the passing of great chiefs to take them to heaven.

Mirages: Optical Confusion

Mirages have been blamed for everything from imaginary waterholes in deserts to sightings of the Loch Ness Monster. They come in two forms: hallucinations or environmental illusions based on tricks of light, shadow, and atmosphere. In April 1977, residents of Grand Haven, Michigan, were able to plainly see the shimmering lights of Milwaukee, Wisconsin, some 75 miles across Lake Michigan. The sighting was confirmed by the flashing pattern of Milwaukee's red harbor beacon. Another rare type of water mirage is the *fata morgana*, which produces a double image that makes mundane objects look gigantic and may account for some reports of sea monsters.

Cobwebs from Heaven?

On their 40-year desert tour with Moses, the Israelites were blessed with a strange substance called manna that fell from the sky. People in other places have also witnessed falls of unknown material, often resembling cobwebs. In October 1881, great quantities of weblike material fell around the cities of Milwaukee, Green Bay, and Sheboygan, Wisconsin. Newspapers speculated that the strong, white strands had come from "gossamer spiders" due to their lightness. The same thing allegedly happened in 1898 in Montgomery, Alabama. Not all falls of unknown material have been so pleasant—a yellowish, smelly substance fell on Kourianof, Russia, in 1832, and something similar was reported in Ireland around 1695.

Quantum Teleportation

Even if you're not a Star Trek fan, you're no doubt aware of how people on the sci-fi series travel from place to place by "beaming" from one location to another. The popular catchphrase "Beam me up, Scotty" (although never actually uttered on the show), has made its way into our lexicon, often used as a way to express a desire to be somewhere else. But the idea of teleporting from one location to another is not as unbelievable as it sounds. In fact, some scientists say that there is nothing in the laws of physics that would render it impossible.

❋ ❋ ❋ ❋

O N STAR TREK, teleportation is made possible by converting the atoms that make up a human into energy, beaming that energy to another location, and then reassembling the atoms. Voila! A reconstructed human. We are definitely not at a point where we can break down humans to an atomic level and reassemble them in another location; for now, that will have to remain science fiction. However, scientists have been able to accomplish something else that, at first glance, seems like it must be fiction. But like so many other amazing things in the scientific world, this is reality.

It's called "quantum teleportation," but unlike *Star Trek*, this is not teleportation of matter, but rather information. Quantum teleportation can become possible due to an interesting, and somewhat strange, property of quantum mechanics called "quantum entanglement." This occurs when particles are linked together in such a way that the state of one particle determines the states of the linked particles, even if they are separated by vast distances.

The classic example used to describe quantum entanglement is called the EPR Paradox, or Einstein-Podolsky-Rosen Paradox, named after physicists Albert Einstein, Boris Podolsky, and Nathan Rosen, who first described it in the 1930s. In the paradox, two entangled particles have an uncertain state until one of them is measured, at which point the state of the other particle is immediately certain. But this would suggest that there is communication between the two particles that is faster than the speed of light, conflicting with Einstein's theory that nothing can travel faster than the speed of light; hence, the paradox.

This paradox was confusing, even for physicists like Einstein. So several years later, physicist David Bohm suggested a more simplified example of the EPR Paradox. In Bohm's example, an unstable particle with a spin of 0 decays into two new particles, Particle A and Particle B, which then travel in different directions. Since the original particle had a spin of 0, the two new particles have a spin of + and - , giving them an entangled property.

The famous "Schroedinger's Cat" thought experiment, dreamed up by physicist Erwin Schroedinger, describes more of the paradoxes of quantum mechanics. Schroedinger envisioned a cat that was placed in a steel box with a vial of poison, a Geiger counter, a hammer, and a radioactive substance. When the radioactive substance decays, it triggers the Geiger counter, the hammer hits the vial of poison, and the cat dies. But radioactive decay is a random process, and there is no way to predict when it will occur. So, according to physicists, the radioactive substance exists in a state known as "superposition," or in a state that is both decayed and not decayed at the same time. Therefore, until an observer actually opens the box, there is no way to know whether or not the cat is alive. It exists, according to Schroedinger, as both "living and dead . . . in equal parts."

Now, setting aside the fact that Schroedinger seemed to really hate cats, this same paradox can be applied to quantum entanglement. Before observing the spins of Particle A and Particle B, they don't have a definite state; rather, they are in a state of superposition, just like Schroedinger's poor cat. Therefore, the spin of Particle A and Particle B is both + and - . But if you measure the spin of Particle A and find it to be + , then you immediately know that the spin of Particle B is - , without even having to measure.

Scientists are already finding practical ways to use quantum entanglement, such as to send and receive information between spacecraft and ground-based receivers, and to create entanglement-enhanced microscopes. But back to quantum teleportation: in order to accomplish this feat, scientists must begin with entangled particles. They must then take whatever information they wish to teleport and include it in the entanglement. The entanglement then becomes the teleportation channel between particles. So far, physicists have been successful in teleporting what is called a spin state, also known as a "qubit," across a quantum communication channel. And in 2017, Chinese scientists successfully teleported the quantum state of a photon from Earth to an orbiting satellite more than 800 miles away.

When the process was first theorized in 1993 by physicists Asher Peres, William Wootters, and Charles Bennett, Peres and Wootters suggested calling it "telepheresis." But Bennett proposed the catchier, much more impressive sounding "quantum teleportation," which has perhaps led to greater interest in the subject. Because who doesn't want teleportation to be possible? While we may not be anywhere close to being able to actually teleport objects, that doesn't mean that quantum teleportation may not have some amazing uses. Quantum mechanics have the potential to make all kinds of new technology possible, such as quantum computers, which could make even today's lightning-fast computers look slow, or a "quantum internet" which can securely send information over long distances without actually traveling those distances.

Teleporting from place to place like a *Star Trek* space explorer may remain fiction for the foreseeable future, but we still have much to learn about the way matter, space, and time work. Properties of the universe that were mysteries a century ago are now explainable, and researchers are continually finding new and amazing things throughout the cosmos. Perhaps we simply haven't found the exact mechanisms to make our science fiction dreams a reality, but one thing is certain: scientists will continue to search the universe and run experiments until we've reached the limits of what's possible. But with an infinite amount of space to study, perhaps those possibilities are as limitless as our universe itself.

The Tunguska Event

What created an explosion 1,000 times greater than the atomic bomb at Hiroshima, destroyed 80 million trees, but left no hole in the ground?

✳ ✳ ✳ ✳

The Event

ON THE MORNING of June 30, 1908, a powerful explosion ripped through the remote Siberian wilderness near the Tunguska River. Witnesses, from nomadic herdsmen and passengers on a train to a group of people at the nearest trading post, reported seeing a bright object streak through the sky and explode into an enormous fireball. The resulting shockwave flattened approximately 830 square miles of forest.

Seismographs in England recorded the event twice, once as the initial shockwave passed and then again after it had circled the planet. A huge cloud of ash reflected sunlight from over the horizon across Asia and Europe. People reported there being enough light in the night sky to facilitate reading.

A Wrathful God

Incredibly, nearly 20 years passed before anyone visited the site. Everyone had a theory of what happened, and none of it good. Outside Russia, however, the event itself was largely unknown. The English scientists who recorded the tremor, for instance, thought that it was simply an earthquake. Inside Russia, the unstable political climate of the time was not conducive to mounting an expedition. Subsequently, the economic and social upheaval created by World War I and the Russian Revolution made scientific expeditions impossible.

Looking for a Hole in the Ground

In 1921, mineralogist Leonid A. Kulik was charged by the Mineralogical Museum of St. Petersburg with locating meteorites that had fallen inside the Soviet Union. Having read old newspapers and eyewitness testimony from the Tunguska region, Kulik convinced the Academy of Sciences in 1927 to fund an expedition to locate the crater and meteorite he was certain existed.

The expedition was not going to be easy, as spring thaws turned the region into a morass. And when the team finally reached the area of destruction, their superstitious guides refused to go any further. Kulik, however, was encouraged by the sight of millions of trees splayed to the ground in a radial pattern pointing outward from an apparent impact point. Returning again, the team finally reached the epicenter where, to their surprise, they found neither a meteor nor a crater. Instead, they found a forest of what looked like telephone poles—trees stripped of their branches and reduced to vertical shafts. Scientists would not witness a similar sight until 1945 in the area below the Hiroshima blast.

Theories Abound

Here are some of the many theories of what happened at Tunguska.

Stony Asteroid: Traveling at a speed of about 33,500 miles per hour, a large space rock heated the air around it to 44,500 degrees Fahrenheit and exploded at an altitude of about 28,000 feet.

Kimberlite Eruption: Formed nearly 2,000 miles below the Earth's surface, a shaft of heavy kimberlite rock carried a huge quantity of methane gas to the Earth's surface where it exploded with great force.

Black Holes & Antimatter: As early as 1941, some scientists believed that a small antimatter asteroid exploded when it encountered the upper atmosphere. In 1973, several theorists proposed that the Tunguska event was the result of a tiny black hole passing through the Earth's surface.

Alien Shipwreck: Noting the similarities between the Hiroshima atomic bomb blast and the Tunguska event, Russian novelist Alexander Kazantsev was the first to suggest that an atomic-powered UFO exploded over Siberia in 1908.

Tesla's Death Ray: Scientist Nikola Tesla is rumored to have test-fired a "death ray" on June 30, 1908, but he believed the experiment to be unsuccessful—until he learned of the Tunguska Event.

Okay, but What Really Happened?

In June 2008, scientists from around the world marked the 100-year anniversary of the Tunguska event with conferences in Moscow. Yet scientists still cannot reach a consensus as to what caused the event. In fact, the anniversary gathering was split into two opposing factions—extraterrestrial versus terrestrial—who met at different sites in the city.

Predictions, Premonitions, and Precognition

Some believe strongly in precognition, while others aren't so sure, but when it arrives it's mighty hard to explain. Here are some freakishly accurate premonitions that might just stand your hair on end.

＊　＊　＊　＊

Cayce at Bat

EDGAR CAYCE (1877–1945) is to prophets what ballplayer Derek Jeter is to the Yankees. As one of the most reliable seers, Cayce, like Jeter, got the job done much of the time. Fittingly referred to as "The Sleeping Prophet," Cayce would enter a trancelike state before issuing his readings. While in this state, Cayce predicted the stock market crash of 1929 six months before it occurred; the beginning of both world wars; the death of President Franklin D. Roosevelt; and the assassination of President John F. Kennedy.

Hoy Foresees Tragedy

On April 19, 1995, during a live radio program in Fayetteville, N.C., clairvoyant Tana Hoy hit prophecy pay dirt when he told the interviewer that there would be a deadly terrorist attack on a building in an American city beginning with the letter "O." He added that the tragedy would occur before the first of May. Just ninety minutes later, the Alfred P. Murrah Federal Building in Oklahoma City was blown up by Timothy McVeigh and other radicals in what was, up to that point, the worst terrorist attack on U.S. soil.

Twain to See

Writer Mark Twain (Samuel Clemons) eerily predicted the deaths of both his brother and himself. In a prophetic dream,

Twain saw his brother laid out in a coffin resting between two folding chairs in his sister's parlor. A few weeks after the unsettling vision, Twain's brother was killed in a boating accident. When Twain entered his sister's living room to pay his last respects to his sibling, his eyes were confronted by a startling sight. Before him lay his brother in a coffin stretched across two folding chairs—precisely as he had envisioned the scene during his dream.

Twain was born in 1835, the year that Halley's Comet was visible. He believed that his life force would be extinguished when Halley's Comet came back for its encore. In 1910, Halley's Comet came back into view. And Mark Twain exited the mortal world. Coincidence?

Rockin' Out in the Afterlife

Twain certainly wasn't alone in predicting his own death. Reports that President Abraham Lincoln witnessed his own assassination in a dream have long made the rounds, but the premonition lacks substantiation and is considered dubious.

Harder to discount is the vision that bassist Mikey Welsh had on September 26, 2011. A former member of the rock band Weezer, Welsh logged onto his Twitter account and issued the following statement: "Dreamt I died in Chicago next weekend (heart attack in my sleep). Need to write my will today."

Then, before signing off Welsh added this: "Correction—the weekend after next."

Two weeks later Welsh travelled to Chicago for Riotfest—an annual rock music festival that was featuring his former band. Unfortunately, he never made it to the show. Staff at the Raffaello Hotel found Welsh's body in his room on October 8, 2011, one day before the scheduled concert. His death came as the result of a drug overdose that in turn led to a heart attack. The time of his passing meshed precisely with his prediction.

Cosmic Microwave Background Radiation

In 1964, Robert Wilson and Arno Penzias, two American radio astronomers working for Bell Telephone Laboratories in Holmdel Township, New Jersey, made an unusual discovery. As Penzias would later say, "we had stumbled upon something big." But at the time, neither Penzias nor Wilson realized just how big. It was, in fact, a revelation that led all the way back to the biggest event in the universe: The Big Bang.

✳ ✳ ✳ ✳

BUT BEFORE DELVING into the story of their discovery, let's think about the universe: First, this giant place that houses our planet and billions of other planets is almost indescribably vast. But if we were to attempt to describe it, we'd have to think about a sphere with a 15-billion light-year radius and picture our tiny Earth somewhere inside it; and that's only the universe we know about. Scientists estimate that we've only begun to scratch the surface of the mysteries of space.

And second, we know that the light we observe emanating throughout the universe is traveling at a fixed speed. The light from the sun, for instance, takes about eight minutes to reach Earth, whereas light from Pluto takes 5.3 hours. So if, theoretically, the sun were to suddenly disappear from the sky, it would take eight minutes before humans on Earth even became aware of that fact! It's also interesting to note that the sun is only about 4.5 billion years old, so its light has only traveled 4.5 billion light-years across the universe; this means that the light from our sun has yet to reach the farthest borders of our known universe.

Back to Wilson and Penzias. The two radio astronomers were tasked with creating a radio receiver for Bell Labs at the company's Crawford Hill location, to be used for radio astronomy and satellite communications experiments. They constructed a microwave radiometer, which is a very sensitive receiver that can detect energy emitted at millimeter or centimeter wavelengths, also known as microwaves. On May 20, 1964, they noticed that their new receiver was picking up a strange noise. It seemed to be a buzzing sound that was coming from everywhere, encompassing all parts of the sky at the same time.

Confused, Wilson and Penzias began looking for a source of the sound. They considered whether it could be interference from nearby New York City, or perhaps even an echo from a nuclear bomb that had been test-detonated over the Pacific years earlier. Or maybe their newly built equipment was faulty; to test this theory, they went so far as to replace parts of the receiver, but the sound remained. But then they more closely inspected the radio receiver, and thought they'd finally found their culprit: pigeons. Two birds had built nests inside the antenna, and pigeon dung was building up on the equipment. Wilson and Penzias removed the birds, cleaned the receiver, and tested their equipment again. To their surprise, the noise remained. So what could cause noise to come from all points of the sky at the same time?

By the 1960s, there were two prevailing theories concerning the origins of the universe. The first was called the "Steady State theory," which hypothesizes that matter is continuously created as the universe expands. This theory also states that the overall density of the universe remains constant, and that the universe has existed forever. The second theory is the "Big Bang theory," which states that the universe began at a point of infinite density and then began to expand outward. Wilson and Penzias theorized that if the second theory was correct, then the universe should be filled with cosmic microwave background radiation left over from the very beginnings of its formation.

After eliminating every other cause of the strange noise (including feathered friends), the two scientists came to a startling conclusion: They had discovered the predicted cosmic microwave background radiation from the Big Bang. Their receiver was picking up a cosmic echo from the very beginnings of the universe's explosive creation, and it was literally coming from everywhere.

This radiation is the oldest light in the universe, dating from about 380,000 years after the Big Bang, which is thought to have occurred around 13.8 billion years ago. After its initial creation, the cosmos was extraordinarily hot, topping out around 273 million degrees above absolute zero. Atoms were quickly broken apart into protons and electrons, and photons of light scattered off into the hot, soupy mix. As the universe began to cool off, the photons, at first as bright and hot as the surface of a star, expanded outward. And, as with all other light in the universe, this light just kept traveling, waiting for someone to discover its presence. Now, this cosmic microwave background radiation has cooled off to a temperature of just 2.73 degrees above absolute zero, or an astoundingly cold negative 456.94 degrees Fahrenheit, and is found quite uniformly throughout the universe.

Wilson and Penzias' discovery immediately lent credence to the Big Bang theory, and the pair was awarded the 1978 Nobel Prize in physics for their work. In 1993, NASA's Cosmic Background Explorer (COBE) mission created a full-sky map of the radiation, which NASA dubbed a "baby picture" of the universe, and other detailed images have been made since then.

Studying the radiation has helped scientists unlock more mysteries of the universe, helping them to pinpoint its age, understand when the first stars were formed, and learn more about the origin of galaxies. There is even some evidence that dark matter and dark energy, mysterious theoretical forces that may affect the laws of gravity throughout the universe, do exist.

It's probably safe to say that when Wilson and Penzias were cleaning pigeon droppings out of their radio receiver, they had no idea that they were on their way to finding the "baby picture" of the universe. But no doubt their discovery inspired new generations of scientists to keep searching for answers to the most perplexing questions in the cosmos.

The Sighting of the Higgs Boson

There's a lot more to the universe than what we see with our eyes.

✳ ✳ ✳ ✳

OUR UNIVERSE IS an incredibly complex place. The Big Bang, dark matter, stars, black holes, photons, galaxies, gamma rays—it's all driven by four "fundamental forces," according to the physicists who spend their lives attempting to unravel the mysteries of our vast cosmos. These forces, which include gravitational force, electromagnetic force, and strong and weak interactions, are said to encompass nearly everything in the known universe, interacting with and influencing the tiniest atoms to the largest planets.

The theory of General Relativity, first proposed by Albert Einstein in 1915, describes the properties of gravity. But the other three forces are included in the Standard Model of particle physics, which has been gradually developed since the latter half of the 20th century by many different scientists around the world. The Standard Model also classifies all elementary particles, which are subatomic particles—particles that are smaller than atoms—with no substructure, meaning they are not made up of other particles. These minute particles are classified as either fundamental fermions, particles which were first observed by physicists Enrico Fermi and Paul Dirac in the mid-1900s, or fundamental bosons. Dirac coined the name "boson" in honor of Indian physicist Satyendra Nath Bose, who, along with Einstein, developed a theory that characterizes elementary particles.

In 1964, a British physicist named Peter Higgs, who was fascinated with these elementary particles, was working on one of the many mysteries of the universe: mass. Or, more precisely, where mass comes from. Mass is the resistance an object exhibits when a force is applied, and most of the time, it seems pretty obvious where that mass comes from. A feather has very little mass, whereas a car has a lot. It makes perfect sense, right? But as we break objects down into their fundamental parts, the source of mass becomes less clear. It may be obvious that an object made up of molecules and atoms has mass; it may even make sense that molecules and atoms themselves have mass, since they are made up of even smaller particles. But the smallest of these—the subatomic particles like bosons—also have mass. And where does the mass of an elementary particle, which is not made up of any other particle, come from?

Strangely, when physicists ran equations to model the behavior of elementary particles, their equations worked perfectly if they assumed the particles had no mass. But when they modified the equations to account for the mass of the particles, the perfection of their calculations fell apart. Higgs suggested that perhaps the scientists were looking at things the wrong way: Instead of assuming that the particles themselves were accounting for mass, he proposed that they were surrounded by a field—which we now call the Higgs field—that was influencing their behavior by exerting a drag force on them. This is not unlike moving a ball underwater—whether moving in air or underwater the ball is unchanged, but it becomes more difficult to move it underwater due to the additional drag.

At first, Higgs' ideas were scorned by the physics community, but over the next couple decades, scientists began to realize that the hypothesis could have merit. By the mid-1980s, most physicists embraced the idea, even confidently teaching college students about the existence of the "Higgs field," even though said existence had never been proven. But it would take another two and a half decades before the technology to test for such an invisible field would come to fruition. In 2008, the Large Hadron Collider (LHC) was completed in Geneva, Switzerland. This 17-mile-long circular tunnel lies hundreds of yards beneath the earth, and is so long that most of its underground "racetrack" is in the neighboring country of France. The LHC is the largest particle collider in the world, built to literally smash particles of matter together. Inside the LHC, protons circle the tunnel in both directions, accelerated by magnets, until they're traveling just short of the speed of light.

The LHC was exactly what Higgs field proponents had been waiting for. The theory was that if the Higgs field existed, then particles colliding together should be able to disrupt it—much like two objects colliding underwater can make the water jiggle. And if these colliding particles did "jiggle" the invisible field around them, a tiny fleck of the field—the Higgs boson particle—should be visible. But calculations predicted that it would also be unstable, almost immediately disintegrating into other particles. Scientists would need to search through the debris of the colliding particles to find a specific area of decay that pointed to the Higgs boson. What's more, the creation of a Higgs boson during particle collisions was deemed to be likely an extremely rare event, occurring only one time in 10 billion collisions. So trillions of collisions needed to be analyzed, to see if a pattern matching up with the Higgs boson particle emerged.

At the end of June 2012, the European Organization for Nuclear Research (also known as CERN), which operates the LHC, announced that they would soon be holding a seminar to discuss research findings. Within a few days, the scientific community was abuzz with rumors; but when news broke that Peter Higgs himself had been asked to travel to Geneva to attend the seminar, physicists knew the news had to be what they'd been all been hoping: the Higgs boson had been found.

On July 4, 2012, CERN announced that two independent experiments, conducted separately and without sharing findings, had both reached the same conclusion: a particle consistent with the Higgs boson had been found. Although it would take several more years of tests and measurements before CERN would officially confirm the finding, scientists around the world were ecstatic, finally having proof that there is so much more to the cosmos than we can see with our naked eyes.

Higgs was awarded the 2013 Nobel Prize in Physics, and since the original discovery, experiments have only strengthened the confirmation of the existence of the Higgs boson. The Higgs field is thought to permeate the entire universe, uniformly existing on Earth, throughout the planets in our solar system, and everywhere else, and many scientists believe it played a pivotal role in the Big Bang, leading some to nickname the Higgs boson "the God particle." No matter what you call it, the discovery of the Higgs boson has drawn us one step closer to understanding our vast and complex universe.

Do You Hear Something?

People who lived just a few miles from Gettysburg did not hear the Civil War battle, but people 50 miles away heard it clearly—due to an unusual phenomenon called acoustic shadow.

✳   ✳   ✳   ✳

THE CIVIL WAR may have taken place in the 19th century, but Winston Churchill once referred to it as "the first 20th century war." Once the ironclad battleships began firing on each other, every navy full of wooden ships in the world was obsolete.

But the generals of the Civil War still lacked things like airplanes that 20th century generals would use for reconnaissance, and both generals and scouts had to rely instead their eyes and ears to get a sense of where the other armies were and what was happening around them. Generals would sometimes send in reinforcements to areas where the sounds of battle seemed to be the "hottest," and wouldn't think to send troops into areas where they could hear see or hear no sign of battle.

But using your eyes and ears wasn't always totally reliable—wind could blow sound swaves around causing all sorts of strange things to happen to the sounds as they echoed through the battlefield. As early as the 1600s, scientists and observers had noted that sounds of naval battles could be heard in some places, but not in others that were the same distance away – or, in some cases, even closer.

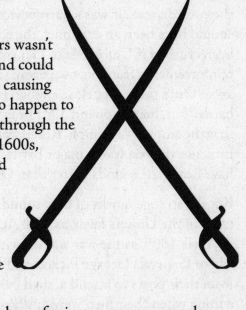

During the Battle of Gettysburg, for instance, many people who lived close enough to the battle to see the flash of the cannons couldn't hear a thing, but people in Pittsburgh, more than 150 miles away, could hear the sound of the battle clearly! This phenomonan is known as an "acoustic shadow," and the bizarre ways that sounds of battles can travel, or not travel, over large areas of terrain created some confusion for generals during the Civil War.

This strange quirk of acoustics is usually caused by high winds carrying sounds to distant areas, but lots of factors in the environment can affect the way sound travels. Trees, hills and other features of the terrain can absorb sounds close to their source, but winds and changes in temperature, which can actually bend the very sound waves themselves, can carry the noises to places far away from the source, away from the features that would absorb them.

There were times when these "shadows" contributed to battlefield decisions and influenced the outcome of the war. At the Battle of Luka in 1862, Union Brigadier General William

Rosencrans's army was attacked and scarcely able to hold off the confederates. It was a narrow victory for the union, but it should have been an easy one; the southern army would have been crushed if Union Major General Edward Ord had sent in reinforcements from his own army, which was only four miles away. Ord's men were close enough to see the smoke from the battle, but, being upwind, Ord heard no sounds, and assumed that the smoke was simply Rosencrans and his men's campfires, not the result of a major battle. People further away might have heard the sounds better than Ord himself did.

But the strange quirks of how sound travels would sometimes work in the Union's favor, as well. At the Battle of Five Forks in April, 1865, as the war was drawing to a close, Confederate Major Generals George Pickett and Fitzhugh Lee were away from their posts to attend a "shad bake" and couldn't hear a thing when their men were attacked by the Union Army barely a mile away. The pine trees between them and the army absorbed the sound, so that even though people further away were allegedly able to hear the sounds, they didn't realize what was happening. Since they didn't have any inkling that they needed to call for reinforcements or help, their armies were decimated, and the resounding defeat was a major factor leading to the collapse of General Lee's army only days later, which was effectively the end of the war.

Though modern technology has made it easier to tell when and where battles are happing, acoustic shadows continued to be observed during later wars, as well. During World War 1, English civilians noted that they could hear the sounds of battle in France duing the summer months, while German civilians heard distant rumbles from France in the winter, due to the ways that the temperature bent the sound waves.

Stormy Weather

Noah's ark is one of the best-known stories from the book of Genesis. Could it have really happened?

✳ ✳ ✳ ✳

SHIPBUILDING IS AN important profession, yet most ship-builders live and die in anonymity. (Raise your hand if you know who designed the *Titanic*. Yeah, didn't think so.) It's a different story, of course, if your name is Noah and your boss is God—then your accomplishments will become one of the most fascinating tales in the Old Testament.

Indeed, practically everyone is familiar with the story of Noah's ark, perhaps the most famous floating menagerie in history. But many people are a little light on the details, so let's take a closer look.

Wickedness Punished

The whole thing started because God was angry. He took a look around and saw only wickedness and violence, so he decided to wipe the earth clean with a global flood and basically start over. Not everyone was wicked, however. God found one righteous man—Noah—and instructed him to build a massive ship out of wood, which he was then to fill with a mated pair of every kind of bird and animal. Noah was also instructed to stock food for all the animals as well as for himself and his family, which included his wife, three sons, and their wives.

The ark itself, as designed by God, was to be 300 cubits long, 50 cubits wide, and 30 cubits high. A cubit is around 17.5 inches, though an Egyptian royal cubit was a little longer, around 20.5 inches. (Noah went to school in Egypt, so he may have used this particular measurement.) As a result, the ark was between 437 and 512 feet long and nearly three stories high—a pretty good-size vessel for the day.

Time-Consuming Project

Building the ark wasn't some weekend project. In fact, if one takes the Bible literally, Noah spent around 120 years constructing it—he was 480 years old when God first spoke to him and 600 when the flood finally occurred. (People lived a *lot* longer back then.)

The flood that followed was a horrifying event. God produced torrential rains for 40 days and 40 nights, enough to flood the entire planet past the mountaintops and kill everyone and everything on it. As the waters receded, the ark came to rest on the mountains of Ararat. However, it took several months more for the world to dry. When finally invited by God to exit the ark, Noah immediately built an altar and worshipped God with burnt offerings. God was pleased, and he promised never to destroy the earth by flood again.

It's a remarkable story, but one that begs a lot of questions. How did Noah fit thousands of birds and animals—plus their food—into the ark? And what about their waste? Feeding the animals and cleaning up after them must have been a Herculean task. The simplest answer, of course, is that God took care of it. After all, the entire event was supernatural in origin, from God instructing Noah on what to do and how to do it to the flood itself.

Fact or Fiction?

Whether the story of Noah's ark is true or not has been the subject of debate for centuries. Some theologians believe it literally, while others posit that the flood did occur, but that it was regional rather than global. And some believe the story is more allegory than fact—a fable designed to illustrate God's intolerance toward wickedness and sin.

Interestingly, some explorers believe that Noah's Ark still rests atop Mount Ararat in eastern Turkey. Over the years, several expeditions have searched the mountain looking for concrete proof of the vessel, though nothing conclusive has been found.

This is a remarkable tale, full of compelling characters and wild adventure, with a simple yet important moral: Righteousness always prevails over wickedness.

The Dog Suicide Bridge

In West Dunbartonshire, Scotland, there sits a 19th century estate known as Overtoun House. Built in the 1860s, the house was originally owned by businessman James White and his family, but in 1938 it was donated to the town of Dunbarton. While the house itself is quite impressive, it hasn't received nearly as much publicity as the strangely unsettling bridge that leads up to the property.

✳ ✳ ✳ ✳

The Devil's in the Details

IN 1891, THE first owner of Overtoun House, James White, passed away and left the property to his son, John. After inheriting the house, John purchased more land and eventually constructed new roads so carriages would be better able to reach the house. This expansion project included the addition of the Overtoun Bridge, which spans a small river at the bottom of a deep gorge. The stone bridge was designed by civil engineer and landscape architect H.E. Milner and was completed in 1895.

For almost a century, the bridge seemed nothing more than a picturesque spot in the countryside, where families would take afternoon strolls, perhaps snapping photos of Overtoun House and the surrounding greenery. But in 1994, the bridge was the site of a horrific tragedy. A man named Kevin Moy was walking across the bridge with his wife and two-week-old son, Eoghan, when suddenly, Moy threw the newborn off the bridge. He then attempted to jump himself, only failing to do so because his screaming wife held him back.

Eoghan died of his injuries the next day, and Moy was arrested for the boy's murder. But it was soon clear that Moy was not in his right mind, as he told investigators that he believed his son was the devil and he himself was the antichrist. He thought the only way to save the world was to kill both his son and himself. At his trial, Moy was found not guilty by reason of insanity, and sent to a psychiatric hospital. Many questioned what would have driven this man to such madness; soon enough, some would be blaming the Overtoun Bridge itself.

"Suicide" or Accident?

In 2005, reports began surfacing about more casualties at the now-infamous bridge. Only this time, the victims weren't human: they were canine. Owners began reporting that their dogs became "possessed" as they crossed the bridge, running to the edge and then, shockingly, jumping off. As researchers

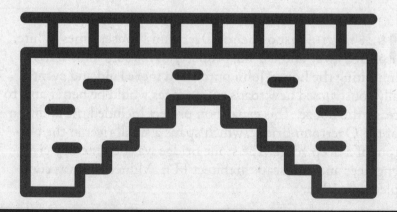

looked into the phenomenon, they discovered claims of these "suicidal dogs" going back to the 1950s. At least 300 dogs have flung themselves off the bridge—some locals insist the number is higher than 600—and 50 are said to have died.

Some researchers believe there are logical explanations for this occurrence. The surrounding foliage tends to hide the view of the 50-foot drop into the gorge, so perhaps the dogs jump over the bridge assuming there is solid ground on the other side. Another theory is that the scent of animals scurrying around in the gorge, like mice, squirrels, and minks, is carried over the bridge, driving the dogs into a frenzy.

The White Lady

But many locals believe the phenomenon has a supernatural explanation. It is said that after John White died in 1908, his grieving widow lived alone for the next 30 years, often wandering the grounds in sadness and despair. Today, the "White Lady of Overtoun" is said to haunt the grounds, often appearing in dark windows of the house or roaming across the bridge. Could this spirit be driving dogs to jump to their deaths?

Whether prompted by something natural or supernatural, investigators continue to try to find the trigger that causes dogs to jump. In the meantime, the best they can do is remind pet owners to be vigilant and to keep their dogs on a leash at all times, especially when they're near the Overtoun Bridge.

CHAPTER 8

PECULIAR PLACES

The Mysterious Blue Hole

State Route 269 hides a roadside attraction of dubious depth and mysterious origin, a supposedly bottomless pool of water that locals simply call the "Blue Hole."

✳   ✳   ✳   ✳

EVERY STATE HAS its tourist traps and bizarre little roadside attractions that are just intriguing enough to pull the car over to see. Back in the day, no roadside attraction brought in the Ohio travelers more than a bottomless pond filled with blue water: the mysterious Blue Hole of Castalia.

The Blue Hole's Origins

The Blue Hole is believed to have formed around 1820, when a dam burst and spilled water into a nearby hole. The ground surrounding Castalia is filled with limestone, which does not absorb groundwater well. The water quickly erodes the limestone, forming cave-ins and sinkholes. It wouldn't be until the late 1870s, however, that most people were made aware of the Blue Hole's existence; the hole was in a very isolated location in the woods. Once the Cold Creek Trout Club opened up nearby, however, its members began taking boat trips out to see the hole, and people all over the area were talking about the mysterious Blue Hole hiding out in Castalia. In 1914, a cave-in resulted in the Blue Hole growing to its current size of almost 75 feet in diameter.

Stop and See the Mystery

The owners of the property where the Blue Hole is situated began promoting it as a tourist stop beginning in the 1920s. It didn't hurt that the entrance to the Blue Hole property was along State Route 269, the same road that people took to get to Cedar Point amusement park. It is estimated that, at the height of its popularity, close to 165,000 people a year came out to take a peek at the Blue Hole.

The Blue Hole was promoted as being bottomless. Other strange stories were often played up as well, including the fact that the water temperature remained at 48 degrees Fahrenheit year-round. Tour guides would point out that regardless of periods of extreme rainfall or even droughtlike conditions, the Blue Hole's water level remained the same throughout.

So What's Up with This Hole, Anyway?

Despite the outlandish claims and theories surrounding the Blue Hole and its origins, the facts themselves are rather mundane. The Blue Hole is really nothing more than a freshwater pond. It isn't even bottomless. Sure, the bright blue surface of the water does indeed make the hole appear infinitely deep, but it's really only about 45 feet to the bottom at its deepest parts.

The blue color of the water is from an extremely high concentration of several elements, including lime, iron, and magnesium. That's the main reason there are no fish in the Blue Hole; they just can't survive with all that stuff in the water.

One Hole or Two?

During the 1990s, the owners of the Blue Hole fell on hard times, forcing them to close the attraction. Families who would show up at the front entrance were forced to stare sadly through a locked gate at the small trail into the woods. That is until several years ago, when the nearby Castalia State Fish Hatchery began clearing land to expand its hatchery. Lo and behold, workers uncovered a second Blue Hole.

Just how this second Blue Hole came to be is still unknown, although the popular belief is that both holes are fed by the same underground water supply. None of that seems to matter to the Blue Hole faithful—they're just thankful to be able to take a gander at a Blue Hole again.

Strange Lights in Marfa

According to a 2007 poll, approximately 14 percent of Americans believe they've seen a UFO. How many of them have been in Marfa?

✳ ✳ ✳ ✳

IF ANYONE IS near Marfa at night, they should watch for odd, vivid lights over nearby Mitchell Flat. Many people believe that the lights from UFOs or even alien entities can be seen. The famous Marfa Lights are about the size of basketballs and are usually white, orange, red, or yellow. These unexplained lights only appear at night and usually hover above the ground at about shoulder height. Some of the lights—alone or in pairs—drift and fly around the landscape.

From cowboys to truck drivers, people traveling in Texas near the intersection of U.S. Route 90 and U.S. Route 67 in southwest Texas have reported the Marfa Lights. And these baffling lights don't just appear on the ground. Pilots and airline passengers claim to have seen the Marfa Lights from the skies. So far, no one has proved a natural explanation for the floating orbs.

Eyewitness Information

Two 1988 reports were especially graphic. Pilot R. Weidig was about 8,000 feet above Marfa when he saw the lights and estimated them rising several hundred feet above the ground.

Passenger E. Halsell described the lights as larger than the plane and noted that they were pulsating. In 2002, pilot B. Eubanks provided a similar report.

In addition to what can be seen, the Marfa Lights may also trigger low-frequency electromagnetic (radio) waves—which can be heard on special receivers—similar to the "whistlers" caused by lightning. However, unlike such waves from power lines and electrical storms, the Marfa whistlers are extremely loud. They can be heard as the orbs appear, and then they fade when the lights do.

A Little Bit About Marfa

Marfa is about 60 miles north of the Mexican border and about 190 miles southeast of El Paso. This small, friendly Texas town is 4,800 feet above sea level and covers 1.6 square miles.

In 1883, Marfa was a railroad water stop. It received its name from the wife of the president of the Texas and New Orleans Railroad, who chose the name from a Russian novel that she was reading. A strong argument can be made that this was Dostoyevsky's *The Brothers Karamazov*. The town grew slowly, reaching its peak during World War II when the U.S. government located a prisoner of war camp, the Marfa Army Airfield, and a chemical warfare brigade nearby. (Some skeptics suggest that discarded chemicals may be causing the Marfa Lights, but searchers have found no evidence of such.)

Today, Marfa is home to about 2,500 people. The small town is an emerging arts center with more than a dozen artists' studios and art galleries. However, Marfa remains most famous for its light display. The annual Marfa Lights Festival is one of the town's biggest events, but the mysterious lights attract visitors year-round.

Widespread Sightings

The first documented sighting was by 16-year-old cowhand Robert Reed Ellison during an 1883 cattle drive. Seeing an odd light in the area, Ellison thought he'd seen an Apache campfire. When he told his story in town, however, settlers told him that they'd seen lights in the area, too, and they'd never found evidence of campfires.

Two years later, 38-year-old Joe Humphreys and his wife, Sally, also reported unexplained lights at Marfa. In 1919, cowboys on a cattle drive paused to search the area for the origin of the lights. Like the others, they found no explanation for what they had seen.

In 1943, the Marfa Lights came to national attention when Fritz Kahl, an airman at the Marfa Army Base, reported that airmen were seeing lights that they couldn't explain. Four years later, he attempted to fly after them in a plane but came up empty again.

Explanations?

Some skeptics claim that the lights are headlights from U.S. 67, dismissing the many reports from before cars—or U.S. 67—were in the Marfa area. Others insist that the lights are swamp gas, ball lightning, reflections off mica deposits, or a nightly mirage.

At the other extreme, a contingent of people believe that the floating orbs are friendly observers of life on Earth. For example, Mrs. W. T. Giddings described her father's early 20th-century encounter with the Marfa Lights. He'd become lost during a blizzard, and according to his daughter, the lights "spoke" to him and led him to a cave where he found shelter.

Most studies of the phenomenon, however, conclude that the lights are indeed real but cannot be explained. The 1989 TV show *Unsolved Mysteries* set up equipment to find an explanation. Scientists on the scene could only comment that the lights were not made by people.

Share the Wealth

Marfa is the most famous location for "ghost lights" and

"mystery lights," but it's not the only place to see them. Here are just a few of the legendary unexplained lights that attract visitors to dark roads in Texas on murky nights.

* In southeast Texas, a single orb appears regularly near Saratoga on Bragg Road.

* The Anson Light appears near Mt. Hope Cemetery in Anson, by U.S. Highway 180.

* Since 1850, "Brit Bailey's Light" glows five miles west of Angleton near Highway 35 in Brazoria County.

* In January 2008, Stephenville attracted international attention when unexplained lights—and perhaps a metallic spaceship—flew fast and low over the town.

The Marfa Lights appear over Mitchell Flat, which is entirely private property. However, the curious can view the lights from a Texas Highway Department roadside parking area about nine miles east of Marfa on U.S. Highway 90. Seekers should arrive before dusk for the best location, especially during bluebonnet season (mid-April through late May), because this is a popular tourist stop.

The Marfa Lights Festival takes place during Labor Day weekend each year. This annual celebration of Marfa's mystery includes a parade, arts and crafts, food, and a street dance.

Blue Light Cemeteries

Under the full moon, some cemeteries in Texas are known for eerie, flashing blue lights and ghostly figures hovering over certain graves.

✳ ✳ ✳ ✳

TEXAS'S MANY INTRIGUING mysteries include "blue light" cemeteries. Many people believe that these blue lights and figures are ghosts, angels, or even demons. Others blame the phenomena on swamp gas or foxfire, a luminescent fungus that glows in the dark. The likely explanation is more simple . . . and perhaps more mystical.

Geologists explain that normal flashes occur when the mineral labradorite is exposed to bright, natural light. Although they can happen at any time, these flashes become especially obvious at night. The effect is so unique, it's called *labradorescence*.

No Need to Be Alarmed

Labradorite is a blue-green stone that's found in Finland, Nova Scotia, Newfoundland, and Labrador. The mineral has been used for gravestones, especially in Louisiana and Texas. Unfortunately, natural cracks and refractions within the mineral cause it to crumble, especially after years in the hot sun.

Thus, in cemeteries throughout Texas, pieces of crumbled labradorite glisten beneath the moon. Those shards reflect moonlight spark ghost stories

Or Is There?

According to folklore, labradorite can connect the living to the spirit world. Some psychics use labradorite to communicate with "the other side." Perhaps labradorite gravestones connect the worlds, too.

One of Texas's most famous blue light cemeteries is just west of Houston near Patterson Road. For more than 20 years, curiosity seekers have ignored poison ivy, spiders, snakes, and barbed wire to explore Hillendahl-Eggling Cemetery. It's been called "Blue Light Cemetery" since the 1940s when the

surrounding German community moved to make room for a Houston reservoir. Other Texas "blue light" cemetery locations include Andice, Cason, and Spring.

Austria's Atmospheric Anomalies

The southern Austrian state of Styria is pretty familiar with the paranormal and—what some local paranormal experts might call—mysterious atmospheric phenomena.

✳ ✳ ✳ ✳

THE SOUTHERN AUSTRIAN state of Styria is pretty familiar with the paranormal and—what some local paranormal experts might call—mysterious atmospheric phenomena. In recent years, there have been dozens of reports about completely amazing and awe striking aerial objects over the Aichfield Basin in southern Austria but no one—even officials—can explain why.

In July of 2014, one of the most witnessed mysterious atmospheric phenomenon took place over the night sky with hundreds of multicolored orbs moving at tremendous speeds. Many observers first believed it to be some type of natural phenomenon because of the objects' multicolored and fluid-like look, but soon rejected that notion as the objects flew in various formations. Not only that, but these high-speed, multicolored orbs—despite their numbers—were silent. Austrians may be used to seeing things in the sky, but this was surely a mysterious atmospheric phenomenon.

Many officials were contacted that evening for answers, but failed to give an adequate explanation even after some saw the phenomena themselves. Local media contacted traffic controllers for a comment about the event, and although they acknowledge they received many reports that night, they could say no more about the situation.

Ohio's Mysterious Hangar 18

An otherwordly legend makes its way from New Mexico to Ohio when the wreckage from Roswell ends up in the Midwest.

Even those who aren't UFO buffs have probably heard about the infamous Roswell Incident, where an alien spaceship supposedly crash-landed in the New Mexico desert, and the U.S. government covered the whole thing up. But what most people don't know is that according to legend, the mysterious aircraft was recovered (along with some alien bodies), secreted out of Roswell, and came to rest just outside of Dayton, Ohio.

✳ ✳ ✳ ✳

Something Crashed in the Desert

WHILE THE EXACT date is unclear, sometime during the first week of July 1947, a local Roswell rancher by the name of Mac Brazel decided to go out and check his property for fallen trees and other damage after a night of heavy storms and lightning. Brazel allegedly came across an area of his property littered with strange debris unlike anything he had ever seen before. Some of the debris even had strange writing on it.

Brazel showed some of the debris to a few neighbors and then took it to the office of Roswell sheriff George Wilcox, who called authorities at Roswell Army Air Field. After speaking with Wilcox, intelligence officer Major Jesse Marcel drove out to the Brazel ranch and collected as much debris as he could. He then returned to the airfield and showed the debris to his commanding officer, Colonel William Blanchard, commander of the 509th Bomb Group that was stationed at the Roswell Air Field. Upon seeing the debris, Blanchard dispatched military vehicles and personnel back out to the Brazel ranch to see if they could recover anything else.

"Flying Saucer Captured!"

On July 8, 1947, Colonel Blanchard issued a press release

stating that the wreckage of a "crashed disk" had been recovered. The bold headline of the July 8 edition of the *Roswell Daily Record* read: "RAAF Captures Flying Saucer on Ranch in Roswell Region." Newspapers around the world ran similar headlines. But then, within hours of the Blanchard release, General Roger M. Ramey, commander of the Eighth Air Force in Fort Worth, Texas, retracted Blanchard's release for him and issued another statement saying there was no UFO. Blanchard's men had simply recovered a fallen weather balloon.

Before long, the headlines that had earlier touted the capture of a UFO read: "It's a Weather Balloon" and "'Flying Disc' Turns Up as Just Hot Air." Later editions even ran a staged photograph of Major Jesse Marcel, who was first sent to investigate the incident, kneeling in front of weather balloon debris. Most of the general public seemed content with the explanation, but there were skeptics.

Whisked Away to Hangar 18?

Those who believe that aliens crash-landed near Roswell claim that, under cover of darkness, large portions of the alien spacecraft were brought out to the Roswell Air Field and loaded onto B-29 and C-54 aircrafts. Those planes were then supposedly flown to Wright-Patterson Air Force Base, just outside of Dayton. Once the planes landed, they were taxied over to Hangar 18 and unloaded. And according to legend, it's all still there.

There are some problems with the story, though. For one, none of the hangars on Wright-Patterson Air Force Base are officially known as "Hangar 18," and there are no buildings designated with the number 18. Rather, the hangars are labeled 1A, 1B, 1C, and so on. There's also the fact that none of the hangars seem large enough to house and conceal an alien spacecraft. But just because there's nothing listed as Hangar 18 on a Wright-Patterson map doesn't mean it's not there. Conspiracy theorists believe that hangars 4A, 4B, and 4C might be the infamous

Hangar 18. As for the overall size of the hangars, it's believed that most of the wreckage has been stored in giant underground tunnels and chambers deep under the hangar, both to protect the debris and to keep it safe from prying eyes. It is said that Wright-Patterson is currently conducting experiments on the wreckage to see if scientists can reverse-engineer the technology.

So What's the Deal?

The story of Hangar 18 only got stranger as the years went on, starting with the government's Project Blue Book, a program designed to investigate reported UFO sightings across the United States. Between 1947 and 1969, Project Blue Book investigated more than 12,000 UFO sightings before being disbanded. And where was Project Blue Book headquartered? Wright-Patterson Air Force Base.

Then in the early 1960s, Arizona senator Barry Goldwater, himself a retired major general in the U.S. Army Air Corps (and a friend of Colonel Blanchard), became interested in what, if anything, had crashed in Roswell. When Goldwater discovered Hangar 18, he first wrote directly to Wright-Patterson and asked for permission to tour the facility but was quickly denied. He then approached another friend, General Curtis LeMay, and asked if he could see the "Green Room" where the UFO secret was being held. Goldwater claimed that LeMay gave him "holy hell" and screamed at Goldwater, "Not only can't you get into it, but don't you ever mention it to me again."

Most recently, in 1982, retired pilot Oliver "Pappy" Henderson attended a reunion and announced that he was one of the men who had flown alien bodies out of Roswell in a C-54 cargo plane. His destination? Hangar 18 at Wright-Patterson. Although no one is closer to a definitive answer, it seems that the legend of Hangar 18 will never die.

Nefertiti Replaced by E.T.

New examinations of Tutankhamun's (King Tut) tomb might lead us to rewrite history to include our extraterrestrial friends in the narrative.

✳ ✳ ✳ ✳

Alien History

THE PROVENANCE OF Egypt's pyramids has been up for debate since their western-world discovery in the 19th century. Researchers and archaeologists have puzzled over how a people without the use of modern technology could construct such humongous edifices. Maybe it was slave labor with the help of gigantic pulleys and ramps that put the three-ton, limestone blocks in place. Or maybe it was with the help of extraterrestrial beings and their sophisticated crafts that did most of the grunt work.

The signs of extraterrestrial activity in King Tut's tomb come from reports by a French archeologist's recent radar scan of the tomb. Archeologist Avril Sap now claims that the myths of Queen Nefertiti's tomb being hidden under King Tut's tomb are false, and that something much more foreign lies within the chamber.

Sap is not alone in her claims. Even the Antiquities Ministry of Egypt has confirmed that what was originally thought to be in there is in fact not in there, and that what is in there is some type of extraterrestrial material that resembles a body. Neither the Antiquities Ministry of Egypt or Sap are confirming that they have found an extraterrestrial's body, but they're not discounting it either.

The tomb has long presented deep secrets to those who have studied it, but this only deepens the mystery. The chamber in question was thought to be the tomb of King Tut's supposed predecessor, Nefertiti, but hidden access into the chamber has prevented archeologists from confirming the rumors. Now, with the recent radar scans of the tomb, the rumors have moved even further away from being confirmed. Sap is now scanning the tomb to find entryways into the chamber but none have been found.

The mysteries of ancient Egypt only continue to grow as what we once thought to be true continues to be disproven. Who really knows how or why King Tut was buried with a blade made from a meteorite? Who knows what really lies within the chamber next to King Tut's tomb? All we know so far is that the Antiquities Ministry of Egypt knows about the extraterrestrial material inside the chamber. Whether or not it's a tomb for an alien is still to be uncovered.

The Great Texas Airship Mystery

Roswell, New Mexico, may be the most famous potential UFO crash site, but did Texas experience a similar event in the 19th century?

✳ ✳ ✳ ✳

ONE SUNNY APRIL morning in 1897, a UFO crashed in Aurora, Texas.

Six years before the Wright Brothers' first flight and 50 years before Roswell, a huge, cigar-shape UFO was seen in the skies. It was first noted on November 17, 1896, about a thousand feet above rooftops in Sacramento, California. From there, the spaceship traveled to San Francisco, where it was seen by hundreds of people.

A National Tour

Next, the craft crossed the United States, where it was observed by thousands. Near Omaha, Nebraska, a farmer reported the ship on the ground, making repairs. When it returned to the skies, it headed toward Chicago, where it was photographed on April 11, 1897, the first UFO photo on record. On April 15, near Kalamazoo, Michigan, residents reported loud noises "like that of heavy ordnance" coming from the spaceship.

Two days later, the UFO attempted a landing in Aurora, Texas, which should have been a good place. The town was almost deserted, and its broad, empty fields could have been an ideal landing strip.

No Smooth Sailing

However, at about 6 A.M. on April 17, the huge, cigar-shape airship "sailed over the public square and, when it reached the north part of town, collided with the tower of Judge Proctor's windmill and went to pieces with a terrific explosion, scattering debris over several acres of ground, wrecking the windmill and water tank and destroying the judge's flower garden."

That's how Aurora resident and cotton buyer S. E. Haydon described the events for *The Dallas Morning News*. The remains of the ship seemed to be strips and shards of a silver-colored metal. Just one body was recovered. The newspaper reported, "while his remains are badly disfigured, enough of the original has been picked up to show that he was not an inhabitant of this world."

On April 18, reportedly, that body was given a good, Christian burial in the Aurora cemetery, where it may remain to this day. A 1973 effort to exhume the body and examine it was successfully blocked by the Aurora Cemetery Association.

A Firsthand Account

Although many people have claimed the Aurora incident was a hoax, an elderly woman was interviewed in 1973 and clearly recalled the crash from her childhood. She said that her parents wouldn't let her near the debris from the spacecraft, in case it contained something dangerous. However, she described the alien as "a small man."

Aurora continues to attract people interested in UFOs. They wonder why modern Aurora appears to be laid out like a military base. Nearby, Fort Worth seems to be home to the U.S. government's experts in alien technology. Immediately after the Roswell UFO crash in 1947, debris from that spaceship was sent to Fort Worth for analysis.

Is There Any Trace Left?

The Aurora Encounter, a 1986 movie, documents the events that began when people saw the spacecraft attempt a landing at Judge Proctor's farm. Today, the Oates gas station marks the area where the UFO crashed. Metal debris was collected from the site in the 1970s and studied by North Texas State University. That study called one fragment "most intriguing": It appeared to be iron but wasn't magnetic; it was shiny and malleable rather than brittle, as iron should be.

As recently as 2008, UFOs have appeared in the north central Texas skies. In Stephenville, a freight company owner and pilot described a low-flying object in the sky, "a mile long and half a mile wide." Others who saw the ship several times during January 2008 said that its lights changed configuration, so it wasn't an airplane. The government declined to comment.

Today, a plaque at the Aurora cemetery mentions the spaceship, but the alien's tombstone—which, if it actually existed, is said to have featured a carved image of a spaceship—was stolen many years ago.

The Seven Wonders of
the Ancient World

It was the ultimate destination guide—seven of the most spectacular hand-built wonders of the world. In fact, the Greek referred to these wonders as theamati, which translates roughly to "must-sees."

✳ ✳ ✳ ✳

THE FIRST COMPREHENSIVE listing of the Seven Wonders has been attributed to Herodotus, a Greek historian dating back to the 5th century B.C. Other versions soon followed— each reflecting the writer's opinion of what was worth mentioning, and often naming many more than seven sights. Most of the earliest lists were lost; the oldest existing version known today was compiled by Antipater of Sidon in 140 B.C. The items on his list, with a few revisions, are the ones that came to forever be known as the Seven Wonders of the Ancient World. Unfortunately, only one of the seven still exists today; all that remains of the other six are descriptions from writers over the centuries.

So What's the Big Deal?

What makes the seven wonders of the world so wonderful? It's a combination of factors: the intricacies of the architecture, the scale of engineering, and the beauty of each project—not to mention the construction technology and available materials in use at the time.

Religion often played a big role in the significance of these structures. Some were built to honor certain gods. Others were built to showcase important rulers, a number of whom had achieved a godlike following.

And the Seven Wonders Are . . .

1. **The Great Pyramid of Giza :** Located on the west bank of the Nile river near Cairo, Egypt, this is the largest of ten

pyramids built between 2600 and 2500 B.C. Built for King Khufu, the Great Pyramid was constructed by thousands of workers toiling over the span of decades (2609 B.C.– 2584 B.C.). The structure consists of more than two million 2.5-ton stones. If the stones were piled on top of each other, the resulting tower would be close to 50 stories high. The base covers an astonishing 13 acres. It's not known exactly how the blocks were lifted. Theories include mud- and water-coated ramps or an intricate system of levers. Not only did the blocks have to be lifted, but they also had to be transported from the quarries. Even the experts can't say exactly how that was done. The mystery is part of the fascination. The pyramid originally stood 481 feet high but has been weathered down to about 450 feet. It was considered the tallest structure on the planet for 43 centuries. The Great Pyramid is the only Wonder of the Ancient World still standing—a testament to one of the mightiest civilizations in history.

2. **The Hanging Gardens of Babylon :** Legend has it the Gardens were built by King Nebuchadnezzar II, ruler of Babylon (near modern Baghdad, Iraq), around 600 B.C. as a present for his wife, Amytis of Media. The gardens consisted of a series of terraces holding trees, exotic plants, and shady pools—all fed by water piped in from the Euphrates River and rising about 60 feet high. References to the Gardens appear as late as the first century B.C., after which they disappear from contemporary accounts. There has been some speculation over whether or not the Gardens ever actually existed.

3. **The Temple of Artemis at Ephesus :** Constructed around 550 B.C. in what is now Turkey, the Temple was built in honor of Artemis (Diana), goddess of hunting and nature. The marble temple measured 377 by 180 feet and had a tile-covered roof held up by at least 106 columns between 40 and 60 feet high. The temple held priceless art and

also functioned as the treasury of the city. It stood until 356 B.C. when it was purposely destroyed by an artist, known in infamy as Herostratus, who burned the Temple merely so his name would be remembered for ages. The outraged Ephesians rebuilt the temple, this time entirely of stone, but the new building was destroyed by invading Goths in A.D. 262. A few surviving sculptures are displayed at the British Museum.

4. **The Statue of Zeus at Olympia :** Even contemporary historians and archaeologists consider the Statue of Zeus at Olympia to be one of the best-known statues in the ancient world. The image, standing 40 feet high with a 20-foot base, was constructed by Phidias around 435 B.C. to honor Zeus, king of the gods. The statue depicted a seated Zeus (made of ivory, though his robes and sandals were made of gold) holding a golden figure of the goddess of victory in one hand and a staff topped with an eagle in the other. Atop his head was a wreath of olive branches. In the flickering lamplight of the temple, the statue seemed almost alive and attracted pilgrims from all over Greece for eight centuries. After the old gods were outlawed by Christian emperor Theodosius, the statue was taken as a prize to Constantinople, where it was destroyed in a fire around A.D. 462.

5. **The Mausoleum of Maussollos :** This white marble tomb, built in what is today southwestern Turkey, was built around 353 B.C. for Maussollos, a Persian king. Around 45 stories tall, the building was covered in relief sculpture depicting scenes from mythology; gaps were filled in with bigger-than-life statues of famous heroes and gods. The very top was capped with a marble statue of Maussollos, pulled in a chariot by four horses. The structure was so impressive that the king's name has been lent to the present-day word mausoleum, now used to refer to an impressive burial place. The tomb remained largely intact until

the 13th century, when it was severely damaged by a series of earthquakes. In 1494, the Knights of Saint John raided its stonework to use as building materials for a castle being constructed nearby, and thus the Mausoleum was lost to history.

6. **The Colossus of Rhodes :** Standing nearly 110 feet tall—rivaling the modern Statue of Liberty, which tops out at 151 feet—the Colossus of Rhodes was a sight to behold. The bronze statue was built near the harbor of Rhodes in the Aegean Sea in honor of the sun god Helios. Construction took 12 years—from approximately 292 B.C. to 280 B.C. The exact pose of the statue is a matter of debate; records say that one arm was raised but are maddeningly silent on other details. The statue stood for only 56 years before it was toppled by an earthquake. It lay on the ground for another 800 years, still a tourist attraction. Accounts say a popular tourist game was to see if a person could encircle one of the fallen statue's thumbs with their arms. Finally, in A.D. 654, Rhodes was captured by invaders who broke up the statue and melted it down for bronze.

7. **The Lighthouse of Alexandria :** The youngest of the ancient wonders was a building with a civic, rather than a spiritual, purpose. The famed lighthouse of Alexandria was built around 250 B.C. to aid ships making the journey into that city's harbor. At 380 feet tall, it was a marvel of ancient engineering. Overshadowed only by two of the tallest Egyptian pyramids, a tower of greater height wouldn't be constructed for centuries. An interior ramp led up to a platform supporting a series of polished bronze mirrors, which would reflect sunlight during the day and firelight at night. The fuel source is uncertain but may have been oil or even animal dung. Some accounts claim the lighthouse could be seen 300 miles from the shore; this is almost certainly exaggerated, but more reasonable claims of 35 miles are impressive enough. It continued to impress travelers into the 1300s, when it was destroyed by an earthquake.

The Mysterious Area 51

Who killed JFK? Did Americans really land on the moon? Conspiracy theorists have been debating these questions for years. But they all agree on one thing—these conspiracies pale in comparison to the mother of all conspiracies: Area 51.

✳ ✳ ✳ ✳

ALIEN AUTOPSIES. COVERT military operations. Tests on bizarre aircraft. These are all things rumored to be going on inside Area 51—a top secret location inside the Nevada Test and Training Range (NTTR) about an hour northwest of Las Vegas. Though shrouded in secrecy, some of the history of Area 51 is known. For instance, this desert area was used as a bombing test site during World War II, but no facility existed on the site until 1955. At that time, the area was chosen as the perfect location to develop and test the U-2 spy plane. Originally known as Watertown, it came to be called Area 51 in 1958 when 38,000 acres were designated for military use. The entire area was simply marked "Area 51" on military maps. Today, the facility is rumored to contain approximately 575 square miles. But you won't find it on a map because, officially, it doesn't exist.

An Impenetrable Fortress

Getting a clear idea of the size of Area 51, or even a glimpse of the place, is next to impossible. Years ago, curiosity seekers could get a good view of the facility by hiking to the top of two nearby mountain peaks known as White Sides and Freedom Ridge. But government officials soon grew weary of people climbing up there and snapping pictures, so in 1995, they seized control of both. Currently, the only way to legally catch a glimpse of the base is to scale 7,913-foot-tall Tikaboo Peak. Even if you make it that far, you're still not guaranteed to see anything because the facility is more than 25 miles away and is only visible on clear days with no haze.

The main entrance to Area 51 is along Groom Lake Road. Those brave (or foolhardy) souls who have ventured down the road to investigate quickly realize they are being watched. Video cameras and motion sensors are hidden along the road, and signs alert the curious that if they continue any further, they will be entering a military installation, which is illegal "without the written permission of the installation commander." If that's not enough to get unwanted guests to turn around, one sign clearly states: "Use of deadly force authorized." Simply put, take one step over that imaginary line in the dirt, and they will get you.

Camo Dudes

And just exactly who are "they"? They are the "Camo Dudes," mysterious figures watching trespassers from nearby hillsides and jeeps. If they spot something suspicious, they might call for backup—Blackhawk helicopters that will come in for a closer look. All things considered, it would probably be best to just turn around and go back home. And lest you think about hiring someone to fly you over Area 51, the entire area is considered restricted air space, meaning that unauthorized aircraft are not permitted to fly over, or even near, the facility.

Who Works There?

Most employees are general contractors who work for companies in the area. But rather than allow these workers to commute individually, the facility has them ushered in secretly and en masse in one of two ways. The first is a mysterious white bus with tinted windows that picks up employees at several unmarked stops before whisking them through the front gates of the facility. Every evening, the bus leaves the facility and drops the employees off.

The second mode of commuter transport, an even more secretive way, is JANET, the code name given to the secret planes that carry workers back and forth from Area 51 and Las Vegas McCarran Airport. JANET has its own terminal, which is located at the far end of the airport behind fences with special security gates. It even has its own private parking lot. Several times a day, planes from the JANET fleet take off and land at the airport.

Bob Lazar

The most famous Area 51 employee is someone who may or may not have actually worked there. In the late 1980s, Bob Lazar claimed that he'd worked at the secret facility he referred to as S-4. In addition, Lazar said that he was assigned the task of reverse engineering a recovered spaceship in order to determine how it worked. Lazar had only been at the facility for a short time, but he and his team had progressed to the point where they were test flying the alien spaceship. That's when Lazar made a big mistake. He decided to bring some friends out to Groom Lake Road when he knew the alien craft was being flown. He was caught and subsequently fired.

During his initial interviews with a local TV station, Lazar seemed credible and quite knowledgeable as to the inner workings of Area 51. But when people started trying to verify the information Lazar was giving, not only was it next to impossible to confirm most of his story, his education and employment history could not be verified either. Skeptics immediately proclaimed that Lazar was a fraud. To this day, Lazar contends that everything he said was factual and that the government deleted all his records in order to set him up and make him look like a fake. Whether or not he's telling the truth, Lazar will be remembered as the man who first brought up the idea that alien spaceships were being experimented on at Area 51.

What's Really Going On?

So what really goes on inside Area 51? One thing we do know is that they work on and test aircraft. Whether they are alien spacecraft or not is still open to debate. Some of the planes worked on and tested at Area 51 include the SR-71 Blackbird and the F-117 Nighthawk stealth fighter. Currently, there are rumors that a craft known only by the codename Aurora is being worked on at the facility.

If you want to try and catch a glimpse of some of these strange craft being tested, you'll need to hang out at the "Black Mailbox" along Highway 375, also known as the Extraterrestrial Highway. It's really nothing more than a mailbox along the side of the road. But as with most things associated with Area 51, nothing is as it sounds, so it should come as no surprise that the "Black Mailbox" is actually white. It belongs to a rancher, who owns the property nearby. Still, this is the spot where people have been known to camp out all night just for a chance to see something strange floating in the night sky.

The Lawsuit

In 1994, a landmark lawsuit was filed against the U.S. Air Force by five unnamed contractors and the widows of two others. The suit claimed that the contractors had been present at Area 51 when large quantities of "unknown chemicals" were burned in trenches and pits. As a result of coming into contact with the fumes of the chemicals, the suit alleged that two of the contractors died, and the five survivors suffered respiratory problems and skin sores. Reporters worldwide jumped on the story, not only because it proved that Area 51 existed but also because the suit was asking for many classified documents to be entered as evidence. Would some of those documents refer to alien beings or spacecraft? The world would never know because in September 1995, while petitions for the case were still going on, President Bill Clinton signed Presidential Determination No. 95–45, which basically stated that Area 51 was exempt from federal, state, local, and interstate hazardous and solid waste laws. Shortly thereafter, the lawsuit was dismissed due to a lack of evidence, and all attempts at appeals were rejected. In 2002, President George W. Bush renewed Area 51's exemptions, ensuring once and for all that what goes on inside Area 51 stays inside Area 51.

So at the end of the day, we're still left scratching our heads about Area 51. We know it exists and we have some idea of what goes on there, but there is still so much more we don't know. More than likely, we never will know everything, but then again, what fun is a mystery if you know all the answers?

Thomas Tresham Ties Triangles Together

Nothing prompts a person to build a bizarre, triangular stone lodge in the middle of nowhere quite like religious persecution. At least, that's how Sir Thomas Tresham felt back in 1593 when he began work on what would become the mysterious Rushton Triangular Lodge, a structure that he hoped would be much more than a place to hang his hat.

✳ ✳ ✳ ✳

But Why?

A T THE END of the 16th century, life wasn't much fun for Catholics living in England, as Tresham could attest. As a devout Catholic, he'd spent 15 years in prison—his faith had made him a criminal in the eyes of the law. Once he was a free man, Tresham figured he'd better keep his mouth shut about his religion, but that didn't keep him from professing his faith in other ways.

Tresham decided to build a secretly Catholic monument near Rushton that would encode messages to keep it safe from Protestant adversaries. The bricks and mortar of his lodge would showcase aspects of his faith without betraying his freedom. The man stuck to his plan so diligently that the details of Rushton Triangular Lodge are downright weird.

The Rule of Three

To represent the Holy Trinity, Tresham designed the building with only three walls. The structure is itself a perfect equilateral triangle, its walls meeting at 60-degree angles. Glorifying the Holy Trinity via the rule of three is repeated (and repeated and repeated) throughout the whole building. Check this out:

* Each of the three walls is 33.3 feet.

* Each floor of the three-story building has three windows.

* Each wall has three gables. Each gable is 3 feet by 3 feet with three-sided pinnacles.

* There are nine gargoyles (three sets of three).

* Friezes run along the walls on each side of the building, containing a phrase in Latin—each phrase contains exactly 33 letters.

* And though the main room on each floor is hexagonal in shape, if you draw three bisecting lines through a hexagon, you get six more equilateral triangles.

* And if all those threes are making you a little dizzy, just wait—Tresham was far from content with a few triangular tricks. The building's ornaments were where Tresham spared no expense to work in secret codes for the glory of the Lord.

Gables, and Windows, and Math, Oh My!

Two of the gables of Tresham's lodge are inscribed with dates. One of the dates is 1641, one is 1626. Indeed, Tresham carved future dates into the side of the building for a reason. If you subtract 1593 (the year he started building) from 1626, you get 33. Subtract 1593 from 1641, and you get 48. Both numbers are divisible by three—no big surprise there—but there's something more. If you add the anno domani (commonly known as "A.D.") you get the years of Jesus' death and the Virgin Mary's death, respectively. The second gable shows the dates 3898 B.C. and 3509 B.C., dates that are said to be the years of the Great Flood and the call of Abraham.

The windows provided another place for Tresham to work in his code magic. The three windows on the first floor are in the shape of a Gothic trefoil, a vaguely triangular-shape Christian symbol that also happened to be the Tresham family crest. The trefoil-shape is carried through to the basement windows as well, all of which are, of course, repeated in threes.

Double Entendres

* As mentioned before, there were three 33-character-long inscriptions on the Rushton Lodge, one on each side. The inscriptions and their respective translations read as follows:

* "Aperiatur terra & germinet salvatorem" means "Let the earth open and let them bring forth a Savior."

* "Quis seperabit nos a charitate Christi" means "Who shall separate us from the love of Christ."

* "Consideravi opera tua domine at expavi" means "I have considered your works and am sorely afraid."

* In addition, if you inspect all the waterspouts at Tresham's place, you'll find a letter above each one. Together, they createan acronym for the first three letters of a Latin mass. An inscription above the main door to the lodge reads *Tres Testiminium Dant*, which means "these three bear witness." But Tresham's wife is said to have called him "Tres" for short; knowing that, one might interpret this as: "Tresham bears witness," which was certainly the point of all this obsessive building.

Even More Hidden Meaning?

Tresham got away with his secretly Catholic building—though it certainly raised a few eyebrows. In fact, the building (which is now maintained as a historical site by the English Heritage organization) is still a source of much discussion. Some people don't think Tresham was über-Catholic at all, that all those numbers and all that funky math were rooted in black magic.

Either way, the building is a great example of the era's love of allegory—using something to represent something else entirely. After the Triangular Lodge was done, Tresham started *another* building full of secret codes and mysterious math called

Lyveden New Bield but died before it was finished. It still sits in England exactly as it was left, half-built and full of its own mystery.

Reward: One Lost Island

Did the legendary island of Atlantis ever really exist? Or did Plato make the whole thing up?

✳   ✳   ✳   ✳

IT'S HARD TO believe that Plato, an early Greek philosopher, was the type to start rumors. But in two of his dialogues, *Timaeus* and *Critias*, he refers to what has become one of the most famous legends of all time: the doomed island of Atlantis.

In *Timaeus*, Plato uses a story told by Critias to describe where Atlantis existed, explaining that it "came forth out of the Atlantic Ocean, for in those days the Atlantic was navigable; and there was an island situated in front of the straits which are by you called the Pillars of Heracles; the island was larger than Libya and Asia put together, and was the way to other islands..." Not only that, but Plato also divulges the details of its fate: "afterwards there occurred violent earthquakes and floods; and in a single day and night of misfortune all your warlike men in a body sank into the earth, and the island of Atlantis in like manner disappeared in the depths of the sea. For which reason the sea in those parts is impassable and impenetrable, because there is a shoal of mud in the way; and this was caused by the subsidence of the island." In *Critias*, the story revolves around Poseidon, the god of the sea, and how the kingdom of Atlantis attempted to conquer Athens.

Although many ascribe Plato's myth to his desire for a way to emphasize his own political theories, historians and writers perpetuated the idea of the mythical island for centuries, both in fiction and nonfiction. After the Middle Ages, the story of the doomed civilization was revisited by such writers as Francis

Bacon, who published *The New Atlantis* in 1627. In 1870, Jules Verne published his classic *Twenty Thousand Leagues Under the Sea*, which includes a visit to sunken Atlantis aboard Captain Nemo's submarine *Nautilus*. And in 1882, *Atlantis: The Antediluvian World* by Ignatius Donnelly was written to prove that Atlantis did exist—initiating much of the Atlantis mania that has occurred since that time. The legendary Atlantis continues to surface in today's science fiction, romantic fantasy, and even mystery stories.

More recently, historians and geologists have attempted to link Atlantis to the island of Santorini (also called Thera) in the Aegean Sea. About 3,600 years ago, one of the largest eruptions in the history of planet Earth occurred at the site of Santorini: the Minoa, or Thera, eruption. This caused the volcano to collapse, creating a huge caldera or "hole" at the top of the volcanic mountain. Historians believe the eruption caused the end of the Minoan civilization on Thera and the nearby island of Crete, most likely because a tsunami resulted from the massive explosion. Since that time, most of the islands, which are actually a complex of overlapping shield volcanoes, grew from subsequent volcanic eruptions around the caldera, creating what is now the volcanic archipelago of islands called the Cycladic group.

Could this tourist hot spot truly be the site of the mythological island Atlantis? Some say that Plato's description of the palace and surroundings at Atlantis were similar to those at Knossos, the central ceremonial and cultural center of the Minoan civilization. On the scientific end, geologists know that eruptions such as the one at Santorini can pump huge volumes of material into the air and slump other parts of a volcanic island into the oceans. To the ancient peoples, such an event could literally be translated as an island quickly sinking into the ocean. But even after centuries of study, excavation, and speculation, the mystery of Atlantis remains unsolved.

Dan Brown's blockbuster novel *The Da Vinci Code* reignited public interest in Atlantis in a roundabout way. Brown's story referenced the Knights Templar, an early Christian military order with a dramatic history that involved bloodshed, exile, and secrets—one of which was that they were carriers of ancient wisdom from the lost city of Atlantis.

Lunar Legacy: The Big Whack?

Here's one thing we know for certain about the moon: It isn't made of cheese. Most everything else, including its origins, is a matter of scientific reasoning and speculation.

✻　✻　✻　✻

Mooning Over the Moon

OUR PLANET'S MOON, our only true natural satellite, has stimulated romance, mystery, and scientific curiosity. And no wonder—besides the sun, the moon is the most noticeable member of our solar system, measuring about one-quarter the size of Earth. Only one side faces our planet, and every month, because of its orbit around us, we watch the moon change phases, from full to quarter to gibbous to new and back again. The moon is also the subject of various origin theories, which alternately laud it as a deity or discount it as a flying chunk of rock, depending on the culture.

Blinded by Science

The list of scientific theories concerning the moon's origin is a bit smaller. One theory suggests that the moon was "captured" by Earth's gravity as it traveled by our planet; another theory posits that our planet and its satellite formed side by side as the solar system developed some 4.56 billion years ago. The moon has simply tagged along with us ever since.

The most recently accepted theory has its origins in the 19th century. In 1879, the son of British astronomer George Darwin (son of Charles Darwin) suggested that a rapidly spinning

Earth threw off material from the Pacific Ocean, creating the moon. The idea drew criticism on and off for decades. But thanks to the advent of modern computers, scientists have created a similar theoretical scenario that makes parts of Darwin's suggestion more reasonable. The data suggests that while Earth was still in a semimolten state, it was hit by a space body—a protoplanet, or planetesimal—almost the size of Mars, or about half the size of Earth. The massive collision would have sent a huge chunk of broken material into orbit around Earth; over time, those larger pieces could have gathered together—thanks to gravity—creating our moon.

It's All Relative?

Why do scientists now agree with the "Moon, daughter of Earth" theory? One of the main reasons is the Apollo program, the U.S. moon missions. Astronauts gathered and delivered more than 800 pounds of lunar material back to Earth. The dates of those rocks—ranging from 3.2 to 4.2 billion years old for material gathered from the flat, dark maria (lava seas) and 4.3 to 4.5 billion years old for rocks from the highlands—along with their composition, have led scientists to believe that the moon is definitely related to Earth.

The evidence is in the fact that the rocks are similar to Earth's mantle material—the moving, molten layer of our planet just under the crust. If a huge planetary body struck our planet, it would make sense that the resulting material would be similar to rock deep below Earth's surface. In addition, moon rocks have exactly the same oxygen isotope composition as Earth's rocks. Materials from other parts of the solar system have different oxygen isotope compositions, which means that the moon probably formed around Earth's neighborhood.

Is the moon our only satellite? Scientists know there are other space bodies circling our planet, but none of the objects can be considered a moon. They are more likely asteroids caught in the Earth's and moon's gravitation. For example, the asteroid 3753 Cruithne looks like it's following Earth in the orbit around the sun; the asteroid 2002 AA29 follows a horseshoe path near Earth. Neither is a moon, and so far neither rock has been in danger of striking our planet. Another object once caught scientists' eyes: Nearby J002E3 was considered a possible new moon of Earth until it was determined to be the third stage of the *Apollo 12* Saturn V rocket.

Legendary Lake Mills

Along the interstate between Madison and Milwaukee is the small town that dubbed itself "Legendary Lake Mills." It's legendary, indeed, and controversial too.

✻ ✻ ✻ ✻

An Underwater Mystery

SINCE THE 1840s, locals have buzzed about "stone tepees" standing at the bottom of Rock Lake. The idea seems plausible. Less than three miles due east is Aztalan State Park, an archeological site where the ancient remains of a Middle-Mississippian village, temple mounds, and ceremonial complex have been restored.

But Native American legend and local folklore, combined with years of third-party research, have not been enough to persuade top scientists that there are pyramids beneath Rock Lake's waters. In fact, the phenomena has been dubbed "North America's most controversial underwater archeological discovery of the 20th century."

One theory holds that Ancient Aztecs believed that their ancestors hailed from a land far north of Mexico, called Aztalan. The legend goes that in 1066, the Aztalans of Lake Mills appealed to the gods for relief from a long drought by building sacrificial pyramids. Rain came down, creating a beautiful lake and submerging the pyramids. They named the lake *Tyranena*, meaning "sparkling waters."

Fast-forward 800 years. When the first white settlers set up camp along Tyranena's banks in the 1830s, the resident Winnebago people shared the story of Tyranena with them. But even the Winnebago didn't quite understand the story, as it came from a "foreign tribe." The lore remained as elusive as the small islands that settlers reported as floating above the water.

Soon after the settlers arrived, a sawmill and a gristmill were built on the lake's edge, subsequently raising the water level. What little was left to see of the supposed pyramids was submerged.

Doubt and Circumstance

Over the next 200 years, the lake would be caught up in a continuous cycle of sensationalism and doubt, false starts, and circumstance. In the early 1900s, two brothers, Claude and Lee Wilson, went out duck hunting one hot, clear day during a drought and were able to reach down and touch the so-called pyramid's apex with an oar. Local residents would find the pyramid again the next day, but by the time a reporter got onto the lake a week later rain had fallen, ending the drought and raising the water level. Through the decades, anglers would declare their belief in the structures when they snagged their lines and nets, but interest waned.

The lore was rekindled in the 1930s when a local school-teacher, Victor Taylor, took it upon himself to canvass residents and dive over the pyramids, without diving equipment. He described four conical underwater structures. With this "evidence," state and national agencies threw money into the effort, even hiring professional divers to explore the underwater structures. But these divers were literally mired by the lake's deteriorating, muddy bottom, mucking up belief in the pyramids once again.

Eventually the controversy would reach an MIT engineer, Max Nohl, the man who invented the first scuba-type device. A master excavator, Nohl made it his personal mission to uncover the truth beneath the lake. He rekindled the town's pyramid fever with his extensive dives and written accounts with detailed measurements.

Debunked?

While Nohl successfully made his case, the curious fact remained that no professional archeologist wanted to be associated with Rock Lake. The establishment theory contends that the lake bottom anomalies are merely glacial castoffs from the last Ice Age. In an article in the September 1962 issue of *The Wisconsin Archeologist*, the pyramids were wholly debunked by the state's academes, who alleged that Native Americans didn't work in stone and that mound-building only began 2,000 years prior, whereas Rock Lake was at least 10,000 years old. Case closed. Or not.

In July 1967, Jack Kennedy, a professional diver from Illinois, was sport diving with friends on Rock Lake. Near the end of the day, after all of his comrades had run out of air, Kennedy took one last dive . . . over a pyramid. Shocked at his discovery, he removed three rocks from its wall. Further analysis revealed the rocks were made of quartzite from a riverbed. The first concrete evidence was now in hand.

Kennedy continued to dive at Rock Lake, eventually making a sketch of a structure 70 feet long, 30 feet wide, and 15 feet tall, which appeared in *Skin Diver* magazine. His discovery led to a resurgence in the exploration of Rock Lake, a summer haven for leisure boaters and beachgoers. Explorers have documented stone rings, tombs, curiously long rock bars, and pyramidal structures in dives, sonic sonar, and aerial photography. In 1998, two Rock Lake enthusiasts, Archie Eschborn and Jack LeTourneau, formed Rock Lake Research Society to "document and help preserve these archeological treasures that could rewrite North American history . . . and persuade state officials to declare Rock Lake a historical site."

History Still Unwritten

Does the Aztalan connection hold water? How does glacial activity fit in the picture?

To date, Rock Lake remains just that, a lake, which is still unprotected as a historical site. But locals continue to believe, if not for the archeological and anthropological truth, then for the opportunities the lore and legend provide. In Lake Mills, you can stay at the Pyramid Motel or throw back a Stone Tepee Pale Ale, made by the city's resident Tyranena Brewing Company. Or perhaps you can head to one of the city's three beaches and try your hand at uncovering the mysteries of the "sparkling waters" yourself.

Sunken Civilizations

Researchers have discovered the tantalizing remains of what appears to be advanced Mesolithic and Neolithic civilizations hidden for millennia under water or sand. But are the ancient cities real, or is it just wishful thinking?

✳   ✳   ✳   ✳

La Marmotta: Stone Age Lakefront

WHAT IS NOW the bottom of Italy's six-mile-wide Lake Bracciano was once a lovely and fertile river floodplain. In 1989, scientists discovered a lost city, which they renamed La Marmotta. Dive teams have recovered artifacts ranging from ancient timbers to uneaten pots of stew, all preserved under ten feet of mud.

The site dates back to about 5700 B.C. around the late Stone Age or Neolithic era. Though not much is known about the people who lived there, scientists do know that the city's residents migrated from the Near East or Greece in 35-foot-long, wooden dugout boats with their families. They had domesticated animals, pottery, religious statues, and even two species of dogs. They laid out their village with large wooden houses.

Items such as obsidian knives and greenstone ax blades show that La Marmotta was a busy Mediterranean trade center. But after 400 years of occupation, it seems the village was hastily abandoned. Why they fled still puzzles researchers.

Atlantis Beneath the Black Sea

Ever since the Greek writer Plato described the lost island of Atlantis in the 4th century B.C., scholars have searched for its location. One oft-suggested candidate is a grouping of underwater settlements northwest of the Black Sea. Researchers claim this advanced Neolithic population center was once situated on shore along a freshwater lake that was engulfed by seawater by 5510 B.C. Ancient landforms in the area seem to have centered around an island that roughly fits the description of Atlantis. Similarities between the lore of Atlantis and this settlement include the use of a form of early writing, the existence of elephants (from eastern trade routes), obsidian used as money, and circular observatory structures.

Japan, Gateway to Mu

According to Japanese geologist Masaaki Kimura, a legendary lost continent called Mu may have been discovered off the coast of Japan. Kimura says underwater formations that were found in 1985 at Yonaguni Island indicate that they were handmade and that they possibly once resembled a Roman city complete with a coliseum, a castle, statues, paved streets, and plazas. Although photos show sharp, step-like angles and flat surfaces, skeptics still argue these "roads" were actually created by forces such as tides or volcanoes. Nevertheless, Kimura maintains his belief that the ruins are the proof of a 5,000-year-old city.

Ancient Alpine Lake Towns

Today, most people would associate the Alps, the mountain region that borders Germany, Switzerland, and Italy, with skiing. But in late Stone Age or Neolithic period (6000–2000 B.C.), the region's lakes dominated the action. A dry spell in the mid-1800s lowered water levels and allowed evidence of ancient villages to surface within many lakes in the region. One site at the Swiss town of Obermeilen yielded exciting finds such as wooden posts, artifacts made from antlers, Neolithic clay objects, and wooden utensils. It is now believed that the posts supported large wooden platforms that sat over the water, serving as docklike foundations for houses and other village structures.

Hamoukar: City of Commerce

Until the mid-1970s, when the ancient settlement of Hamoukar was discovered in Syria, archaeologists believed the world's oldest cities—dating back to 4000 B.C.—were in present-day Iraq. But the massive, 750-acre Hamoukar, surrounded by a 13-inch-thick wall and home to an estimated 25,000 people, was already a prosperous and advanced city by 4000 B.C.

Situated in the land between the Tigris and Euphrates rivers, Hamoukar was sophisticated enough to support commercial bakeries and large-scale beer breweries. People used clay seals as "brands" for mass-produced goods, including delicate pottery, jewelry, and stone goods. The city was also a processing area for obsidian and later, copper. The settlement was destroyed in a fierce battle around 3500 B.C., leaving more than 1,000 slingshot bullets in the city's ruins.

The Great Danes

They sure ate a lot of shellfish—that much is known about the Mesolithic European culture that lived along the coast of what is now Denmark between 5600 and 4000 B.C. The now-underwater cities were investigated in the 1970s; the first is known as Tybrind Vig and its people are called the Ertebölle. The Ertebölle skeletons resemble those of modern Danes, but some also show Cro-Magnon facial features such as protruding jaws and prominent brow ridges. Archaeologists have found implements made of antler, bone, and stone sticking out of the Danish sea floor. They also found large piles of shellfish at the oldest sites, indicating that the inhabitants loved seafood. Preserved remains of acorns, hazelnuts, and other plants showed their diet was well rounded.

The Ertebölle made clever use of local materials. They lived in wattle or brush huts; "knitted" clothing from plant fibers; made ceramic pots decorated with impressions of grains, cord, and bones; and created art from polished bone and amber. Eventually, it is assumed, the Ertebölle hunter-gatherers either evolved into or were replaced by people with farming skills.

Mystery of the Bimini Blocks

The reason adventurers Robert Ferro and Michael Grumley traveled to the Bahamas was that they had read psychic Edgar Cayce's 1936 prediction that Atlantis would be found in the late 1960s off Bimini Island in the Bahamas. Needless to say, their discovery in the late '60s of giant rows of flat, rectangular blocks resembling a road off northern Bimini was a tad controversial.

The sunken, geometrically arranged rocks stretched for an estimated 700 to 1,000 feet. Several investigators estimated the "structure" dated back to 10,000 B.C. Since then, other explorers have claimed to find additional stones that may have once formed part of an encircling wall around the entire island. Author Charles Berlitz observed that the stones resembled work by pre-Incan Peruvians.

However, geologists have noted that island shore rocks may split into regular planes due to a combination of solar exposure and shifting subsoil—formations resembling the Bimini Blocks also exist off the coast of Australia.

The Library of the Muses

By far the most famous library in history, the Library of Alexandria held an untold number of ancient works. Its fiery destruction meant the irrecoverable loss of a substantial part of the world's intellectual history.

✳ ✳ ✳ ✳

The Library's Beginnings

THE CITIES OF ancient Mesopotamia (e.g., Uruk, Nineveh, Babylon) and Egypt (e.g., Thebes, Memphis) had cultivated archives and libraries since the Bronze Age, but the idea for a library as grand as Alexandria did not occur in Greek culture until the Hellenistic Age, when Alexander the Great's conquests brought both Greece and these former civilizations under Macedonian rule. Previous Greek libraries were owned by individuals; the largest belonged to Aristotle (384–322 B.C.), whose work and school (the Lyceum) in Athens were supported by Alexander.

When Alexander died suddenly in 323 B.C., his generals carved his empire into regional dynasties. The Hellenistic dynasties competed with each other for three centuries (until each was in turn conquered by either Rome or Parthia). Each dynasty desired cultural dominance, so they invited famous artists, authors, and intellectuals to live and work in their capital cities. Alexander's general Ptolemy, who controlled Egypt, decided to develop a collection of the world's learning (the Library) and a research center, the Mouseion (the Museum, or "Temple of the Muses"), where scholars on subsidy could study and add their research to the collection. This idea may well have come from Demetrius of Phaleron (350–280 B.C.), Ptolemy's advisor and the former governor of Athens, who had been a pupil at the Lyceum, but the grand project became one of the hallmarks of the Ptolemaic dynasty. Under the first three Ptolemies, the Museum, a royal library, and a smaller "daughter" library at the Temple of Serapis (the Serapeum) were built and grew as Alexandria became the intellectual, as well as commercial, capital of the Hellenistic world.

Egypt and Alexandria offered the Ptolemies distinct advantages for accomplishing their goals. Egypt was not only immensely rich, which gave it the wealth to purchase materials and to bring scholars to Alexandria, but it was the major producer of papyrus, a marsh reed that was beaten into a flat surface and made into scrolls for writing and copying. Alexandria was also the commercial hub of the Mediterranean, and goods and information from all over the world passed through its port.

Bibliomania: So Many Scrolls, So Little Time

Acquiring materials for the libraries and Museum became somewhat of an obsession for the Ptolemies. Although primarily focused on Greek and Egyptian works, their interests included translating other traditions into Greek. Among the most important of these efforts was the production of the Septuagint, a Greek version of the Jewish scriptures. Besides employing agents to scour major book markets and to search out copies of works not yet in the library, boats coming into Alexandria were required to declare any scrolls on board. If they were of interest, the scrolls were confiscated and copied, and the owners were given the copies and some compensation. Ptolemy III (285–222 B.C.) may have acquired Athens' official state collection of the plays of Aeschylus, Sophocles, and Euripides in a similar way—putting up 15 talents of silver as a guarantee while he had the plays copied, then foregoing the treasure in favor of keeping the originals. Whether or not this is true, it speaks to the value he placed on getting important works and the resources he had at his disposal to do so.

Alexandria's efforts were fueled by a fierce competition with the Hellenistic kingdom of Pergamum (modern Bergamo, Turkey), which created its own library. Each library sought to claim new finds and to produce new editions, leading at times to the acquisition of forgeries and occasional embarrassment. Alexandria finally tried to undercut its rival by cutting off papyrus exports, but Pergamum perfected a method for making writing material out of animal skins (now called "parchment" from the Latin pergamina) and continued to build its holdings. Eventually, however, Alexandria got the upper hand when the Roman general Marcus Antonius (Mark Antony) conquered Pergamum and made a present of its library to his lover, the Ptolemaic Queen Cleopatra.

Estimates as to the number of volumes in the Alexandrian library ranged wildly even in antiquity, generally between 200,000 and 700,000. Estimates are complicated by the fact that it isn't clear whether the numbers originate from works or scrolls: Some scrolls contained one work, some multiple works, and long works like the Iliad took multiple scrolls. Over time, a complex cataloguing system evolved, which culminated in a bibliographic survey of the library's holdings called the Pinakes. The survey was put together by the great Hellenistic scholar and poet Callimachus of Cyrene (305–240 B.C.). Unfortunately, this important work only exists in fragments today.

Burning Down the House

The Royal Library and its holdings were accidentally set aflame in 48 B.C. when Caesar (who had taken Cleopatra's side in her claim to the throne against her brother) tried to burn his way out of being trapped in the port by opposing forces. Further losses probably occurred in A.D. 271 when Emperor Aurelian destroyed part of the Museum while recapturing Alexandria from Queen Zenobia's forces. The "daughter" library of the Serapeum was finally destroyed by Christians under Emperor Theodosius near the end of the 4th century. But by then, much of the contents (like the contents of other great civic libraries of antiquity) had decayed or found their way into other hands, leaving the classical heritage scattered and fragmented for centuries. Much later, Christians dramatically blamed the burning of the library holdings on Muslim conquerors. Although this made for a good story, the legendary contents of the library were already long gone.

Sandstone Gateway to Heaven

For hundreds of years, rumors of the lost city of Angkor spread among Cambodian peasants. On a stifling day in 1860, Henri Mahout and his porters discovered that the ancient city was more than mere legend.

✳ ✳ ✳ ✳

FRENCH BOTANIST AND explorer Henri Mahout wiped his spectacles as he pushed into the Cambodian jungle clearing. Gasping for breath in the rain forest's thick mists, he gazed down weed-ridden avenues at massive towers and stone temples wreathed with carvings of gods, kings, and battles. The ruins before him were none other than the temples of Angkor Wat.

Although often credited with the discovery of Angkor Wat, Mahout was not the first Westerner to encounter the site. He did, however, bring the "lost" city to the attention of the European public when his travel journals were published in 1868. He wrote: "One of these temples—a rival to that of Solomon, and erected by some ancient Michelangelo— might take an honorable place beside our most beautiful buildings."

Mahout's descriptions of this "new," massive, unexplored Hindu temple sent a jolt of lightning through Western academic circles. Explorers from western Europe combed the jungles of northern Cambodia in an attempt to explain the meaning and origin of the mysterious lost shrine.

The Rise of the Khmer

Scholars first theorized that Angkor Wat and other ancient temples in present-day Cambodia were about 2,000 years old. However, as they began to decipher the Sanskrit inscriptions, they found that the temples had been erected during the 9th through 12th centuries. While Europe languished in the Dark Ages, the Khmer Empire of Indochina was reaching its zenith.

The earliest records of the Khmer people date back to the middle of the 6th century. They migrated from southern China and settled in what is now Cambodia. The early Khmer retained many Indian influences from the West—they were Hindus, and their architecture evolved from Indian methods of building.

In the early 9th century, King Jayavarman II laid claim to an independent kingdom called Kambuja. He established his capital in the Angkor area some 190 miles north of the modern Cambodian capital of Phnom Penh. Jayavarman II also introduced the cult of devaraja, which claimed that the Khmer king was a representative of Shiva, the Hindu god of chaos, destruction, and rebirth. As such, in addition to the temples built to honor the Hindu gods, temples were also constructed to serve as tombs when kings died.

The Khmer built more than 100 stone temples spread out over about 40 miles. The temples were made from laterite (a material similar to clay that forms in tropical climates) and sandstone. The sandstone provided an open canvas for the statues and reliefs celebrating the Hindu gods that decorate the temples.

Home of the Gods

During the first half of the 12th century, Kambuja's King Suryavarman II decided to raise an enormous temple dedicated to the Hindu god Vishnu, a religious monument that would subdue the surrounding jungle and illustrate the power of the Khmer king. His masterpiece—the largest temple complex in the world—would be known to history by its Sanskrit name, "Angkor Wat," or "City of Temple."

Pilgrims visiting Angkor Wat in the 12th century would enter the temple complex by crossing a square, 600-foot-wide moat that ran some four miles in perimeter around the temple grounds. Approaching from the west, visitors would tread the moat's causeway to the main gateway. From there, they would follow a spiritual journey representing the path from the outside world through the Hindu universe and into Mount Meru, the home of the gods. They would pass a giant statue of an eight-armed Vishnu as they entered the western gopura, or gatehouse, known as the "Entrance of the Elephants." They would then follow a stone walkway decorated with nagas (mythical serpents) past sunken pools and column-studded buildings once believed to house sacred temple documents.

At the end of the stone walkway, a pilgrim would step up to a rectangular platform surrounded with galleries featuring six-foot-high bas-reliefs of gods and kings. One depicts the Churning of the Ocean of Milk, a Hindu story in which gods and demons churn a serpent in an ocean of milk to extract the elixir of life. Another illustrates the epic battle of monkey warriors against demons whose sovereign had kidnapped Sita, Rama's beautiful wife. Others depict the gruesome fates awaiting the wicked in the afterlife.

A visitor to King Suryavarman's kingdom would next ascend the dangerously steep steps to the temple's second level, an enclosed area boasting a courtyard decorated with hundreds of dancing apsaras, female images ornamented with jewelry and elaborately dressed hair.

For kings and high priests, the journey would continue with a climb up more steep steps to a 126-foot-high central temple, the pinnacle of Khmer society. Spreading out some 145 feet on each side, the square temple includes a courtyard cornered by four high conical towers shaped to look like lotus buds. The center of the temple is dominated by a fifth conical tower soaring 180 feet above the main causeway; inside it holds a golden statue of the Khmer patron, Vishnu, riding a half-man, half-bird creature in the image of King Suryavarman.

Disuse and Destruction

With the decline of the Khmer Empire and the resurgence of Buddhism, Angkor Wat was occupied by Buddhist monks, who claimed it as their own for many years. A cruciform gallery leading to the temple's second level was decorated with 1,000 Buddhas; the Vishnu statue in the central tower was replaced by an image of Buddha. The temple fell into various states of disrepair over the centuries and is now the focus of international restoration efforts.

World of Wonder!

The laws of nature appear unenforceable at Mystery Hill, a popular tourist attraction in Marblehead.

✳ ✳ ✳ ✳

MYSTERY HILL IS located near a limestone quarry that, for years, shipped rock throughout the Great Lakes. However, the small area of the quarry upon which Mystery Hill is located was never excavated and remained untouched. The plot was sold, and in 1953 a house was built there. Today, that's where visitors can marvel at what appears to be nature run amok. Water flows uphill, balls refuse to roll downhill, and chairs easily balance on two legs. Visitors comfortably lean at an almost 45-degree angle without falling over.

The Forest Inside the Hill

Mystery Hill is part of a larger attraction that also includes Prehistoric Forest, a trip back in time to when dinosaurs still ruled. Sure, they're brightly painted plastic dinosaurs, but they're life-size and still pretty impressive—especially when they roar.

Visitors to Prehistoric Forest enter through a volcano and walk under a thundering waterfall where a huge serpent lies in wait. The 10-acre park is a tranquil natural forest that harkens back to Ohio's earliest days. Dinosaurs and other prehistoric creatures lurk among the trees, ready to give guests a fright, and there's also a dig site where youngsters can search for plastic dinosaur bones. Further exploration will reveal such ancient mysteries as Water Wars and miniature golf. There are other bizarre, gravity-defying locations found in Lake Wales, Florida, and Santa Cruz, California, among others. But at Mystery Hill, as it is with much of the unexplained phenomena in Ohio, the mystery and wonder of the natural world can't overcome an Ohioan's entrepreneurial spirit.

The Serpent Mound

It may be just a mound of dirt to some, or an eerie formation to anyone with a phobia of reptiles, but Ohio's serpentine structure has a serious history.

✳ ✳ ✳ ✳

THOSE AFRAID OF snakes should think twice before visiting Adams County. There's a whopper of a serpent hanging out there—all 1,300-plus feet of it. This isn't a real snake, however; it's the Serpent Mound. And just who built it, and why, is a mystery that has puzzled scientists for years.

Mysterious from Any Angle

From the ground, the Serpent Mound looks like a three-foot-tall lump of ground meandering its way across a field. But from the air, the landscape takes on a whole different look: That lumpy ground resembles the shape of a massive snake. At one end, the snake's tail ends in a multicoiled rattle; at the other, its mouth appears ready to devour an oval-shaped object, which some believe is supposed to represent an egg.

While not much is known about the mound, it's fairly certain that it was not used as a burial mound—no remains were found during excavations. Some claim that the snake is aligned with the summer solstice and was designed as a calendar of sorts. Others believe that a group of ancient peoples saw a meteor with a snakelike tail (or possibly Halley's Comet) streak across the night sky and created the Serpent Mound as a memorial to what they had seen.

Finding out who built the Serpent Mound is just as big a riddle. Scientists believe it was constructed by either the Adena culture or the Fort Ancient culture—though there is little concrete evidence to support either theory. Ultimately, no one can say for certain who built the Serpent Mound or why. As far as Ohioans are concerned, there's nothing wrong with some things remaining a mystery.

Three Sides to Every Story

Few geographical locations on Earth have been discussed and debated more than the three-sided chunk of ocean between the Atlantic coast of Florida and the regions of San Juan, Puerto Rico, and Bermuda known as the Bermuda Triangle.

✳   ✳   ✳   ✳

OVER THE CENTURIES, hundreds of ships and dozens of airplanes have mysteriously disappeared while floating in or flying through the region commonly called the Bermuda Triangle. Myth mongers propose that alien forces are responsible for these dissipations. Because little or no wreckage from the vanished vessels has ever been recovered, paranormal pirating has also been cited as the culprit. Other theorists suggest that leftover technology from the lost continent of Atlantis—mainly an underwater rock formation known as the Bimini

Road (situated just off the island of Bimini in the Bahamas)—
exerts a supernatural power that grabs unsuspecting intruders
and drags them to the depths.

A Deadly Adjective

Although the theory of the Triangle had been mentioned
in publications as early as 1950, it wasn't until the '60s that
the region was anointed with its three-sided appellation.
Columnist Vincent Gaddis wrote an article in the February
1964 edition of *Argosy* magazine that discussed the various
mysterious disappearances that had occurred over the years
and designated the area where myth and mystery mixed as the
"Deadly Bermuda Triangle." The use of the adjective *deadly*
perpetrated the possibility that UFOs, alien anarchists, supernatural beings, and metaphysical monsters reigned over the
region. The mystery of Flight 19, which involved the disappearance of five planes in 1945, was first noted in newspaper articles that appeared in 1950, but its fame was secured
when the flight and its fate were fictitiously featured in Steven
Spielberg's 1977 alien opus, *Close Encounters of the Third Kind*.
In Hollywood's view, the pilots and their planes were plucked
from the sky by friendly aliens and later returned safely to terra
firma by their abductors.

In 1975, historian, pilot, and researcher Lawrence David
Kusche published one of the first definitive studies that dismissed many of the Triangle theories. In his book *The Bermuda
Triangle Mystery—Solved*, he concluded that the Triangle
was a "manufactured mystery," the result of bad research and
reporting and, occasionally, deliberately falsified facts. Before
weighing anchor on Kusche's conclusions, however, consider
that one of his next major publications was a tome about exotic
popcorn recipes.

Explaining Odd Occurrences

Other pragmatists have insisted that a combination of natural
forces—a double whammy of waves and rain that create the

perfect storm—is most likely the cause for these maritime misfortunes. Other possible "answers" to the mysteries include rogue waves (such as the one that capsized the *Ocean Ranger* oil rig off the coast of Newfoundland in 1982), hurricanes, underwater earthquakes, and human error. The Coast Guard receives almost 20 distress calls every day from amateur sailors attempting to navigate the slippery sides of the Triangle. Modern-day piracy—usually among those involved in drug smuggling—has been mentioned as a probable cause for odd occurrences, as have unusual magnetic anomalies that screw up compass readings. Other possible explanations include the Gulf Stream's uncertain current, the high volume of sea and air traffic in the region, and even methane hydrates (gas bubbles) that produce "mud volcanoes" capable of sucking a ship into the depths.

Other dramatic and disastrous disappearances amid the Bermuda Triangle include the USS *Cyclops*, which descended to its watery repository without a whisper in March 1918 with 309 people aboard. Myth suggests supernatural subterfuge, but the reality is that violent storms or enemy action were the likely culprits. The same deductions had been discussed and similar conclusions reached in 1812 when the sea schooner *Patriot*, a commercial vessel, was swept up by the sea with the daughter of former vice president Aaron Burr onboard.

The Legend of Gore Orphanage

Though it's not much to look at today —in fact, there's nothing left to see—an old sign and an abandoned mansion add up to a long legend in Vermilion.

✳ ✳ ✳ ✳

Travelers who find themselves on the outskirts of the town of Vermilion should keep their eyes peeled for a road sign that has given rise to one of Ohio's longest-standing legends. The green sign simply reads, "Gore Orphanage Road."

The Legend

Not surprisingly, there was at one point an orphanage located along what is now Gore Orphanage Road. The story goes that "Old Man" Gore, the man who ran the orphanage, was rather wicked and often mistreated the children. It is claimed that one night, in a fit of rage, he even burned down the orphanage, with all of the children still inside. (In an alternate version of the story, a mysterious "old man" living in the woods is blamed for the fire.)

Few visitors make their way to the ruins of the orphanage, but it is said that those who do will hear all sorts of strange noises coming from within—perhaps the screams of the children as they are being burned alive. If curiosity seekers are really lucky, they'll catch a glimpse of ghostly children running through the woods, burning. But even if the ephemeral children aren't seen, they might still make their presence known by leaving tiny handprints all over the cars of those who park there.

The Facts

An orphanage was indeed located along Gore Orphanage Road. The Reverend John Sprunger started the Light of Hope Orphanage around 1902. Sprunger and his wife ran the orphanage for roughly a dozen years until Sprunger passed away. Mrs. Sprunger was eventually forced to sell off everything and move away; orphans who remained were sent to live with relatives or found homes in the community. There is nothing in the records about any children dying in a fire. Some of the outbuildings may have ultimately burned down, but that was many years after they had been abandoned.

If there was no Gore Orphanage, where did the name of the road come from? Simple: A *gore* is a surveyor's term used to describe a triangular piece of land. In other words, the road ran through the gore that was near the orphanage.

Swift Mansion

There even seems to be some confusion as to where the

actual orphanage was located. In reality, the Light of Hope Orphanage was made up of several buildings. There are ruins of a burned building on Gore Orphanage Road, but they are the ruins of the Swift Mansion. In the early 1840s, wealthy farmer Joseph Swift created a farm at the bottom of the ravine, causing all of the townsfolk to nickname the mansion he erected "Swift's Folly." Swift operated the farm for several years until some bad investments forced him to sell the mansion and land to Nicholas Wilber. And with that transaction, the final piece of the Gore Orphanage legend fell into place.

The Wilbers were apparently very interested in spiritualism. So when several Wilber grandchildren sadly fell victim to the diphtheria epidemic that swept through the area in early 1893, as legend has it, the Wilbers would hold seances in the Swift Mansion to contact them. When Nicholas died in 1901, the mansion was left empty and soon acquired the reputation of being haunted, possibly by the ghosts of the Wilber children. Years later, the mansion fell victim to arson, which may be what brought about the legend of ghosts of burning children.

Haunting the Sea: Oregon's Ghost Forests

The gnarled, twisted shapes rising up from Oregon's coastline are macabre memorials to the magnificent forests that stood here ages ago. Like a ghost town eerily preserved in time, these "ghost forests" are shrouded in mystery: What caused the mighty trees to fall? Why are they still here? And where are they going?

* * * *

An Eerie Appearance

THESE GROVES OF ancient tree stumps—called "ghost forests" because of their age (approximately 1,000 to 4,000 years old) and bleak appearance—emerge along the 46-mile stretch between Lincoln City and Tillamook. For years, tourists and scientists alike have been perplexed by the forests' strange beauty. Some trees extend out of the sand like angular sculptures; others are just visible as tiny tips poking through the water.

All are remnants of the giant Sitka spruce forests, which towered 200 feet above Oregon's coastline for years. That is, until something knocked them down.

A Cataclysmic Collapse

No one knows for sure just what that "something" was, but experts agree that for such forests to be preserved, the trees must have been very suddenly submerged in sand, clay, or mud. This submersion would not only kill the trees but also keep them frozen in time by shutting off their oxygen.

The original (and still widely held) belief is that a giant earthquake, which suddenly dropped the ground 25 feet below sea level and immersed the trees in sand and water, toppled the forests. Another theory is that it wasn't an earthquake but a tsunami that struck, drowning the trees under a massive tidal wave. A third theory suggests that it was a combination of the two—an earthquake buried the trees and then caused a tsunami that lopped off the tree tops, leaving only stumps behind.

A newer theory is that the trees died as a result of sudden landscape changes, with sand levels rising over the course of a few decades (that's "sudden" when you're speaking in geologic terms) to eventually overwhelm the forest.

Seasonal Specters

For decades, ghost forests were seen only occasionally during the harsh winter months, when violent waves strip away layers of sand, exposing the tree stumps just briefly before the calmer waves of spring and summer carry sand back to the shores and bury them once again.

But lately, the ghost forests have become less of a rarity. Since 1998, more and more spooky spruces have been popping up—

the result of a decade of rough winters, washing away as much as 17 feet of sand in some areas, combined with less sand recovery in the spring and summer.

In 2007, Arch Cape saw stumps for the first time in 40 years, along with the mud-cliff remains of a forest floor, and in the winter of 2008, an unprecedented 10-foot drop in sand level revealed a new forest at Cape Kiwanda.

Just a few miles away at Hug Point, the waves uncovered stumps that could date back 80,000 years to the Pleistocene era, when woolly mammoths and saber-toothed tigers roamed the earth. And the remains of roots marred by saws at Moolack Beach show that early European settlers harvested the trees for fire and shelter. Oregon's most impressive and most famous ghost forest is found at Neskowin, where 100 twisted shapes can be seen poking through the water year-round.

Grim Tide-ings

But the erosion that has newly exposed these phantom forests may also be destroying them. The stumps at Neskowin and Cape Lookout are reportedly showing so much that waves are ripping them out by the roots.

Some experts believe this increased erosion means the coastline is gradually disappearing—and taking the ghost forests with it. Perhaps soon, the ghost forests of Oregon will haunt only our memories.

CHAPTER 9

WHO ARE YOU?

The Clairvoyant Crime-Buster

Before there were TV shows like Ghost Whisperer *and* Medium, *which make the idea of solving crimes through ESP seem almost commonplace, there was psychic detective Arthur Price Roberts. And his work was accomplished in the early 1900s, when high-tech aids like electronic surveillance and DNA identification were still only far-fetched dreams. Police in those times often used psychics to help solve many cases.*

✳   ✳   ✳   ✳

"I See Dead People"

A MODEST MAN BORN in Wales in 1866, Roberts deliberately avoided a formal education because he believed too much learning could stifle his unusual abilities. He moved to Milwaukee, Wisconsin, as a young man where, ironically, the man who never learned to read was nicknamed "Doc."

One of his earliest well-known cases involved a baffling missing person incident in Peshtigo, a small town about 160 miles north of Milwaukee. A man named Duncan McGregor had gone missing in July 1905, leaving no clue as to his whereabouts. The police searched for him for months, and finally his desperate wife decided to go to the psychic detective who had already made a name for himself in Milwaukee. She didn't even have to explain the situation to Roberts; he knew immediately upon meeting her who she was.

Roberts meditated on the vanished husband, then sadly had to tell Mrs. McGregor that he'd been murdered and that his body was in the Peshtigo River, caught near the bottom in a pile of timber. Roberts proved correct in every detail.

Mystery of the Mad Bombers

Roberts solved numerous documented cases. He helped a Chicago man find his brother who had traveled to Albuquerque and had not been heard from for months; Roberts predicted that the brother's body would be found in a certain spot in Devil's Canyon, and it was.

After coming up with new evidence for an 11th hour pardon, Roberts saved a Chicago man named Ignatz Potz, who had been condemned to die for a murder he didn't commit. But his most famous coup came in 1935 when he correctly predicted that the city of Milwaukee would be hit by six large dynamite explosions, losing a town hall, banks, and police stations. People snickered; such mayhem was unheard of in Milwaukee. Roberts made his prediction on October 18 of that year. In about a week, the Milwaukee area entered a time of terror.

First, a town hall in the outlying community of Shorewood was blasted, killing two children and wounding many other people. A few weeks later, the mad bombers hit two banks and two police stations. Federal agents descended upon the city, and several local officers were assigned to work solely on solving the bombings. Finally, the police went to Roberts to learn what was coming next. Roberts told them one more blast was in the works, that it would be south of the Menomonee River, and that it would be the final bomb. Police took him at his word and blanketed the area with officers and sharpshooters.

And sure enough, on November 4, a garage in the predicted area blew to smithereens in an explosion that could be heard as far as eight miles away. The two terrorists, young men 18 and 21 years old, had been hard at work in the shed assembling 50 pounds of dynamite when their plan literally backfired. Few people argued with Roberts's abilities after that.

His Final Fortune

Roberts's eeriest prediction, however, may have been that of his own death. In November 1939, he told a group of assembled friends that he would be leaving this world on January 2, 1940. And he did, passing quietly in his own home on that exact date. Many of his most amazing accomplishments will probably never be known because a lot of his work was done secretly for various law enforcement agencies. But "Doc" Roberts had an undeniable gift, and he died secure in the knowledge that he had used it to help others as best he could.

The Bard vs. Bacon: Who Wrote Shakespeare?

"What's in a name? That which we call a rose, by any other name, would smell as sweet." But would that which we call prose, by any other name, read as neat?

✳   ✳   ✳   ✳

THE QUOTE ABOVE was penned by William Shakespeare—or was it? Many scholars have raised doubts as to whether he really wrote some of the finest words in Western literature. Did other writers actually do the deed? Both sides believe they have the evidence to prove their point.

Meet Bill

William Shakespeare was born in Stratford-upon-Avon, England, in April 1564—the exact date is unknown. This and many other details of his life are vague, which has fueled the rampant speculation about authorship. It is generally accepted that he was the first in his family to read and write, although the extent of his education has been widely questioned. His father was involved in local politics, so it is likely that Shakespeare attended school until his early teens to study Latin and literature. At age 18, Shakespeare married Anne Hathaway, who was eight years older than he was and three months pregnant with their first child, Susanna. Twins Hamnet and Judith were born two years later.

The Bard's life story seems to disappear into the mist for more than seven years at this point, resurfacing in 1592, when he became involved in London theater. As a playwright and actor, he founded a performing troupe that was soon part of the court of King James I. Shakespeare retired in 1613, returning to his hometown with some wealth. He died in 1616 and was laid to rest in the Holy Trinity Church of Stratford-upon-Avon.

The Play's the Thing

While Shakespeare's plays were performed during his lifetime, they were not collected and published in book form until seven years after his death; *The First Folio* contained 36 of his theatrical works. Editors John Heminge and Henry Condell categorized the plays as tragedies, comedies, and histories. Many of Shakespeare's works, such as Hamlet and King Lear, were based on writings of former playwrights or even of Shakespeare's contemporaries—a common practice of the time. He also penned more than 150 sonnets, which often focused on love or beauty.

The diversity of this amazing body of work is what leads many to wonder whether Shakespeare had the education or ability to write it all. Certainly, they insist, others with better backgrounds and academic credentials were more likely to have actually written such great and timeless works of literature. Furthermore, they say, many of the plays displayed the acumen of a well-traveled writer—something Shakespeare was most likely not—someone who had a great knowledge of foreign languages, geography, and local customs. Who could have written such worldly plays?

Bringing Home the Bacon

Francis Bacon was born into a royal London family in 1561. Fragile as a young child, Bacon was schooled at home. He spent three years at Trinity College at Cambridge and traveled to Paris at age 15. Bacon became a lawyer and a member of the British Parliament in 1584. He soon joined the court of Queen Elizabeth and was knighted by King James I in 1603. Bacon eventually ascended to the positions of solicitor general and attorney general of the British government. He died of bronchitis in 1626.

Bacon is best remembered for his part in developing the scientific method, a process of systematic investigation. This standard prescribes defining a question, performing diligent research about the subject, forming a hypothesis, experimenting and collecting data, analyzing the results, and developing a conclusion. The progression has become commonplace in all types of scientific work, from grade school projects to research labs, and is still used today. But the multitalented Bacon was also a writer and essayist who once observed that "knowledge is power." His works include *Novum Organum*, *Astrologia Sana*, and *Meditationes Sacrae*. But could the man who penned these works be diverse and capable enough to also write *Much Ado About Nothing*, *Romeo and Juliet*, and words such as "If music be the food of love, play on"?

Something Is Rotten in the State of . . . Authorship

Speculation about the origin of Shakespeare's work began in the mid-1800s, as writers and scholars sought to demystify the works of the Bard. By the early 1900s, even the great American humorist Mark Twain had weighed in and questioned the authenticity of Shakespeare's plays and sonnets, albeit in his own way. In *Is Shakespeare Dead?*, Twain parodied those intellectuals who tried to discredit the man from Stratford-upon-Avon. The satiric piece questioned how biographers could write such detailed stories about their subject when so little solid information existed in the first place. But Twain also raised the question of whether Shakespeare could even write.

Similarities between the writings of Shakespeare and Bacon are abundant, and perhaps a bit too coincidental. For example, Shakespeare's Hamlet offers, "To thine own self be true . . . Thou canst not then be false to any man." In *Essay of Wisdom*, Bacon wrote, "Be so true to thyself as thou be not false to others." Plagiarism? Who can really say? In *Julius Caesar*, Shakespeare wrote, "Cowards die many times before their deaths." In Bacon's *Essay of Friendship*, he offered, "Men have their time, and die many times." Coincidence? Sure, maybe. The Bard wrote, "Tomorrow, and tomorrow, and tomorrow/ Creeps in this petty pace from day to day" in *Macbeth*. Bacon observed in *Religious Meditations*, "The Spanish have a proverb, 'To-morrow, to-morrow; and when to-morrow comes, tomorrow.'" Is it possible that Shakespeare knew of the same Spanish proverb? Certainly. While other similarities and questions proliferate, enough disbelief and lack of concrete evidence remain to thrill the world's doubting Thomases.

Parting Is Such Sweet Sorrow

Amid the swirl of controversy, most academics are convinced that Shakespeare himself wrote the plays and sonnets that made him famous. Of course, that conviction has done little to discourage those who have their doubts.

Stranger than Fiction: Doppelgängers

A perplexing number of people have reported encountering their doppelgängers. Read on for some of the more famous (and creepy) examples.

✳ ✳ ✳ ✳

Haven't We Met Before?

ACCORDING TO MANY sources, *doppelgänger* is a German word meaning "double goer" or "double walker." Essentially, a doppelgänger is defined as a person's twin, although not in a Doublemint Gum sense. Rather, a doppelgänger is often described as a very pale, almost bloodless version of the person. Its appearance usually means impending danger or even death for its human counterpart, although there have been instances in which the doppelgänger foretold the future or simply showed up and didn't cause any harm.

Interestingly, the doppelgänger is such a constant phenomenon that Sigmund Freud tackled it in a paper titled "The Uncanny." In it, he theorized that the doppelgänger is a denial of mortality by people. Once they leave that denial behind, the double remains as "the ghastly harbinger of death."

Deathly Doppelgängers

Many famous people have reported seeing their doppelgänger, and most of the time it wasn't a good thing. One of the most famous instances was U.S. President Abraham Lincoln, who reported seeing his doppelgänger in a mirror in 1860, just after his election. As he supposedly described it to his friend Noah Brooks, the double was "five shades" paler than himself. Lincoln's wife interpreted this as an omen that he would be elected to a second term but would not live through it. She was eerily on the mark.

At the very end of her long reign, Queen Elizabeth I of England reportedly saw a pale and wizened double of herself laid out on her bed. She died soon afterward in 1603. Renowned poet Percy Bysshe Shelley supposedly encountered his doppelgänger in Italy. The figure pointed toward a body of water. Shortly after, Shelley drowned while sailing on July 8, 1822.

In 1612, English poet John Donne was traveling abroad in Paris when suddenly appearing before him was the doppelgänger of his pregnant wife. Although the double was holding a newborn baby, she appeared incredibly sad. "I have seen my dear wife pass twice by me through this room, with her hair hanging about her shoulders, and a dead child in her arms,"

Donne told a friend. He later found out that at the precise moment the apparition appeared to him, his wife had given birth to a stillborn child.

Sometimes a person won't see his or her doppelgänger, but somebody else will, often with the same unfortunate result. That was the case with Pope Alexander VI who was a man given to murder, incest, and other manner of foul deeds. According to some stories, Alexander plotted to kill a church cardinal for his money. He brought poisoned wine to a dinner with the cardinal but forgot to bring an amulet he owned that he believed made him invulnerable to poison. According to lore, Alexander sent a church official back to get it. When the official entered Alexander's room, he saw a perfect image of the pope lying atop a funeral bier in the middle of the room. That night at dinner Alexander drank his own poison by mistake. He died a few days later on August 18, 1503.

Hello, It's . . . Me?

Not all doppelgängers sound Death's clarion call. In 1905, a severe influenza outbreak prevented a member of the British Parliament named Sir Frederick Carne Rasch from attending a session. However, during the session a friend, Sir Gilbert Parker, looked over and saw Rasch sitting there. Another member also reported briefly seeing Rasch, who, as it turned out, had never left his home. (When Rasch finally returned to Parliament, he became annoyed whenever someone poked him in the ribs to make certain it was really him.)

In 1771, while traveling to a city, Wolfgang von Goethe encountered himself, wearing unfamiliar clothes, heading in the opposite direction. Eight years later, Goethe found himself traveling the same road, heading in the same direction as his double had—and wearing the same clothes that before had seemed unfamiliar. Ninteenth-century French writer Guy de Maupassant once watched as his double sat down across from him and dictated what he was writing. Maupassant's doppelgänger experiences became so common that he wrote about them in his short story "Lui."

Twin Teachers

One of the most celebrated cases in doppelgänger lore occurred in 1845 in Latvia. Emilie Sagée was a popular French teacher at a school for upper-class girls. The students often talked about how Sagée seemed to be in two places at once: One student would report seeing her in a hallway, but another girl would shake her head and say no, she had just seen Sagée in a classroom.

One day, while Sagée was writing on the blackboard, her double appeared right beside her, moving its hand in exact unison with the teacher. Another time, as Sagée helped a young girl dress for a party, the girl looked in the mirror to see two Sagées moving in perfect harmony, working on the girl's dress.

Sagée's doppelgänger was resistant to touch at times, while at other times a person could walk right through it. Oddly, her double would appear healthy and energetic when Sagée was ill.

While reports like these and similar incidents involving Sagée didn't seem to distress the students, it freaked out their parents, who began pulling their children out of the school. According to some stories, the headmaster decided that he would have to let Sagée go. When told of this, the teacher reportedly lamented that she had lost nearly two dozen teaching positions throughout her career for the same reason.

Who Was Davy Crockett?

Just who exactly was Davy Crockett? Was he a rough-and-tumble pioneer, a man whose fearless exploits helped tame the wilderness? Or was he an ambitious and self-promoting politician, made famous by a well-orchestrated public relations campaign and a little help from Hollywood?

✳ ✳ ✳ ✳

A Man from Tennessee

SOME ASPECTS OF David "Davy" Crockett's life are not in dispute, though much of it is. We know that he was born on August 17, 1786, in eastern Tennessee. His first wife was Mary "Polly" Finley, who died in 1815. He soon remarried, taking the widow Elizabeth Patton to be his bride.

Crockett was an excellent hunter. Often his rifle enabled him to provide food for his wife and five children. But he wasn't entirely an outdoorsman: He was elected to the Tennessee legislature in 1821, then the United States House of Representatives in 1827. For the next decade he was in and out of Congress, and when he found himself in a hard-fought battle for the Congressional seat in 1835, he threatened that if he lost the election he would tell his constituents "to go to hell" and move to Texas. He lost the vote and kept his word, departing to Texas, where he met his end at the Alamo on March 6, 1836.

Two Men the Same—Two Men Different

Crockett is always lumped together with Daniel Boone as one of the two premier American frontiersmen, blazing trails through untamed wilderness. Without question, Boone was the real deal. He explored Kentucky when it was populated almost primarily by Native Americans, built the Wilderness Road to provide greater access to the region, led settlers into Kentucky when it was just a howling wilderness, and narrowly escaped death numerous times.

Crockett's life followed a different path. Bitten by the political bug upon his first foray into elected office, he progressed from justice of the peace to U.S. Congressman in a remarkably short time, particularly because political campaigns then—as now— cost money, and Crockett's low-budget campaigns would have embarrassed a shoestring.

Crockett was a natural for politics. Independent-minded and loyal to his backwoods constituents, he was also gregarious, quick-witted, and personable. Once, a flock of guinea hens showed up at an outside political debate and squawked so loudly that his opponent was completely unnerved. Crockett, however, joked that the birds had actually been chanting "Crockett, Crockett, Crockett," which is why the other candidate was spooked. He won the debate and the election.

Contrast that with the stoic and reclusive Boone, who probably would have preferred to swim the entire length of the Mississippi River rather than hobnob and glad-hand. As one story has it, Boone once welcomed a visitor to his cabin and in conversation asked where the man lived. When informed that he resided about 70 miles from Boone's home, Boone turned to his wife and said, "Old woman, we must move, they are crowding us."

A Lion with a Touch of Airth-Quake

Crockett enjoyed his reputation as a humble backwoodsman in sophisticated Washington, D.C. This reputation was spread even further by the wildly popular 1831 play *The Lion of the West*. The main character, obviously based on Crockett, is a Congressman from Kentucky named Nimrod Wildfire, who boasts that he's "half horse, half alligator, a touch of the airth-quake, with a sprinkling of the steamboat." Beginning in 1835, with the publication of the so-called *Crockett Almanacs*, he was portrayed in an even more sensational light—as biographer Mark Derr calls him, a "comic Hercules."

Thanks to Walt Disney in the mid-1950s, Crockett became one

of the first media sensations of the modern age. By the time Disney was finished with his legend, people everywhere were singing about Tennessee mountaintops and wearing coonskin caps (which Crockett never wore). From then on, Crockett's image as an authentic American hero was set.

A Little of This, a Little of That

So who was Davy Crockett? Like all of us, he's hard to pin down—a combination of different factors that make a characterization difficult. Part frontiersman and part politician mixed with a keen wit, unabashed honesty, and a friendly nature, Davy Crockett in the end was 100 percent uniquely American.

Controversial Queen

In establishing the identity of the Egyptian queen Nefertiti, scholars find themselves up to their necks in conflicting info.

✳ ✳ ✳ ✳

LIKE CLEOPATRA, NEFERTITI is one of the most famous queens of ancient Egypt. She's also often referred to as "The Most Beautiful Woman in the World," largely due to the 1912 discovery of a painted limestone bust of Nefertiti depicting her stunning features: smooth skin, full lips, and a graceful swanlike neck—quite the looker! Now housed in Berlin's Altes Museum, the likeness has become a widely recognized symbol of ancient Egypt and one of the most important artistic works of the pre-modern world. But the bust, like almost everything about the famous queen, is steeped in controversy.

Conflicting Accounts

It wasn't until the bust surfaced in the early 20th century that scholars began sorting out information about Nefertiti's life. Her name means "the beautiful one is come," and some think she was a foreign princess, not of Egyptian blood. Others believe she was born into Egyptian royalty, that she was the niece or daughter of a high government official named Ay, who later became pharaoh. No one knows her origins for sure.

When the beautiful one was age 15, she married Amenhotep IV, who later became king of Egypt. Nefertiti was thus promoted to queen. No one really knows when this happened—other than it was in the 18th Dynasty—but it's safe to say that it was a really long time ago (as in, the 1340s B.C.). Nefertiti appears in many reliefs of the period, often accompanying her husband in various ceremonies—a testament to her power.

An indisputable fact about both Nefertiti and Amenhotep IV is that they were responsible for bringing monotheism to ancient Egypt. Rather than worship the vast pantheon of Egyptian gods—including the supreme god, Amen-Ra—the couple devoted themselves to exclusively worshipping the sun god Aten. In fact, as a sign of this commitment, Amenhotep IV changed his named to Akhenaten. Similarly, Nefertiti changed her name to Neferneferuaten-Nefertiti, meaning, "The Aten is radiant of radiance [because] the beautiful one is come." (But we're guessing everyone just called her "Nef.") Again, it's unclear as to why the powerful couple decided to turn from polytheism. Maybe there were political reasons. Or perhaps the two simply liked the idea of one universal god.

Disappearance/Death?

In studying Egyptian history, scholars discovered that around 14 years into Akhenaten's reign, Nefertiti seems to disappear. There are no more images of her, no historical records. Perhaps there was a conflict in the royal family, and she was banished from the kingdom. Maybe she died in the plague that killed half of Egypt. A more interesting speculation is that she disguised herself as a man, changed her named to Smenkhkare, and went on to rule Egypt alongside her husband. But—all together now—*no one knows for sure!*

During a June 2003 expedition in Egypt's Valley of the Kings, an English archeologist named Joann Fletcher unearthed a mummy that she suspected to be Nefertiti. But despite the fact that the mummy probably is a member of the royal family from the 18th Dynasty, it was not proven to be female. Many Egyptologists think there is not sufficient evidence to prove that Fletcher's mummy is Nefertiti. So, that theory was something of a bust.

In 2009, Swiss art historian Henri Sierlin published a book suggesting that the bust is a copy. He claimed that the sculpture was made by an artist named Gerard Marks on the request of Ludwig Borchardt, the German archeologist responsible for discovering the bust in 1912. Despite the mysteries surrounding Nefertiti, there's no question that she was revered in her time. At the temples of Karnak are inscribed the words: "Heiress, Great of Favours, Possessed of Charm, Exuding Happiness . . . Great King's Wife, Whom He Loves, Lady of Two Lands, Nefertiti."

The Woman Behind the Beguiling Smile

It's been one of history's great mysteries: Who posed for Leonardo da Vinci when he painted art's most famous face, the Mona Lisa, in the early 1500s?

✳ ✳ ✳ ✳

The Possibilities

YOU WOULD THINK that the missing eyebrows would be a dead giveaway as to the identity of the woman who posed for the *Mona Lisa*. How many eyebrow-less ladies could have been wandering around Italy back then? As it turns out, quite a few—it was a popular look at the time. Those crazy Renaissance women.

The leading theory has always been that Lisa is Lisa Gherardini, the wife of wealthy Florentine silk merchant Francesco del Giocondo. Sixteenth-century historian Giorgio Vasari made this claim in *The Lives of the Artists*, noting that the untitled painting was often called "La Gioconda," which literally means "the happy woman" but can also be read as a play on the name Giocondo. (If you're wondering what the more popular title means, "Mona" is simply a contraction of *ma donna*, or "my lady," in Italian; the title is the equivalent of "Madam Lisa" in English.)

Vasari was infamous for trusting word of mouth, so there's a possibility that he got it wrong. Therefore, historians have proposed many alternative Lisas, including Leonardo da Vinci's mom, various Italian noblewomen, a fictitious ideal woman, and a prostitute. Some have believed that the painting is a disguised portrait of Leonardo himself, noting that his features in other self-portraits resemble Lisa's. Hey, maybe the guy wanted to see what he would look like as a woman—nothing wrong with that.

Lisa Gherardini

In 2005, Armin Schlecter, a manuscript expert at Heidelberg University Library in Germany, closed the case. While looking through one of the books in the library's collection—a very old copy of Cicero's letters—Schlecter discovered notes in the margin that were written in 1503 by Florentine city official Agostino Vespucci. Vespucci, who knew Leonardo, described some of the paintings on which the artist was working at the time. One of the notes mentions a portrait of Lisa del Giocondo, a.k.a. Lisa Gherardini, which proves fairly conclusively that Vasari had the right Lisa.

Historians know a bit about Lisa's life. She was Francesco's third wife; she married him when she was sixteen and he was thirty, a year after his second wife had died. They lived in a big house, but it was in the middle of the city's red-light district. She likely sat for the portrait soon after the birth of her third child, when she was about twenty-four. She had five children altogether and died at age 63.

Now that this one seems to be solved, we can move on to other art mysteries, such as this: How did those dogs learn how to play poker?

Possible Authors of the Gospels

Seems pretty simple; each Gospel was written by the book's namesake, as direct testament of that writer's experiences with Jesus Christ. Indeed, for most of the history of Christianity, this was the unquestioned interpretation. But in the past two centuries, biblical scholars have begun to question these assumptions.

✳ ✳ ✳ ✳

PART OF THE problem in finding the authors is the phenomenon of "pseudoepigraphy"—falsely attributing a book to an author, often as a means to validate the work. Pseudoepigraphy is common throughout the world and throughout history, but it was especially common in ancient times. Another problem is that most biblical scholars agree that the original Gospels were written in Greek—unlikely if the authors were poor disciples of Jesus who spoke Hebrew or Aramaic. So who were the authors of these important works?

Gospel of Matthew

Until the 18th century, the unquestioned author of the Gospel of Matthew was the apostle Matthew. Matthew was also considered the first Gospel written. By the 19th century, biblical scholars began to question this authorship. Today, the majority of scholars believe the Gospel of Matthew was written by an anonymous Jewish Christian toward the end of the first century. The case for Matthew:

✳ Early Christian scholars say it is so. Papias of Hierapolis, an early Christian writer, states that Matthew wrote a Gospel in Hebrew. Though the Gospel of Matthew was written in Greek, some modern scholars believe the Hebrew book may have been a prototype. Unfortunately, Papias, who is one of the primary sources for much of what we know about early Christian writing, was considered "a man of meager intelligence" by his contemporaries.

* The writer was probably Jewish. Textual clues in the narrative, such as a familiarity with Jewish customs and local geography, as well as a familiarity with the Old Testament, indicate the writer was Jewish.

* The writer didn't like Pharisees. The Pharisees are depicted in a dim light in Matthew. The Pharisees were hard on tax collectors, and Matthew was a tax collector.

* Matthew copied Mark. Though presented first in the New Testament, biblical scholars agree that Matthew was actually written after Mark, using Mark as a source. Evidence for this includes the fact that Matthew incorporates passages from Mark wholesale. Why would an apostle, who was an eyewitness, need to copy from Mark, who was writing everything down secondhand?

* The book was written in Greek. Not only was the Gospel written in Greek, but it was an eloquent Greek. Very few people could write at this time, much less in a nonnative language.

Gospel of Mark

Traditionally, the Gospel of Mark was associated with John Mark the Evangelist. The Gospel was written not as an eyewitness account, but as a summary of what Mark had heard from Peter's preaching in Rome. Of all the Gospels, Mark's authorship of the Gospel bearing his name is the one that is most widely accepted. The case for Mark:

* Church fathers didn't ascribe the Gospel to an apostle. It would make sense for the early church fathers to ascribe the most important accounts of Jesus' life to apostolic sources— as they did with Matthew and John—to provide added credibility to the text. There is no reason to give credit to Mark,

who is a minor character in the New Testament.

* The book displays an ignorance of Palestine. An apostle of Jesus would be intimately familiar with Palestine, including its geography. Time and again the author of Mark bungles basic details, which shows that the author probably was not a Jew and was hearing it second-hand.

* The Gospel seems to be written for gentiles. The book is written for a gentile audience and seems to be designed to bolster the faith of those under threat of persecution—as Christians were in Rome during the time Mark was there.

* Persecution was widespread. Just because the Gospel seemed concerned about persecution doesn't mean it was written in Rome, a main contention of pro-Mark scholars. Skeptics suggest this indicates the writer *could* have been someone other than Mark.

Gospel of Luke

The author of the Gospel of Luke has been assumed to be Luke the Evangelist, during the first century. Luke was a companion of Paul, and so the Gospel is not an eyewitness account. The case for Luke:

* All early writings attribute the Gospel to Luke. The oldest surviving manuscript referencing the Gospel, dating back to A.D. 200, attributes the book to Luke.

* Luke spoke fluent Greek. The Gospel of Luke was originally written in an eloquent Greek of the sort a highly educated physician might use.

* The Gospel of Luke and Acts of the Apostles is written by the same person. Both books exhibit the same writing style and are dedicated to the same patron, Theophilus.

* Textual clues indicate Luke wrote Acts, and therefore Luke. At several places in Acts the writer refers to Paul and his companions as "we." Scholars determined that the "we" passages correspond to times when Luke was in Paul's company.

* Contradictions between Acts and Paul's letters. Multiple contradictions occur in Acts. These contradictions cause skeptics to suggest Luke the physician did not write Acts, since the real Luke, a companion of Paul, would not have made such errors. And since he didn't write Acts, he could not have written the Gospel of Luke.

Gospel of John

The authorship of John is the most hotly debated. Traditionally, the Gospel was ascribed to John the Apostle. The book was said to have been written to refute the heretical writings of the gnostic scholar Cerinthus, who taught that Jesus was separate from Christ. Today most scholars agree that John the Apostle was most likely not the author of the Gospel. The case for John:

* Every existing manuscript attributes it to him. While this is not evidence that John wrote the Gospel, it is worth noting that none of the manuscripts we have containing early versions of the Gospel suggest otherwise.

* The author claims to be an eyewitness. The manuscript indicates intimate familiarity with Jesus and the other disciples.

* The book was written well after John's death. Scholars' best estimates peg the writing of John as A.D. 70. This would be difficult for the apostle John, considering that some scholars believe he was martyred with his brother James decades before.

* Contradictions with the other Gospels. John's Gospel is littered with details that are at odds with the synoptic (Matthew, Mark, and Luke) Gospels.

* John was probably illiterate. Most scholars now agree that John was illiterate.

So who *did* write the Gospel of John? Over the years, various scholars have put forth theories:

* Cerinthus: Cerinthus was a 1st-century gnostic writer who is the author of several important pieces of early Christian writing. The Alogi, a 2nd century Christian sect, attributed the Gospel to him.

* Mary Magdalene: Mary Magdalene was not one of the 12 apostles, but she could be interpreted as the "beloved disciple" referred to in John. Additionally, Ephesus, where Mary Magdalene was from, is considered the likely place of origin for the Gospel.

* John the Elder: Papias of Hierapolis claims that the Gospel of John is written by "the elder John," leading some to believe that John the Elder is the actual author of the Gospel.

* Multiple authors: One of the most popular interpretations is that the Gospel of John was a composite work. The theory holds that the work originated with John's recollections, which were then expanded and formed by multiple authors over several years into the Gospel we have today.

...and Q

Most might associate Q with James Bond, but the Q of the Gospels is more intriguing—a hypothetical, lost source book from which the authors of Matthew and Luke drew inspiration.

The possibility of this book was first proffered in the early 19th century. The term Q, which stands for the German word *Quelle* ("source"), was first proffered by German theologian Johannes Weisse in the late 1800s and is theorized to have been a collection of Jesus' sayings.

Coming to America

This land is your land, this land is my land . . . But who was here "first"? Although the Vikings (A.D. 1000) and 15th- and 16th-century Europeans claimed to be among the first to inhabit North America, this legacy actually belongs to the Native Americans. But where did THEY come from?

✳   ✳   ✳   ✳

Northeast Asia?

NATIVE AMERICANS AND Eastern Asians have several strong similarities—hair and skin color, little or no facial and body hair, and extremely distinctive dental shapes. Even sophisticated DNA studies show common links between the two groups. This evidence lends credence to the theory that a migration from Eastern Asia into North America (what is now Alaska and Canada) occurred via a land bridge. At the time of the last Ice Age—about 10,000 to 12,000 years ago—a large glacier formed across much of North America. The ice drew from the waters between Siberia and Alaska. The result was a dry ocean bed nearly 1,000 miles wide called Beringia. Small, nomadic bands of Asians—known as "hunter-gatherers"— began moving across Beringia in a constant search for food, such as small game animals, nuts, berries, and roots. Seasonal changes continued to push these visitors down the Pacific Coast and inland to what are now the Rocky Mountain states. As the ice melted, Beringia slowly began to shrink, returning to its watery origins within about 4,000 years.

According to anthropologist Paul Martin, the migration across the Americas continued at a rate of about eight miles per year. It took nearly 1,000 years to reach the southern tip of South America.

Japan or Southeast Asia?

Another theory of migration suggests that a group of Japanese fishermen or sailors were caught in a mighty sea current some

3,000 to 4,000 years ago. They followed the tides from mainland Japan to the western coast of Ecuador in South America called Valdivia. Sound impossible? Consider the anthropological evidence: Ecuadorian pottery was found to be identical to the Jomon styles that existed in Japan at the very same time. Yet many experts suggest it is merely coincidence, and the source of the pottery is more likely Columbia than the Far East.

The famous finds of arrowheads near Clovis, New Mexico, in the 1930s showed that these Americans may have lived nearly 14,000 years ago—2,000 years earlier than those who crossed Beringia. More recent finds show that the early inhabitants from that area (and south, all the way to Brazil) resemble ancient Australian Aborigines. Other skeletal finds in contemporary times point to possible origins in Polynesia.

Europe or Africa?

Long before 1492, when Columbus sailed the ocean blue, plant forms known to be native to Europe and Africa somehow made their way onto North American soil. Cotton and the bottle gourd were already here in America when Columbus hit the beach in the Bahamas. What's more, the Topper archeological site in South Carolina offered artifacts that predate Clovis by as much as 35,000 years!

Though little hard evidence exists to suggest the origin of the Topper inhabitants, many doubt any connection to Asia or South America—leaving Europe and/or Africa as the possible homes of these early travelers to the New World.

Who Downed the Red Baron? The Mystery of Manfred von Richthofen

He was the most successful flying ace of World War I—the conflict that introduced the airplane as a weapon of war. Yet, his demise has been credited to a number of likely opponents, both in the sky and on the ground.

✳ ✳ ✳ ✳

A Precious Little Prussian

MANFRED VON RICHTHOFEN was born in Silesia, Prussia (now part of Poland), in May 1892. Coming from a family steeped in nobility, the young von Richthofen decided he would follow in his father's footsteps and become a career soldier. At 11 years old, he enrolled in the cadet corps and, upon completion, became a member of a Prussian cavalry unit.

Up, Up, and Away

The Germans were at the forefront in using aircraft as offensive weapons against the British, French, and Russians during World War I. Von Richthofen was recruited into a flying unit as an "observer"—the second occupant of a two-seat plane who would direct the pilot over areas to gather intelligence. By 1915, von Richthofen decided to become a pilot himself, having already downed an enemy aircraft as an observer.

The young and green pilot joined a prestigious flying squad, one of the premier German jagdstaffeln—literally "hunting squadrons." In late 1916, von Richthofen's aggressive style brought him face-to-face with Britain's greatest fighter pilot, Major Lanoe Hawker. After a spirited battle in the sky, the German brought Hawker down in a tailspin, killing him. Von Richthofen called Hawker "a brave man and a sportsman." He later mounted the machine gun from the British plane over the door of his family home as a tribute to Hawker. The bold flying ace often showed a great deal of respect and affinity for his foes, once referring to his English dogfight opponents as "waltzing partners." Yet, he remained ruthless, even carrying with him a photograph of an Allied pilot he had viciously blown apart.

Creating an Identity

Von Richthofen quickly became the most feared, and respected, pilot in the skies. As he sought faster and more nimble aircraft, he decided he needed to be instantly recognizable. He ordered his plane to be painted bright red, with the German Iron Cross emblazoned on the fuselage. The "Red Baron" was born.

The End—But at Whose Hands?

By the spring of 1918, the Red Baron had shot down an amazing 80 Allied airplanes. This feat earned him the distinguished "Blue Max" award, and he assembled his own squadron of crack-shot pilots known as "the Flying Circus." But the celebrated pilot was not without his failures.

Von Richthofen suffered a head wound during an air battle in July 1917, which may have left an open wound exposing a small portion of his skull until his death. There are theories that this injury resulted in brain damage—if so, it would have caused the Red Baron to make some serious errors in judgment that may have led to his death on April 21, 1918.

On that day, von Richthofen was embroiled in a deadly dogfight with British Royal Air Force Sopwith Camels. As the Red Baron trained his machine-gun sights on a young pilot, enemy fire came seemingly from nowhere, striking his red Fokker. Von Richthofen crashed in an area of France occupied by Australian and Canadian allies. He was buried with full military honors by a respectful British Royal Air Force (RAF).

However, questions remain to this day as to who exactly killed von Richthofen. He suffered a fatal bullet wound through his chest. The RAF credited one of their pilots, but another story tells of Canadian soldiers who pounced on the plane crash and literally murdered the Red Baron. Still other tales claim von Richthofen was shot from the ground by rifle or machine-gun fire as he flew overhead.

The answer remains lost, perhaps forever. But there is no question as to the identity of the greatest flying ace of the First World War. That honor belongs to the Red Baron.

Vlad the Impaler: The Original Dracula

Most people are aware of Bram Stoker's Dracula and the many cultural reincarnations that the title character has gone through. But the fictional character of Dracula was based on a human being far more frightening than his fictional avatar.

❋ ❋ ❋ ❋

Background

THE LATE 1300s and early 1400s were a dramatic time in the area now known as Romania. Three sovereign states—Transylvania, Moldavia, and Wallachia—held fast to their independence against the Ottoman Empire. Wallachia was an elective monarchy, with much political backstabbing between the royal family and the boyars, the land-owning nobles.

Vlad III, known after his death as Vlad the Impaler, was born in the latter half of 1431 in the citadel of Sighisoara, Transylvania. His family was living in exile when he was born, ousted from their native Wallachia by pro-Turkish boyars. He was the son of a military governor who himself was a knight in the Order of the Dragon, a fraternity established to uphold Christian beliefs and fight Muslim Turks. Vlad II was also known as Vlad Dracul—Dracul meaning devil in Romanian. The a at the end of Dracul means "son of."

The throne of Wallachia was tossed from person to person, much like a hot potato, but with a lot more bloodshed. In

1436, Vlad Dracul took over the throne of Wallachia, but two years after that, he formed an alliance with the dreaded Turks, betraying his oath to the Order of the Dragon. He was assassinated in 1447 for his treachery.

Unfortunately for Vlad the Impaler, while his father was negotiating deals with the sultan of the Ottoman Empire, he traded his sons as collateral for his loyalty. While in captivity, Vlad the Impaler was frequently beaten and tortured.

Battleground

Released by the Turks after his father was killed, Vlad the Impaler showed up in Wallachia and defeated the boyars who had taken over the throne. He ruled for a brief time during 1448, but Vlad was quickly kicked out when the man who assassinated his father appointed someone else to fill the kingly duties. Vlad the Impaler bided his time, and in 1456, he not only took back the throne of Wallachia but also killed his father's murderer. He ruled Wallachia until 1462, but he was not a happy monarch.

Vlad the Impaler had a habit of killing huge numbers of people—slaves who didn't work hard enough, weak people who he felt were wasting space in his kingdom, and of course, criminals—you really did not want to be a criminal in Vlad's kingdom. Mostly, as might be guessed from his nickname, Vlad liked impaling people and then perching them in circles around town, an example of what would happen if citizens stepped out of line. In addition, he was rumored to drink the blood of those he had killed. On the upside, however, the crime rate in Wallachia was impressively low.

Breakdown

In 1461, Vlad the Impaler took on the Turks but was run out of Wallachia the next year. He lost the throne to Sultan Mehmed II's army and eventually sought refuge in Transylvania. The sultan installed Vlad's brother Radu on the throne of Wallachia. Once again, Vlad the Impaler was not happy. In 1476, with help from his Transylvanian pals, he launched a campaign to take back the throne of Wallachia, and he succeeded, impaling up a storm along the way. The Turks retaliated, and even though Vlad tried to organize an army to fight them, he couldn't raise a battalion large enough to defeat the Turks permanently. In his final battle, Vlad was killed, though the manner of his death is unknown. Some say that he was mistakenly killed by his own army, while others say that he was killed and decapitated by the Turks. One thing is known, however: Unlike the hundreds of thousands he killed, Vlad the Impaler was never one of the impalees.

Cleopatra: Stranger Than Fiction

In his work, Antony and Cleopatra, the immortal William Shakespeare gave the Egyptian queen the following line: "Be it known that we, the greatest, are misthought." These "misthoughts" could be the myths, untruths, and fallacies that seem to surround Cleopatra. Though movies and the media tend to focus on these misconceptions, the true stories are equally fascinating.

✳   ✳   ✳   ✳

MYTH: Cleopatra was Egyptian.

FACT: Cleopatra may have been the queen of Egypt, but she was actually Greek. Though her family had called Egypt home for hundreds of years, their lineage was linked to a general in Alexander the Great's army named Ptolemy who had come from Macedonia, an area in present-day Greece.

MYTH: Cleopatra was a vision of beauty.

FACT: Beauty, of course, is in the eye of the beholder. In ancient times, there were no cameras, but a person of Cleopatra's stature and wealth could have their likeness sculpted. If the image on an ancient Roman coin is believed to be accurate, then Cleopatra was endowed with a large, hooked nose and was as cheeky as a chipmunk.

MYTH: Cleopatra dissolved a pearl earring in a glass of vinegar and drank it. As the story goes, upon meeting Marc Antony, Cleopatra held a series of lavish feasts. On the eve of the final gala, Cleopatra bet Antony that she could arrange for the costliest meal in the world. As the banquet came to a close, she supposedly removed an enormous pearl from her ear, dropped it into a goblet of wine vinegar, then drank it down, with Antony admitting defeat.

FACT: Scientifically speaking, calcium carbonate—the mineral of which pearls are composed—will dissolve in an acid such as vinegar. However, based on the description of the pearl in question, it is likely that the short dip in vinegar resulted in nothing more than a soggy gem, as it would have taken a very long time for that amount of calcium carbonate to dissolve.

MYTH: Julius Caesar allowed Cleopatra to remain queen of Egypt because he loved her.

FACT: Though not married, Cleopatra did bear Caesar a son, Caesarion. However, that was hardly reason enough to hand over an entire country to her. Most likely, Caesar felt that any male ruler would pose a formidable threat to his empire, whereas Cleopatra was a safer alternative to rule Egypt.

MYTH: Cleopatra died from the bite of an asp after learning of Marc Antony's death.

FACT: It's unclear exactly how or why Cleopatra committed suicide. According to legend, after hearing of the death of her lover, she had two poisonous asps brought to her in a basket of

figs. The person who found the expired Cleopatra noted two small marks on her arm, but the snakes in question were never located. Cleopatra may very well have been distraught about her lover's demise, but it is likely that rumors she was about to be capture, and exhibited in the streets of Rome drove her to suicide.

Are You Related to Genghis Khan?

Your DNA may carry the stuff you need to conquer the world.

✳ ✳ ✳ ✳

From Riches To Rags To Riches

GENGHIS KHAN WAS one of the first self-made men in history. He was born to a tribal chief in 1162, probably at Dadal Sum, in the Hentii region of what is now Mongolia. At age 9, Genghis was sent packing after a rival tribe poisoned his father. For three years, Genghis and the remainder of his family wandered the land living from hand to mouth.

Genghis was down, but not out. After convincing some of his tribesmen to follow him, he eventually became one of the most successful political and military leaders in history, uniting the nomadic Mongol tribes into a vast sphere of influence. The Mongol Empire lasted from 1206 to 1368 and was the largest contiguous dominion in world history, stretching from the Caspian Sea to the Sea of Japan. At the empire's peak, it encompassed more than 700 tribes and cities.

A Uniter, Not A Divider

Genghis gave his people more than just land. He introduced a writing system that is still in use today, wrote the first laws to govern all Mongols, regulated hunting to make sure everybody had food, and created a judicial system that guaranteed fair trials. His determination to create unity swept old tribal rivalries aside and made everyone feel like a single people, the "Mongols."

Today, Genghis Khan is seen as one of the founding fathers of Mongolia. However, he is not so fondly remembered in Asia, the Middle East, and Europe, where he is regarded as a ruthless and bloodthirsty conqueror.

Who's Your Daddy?

It seems that Genghis was father of more than the Mongol nation. Recently, an international team of geneticists determined that one in every 200 men now living is a relative of the great Mongol ruler. More than 16 million men in central Asia have been identified as carrying the same Y chromosome as Genghis Khan.

A key reason is this: Genghis's sons and other male descendants had many children by many women; one son, Tushi, may have had 40 sons of his own, and one of Genghis's grandsons, Chinese dynastic ruler Kublai Khan, fathered 22 sons with recognized wives and an unknown number with the scores of women he kept as concubines.

Genetically speaking, Genghis continues to "live on" because the male chromosome is passed directly from father to son, with no change other than random mutations (which are typically insignificant). When geneticists identify those mutations, called "markers," they can chart the course of male descendants through centuries.

Is the world large enough for 16 million personal empires? Time—and genetics—will reveal the answer.

The Mound Builders: Mythmaking In Early America

The search for an improbable past, or, how to make a mountain out of a molehill.

✳ ✳ ✳ ✳

IN THE EARLY 1840s, the fledgling United States was gripped by a controversy that spilled from the parlors of the educated men in Boston and Philadelphia—the core of the nation's intellectual elite—onto the pages of the newspapers printed for mass edification. In the tiny farming village of Grave Creek, Virginia (now West Virginia), on the banks of the Ohio River stood one of the largest earthen mounds discovered during white man's progress westward. The existence of these mounds, spread liberally throughout the Mississippi Valley, Ohio River Valley, and much of the southeast, was commonly known and had caused a great deal of speculative excitement since Europeans had first arrived on the continent. Hernando de Soto, for one, had mentioned the mounds of the Southeast during his wandering in that region.

Money Well Spent

The colonists who settled the East Coast noticed that the mounds, which came in a variety of sizes and shapes, were typically placed near excellent sites for villages and farms. The Grave Creek mound was among the first of the major earthworks discovered by white men in their westward expansion. By 1838, the property was owned and farmed by the Tomlinson family. Abelard B. Tomlinson took an interest in the mound on his family's land and decided to open a vertical shaft from its summit, 70 feet high, to the center. He discovered skeletal remains at various levels and a timbered vault at the base containing the remains of two individuals. More importantly, he discovered a sandstone tablet inscribed with three lines of characters of unknown origin.

Who Were the Mound Builders?

Owing to the general belief that the aborigines were lazy and incapable of such large, earth-moving operations and the fact that none of the tribes who dwelt near the mounds claimed any knowledge of who had built them, many 19th-century Americans believed that the mound builders could not have been the ancestors of the Native American tribes they encountered. Wild and fantastic stories arose, and by the early 19th century, the average American assumed that the mound builders had been a pre-Columbian expedition from the Old World—Vikings, Israelites, refugees from Atlantis—all these and more had their champions. Most agreed, however, that the New World had once hosted and given rise to a civilization as advanced as that of the Aztecs and Incas who had then fallen into disarray or been conquered by the savage barbarians that now inhabited the land. Speculation on the history of the mound builders led many, including Thomas Jefferson, to visit mounds and conduct their own studies.

Mormons and the Mounds

Meanwhile, the Grave Creek tablet fanned the flames of a controversy that was roaring over the newly established, and widely despised, Church of Jesus Christ of Latter Day Saints, founded by Joseph Smith. The Mormon religion is based upon the belief that the American continent was once inhabited by lost tribes of Israel who divided into warring factions and fought each other to near extinction. The last surviving prophet of these people, Mormon, inscribed his people's history upon gold tablets, which were interred in a mound near present-day Palmyra, New York, until they were revealed to 15-year-old Joseph Smith in 1823. Though many Americans were ready to believe that the mounds represented the remains of a nonaboriginal culture, they were less ready to believe in Smith's new religion. Smith and his adherents were persecuted horribly, and Smith was killed by an angry mob while leading his followers west. Critics of the Saints (as the Mormons prefer to be called) point to the early 19th-century publication of several popular books purporting that the earthen mounds of North America were the remains of lost tribes of Israel. These texts claimed that evidence would eventually be discovered to support their author's assertions. That the young Smith should have his revelation so soon after these fanciful studies were published struck many observers as entirely too coincidental. Thus, Abelard Tomlinson's excavation of the sandstone tablet with its strange figures ignited the passions of both Smith's followers and his detractors.

Enter the Scholar

Into this theological, and ultimately anthropological, maelstrom strode Henry Rowe Schoolcraft, a mineralogist whose keen interest in Native American history had led to his appointment as head of Indian affairs. While working in Sault

Ste. Marie, Schoolcraft married a native woman and mastered the Ojibwa language. Schoolcraft traveled to Grave Creek to examine Tomlinson's tablet and concluded that the figures were indeed a language but deferred to more learned scholars to determine just which language they represented. The opinions were many and varied—from Celtic runes to early Greek; experts the world over weighed in with their opinions. Nevertheless, Schoolcraft was more concerned with physical evidence and close study of the mounds themselves, and he remained convinced that the mounds and the artifacts they carried were the products of ancestors of the Native Americans. Schoolcraft's theory flew  in the face of both those who sought to defend and those who sought to debunk the Mormon belief, and it would be more than three decades until scholarship and the emergence of archeological techniques began to shift opinion on the subject.

Answers Proposed, but Questions Still Abound

History has vindicated Schoolcraft's careful and thoughtful study of the mounds. Today, we know that the mound builders were not descendants of Israel, nor were they the offspring of Vikings. They were simply the ancient and more numerous predecessors of the Native Americans, who constructed the mounds for protection from floods and as burial sites, temples, and defense strongholds. As for the Grave Creek tablet: Scholars today generally agree that the figures are not a written language but simply a fanciful design whose meaning, if ever there was one, has been lost to the ages. Though the Smithsonian Institute has several etchings of the tablet in its collection, the whereabouts of the actual tablet have been lost to the ages.

Rasputin: Depraved Sex Freak or Maligned Holy Man?

We know this much: Grigori Yefimovich Rasputin, a barely literate Russian peasant, grew close to the last tsaritsa—close enough to cost him his life. Incredibly lurid stories ricocheted off the walls of the Winter Palace: drunken satyr, faith healer, master manipulator. What's true? And why does Rasputin fascinate us even today?

✳ ✳ ✳ ✳

THE RASPUTIN SAGA began on January 22, 1869, in the grubby peasant village of Pokrovskoe, Russia. Baby Rasputin was born on the day of the Orthodox saint Grigori, and was thus named after him. There wasn't much to distinguish little Grigori from tens of millions of Russian peasant kids, and he grew up a rowdy drunk. He married a peasant woman named Praskovia, who hung back in Pokrovskoe raising their five kids in Rasputin's general absence.

At 28, Rasputin was born again, rural Russian style. He sobered up—a small miracle in itself—and wandered between monasteries seeking knowledge. Evidently, he fell in with the khlysti—a secretive, heretical Eastern Orthodox sect swirling with rumors of orgies, flagellation, and the like. He gained a mystical aura, and his behavior reflected a sincere spiritual search.

In 1903, he wandered to the capital, St. Petersburg, where he impressed the local Orthodox clergy. Word spread. The ruling Romanov family soon heard of Rasputin.

The Romanovs held a powerful yet precarious position. Ethnically, they were more German than Russian, a hot-button topic for the bona fide Slavs they ruled. Greedy flatterers and brutal infighters made the corridors of power a steep slope with weak rock and loose mud: As you climbed, your prestige and influence grew—but woe to you if you slipped (or were pushed). In that event, the rest would step aside and let you fall—caring only to get out of your way. This was no safe place for a naive peasant—however spiritually inclined. Even the Romanovs lived in fear, for tsars tended to die violent deaths. They ruled a dirt-poor population that was seething with resentment. Tsaryevich ("tsar's son") Alexei, the heir apparent, was a fragile hemophiliac who could bleed out from a skinned knee, aptly symbolic of the blood in the political water in St. Petersburg in those final days of the last tsar, Nikolai II.

As the tsaritsa worried over gravely ill Alexei in 1906, she thought of Rasputin and his healing reputation. He answered her summons in person, blessed Alexei with an Orthodox ikon and left. Alexei improved, and Tsaritsa Aleksandra was hooked on Rasputin. She consulted him often, promoted him to her friends, and pulled him onto that treacherous slope of imperial favor. For his final ten years, Rasputin became a polarizing figure as he grew more influential. His small covey of upper-crust supporters (mostly female) hung on his every word, even as a growing legion of nobles, peasants, and clergy saw in Rasputin all that was wrong with the monarchy.

What few ask now is: What was Rasputin thinking? What was he feeling? His swift rise from muddy fields to the royal palace gave him an understandable ego trip. He was a peasant but not an idiot; he realized his rise would earn him jealous enemies. The sheer fury of their hatred seems to have surprised, frightened, and saddened him, for he wasn't a hateful man. He certainly felt duty-bound to the tsaritsa, whose unwavering favor deflected most of his enemies' blows. Rasputin's internal spiritual struggle (against sin, toward holiness) registers authentic, at least until his last year or so of life—but he made regular visits to prostitutes long before that. Defenders claim that he was only steeling himself against sexual temptation; you can imagine what his enemies said.

Life worsened for Rasputin in 1914, when he was stabbed by a former prostitute. He survived, but the experience shook him. After recuperating, he abandoned any restraint he'd ever exercised. Rasputin better acquainted himself with the bottoms of liquor bottles—and those of his visitors. Most likely he expected death and gave in to natural human desires: Cartoons portrayed him as a cancer infecting the monarchy, especially after Russia went to war with Germany. Military setbacks left Russians with much to mourn and resent. A wave of mandatory patriotism swept Russia, focusing discontent upon the royal family's Germanic ties.

In the end, clergy and nobility agreed with the media: down with Rasputin.

Led by a fabulously rich libertine named Felix Yusupov, a group of Rasputin's enemies lured him to a meeting on December 29, 1916. The popular story is that he scarfed a bunch of poisoned food and wine, somehow didn't die, was shot, got up, was beaten and shot some more, then was finally tied up and thrown alive through the ice of a frozen river. What is sure: Rasputin was shot, bound, and dumped into freezing water to die. Whether or not he was still alive when dumped and whether or not he actually partook of the cyanide munchies, he was found with at least one fatal bullet wound.

The tsaritsa buried her advisor on royal property. After the Romanovs fell, a mob dug up Rasputin and burned his corpse. To our knowledge, nothing remains of him.

Rasputin had predicted that if he were slain by the nobility, the Russian monarchy wouldn't long survive him. His prophecy came true: Less than a year after his death, the Russian Revolution deposed the tsar. The Reds would soon murder the entire royal family; had they captured Rasputin, it's hard to imagine him being spared. For the "Mad Monk" who was neither mad nor monastic, the muddy road of life had dead-ended in the treacherous forest of imperial favor.

Nostradamus: Seer of Visions

Nostradamus was born in December 1503 in Saint-Rémy-de-Provence, a small town in southern France. Little is known about his childhood except that he came from a very large family and that he may have been educated by his maternal great-grandfather. In his teens, Nostradamus entered the University of Avignon but was only there for about a year before the school was forced to close its doors due to an outbreak of the plague. He later became a successful apothecary and even created a pill that could supposedly protect against the plague.

✳ ✳ ✳ ✳

Looking to the Future

IT IS BELIEVED that some time in the 1540s, Nostradamus began taking an interest in the occult, particularly in ways to predict the future. His preferred method was scrying: gazing into a bowl of water or a mirror and waiting for visions to appear.

Nostradamus published a highly successful almanac for the year 1550, which included some of his prophecies and predictions. This almanac was so successful that Nostradamus wrote more, perhaps even several a year, until his death in 1566. Even so, it was a single book that caused the most controversy, both when it was released and even today.

Les Prophéties

In addition to creating his almanacs, Nostradamus also began compiling his previously unpublished prophecies into one massive volume. Released in 1555, *Les Prophéties* (*The Prophecies*) would become one of the most controversial and perplexing books ever written. The book contained hundreds of quatrains (four-line stanzas or poems), but Nostradamus worried that some might see his prophecies as demonic, so he encoded them to obscure their true meanings. To do this, Nostradamus did everything from playing with the syntax of the quatrains to switching between French, Greek, Latin, and other languages.

When first released, some people did think that Nostradamus was in league with the devil. Others simply thought he was insane and that his quatrains were nothing more than the ramblings of a delusional man. As time went on, though, people started looking to Nostradamus's prophecies to see if they were coming true. It became a common practice that after a major event in history, people would pull out a copy of Les Prophéties to see if they could find a hidden reference to it buried in one of Nostradamus's quatrains. It is a practice that has continued to this day and is more and more common as the years go by.

Lost in Translation

One of the interesting and frustrating things about Nostradamus's *Les Prophéties* is that due to the printing procedures in his time, no two editions of his book were ever alike. Not only were there differences in spelling or punctuation, but entire words and phrases were often changed, especially when translated from French to English. Presently, there are more than 200 editions of *Les Prophéties* in print, all of which have subtle differences in the text. So it's not surprising that people from all over the world have looked into their version and found references to the French Revolution, Napoleon, the rise of Hitler, the JFK assassination, even the Apollo moon landing. But of all the messages reportedly hidden in Nostradamus's quatrains, the most talked about recently are those relating to the terrorist attacks on September 11, 2001.

Soon after the Twin Towers fell, an e-mail started making the rounds, which claimed that Nostradamus had predicted the events and quoted the following quatrain as proof:

In the City of God there will be a great thunder,

Two Brothers torn apart by Chaos,

While the fortress endures,

The great leader will succumb,

The third big war will begin when the big city is burning.

—Nostradamus, 1654

Anyone reading the above can clearly see that Nostradamus is describing September 11, the Twin Towers ("Two Brothers") falling, and the start of World War III. Pretty chilling, except Nostradamus never wrote it. It's nothing more than an Internet hoax that spread like wildfire. It's a pretty bad hoax, too. First, Nostradamus wrote quatrains, which have four lines. This one has five. Also, consider that the date Nostradamus supposedly penned this—1654—was almost 90 years after he died. Nostradamus might have been able to see the future, but there's no mention of him being able to write from beyond the grave.

However, others believe Nostradamus did indeed pen a quatrain that predicted September 11. It is quatrain I.87, which when translated reads:

Volcanic fire from the center of the earth

Will cause tremors around the new city;

Two great rocks will make war for a long time

Then Arethusa will redden a new river.

Those who believe this quatrain foresaw September 11 believe that the "new city" is a thinly-veiled reference to New York City. They further state that Nostradamus would often use rocks to refer to religious beliefs and that the third stanza refers to the religious differences between the United States and the terrorists. Skeptic James Randi, however, believes that the "new city" referred to is Naples, not New York. So who's right? No one is really sure, so for now, the debate continues . . . at least until the next major catastrophe hits and people go scrambling to the bookshelves to see what Nostradamus had to say about it.

Enrico Caruso: The Superstitious Songster

One of the most famous tenors of all time, Italian opera singer Enrico Caruso played many unusual roles in his day, but none were as eccentric as Caruso himself.

✳ ✳ ✳ ✳

DETAILS OF CARUSO'S birth in Naples on February 25, 1873, vary widely, but sources say he was the 18th of 21 children in a family that included 19 brothers and one lone sister; most of his siblings died in infancy. Because his mother was too ill, Enrico was nursed by Signora Rosa Baretti. He believed her milk caused him to be different from the rest of his family.

The Caruso family was quite poor—Enrico's father was a mechanic and he encouraged his son to become one as well. Instead, Enrico began singing in churches and cafés at age 16 to help support himself and his family. It may have been his impoverished youth or his need for order that led to his habit of obsessively recording even the most minor purchases in carefully tended books. And yet Caruso was extremely generous, dispensing handouts to almost everyone who asked. He also saved every newspaper clipping about his performances.

Caruso moved to the United States after making a big splash at New York's Metropolitan Opera in Rigoletto in 1903. Later, while touring with the Met, he found himself smack in the middle of the 1906 San Francisco earthquake. Although he escaped unscathed, the experience incited him to vow never to return. Upon his departure from the city, he is famously known to have shouted, "Give me Vesuvius!" (the explosive volcano of his native Italy that had erupted two weeks earlier).

The Weird Tenor's Tenets

Caruso regulated his life with a rigid set of curious and unexplained superstitions. In her account of Caruso's life, his wife, Dorothy Park Benjamin, revealed that he considered it bad luck to wear a new suit on a Friday, and he shunned the phrase, "Good luck!" for fear it would produce the opposite effect. For reasons unknown, he also refused to start any new undertakings on either a Tuesday or a Friday.

Like many artistic geniuses, he was germ-phobic and bathed twice daily, often changing all of his clothes many times a day. As might be expected, some of Caruso's strongest and most peculiar beliefs were related to his magnificent voice. Before going on stage, he performed the following ritual:

1. Smoked a cigarette in a holder so as not to dirty his hands

2. Gargled with salt water to clean his throat

3. Sniffed a small amount of snuff

4. Sipped a cup of water

5. Ate precisely one quarter of an apple

6. Asked his deceased mother to help him sing

Caruso also believed he could enhance his vocal prowess by wearing anchovies around his neck and smoking two packs of cigarettes a day.

The Final Crazy Curtain

Enrico Caruso died in 1921 from complications of bronchial pneumonia. After his death, the Naples Museum in Italy claimed he had left them his throat for examination, and newspapers in Rome printed a diagram of what was supposedly the singer's internal sound system. According to *The New York Times*, doctors said Caruso had vocal cords twice as long as normal, a supersized epiglottis, and the lung power of a "superman." But the *Times* also printed his wife's denial that any organs had been removed from her husband.

Despite the strange circumstances of his life, Caruso left an almost superhuman legacy to the world of music. With nearly 500 recordings of his stupendous voice, he remains one of the top-selling artists of record company RCA more than 80 years after his death.

Identities Lost: The Druids and the Picts

What do you know about the Druids? How about the Picts? Chances are, what you know (or think you know) is wrong. These two "lost" peoples are saddled with serious cases of mistaken identity.

✳ ✳ ✳ ✳

MOST CONTEMPORARY PERCEPTIONS of the Druids and Picts tend to be derived from legend and lore. As such, our conceptions of these peoples range from erroneous and unlikely to just plain foolish.

Let's start with the Druids. They are often credited with the building of Stonehenge, the great stone megalith believed to be their sacred temple, as well as their arena for savage human sacrifice rituals. True or False?

False. First of all, Stonehenge was built around 2000 B.C.— 1,400 years before the Druids emerged. Second, though we know admittedly little of Druidic practice, it seemed to be traditional and conservative. The Druids did have specific divinity-related beliefs, but it is not known whether they actually carried out human sacrifices.

What about the Picts? Although often reduced to a mythical race of magical fairies, the Picts actually ruled Scotland before the Scots.

So who were the Druids and the Picts?

The Druids—The Priestly Class

As the priestly class of Celtic society, the Druids served as the Celts' spiritual leaders—repositories of knowledge about the world and the universe, as well as authorities on Celtic history, law, religion, and culture. In short, they were the preservers of the Celtic way of life.

The Druids provided the Celts with a connection to their gods, the universe, and the natural order. They preached of the power and authority of the deities and taught the immortality of the soul and reincarnation. They were experts in astronomy and the natural world. They also had an innate connection to all things living: They preferred holding great rituals among natural shrines provided by the forests, springs, and groves.

To become a Druid, one had to survive extensive training. Druid wannabes and Druid-trained minstrels and bards had to endure as many as 20 years of oral education and memorization.

More Powerful Than Celtic Chieftains

In terms of power, the Druids took a backseat to no one. Even the Celtic chieftains, well-versed in power politics, recognized the overarching authority of the Druids. Celtic society had well-defined power and social structures and territories and property rights. The Druids were deemed the ultimate arbiters in all matters relating to such. If there was a legal or financial dispute between two parties, it was unequivocally settled in special Druid-presided courts. Armed conflicts were immediately ended by Druid rulings. Their word was final.

In the end, however, there were two forces to which even the Druids had to succumb—the Romans and Christianity. With the Roman invasion of Britain in A.D. 43, Emperor Claudius decreed that Druidism throughout the Roman Empire was to be outlawed. The Romans destroyed the last vestiges of official Druidism in Britain with the annihilation of the Druid stronghold of Anglesey in A.D. 61. Surviving Druids fled to unconquered Ireland and Scotland, only to become marginalized by the influence of Christianity within a few centuries.

Stripped of power and status, the Druids of ancient Celtic society disappeared. They morphed into wandering poets and storytellers with no connection to their once illustrious past.

The Picts—The Painted People

The Picts were, in simplest terms, the people who inhabited ancient Scotland before the Scots. Their origins are unknown, but some scholars believe that the Picts were descendents of the Caledonians or other Iron Age tribes who invaded Britain.

No one knows what the Picts called themselves; the origin of their name comes from other sources and probably derives from the Pictish custom of tattooing or painting their bodies. The Irish called them Cruithni, meaning "the people of the designs." The Romans called them Picti, which is Latin for "painted people"; however, the Romans probably used the term as a general moniker for all the untamed peoples living north of Hadrian's Wall.

A Second-Hand History

The Picts themselves left no written records. All descriptions of their history and culture come from second-hand accounts. The earliest of these is a Roman account from A.D. 297 stating that the Picti and the Hiberni (Irish) were already well-established enemies of the Britons to the south.

The Picts were also well-established enemies of each other. Before the arrival of the Romans, the Picts spent most of their time fighting amongst themselves. The threat posed by the Roman conquest of Britain forced the squabbling Pict kingdoms to come together and eventually evolve into the nation-state of Pictland. The united Picts were strong enough not only to resist conquest by the Romans, but also to launch periodic raids on Roman-occupied Britain.

Having defied the Romans, the Picts later succumbed to a

more benevolent invasion launched by Irish Christian missionaries. Arriving in Pictland in the late 6th century, they succeeded in converting the polytheistic Pict elite within two decades. Much of the written history of the Picts comes from the Irish Christian annals. If not for the writings of the Romans and the Irish missionaries, we might not have knowledge of the Picts today.

Despite the existence of an established Pict state, Pictland disappeared with the changing of its name to the Kingdom of Alba in A.D. 843, a move signifying the rise of the Gaels as the dominant people in Scotland. By the 11th century, virtually all vestiges of them had vanished.

The Brain of the Confederacy

Mystery surrounds the life of Judah P. Benjamin, a Confederate leader subjected to anti-Semitism and suspicion despite his loyalty to the Southern cause.

✳   ✳   ✳   ✳

EVEN BEFORE BECOMING Jefferson Davis's most trusted confidant, Senator Judah P. Benjamin had made an exceptional career for himself. The Sephardic Jew who devoted his powers of oratory to the cause of slavery was a novelty in the prewar Senate. Admirers claimed that intelligence blazed from his eyes. He enchanted allies with his disarming wit, his old-world sophistication, and, as one lawmaker recalled, a voice "as musical as the chimes of silver bells."

Representing Louisiana in the Senate, he withdrew from that body when Louisiana left the Union. The newly formed Confederate government put his smiling face on its two-dollar bill and his quick mind to work as secretary of war. The wife of Confederate President Jefferson Davis reported that Benjamin was at Davis's side 12 hours a day. One biography asserts that his workdays began at 8:00 A.M. and lasted until the crack of dawn the next morning. But even as a powerful Confederate, he remained an outsider in his own South. Plantation society repaid Benjamin's devotion to the Confederacy with anti-Semitism and suspicion. One way he coped with this predicament was through humor. In one instance when Davis was headed for a service at an Episcopal church and Benjamin realized he was obliged to accompany his president, Benjamin joked, "May I not have the pleasure of escorting you?"

Humble Beginnings

Judah Philip Benjamin was born in the present-day Virgin Islands to a dry-goods seller who founded one of America's first reform synagogues. After growing up in the Carolinas, the immigrant son attended Yale at only 14 years old, but he was expelled under cloudy circumstances. A newspaper piece published just before the Civil War claimed that his expulsion had been for playing cards and pickpocketing, a charge that Benjamin dismissed as libel by a man who falsely claimed to be his classmate.

Fortunately for the young Benjamin, one could become a self-trained lawyer in the 19th century. Harvard was the only law school at that time, so most lawyers—including Abraham Lincoln—were self-taught. Benjamin's facile legal mind readily cut to the heart of a case, and clients paid him handsomely. In this way, he achieved one of his aims, that of owning a plantation. His climb up the social ladder accelerated when he married Natalie St. Martin, a stunning Creole beauty from a well-to-do Catholic Louisiana family. The marriage was somewhat mysterious, characterized by long periods of separation and rumors that Mrs. Benjamin sometimes looked elsewhere for love. She spent most of her married life in Paris.

A Future in Politics

Benjamin sold off his plantation and about 140 slaves in 1850. His rising political career took him to the Senate two years later. President Millard Fillmore considered appointing

Benjamin to the Supreme Court, but the senator chose to stay in Congress instead. He also wrote books and was a walking encyclopedia on everything from techniques for planting sugar to the French language, his wife's native tongue. For relaxation, he regaled friends with suspenseful ghost stories and verses by his favorite poet, Lord Alfred Tennyson.

Benjamin had a knack for enraging abolitionist enemies such as Senator Ben Wade of Ohio, who disdainfully called him "an Israelite in Egyptian clothing" for defending the right to own slaves. Benjamin took what might be called a libertarian view of slavery. To him, the pro-abolitionist positions of the Republican party were violating the sacred American right of property. In one speech, he asked how the North would like it if animal-rights fanatics, believers in "the sinfulness of subjecting the animal creation to the domination and service of man," were to steal cattle and descend on farms with torches, making "the night lurid with the flames of their barns and granaries."

There is no record of Benjamin being religious, but he was quick to confront any attack on his heritage with devastating oratorical parries. "It is true that I am a Jew," he snapped back at Wade, "and when my ancestors were receiving their Ten Commandments from the immediate Deity, amidst the thunderings and lightnings of Mt. Sinai, the ancestors of my opponent were herding swine in the forests of Great Britain." Known for his attacks, he was well-known for the ease with which he'd patch up the injury, using courtesy and tricks such as allowing his adversary to win a round of ten-pin bowling.

The election of Abraham Lincoln and the secession of Southern states that followed it found Benjamin declaring his enemies beyond reconciliation. In an address to the Senate on December 31, 1860, he told Northerners to wild applause, "You may carry desolation into our peaceful land, and with torch and fire you may set our cities in flames . . . but you never can subjugate us; you never can convert the free sons of the soil into vassals, paying tribute to your power . . . Never! Never!"

The Davis Connection

When the Confederacy was formed, Jefferson Davis tapped Benjamin to be attorney general. To anyone who saw how they bickered in the Senate, their friendship seemed unlikely. Benjamin had been speaking on an army appropriations bill when Davis snidely interrupted to complain that he'd had no idea he'd have to listen to "the arguments of a paid attorney in the Senate chamber." Benjamin demanded an apology. To avert the duel that was expected in those days, Davis admitted his error and apologized on the Senate floor. From that point, the two gradually came to be close allies in the Southern cause. From attorney general, Davis moved Benjamin over to Confederate secretary of war, but he soon ran into trouble in that post. In February 1862, Roanoke Island, off the coast of North Carolina, was lost to General Ambrose Burnside's forces after the rebel government failed to send reinforcements. Benjamin scored loyalty points by shouldering responsibility. Had he been less faithful, he might have embarrassed the President by revealing the real reason for the defeat: He had no troops to send.

Benjamin couldn't continue as secretary of war under the circumstances, but he remained in the Confederate Cabinet by sliding to a new role as secretary of state. He worked hard to lure the British into the war, an effort that ultimately failed. The Confederates hoped to entice European allies with promises of cotton, but that scheme proved no more successful than another idea he promoted. In late 1864 and early 1865, Benjamin devised a desperate plan to impress the United Kingdom and shore up Southern forces by freeing the slaves—if they joined the gray army. "Let us say to every Negro who wishes to go into the ranks, 'Go and fight—you are free!'" Benjamin said, and General Robert E. Lee agreed. It was, however, a plan that came too late in the war to come to fruition.

New Country, New Life

When the South lost the war, Benjamin disguised himself and

escaped to England, where he again took up his career as an attorney. Back at home, on both sides of the Mason-Dixon line, anti-Semitic conspiracy theories had sprouted to blame "Judas" Benjamin for scuttling the Confederate war effort, running off with the Southern treasury, or plotting the death of Lincoln in his capacity as Southern spy chief. For that last accusation, Benjamin and Davis both feared that Benjamin would be arrested and hanged. Later investigation and scholarship has determined that Benjamin was not involved in the Lincoln assassination.

The popular memory Benjamin left behind was captured in poet Stephen Vincent Benet's 1928 depiction of a lonely but malevolent outsider—"Seal-sleek, black-eyed, lawyer and epi-cure/Able, well-hated, face alive with life"—who is haunted by the question: "I am a Jew. What am I doing here?"

Benjamin died in 1884 in Paris and was buried under a head-stone that read, "Phillipe Benjamin." His personal letters had been burned, leaving historians with the mystery of what it was really like to be a Jewish leader of the Confederacy.

The Story of the Tasaday

A 1972 National Geographic article announced the discovery of a gentle, pristine Stone Age people in the Philippines: the Tasaday. Skeptics say the Tasaday were a hoax perpetrated by the Marcos government—but are they right?

✳ ✳ ✳ ✳

IN 1971, STRONGMAN Ferdinand Marcos was dictator of the Philippines. His wealthy crony, Manuel Elizalde, Jr., was head of Panamin, a minority-rights watchdog agency. In a nation with 7,107 islands, 12 major regional languages, and hundreds of ethnic groups, such an agency has its work cut out for it.

The Discovery
The Philippines' second largest island, Mindanao, is bigger than

Maine, with lots of jungle. According to Elizalde, a western Mindanao tribesman put him in contact with the Tasaday. The tribe numbered only a couple dozen and lived amid primitive conditions. Their language bore relation to nearby tongues but lacked words for war and violence. They seemed to be living in gentle simplicity, marveling at Elizalde as a deity and protector. For his part, Elizalde clamped the full power of the Philippine state into place to shield his newfound people. One of the few study groups permitted to examine the Tasaday was from *National Geographic*, which introduced the Tasaday to the world in 1972.

After Marcos fell from power in 1986, investigators studying the lives of the Tasaday revealed that it was all a fraud. According to reports, Elizalde had recruited the Tasaday from long-established local tribes and forced them to role-play a Stone Age lifestyle. The Tasaday eventually became the "Tasaday Hoax."

A Scam Revealed?

A couple of Tasaday told a sad story: They normally farmed nearby, living in huts rather than caves, but Elizalde made them wear loincloths and do dog-and-pony shows for paying visitors. The poorer and more primitive they looked, the more money they would get. In one instance, a group of German journalists who set out to document the Tasaday found them dressed primitively—sort of. They were wearing leaves, but they had stuck them onto their clothing, which was visible beneath the foliage. Scientific skepticism soon surfaced as well: How could they have remained that isolated for so long, even on Mindanao? Why didn't modern disease now decimate them? Why did their tools show evidence of steel-knife manufacturing?

Elizalde didn't back down easily. In an attempt to keep up the charade, he flew a few Tasaday to Manila to sue the naysayers for libel. With Marcos ousted, however, Elizalde was less able to influence investigators or control what they had access to.

Eminent linguist Lawrence Reid decided that the Tasaday were indeed an offshoot of a regional tribe—but one that had been living in the area for only 150 years, not more than a thousand as was claimed. Likely as confused as everyone else at this point, previous Tasaday whistleblowers now confessed that translators had bribed them to say the whole thing was a hoax.

The Aftermath

Elizalde later fled to Costa Rica, squandered his money, and died a drug addict. If he had indeed fabricated the history of the Tasaday, what was his motivation? It could have been a public-relations ploy, because the Marcos government had a well-earned reputation for repression. A strong minority-rights stance in defense of the Tasaday could be expected to buff some tarnish off the government's image. Commerce likely played a role, for the Tasaday episode denied huge tracts of jungle to logging interests. Perhaps those interests hadn't played ball with Marcos and/or Elizalde.

Elizalde did not "discover" the Tasaday, but that doesn't mean they were total fakes. What is clear is that they were pawns in a sociopolitical chess game far greater than the jungle of Mindanao.

The World's First Civilization

The fame of the ancient Egyptians—pyramids, pharaohs, eye makeup!—has led to the common misconception that ancient Egypt was the world's first civilization.

✳ ✳ ✳ ✳

MOST WESTERN SCHOLARS agree that the Sumerian civilization in Mesopotamia, located between the Tigris and Euphrates rivers in modern-day Iraq, was the first. Yet a deeper look reveals that there is a whole pageant of contenders for that coveted prize.

The Contestants

1. Ancient Sumer. The first civilization is believed to have begun around 4000 B.C. The great city of Ur, associated with Sumer, is possibly the world's first city. Archaeological evidence suggests that "pre-civilized" cultures lived in the Tigris and Euphrates river valleys long before the emergence of Sumer.

2. The Harappan. Next in line are the ancient Indus Valley civilizations, located in the Indus and Ghaggar-Hakra river valleys in modern-day Pakistan and western India. The first mature civilization associated with this area is called the Harappan, generally cited as beginning around 3500 B.C., thus placing it in time after Sumer. However, it is clear that agricultural communities had inhabited the area since at least 9000 B.C.

3. Ancient Egypt. Located in Africa's Nile Valley, it is generally cited as beginning in 3200 B.C. But as with the Indus Valley civilization, it is difficult to establish a firm beginning date because agricultural societies had settled in the Nile River Valley since the 10th millennium B.C.

4. and 5. Ancient China and Elam. The final two, and least known, contestants (from the Western perspective) are the ancient Chinese civilizations and the Elam civilization of modern-day Iran. The Elamite kingdom began around 2700 B.C., though recent evidence suggests that a city existed in this area at a far earlier date—perhaps early enough to rival Sumer. Meanwhile, the ancient Chinese civilizations, located in the Yangtze and Yellow river valleys, are said to have begun around 2200 B.C.

The Criteria

The most salient feature of a civilization is a city, which, unlike a village, should have large religious and government buildings, evidence of social stratification (mansions for the rich and shacks for the poor), and complex infrastructure such as roads and irrigation. Civilizations are also defined by elaborate social systems, organized trade relations with outside groups, and the development of writing.

Marking a "civilization" is difficult because in all five possible cradles of civilization described above, complex societies lived in the same areas long before true civilization emerged. In fact, this is surely why civilizations first developed in these regions—human groups lived in the areas before the development of agriculture. Human populations have roamed the sprawling Eurasian continent for at least 100,000 years.

The emergence of civilization can be seen as the result of culture after culture living in one geographic area for countless generations until something happened that set these seminomadic groups on the path to civilization.

There's More to Know About Tycho

A golden nose, a dwarf, a pet elk, drunken revelry, and . . . astronomy? Read about the wild life of this groundbreaking astronomer.

✳ ✳ ✳ ✳

Look to the Stars

TYCHO BRAHE WAS a Dutch nobleman who is best remembered for blazing a trail in astronomy in an era before the invention of the telescope. Through tireless observation and study, Brahe became one of the first astronomers to fully understand the exact motions of the planets, thereby laying the groundwork for future generations of star gazers.

In 1560, Brahe, then a 13-year-old law student, witnessed a partial eclipse of the sun. He reportedly was so moved by the event that he bought a set of astronomical tools and a copy of Ptolemy's legendary astronomical treatise, *Almagest,* and began a life-long career studying the stars. Where Brahe would differ from his forbearers in this field of study was that he believed that new discoveries in the field of astronomy could be made, not by guesswork and conjecture, but rather by rigorous and repetitious studies. His work would include many publications and even the discovery of a supernova now known as SN 1572.

Hven, Sweet Hven

As his career as an astronomer blossomed, Brahe became one of the most widely renowned astronomers in all of Europe. In fact, he was so acclaimed that when King Frederick II of Denmark heard of Brahe's plans to move to the Swiss city of Basle, the King offered him his own island, Hven, located in the Danish Sound.

Once there, Brahe built his own observatory known as Uraniborg and ruled the island as if it were his own personal kingdom. This meant that his tenants were often forced to supply their ruler (in this case Brahe) with goods and services or be locked up in the island's prison. At one point Brahe imprisoned an entire family—contrary to Danish law.

Did We Mention That He Was Completely Nutty?

While he is famous for his work in astronomy, Brahe is more infamous for his colorful lifestyle. At age 20, he lost part of his nose in an alcohol-fueled duel (reportedly using rapiers while in the dark) that ensued after a Christmas party. Portraits of Brahe show him wearing a replacement nose possibly made of gold and silver and held in place by an adhesive. Upon the exhumation of his body in 1901, green rings discovered around the nasal cavity of Brahe's skull have also led some scholars to speculate that the nose may actually have been made of copper.

While there was a considerable amount of groundbreaking astronomical research done on Hven, Brahe also spent his time hosting legendarily drunken parties. Such parties often featured a colorful cast of characters, including someone named Jepp who dwelled under Brahe's dining table and functioned as something of a court jester; it is speculated that Brahe believed that Jepp was clairvoyant. Brahe also kept a tame pet elk, which stumbled to its death after falling down a flight of stairs—the animal had gotten drunk on beer at the home of a nobleman.

Brahe also garnered additional notoriety for marrying a woman from the lower classes. Such a union was considered shameful for a nobleman such as Brahe, and he was ostracized because of the marriage. Thusly all of his eight children were considered illegitimate.

However, the most lurid story of all is the legend that Brahe died from a complication to his bladder caused by not urinating, out of politeness, at a friend's dinner party where prodigious amounts of wine were consumed. The tale lives on, but it should be pointed out that recent research suggests this version of Brahe's demise could be apocryphal: He may have died of mercury poisoning from his own fake nose.

The Rise and Fall of the Knights Templar

The Crusades, Christendom's quest to recover and hold the Holy Land, saw the rise of several influential military orders. Of these, the Knights Templar had perhaps the greatest lasting influence—and took the hardest fall.

✳ ✳ ✳ ✳

JULY 15, 1099: On that day, the First Crusade stormed Jerusalem and slaughtered everyone in sight—Jews, Muslims, Christians—didn't matter. This unleashed a wave of pilgrimage, as European Christians flocked to now-accessible Palestine and its holy sites. Though Jerusalem's loss was a blow to Islam, it was a bonanza for the region's thieves, from Saracens to lapsed Crusaders: a steady stream of naive pilgrims to rob.

Defending the Faithful

French knight Hugues de Payen, with eight chivalrous comrades, swore to guard the travelers. In 1119, they gathered at the Church of the Holy Sepulchre and pledged their lives to poverty, chastity, and obedience before King Baldwin II of Jerusalem. The Order of Poor Knights of the Temple of Solomon took up headquarters in said Temple.

Going Mainstream

The Templars did their work well, and in 1127 Baldwin sent a Templar embassy to Europe to secure a marriage that would ensure the royal succession in Jerusalem. Not only did they succeed, they became rock stars of sorts. Influential nobles showered the Order with money and real estate, the foundation of its future wealth. With this growth came a formal code of rules. Some highlights include:

* Templars could not desert the battlefield or leave a castle by stealth.

* They had to wear white habits, except for sergeants and squires who could wear black.

* They had to tonsure (shave) their crowns and wear beards.

* They had to dine in communal silence, broken only by Scriptural readings.

* They had to be chaste, except for married men joining with their wives' consent.

A Law Unto Themselves

Now with offices in Europe to manage the Order's growing assets, the Templars returned to Palestine to join in the Kingdom's ongoing defense. In 1139, Pope Innocent II decreed the Order answerable only to the Holy See. Now exempt from the tithe, the Order was entitled to accept tithes! The Knights Templar had come far.

By the mid-1100s, the Templars had become a church within a

church, a nation within a nation, and a major banking concern. Templar keeps were well-defended depositories, and the Order became financiers to the crowned heads of Europe—even to the Papacy. Their reputation for meticulous bookkeeping and secure transactions underpinned Europe's financial markets, even as their soldiers kept fighting for the faith in the Holy Land.

Downfall

Templar prowess notwithstanding, the Crusaders couldn't hold the Holy Land. In 1187, Saladin the Kurd retook Jerusalem, martyring 230 captured Templars. Factional fighting between Christians sped the collapse as the 1200s wore on. In 1291, the last Crusader outpost at Acre fell to the Mamelukes of Egypt. Though the Templars had taken a hosing along with the other Christian forces, their troubles had just begun.

King Philip IV of France owed the Order a lot of money, and they made him more nervous at home than they did fighting in Palestine. In 1307, Philip ordered the arrest of all Templars in France. They stood accused of apostasy, devil worship, sodomy, desecration, and greed. Hideous torture produced piles of confessions, much like those of the later Inquisition. The Order was looted, shattered, and officially dissolved. In March 1314, Jacques de Molay, the last Grand Master of the Knights Templar, was burned at the stake.

Whither the Templars?

Many Templar assets passed to the Knights Hospitallers. The Order survived in Portugal as the Order of Christ, where it exists to this day in form similar to British knightly orders. A Templar fleet escaped from La Rochelle and vanished; it may have reached Scotland. Swiss folktales suggest that some Templars took their loot and expertise to Switzerland, possibly laying the groundwork for what would one day become the Swiss banking industry.

Canada's Cryptic Castaway

This mute amputee has a foothold in Nova Scotian folklore—
nearly a century after his death.

✳ ✳ ✳ ✳

Who Is This Man?

ON SEPTEMBER 8, 1863, two fishermen in Sandy Cove,
Nova Scotia, discovered an unusual treasure washed
ashore: a lone man in his twenties with newly amputated legs,
left with just a loaf of bread and jug of water.

There were a few clues, such as his manner of dress, that led the
townspeople to speculate on whether the fellow was a gentleman, an aristocrat. But there was no point in asking him—he
didn't speak. In fact, he was said to have uttered only three
words after being found: "Jerome" (which the villagers came
to call him), "Columbo" (perhaps the name of his ship), and
"Trieste," an Italian village.

Based on these three words, the villagers theorized he was
Italian and concocted various romantic stories about his fate:
that he was an Italian nobleman captured and mutilated by
pirates (or perhaps a pirate himself), a seaman punished for
threatening mutiny, or maybe he was an heir to a fortune who
had been crippled and cast away by a jealous rival.

Charity Case

Jerome was taken to the home of Jean and Juliette Nicholas, a
French family who lived across the bay in Meteghan. There was
still a chance Jerome could be French and Jean was fluent in five
languages. (Although none of which proved successful in communicating with Jerome.)

In 1870, the Nicholases moved away. The town, enthralled
with their mysterious nobleman, rallied together and paid the
Comeau family $140 a year to take him in. On Sundays after
mass, locals would stop by and pay a few cents for a look at

the maimed mute. Jerome lived with the Comeaus for the next 52 years until his death on April 19, 1912.

Records suggest Jerome was no cool-headed castaway. Though he never spoke intelligibly, hearing certain words (specifically "pirate") would send him into a rage. It's also been said that he was particularly anxious about the cold, spending winters with his leg stumps shoved under the stove for warmth. Though in his younger days he enjoyed sitting in the sun, he allegedly spent the last 20 years of his life as a complete shut-in, huddled by the stove.

Mystery Revealed

Jerome's panic about the cold makes sense—if the latest hypotheses about him are true. Modern historians have posited a couple of different theories, both of which trace Jerome to New Brunswick.

One group of scholars uncovered a story in New Brunswick about a man who was behaving erratically and couldn't (or wouldn't) speak. To rid themselves of the weirdo, members of his community put him on a boat to New England—but not without first chopping off his legs. The man never made it to New England but instead wound up on the beach at Sandy Cove.

Another theory links Jerome to a man—believed to be European—who was found in 1861, pinned under a fallen tree in Chipman, New Brunswick, with frozen legs that had to be amputated. Without a doctor nearby, the man was sent down the St. John River to Gagetown and then shipped back to Chipman, where he was supported for two years by the parish and nicknamed "Gamby" by the locals (which means "legs" in Italian). At that point, the parish got tired of taking care of him and paid a captain to drop him across the bay in Nova Scotia. Another account suggests that after the surgery, the man wasn't returned to Gagetown but put directly on a boat.

Regardless of which theory is more accurate, all suggest that the reason for Jerome's arrival in Nova Scotia is that an entire town disowned him.

But New Brunswick's loss has been Nova Scotia's gain. There, Jerome is a local legend. He has been the subject of a movie (1994's *Le secret de Jérôme*), and a home for the handicapped bears his name. Tourists can even stop by his grave for a quick snapshot of the headstone, which reads, quite simply, "Jerome."

Forty Days On the Rio Grande

Alonso Álvarez de Pineda was the first known European visitor to Texas. In 1519, he and his company explored and mapped the Texas coast, occupying the mouth of the Rio Grande for more than a month while repairing their ships. Despite his map—Texas history's earliest document—surprisingly little is known about Álvarez de Pineda beyond the nature of his grisly death.

✳ ✳ ✳ ✳

UNDER ORDERS FROM Francisco de Garay, the Spanish governor of Jamaica, Alonso Álvarez de Pineda embarked on a reconnaissance trip in March 1519. His four ships carried his party of 270 and sailed from Jamaica to explore the gulf coast in the hope of finding a strait leading directly to the Atlantic Ocean. Many historians believe that Álvarez de Pineda's company sailed north along the gulf coast of Florida before attempting to turn east. If that sounds strange, it is due to the erroneous reports of earlier Spanish explorer Juan Ponce De León. In 1513, De León reported a northern passage that separated Florida from the North American mainland. Therefore, Álvarez de Pineda fully expected to be the first to prove that Florida was an island.

Never coming upon a point at which to turn east, Álvarez de Pineda's company instead headed west along today's Florida panhandle and Alabama coastline. While there is some dispute among historians, it appears that around the time of the feast day of Espíritu Santo, or Pentecost, on June 2, 1519, Álvarez de Pineda became the first European to see the Mississippi River. He named it Río del Espíritu Santo in reference to the religious holiday and managed to sail upstream for several miles before continuing his voyage along the gulf coast.

First into Texas

Álvarez de Pineda mapped the outer islands off the coast of current-day Corpus Christi, Texas, claiming the bay and the land beyond for his king and naming it with the Spanish term meaning "body of Christ." After mapping the entire Texas coastline, Álvarez de Pineda finally made land. His fleet landed slightly south of Boca Chica, at the mouth of the Rio Grande, making his party the first Europeans to set foot in Texas. The Spaniards explored the region for 40 days, the time it took to overhaul their ships and conduct repairs after the extensive voyage. This also means that the Rio Grande was the second place to be visited by Europeans in what is now the United States.

Grisly Demise

Álvarez de Pineda sailed on down the Gulf of Mexico to the mouth of the Panuco River, near where Cortés would later found the town of Tampico, in what is now the Mexican state of Tamaulipas. Here, Álvarez de Pineda's company appears to have suffered a heavy defeat at the hands of the Aztecs. Some reports indicate that Álvarez de Pineda and many of his crew were killed, flayed, and eaten; their skins were then displayed as trophies in the Aztec temples. The Aztecs also burned some of Álvarez de Pineda's fleet; only one ship, under the command of Diego de Camargo, managed to leave successfully.

Álvarez de Pineda's Legacy

Álvarez de Pineda's map of the entire gulf coast made it to safety with Camargo and was presented to Governor Garay, who went on to take all the credit for the expedition and obtain a grant for the territory it explored. Still, it was Alonso Álvarez de Pineda who discovered that there was no strait linking the Gulf of Mexico to the Atlantic Ocean. While many details of his voyage remain shrouded in mystery, there is little doubt that he was the first European to set foot in Texas.

✳ Early goths? Men of the Karankawa, an early Gulf Coast civilization, wore cane piercings through their nipples and lower lips. Some of them also wore no clothing most of the time, probably because they spent a good portion of their days in or on the water searching for food.

Naked Man Running

Mark's Gospel tells us that at the time of Jesus' arrest, soldiers grab a young man by his garment, but the man manages to disengage and run off naked. Who is this guy?

✳   ✳   ✳   ✳

TWO PUZZLING VERSES in the Gospel of Mark present a person who is not otherwise mentioned in the Bible—or so it seems. When Jesus is arrested in the Garden of Gethsemane, his followers desert him. According to a brief passage in the Gospel of Mark, this includes an unidentified young man. The passage reads: "A certain young man was following him [Jesus], wearing nothing but a linen cloth. They caught hold of him, but he left the linen cloth and ran off naked" (Mark 14:51–52). Who is this young man and why is he in the garden wearing nothing but a linen cloth? It's an intriguing puzzle with intriguing possible solutions.

What's It All About?

The first thing the situation brings to mind is how the patriarch Joseph, while a young slave, escaped the sexual advances of his master's wife by running from her and losing his garment in the process. But Joseph was acting heroically, while the young man in the garden was not. It is hard to see why Mark would have introduced the memory of Joseph here. Clearly the answer lies elsewhere. Some scholars see the incident as an allusion to an Old Testament end-time prophecy: "And those who are stout of heart among the mighty shall flee away naked in that day, says the Lord" (Amos 2:16). Others speculate that the young man is either the Gospel's author or someone he knows, and he is adding a personal recollection here. Still others see the young man as a negative counterpart to the ideal disciple, who leaves everything to follow Jesus. But this seems unlikely, as Jesus' true disciples also leave Jesus at this time.

A Secret Gospel

Possibly the most interesting theory about the young man involves an earlier edition of Mark's Gospel. There is good reason to believe that Mark's Gospel went through several editions before reaching the revered text now in the Bible.

In addition, one of the earlier editions was known as the Secret Gospel of Mark because it contained material that was meant only for mature Christians—material that may be misunderstood by spiritual neophytes. In order to make the Gospel safe for all Christians, this material was later excised and all of it was lost—well, maybe not all.

Surviving Fragments

Some of the lost material appears in an 18th century copy of a letter from the Church Father Clement of Alexandria. In his letter, Clement defends the authenticity of both the canonical Gospel and the Secret Gospel against a falsified version. When Mark died, the letter claims, he left the Secret Gospel to the church at Alexandria, Egypt, where it is "read only to those being initiated into the greater mysteries." In discussing the Secret Gospel, Clement reproduces passages about a rich young man from Bethany who brings to mind both the naked man in Gethsemane and Lazarus, whom Jesus had earlier raised from the dead.

According to the cited passages, when the young man dies, Jesus raises him from the dead at the request of the man's sister.

At his rising, the young man looks upon Jesus and loves him. Six days later, he comes to Jesus, wearing only a linen cloth on his naked body (possibly as a baptismal garment). Jesus then teaches him the mystery of the kingdom of God.

Conclusions

Scholars who have studied the passages in Clement's letter believe they predate the Gospel we know. If this is so, they may preserve an early telling of the story of the raising of Lazarus, as later told in John's Gospel. In addition, the texts bring to mind the young man who runs off naked at Jesus' arrest. If the Secret Gospel passages are authentic, then the young man at Gethsemane may be a part of the story of the young man in the Secret Gospel. It is possible that the editor charged with deleting this story from the Gospel overlooked these two brief verses, which then remained in the final text of Mark's Gospel to mystify us.

Why Didn't the Vikings Stay in North America?

Because they weren't particularly good guests, and the Native Americans threw them out.

* * * *

ACCORDING TO ANCIENT Norse sagas that were written in the thirteenth century, Leif Eriksson was the first Viking to set foot in North America. After wintering at the place we now call Newfoundland in the year 1000, Leif went home. In 1004, his brother Thorvald led the next expedition, composed of thirty men, and met the natives for the first time. The Vikings attacked and killed eight of the nine native men they encountered. A greater force retaliated, and Thorvald was killed. His men then returned home.

Six years later, a larger expedition of Viking men, women, and livestock set up shop in North America. They lasted two years, according to the sagas. The Vikings traded with the locals initially, but they started fighting with them and were driven off. There may have been one further attempt at a Newfoundland settlement by Leif and Thorvald's sister, Freydis.

In 1960, Norse ruins of the appropriate age were found in L'Anse aux Meadows, Newfoundland, by Norwegian couple Helge and Anne Stine Ingstad. The Vikings had been there, all right. Excavations over the next seven years uncovered large houses and ironworks where nails and rivets were made, as well as woodworking areas. Also found were spindlewhorls, weights that were used when spinning thread; this implies that women were present, which suggests the settlement was more than a vacation camp.

The ruins don't reveal why the Vikings left, but they do confirm what the sagas claimed: The Vikings were in North America.

The sagas say that the settlers fought with the local *Skraelings*, a Norse word meaning "natives," until the *Skraelings* came at them in large enough numbers to force the Vikings out.

This sounds plausible, given the reputation of the Vikings—they'd been raiding Europe for centuries—and the Eriksson family's history of violence. Erik the Red, the father of Leif, founded a Greenland colony because he'd been thrown out of Iceland for murder, and Erik's father had been expelled from Norway for the same reason.

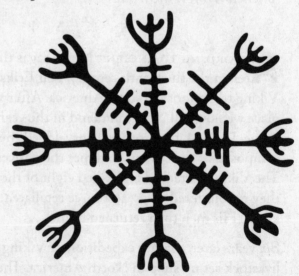

Demonized by Mythology: Lucrezia Borgia

In public perception, she rates alongside Jezebel and Messalina for conniving promiscuity. But who was the real Lucrezia Borgia, and how depraved was she?

✳ ✳ ✳ ✳

Backdrop

LUCREZIA BORGIA'S LIFE was orchestrated by the intense political and military competition of the Italian Renaissance. Italy was a gaggle of city-states and noble families, with foreign neighbors butting in, all jostling for advantage in a sleazy multiplayer chess game of shifting alliances, fiefdom grants, political marriages, excommunication, and warfare. The Vatican sat at that chessboard, and Lucrezia was a pawn.

The Borgia Family

Lucrezia's father was Cardinal Rodrigo Borgia, later Pope Alexander VI, the poster boy for corrupt, lascivious popes. His Holiness fathered Lucrezia and her three brothers with a mistress; her most prominent brother, Cesare, was ambitious and ruthless even by the inflated standards of the Renaissance. Lucrezia had the misfortune of being born into a family whose name evoked fear and loathing, with good cause.

Lucrezia's Marital Career

When Lucrezia reached the age of 13 in 1493, her father married her off to Giovanni Sforza to cement an alliance with Sforza's powerful Milanese clan, thus boosting Cesare's fortunes. When Alexander no longer needed to make nice with the Sforzas, he had Lucrezia's marriage to Giovanni annulled.

It was rumored that Lucrezia had a love affair and bore a son out of wedlock. In 1498, she entered an arranged marriage to Alfonso of Bisceglie, this time to ingratiate Cesare with the king of Naples. When that notion soured, mulitple "unknown assailants" (probably her brother Cesare's henchmen) assassinated Alfonso.

In 1501, Alexander brokered Lucrezia's marital hand to Alfonso d'Este, Prince of Ferrara. The new bride's sister-in-law, Isabella, delighted in snubs and snippy comments, but Lucrezia now knew the game. While keeping up appearances as a noble, dutiful Ferrarese matron, she carried on with Isabella's husband. After the deaths of Alexander (1503) and then Cesare (1507), Lucrezia could finally settle down. She died on June 24, 1519, at the age of 39, of complications from childbirth.

Heinous Allegations

Detractors love to paint Lucrezia as a Renaissance floozy with a poison-filled ring who had incestuous relations with her father and brother. It makes lurid reading, but the sliver of truth in such allegations is rather dull and tame. She did have lovers between marriages and outside of wedlock, as did many in her time. Living as a political pawn, can anyone blame her for wanting romantic flings? It would be peculiar if she hadn't.

There's no evidence supporting the incest slander—but there is good reason to reject it. Unlike her father and Cesare, Lucrezia had authentic religious scruples. Her consent would be unthinkable. She remained fond of each unto his death and mourned both. Would she have lamented those who'd traumatized her? Her later life is inconsistent with childhood molestation: She adjusted well, had a healthy love life when she could, and was never self-destructive.

The Origins of Slurs

Some aspersions were bandied during her life, mainly as weapons against the Borgias, spurred by Cesare's atrocious conduct. In 1833, Victor Hugo wrote a play that painted Lucrezia as a princess of poison, reveling in each toxic takedown. This, not actual history, has adhered to the public perception. It libels a pleasant, loving woman whose fortunes were dictated mainly by men of great power and limitless greed.

The Amazons: Man-Eaters of the Ancient World

They were the ultimate feminists—powerful, independent women who formed female-only societies that had no use for men beyond procreation. They were the epitome of girl power, fierce mounted warriors who often emasculated the best male fighters from other societies. They were the Amazons—man-eaters of the ancient world.

* * * *

THE ANCIENT GREEKS were enthralled by the Amazons. Greek writers, like today's Hollywood gossip columnists, relished lurid tales of love affairs between Amazon queens and their Greek boy toys. Others wrote of epic battles between Amazon warriors and the greatest heroes of Greek mythology.

Given their prominent place in Greek lore, the story of the Amazons has generally been considered the stuff of legend. But recent archeological finds suggest that a race of these warrior über-women actually did exist.

The Amazons According to the Greeks

History's first mention of the Amazons is found in Homer's Iliad, written in the 7th or 8th century B.C. Homer told of a group of women he called Antianeira ("those who fight like men"), who fought on the side of Troy against the Greeks. They were led by Penthesilea, who fought Achilles and was slain by him. According to some accounts, Achilles fell in love with her immediately afterward. Achilles was highly skilled in the art of warfare, but it seems he was sorely lacking in the intricacies of courtship.

From then on, the Amazons became forever linked with the ancient Greeks. Their very name is believed to derive from the Greek a-mazos, meaning "without a breast." This referred to the Amazon practice of removing the right breast of their young girls so that they would be unencumbered in the use of the bow and spear. Draconian, yes, but no one could accuse the Amazons of being anything less than hardcore. This may have made Greek, Roman, and European artists a bit squeamish because their depictions of Amazons showed them with two breasts, though the right breast was often covered or hidden.

According to Greek mythology, the Amazons were the off-spring of Ares, god of war, who was the son of the mightiest of the Greek gods, Zeus. Though the Amazons may have had Greek roots, they didn't want anything to do with them. Like young adults eager to move from their parents' homes, the Amazons established their realm in a land called Pontus in modern-day northeastern Turkey, where they founded several important cities, including Smyrna.

The Greeks paint a picture of the Amazons as a female-dominated society of man-haters that banned men from living among them. In an odd dichotomy between chastity and promiscuity, sexual encounters with men were taboo except for once a year when the Amazons would choose male partners from the neighboring Gargareans strictly for the purposes of procreation. Female babies were kept; males were killed or sent back with their fathers. Females were raised to do everything a man could do—and to do it better.

Soap Opera Encounters with Greek Heroes

The Greeks and the Amazons interacted in a turbulent love-hate relationship resembling something from a Hollywood soap opera. Hercules, as one of his labors, had to obtain the girdle of the Amazon queen Hippolyte. He was accompanied in his task by Theseus, who stole Hippolyte's sister Antiope. This led to on-going warfare between the Greeks and Amazons as well as several trysts between members of the two societies. One account has Theseus and Antiope falling in love, with her dying by his side during a battle against the Amazons. Another account has Theseus and Hippolyte becoming lovers. Stories of

Hercules have him alternately wooing and warring with various Amazonian women.

Jason and the Argonauts met the Amazons on the island of Lemnos. Completely unaware of the true nature of the island's inhabitants, Jason queried the Amazons as to the whereabouts of their men. They told him their men were all killed in an earlier invasion. What the Argonauts didn't realize was that the Amazons themselves were the killers. The Amazons, anticipating another opportunity for manslaughter, invited the Argonauts to stay and become their husbands. But Jason and the boys, perhaps intimidated by the appearance of the Amazons in full battle dress, graciously declined and hightailed it off the island.

More Than Myth?

The Greek historian Herodotus perhaps provides the best connection of the Greeks to what may be the true race of Amazons. Writing in the 5th century B.C., Herodotus chronicles a group of warrior women who were defeated in battle by the Greeks. These Androktones ("killers of men"), as he called them, were put on a prison ship, where they happily went about killing the all-male Greek crew. Hellcats on land but hopeless on water, the women drifted to the north shores of the Black Sea to the land of the Scythians, a people of Iranian descent.

Here, says Herodotus, they intermarried with the Scythian men on the condition that they be allowed to keep their traditional warrior customs. They added a heartwarming social tenet that no woman could wed until she had killed a man in battle. Together, they migrated northeast across the Russian steppes, eventually evolving into the Sarmatian culture, which featured a role for women hunting and fighting by the sides of their husbands. The men may have given their wives the loving pet name ha-mazan, the Iranian word for "warrior."

Though the Amazons are still mostly perceived as myth, recent archeological discoveries lend credence to Herodotus's account and help elevate the Amazons from the pages of Greek legend to historical fact. Excavations of Sarmatian burial grounds found the majority of those interred there were heavily armed women, all of whom got the very best spots in the site.

Was *The Exorcist* Really Based on a True Story?

Almost everyone is familiar with the movie The Exorcist. *The 1973 film stars Ellen Burstyn, Jason Miller, and—most memorably—Linda Blair as a young girl who is possessed by a demon. Naturally, everyone wants to know if the story—which was based on a best-selling novel by William Peter Blatty—is true. The answer to that question is . . . maybe.*

✳ ✳ ✳ ✳

I N JANUARY 1949, a 13-year-old boy named Roland (some sources say that his name was Robbie) and his family—who lived in Mount Rainier, Maryland—began hearing scratching sounds from behind the walls and inside the ceiling of their house. Believing that their home was infested with mice, Roland's parents called an exterminator. However, the exterminator found no evidence of rodents in the house. After that, the family's problem got worse: They began to hear unexplained footsteps in the home, and objects such as dishes and furniture seemed to relocate on their own.

But these incidents would seem minor compared to what came next: Roland claimed that an invisible entity attacked him and that his bed shook so violently that he couldn't sleep. The sheets and blankets were repeatedly ripped from his bed and tossed onto the floor. One time, Roland tried to grab them, but he was yanked onto the floor with the bedcovers still clenched in his fists.

Roland liked board games, and his aunt "Tillie"—a woman who had a strong interest in the supernatural—had taught him how to use a Ouija board before she died. Some blamed the Ouija board for causing the trouble, claiming that it had allowed a demonic being to enter the home and target Roland.

Not Such Good Vibrations

By this time, the family was convinced that an evil entity was afoot, so they appealed to a Lutheran minister named Schulze for help. Reverend Schulze prayed for Roland and had his congregation do so as well. He even took Roland to his own home so the boy could get some sleep. However, both the bed and an armchair that Roland tried to sleep in there vibrated and moved, allowing the boy no rest. Schulze noted that Roland seemed to be in a trance while these incidents occurred.

If Schulze had any doubt that it was time to call in the cavalry, he was certainly convinced when scratches mysteriously materialized on Roland's body. These marks were then replaced by words that appeared to be made by claws. The word *Louis* was clearly visible, which was interpreted as St. Louis—Roland's mother's hometown. With all signs pointing to the need for an exorcism, Father Edward Albert Hughes of St. James Catholic Church was summoned.

Truth or Fiction?

At this point, accounts of the story begin to splinter, as no two versions are alike. According to the version that has been more or less accepted as fact, Father Hughes went to see Roland and was disturbed when the boy addressed him in Latin—a language that was unknown to the youth. Hughes decided to perform an exorcism, during which a loose bedspring slashed him. The priest was supposedly so shaken by the ordeal that he was never the same again. (However, according to some sources, this part of the story never happened; they say that Hughes only saw Roland once at St. James, Roland never spoke in Latin, and Hughes never performed an exorcism on the boy, nor was he physically or emotionally affected by it. It is unclear why someone felt that dramatic license needed to be taken here, because the actual events are strange enough.)

During Roland's visit to Hughes, the priest suggested using blessed candles and special prayers to help the boy. But when Roland's mother did this, a comb flew across the room, hitting the candles and snuffing them out. Other objects also flew around the room, and at one point, a Bible was thrown at the boy's feet. Supposedly, Roland had to stop attending school because his desk shook so badly.

It seems that an attempt was made to baptize Roland into the Catholic faith as a way of helping him. However, this didn't work out so well: As his uncle drove him to the ceremony, the boy grabbed him by the throat and screamed that the baptism wouldn't work.

The Battle of St. Louis

Finally, at their wits' end, the family decided to stay with relatives in the St. Louis area. Unfortunately, the distance between Maryland and Missouri proved to be no deterrent to the invisible entity, and the assaults on Roland continued. In St. Louis, a relative introduced the boy and his family to Jesuit priest Father William Bowdern, who, in turn, employed Father Raymond J. Bishop, a pastor at St. Francis Xavier Church in St. Louis, in his efforts to help the family.

Father Bishop made several attempts to stop the attacks on the boy but to no avail. After Bishop sprinkled the boy's mattress with holy water in the shape of a cross, the attacks ceased. However, after Bishop left the room, the boy suddenly cried out in pain; when his pajama top was pulled up, Roland had numerous scratches across his abdomen. He could not have done it to himself, as he was in the presence of several witnesses at all times.

After more nights of violence against Roland, Father Bishop returned—this time with Father Bowdern. They prayed in the boy's room and then left. But as soon as they departed, loud noises began emanating from the room. When family members investigated, they found that an extremely heavy bookcase had swiveled around, a bench had overturned, and the boy's mattress was once again shaking and bouncing. It was at this point that another exorcism was deemed the only sensible course of action left.

The exorcism was a desperate battle that was waged over the course of several months. Some of it took place in the rectory at St. Francis Xavier Church, some of it at a hospital, and some of it at Roland's home; one source says that the boy was exorcised no less than 20 times. During this time, practically everything and anything typically associated with an exorcism occurred: Roland's body jerked in uncontrollable spasms, he experienced projectile vomiting, and he spit and cursed at the priests; he also conveyed information that he couldn't possibly have known. However, his head didn't spin completely around like Linda Blair's did in *The Exorcist*.

Gone, but Certainly Not Forgotten

Eventually, Bowdern's persistence paid off. He repeatedly practiced the ritual and ignored the torrent of physical and verbal abuse hurled at him by the entity that was residing inside the boy. Finally, in mid-April 1949, Roland spoke with a voice that identified itself as St. Michael. He ordered Satan and all demons to leave the boy alone. For the next few minutes,

Roland went into a titanic rage, as if all the furies of the world were battling inside of him. Suddenly, he became quiet, turned to the priests, and simply said, "He's gone."

The entity *was* gone, and fortunately, Roland remembered little about the ordeal. Some months later, a 20-year-old Georgetown University student named William Peter Blatty spotted an article in *The Washington Post* about Roland's experience. He let the idea of demonic possession percolate in his brain for years before finally writing his book, which became a best seller. Out of privacy concerns, Blatty changed so many details from the actual case that the source was virtually unrecognizable—until the intense publicity surrounding the movie forced the "real" story out.

Over the years, numerous theories regarding the incident have been suggested: Some say that it was an elaborate hoax gone too far, while others claim that it was the result of poltergeist activity or an actual possession. Regardless, this case continues to resonate in American culture.

On July 24, 1915, hundreds of people died in the Chicago River when the Eastland, a steamer that was overloaded with passengers who were on their way to a company picnic, capsized just a few feet from the dock.

There are many stories of hauntings related to the Eastland disaster, but none are more famous than the phenomena experienced at Oprah Winfrey's Harpo Studios. At the time of the Eastland disaster, the building served as the Second Regiment Armory and was used as a temporary morgue for the victims. Some Harpo employees have heard odd sounds, such as children's laughter, old-time music, clinking glasses, whispering voices, footsteps, slamming doors, sobbing, and muffled screams. Others have seen a spectral woman in a long gray dress who walks the corridors and then mysteriously vanishes into the wall.

The Bordentown Bonaparte

Not many people know that after the Battle of Waterloo in June 1815, Napoleon Bonaparte had the chance to flee to America. Though he didn't flee—at least not then—his older brother Joseph did, and wound up in . . . New Jersey.

✳ ✳ ✳ ✳

Born to Run?

A S ALL OF Napoleon's dreams and ambitions were crashing down around him, in July 1815, the general and his brother Joseph met at Rochefort on the Atlantic coast of France. The men needed to make a big decision. Joseph urged his brother to flee to the United States, but Napoleon was unwilling to run like a common criminal. He remained behind, while Joseph set sail for America.

Joseph tried living in New York City and then Philadelphia, but found that he could not blend into the crowded city background without meeting someone who knew him. What he needed was an isolated country estate. What he found was Point Breeze in Bordentown, New Jersey.

Peace and Quiet

Situated between Crosswicks Creek and the Delaware River, Point Breeze was a 211-acre estate that gave Joseph ample opportunity to indulge his passion for landscaping, gardening, and building. Joseph closed on the property in either 1816 or 1817 (sources differ), paying $17,500. The total property eventually included 1,000–1,800 acres.

Having ruled as both King of Naples and Sicily (1806–1808) and King of Spain (1808–1813), Joseph had developed a love of finery, and so he began building a house to be second only to the White House. He had hated the politics thrust upon him in Europe, and so he reveled in the peace of Point Breeze. "This country in which I live is very beautiful," he wrote. "Here one can enjoy perfect peace . . . the people's way of life is perfect."

Joseph spent hours roaming his estate and beautifying the grounds. He created artificial lakes and planted many trees and a great lawn in front of his house bordered with rhododendrons and magnolia bushes. He covered the grounds with miles of winding carriage lanes, placed sculpture, and built cabins.

He didn't neglect the magnificent house he was building either. He filled it with valuable furniture, fine works of art and sculpture, and thousands of books. When all was done, Joseph had a house that rivaled the finest in America.

Then, on January 4, 1820, the house burned to the ground.

Joseph, in New York at the time, hurried home to find that many of his treasures had been saved by the townspeople. Not used to this sort of kindness and honesty in his previous life of war and intrigue, he wrote a letter gratefully thanking the residents of Bordentown.

Joseph built an even more fabulous home, with great fireplaces, marble mantels, and winding staircases. He employed many locals, which endeared him to the residents. He filled the grounds on his property with pheasants, hares, and swans. Local children played on the deer and lion statues in the park and went ice-skating on his lakes in winter.

Mystery Man

But much like Joseph, his estate was more than met the eye. He had also built a network of tunnels underneath the house. Ostensibly built to bring supplies into the house, and for the convenience of females to move between buildings in foul weather, later the tunnels gave rise to speculation that they were built so Joseph could escape capture by anti-Bonaparte forces.

In 1914, *The World Magazine* had a better theory: Perhaps Napoleon did not die at St. Helena in 1821, but escaped to America—and to Joseph.

"He could have been rowed from the Delaware River directly

into his brother's house," postulated the writer. "And during the years that he was watching for a chance to return to power, he could have had the freedom, through a labyrinth of secret underground passages, of one of the most beautiful estates in America."

Eventually Joseph abandoned Point Breeze and returned to Europe, where he died in 1844. Did his brother live with him in New Jersey? Unfortunately, we may never know—though the idea of Napoleon prowling the streets of tiny Bordentown late at night is too intriguing to completely dismiss.

The Catcher Was a Spy

When it comes to character assessments, you gotta listen to Casey Stengel. And the Ol' Perfessor claimed Moe Berg was "the strangest man ever to put on a baseball uniform." But Berg wasn't just strange in a baseball uniform, he was strange and mysterious in many ways—some of them deliberate.

✳ ✳ ✳ ✳

MOE BERG LIVED a life shrouded in mystery and marked by contradictions. He played alongside Babe Ruth, Lefty Grove, Jimmie Foxx, and Ted Williams; he moved in the company of Norman Rockefeller, Albert Einstein, and international diplomats; and yet he was often described as a loner. He was well-liked by teammates but preferred to travel by himself. He never married, and he made few close friends.

"The Brainiest Guy in Baseball"

Moe was a bright kid from the beginning, with a special fondness for baseball. As the starting shortstop for Princeton University, where he majored in modern languages, Moe was a star. He was fond of communicating with his second baseman in Latin, leaving opposing baserunners scratching their heads.

He broke into the majors in 1923 as a shortstop with the Brooklyn Robins (later the Dodgers). He converted to catcher and spent time with the White Sox, Senators, Indians, and Red Sox throughout his career. A slow runner and a poor fielder, Berg nevertheless eked out a 15-season big-league career. Pitchers loved him behind the plate: They praised his intelligence and loved his strong, accurate arm. And while he once went 117 games without an error, he rarely nudged his batting average much past .250. His weak bat often kept him on the bench and led sports writers to note, "Moe Berg can speak 12 languages flawlessly and can hit in none." He was, however, a favorite of sportswriters, many of whom considered him "the brainiest guy in baseball."

He earned his law degree from Columbia University, attending classes in the off-seasons and even during spring training and partial seasons with the White Sox. When Berg was signed by the Washington Senators in 1932, his life took a sudden change. In Washington, Berg became a society darling, delighting the glitterati with his knowledge and wit. Certainly it was during his Washington years that he made the contacts that would serve him in his espionage career.

Time in Tokyo and On TV

Berg first raised eyebrows in the intelligence community at the start of World War II when he shared home movies of Tokyo's shipyards, factories, and military sites, which he had secretly filmed while on a baseball trip in 1934. While barnstorming through Japan along with Ruth, Lou Gehrig, and Foxx, Berg delighted Japanese audiences with his fluency in their language and familiarity with their culture. He even addressed the Japanese parliament. But one day he skipped the team's scheduled game and went to visit a Tokyo hospital, the highest building in the city. He sneaked up to the roof and took motion picture films of the Tokyo harbor. Some say those photos were used by the U.S. military as they planned their attack on Tokyo eight years later. Berg maintained that he had not been sent to Tokyo on a formal assignment, that he had acted on his own initiative to take the film and offer it to the U.S. government upon his return. Whether or not that was the case, Berg's undercover career had begun.

On February 21, 1939, Berg made the first of several appearances on the radio quiz show *Information, Please!* He was an immense hit, correctly answering nearly every question he was asked. Commissioner Kenesaw Mountain Landis was so proud of how intelligent and well-read the second-string catcher was that he told him, "Berg, in just 30 minutes you did more for baseball than I've done the entire time I've been commissioner." But Berg's baseball time was winding down; 1939 was his last season.

Secret Agent Man

Berg's intellect and elusive lifestyle were ideal for a post-baseball career as a spy. He was recruited by the Office of Strategic Services (predecessor to the CIA) in 1943 and served in several capacities. He toured 20 countries in Latin America early in WWII, allegedly on a propaganda mission to bolster the morale of soldiers there. But what he was really doing was trying to determine how much the Latin countries could help the U.S. war effort.

His most important mission for the OSS was to gather information on Germany's progress in developing an atomic bomb. He worked undercover in Italy and Switzerland and reported infor mation to the States throughout 1944. One of his more daring assignments was a visit to Zurich, Switzerland, in December 1944, where he attended a lecture by German nuclear physicist Werner Heisenberg. If Heisenberg indicated the Germans were close to developing nukes, Berg had been directed to assassinate the scientist. Luckily for Heisenberg, Berg determined that German nuclear capability was not yet within the danger range.

Life After the War

On October 10, 1945, Berg was awarded the Medal of Freedom (now the Presidential Medal of Freedom) but turned it down without explanation. (After his death, his sister accepted it on his behalf.)

After the war he was recruited by the CIA. It is said that his is the only baseball card to be found in CIA headquarters. After his CIA career ended, Berg never worked again. He was often approached to write his memoirs. When he agreed, in 1960 or so, the publisher hired a writer to provide assistance. Berg quit the project in fury when the writer indicated he thought Berg was Moe Howard, founder of *The Three Stooges*. But his unusual career turns were later immortalized in the Nicholas Dawidoff book *The Catcher Was a Spy*. At age 70, Berg fell, injuring himself. He died in the hospital. His last words were to ask a nurse, "What did the Mets do today?"

Pancho Villa: The Man with Two Faces

Hero or criminal? You decide.

✳   ✳   ✳   ✳

T HE MAN THE world knew as Pancho Villa led a contradictory life that caused some to venerate him as a saint and others to loathe him as a fiend. Certainly, Pancho Villa was a man of bold action with an uncanny sense of destiny whose exploits—whether actual or mythical, inherently good or evil—have become the stuff of legend. Even in his own time, he was celebrated as a living folk hero by Mexicans and Americans alike. In fact, film companies sent crews to revolutionary Mexico to chronicle his exploits—a circumstance that pleased the wily Villa, if for no other reason than the gold the directors brought with them. Journalists, novelists, friends, and enemies all conspired to create the image of a man whose true nature remained elusive. To the present day, the name of Francisco "Pancho" Villa continues to inspire both admiration and scorn with equal fervor . . . depending on whom you ask.

General Pancho Villa: Hero of the People

Pancho Villa was born Doroteo Arango in Durango, Mexico, either in 1877 or 1879. As the son of a peasant family working for a hacienda owner, he realized that he would eventually inherit his father's debt and work the land until the day he died. At age 16, however, Doroteo returned home to find his sister fending off the lecherous advances of a local don. Unable to countenance the dishonoring of his beloved sister, Villa obtained a pistol, shot and killed the offending "gentleman," and escaped to the hills. For nearly ten years, he lived as a bandit, robbing the rich and giving to the poor men who joined him. With the start of the Mexican Revolution, Villa came down from the mountains to form an army in support of the populist platform espoused by Francisco Madero.

As a general, Villa staged bold cavalry charges that overwhelmed his opponents even at great risk to his own life. General Villa was very popular with the ladies (purportedly marrying 26 times) and loved to dance. However, he did not drink and once famously choked on a dram of brandy offered him by fellow revolutionary General Emiliano Zapata. As the Mexican Revolution ground through a series of corrupt leaders, Villa remained true to his populist ideology.

When his political rival, Venustiano Carranza, came to power, Villa became a wanted man again, this time in both Mexico and the United States. As in his youth, he took to the mountains, evading capture for several years until, weary of life on the run, he surrendered in 1920. Villa purchased a former hacienda known as La Purísima Concepción de El Canutillo and moved there with about 400 of his soldiers and their families. Rather than become like the wealthy landowners he despised, however, Villa used the hacienda to form an agricultural community that soon swelled to approximately 2,000 men, women, and children who received an education and shared in the profits.

Pancho Villa: Murderous Thug

When American President Woodrow Wilson chose to support the presidency of Villa's rival Venustiano Carranza, Villa retaliated. On January 11, 1916, Villa and a group of his men stopped a train in Santa Ysabel, Mexico, and brutally killed 18 Texas businessmen. Murder and banditry were nothing new to Villa; as a young man he had made his living stealing cattle and was a murderer before he reached 20. As a revolutionary general, he ordered executions for specious reasons, robbed herds of cattle to sell north of the border, and shot merchants who refused to take the money he had printed for his army. His cattle thieving incensed powerful newspaper magnate William Randolph Hearst who conducted a long-term smear campaign against the bandit, which, among other things, led to the criminalization of marijuana in the United States.

Pancho Villa's greatest moment of infamy, however, came at 2:30 A.M. on March 9, 1916, when he led a band of 500 horse-mounted followers against the 13th U.S. Cavalry and then into Columbus, New Mexico, where the bandits killed indiscriminately and destroyed property. When the Villistas departed at 7:00 A.M., 14 American soldiers, 10 civilians, and scores of bandits lay dead. President Wilson ordered Brigadier General John J. Pershing to lead a punitive cavalry expedition into Mexico to capture Villa but multiple, costly attempts to corner the cunning outlaw proved fruitless. Soon, the nuisance of Pancho Villa was replaced in the national consciousness by the United States' entry into the war raging in Europe.

The End of the Man, the Start of the Legend

Pancho Villa was assassinated by unknown persons while visiting the village of Parral in 1923. After Villa's death, one of his officers allegedly opened his tomb in Parral and removed his head to sell to a Chicago millionaire who collected skulls. Villa's body was later moved to Mexico City and interred in the Tomb of the Illustrious, but many believe that it was simply a headless decoy and his true resting place remains in Northern Mexico.

Thus, even the final resting place of Villa's body has become obscured by speculation and doubt.

Houdini Unbound

Magic still thrives, thanks to the mystifying antics of entertainers such as David Blaine and Criss Angel. But none hold a candle to the great Harry Houdini, master magician and escape artist extraordinaire.

✳   ✳   ✳   ✳

The Early Years

HOUDINI WAS BORN Ehrich Weisz on March 24, 1874, in Budapest, Hungary. His family immigrated to the United States when Ehrich was about four years old, settling in Appleton, Wisconsin. A precocious youngster, Ehrich started performing magic at age 12, billing himself as Eric the Great. He ran away from home to entertain at fairs and circuses, but he rejoined his family at their new home in New York City a year later.

When he was 15, Ehrich read a biography of famed French magician Jean Robert-Houdin. The book changed his life. In honor of his hero, he took the stage name Harry Houdini. He performed solo for a while, and then, in 1892, teamed up with his brother Theo. As the Houdini Brothers, the duo performed at a variety of venues, including Coney Island and the 1893 Chicago World's Fair. In 1894, Houdini married Wilhelmina Rahner, who replaced Theo in the act.

The Escape Artist

Houdini was skilled at magic, card tricks, and escape artistry, but widespread fame eluded him until he took the advice of renowned vaudeville booking agent Martin Beck, who encouraged Houdini to eschew the small stuff and concentrate on illusions and escapes. Beck put Houdini on the vaudeville Orpheum circuit, which took him throughout the country. To generate publicity in each town he visited, Houdini would ask the local police department to lock him in their sturdiest cell—from which he would promptly escape.

Houdini traveled to Europe in 1900, and it was there that he really made his reputation, routinely escaping from the seemingly inescapable. Soon he was the highest-paid entertainer on the continent, raking in $2,000 a week. When he returned to the United States, the master magician set out to prove that there was virtually nothing from which he could not escape, including padded cells; burglar-proof safes; a diving suit; a water-filled, padlocked milk pail; and the Washington, D.C., jail cell that had once held Charles Guiteau, assassin of President James Garfield. Several of Houdini's stunts were literally death-defying: One time he came frighteningly close to suffocating while escaping from a buried coffin.

In 1918, Houdini created a magic act that would become a staple for later magicians such as David Copperfield—he made a live elephant disappear at the famed Hippodrome in New York City. He also introduced another fan favorite, swallowing several needles and a piece of string, then pulling the string from his throat with the needles threaded. "My professional life has been a constant record of disillusion," said Houdini, "and many things that seem wonderful to most men are the everyday commonplaces of my business."

More than a Magician

Houdini became the planet's premier magician and escape artist, but he was also much more. In 1910, he became the first person ever to make a sustained plane flight on the continent of Australia, and in 1919 he appeared in several motion picture thrillers. (He later produced two movies in which he was the star.) Houdini also was a prolific writer and lecturer.

In the 1920s, Houdini established himself as a debunker of fake spiritualists, testifying before a congressional committee on the subject in 1926. As a magician, he knew the tricks of the trade, and would often don a disguise to visit "spiritualists" who claimed to be able to talk to the dead. Once they'd gone through their act, Houdini would reveal how the tricks were done. It was Houdini's way of giving back—he hated charlatans who preyed on grieving families.

Houdini died on October 31, 1926—not in a failed escape attempt, as some legends have it—but from complications from a ruptured appendix. There is some debate regarding the details leading up to his death, which almost certainly involved an incident in which he was punched in the stomach by a student at McGill University in Montreal. Houdini's funeral was held on November 4th in New York, attended by more than 2,000 mourners.

The Real "Man Who Never Was"

When a drowned corpse washed ashore in Spain holding a briefcase of plans to invade Sardinia and Greece, the Nazis thought they'd made an astounding catch. They couldn't have been more wrong.

✳ ✳ ✳ ✳

THE ROUGH TIDES slapped against the southern Spanish coast in the spring of 1943, carrying the mangled corpse of a British major who appeared to have drowned after his plane crashed into the sea. The body, one of thousands of military men who had met their end in the Mediterranean waters, floated atop a rubber life jacket as the current drifted toward Huelva, Spain. With a war raging in Tunisia across the sea, a drifting military corpse was not such an unusual event.

But this body was different, and it drew the immediate attention of Spanish authorities sympathetic to German and Italian Fascists. Chained to the corpse was a briefcase filled with dispatches from London to Allied Headquarters in North Africa concerning the upcoming Allied invasions of Sardinia and western Greece. The information was passed on to the Nazis, who accepted their apparent stroke of good luck, and now anticipated an Allied strike on the "soft underbelly of Europe."

Unfortunately for them, the whole affair was a risky, carefully contrived hoax.

Rigging the "Trojan Horse"

Operation Mincemeat was conceived by British intelligence agents as a deception to convince the Italians and Germans that the target of the next Allied landings would be somewhere other than Sicily, the true target. To throw the Fascists off the trail, British planners decided to find a suitable corpse—a middle-aged white male—put the corpse in the uniform of a military courier, and float the corpse and documents off the coast of Huelva, Spain, where a local Nazi agent was known to be on good terms with local police.

The idea of planting forged documents on a dead body was not new to the Allies. In August 1942, British agents planted a corpse clutching a fake map of minefields in a blown-up scout car. The map was picked up by German troops and made its way to Rommel's headquarters. He obligingly routed his panzers away from the "minefield" and into a region of soft sand, where they quickly bogged down.

This deception, however, would be much grander. If the planted documents made their way up the intelligence chain, Hitler and Mussolini would be expecting an invasion far from the Sicilian coast that Generals Eisenhower, Patton, and Montgomery had targeted for invasion in July 1943.

The Making of a Major

Operation Mincemeat, spearheaded by Lieutenant Commander Ewen Montagu, a British naval intelligence officer, and Charles Cholmondeley of Britain's MI5 intelligence service, found its "host" in early 1943 when a Welshman living in London committed suicide by taking rat poison. The substance produced a chemical pneumonia that could be mistaken for drowning. The two operatives gave the deceased man a new, documented identity: "Major William Martin" of the Royal Marines. They literally kept the "major" on ice while arrangements for his new mission were made. To keep Spanish authorities from conducting an autopsy—which would give away the body's protracted post-mortem condition—the agents decided to make "Major Martin" a Roman Catholic, giving him a silver cross and a St. Christopher medallion. They dressed the body, complete with Royal Marine uniform and trench coat, and gave him identity documents and personal letters (including a swimsuit photo of his "fiancée," an intelligence bureau secretary). With a chain used by bank couriers, they fixed the briefcase to his body.

Martin's documents were carefully prepared to show Allied invasions being planned for Sardinia and Greece (the latter bearing the code name Operation Husky). They also indicated that an Allied deception plan would try to convince Hitler that the invasion would take place in Sicily (the site of the real Operation Husky). With everything in order, the agents carefully placed the corpse into a sealed container—dry ice kept the body "fresh" for the ride out to sea.

The submarine HMS *Seraph* carried "Major Martin" on his final journey. On April 28, the *Seraph* left for the Andalusian coast, and two days later the body of a Royal Marine officer washed ashore. Within days, photographs of the major's documents were on their way to intelligence agents in Berlin.

Taking the Bait

Abwehr, Hitler, and the German High Command swallowed the story. After the war, British intelligence determined that Martin's documents had been opened and resealed before being returned by the Spanish. The German General Staff, believing the papers to be genuine, had alerted units in the Mediterranean to be ready for an invasion of Sardinia and

Greece. They moved one panzer division and air and naval assets off the Peloponnese, and disputed Italian fears of an impending invasion of Sicily.

The Allies captured Sicily in July and August 1943, and after the war, Commander Montagu wrote a bestselling account of Operation Mincemeat titled *The Man Who Never Was*. The book was made into a film thriller a few years later.

Who was Major William Martin? The original body appears to have been a 34-year-old depressed Welsh alcoholic named Glyndwr Michael, and "Major Martin's" tombstone in Spain bears Michael's name. Historians have debated the identity of "Major Martin," however, theorizing that a "fresher" corpse from a sunken aircraft carrier was substituted closer to the launch date.

Whoever the real "Major Martin" may have been, one thing is certain: He saved thousands of lives, and became a war hero and action movie star in the process—quite an accomplishment for a dead man!

The Gangster's Treasure

Arthur Simon Flegenheimer—better known as Dutch Schultz— was a mobster in the 1920s and 30s who was eventually gunned down by the mafia. While he may have left behind a legacy of bootlegging and racketeering, Schultz is more often remembered for something else he left behind: $7 million in cash and bonds, reportedly hidden somewhere in the Catskill Mountains.

✳   ✳   ✳   ✳

Rising Through the Ranks

Born to German Jewish immigrants on August 6, 1901, Arthur Simon Flegenheimer turned to a life of crime at an early age. After his father abandoned his family, Arthur was forced to drop out of school to find work, and soon after, he began stealing and burglarizing homes. He was caught breaking into an apartment at the age of 18 and sent to prison, but was released in December 1920, just as Prohibition began.

Arthur then went to work for a company called Schultz Trucking in the Bronx, which began smuggling liquor into the United States from Canada. Instead of leaving his criminal deeds in the past, Arthur started associating more with members of organized crime, who gave him the nickname "Dutch," a variant of his "Deutsch" heritage, and "Schultz," in homage to the trucking company. Soon after, he left the trucking company and went to work for a competitor; but the name "Dutch Schultz" stuck for the rest of his life.

Prohibition turned out to be very lucrative for Schultz, who began running his own bootlegging operation with a gangster named Joey Noe. Schultz and Noe had a successful run in the Bronx, so much so that they were able to rival the famous Five Families of the Italian American Mafia. But their success came with a price, when rival gangsters shot and killed Noe outside a speakeasy in 1928.

Tax Trouble and Betrayal

For Schultz, the years that followed were a tumultuous collection of gang wars, racketeering, and mingling with organized crime members with nicknames like "Legs," "Lucky," and "Abbadabba." And then, in the mid-1930s, the U.S. Attorney for the Southern District of New York, Thomas Dewey, targeted Schultz for tax evasion. Originally found guilty at a court in Manhattan, the verdict was overturned on appeal. A second trial was held in the small town of Malone, in upstate New York, where Schultz's lawyers felt he would get a fairer trial.

The ploy paid off, and in the summer of 1935, Schultz was acquitted of tax evasion. However, in order to pay his mounting legal costs, Schultz had been cutting back commissions to his gang members, a tactic that caused upheaval within his organized crime community. In fact, Charlie "Lucky" Luciano, the head of the Commission—the governing body of the American mafia—was secretly planning to take over Schultz's territory.

Disgruntled from his tax evasion trials, Schultz proposed to the National Crime Syndicate that Dewey be assassinated. But Luciano felt that this would bring unneeded attention from law enforcement. Instead, in a secret meeting, Luciano and the Commission agreed on another target: Dutch Schultz. On October 23, 1935, two hitmen entered the Palace Chop House in Newark, New Jersey, where Schultz was dining with three associates, and opened fire. Schultz and the other men were all mortally wounded. Schultz survived for a day, ultimately dying of Peritonitis on October 24.

Treasure in the Catskills?

But this is not where Dutch Schultz's story ends. Just before his assassination, Schultz was feeling the pressure of the ongoing tax evasion investigation that Dewey was conducting. Fearing a prison sentence, he had an airtight, waterproof safe constructed and placed $7 million in cash and bonds inside, so the authorities would be unable to seize his wealth if he was incarcerated. He and his personal bodyguard, Bernard "Lulu" Rosenkrantz, then drove the safe into upstate New York and buried it in an unknown location. Since Rosenkrantz was also killed in the Palace Chop House shooting, the location of the safe's whereabouts was lost.

Of course, this has not stopped treasure hunters from searching. It was well known that Schultz and Rosenkrantz had visited the small town of Phoenicia, New York, during his trial. This area of the Catskill Mountains is believed to be the most likely spot for Schultz's buried safe. Rumors have surfaced that Rosencrantz even drew a map for his nurse right before he died, which pinpointed Phoenicia.

Devilish Last Words

Many treasure seekers have looked to Schultz's last words for clues. As he lay dying, a police stenographer recorded everything Schultz said. Most of it seemed to be incoherent rambling, but some believe that Schultz's words revealed hints to the safe's location. Especially interesting were the words "don't let Satan draw you too fast." While they don't seem to make much sense at first glance, they take on more meaning after learning a bit about Phoenicia. The town is known for two "devilish" natural attractions, including a rock outcropping called the Devil's Face and a huge boulder known as the Devil's Tombstone. Could Schultz's reference to "Satan" have been a suggestion that the treasure is somewhere near one of these locations?

Some historians believe that the story of Dutch Schultz's treasure is just a story. There has never been any evidence that the gangster did, in fact, bury a safe anywhere. But that certainly hasn't stopped hopeful treasures seekers from looking. Reportedly, even Schultz's gangster rivals spent the rest of their lives looking for the safe. To this day, curious tourists, documentary filmmakers, groups of friends, and treasure hunting clubs descend on the Catskills with shovels and metal detectors, often year after year, hoping to one day strike it rich.

Who Was the Zodiac Killer?

On the evening of December 20, 1968, 17-year-old David Faraday and 16-year-old Betty Lou Jensen headed out on their first date in Benicia, California. Late that night, a passing motorist noticed two lifeless bodies lying next to a car at a "lover's lane" parking spot. It was Faraday and Jensen, who had both been shot to death. The unwitting couple became the first official victims of the Zodiac Killer, who would spend the next six years taunting the police and frightening the public.

✳ ✳ ✳ ✳

Senseless Killings

THE MURDERS OF Faraday and Jensen stumped investigators. There appeared to be no motive, and forensic data of the time yielded few clues. Why would someone gun down two teenagers who were merely out having fun? No leads developed, and the case quickly grew cold.

Months later, just before midnight on July 4, 1969, another young couple, Michael Mageau and Darlene Ferrin, were in their car at Blue Rock Springs Park in Vallejo, about four miles from where Faraday and Jensen were murdered. As they sat in the car, another car pulled up behind them and the driver exited, approaching their car with a flashlight. The stranger shined the bright light in their faces, and then, without warning, began shooting. When it was all over, Ferrin was dead; but Mageau, despite being shot three times, somehow survived.

About an hour later, at 12:40 A.M. on July 5, a man called the Vallejo Police Department saying he wanted to "report a murder," giving the dispatcher the location of Mageau and Ferrin's car. Using a calm, low voice, he also confessed that he had "killed those kids last year." It was the first contact anyone had with the killer, but it wouldn't be the last.

Clues and Codes

Mageau was able to describe his attacker as a white male with curly brown hair, around 200 pounds, 5 feet 8 inches tall, in his late 20s. It was little to go on, but it was a start. Then, on August 1, three Northern California newspapers—the *Vallejo Times-Herald*, *San Francisco Chronicle*, and *San Francisco Examiner*—all received virtually identical handwritten letters that contained crime details that only the killer could know. Each newspaper also received one third of a three-part coded cipher that the writer claimed would reveal his identity. The letters all ended with the same symbol: a circle with a cross through it.

The killer demanded that the ciphers be published on the front pages of each paper, otherwise he threatened to go on another killing spree. But investigators were not convinced that the letters came from the actual killer, so the *Chronicle* published

its part of the code on page four, along with a quote from the Vallejo chief of police asking for more proof.

The promised killing spree never materialized, and all three sections of the cipher were published over the next week. Then, on August 7, the *Examiner* received another letter that began with, "Dear Editor This is the Zodiac speaking." The killer now had a nickname which would soon become infamous. In the letter, the Zodiac Killer described details of the crimes known only to police, and taunted them for not yet solving his code, saying that once they did, they "will have me."

The very next day, a high school teacher named Donald Harden and his wife, Bettye, solved the cipher. The disturbing message began with the words "I like killing people because it is so much fun." The Zodiac then said that he was killing people to act as his "slaves" in the afterlife, in a rambling message full of misspellings and typos. But nowhere did the note reveal, or even hint, at the killer's identity.

A Killer Unchecked

On September 27, 1969, the Zodiac Killer struck again. A man wearing a black hood with a circle and cross symbol on his chest attacked college students Bryan Hartnell and Cecelia Shepard as they were picnicking at Lake Berryessa, tying them up and then stabbing them repeatedly. The attacker then drew the circle and cross symbol on Hartnell's car, along with the dates of each murder. Once again, he called the police—this time the Napa County Sheriff's Office—to report his own crime. And once again, the killer left behind a witness, when

Hartnell survived the attack. Police were able to lift a palm print from the pay phone where the killer had called the police, but were unable to match it to a perpetrator.

Even with two witnesses, a description of the attacker, fingerprints, and handwritten letters, the identity of the Zodiac Killer remained frustratingly elusive. The last confirmed Zodiac Killer murder occurred on October 11, 1969, when he shot taxi driver Paul Stine in the head and then ripped off part of Stine's bloodstained shirt. The Zodiac Killer then sent another letter to the *Chronicle*, along with a piece of Stine's shirt, in which he mocked police for failing to catch him and threatened to shoot school children on a bus.

More Letters, But No Answers

Over the next few years, the Zodiac Killer kept up a strange correspondence with Bay Area newspapers, hinting at numerous other victims, making bomb threats, and demanding that people begin wearing buttons featuring his circle and cross symbol. Some of the letters included codes or strange references, including a 340-character cipher sent to the *Chronicle* on November 8, 1969, that has never been solved. He would often end his letters with a "score" claiming "SFPD = 00 while the Zodiac's "score" continued to climb, suggesting he continued his killing spree.

The final letter thought to be from the Zodiac Killer was sent on January 29, 1974; the killer then simply seemed to disappear. But the investigation into his identity continues to this day. More than 2,500 suspects have been considered—including the "Unibomber," Ted Kaczynski—but no one has ever been arrested. Law enforcement agencies hope that modern DNA testing may one day yield clues to his identity. Until then, the closing line of the Zodiac's final letter still haunts investigators: "Me – 37; SFPD – 0."

CHAPTER 10

CREEPY CREATURES

Fireball in the Sky

What's that thing up there in that ocean of blue?

✳ ✳ ✳ ✳

WHILE PLAYING FOOTBALL on the afternoon of September 12, 1952, a group of boys in Flatwoods, West Virginia, saw a large fireball fly over their heads. The object seemed to stop near the hillside property of Bailey Fisher. Some thought the object was a UFO, but others said it was just a meteor. They decided to investigate.

Darkness was falling as the boys made their way toward the hill, so they stopped at the home of Kathleen May to borrow a flashlight. Seeing how excited the boys were, May, her two sons, and their friend, Eugene Lemon, decided to join them. The group set off to find out exactly what had landed on the hill.

Walking Through the Darkness

As they neared the top of the hill, the group smelled a strange odor that reminded them of burning metal. Continuing on, some members of the group thought they saw an object that resembled a spaceship. Shining their flashlights in front of them, the group was startled when something not of this world moved out from behind a nearby tree.

The Encounter

The description of what is now known as the Flatwoods

Monster is almost beyond belief. It stood around 12 feet tall and had a round, reddish face from which two large holes were visible. Looming up from behind the creature's head was a large pointed hood. The creature, which appeared to be made of a dark metal, had no arms or legs and seemed to float through the air. Looking back, the witnesses believe what they saw was a protective suit or perhaps a robot rather than a monster.

When a flashlight beam hit the creature, its "eyes" lit up and it began floating toward the group while making a strange hissing noise. The horrible stench was now overpowering and some in the group immediately felt nauseous. Because she was at the head of the group, Kathleen May had the best view of the monster. She later stated that as the creature was moving toward her, it squirted or dripped a strange fluid on her that resembled oil but had an unusual odor to it.

Terrified beyond belief, the group fled down the hillside and back to the May house, where they telephoned Sheriff Robert Carr, who responded with his deputy, Burnell Long. After talking with the group, they gathered some men and went to the Fisher property to investigate. But they only found a gummy residue and what appeared to be skid marks on the ground. There was no monster and no spaceship. However, the group did report that the heavy stench of what smelled like burning metal was still in the air.

The Aftermath

A. Lee Stewart, a member of the of the search party and copublisher of the *Braxton Democrat*, knew a good story when he saw one, so he sent the tale over the news wire, and almost immediately, people were asking Kathleen May for interviews. On September 19, 1952, May and Stewart discussed the Flatwoods Monster on the TV show *We the People*. For the show, an artist sketched the creature based on May's description, but he took some liberties, and the resulting sketch was so outrageous that people started saying the whole thing was a hoax.

Slowly, though, others came forward to admit that they too had seen a strange craft flying through the sky near Flatwoods on September 12. One witness described it as roughly the size of a single-car garage. He said that he lost sight of the craft when it appeared to land on a nearby hill.

Since that night in 1952, the Flatwoods Monster has never been seen again, leaving many people to wonder what exactly those people encountered. A monster? An alien from another world? Or perhaps nothing more than a giant owl? One thing is for sure: There were far too many witnesses to deny that they stumbled upon something strange that night.

Beyond Bigfoot: Cryptozoological Creatures

Cryptozoology is the study of creatures that are rumored to exist. But for true believers and alleged eyewitnesses, these "cryptids" are alive and well and lurking among us.

✳ ✳ ✳ ✳

Marozi: With a maned lion's face fronting a jaguarlike body, the Marozi (also known as the spotted lion) was reported several times in the 1930s in Kenya's mountains but hasn't been mentioned much since. The Natural History Museum in Great Britain is said to be in possession of the spotted skin of a marozi, but many experts think the specimen represents a jaguar that bred with common spotless plains lions.

Kamchatka Giant Bear: Swedish zoologist Sten Bergman, working in Russia's Kamchatka Peninsula in the 1920s, discovered a paw print that measured a full square foot, suggesting a bear of remarkable size. Similar sightings tell of an ursine almost twice the size of a typical North American grizzly bear, measuring six feet at the shoulder. Some Russian biologists believe there is a small group of Kamchatka Giant Bears that survived the most recent ice age.

Skunk Ape: Bigfoot's smelly Southern cousin has been reported a number of times in Florida's swamps, most convincingly in 2000 by a couple who took an excellent snapshot of what looked to be a six-foot-six orangutan. The picture didn't capture its scent, of course, but the couple attested to its atrocity.

Lizard Man: This scaly green hominid, the resident mysterious beast of Escape Ore Swamp in South Carolina, has long been at the center of local lore. While many consider the creature a hoax, others swear they've encountered it face to face. Lizard Man has had several brushes with fame: A local radio station once offered $1 million for a live capture, and in 1988, a South Carolina Republican leader labeled Lizard Man a staunch Democrat.

Jersey Devil: According to most reports, New Jersey's crypto-zoological curiosity has wings, a horse's face, a pig's hooves, and a kangaroo's body. The legend of the Jersey Devil was born in the 1700s—based on a tale of a cursed baby-turned-demon that flew off into the night—and boomed in the early 1900s, with supposed sightings all over the state. To this day, people report Devil sightings, mostly in the spooky Pine Barrens of southern New Jersey. While some locals think the creature is truly a supernatural beast, others say it's probably a misidentified sandhill crane.

El Chupacabra: Puerto Rico's legendary "goat sucker" is a fanged and clawed beast that performs vampirism on livestock. The first accounts of its victims—often goats, chickens, horses, and cows—were reported in the 1950s by farmers who found animals drained of blood, with several large puncture marks. Some who have allegedly sighted the creature describe it as a short, kangaroolike monster with oversize teeth and an oval head, but others liken it to a large reptile or bat.

Tessie: Deep in Lake Tahoe on the California–Nevada border lurks a storied sea creature that's the Sierra Nevada cousin of the Loch Ness Monster. It's alleged that after a submarine expedition, undersea explorer Jacques Cousteau said, "The world isn't ready for what's down there." (He could, of course, have been referring to anything odd.) Popular descriptions portray Tessie as either a freshwater relative of a whale or a 20-foot sea serpent with a humped back.

Champ: Like Tessie, Champ is named for the body of water in which it purportedly lurks, in this case New York's Lake Champlain. Several hundred recorded sightings typically describe the beast as an angular black sea monster measuring about 50 feet in length. One investigative group believes the often-sighted Champ is actually a surviving plesiosaur, a dinosaur that died off 60 million years ago.

Spotting Sasquatch

Throughout the world, it's called Alma, Yeti, Sasquatch, the Abominable Snowman, Wildman, and Bigfoot. Whatever the name, people agree that it's tall, hairy, doesn't smell good, and has a habit of showing up in locations around the globe—especially in North America.

✳ ✳ ✳ ✳

Jasper, Alberta, Canada (1811)

THIS WAS THE first known Bigfoot evidence found in North America. An explorer named David Thompson found 14-inch footprints in the snow, each toe topped by a short claw. He and his party didn't follow the tracks, fearing their guns would be useless against such a large animal. In his journal he wrote that he couldn't bring himself to believe such a creature existed.

British Columbia, Canada (1924)

In 1957, prospector Albert Ostman was finally able to come forward about a chilling event that happened to him more than 30 years prior. While camping at the head of Toba Inlet near Vancouver Island, Ostman was snatched up, still in his sleeping bag, and taken to a small valley where several Bigfoot were living. Held captive for several days, Ostman was only able to escape when one of the larger creatures tried to eat his snuff and chaos ensued.

Wanoga Butte, Oregon (1957)

After a long, uneventful morning hunting, Gary Joanis and Jim Newall were ecstatic when Joanis felled a deer with a single shot. But when a hairy creature "not less than nine feet tall" emerged from the woods, threw the deer over its shoulder, and lumbered off, the two men were left speechless.

Monroe, Michigan (1965)

On August 13, Christine Van Acker and her mother were driving when a large, hairy creature came out of the nearby woods. Frightened by the creature, the mother lost control of the car and grazed the beast. The car stalled and while the mother struggled to start it, the creature put its arm through the window, struck Christine in the face and slammed her mother's head against the car door, leaving both women with black eyes, photos of which were widely circulated in the press.

Bluff Creek, California (1967)

The famous sighting by Roger Patterson and Bob Gimlin yielded the first home-movie footage of Bigfoot. Although critics said it was obviously a man in a gorilla suit, Patterson denied the hoax allegations until his death in 1972. As of 2008, Gimlin still contends that the footage wasn't faked.

Spearfish, South Dakota (1977)

Betty Johnson and her three daughters saw two Bigfoot in a cornfield. The larger of the two was eight-feet tall; the other, slightly smaller. They both appeared to be eating corn and making a whistling sound.

Paris Township, Ohio (1978)

Herbert and Evelyn Cayton reported that a seven-foot-tall, 300-pound, fur-covered creature appeared at their house so frequently that their daughter thought it was a pet.

Jackson, Wyoming (1980)

On June 17, Glenn Towner and Robert Goodrich went into the woods on Snow King Mountain to check out a lean-to built by a friend of theirs. After hearing moaning and growling, the pair was chased out of the woods by a 12-foot-tall creature covered in hair. The creature followed them back to civilization, where it was last spotted standing briefly beneath a streetlight before vanishing back into the woods.

Crescent City, California (1995)

A TV crew was driving in their RV, filming the scenery in Jedediah Smith Redwoods State Park, when an eight-foot-tall hairy giant crossed their path and was caught on tape.

Cotton Island, Louisiana (2000)

Bigfoot surprised lumberjacks Earl Whitstine and Carl Dubois while they were clearing timber. The hairy figure returned a few days later, leaving behind footprints and hair samples.

Selma, Oregon (2000)

While hiking with his family near the Oregon Caves National Monument on July 1, psychologist Matthew Johnson smelled a strange musky odor. Hearing odd grunting noises coming from behind some trees, Johnson went to investigate and saw something very tall and hairy walking away. When asked to describe it, Johnson said that it could be "nothing else but a Sasquatch."

Granton, Wisconsin (2000)

As James Hughes was delivering newspapers early one morning, he saw a shaggy figure, about eight feet tall, carrying a goat. However, sheriffs called to the scene couldn't find any footprints or missing goats.

Mt. St. Helens, Washington (2002)

Jerry Kelso made his wife and two-year-old child wait in the car, while he chased what he thought was a man in a gorilla suit. When he was about 100 feet away, he realized that it wasn't a gorilla suit and that the seven-foot-tall creature was carrying a club.

Cranbrook, British Columbia, Canada (2007)

Snowplow driver Gord Johnson drove by a large, hairy figure with a "conical head" walking along a snowy road.

Mythical Creatures

From the time man first began telling tales around the campfire, every human culture has described creatures with characteristics quite different from run-of-the-mill animals. The legends of horses and snakes with wings, behemoths with horns in odd places, or other conglomerations live on to tease us with questions of their existence.

✻   ✻   ✻   ✻

Dragons: Real Scorchers

ONE OF THE oldest and most universal mythical creatures is the dragon. Huge, winged lizards or serpents with greenish scales and flaming breath are found in tales from ancient China to medieval Europe.

In China, the dragon originally represented the rising sun, happiness, and fertility. Sumerians included dragons in their religious art as early as 4000 B.C. The ancient Greeks called their dragon *Draco* and pictured it as a massive, winged snake emitting light and squeezing victims to death in its coils.

In the British Isles, dragons were associated with the legendary King Arthur and St. George, and though it is generally accepted that dragons do not exist, some think ancient man's glimpses of giant sea snakes may have inspired dragon myths.

People Acting Fishy: Mermaids and Mermen

The ancient Babylonians worshipped a half-human/half-fish creature named Oannes who gave them the gift of civilization. The contemporary mermaid, a beautiful woman with the lower body of a fish, may have been popularized by Danish writer Hans Christian Andersen's tale *The Little Mermaid*. Some think that mermaids spotted at sea by lonesome sailors are nothing more than manatees—large flat-tailed mammals.

Unicorns: Creatures that Make a Point

Variations of the unicorn, a horse with a single, long horn growing out of its forehead, appear in myths worldwide. It is possible that a similar, actual creature may have appeared at one time to inspire these myths. In the 1800s, a French woman grew a single, ten-inch horn from her forehead. A wax casting of the horn is preserved in Philadelphia's Mütter Museum. In 2003, a 95-year-old Chinese woman began growing a similar horn. By May 2007, it was five inches long. These are called cutaneous (skin-related) horns and, if possible in humans, could also logically occur in other large mammals. Unicorns are usually portrayed as snow white, gentle, noble creatures—each with a very long, twisted horn that comes to a sharp point.

Pegasus: Cloud Galloper

Greek legend has it that when Poseidon, god of the sea, got together with Medusa, the gorgon with the snake-infested hair, their offspring was Pegasus, a great white horse with wings. Pegasus became the mount of the hero Bellerophon, and together they slew the bizarre Chimera (a fire-breathing monster with the head of a lion, body of a goat, and tail of a snake). Pride in the great deed made Bellerophon think he could ride Pegasus to Mt. Olympus, home of the gods, so he sprang away for the heavens. But the mortal Bellerophon was thrown back to Earth by Zeus, who kept the winged horse for himself. There is a constellation named for Pegasus.

Cyclops: Keeping an Eye Out

They were not pretty, according to Greek legend. The small group of grotesque, one-eyed giants called Cyclopes (in the plural) was warlike and given to eating human flesh. Their one skill was an astonishing talent for creating weapons for the gods, such as swords and arrows. Could such people ever have existed? Humans inflicted with an endocrine disorder known as gigantism have been known to reach a height of eight feet, and very rarely humans may also be born with a birth defect that gives them a single eye.

Having a Lot of Faun

Very similar to goat-man creatures called satyrs but not at all related to baby deer (fawns), fauns looked like men from the navel up, except for the goat horns sprouting from their temples. They also bounded about on goat legs and hooves. Fathered by the Greek god Faunus, fauns protected the natural world, especially fields and woods. They were also similar in appearance to Pan, Greek god of nature, who gave us the word panic for the fright he could inspire by blowing on his magical conch shell. Mr. Tumnus from C. S. Lewis's *The Lion, the Witch, and the Wardrobe* was a faun.

Centaurs: When Horse and Rider are Truly One

A skilled rider will often appear as one with his or her galloping steed, so it isn't hard to see how ancient Greeks may have envisioned a creature that was humanlike from the trunk up but with the legs and body of a stallion—it makes for truly seamless horsemanship. Centaurs were meat-eating revelers who loved to drink, according to Greek legend, except for one gentle man-horse named Chiron known for his wisdom and teaching abilities. Chiron lives on as the centaur constellation Sagittarius, and centaurs are still seen on the coats of arms of many old European families.

Trolls: Mammoth Mountain Men

Although the descriptions of these ugly, manlike beings vary from country to country, trolls originated in Scandinavian lands, where they were said to be gigantic, grotesque humanoids who lived in the hills or mountains, mined ore, and became wondrous metalsmiths. Trolls could turn to stone if caught in the sun, and Norway's ancient rock pillars are said to be evidence of this belief. But perhaps legends of trolls are based on a few individuals with a disorder that would not have been understood in ancient times. A rare hormonal disorder called gigantism causes excessive growth of the long bones, and, thus, greatly increased height.

Griffins: In the Cat-Bird Seat?

Depictions of these folk monsters can be found in artwork from ancient Egypt and other cradles of civilization as early as 3300 B.C. Mainly a lion-eagle combo, griffins featured a lion's body and an eagle's wings, head, and legs. But they also sported big ears and fierce, ruby-colored eyes. Griffins often guarded rich treasure troves and viciously defended their turf with their sharp beaks and talons. They have survived in modern fantasy fiction, including Lewis Carroll's *Alice's Adventures in Wonderland.*

Fairies: Not Always Tinkerbell

Fairies, also known as wood nymphs, sprites, pixies, and many other names in cultures around the world, are usually thought of as attractive little spirit beings, proportioned like humans and charmingly dressed in wildflowers and acorns. In modern times, they are often depicted as sweet little beings with translucent wings. But in medieval times, the *fée* or *fay*, as they were called in Old French or English, could be naughty or nice.

One Irish tradition maintains that fairies often stole babies, substituting an old, wrinkled fairy or even a bundled log in place of the infant. Some European folk traditions believed fairies were descended from an old, superior race of humanoid creatures, and others thought they were fallen angels that had landed in woods or meadows. Shakespeare's play, *A Midsummer Night's Dream,* with its royal fairies Oberon and Titania, helped popularize the notion of fairies as small, magical people living in their own kingdom among humans. And folk belief worldwide still insists that these little people must be treated respectfully and given offerings and gifts to keep them from pulling nasty tricks on their human neighbors.

Monsters Across America

Dracula, Frankenstein, the Wolf Man—these are the monsters who strike fear into the hearts of children—the same ones that parents chase away and tell their kids there's no such thing as monsters. But are they wrong?

✳ ✳ ✳ ✳

Dover Demon

FOR TWO DAYS in 1977, the town of Dover, Massachusetts, was under attack from a bizarre creature that seemed to be from another world. The first encounter with the beast—nick-named the Dover Demon—occurred on the evening of April 21. Bill Bartlett was out for a drive with some friends when they saw something strange climbing on a stone wall. The creature appeared to be only about three feet tall but had a giant, oversize head with large, orange eyes. The rest of the body was tan and hairless with long, thin arms and legs.

Several hours later, the same creature was spotted by 15-year-old John Baxter, who watched it scurry up a hillside. The following day, a couple reported seeing the Demon, too. When authorities asked for a description, the couple's matched the ones given by the other witnesses except for one difference: The creature the couple encountered appeared to have glowing green eyes. Despite repeated attempts to locate it, the creature was never seen again.

Momo

In the early 1970s, reports came flooding in of a strange creature roaming the woods near the small town of Louisiana, Missouri. Standing nearly seven feet tall, Momo (short for Missouri Monster) was completely covered in black fur with glowing orange eyes. The first major report came in July 1971 when Joan Mills and Mary Ryan claimed to have been harassed by a "half ape, half man" creature that made bizarre noises at them as they passed it on Highway 79. Even though the creature didn't make physical contact with them, both women believed it would have harmed them had it been given the chance. That seemed to be confirmed the following year when, on July 11, 1972, brothers Terry and Wally Harrison spotted a giant, hairy beast carrying a dead dog. The boys screamed, alerting family members, who caught a sight of the creature before it disappeared into the woods. Sightings continued for a couple of weeks, but Momo hasn't been seen since.

Lawndale Thunderbird

If you're ever in Lawndale, Illinois, keep an eye out for giant birds lest they sneak up on you and whisk you away. That's what almost happened in 1977 when Lawndale residents noticed two large black birds with white-banded necks and 10- to 12-foot wingspans flying overhead. The birds, though enormous, seemed harmless enough. That is, until they swooped down and one of them reportedly tried to take off with ten-year-old Marlon Lowe while he played in his yard. The boy was not seriously injured, but the thunderbird did manage to lift the terrified boy several feet off the ground and carry him for nearly 40 feet before dropping him. Over the next few weeks, the birds were seen flying over various houses and fields in nearby towns, but, thankfully, they did not attack anyone else. And though they appear to have left Lawndale for good, reports of thunderbird sightings continue across the United States.

Ohio Bridge Trolls

In May 1955, a man driving along the Miami River near Loveland, Ohio, came across a frightening sight. Huddled under a darkened bridge were several bald-headed creatures, each three to four feet tall. Spellbound, the man pulled over and watched the creatures, which he said had webbed hands and feet. Though they made no sound, the man said the creatures appeared to be communicating with each other and did not notice him watching them. However, when one of the creatures held up a wand or rod that began emitting showers of sparks, the man quickly left. He drove straight to the local police station, which dispatched a car to the bridge. A search of the area turned up nothing, and, to this day, there have been no more reported sightings of these strange creatures.

Maryland's Goatman

Think goats are cute and fuzzy little creatures? If so, a trip through Prince George's County in Maryland just might change your mind. Since the 1950s, people have reported horrifying encounters with a creature known only as the Goatman. From afar, many claim to have mistaken the Goatman for a human being. But as he draws nearer, his cloven feet become visible, as do the horns growing out of his head. If that's not enough to make you turn and run, reports as recent as 2006 state that the Goatman now carries an ax with him.

Gatormen

The swamplands of Florida are filled with alligators, but most of them don't have human faces. Since the 1700s, tales of strange half-man, half-alligator creatures have circulated throughout the area. Gatormen are described as having the face, neck, chest, and arms of a man and the midsection, back legs, and tail of an alligator. Unlike most other monsters and strange beasts, Gatormen reportedly prefer to travel and hunt in packs and even appear to have their own verbal language. What's more, recent sightings have them traveling outside the state of Florida and taking up residence in the swamplands of Louisiana and swimming around a remote Texas swamp in 2001.

Skunk Ape

Since the 1960s, a creature has been spotted in the Florida Everglades that many call Bigfoot's stinky cousin: the skunk ape. The beast is said to closely resemble Bigfoot with one minor difference—it smells like rotten eggs. In late 2000, Sarasota police received an anonymous letter from a woman who complained that an escaped animal was roaming near her home at night. Included with the letter were two close-up photographs of the creature—a large beast that resembled an orangutan standing behind some palmetto leaves, baring its teeth.

Lizard Man

At around 2:00 A.M. on June 29, 1988, Christopher Davis got a flat tire on a back road near the Scape Ore Swamp in South Carolina. Just as the teen finished changing the tire, he was suddenly attacked by a seven-foot-tall creature with scaly green skin and glowing red eyes. Davis was able to get back into his car and drive away but not before the Lizard Man managed to climb onto the roof and claw at it, trying to get inside. As he drove, Davis could see the creature had three claws on each of its "hands." Eventually, the creature fell from the car and Davis was able to escape. A search of the scene later that day turned up nothing. Despite numerous subsequent sightings, the creature has yet to be apprehended.

Devil Monkeys

Far and away, some of the strangest creatures said to be roaming the countryside are the Devil Monkeys. Take an adult kangaroo, stick a monkey or baboon head on top, and you've got yourself a Devil Monkey. By most accounts, these creatures can cover hundreds of feet in just a few quick hops. They're nothing to tangle with, either. Although Devil Monkeys have traditionally stuck to attacking livestock and the occasional family pet, some reports have them attempting to claw their way into people's homes. Originally spotted in Virginia in the 1950s, Devil Monkeys have now been spotted all across the United States. On a related note, in May 2001, residents of New Delhi, India, were sent into a panic when a four-foot-tall half-monkey, half-human creature began attacking them as they slept.

The Champion of American Lake Monsters

In 1609, French explorer Samuel de Champlain was astonished to see a thick, eight- to ten-foot-tall creature in the waters between present-day Vermont and New York. His subsequent report set in motion the legend of Champ, the "monster" in Lake Champlain.

✳ ✳ ✳ ✳

Eerie Encounters

EVEN BEFORE CHAMPLAIN'S visit, Champ was known to Native Americans as Chaousarou. Over time, Champ has become one of North America's most famous lake monsters. News stories of its existence were frequent enough that in 1873, showman P. T. Barnum offered $50,000 for the creature, dead or alive. That same year, Champ almost sank a steamboat, and in the 1880s, a number of people, including a sheriff, glimpsed it splashing playfully offshore. It is described as dark in color (olive green, gray, or brown) with a serpentlike body.

Sightings have continued into modern times, and witnesses have compiled some film evidence that is difficult to ignore. In 1977, a woman named Sandra Mansi photographed a long-necked creature poking its head out of the water near St. Albans, Vermont, close to the Canadian border. She estimated the animal was 10 to 15 feet long and told an investigator that its skin looked "slimy" and similar to that of an eel. Mansi presented her photo and story at a 1981 conference held at Lake Champlain. Although she had misplaced the nega-tive by then, subse-

quent analyses of the photo have generally failed to find any evidence that it was manipulated.

In September 2002, a researcher named Dennis Hall, who headed a lake monster investigation group known as Champ Quest, videotaped what looked like three creatures undulating through the water near Ferrisburgh, Vermont. Hall claimed that he saw unidentifiable animals in Lake Champlain on 19 separate occasions.

In 2006, two fishermen captured digital video footage of what appeared to be parts of a very large animal swimming in the lake. The images were thoroughly examined under the direction of ABC News technicians, and though the creature on the video could not be proved to be Champ, the team could find nothing to disprove it, either.

Champ or Chump?

As the sixth-largest freshwater lake in the United States (and stretching about six miles into Quebec, Canada), Lake Champlain provides ample habitat and nourishment for a good-size water cryptid, or unknown animal. The lake plunges as deep as 400 feet in spots and covers 490 square miles.

Skeptics offer the usual explanations for Champ sightings: large sturgeons, floating logs or water plants, otters, or an optical illusion caused by sunlight and shadow. Others think Champ could be a remnant of a species of primitive whale called a zeuglodon or an ancient marine reptile known as a plesiosaur, both believed by biologists to be long extinct. But until uncontestable images of the creature's entire body are produced, this argument will undoubtedly continue.

Champ does claim one rare, official nod to the probability of its existence: Legislation by both the states of New York and Vermont proclaim that Champ is a protected—though unknown—species and make it illegal to harm the creature in anyway.

Werewolves in Wisconsin?

Do you believe in werewolves? If you head out to southeastern Wisconsin, you might just meet one face-to-fang.

✳   ✳   ✳   ✳

Meeting the Beast

THE FIRST RECORDED sighting of the Beast came in 1936, long before it even had a name. Security guard Mark Schackelman was walking the grounds of a convent near Jefferson shortly before midnight when he saw a strange creature digging on top of a Native American burial mound. As Schackelman got closer, the creature ran off into the darkness. The scene repeated itself the following night, but this time, the creature stood up on its hind legs, growled at the shocked security guard, and simply walked away.

Encounters like this have continued through the years. Most people describe the creature as six to eight feet tall. It gets around on all fours but can also walk on two feet. Its entire body is covered with fur (similar to Bigfoot), but this Beast also has clawed hands, the head of a wolf, and bright yellow eyes. With a description like that, it's easy to see why some people believe that the creature is a werewolf. But several people have seen the Beast in broad daylight.

The Beast Gets a Name

In the early 1990s, an outbreak of Beast sightings in southeastern Wisconsin—specifically, along an isolated stretch of Bray Road, just outside the town of Elkhorn—led a local reporter to dub the creature "The Beast of Bray Road."

Today, the Beast continues to linger around southeastern Wisconsin, but it's seldom seen on Bray Road anymore. It was, however, spotted in Madison in 2004. So if you're ever driving through the area, keep an eye out for what might be lurking around the bend.

The Black Dog of Moeraki

Moeraki, New Zealand is home to the frightening Maori legend of the Black Dog.

✳ ✳ ✳ ✳

Long Ago

BEFORE EUROPEANS CAME to New Zealand's South Island, seafaring Maori were its sole human residents. One tribal group lived on the Moeraki peninsula in the modern Otago Region, noted for its round granite boulders and wave-bashed coast. The Maori kept dogs, mostly for guard purposes.

Maori legend tells that the Kuia (wisewoman) of Moeraki loved her huge, fierce black dog. One night, the chief tripped over her dog in the dark, injuring his leg and getting a nasty bite from the startled canine. Enraged, the chief ordered the Kuia's dog served for dinner without telling her. At mealtime, seeking to share some scraps with her dog, she asked the chief where Rover was. He told her: "You're eating him." She pronounced a curse on the chief, and a ban on harming black dogs. The story goes that he choked on a bone and died that night. From that day forward, the Maori of Moeraki considered large black dogs ill omens.

The Legend Today

Europeans came to Moeraki in 1836 and built a whaling village. Many intermarried with the Maori, who probably taught the newcomers the Black Dog legend. Locals and visitors have reported seeing the animal, which has two reported behavior patterns: one benign, one not.

Some persons lost in the dark have reported the dog calmly walking a straight path, leading them safely home; this version of the Black Dog was calm and helpful. In other cases, the story grows more sinister, with the dog taking an irregular and disturbed path while barking and growling. Those attempting to follow it have reported stumbling and falling, with the dog agitated by something they couldn't discern.

If the Black Dog doesn't go straight, don't follow it!

Strange Doings Beneath the Sea

Most sea creatures are quite comfortable with habitats and relationships that human land-dwellers find rather odd. They're flexible about how they look, where they live, and even what gender they claim as their own.

✳ ✳ ✳ ✳

No-Brainers

SEA SQUIRTS—SO NAMED because they squirt water at whatever annoys them—are small, blobby creatures that appear in all oceans and seas. Many are short and fat, while others are elongated. Sea squirts can grow to the size of an egg, though most are much smaller. Some live alone and some form colorful colonies that look like flowers blooming on the ocean floor. Although usually found in shallow water, sea squirts also turn up as deep as 28,000 feet.

Sea squirts are categorized as chordates, the same phylum that humans belong to. That's because the larval stage has a notochord (a flexible skeletal rod) and a simple nervous system. With a head, mouth, sucker, and tail, the young sea squirt looks and moves like a tadpole. But this adolescent goes through some major changes as it grows up—more than a human teenager.

Attaching itself to a piling, a seashell, a sandy bottom, gravel, algae, or even the back of a big crab, the youngster absorbs its own tail and nervous system. The mature sea squirt is a spine-less, sedentary, immobile glob. Science philosopher Daniel C. Dennett put it this way: "When it finds its spot and takes root, it doesn't need its brain anymore, so it eats it! (It's rather like getting tenure.)"

Sex-Shifters

Worldwide, the oceans' coral reefs harbor about 1,500 species of fish, including some with adaptable sexual identities. Wrasses, parrotfish, and other reef fish start out female and eventually become male. However, other types of reef fish change sex according to the needs of the group. If there aren't enough males or females, the problem is easily taken care of.

Gobies that live in Japan's coral reefs can change back and forth as need dictates. If the dominant male dies or leaves, a female will become male, changing gender in about four days. If a larger male shows up, the gobie that changed simply switches back to female. Many fish that change sex do so quickly. A particular variety of sea bass found in reefs from North Carolina to Florida and in the northern Gulf of Mexico are both female when they meet for mating. One switches to male, they mate, then both switch sex and they mate again. This toggling between sexes is accompanied by color changes; the female is blue, and the male is orange with a white stripe.

Dual Sexuality

The belted sandfish (a coastal sea bass) is a hermaphrodite, with active male and female organs. It can theoretically self-fertilize, meaning that a single individual can release eggs, then shift to its male self (in about 30 seconds) and release sperm. More often, two fish take turns fertilizing each other's eggs. Hermaphroditic sea slugs are underwater snails without shells. The Navanax inermis variety, found off the coast of California and Mexico and in the Gulf of Mexico, have male sex organs on one end and female sex organs on the other. They sometimes mate in chains of three or more, with suitable ends attached. The slugs in the middle of the line act as male and female simultaneously.

The Perfect Couple?

Seahorses, those bony little fish that swim upright, live in sea grasses, mangrove roots, corals, and muddy bottoms in both tropical and temperate oceans and lagoons. They keep the sex they were born with, and seahorse couples tend to remain monogamous throughout a mating season. Couples perform a little dance when they meet, joining tails, swimming around together, and circling each other. It's the male seahorse that gets pregnant. After he opens a special pouch in his body, the female aligns with the opening and lays her eggs. The male fertilizes the eggs, his pouch swells, and two weeks later he gives birth to as many as 1,500 live offspring. Male seahorses sometimes experience false pregnancies; the pouch swells but no eggs or babies are present. Males can even die of postpartum complications such as infections caused by dead, unborn ponies.

Partners Forever

Far down in the ocean, between 3,000 and 10,000 feet, is a cold, dark world of sharp-toothed hunters. There, many fish use built-in lights to confuse pursuers, to signal a mate, or to bait a trap. Among these deep-sea hunters are anglerfish that grow a "fishing rod" with deceptive "bait" dangling from it. They move about slowly, waving their glowing lures to attract potential meals toward their big toothy mouths. However, only the female anglerfish grows a lure—the male doesn't need one. He's also born without a digestive system, because he isn't going to need that either.

When a young male anglerfish is just a few inches long, he searches out a (much larger) female and sinks his teeth into her. His jaws begin to grow into her skin, and after a few weeks he is unable to let go. The male's eyes get smaller and eventually disappear. Most of his internal organs also disappear. His blood vessels connect to those of the female, so he gets nutrition from whatever she eats. The male grows a little larger, but the gain is all in testes. Finally, he's the sex object he was destined to be—a producer of sperm and little else. The female gains a mate that's literally attached to her forever. Sometimes she doesn't settle for just one but drags several males along through life.

The Sea Creature with 1,000 Stomachs

The longest of all ocean-dwellers, the praya, assigns sex to small entities that are also its body parts. A praya is a "colonial" animal called a siphonophore, made up of many individuals called polyps. Each polyp is adapted for a special duty: some breed, some swim, and some are just stomachs.

In a praya, the various kinds of polyps are strung together into a well-coordinated monster that moves through the water like a snake on a roller coaster. It roams the ocean vertically, from near the surface to depths of 1,500 feet. Though only as thick as a finger, a praya can grow to be 130 feet long. A mere six-foot siphonophore can have more than 100 stomach polyps, and a large praya might have 1,000 stomachs.

Red Eyes Over Point Pleasant: The Mysterious Mothman

In 1942, the U.S. government took control of several thousand acres of land just north of Point Pleasant, West Virginia. The purpose was to build a secret facility capable of creating and storing TNT that could be used during World War II. For the next three years, the facility cranked out massive amounts of TNT, shipping it out or storing it in one of the numerous concrete "igloo" structures that dotted the area. In 1945, the facility was shut down and eventually abandoned, but it was here that an enigmatic flying creature with glowing red eyes made its home years later.

✳   ✳   ✳   ✳

"Red Eyes on the Right"

ON THE EVENING of November 15, 1966, Linda and Roger Scarberry were out driving with another couple, Mary and Steve Mallette. As they drove, they decided to take a detour that took them past the abandoned TNT factory.

As they neared the gate of the old factory, they noticed two red lights up ahead. When Roger stopped the car, the couples were horrified to find that the red lights appeared to be two glowing red eyes. What's more, those eyes belonged to a creature standing more than seven feet tall with giant wings folded behind it. That was all Roger needed to see before he hit the gas pedal and sped off. In response, the creature calmly unfolded its wings and flew toward the car. Incredibly, even though Roger raced along at speeds close to 100 miles per hour, the red-eyed creature was able to keep up with them without much effort.

Upon reaching Point Pleasant, the two couples ran from their car to the Mason County Courthouse and alerted Deputy Millard Halstead of their terrifying encounter. Halstead couldn't be sure exactly what the two couples had seen, but whatever it was, it had clearly frightened them. In an attempt to calm them down, Halstead agreed to accompany them to the TNT factory. As his patrol car neared the entrance, the police radio suddenly emitted a strange, whining noise. Other than that, despite a thorough search of the area, nothing out of the ordinary was found.

More Encounters

Needless to say, once word got around Point Pleasant that a giant winged creature with glowing red eyes was roaming around the area, everyone had to see it for themselves. The creature didn't disappoint. Dubbed Mothman by the local press, the creature was spotted flying overhead, hiding, and even lurking on front porches. In fact, in the last few weeks of November, dozens of witnesses encountered the winged beast. But Mothman wasn't the only game in town. It seems that around the same time that he showed up, local residents started noticing strange lights in the evening sky, some of which hovered silently over the abandoned TNT factory. Of course, this led some to believe that Mothman and the UFOs were somehow connected. One such person was Mary Hyre of *The Athens Messenger*, who had been reporting on the strange activities in Point Pleasant since they started. Perhaps that's why she became the first target.

Beware the Men in Black

One day, while Mary Hyre was at work, several strange men visited her office and began asking questions about the lights in the sky. Normally, she didn't mind talking to people about the UFO sightings and Mothman. But there was something peculiar about these guys. For instance, they all dressed exactly the same: black suits, black ties, black hats, and dark sunglasses. They also spoke in a strange monotone and seemed confused by ordinary objects such as ballpoint pens. As the men left, Hyre wondered whether they had been from another planet. Either way, she had an up-close-and-personal encounter with the legendary Men in Black.

Mary Hyre was not the only person to have a run-in with the Men in Black. As the summer of 1967 rolled around, dozens of people were interrogated by them. In most cases, the men showed up unannounced at the homes of people who had recently witnessed a Mothman or UFO sighting. For the most part, the men simply wanted to know what the witnesses had seen. But sometimes, the men went to great lengths to convince the witnesses that they were mistaken and had not seen anything out of the ordinary. Other times, the men threatened witnesses. Each time the Men in Black left a witness's house, they drove away in a black, unmarked sedan. Despite numerous attempts to determine who these men were and where they came from, their identity remained a secret. And all the while, the Mothman sightings continued throughout Point Pleasant and the surrounding area.

The Silver Bridge Tragedy

Erected in 1928, the Silver Bridge was a gorgeous chain suspension bridge that spanned the Ohio River, connecting Point
Pleasant with Ohio. On December 15, 1967, the bridge was
busy with holiday shoppers bustling back and forth between
West Virginia and Ohio. As the day wore on, more and more
cars started filling the bridge until shortly before 5:00 P.M.,
when traffic on the bridge came to a standstill. For several
minutes, none of the cars budged. Suddenly, there was a loud
popping noise and then the unthinkable happened: The Silver
Bridge collapsed, sending dozens of cars and their passengers
into the freezing water below.

Over the next few days, local authorities and residents searched
the river hoping to find survivors, but in the end, 46 people
lost their lives in the bridge collapse. A thorough investigation
determined that a manufacturing flaw in one of the bridge's
supporting bars caused the collapse. But there are others who
claim that in the days and weeks leading up to the collapse,
they saw Mothman and even the Men in Black around, on,
and even under the bridge. Further witnesses state that while
most of Point Pleasant was watching the Silver Bridge collapse,
bright lights and strange objects were flying out of the area and
disappearing into the winter sky. Perhaps that had nothing to
do with the collapse of the Silver Bridge, but the Mothman has
not been seen since . . . or has he?

Mothman Lives!

There are reports that the Mothman is still alive and well and
has moved on to other areas of the United States. There are
even those who claim that he was spotted flying near the Twin
Towers on September 11, 2001, leading to speculation that
Mothman is a portent of doom and only appears when disasters are imminent. Some believe Mothman was a visitor from
another planet who returned home shortly after the Silver
Bridge fell. Still others think the creature was the result of the
toxic chemicals eventually discovered in the area near the TNT

factory. And then there are skeptics who say that the initial sighting was nothing more than a giant sand crane and that mass hysteria took care of the rest.

Nessie: Shock in the Loch

The legend of Nessie, the purported inhabitant of Scotland's Loch Ness, dates back to the year 565 when a roving Christian missionary named St. Columba is said to have rebuked a huge water monster to save the life of a swimmer. Rumors persisted from that time on, but it wasn't until the 20th century that the creature became internationally famous.

❋ ❋ ❋ ❋

Monster Ahoy

IN 1933, ONE witness said he saw the creature three times; that same year, a vacationing couple claimed they saw a large creature with flippers and a long neck slither across the road and then heard it splash into the lake. These incidents made news around the world, and the hunt for Nessie was on.

Sightings multiplied and became more and more difficult to explain away. In 1971, a priest named Father Gregory Brusey saw a speedy long-necked creature cruising through the loch. One investigator estimates that more than 3,000 people have seen Nessie. The witnesses come from every walk of life, including teachers, doctors, police officers, and scientists.

Monster Media Madness

As technology has advanced, Nessie has been hunted with more sophisticated equipment, often with disappointing results. In 1934, a doctor snapped the famous "Surgeon's Photo," which showed a dinosaurlike head atop a long neck sticking out of the water. It has since been proven a hoax and what was thought to be Nessie was actually a picture of a toy submarine. Many other photos have been taken, but all are inconclusive.

Since 1934, numerous expeditions have been mounted in search of Nessie. Scuba divers and even submarines have scoured the lake to no avail because the amount of peat in the water makes visibility extremely poor.

In 2003, the British Broadcasting Corporation undertook a massive satellite-assisted sonar sweep of the entire lake, but again with no results. And in 2007, cameras were given to 50,000 people attending a concert on the lake's shore in hopes that someone might get lucky and snap a shot of Nessie. But apparently she doesn't like rock music—Nessie was a no-show.

The Nessessary Debate

Theories about Nessie's true nature abound. One of the most popular ideas, thanks to the oft-reported long neck, flippers, and bulbous body, is that Nessie is a surviving plesiosaur—a marine reptile thought to have gone extinct 65 million years ago. Critics insist that even if a cold-blooded reptile could exist in the lake's frigid waters, Loch Ness is not large enough to support a breeding population of them. Other theories suggest that Nessie is a giant eel, a string of seals or otters swimming in formation, floating logs, a porpoise, or a huge sturgeon.

Locals have hinted that the creature is actually a demon. Stories of devil worship and mysterious rituals in the area have gone hand in hand with rumors of bodies found floating in the loch. In the early 1900s, famed occultist Aleister Crowley owned a home on the lake's southern shore where he held "black masses" and conducted other ceremonies that may have aimed to "raise" monsters. And for centuries, Scots have repeated folktales of the kelpie, or water horse, a creature that can shape-shift in order to lure the unwary into the water.

Whatever the truth about Nessie, she has made quite a splash as a tourist attraction. Every year thousands of people try their luck at spotting and recording the world's most famous monster.

The Devil Is Alive . . . and Living in New Jersey

The Pine Barrens consist of more than a million acres of forested land in central and southern New Jersey. So named because the area's sandy, acidic soil is bad for growing crops, it has proven a fertile home for an amazing collection of trees and plants. Of course, if the stories are true, the area is also home to a bizarre winged creature known as the Jersey Devil.

✳ ✳ ✳ ✳

Birth of the Devil

THERE ARE MANY legends concerning the origin of the Jersey Devil. The most popular involves the Leeds family, who came to America from Europe in the 1730s and settled in the southern area of the Pine Barrens. The Leeds family quickly grew by leaps and bounds, and before long, their house was filled with a dozen children. Needless to say, when Mother Leeds found out she was pregnant with child number 13, she was less than enthusiastic. In fact, she supposedly yelled out that she was done having children and that this child "could be the devil" for all she cared. Apparently someone was listening, for when the 13th child was born, it allegedly resembled a devil, complete with wings, a tail, and cloven hooves. Once born, the child devoured its 12 siblings and its parents, then promptly disappeared into the Pine Barrens, where it still lives to this day.

The First Sightings

One of the first, and most intriguing, sightings of the Jersey Devil took place in the early 1800s when Commodore Stephen Decatur saw a bizarre creature flying overhead as he was test-firing cannons at the Hanover Iron Works. Perhaps wishing to test the accuracy of the cannons, Decatur took aim and fired upon the creature overhead, striking one of its wings. To the amazement of Decatur and the other onlookers, the creature didn't seem to care that it had just been shot by a cannonball and casually flew away.

From the mid-1800s until the early 1900s, there were numerous sightings of the Jersey Devil throughout the Pine Barrens and beyond. Those who actually witnessed it described it as being everything from short and hairy to tall and cranelike. But there was one thing everyone agreed upon—whatever the creature was, it was not of this earth.

1909: The Year of the Devil

At the beginning of 1909, thousands of people encountered the beast in the span of a week. On Saturday, January 16, a winged creature believed to be the Jersey Devil was spotted flying over the town of Woodbury, New Jersey. The following day, residents of Bristol, Pennsylvania, also reported seeing something strange flying in the sky. Later the same day, bizarre tracks were discovered in the snow. Then on Monday, January 18, residents of Burlington, New Jersey, and neighboring towns were perplexed by the strange tracks in the snow on their rooftops. They had no clue as to who or what left them. All the while, reports kept coming in of something strange flying overhead with a head resembling a horse and hooves for feet.

In the early morning hours of January 19, Nelson Evans and his wife got up close and personal with the Jersey Devil outside their Gloucester, New Jersey, home. At approximately 2:30 A.M., a creature standing more than eight feet tall with a "head like a collie dog and a face like a horse" peered into the Evanses' window. Although they were petrified, Nelson mustered up the courage to open the window and yell at the creature. Startled, the creature turned, made a barking sound, and then flew off. Later that day, two Gloucester hunters claimed they had tracked strange footprints in the snow for nearly 20 miles. They noticed that whatever this creature was, it not only had the ability to fly or leap over large areas, but it could also squeeze underneath fences and through small spaces.

By Wednesday, January 20, local towns were forming posses

intent on tracking down the Jersey Devil. They were all unsuccessful, although they did have several sightings of the winged
creature flying toward neighboring towns. Then on Thursday,
things really got out of hand. The day began with the Devil
reportedly attacking a trolley car in Haddon Heights. It was
also during this time that local farmers reported finding some
of their livestock missing or dead. And in Camden, New Jersey,
a dog was attacked by the Jersey Devil and only managed to
survive when its owner chased the beast away.

By Friday, the Devil had been spotted all over New Jersey and
in parts of Pennsylvania. During that time, the creature had
been shot at (and was supposedly struck by several bullets) and
was even hosed down by a local fire department, but this didn't
seem to phase the beast at all.

Sightings Continue

As news of the Jersey Devil spread, it seemed that the entire
nation descended upon New Jersey in an attempt to catch a
glimpse of or, better yet, capture, the creature. But despite all
the searching and even a $10,000 reward for the beast's capture,
it was never caught.

It appears that after its very busy week in 1909, the Jersey
Devil decided to lay low. In fact, though sightings did continue
through the years, they were few and far between. Because of
this, people started to believe that the Jersey Devil was a harbinger of doom and would only be sighted when something
bad was going to happen. Of course, this did not stop hundreds of people from wandering through the Pine Barrens in
search of the beast. But no matter how hard people looked,
not a single photograph or piece of video exists of the creature.
Part of the reason certainly has to be that the Pine Barrens has
remained virtually the same vast and undeveloped area, making it the perfect place for a devil to hide. So for now, the Pine
Barrens is keeping its secret.

The Weird Animals of Texas

Texas is full of unusual critters. Here are some of its strangest.

✳ ✳ ✳ ✳

Texas State Small Mammal: The Texas state small mammal is the nine-banded armadillo, an insect-eating relative of sloths and anteaters. Originating in South America, the armadillo migrated to Texas via Mexico in the 19th century. Its fear response is to jump in the air, which is why so many are found dead on Texas highways. Selling armadillos is illegal in Texas because they're the only animal besides humans to carry leprosy.

Horned Toad: The horned toad, horny toad, or horned frog is really a horned lizard and the Texas state reptile. The mistaken identities come from the lizard's round body and blunt snout, and the name comes from the scaly spikes on its back, sides, and head. Unrelated to the name, the male also has two sexual organs.

Houston Toad: The Houston Toad is an endangered toad species discovered in and around Houston in the late 1940s. Only between a few hundred to a few thousand remain, and they're gone from the city that gave them their name. The largest group of these loud amphibians is in Bastrop State Park.

Longhorn Cattle: When people think of Texas, they often think of the longhorn. Longhorn cattle are a hybrid descended primarily from the first cattle brought to the United States by the Spanish and mixed with English cattle. The horns can measure 120 inches tip to tip for steers (which are castrated males) and up to 80 inches for cows and bulls. Longhorns might have been bred out of existence if not for members of the U.S. Forest Service who saved a herd of breeding stock in 1927.

Whooping Crane: At five feet in height, the whooping crane is North America's tallest bird and an endangered species. An estimated 340 exist in the wild. The largest group spends the summers in Wood Buffalo National Park in Alberta, Canada, and migrates south in the winter to the Texas Gulf Coast, settling primarily near Corpus Christi on the Aransas National Wildlife Refuge and Matagorda Island.

Guadalupe Bass: Found only in the Guadalupe and a few other Texas rivers, the Guadalupe bass is the Texas state fish. A black bass and member of the sunfish family, the Guadalupe bass is called the "Texas trout" by fishers because of its fighting ability.

Mexican Free-Tailed Bats: These bats live in caves across the western and southern United States, but the largest colony—nearly 20 million bats—hangs out in Bracken Cave, north of San Antonio. Another huge colony of 1.5 million free-tails spends its summers under the Congress Avenue Bridge in Austin, just ten blocks from the state capitol building, making it the largest urban bat colony in North America. Those numbers helped make the Mexican free-tailed bat the official "flying mammal" of Texas.

Greater Roadrunner: The greater roadrunner, a member of the cuckoo family, believe it or not, is a year-round resident of Texas, although it can be found in other southwestern deserts, as well. It can fly if necessary, but it prefers to stay on the ground, where it can reach speeds of more than 15 miles per hour. Although roadrunners try to stay clear of coyotes, they are willing to attack a snake for a nice meal.

Texas Leafcutter Ant: At the small end of the Texas critters scale, the Texas leafcutter ant is a fungus-farming ant species that likes to dine on more than 200 types of plants. Considered a major pest by Texas farmers, leafcutter colonies can contain as many as 2 million ants, and one colony with high hopes can strip a citrus tree of its leaves in less than a day.

Chupacabra: It sounds strange, but many Texans, particu-

larly goat farmers, fear a creature known as the Chupacabra—
Spanish for "goat sucker"—because of its reputation for
attacking goats and other livestock and then drinking their
blood. Unexplained livestock disappearances are often blamed
on this creature, which is said to be the size of a small bear
with fangs and huge claws, have spines down its hairless leathery back, and be bluish-greenish-gray in color. In 2004, a
San Antonio rancher killed a creature many believed to be a
Chupacabra, but DNA analysis identified it as a coyote with
a mange problem. Even though no credible evidence of such a
creature exists, it has built up quite a reputation.

Dino Mix-Ups

*The field of paleontology, once the realm of dusty fossils
displayed in museums, has in recent years become a hot field of
study. New methods of testing, using DNA analysis, CAT scans,
and MRI imaging, allow researchers to study fossil findings in
new ways. However, one result of this current wave of research
is the unearthing of mixed-up fossils, scientific wrong turns, and
mistaken identities.*

✳   ✳   ✳   ✳

You Say *Brontosaurus*, I Say *Apatosaurus*

O NE OF THE earliest dino-bloopers was the case of the
Brontosaurus. In 1877, paleontologist O. C. Marsh identified a specimen as being of the species type, *Apatosaurus ajax*.
A few years later, he found a more complete sample of the
same dinosaur. In the paper following this find, Marsh called
the beast a *Brontosaurus*, setting off decades of confusion. The
two names actually mean the same thing, but over time they
began to be thought of as two different dinosaurs. According to
the rules for naming new species, the older name takes prece-
dence; to put a halt to the confusion, *Brontosaurus* was officially
dropped as the dino's name. Despite this, the *Brontosaurus* is
still one of the most recognized names of dinosaurs.]

Big, Bigger, Much Bigger

At an estimated 90 feet long and weighing 11 tons, the long-necked, plant-eating *Diplodocus* was considered to be the largest animal ever to have lived. It enjoyed that distinction for nearly a century until someone discovered the 100- to 130-foot-long *Supersaurus* in 1972. Then the *Seismosaurus*, at 150 feet long and weighing 85 tons, was uncovered in 1979. As more research emerges, museums around the world continue to rewrite the identification cards for these long-necked beasts. It is now thought that while the *Seismosaurus* probably made tremor-like sounds when stamping through the forest, and the *Supersaurus* was without question very, very big, they were not separate species. In fact, both were just large specimens of the *Diplodocus*.

Plateosaurus Puzzler

It is remarkable that scientists can make any sense out of the jumble of bones that they discover. It's something like putting together a puzzle—one that is sure to have missing pieces, broken parts, and no picture on the box to show how it should look in the end. It is not surprising that the pieces would get mixed up at times, as in the case of the *Plateosaurus*. In the late 1800s, German fossil hunters found the skeleton of a dinosaur that had the razor teeth of a meat eater. This was named *Teratosaurus* ("monster reptile") and was thought of as a slow-moving, long-necked carnivore. It took almost 100 years for paleontologists to sort out the fact that the *Teratosaurus* was actually the remains of a plant-eating *Plateosaurus*, whose skull was mixed up with that of the crocodile-like creature that ate it. This beast, one of the top predators of the time, was actually not a dinosaur at all. Even so, it got to keep the name *Teratosaurus*.

Oviraptor: Falsely Accused

When the first *Oviraptor* specimens were discovered in Mongolia, they were found near fossilized eggs. It was assumed at the time that the eggs were from the *Protoceratops*, and since the new dinosaur was found to be toothless, it made sense to assume the eggs were a part of its diet. This theory led to its name: *Oviraptor* ("egg thief"). However, it was not until the 1990s when excavations in China cleared the *Oviraptor's* name. At the site, *Oviraptor* specimens were found, as they had been in the past, near eggs. Thanks to new technologies, this time scientists were able to examine the inside of the fossilized eggs. What they found was the embryo of an *Oviraptor*—the "egg thieves" were actually very good parents, protecting their nests and their young with their lives.

The Kuano River Boy

Around the world, feral (or wild) children have reportedly been raised by wolves, monkeys, and even ostriches, but a boy seen splashing about the banks of a river in northern India in the 1970s was rumored to have been raised by fish or lizards.

✳ ✳ ✳ ✳

From the Black Lagoon

THE BOY, ABOUT 15 years old when first discovered in 1973 by residents of the small town of Baragdava, had blackish-green skin and no hair. His head appeared malformed in a strange bullet shape, and he was entirely naked. "Lizard people" complete with green scales have been reported from time to time around the world, but this boy lacked scales, gills, or even webbed toes.

He lived amid the crocodiles in the Kuano River without fear of attack and was able to hold his breath and stay underwater longer than thought humanly possible. But strangest of all, hundreds of people, including police and reporters, saw him run across the surface of the water. This may have been explained by the slightly submerged dam surface. A person dashing across it might have appeared to be running on water to observers at a distance. Either way, there was no question that the boy was strangely at home in the river habitat.

Son of a Water Spirit

Although his initial appearance was a shock, a village woman named Somni, who found the boy lying in a field one day, noticed a birthmark on his back that was identical to that of the infant son she had lost in the swirling river several years earlier. Somni even had an explanation for why her son, whom she'd named Ramchandra, ended up as a "merman." Somni claimed that she had been raped and impregnated by a giant water spirit during a rainstorm. Villagers accepted Somni's story; however, her husband displayed the same bullet-shape skull as the River Boy.

The Amphibious Life

Although Ramchandra, if that was indeed his true identity, preferred to remain in the river most of the time, he did seem curious about the human villagers living nearby and would sometimes approach them. Several times he was captured and brought to the village by force. He enjoyed eating vegetables left for him along the riverbank, although his main sustenance came from raw fish and frogs that he gulped from the river without using his hands.

Not Easy Being Green

For nine years, the River Boy interacted with the villagers of Baragdava, but eventually he came to a terrible end. In 1982, after two policemen tried to catch him, he made an escape from what had been his home village and swam to another river town about 12 miles away. There he approached a woman tending a small tea shop. The woman was so frightened by his naked, greenish appearance that she doused him with a pan of boiling water. Ramchandra ran back to the river where he died from severe burns. His body was eventually retrieved floating on the water. The Kuano River Boy's age at the time of his tragic death was estimated at 24.

The River Boy's green-tinted skin was never definitively explained, although it was presumed to have been from longtime contact with the river water and perhaps algae. But strangely, there are records of other green children of unknown origin. In 1887, some field workers observed a boy and a girl as they timidly emerged from a cave in Banjos, Spain. The skin of both children was bright green, and they wore clothing made from an unrecognizable fabric. They spoke a language no one understood, but when the girl learned some Spanish, she told the villagers that a whirlwind had brought them to the cave from another land where the sun was never seen. Both children perished young—the boy after some days and the girl after about five years—but their skin turned a paler and paler green the longer they were out of the cave.

The Mystery of the Loveland Frog

If anyone ever runs into a four-foot-tall humanlike creature with a frog's face and webbed feet, for the love of Kermit, take a picture. The legend of the Loveland Frog dates back decades—yet, like so many other unusual creatures in American folklore, no firm evidence of its existence has ever been found.

✳   ✳   ✳   ✳

THE LOVELAND FROG was supposedly spotted in the town of Loveland (hence the name). As the story goes, chatter of the leathery-skinned croaker first came up when French explorers began colonizing the region. Indians native to the area warned the pioneers about the immortal beast they called "Shawnahooc," or "demon of the river."

Actual sightings were not reported until the mid-1950s. That's when, in May 1955, someone reported seeing three frog-people just chilling on a bridge over the Little Miami River. One was said to be carrying some sort of bar that was sending off blue sparks. The observer, a local businessman, noted that the creatures' chests were lopsided, their lips froglike, and their scent a mix of alfalfa and almonds. Sounds lovely, eh?

The Loveland Frog's next alleged appearance came in 1972, when a police officer named Ray Shockey said he spotted a short person with a frog's face sitting on a guardrail in the same vicinity. Two weeks later, another officer, Mark Matthews, was said to have seen the same thing lying in the road. Of course, when the officer tried to approach it (and shoot it), Mr. L. F. leapt into the river, never to be seen again.

Legacy in Loveland

The Loveland Frog may not have been seen in a while, but its tall tale lives on among the locals in the clearly action-packed town of Loveland. One man told a local newspaper he and his friends spent entire summers searching for signs of the amphibian hybrid.

"For the whole summer in '72, me and my friends, we went through the river at night with frog gigs and shotguns, looking for the thing," he said. "Every now and then, we seen something across the river. All we managed to catch, though, were red-horse suckers." (Redhorse suckers are sucker fish with red-tinted fins.)

Fact or Fiction?

So is the Loveland Frog real, or is it little more than misguided myth? It all depends on whom you ask. Mark Matthews, the second officer who supposedly spotted the beast, told *X-Project Paranormal Magazine* in 2001 that the reports had been greatly exaggerated over the years. "There is absolutely nothing to the incident that relates to 'monsters' or the 'paranormal,'" he said. "This entire thing has been habitually blown out of proportion."

According to Matthews's interview, the Loveland Frog was not a monster, wasn't leathery, and didn't even stand on two feet. Rather, Matthews clarifies, the animal was some sort of lizard that likely escaped from somewhere nearby.

"It was less than 3 feet in length, ran across the road, and was probably blinded by my headlights. It presented no aggressive action," he said.

That may be. Still, if those who find themselves strolling around the river near the town of Loveland notice a bizarre "ribbit" sound filling the air, they should grab their camera— they could become very, very rich.

Arf! Dog-Men in History

Dog may be man's best friend, but he's also been invoked to explain the unexplainable, and even to denigrate enemies— reasons why tales of men with the heads of dogs are not uncommon throughout the historical record.

✳   ✳   ✳   ✳

Dog-Headed Foreigners

ANCIENT STORIES ABOUT dog-headed men unwittingly reveal an apprehensiveness about the power of canines. We love our pooches, but let's face it: They have claws and sharp teeth, they run faster than we do, and they can eat our faces if they feel like it. Historically, this small bit of disquiet bubbling beneath our adoration has encouraged cultures to invoke dog-like creatures for diverse purposes, sometimes as gods, such as Egypt's Anubis, and frequently to belittle other cultures.

Whatever the motives, the eventual effect of these pervasive tales was to make fantastical dog-men seem very real. Most imaginative of all, though, were ancient writers from China, India, and Europe, who relayed purportedly true stories of human beings who literally had the heads of dogs.

Sit, Cynocephali!

Dog-headed peoples are often referred to as *Cynocephali*, Greek for "dog-head." In the 5th century B.C., Greek historian Herodotus described a distant country inhabited by "huge snakes and the lions, and the elephants and bears and asps, the Kunokephaloi (Dog-headed) and the Headless Men that have their eyes in their chests."

Herodotus was not alone in his testimony about dog-headed

peoples. Fellow Greek historian Ctesias claimed that on the mountains in distant India, "there live men with the head of a dog, whose clothing is the skin of wild beasts."

In accounts of this nature, it's difficult to sort out myth from fact. Like many of today's bloggers, ancient historians made implausible claims based on hearsay rather than direct observation. Writers played so fast and loose with the available facts that many believed—and made their readers believe—that some foreign societies barked rather than spoke.

Some historians tried to legitimize their claims by skipping down the road of pseudo-science. The second-century Greek historian Aelian included the Cynocephali in his book of animals. He declared that beyond Egypt one encounters the "human Kynoprosopoi (Dog faces)... they are black in appearance, and they have the head and teeth of a dog. And since they resemble this animal, it is very natural that I should mention them here [in a book about Animals]."

Racism Collides with Legend

Many present-day historians charge that these accounts of dog-headed tribes aren't simply reflections of a fear of foreigners, but racist ignorance. Repeated accounts of dog-headed groups in northern Africa suggest that race did indeed help encourage some dog-driven tales. These groups were often referred to as the Marmaritae, who engaged in on-again off-again warfare with the Romans. Legend has it that St. Christopher was a captured dog-headed slave from a Marmaritae tribe—paintings that depict the saint with the head of a brown dog still exist. According to lore, Christopher's dog head was replaced with a human head after he was baptized.

Modern scholars believe that historical references to dog-headed tribes derived from the lore created by many tribes in Central Asia, who described their own origins as having roots in the progeny of a human female who mated with a male dog. Biology this startling certainly would have tickled the imaginations of outsiders, and reinforced the notion that dog-headedness signified a profound and culturally expedient "otherness" of foreigners.

Baffling Baboons

And then there's the issue of *Papio cynocephalus*, central Africa's yellow baboon, whose head is curiously doglike. Foreigners' accounts of Africa often remarked on this intriguing animal with zeal. In fact, during the mad European scramble to colonize the African continent in the 19th century, baboons were shipped to the West for exhibition in circuses and freak shows as exotic dog-men. One such circus claimed that its baboon-man had been captured from an ancient African tribe. Marveling audiences failed to see the baboon face on the baboon, just as people failed to see the legitimate uniqueness of persons who didn't look or act as they did.

Bigfoot: The King of All Monsters

Let's face it—if you had to pick one monster that stands head (and feet) above all others, it would be Bigfoot. Not only is it the stuff of legends, but its likeness has also been used to promote everything from pizza to beef jerky.

✳ ✳ ✳ ✳

Early Sightings

FOLKTALES FROM NATIVE American tribes throughout the Northwest, the area that Bigfoot traditionally calls home, are filled with references to giant, apelike creatures roaming the woods. They described the beast as between seven and ten feet tall and covered in brown or dark hair. (Sasquatch, a common term used for the big-footed beast, is actually an anglicization of a Native American term for a giant supernatural creature.)

Walking on two legs, there was something humanlike about Sasquatch's appearance, although its facial features more closely resembled that of an ape, and it had almost no neck. With looks like that, it's not surprising that Native American folklore often described the creature as cannibalistic, supernatural, and dangerous. Other tales, however, said Sasquatch appeared to be frightened of humans and mostly kept to itself.

It wasn't until the 1900s, when more and more woodlands were being devoured in the name of progress, that Sasquatch sightings started to increase. It was believed that, though generally docile, the beast did have a mean streak when feeling threatened. In July 1924, Fred Beck and several others were mining in a mountainous area of Washington State. One evening, the group spotted and shot at what appeared to be an apelike creature. After fleeing to their cabin, the group was startled when several more hairy giants began banging on the walls, windows, and doors. For several hours, the creatures pummeled the cabin and threw large rocks at it before disappearing shortly before dawn. After several such encounters in the same general vicinity, the area was renamed Ape Canyon.

My, What Big Feet You Have!

In August 1958, Jerry Crew, a bulldozer operator, showed up for work at a wooded site in Bluff Creek, California. Walking up to his bulldozer, which had been left there overnight, Crew found giant footprints in the dirt. At first, they appeared to be the naked footprints of a man, but with one major difference—these feet were huge! After the tracks appeared on several occasions, Crew took a cast of one of them and brought it to *The Humboldt Times* in Eureka, California. The following day, the newspaper ran a front-page story, complete with photos of the footprint and a name for the creature: Bigfoot. The story and photographs hit the Associated Press, and the name stuck.

Even so, the event is still rife with controversy. Skeptics claim that it was Ray Wallace, not Bigfoot, who made the tracks as a practical joke on his brother Wilbur, who was Crew's supervisor. Apparently the joke backfired when Crew arrived at the site first and saw the prints before Wilbur. However, Ray Wallace never admitted to faking the tracks or having anything to do with perpetrating a hoax.

Video Evidence?

In 1967, in response to numerous Bigfoot sightings in northern California, Roger Patterson rented a 16mm video camera in hopes of filming the elusive creature. Patterson and his friend, Robert Gimlin, spent several days on horseback traveling though the Six Rivers National Forest without coming across as much as a footprint.

Then, on October 20, the pair rounded a bend and noticed something dark and hairy crouched near the water. When the creature stood up on two legs and presented itself in all its hairy, seven-foot glory, that's when Patterson said he knew for sure he was looking at Bigfoot. Unfortunately, Patterson's horse saw the creature, too, and suddenly reared up. Because of this, it took Patterson several precious seconds to get off the horse and remove the video camera from his saddlebag. Once he did that, he ran toward the creature, filming as he went.

As the creature walked away, Patterson continued filming until his tape ran out. He quickly changed his film, and then both men retrieved their frightened horses and attempted to follow Bigfoot further before eventually losing sight of it.

When they arrived back in town, Patterson reviewed the film. Even though it was less than a minute long and extremely shaky in spots, the film appeared to show Bigfoot running away while occasionally looking toward the camera. For most Bigfoot enthusiasts, the Patterson–Gimlin film stands as the Holy Grail of Bigfoot sightings—physical proof captured on video. Skeptics, however, alleged that Patterson and Gimlin faked the entire incident and filmed a man in an expensive monkey suit. Nevertheless, more than 40 years after the event occurred, the Patterson–Gimlin film is still one of the most talked about pieces of Bigfoot evidence, mainly because neither man ever admitted to a hoax and the fact that no one has been able to figure out how they faked it.

Gone Sasquatching

The fact that some people doubt the existence of Bigfoot hasn't stopped thousands of people from heading into the woods to try to find one. Even today, the hairy creature makes brief appearances here and there. Of course, sites like YouTube have given rise to dozens of "authentic" videos of Bigfoot, some of which are quite comical.

Still, every once in a while, a video that deserves a second look pops up. For example, in 2005, ferry operator Bobby Clarke filmed almost three minutes of video of a Bigfoot-like creature on the banks of the Nelson River in Manitoba.

Snakes Alive!

Residents of the town of Peninsula reported seeing a giant snake in several different places over a series of months in 1944. But was the "Peninsula Python" a real-life monster or just a hoax?

✳   ✳   ✳   ✳

GIANT SNAKES ARE no fantasy. Pythons ten feet or more in length are commonly found in South America. Closer to home, South Florida is seeing more than its share of sensationally large serpents as owners cast unwanted pets into the wild.

Unlike Florida, Ohio isn't famous for its weird flora and fauna. However, one of the state's most enduring legends is the so-called "Peninsula Python," a snake of frightening proportions that terrorized the town of Peninsula in the mid-1940s, and whose offspring, some believe, still inhabit the region's forests and marshes.

No Ordinary Snake

The Peninsula Python first made headlines in June 1944, when a farmer named Clarence Mitchell reported seeing it slithering across his cornfield. According to Mitchell, what he witnessed was no ordinary corn snake—it was at least 18 feet long, and so big around that its trail was the width of a tire track.

Two days later, the snake appeared again, this time leaving its huge track across Paul and John Szalay's fields. Two days after that, Mrs. Roy Vaughn called the fire department to report that some sort of giant reptile had climbed a fence, entered her henhouse, and devoured one of her chickens.

By then, the residents of Ohio had accepted the snake as real, and both the Cleveland and Columbus zoos offered a reward for its live capture. To calm fears, the Peninsula mayor's office formed a posse to hunt down the snake and bring it in—dead or alive.

Python Fever

Because giant pythons aren't exactly indigenous to Ohio, people speculated as to where the snake may have come from. The most popular theory was that it had escaped from a crashed carnival truck, a common explanation for unusual animal sightings.

The town of Peninsula quickly became "snake happy" as sightings of the Peninsula Python continued. On June 25, sirens alerted the posse to a sighting near Kelly Hill, but after searching through the prickly brush for a while, they were told it was a false alarm. Then, on June 27, Mrs. Pauline Hopko told authorities that the giant snake had leaped from a willow tree, frightening her, her dogs, and her milk cows, which broke their harnesses and hightailed it for fields afar. On the same day, a group of boys playing also reported seeing the snake.

Sightings became almost commonplace over the next few days. Mrs. Ralph Griffin said the snake reared up in the middle of her backyard, and Mrs. Katherine Boroutick alleged the behemoth fell from her butternut tree while she was getting rid of some trash down by the river. But every time the mayor's posse arrived at the scene of a reported sighting, the snake was nowhere to be found.

Myth or Real Creature?

The Peninsula Python continued to terrorize the residents of Peninsula through the summer and into the fall, when reports suddenly ceased. It was assumed that the bitter Ohio winter ultimately did the snake in, but no evidence of its remains was ever discovered.

Was the Python real? Many residents believe so, but others suspect that the whole thing was just a hoax perpetrated by writer Robert Bordner, a local resident whose account of the snake's mysterious appearance was published in the November 1945 issue of *Atlantic Monthly*.

Regardless, the town of Peninsula has heartily embraced the snake, and now celebrates the legend with an annual Peninsula Python Day. The celebration includes food, fun, and festivities such as a Python Scavenger Hunt, face painting, and a display of live snakes from the Akron Zoo—all of which are of normal size.

Local Legends

These alligator tales will have you crawling under your skin.

✳ ✳ ✳ ✳

THE MYTH THAT albino alligators sightlessly prowl the New York City sewer system has its roots in an alleged decades-old fad. Some say vacationers brought the infant 'gators home from Florida, while others insist that New York pet shops enjoyed a thriving trade in such babies (the reptiles sometimes sold in stores today are actually caimans, crocodilians from South America). When these 'gator tots grew too large for apartment dwelling, they were supposedly dispatched by flushing down the toilet—a trip these hardy creatures survived all the way down to the sewers, where, it was claimed, they evolved over the years, adapting to their new environment by becoming blind and losing their pigmentation. The legend grew legs, as it were, when an alleged eyewitness—a retired sewer official who swore he'd seen a colony of the things back in the 1930s—was quoted in a 1959 book entitled *The World Beneath the City.* Thomas Pynchon also wrote of them in his 1963 novel .

Reports of regular alligators in New York City might be a little

bit more believable.
In 1932, "swarms"
of alligators were
reportedly spotted
in the Bronx River,
and on February
10, 1935, the *New
York Times* wrote
that several urban
teens had pulled a
seven-footer from an
open manhole while
clearing snow—and
had beaten the beast

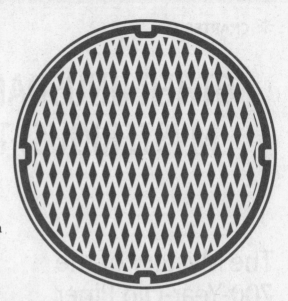

to death after it snapped at them. The paper suggested that perhaps the animal had escaped from a ship "from the mysterious
Everglades." Even before this—a full century earlier in 1831—a
little-known paper called *The Planet* noted a 'gator sighting in
the East River.

However, any herpetologist worth his or her scales will tell
you that it's impossible for the tropical-thriving 'gator to get
through a New York City winter, in polluted waters, no less.
One explained that alligators can't digest food when they're
cold. Plus, living without sun destroys their ability to utilize
calcium, which would result in too soft of a skeletal structure
for the creature to survive. As one spokesperson for the city's
Department of Environmental Protection, who has been deny-
ing the rumors for 30 years, wearily sighed: "Sewers simply are
not a prime environment for alligators."

But you're still going to check before you sit down,
though—right?

CHAPTER 11

OTHER UNUSUAL (AND MYSTERIOUS) TALES

The Mystery of the 700-Year-Old Piper

It's an intriguing story about a mysterious piper and more than 100 missing children. Made famous by the eponymous Brothers Grimm, this popular fairy tale has captivated generations of boys and girls. But is it actually more fact than fiction?

✳   ✳   ✳   ✳

THE LEGEND OF The Pied Piper of Hameln documents the story of a mysterious musician who rid a town of rats by enchanting the rodents with music from his flute. The musician led the mesmerized rats to a nearby river, where they drowned. When the townsfolk refused to settle their debt, the rat catcher returned several weeks later, charmed a group of 130 children with the same flute, and led them out of town. They disappeared—never to be seen again.

It's a story that dates back to approximately A.D. 1300 and has its roots in a small German town called Hameln. Several accounts written between the 14th and 17th centuries tell of a stained-glass window in the town's main church. The window pictured the Pied Piper with hands clasped, standing over a group of youngsters. Encircling the window was the following verse (this is a rough translation): "In the year 1284, on John's and Paul's day was the 26th of June. By a piper, dressed in all kinds of colors, 130 children born in Hameln were seduced and lost at the calvarie near the koppen."

The verse is specific: precise month and year, exact number of children involved in the incident, and detailed place names. Because of this, some scholars believe this window, which was removed in 1660 and either accidentally destroyed or lost, was created in memory of an actual event. Yet, the verse makes no mention of the circumstances regarding the departure of the children or their specific fate. What exactly happened in Hameln, Germany, in 1284? The truth is, no one actually knows—at least not for certain.

Theories Abound

Gernot Hüsam, a chairman of the Coppenbrügge Castle Museum, believes the word "koppen" in the inscription may reference a rocky outcrop on a hill in nearby Coppenbrügge, a small town previously known as Koppanberg. Hüsam also believes the use of the word "calvarie" is in reference to either the medieval connotation of the gates of hell—or since the Crusades—a place of execution.

One theory put forward is that Coppenbrügge resident Nikolaus von Spiegelberg recruited Hameln youth to emigrate to areas in Pomerania near the Baltic Sea. This theory suggests the youngsters were either murdered, because they took part in summertime pagan rituals, or drowned in a tragic accident while in transit to the new colonies.

But this is not the only theory. In fact, theories concerning the fate of the children abound. Here are some ideas about what really happened:

* They suffered from the Black Plague or a similar disease and were led from the town to spare the rest of the population.

* They were part of a crusade to the Holy Land.

* They were lost in the 1260 Battle of Sedemünder.

* They died in a bridge collapse over the Weser River or a landslide on Ith Mountain.

* They emigrated to settle in other parts of Europe, including Maehren, Oelmutz, Transylvania, or Uckermark.

* They were actually young adults who were led away and murdered for performing pagan rituals on a local mountain.

Historians believe that emigration, bridge collapse/natural disaster, disease, or murder are the most plausible explanations.

Tracing the Piper's Path

Regardless of what actually happened in Hameln hundreds of years ago, the legend of the Pied Piper has endured. First accounts of the Piper had roots to the actual incident, but as time passed, the story took on a life of its own.

Earliest accounts of the legend date back to 1384, at which time a Hameln church leader, Deacon von Lude, was said to be in possession of a chorus book with a Latin verse related to the legend written on the front cover by his grandmother. The book was misplaced in the late 17th century and has never been found.

The oldest surviving account—according to amateur Pied Piper historian Jonas Kuhn—appears as an addition to a 14th-century manuscript from Luneburg. Written in Latin, the note is almost identical to the verse on the stained-glass window and translates roughly to:

"In the year of 1284, on the day of Saints John and Paul on the 26th of June 130 children born in Hamelin were seduced By a piper, dressed in all kinds of colors, and lost at the place of execution near the koppen."

Sixteenth-century physician and philosopher Jobus Fincelius believed the Pied Piper was the devil. In his 1556 book

Concerning the Wonders of His Times, Fincelius wrote: "It came about in Hameln in Saxony on the River Weser . . . the Devil visibly in human form walked the lanes of Hameln and by playing a pipe lured after him many children . . . to a mountain. Once there, he with the children . . . could no longer be found."

In 1557, Count Froben Christoph von Zimmern wrote a chronicle detailing his family's lineage. Sprinkled throughout the book were several folklore tales including one that referenced the Pied Piper. For some unknown reason, the count intro- duced rats into his version of the story: "He passed through the streets of the town with his small pipe . . . immedi- ately all the rats . . . collected outside the houses and followed his footsteps." This first insertion of rodents into the legend led other writers to follow suit.

In 1802, Johan Wolfgang Goethe wrote "Der Rattenfanger," a poem based on the legend. The monologue was told in the first person through the eyes of the rat catcher. Goethe's poem made no direct reference to the town of Hameln, and in Goethe's ver- sion the Piper played a stringed instrument instead of a pipe. The Piper also made an appearance in Goethe's *Faust*.

Jacob and Wilhelm Grimm began collecting European folk- tales in the early 1800s. Best known for a series of books that documented 211 fairy tales, the brothers also published two volumes between 1816 and 1818 detailing almost 600 German folklore legends. One of the volumes contained the story of Der Rattenfanger von Hameln.

The Grimm brothers' research for The Pied Piper drew on 11 different sources, from which they deduced two children were left behind (a blind child and a mute child); the piper led the children through a cave to Transylvania; and a street in Hameln was named after the event.

No End in Sight

While the details of the historical event surrounding the legend of The Piped Piper have been lost to time, the mystique of the story endures. Different versions of the legend have even appeared in literature outside of Germany: A rat catcher from Vienna helped rid the nearby town of Korneuburg of rats. When he wasn't paid, he stole off with the town's children and sold them as slaves in Constantinople. A vagabond rid the English town of Newton on the Isle of Wight of their rats, and when he wasn't paid, led the town's children into an ancient oak forest where they were never seen again. A Chinese version had a Hangchow district official use magic to convince the rats to leave his city.

The legend's plot has been adapted over time to fit whichever media is currently popular and has been used as a story line in children's books, ballet, theatre, and even a radio drama. The intriguing story of the mysterious piper will continue to interest people as long as there is mystery surrounding the event.

Ahead of His Time

It's long been claimed that Dr. Joseph-Ignace Guillotin, the presumed creator of the guillotine, was put to death during the French Revolution by the decapitating contraption that bears his name. It would be the ultimate irony—if the story were true.

✳ ✳ ✳ ✳

BEFORE WE TAKE a closer look at this long-lived myth, we should probably clear up a larger misconception: Joseph Guillotin did not invent the guillotine. Mechanical beheading devices had long been used in Germany, Italy, Scotland, and elsewhere, though it was the French who made them famous.

The Good Doctor

Guillotin, a respected physician and member of the French National Assembly, opposed the death penalty. However, he realized that public executions weren't about to go out of style anytime soon, so he sought a more "humane" alternative to being drawn and quartered, which was the usual way that impoverished criminals were put to death.

A quick beheading, Guillotin argued, was far more merciful than being hacked apart by a dull ax. And it had the benefit of making executions socially equal, since beheading had been, until that time, the method of execution only for aristocratic convicts who could buy themselves a quicker, kinder death.

Guillotin hooked up with a German engineer and harpsichord maker named Tobias Schmidt, who built a prototype of the guillotine as we know it today. For a smoother cut, Schmidt suggested a diagonal blade rather than the round blade.

Heads Will Roll

The guillotine's heyday followed the French Revolution in 1789. After King Louis XVI had been imprisoned, the new civilian assembly rewrote the penal code to make beheading by guillotine the official method of execution for all convicted criminals—and there were a lot of them.

The first person to lose his head was Nicolas Jacques Pelletie, who was guillotined at Place de Greve on April 25, 1792. King Louis XVI felt the blade a year later, and thousands more followed. The last person to be publicly guillotined was convicted murderer Hamida Djandoubi, who died on September 10, 1977, in Marseilles.

Joseph Guillotin survived the French Revolution with his head attached, though he was forever stigmatized by his connection with the notorious killing machine. He died in 1814 from an infected carbuncle on his shoulder, and his children later petitioned the government for the right to change their last name, not wanting to be associated with their father's grisly past.

A common belief often associated with the guillotine is that people who are beheaded remain conscious for several agonizing seconds—and even respond to stimulus. Whether or not this is true remains open to debate. Many scientists believe that death is almost instantaneous, while others cite anecdotal evidence that suggests the deceased are well aware of what has happened to them.

Indeed, stories abound of "experiments" during the height of the guillotine boom in which doctors and others made agreements with condemned prisoners to determine once and for all if the head "lived" on for moments after being severed.

One story claims that Charlotte Corday, who was guillotined for killing Jean-Paul Marat, looked indignant when the executioner held her severed head aloft and slapped her across the face. However, it was also claimed that her cheeks reddened as a result of the slap, which seems unlikely given the loss of blood. It's been said that other severed heads have blinked or moved their eyes when spoken to, and some have allegedly bitten their executioners.

Most doctors agree that the brain may remain active for as long as 15 seconds after a beheading. Whether the individual is actually aware of what has transpired remains a medical mystery that likely will never be answered.

A Sewer Story

The moral of this tale? Don't flush unwanted pets down the toilet.

❊ ❊ ❊ ❊

THE URBAN LEGEND goes like this: In the early 20th century, some denizens of Gotham thought that baby alligators made great gifts for kids. Apparently, these knuckleheads couldn't foresee that cute baby alligators would become ugly, adult limb-manglers.

When the gators grew and became dangerous, these New Yorkers flushed the animals into the city's sewer system. There, these warm-climate amphibians found a friendly enough environment, and abandoned alligators, it was said, formed a thriving colony beneath the Manhattan streets.

Fueling the legend was Robert Daley's 1959 book *The World Beneath the City*. According to the book, Teddy May, a former sewer superintendent, claimed that in the 1930s he saw gators as long as two feet in the sewer tunnels. May said that he ordered his charges to kill the reptiles and that it took a few months to complete the job.

Indeed, the 1930s were a golden age for news stories of alligator sightings in and around the city. Oddly, accounts involving the sewer system were rare. Most reports involved surface-level encounters, and the critters in question are believed to have been escaped pets. A February 1935 article in the *New York Times* told of a group of boys who discovered that the manhole into which they were shoveling snow contained an alligator. They used a clothesline to drag the reptile up to the street, then beat it to death with their shovels. Welcome to the Big Apple.

Curiously, no contemporary news coverage of Teddy May's extended alligator hunt can be found. Subsequent published reports painted May as a bit of a raconteur who quite possibly was having some fun at the expense of author Daley. We're not saying you won't encounter some sort of underground wildlife in NYC, but you're more likely to find it on the subway than in the sewers.

Ezekiel's Wheel: What in the World? Vision? UFO?

This scriptural passage is responsible for some of the most interesting speculation in the Bible's history. What was Ezekiel seeing?

✳ ✳ ✳ ✳

Scriptural Description

GOING TO THE source (Ezekiel 1), first the prophet describes some extremely strange living creatures in a fiery cloud: humanoids with four faces (human, eagle, ox, lion), four wings, bronze bodies, surrounding something like fiery coals. Then (verses 15–21):

As I looked at the living creatures, I saw a wheel on the earth beside the living creatures, one for each of the four of them. As for the appearance of the wheels and their construction: their appearance was like the gleaming of beryl; and the four had the same form, their construction being something like a wheel within a wheel. When they moved, they moved in any of the four directions without veering as they moved. Their rims were tall and awesome, for the rims of all four were full of eyes all around. When the living creatures moved, the wheels moved beside them; and when the living creatures rose from the earth, the wheels rose. Wherever the spirit would go, they went, and the wheels rose along with them; for the spirit of the living creatures was in the wheels. When they moved, the others moved; when they stopped, the others stopped; and when they rose from the earth, the wheels rose along with them; for the spirit of the living creatures was in the wheels.

Any lesser person than an Old Testament prophet of God might take a few aspirin and swear off "drink" for life.

Otherworldly Interpretations

Plenty of artists have tried to depict Ezekiel's wheel. Most efforts look like gyroscopes: two shining circles intersecting. Picture a globe with a steel-blue ring around the equator. Imagine another metallic ring at a right angle to the first, passing through the North and South Poles. Subtract the globe. Could this be an ancient spaceship? All we have going for us is our science-fiction ideas of alien spacecraft. Some very educated minds suggest that Ezekiel is indeed describing a credible alien spaceship. We can't prove either way.

One book that fueled much of the speculation was *Chariots of the Gods* (1968, Erich von Däniken). Von Däniken's thesis— that many ancient writings about gods, including the Bible, refer to contact with aliens—is unacceptable to most believers. Therefore, his thesis hasn't gained lasting traction with Jews and Christians. Nevertheless, some suspect that, with regard to Ezekiel 1, von Däniken had a grain of the truth.

Non-Science-Fiction Views

Since we can only speculate, let's do so: The simplest explanation might be an angelic vision of the Lord's might. Ezekiel seems to have thought so (see Ezekiel 10) when he reflected on the matter. Perhaps the four forms represent archangels. They could also represent the four Gospels, identifying Matthew with the lion, Mark with the ox, Luke with the man, and John with the eagle.

Considering that Ezekiel's vision came from God, one might consider the "rims . . . full of eyes all around" to mean that God sees everything in all directions. One supposes that Ezekiel, as a believer, wouldn't normally need a reminder of this—but perhaps the Lord felt he did, or he wanted to dramatize it. That veers into trying to guess God's motives, which is problematic for the human mind.

One mainstream Jewish view, according to rabbinic wisdom and analysis, is that Ezekiel saw a heavenly chariot/throne bearing *Hashem* (God). It represented a vision of the Lord, a symbol of his ultimate generosity in showing his glory to his people. Given the location—near Babylon (modern Iraq)—it could foretell the equipment the region's main product (oil) would fuel someday.

We don't know. We can, however, compare the theories of the learned and determine for ourselves with the minds God gave us.

Time Travelers

Hold on to your hat—you're in for a wild, mind-blowing ride back and forth through the realms of time!

✳   ✳   ✳   ✳

IN 2013, MANY people didn't believe President Obama when he claimed that he often fired guns on the skeet shooting range at Camp David. But others believed that Obama had actually come close to revealing the "real" truth: that he has been working for the CIA for more than 30 years, and that he had personally used the CIA's top secret "jump room" to visit Mars on several occasions as a young man.

However, there's at least one witness who claims to have known the future president in his Mars-hopping days: a Seattle attorney named Andrew Basiago, who also only claims to have been to Mars himself as an Earth ambassador to a Martian civilization in the early 1980s.

But by then, Basiago says, he was an old hand with the CIA: some years before, when he was only 12, he was a participant in a top secret initiative called "Project Pegasus," an elite force that used "radiant energy" principles discovered in the papers of inventor Nikola Tesla to travel through time.

Basiago claims that he traveled through time using eight different technologies as a boy, but mainly using a teleporter that consisted of two "elliptical booms" that stood eight feet tall, positioned about ten feet apart and separated by a curtain of "radiant energy." Participants would jump through the curtain and enter a "vortal tunnel" that took them through time and space. By jumping though, Basiago claims to have attended Ford's Theatre on the night Abraham Lincoln was shot more than once - often enough that on a few occasions, he saw himself, on other trips, among the crowd. Oddly, though this would imply that each "jump" took him to the same "timeline," he says that every time he attended the theatre, the events of the night came off slightly differently, as though he were going to different "timelines" on each trip.

But Lincoln's assassination wasn't the only historic event Basiago claims to have attended. In 1972, he says, he used a "plasma confinement chamber" in East Hanover, New Jersey, to travel back to 1863 to see the Gettysburg Address. Basiago even claims that photographic evidence of this exists; In the foreground of the one photograph of Lincoln at Gettysburg that exists stands a young boy in oversized men's shoes, standing casually outside of the crowd in the background. Basiago says that the boy is him.

Basiago told his story over the course of several appearances on Coast to Coast AM, a radio program where conspiracies, UFOs, hauntings, and other strange phenomena are discussed during late night broadcasts. The online forums on which listeners discuss the topics spoken about on the show once brought forth the story of another alleged time traveler: the story of John Titor, who began posting on the forum in 2000 and claimed to be a time traveler from 2036. Physicists tried to drill him on the mathematics and theories behind time travel, and he seemed to pass every test.

Titor claimed that he was a soldier based in Tampa who was visiting year 2000 for personal reasons—perhaps to collect old family photos that had been destroyed by his time. He even posted schematics showing the devices he used to travel in time, and many became convinced that he was telling the truth.

However, the stories he told about the future of the United States failed to come to pass. In 2001, he claimed that unrest in America surrounding the 2004 presidential election would gradually build up until it became a full-on Civil War, broadly defined as a war between urban and rural parts of the country eventually splitting the United States into five regions. In 2011, he claimed, he was a young teenage soldier for a group called The Fighting Diamondbacks fighting for the rural armies. But the war, he said, would end in 2015 when Russia launched a nuclear assault destroying most American cities, killing as many as half of the people in the country and creating a "new" America in which Omaha, Nebraska served as the nation's capital. Titor said there was an upside to this: in many ways, he said, the world was better with half of the people gone.

Titor's odd story found a lot of supporters when it was first posted, and the events of September 11, 2001 convinced many people that World War III was, in fact, at hand. However, the 2004 election came and went without anything happening in the United States that could ever reasonably be called a civil war breaking out. There was still no such war going in 2008, either, by which time Titor claimed that the war would be fully raging and undeniable.

Fans of Coast to Coast AM are certainly not the only people who claim to have traveled through time, though, and some of the supposed time travelers have far more bona fide military credentials than Titor, who eventually disappeared from the forums. In 1935, Sir Victor Goddard, an air marshall in the Royal Air Force, claimed that he flew into a strange storm while flying his plane above an airfield in Scotland. The turbulence was so bad that he nearly crashed, and he emerged from the storm to find that the landscape beneath him now contained strange-looking aircraft in hangars that weren't there before, all attended by officers wearing blue uniforms instead of the brown ones the RAF normally used. Four years later, the RAF officially changed the uniforms from brown to blue and began using planes like the ones he had seen after the "storm."

This wasn't Goddard's only brush with the unknown. A decade later, he overheard an officer telling of a dream he'd had in which Air Marshall Goddard had died in a wreck when the plane he was flying in iced over and crashed on a beach. That night, Goddard's plane did, indeed, ice over, and an emergency landing was forced on a beach. Though the dream had ended with Goddard dead, Goddard, having had a sort of early warning, kept his cool and brought the plane safely down. The dream he overheard may very well have saved his life.

Space Ghosts

Shortly after the Soviet Union successfully launched Sputnik 1 on October 4, 1957, rumors swirled that several cosmonauts had died during missions gone horribly wrong, and their spacecraft had drifted out of Earth's orbit and into the vast reaches of the universe.

✳ ✳ ✳ ✳

IT WAS EASY to believe such stories at the time. After all, the United States was facing off against the Soviet Union in the Cold War, and the thought that the ruthless Russians would do anything to win the space race—including sending cosmonauts to their doom—seemed plausible.

However, numerous researchers have investigated the stories and concluded that, though the Soviet space program was far from perfect and some cosmonauts had in fact died, there are no dead cosmonauts floating in space.

According to authors Hal Morgan and Kerry Tucker, the earliest rumors of deceased cosmonauts even mentioned their names and the dates of their doomed missions: Aleksei Ledovsky in 1957, Serenti Shiborin in 1958, and Mirya Gromova in 1959. In fact, by the time Yuri Gagarin became the first human in space in April 1961, the alleged body count exceeded a dozen.

Space Spies

So prevalent were these stories that no less an "authority" than *Reader's Digest* reported on them in its April 1965 issue. Key to the mystery were two brothers in Italy, Achille and Giovanni Battista Judica-Cordiglia, who operated a homemade listening post with a huge dish antenna. Over a seven-month period, the brothers claimed to have overheard radio signals from three troubled Soviet spacecraft:

* On November 28, 1960, a Soviet spacecraft supposedly radioed three times, in Morse code and in English, "SOS to the entire world."

* In early February 1961, the brothers are alleged to have picked up the sound of a rapidly beating heart and labored breathing, which they interpreted to be the final throes of a dying cosmonaut.

* On May 17, 1961, two men and a woman were allegedly overheard saying, in Russian, "Conditions growing worse. Why don't you answer? We are going slower . . . the world will never know about us."

The Black Hole of Soviet PR

One reason rumors of dead cosmonauts were so believable was the extremely secretive nature of the early Soviet space program. Whereas the United States touted its program as a major advance in science and its astronauts as heroes, the Soviet Union revealed little about its program or people involved.

It's not surprising, then, that the Soviet Union did not report to the world the death of Valentin Bondarenko, a cosmonaut who died tragically in a fire after he tossed an alcohol-soaked cotton ball on a hot plate and ignited the oxygen-rich chamber in which he was training. He died in 1961, but it wasn't revealed publicly until 1986.

Adding to the rumors was the fact that other cosmonauts had been mysteriously airbrushed out of official government photographs. However, most had been removed because they had been dropped from the space program for academic, disciplinary, or medical reasons—not because they had died during a mission. One cosmonaut, Grigoriy Nelyubov, was booted from the program in 1961 for engaging in a drunken brawl at a rail station (he died five years later when he stepped in front of a train). Nelyubov's story, like so many others, was not made public until the mid-1980s.

Only one Soviet cosmonaut is known to have died during an actual space mission. In 1967, Vladimir Komarov was killed when the parachute on his *Soyuz 1* spacecraft failed to open properly during reentry. A Russian engineer later acknowledged that Komarov's mission had been ordered before the spacecraft had been fully debugged, likely for political reasons.

Ghostly Encounters by the Average Joe

There's something fascinating about a ghost story. And sometimes the scariest, eeriest, and most mysterious tales are about the personal encounters that regular people—people just like you—have with the paranormal. The following accounts were shared on the television show My Ghost Story; *they'll leave you wondering what you'd do if you encountered a ghost.*

✳ ✳ ✳ ✳

Footprints on the Bed

UNEXPLAINED NOISES AND cabinet doors opening on their own were the first clues that Marci Smith's home in rural Maryland might be haunted. And it only got worse from there. She felt something move across her feet at night, but there were no signs of rodents, so she set up a video camera to record her bedroom while she was sleeping. What she captured convinced her that something otherworldly was sharing her house. A misty figure that looked like a phantom cat was seen jumping onto the bed. Later in the video, the blankets depressed as if an unseen presence was walking across the bed.

Marci called in paranormal investigators, who set up audio and video recorders in the house. Several voices were captured, ranging from children to elderly people. Marci said that the house seems perfectly normal during the daytime. But at night? Well, let's just say that she's never really alone.

One Cool Spirit

If anyone would be safe from a ghostly encounter, it would surely be someone in the security business, right? Wrong. A policeman of nearly 24 years, Ron Colbert had a supernatural experience while working security for the city of Anderson, South Carolina. One night, while monitoring security cameras in Anderson's municipal building with IT Director Mark Cunningham, Colbert saw a ghostly orb move across the deserted lobby of the city's credit union. The pair cleaned the camera, adjusted the blinds, moved a chair, and finally replaced the camera in an effort to explain the phenomenon, but the orb kept coming back, and employees became spooked. Incidentally, the lobby was the coldest room in the building, with temperatures never rising above 60 degrees. Perhaps the spirit was cold-hearted because after space heaters were brought in to warm up the room, the orb was never seen again.

The Spirited Giraffe

When Nicholas Honkoski's father acquired a two-foot-tall porcelain giraffe statue from Africa, life started to get a little weird in the family's house in San Gabriel, California. Nick and his cousin Cody heard strange noises, so they decided to set up a video camera to record while they were sleeping. They were astounded by what they saw when they reviewed the footage: The giraffe was moving across the floor by itself! They even captured a partial apparition: a ghostly arm that reached out to grab Cody. The pair also picked up EVPs (electronic voice phenomena), and Cody saw the reflection of Nick's deceased grandfather in a mirror. One morning, the giraffe figurine was mysteriously found shattered; after that, everything returned to normal. The cousins never did figure out the connection between the giraffe and the spirit world, but they weren't sad when the haunting ceased.

An Ordinary Guy Meets a Long-Dead Actress

After David Oman built a house next to the Los Angeles–area dwelling where five people were murdered by the Manson Family in 1969, he was "welcomed" by a few uninvited guests. During his first night in his new home, he awoke to see the full-bodied apparition of a man. He got up to investigate, and when he asked who was there, he was shocked to hear, "It's Sharon." That would be Sharon Tate, the actress who was eight-and-a-half months pregnant when she was brutally murdered by Charles Manson's followers. Items that disappear and reappear in other places, objects that crash to the ground on their own, a palpable energy, and a photo showing an orb within an orb (which indicates a pregnant spirit) are just some of the phenomena David has encountered there. He said that he has learned to live with his invisible roommates, but his friends prefer to gather elsewhere.

Aesop: Was the Fantastic Fabler a Fable Himself?

Aesop's tales of talking animals—the industrious ant and the irresponsible grasshopper, or the fast but arrogant rabbit and the plodding but persistent tortoise—have been a staple of traditional folklore for centuries. But as it turns out, Aesop himself may have been as much a fable as his famous tales.

✳ ✳ ✳ ✳

I T'S FUN TO tell Aesop's tales—especially since many of them take the air out of someone else's inflated ego or show the comic consequences of someone else's bad behavior. And with talking animals to boot! What's not to love?

Who Was Aesop?

By various traditions, Aesop (620–560 B.C.?) was a slave from Phrygia (central Turkey), Thrace (northern Greece), Sardis (western Turkey), or Ethiopia (horn of Africa), who was brought to the Greek island of Samos in the early 6th century B.C. and was eventually set free because of his wit and wisdom.

What we actually know of his life may be as fictional as his stories. Aesop's first official biography wasn't composed until the 14th century, and it was composed for the purposes of entertainment—not history. In it, Aesop appears as an unsightly, ungainly, and clever rogue who is always undermining and outwitting his master with his clever use of language. In one instance, when his master Xanthus has given precise directions for fixing "a lentil soup" for a special dinner party, Aesop fixes one boiled lentil and then avoids punishment by forcing the embarrassed Xanthus to admit that Aesop was only following his directions. In this version, Aesop the fabler is a subversive figure who turns the tables on the powerful—a trickster as common to folklore around the world as animal stories. Later biographies frame Aesop as a serious moral teacher and take most of the fun out of him. He becomes, after meritoriously winning freedom, a famous personality of the court of the Lydian King Croesus in Sardis (modern Sart, Turkey). Besides amazing the king and all the wisest men of the day, Aesop traveled about Greece instructing the powerful with his fables.

Even Aesop's death became a fable with as pointed a moral as any of his tales. He was framed and executed by dishonest men at Delphi (a famous Greek shrine) when he refused to distribute some of Croesus's gold (which the king had sent to the shrine as a gift) because of the men's greed. However, ensuing disasters forced the guilty to fess up, and so the "the blood of Aesop" became a proverb for dishonest deeds that eventually come to light and come home to roost.

So, Was There an Aesop?

Well, perhaps. The Greeks and Romans certainly thought there was. But, as with Homer, the famous bard who traditionally composed the *Iliad* and *Odyssey*, whether the author created the works or the works created the author is open for debate. Just as Demodocus, the blind bard who appears in Book Eight of the *Odyssey*, may have suggested the tradition that Homer was blind, so too the sly and satirical characters of the fables may have helped to create the character that became Aesop. In any case, both Aesop's fables and life make for "fabulous" reading.

A Railroad to Nowhere

When we think of scandals, the Union Pacific Railroad probably isn't the first thing to come to mind. But this 32,000-mile freight hauling system was part of one of the earliest American political corruption controversies.

✳ ✳ ✳ ✳

A Railroad to Nowhere?

IN THE 1860s, the federal government agreed to provide the Union Pacific Railroad with $100 million in capital to help build a transcontinental rail line from the Missouri River to the Pacific coast. The project was daunting: it would require 1,750 miles of rail construction through some of the harshest environments in the country. And once finished, the route would be unpopular with travelers, as the western United States was mostly undeveloped east of the California border. In fact, many who opposed the new railway called it a "railroad to nowhere" and saw it as an unprofitable venture.

A Company within a Company

Because of the predicted difficulties and the fact that few passengers would likely pay to use the new railway, private financers refused to invest in the project. So, Union Pacific corporate leaders, including entrepreneur George Francis Train and Union Pacific vice president Thomas C. Durant, came up with an idea. They formed a business called Credit Mobilier of America in 1864 and portrayed it as a construction company. The group convinced not only the general public but also the government that this fake company had agreed to be the principle contractor for the railroad project. Union Pacific representatives then made agreements with Credit Mobilier to construct the new railway at rates that were significantly higher than the actual cost.

Union Pacific billed the U.S. government with the invoices from Credit Mobilier, which reflected the inflated prices. Since the two companies were presumably independent of one another, no one questioned the costs. While the operating costs of the construction added up to $50,720,959, the U.S. government paid a total of $94,650,287, a profit of $43,929,328 for Credit Mobilier. This "profit" made the fake company a huge success, and their stock began to soar.

Congressional Complicity

But there's even more to the story. In 1867, Credit Mobilier replaced Thomas C. Durant with Massachusetts Congressman Oakes Ames. Ames began to offer members of Congress Credit Mobilier stock at par value, which was much cheaper than its market value. The congressmen could then sell their shares at market value to investors eager to own stock in the "successful" company. In return, the members of Congress granted Credit Mobilier generous government subsidies and land grants.

Participants in the corruption barely tried to hide it, with both Union Pacific and Credit Mobilier stockholders getting rich off the scheme. So it's not surprising that public suspicion began to grow, and in 1872, the New York City newspaper *The Sun* broke the story of the scandal. The paper reported that Credit Mobilier had received far more money for the railroad than it had actually cost to build, and many investors were bankrupt.

Congress investigated 13 lawmakers who were accused in the scam. These included the incoming Vice President Henry Wilson—who was able to prove that he had paid for stock in his wife's name and with her money—and James A. Garfield, who denied any involvement and was later elected president. Also accused was Vice President Schuyler Colfax, who subsequently left politics and never ran for office again. In a strange twist of fate in this train tale, Colfax died in 1885–after he suffered a heart attack while running to catch a train.

Nancy Drew and the Hardy Boys: The Mystery of the Ghostwriters

Nancy Drew and the Hardy Boys may be aces at uncovering secrets, but the real secret lies in the origins of these teen detective novels. The credited authors—Carolyn Keene and Franklin W. Dixon—are as fictitious as the teen sleuths themselves. And all are the brainchildren of early 20th-century children's literature magnate Edward Stratemeyer.

✳ ✳ ✳ ✳

Fiction Factory

EDWARD STRATEMEYER WAS a successful juvenile fiction writer—so successful that he didn't have time to finish all of the books assigned to him. So he assembled a group of ghostwriters to help, and around 1904–1906 (sources vary), Stratemeyer Syndicate was born.

The process functioned like an assembly line: Stratemeyer developed the outlines and character descriptions, farmed them to ghostwriters who worked under the pseudonym assigned to each series, and then he edited each story to ensure consistency across the series. The ghostwriters received a meager $75 to $150 and gave up "all right, title and interest" as well as "use [of] such pen name in any manner whatsoever."

Mystery Makers

Following the syndicate's first successful ventures—the Bobbsey Twins and Tom Swift—Stratemeyer masterminded what would become his greatest legacies.

In 1927, mystery-solving teen brothers Frank and Joe Hardy, aka the Hardy Boys, debuted, authored primarily by Canadian writer Leslie McFarlane under the pseudonym Franklin W. Dixon. Two years later, all-American girl sleuth Nancy Drew hit the scene, written mostly by Mildred Wirt under the pen name Carolyn Keene.

Unfortunately, Stratemeyer would not live to see the success of Nancy Drew; he died just two weeks after the first books, *The Secret of the Old Clock*, *The Hidden Staircase*, and *The Bungalow Mystery*, hit stands in April 1930.

Initially, Stratemeyer's daughters, Edna and Harriet, hoped to sell the syndicate, but it was the height of the Great Depression, and buyers were scarce. So the two sisters—primarily Harriet—took over the business. They managed the ghostwriters and, above all, endeavored to keep their authors' identities secret.

Ghostbusters

In 1958, the syndicate's publisher, Grossett & Dunlap, requested an update of the books for contemporary audiences. Harriet, who had severed the syndicate's ties with Mildred Wirt five years earlier, assumed the rewriting of Nancy Drew herself and even added new titles to the series. Suddenly, despite her previous reticence, Harriet began claiming publicly that she was the real Carolyn Keene and always had been.

In 1980, Harriet sold the Nancy Drew series to Simon & Schuster, who made national fanfare over the series' 50th anniversary, touting Harriet as the originator. Wirt, along with Grossett & Dunlap, promptly sued—and promptly lost. The media had a field day with the "real" Carolyn Keene.

Simon & Schuster subsumed the entire syndicate following Harriet's death in 1982. Despite evidence to the contrary, her obituary lamented the passing of the real Carolyn Keene. Twenty years later, Mildred Wirt's did the same.

* Stratemeyer initially named his heroine Stella Strong, with alternate suggestions of Diana Drew, Diana Dare, Nan Nelson, Nan Drew, and Helen Hale. Not a fan of the name Stella, Grosset & Dunlap chose Nan Drew and lengthened it to Nancy.

* The original rules for the series included "no smooching." Neither Frank, Joe, nor Nancy enjoyed so much as a peck until the 1980s, after Simon & Schuster took over. However, Nancy does faint into "the strong arms" of her boyfriend, Ned Nickerson.

* In 1959, Nancy's car was updated from a roadster to a convertible. Today, she drives a hybrid.

The Smurl Incident

In the 1970s, the "Amityville Horror" story ignited a firestorm of controversy that's still debated today. The Smurl haunting is another incident that's not as well known but is equally divisive.

✳ ✳ ✳ ✳

Spirit Rumblings

I N 1973, JACK and Janet Smurl and their daughters Dawn and Heather moved into a duplex in West Pittston, Pennsylvania. Jack's parents occupied half of the home and Jack and Janet took the other. Nothing out of the ordinary occurred during the first 18 months that they lived there, but then odd things started to happen: Water pipes leaked repeatedly, even though they had been soldered and resoldered; claw marks were found on the bathtub, sink, and woodwork; an unexplained stain appeared on the carpet; a television burst into flames; and Dawn saw people floating in her bedroom.

In 1977, Jack and Janet welcomed twin daughters Shannon and Carin to the family. By then, the home had become Spook Central: Unplugged radios played, drawers opened and closed with no assistance, toilets flushed on their own, empty porch chairs rocked back and forth, and putrid smells circulated throughout the house.

Unfortunately, by 1985, events at the Smurl home had taken a dangerous turn. The house was always cold, and Jack's parents often heard angry voices coming from their son's side of the duplex, even though Jack and Janet were not arguing.

In February of that year, Janet was alone in the basement doing laundry when something called her name several times. A few days later, she was alone in the kitchen when the room became frigid; suddenly, a faceless, black, human-shaped form appeared. It then walked through the wall and was witnessed by Jack's mother.

At this point, the situation became even more bizarre. On the night Heather was confirmed into the Catholic faith, Shannon was nearly killed when a large light fixture fell from the ceiling and landed on her. On another night, Janet was violently pulled off the bed as Jack lay next to her, paralyzed and unable to help his wife as a foul odor nearly suffocated him. Periodically, heavy footsteps were heard in the attic, and rapping and scratching sounds came from the walls. Not even the family dog escaped: It was repeatedly picked up and thrown around.

"Who You Gonna Call?"

Unwilling to be terrorized out of their home, in January 1986, the Smurls contacted psychic researchers and demonologists Ed and Lorraine Warren, who confirmed that the home was haunted by four evil spirits, including a powerful demon. The Warrens theorized that the emotions generated as the older Smurl daughters entered puberty had somehow awoken a dormant demon.

The Warrens tried prayer and playing religious music, but this only angered the demon even more. It spelled out "You filthy bastard. Get out of this house" on a mirror, violently shook drawers, filled the TV set with an eerie white light, and slapped and bit Jack and Janet.

One day, Janet decided to try communicating with the demon on her own. She told it to rap once for "yes" if it was there to harm them; it rapped once. Next, the entity unleashed a new weapon: sexual assault. A red-eyed, green-gummed succubus with an old woman's face and a young woman's body raped Jack. An incubus sexually assaulted Janet, Dawn was nearly raped, and Carin fell seriously ill with a high fever. Pig noises—which supposedly signal a serious demonic infestation—emanated from the walls.

The Smurls could not escape even by leaving their home. The creature followed them on camping trips and even bothered Jack at his job, giving new meaning to the phrase "work is hell." The family appealed to the Catholic Church for help but to no avail. However, a renegade clergyman named Robert F. McKenna did try to help the Smurls by performing an exorcism in the spring of 1986, but even that didn't help.

Going Public

Finally, in August 1986, the family went to the media with their story. The incidents continued, but the publicity drew the attention of Paul Kurtz, chairman of the Buffalo-based Committee for the Scientific Investigation of Claims of the Paranormal (CSICOP). He offered to investigate, but the Smurls turned him down, stating that they wanted to stay with the Warrens and the Church. They were also concerned that CSICOP had already decided that their story was a hoax.

The Smurls did, however, contact a medium, who came to the same conclusion as the Warrens—that there were four spirits in the home: One she couldn't identify, but she said that the others were an old woman named Abigail, a murderer named Patrick, and a very strong demon.

Another exorcism was performed in the summer of 1986, and that seemed to do the trick because the incidents stopped. But just before Christmas of that year, the black form appeared again, along with the banging noises, foul odors, and other phenomena.

Surrender

The Smurls finally moved out of the home in 1988; the next owner said that she never experienced any supernatural events while she lived there.

That same year, *The Haunted*, a book based on the Smurl family's experiences, was released. And in 1991, a TV movie with the same title aired.

But the controversy surrounding the alleged haunting was just beginning. In an article written for *The Skeptical Inquirer*, CSICOP's official magazine, Paul Kurtz cited financial gains from the book deal as a reason to doubt that the incidents were authentic. He also said that for years, residents in the area had complained about foul odors coming from a sewer pipe. He cited other natural explanations for some of the incidents and raised questions about Dawn Smurl's accounts of some of the events. He further claimed that the Warrens gave him a number of conflicting reasons for why he couldn't see the video and audio evidence that they said they'd compiled.

And that's where matters stand today, with the true believers in the Smurl family's account on one side and the doubters on the other. Like the Amityville incident, the Smurl haunting is likely to be debated for a long time to come.

Samuel Clemens's Psychic Dream

One night in the late 1850s, Samuel Clemens—better known as Mark Twain—woke up clutching the sheets on his bed; his palms were sweaty and his heart was pounding. It had been so real, he thought . . . so vivid. Had it really been just a dream, or did it actually happen? And if it was indeed a dream, it was more like a nightmare.

✳ ✳ ✳ ✳

IN THE LATE 1850s—before he was world-renowned author and humorist Mark Twain—Samuel Clemens worked as an apprentice riverboat pilot on the *Pennsylvania*. His younger brother Henry also worked on the vessel as a "mud clerk"—a hard and dreary job that was barely one step above indentured servitude. But Henry stuck with it, enticed by the possibility of a promotion to a superior position on the steamboat.

While the ship was docked in St. Louis, Samuel stayed with his sister and brother-in-law, who lived in town, and Henry would often drop by to visit before returning to his shipboard duties. In May 1858, Henry was unusually solemn as he prepared to return to the *Pennsylvania*; it was not like him to be so somber.

Did That Really Just Happen?

That night, Samuel saw images in a dream that was frighteningly realistic. He saw Henry lying in a coffin that was balanced on two chairs in the sitting room of their sister's house. Henry was wearing a suit of Samuel's, and in his hands—which were folded on his chest—he held a bouquet of white roses with one red rose in the middle.

When Samuel awoke, he didn't know whether he had just had a dream or if the events were real. Was his brother dead? His mind spun; he decided that he must find out. Samuel leaped out of bed and charged into the sitting room where he had seen the coffin during his dream. To his relief, the room was empty.

Later that day, as he piloted the *Pennsylvania* down the Mississippi River to New Orleans, Samuel couldn't get the dream out of his mind. Unfortunately, on the trip downriver, Samuel got into an argument with the owner of the steamer and was relieved of his duties when the *Pennsylvania* reached New Orleans; however, Henry remained on board.

A Nightmare Becomes Reality

Several days later, the *Pennsylvania* left on its return trip to St. Louis. As it approached Memphis, the boat's boilers exploded with a roar. Dozens of people were killed and wounded.

Samuel heard about the horrible accident and quickly made his way to Memphis. After he arrived, he searched high and low for his brother until he found him on a mattress in a warehouse that had been turned into a hospital to treat accident victims. Henry had inhaled red-hot steam and was not expected to live. But he fought back, and his condition slowly improved.

One night, the agonizing screams of those in the makeshift hospital were getting the best of Henry, so a physician ordered a small dose of morphine to help him sleep. But the person who administered the drug gave Henry too much: He overdosed and died before morning broke.

The body of Henry Clemens was dressed in one of Samuel's suits, placed in a coffin, and displayed in a viewing room at the makeshift hospital. As Samuel was mourning near his brother's casket, a woman placed a bouquet of white roses with one red rose in the center in his dead brother's hands.

Samuel was stunned. His chilling dream—or rather nightmare—had come true.

Henry's coffin was sent back to his sister's house in St. Louis. Samuel arrived there just before the coffin was placed in the sitting room. There, two chairs sat spaced apart, waiting to receive the coffin. It was the final detail of Samuel's psychic dream come true.

Samuel Clemens was so deeply affected by his prophetic dream that foreshadowed his brother's death that 24 years later, he joined the Society for Psychical Research, a British group of supporters of paranormal studies.

Ten Alleged Cases of Feral Children

According to legend, ancient Rome was founded by twin brothers Romulus and Remus, who had both been nursed by a female wolf. Since then, there have been hundreds of stories about children being raised by animals. Some of these reports are simply hoaxes. In other cases, the children are not literally feral but are the victims of abusive parents. There are, however, some surprising incidents in recent history that could give the phrase "a walk on the wild side" a whole new meaning.

✳   ✳   ✳   ✳

1. In 2007, a young boy was reported to be living among wolves in the Kaluga Region of Central Russia. He was captured and sent to an orphanage in Moscow, but he managed to escape and is thought to be living in the wild.

2. Traian Caldarar of Brasov, Romania, became lost and lived among stray dogs between the ages of four and seven. In 2002, he was discovered and returned to his mother. He eventually relearned human language and became a normal boy again.

3. In 2004, social workers found seven-year-old Andrei Tolstyk living in an abandoned house in Bespalovskoya, Siberia, with only a dog for company. They believe he had survived there for almost seven years after his alcoholic parents deserted him when he was an infant. He was placed in an orphanage but reportedly never learned to speak.

4. One of Russia's most famous "wild boys" not only lived

with dogs, he actually became leader of his pack. In 1998, six-year-old Ivan Mishukov was finally separated from his beloved pack of stray dogs and placed in a Moscow orphanage. Because he had only been living among the dogs for two years, he was able to relearn language fairly rapidly.

5. Abandoned by her parents at age three, Oxana Malaya of the Ukrainian village of Novaya Blagoveschenka spent five years among wild dogs. Rescued at the age of eight in 1991, she eventually acquired language skills and was featured in a 2004 Discovery Channel documentary on feral children.

6. In 2000, ten-year-old Alex Rivas was found among a pack of 15 wild dogs on the outskirts of Talcahuano, Chile. Social workers believe he had been living with the pack for about two years and may have even suckled milk from one of the female dogs. At the childcare center, he could communicate in basic Spanish. He also liked to draw pictures of his favorite subject—dogs.

7. Not all feral children live among canines. Several have been discovered in the company of nonhuman primates. A seven-year-old girl known only by the name Baby Hospital was discovered living among wild chimpanzees in Sierra Leone in 1984. She reportedly never learned how to speak, though she did cry—a trait unusual in feral children.

8. Saturday Mifune of Kwazulu-Natal, South Africa, lived with a tribe of wild chimpanzees for at least a year. Found in 1987 at the age of five, he was placed in an orphanage. Even after living among humans for a decade, he still behaved in a chimplike fashion, leaping from furniture and clapping his hands to his head when disturbed. He died in 2005 of unreported causes.

9. Two-year-old Bello of Nigeria lived with chimpanzees for a year after his parents abandoned him. In 1996, villagers discovered him and placed him in an orphanage. Reports indicate that he never learned how to speak.

10. John Ssabunnya lived with African Green Monkeys after his parents died in the Ugandan civil war. He was found in 1991, at the age of six, and placed in an orphanage. At 14, he joined the Pearl of Africa Children's Choir, a group dedicated to raising funds for Africa's orphans.

Elephant Graveyard

Do dying elephants actually separate themselves from their herd to meet their maker among the bones of their predecessors?

✳ ✳ ✳ ✳

JUST AS SEARCHING for the Holy Grail was a popular pastime for crusading medieval knights, 19th-century adventurers felt the call to seek out a mythical elephant graveyard. According to legend, when elephants sense their impending deaths, they leave their herds and travel to a barren, bone-filled wasteland. Although explorers have spent centuries searching for proof of these elephant ossuaries, not one has ever been found, and the elephant graveyard has been relegated to the realm of metaphor and legend.

Elephants Never Forget

Unlike most mammals, elephants have a special relationship with their dead. Researchers from the United Kingdom and Kenya have revealed that elephants show marked emotion— from actual crying to profound agitation—when they encounter the remains of other elephants, particularly the skulls and tusks. They treat the bones with unusual tenderness and will cradle and carry them for long periods of time and over great distances. When they come across the bones of other animals, they show no interest whatsoever. Not only can elephants distinguish the bones of other elephants from those of rhinoceroses or buffalo, but they appear to recognize the bones of elephants they were once familiar with. An elephant graveyard, though a good way to ensure that elephants wouldn't be upset by walking among their dead on a daily basis, does not fit with the elephants' seeming sentiment toward their ancestors.

Honor Your Elders

The biggest argument against an elephant burial ground can be found in elephants' treatment of their elders. An elephant would not want to separate itself from the protection of its herd during illness or infirmity, nor would a herd allow such behavior. Elephants accord great respect to older members of a herd, turning to them as guiding leaders. They usually refuse to leave sick or dying older elephants alone, even if it means risking their own health and safety.

But What About the Bones?

Although there is no foundation for the idea that the elephant graveyard is a preordained site that animals voluntarily enter, the legend likely began as a way to explain the occasional discovery of large groupings of elephant carcasses. These have been found near water sources, where older and sickly elephants live and die in close proximity. Elephants are also quite susceptible to fatal malnutrition, which progresses quickly from extreme lethargy to death. When an entire herd is wiped out by drought or disease, the remaining bones are often found en masse at the herd's final watering hole.

There are other explanations for large collections of elephant bones. Pits of quicksand or bogs can trap a number of elephants; flash floods often wash all debris (not just elephant bones) from the valley floor into a common area; and poachers have been known to slay entire herds of elephants for their ivory, leaving the carcasses behind.

In parts of East Africa, however, groups of elephant corpses are thought to be the work of the *mazuku*, the Swahili word for "evil wind." Scientists have found volcanic vents in the earth's crust that emit carbon monoxide and other toxic gases. The noxious air released from these vents is forceful enough to blow out a candle's flame, and the remains of small mammals and birds are frequently found nearby. Although these vents have not proved to be powerful enough to kill groups of elephants, tales of the *mazuku* persist.

The Term Trudges On

Although no longer considered a destination for elephants, the elephant graveyard exists as a geologic term and as a figure of speech that refers to a repository of useless or outdated items. Given how prominent the legend remains in popular culture, it will be a long time before the elephant graveyard joins other such myths in a burial ground of its own.

"Ford to City: 'Drop Dead'"

Two words may have killed a U.S. president's reelection chances— but did he really say them?

✳   ✳   ✳   ✳

WHEN A REQUEST for help is met with a nasty refusal, it's hard to take, especially if it's from a good friend or a close relative. However, when that dose of tough love is doled out by the president of the United States, it can be an even more bitter pill to swallow.

In 1975, New York City was broke. Following years of fiscal mismanagement, a downturn in the national economy pushed the Big Apple to the brink of disaster. While its lawyers filed a bankruptcy petition in the State Supreme Court, Mayor Abraham Beame was forced to beg the White House for a bailout. On October 29, in a speech before the National Press Club, President Gerald R. Ford likened the city's profligate spending to "an insidious disease" and asserted that he was "prepared to veto any bill that has as its purpose a federal bailout of New York City to prevent a default."

Hooked on Heroin?

Meanwhile, Ford's press secretary, Ron Nessen, compared the city to "a wayward daughter hooked on heroin. You don't give her $100 a day to support her habit." None of this sat well with Mayor Beame, who accused the President of "writing off New York City in one speech." The next day, a banner headline on the front page of New York's Daily News announced: "FORD TO CITY: 'DROP DEAD.'"

Those two words, although never uttered by the President, did capture the essence of his remarks—at least, as perceived by many New Yorkers. Yet, even the President did an about-face just two months later, signing legislation for federal loans. But the damage had been done, and Ford later acknowledged that the *Daily News* interpretation of his thoughts probably cost him the 1976 election, when Jimmy Carter narrowly carried New York State. Galvanized by the President's speech, a defiant New York City never did drop dead.

Babe Ruth's Called Shot: Did He or Didn't He?

Whether Ruth called a home run in the 1932 World Series remains one of baseball's greatest mysteries.

* * * *

This much is known. The Yankees had already won the first two games of the '32 fall classic when they met the Cubs at Wrigley Field for Game 3. Although Chicago players were understandably frustrated, there was bad blood between the teams that extended beyond the norm. In August, the Cubs had picked up former Yankee shortstop Mark Koenig from the Pacific Coast League to replace injured starter Billy Jurges, and Koenig hit .353 the rest of the season. Despite these heroics, his new teammates had only voted him a half-share of their World Series bonus money—a slight that enraged his old colleagues. The Yanks engaged in furious bench-jockeying with their "cheapskate" opponents the entire series, and Chicago players and fans shouted back, jeering that Ruth was old, fat, and washed-up.

Up to bat. When Ruth stepped up to bat in the fifth inning of Game 3, the taunts started as usual. A few people threw lemons at Babe from the stands, and he gestured toward the crowd before settling in at the plate. Charlie Root's first pitch was a called strike, and Ruth, looking over at the Chicago dugout, appeared to hold up one finger—as if to say, "That's only one." He did the same thing with two fingers after taking the second pitch, another strike. Then, some eyewitnesses recalled, he pointed toward dead center field. Others didn't remember this act, but there was no mistaking what happened next: Ruth slammed Root's third offering deep into the edge of the right-field bleachers. Onlookers recalled him laughing as he rounded the bases. And, as shown in a much-published photo, he and on-deck batter Lou Gehrig laughed and shook hands back at home plate.

What really happened? Here is where the facts end and speculation begins. Those among the 49,986 fans on hand who noticed Ruth's display likely assumed it was just another round in the ongoing feud between the two clubs, and most sportswriters made nothing out of it in their accounts of New York's 7 –5 victory. The homer was not a game-winner; it was just one (in fact, the last) of 15 home runs Ruth hit in World Series play during his career. He had already taken Root deep earlier in the same contest, and Gehrig also had two in the game. The Yanks finished their four-game sweep the next day.

This being Babe Ruth, however, it only took a few speculative accounts from among the many reporters present to get the ball rolling. "Ruth Calls Shot" read the headline in the next day's New York World Telegram, and soon sports fans everywhere were wondering. Gehrig claimed he heard Ruth yell to Root, "I'm going to knock the next one down your goddamned throat" before the fateful pitch, while Cubs catcher Gabby Hartnett recalled the remark as "It only takes one to hit." Root and Cubs second baseman Billy Herman denied any gesture to the outfield, and grainy film footage that surfaced in 1999 was unclear either way. Ever the diplomat, Ruth granted interviews in which he substantiated the claim, and others in which he denied it.

So did he or didn't he? We may never know for sure, but perhaps it's better that way. When the subject is Babe Ruth, facts are only half the fun.

The First Spark of War

In 1775, the original Thirteen Colonies in America were growing restless and increasingly frustrated by their strained relationship with their British rulers. When the tension finally snapped, someone fired a shot that marked the beginning of war. The question is, who fired first?

❈ ❈ ❈ ❈

An "Intolerable" Situation

IN 1768, THE British Army's infantry, nicknamed "redcoats" by the American colonists, arrived in Boston to maintain order. By 1774, they were joined by the British navy and marines to ensure compliance of what the colonists called the "Intolerable Acts." These were punitive laws put in place by the British Parliament after the infamous Boston Tea Party protest. The Intolerable Acts punished Massachusetts colonists by taking away their right to self-govern. The British Parliament hoped that by making an example of Massachusetts, the other colonies would be deterred from any rebellion.

But by February of 1775, it was clear that the implementation of the Intolerable Acts had backfired on Great Britain, and King George III was warned that rebellion was growing, not only in Massachusetts but in other colonies. There were already around 3,000 British forces stationed in Boston, led by General Thomas Gage, and in April of 1775, Gage was given the go-ahead to begin disarming and imprisoning rebel leaders.

Mustering the Troops

Throughout the day on April 18, Gage attempted to organize

a secret raid on Concord, giving orders to Lieutenant Colonel Francis Smith to hurry to the town and destroy any military stores he found there. But Gage's wife, Margaret, who had been born in New Jersey and sympathized with the colonists, tipped them off, resulting in Paul Revere's "midnight ride" to Concord to warn the town that British troops were on the way. Concord, in turn, warned nearby towns, and that very night militias in the area began to muster.

Meanwhile, Gage received official orders from the British Parliament to "take action" against the colonists. He organized about 700 British troops, under the command of Smith.

In 1775, the original Thirteen Colonies in America were growing restless and increasingly frustrated by their strained relationship with their British rulers. When the tension finally snapped, someone fired a shot that marked the beginning of war. The question is, who fired first?

An "Intolerable" Situation

In 1768, the British Army's infantry, nicknamed "redcoats" by the American colonists, arrived in Boston to maintain order. By 1774, they were joined by the British navy and marines to ensure compliance of what the colonists called the "Intolerable Acts." These were punitive laws put in place by the British Parliament after the infamous Boston Tea Party protest. The Intolerable Acts punished Massachusetts colonists by taking away their right to self-govern. The British Parliament hoped that by making an example of Massachusetts, the other colonies would be deterred from any rebellion.

But by February of 1775, it was clear that the implementation of the Intolerable Acts had backfired on Great Britain, and King George III was warned that rebellion was growing, not only in Massachusetts but in other colonies. There were already around 3,000 British forces stationed in Boston, led by General Thomas Gage, and in April of 1775, Gage was given the go-ahead to begin disarming and imprisoning rebel leaders.

Mustering the Troops

Throughout the day on April 18, Gage attempted to organize a secret raid on Concord, giving orders to Lieutenant Colonel Francis Smith to hurry to the town and destroy any military stores he found there. But Gage's wife, Margaret, who had been born in New Jersey and sympathized with the colonists, tipped them off, resulting in Paul Revere's "midnight ride" to Concord to warn the town that British troops were on the way. Concord, in turn, warned nearby towns, and that very night militias in the area began to muster.

Meanwhile, Gage received official orders from the British Parliament to "take action" against the colonists. He organized about 700 British troops, under the command of Smith and Major John Pitcairn, and at 2 A.M. on the morning of April 19, 1775, they set out on foot for the 17-mile journey from Boston to Concord.

Around 4:15 A.M., the British troops marched into Lexington, about two-thirds of the way to Concord. About 80 militiamen, led by Captain John Parker, stood in the village common, with dozens of spectators watching from the side of the road. According to one of the militiamen, as the British approached, Parker said, "Stand your ground; don't fire unless fired upon, but if they mean to have a war, let it begin here."

The First Shot of Many

The British weren't expecting armed men to meet them in Lexington. Instead of bypassing the village common and continuing on to Concord, the British took the scene as a challenge. Taunts began to pass back and forth between the groups as Parker, Smith, and Pitcairn attempted to diffuse the situation. Pitcairn waved his sword and ordered the militiamen to disperse; suddenly, a shot rang out. Another shot was fired in response, and the two sides began trading fire. By the time officers regained control of their troops, eight colonists were dead and nine were wounded. Only one British troop was injured.

The details of who fired that first shot at Lexington have remained unclear for centuries. One member of Parker's militiamen swore that none of the colonists had fired their muskets, and one witness said a British officer on horseback fired first. But many of the British troops claimed that one of the onlookers, a man either hiding behind a hedge or in a nearby tavern, fired the shot. Another theory states that the shot wasn't fired at either side, but rather at a prisoner who was marching with the British troops and attempted to escape.

We may never know for certain who fired the first shot, but by the end of that day, 15,000 militiamen had gathered in Boston, with more arriving from New Hampshire, Rhode Island, and Connecticut over the next few days. The Revolutionary War had begun.

The End of an Era

It was called the "Bronze Age" for a reason: This historical period, which began around 3300 B.C., was characterized by its widespread use of bronze, a metal that was much stronger and more durable than other metals available at the time. But as the Bronze Age segued into the Iron Age, a strange shift occurred, leaving an inexplicable wake of collapse and destruction behind.

❊ ❊ ❊ ❊

Human Innovation

THE OLDEST BRONZE artifacts discovered date back to 4500 B.C. and were found at an archaeological site in Serbia. Before this point in time, artifacts were most commonly made of materials like stone and wood, and for good reason: Creating bronze requires a certain amount of knowledge and skill, unfamiliar to earlier humans. The metal consists of mostly copper, with between 5 and 15 percent of another metal—usually tin—mixed in. The tin must be mined and melted down separately, then added to the melted copper.

Over the millennium between 4500 and 3500 B.C., this technique became more common throughout the Mediterranean. By 3300 B.C., the region had also made advancements in culture, art, architecture, politics, warfare, and trade, and began to develop writing systems. Now-famous structures like the Pyramids of Giza and the Temple of Karnak were soon constructed, and civilizations including Anatolia, Cyprus, Syria, and Greece flourished. The Bronze Age had begun.

But sometime between the 13th and 12th centuries B.C., this age of prosperity and advancement suddenly—and, many believe, violently—fell apart. Within 50 years, cities were destroyed or abandoned, trade routes collapsed, and the newly acquired literacy in the area was severely diminished. What could cause such an abrupt turnaround in what had seemed an era of innovation and progress?

Evidence of Catastrophe

Throughout the Mediterranean, there is evidence that something catastrophic occurred at the end of the Bronze Age. In Anatolia, archaeologists have found a destruction layer, or a layer within the rock or soil that shows evidence of disaster, in every major site uncovered. The Hittite capital of Hattusa was burned, abandoned, and never reoccupied. The city of Karaoglan, near what is today Ankara, was not only burned, but its dead were left behind, unburied. And the famed city of Troy was destroyed not once but twice, before finally being abandoned altogether.

Cities on the isle of Cyprus were sacked, burned and abandoned, or were simply abandoned for unknown reasons. Archaeologists found valuable items in many of these sites, some of them apparently hidden before residents left, suggesting they expected to return one day. But no one ever returned to claim the valuables, leading to more questions: Why did the residents never come back? Were the citizens of these cities killed or enslaved?

Syria appeared to be a battleground for conflicts between many of the cultures in the region, including the so-called "Sea Peoples," an unidentified seafaring army that attacked many areas in the Mediterranean during the Late Bronze Age collapse. And in Greece, palaces were sacked and destroyed, with 90 percent of the settlements on the Peloponnese peninsula abandoned.

A Perfect Storm?

When archaeologists first began to attempt to explain the sudden collapse of all these civilizations, they assumed the causes occurred in a linear sequence. Earthquakes, climate change, and famine could have led to social and political instability, which in turn led to mass migrations. The huge relocating populations then uprooted other settled areas, and eventually the disruptions caused a collapse within the entire region.

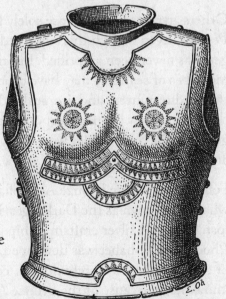

But not all researchers buy into this theory. After all, these civilizations had survived calamities, like earthquakes and invasions, before, so why would this time be different? Some scientists believe the more likely scenario is that the region was not dealt these blows in a linear sequence, but rather all at once. A city may be able to survive an earthquake and then later fight off foreign invaders, but what if they must handle an earthquake, a famine, and an invasion in a short amount of time?

This theory is supported by Eric H. Cline, a professor of archaeology and ancient history at George Washington University in Washington, D.C., who calls is a "perfect storm of calamities." If all of these disasters were to hit a particular area at once, they could cause a "domino effect," leading to the fall of other civilizations over time.

Drought, Invaders, and Rebirth

But the "perfect storm" hypothesis isn't the only theory suggested by experts. Some make the case for a widespread drought that forced relocation. There is evidence that tree growth in the Mediterranean had slowed at the end of the Bronze Age, and sea levels in the Dead Sea region were 50 meters below normal. A long-term drought certainly could've caused crop failures and instability in the region, leading to migrations and invasions.

Others attribute the collapse solely to the mysterious "Sea Peoples," even though this supposed group of naval warmongers has never been identified. But there is evidence that roaming tribes of seafarers may have brought destruction to parts of the Mediterranean, and, ironically, that they were bolstered by their use of new bronze weapons. But evidence seems to suggest that the Sea Peoples were a migratory group of sailors who arrived at foreign shores with wives and children in tow.

Following the Late Bronze Age collapse, the region fell into what was known as the Dark Ages; however, all was not lost. Gold and silver craftsmanship joined bronze work, the Phoenician alphabet was developed, and eventually the peoples of the Mediterranean rebuilt their civilization. We may never know the true cause of the Bronze Age collapse, but out of the ashes of so much destruction came a renewed push toward advancement and the inspiration of unfailing human spirit.

A Mystery Is Afoot

Beaches can be great for collectors. Shells, rocks, and sea glass line the shore, and more treasures can be found buried beneath the sand. But some beaches in the Pacific Northwest are accumulating a collection that is much too macabre for the casual hobbyist.

✳ ✳ ✳ ✳

Disturbing Discoveries

ON AUGUST 20, 2007, a girl and her family from Washington State were visiting Jedediah Island Marine Provincial Park, a 600-acre island in British Columbia, Canada. Among the sea lions, rocks, and driftwood, the girl found something unusual—a size 12, white and blue, Adidas running shoe with a sock inside. But when the girl opened the sock, she made a horrifying discovery. A severed human foot was still inside the shoe.

The finding was unsettling enough; but since that day in 2007, human feet have continued to wash up on beaches in the Pacific Northwest, from British Columbia in the north, to Seattle and Tacoma in the south. One severed foot on a beach, while gruesome, could be written off as an anomaly; two or three would be very strange; but as of 2020, no fewer than 21 human feet have shown up in this area. The feet have belonged to both men and women, and have been from people of various ages and sizes, but they almost always show up encased in running shoes. To make matters more bizarre, no other body parts have ever washed ashore. To paraphrase a common saying: the mystery is afoot!

Serial Killer or Suicides?

What is the source of these morbid disembodied feet? Throughout the years, many theories have been proposed. Could they be from victims of the 2004 Indian Ocean tsunami which killed more than 227,000 people? Tens of thousands of people remain missing after the disaster, so it may not be unusual for body parts to randomly show up, even thousands of miles away and decades later.

Others have worried that the feet may be the work of a serial killer or some kind of organized crime ring operating right in their own backyards. In the mid-2000s, dozens of men went missing from the Vancouver, British Columbia, area and were never found, a fact that seems to bolster this hypothesis. Perhaps a killer (or killers) is lurking in the misty fog of the Pacific Northwest. But another theory proposes that the feet may be from victims of a plane crash or a similar tragedy, and foul play has nothing to do with them.

There have been breaks in the case of the disembodied feet over the years that have put at least some of the speculation to rest. The Jedediah Island foot, the first to be discovered, was eventually identified through DNA analysis as belonging to a man who went missing in 2004. Likewise, DNA testing has linked several of the other feet to missing persons, some of whom suffered from depression and are assumed to have taken their own lives. In fact, two of the feet—one of the rare pairs of feet that came from the same person—were identified as belonging to a woman who died by suicide by jumping from the Pattullo Bridge in Surrey, British Columbia. This discovery led to a new theory: Perhaps all of the feet could belong to people who have jumped from the bridge. It would explain why so many of the appendages have washed ashore in similar locations.

Some Answers, Lingering Questions

But experts say that the bizarre instances of severed feet may not be as strange as it seems. For one thing, the feet have not actually been severed—none of the feet show evidence of cutting or slicing. Rather, as disturbing as it sounds, a decomposing body in the water tends to come apart at the joints. This would result in the hands and feet separating. But why have no hands washed ashore? According to scientists, the shoes

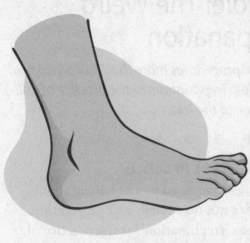

are the key. Although there have been at least two cases where a foot was found in a hiking boot, the vast majority of feet have been found in running shoes, such as the kind made by Nike or New Balance. The shoes protect the feet from underwater scavengers, and the rubber soles are surprisingly buoyant. If an air pocket gets trapped within the shoe, the entire shoe—foot and all—floats to the surface.

While this may explain the mechanics of what is occurring, it still doesn't answer the most basic questions: Why are so many feet washing ashore in such a localized area? And even if the shoes make it easier for the feet to float in the water, why, in almost fifteen years, has no one ever found another body part? Richard Thompson, an oceanographer with the Institute of Ocean Sciences, believes the answer to the first question has to do with ocean currents. The Pacific Northwest consists of a "semi-enclosed basin," where water is constantly recirculated in the same region. Because of the water flow, things that are floating in the water don't go very far; they are simply tossed around in the same general location, until they wind up on shore.

But even experts don't have an answer for the second question. Finding such a high quantity of disembodied feet, without ever locating another body part, is highly unusual. And since we have no other evidence, we can only speculate on what happened to these people. While it's possible that they all died by suicide, or died of other natural causes, it's just as possible that something sinister is occurring, and the people of the Pacific Northwest should watch their backs. And, obviously, their feet.

Head Like a Hole: The Weird History of Trepanation

There aren't many medical procedures more than 7,000 years old that are still practiced today. Trepanation, or the practice of drilling a hole in the skull, is one of the few.

✳   ✳   ✳   ✳

An Ancient Practice

HAS ANYONE EVER angrily accused you of having a hole in your head? Well, it's not necessarily an exaggeration. *Trepanation* (also known as "trephination") is the practice of boring into the skull and removing a piece of bone, thereby leaving a hole. It is derived from the Greek word *trypanon*, meaning "to bore." This practice was performed by the ancient Greeks, Romans, and Egyptians, among others.

Hippocrates, considered the father of medicine, indicated that the Greeks might have used trepanation to treat head injuries. However, evidence of trepanning without accompanying head trauma has been found in less advanced civilizations; speculation abounds as to its exact purpose. Since the head was considered a barometer for a person's behavior, one theory is that trepanation was used as a way to treat headaches, depression, and other conditions that had no outward trauma signs. Think of it like a pressure release valve: The hole gave evil spirits inside the skull a way out of the body. When the spirits were gone, it was hoped, the symptoms would disappear.

How to Trepan

In trepanning, the Greeks used an instrument called a *terebra*, an extremely sharp piece of wood with another piece of wood mounted crossways on it as a handle and attached by a thong. The handle was twisted until the thong was extremely tight. When released, the thong unwound, which spun the sharp piece of wood around and drove it into the skull like a drill.

Although it's possible that the terebra was used for a single hole, it is more likely that it was used to make a circular pattern of multiple small holes, thereby making it easier to remove a large piece of bone. Since formal anesthesia had not yet been invented, it is unknown whether any kind of numbing agent was used before trepanation was performed.

The Incas were also adept at trepanation. The procedure was performed using a ceremonial tumi knife made of flint or copper. The surgeon held the patient's head between his knees and rubbed the tumi blade back and forth along the surface of the skull to create four incisions in a crisscross pattern. When the incisions were sufficiently deep, the square-shaped piece of bone in the center was pulled out. Come to think of it, perhaps the procedure hurt more than the symptom.

Trepanation Today

Just when you thought it was safe to assume that the medical field has come so far, hold on—doctors still use this procedure, only now it's called a craniotomy. The underlying methodology is similar: It still involves removing a piece of skull to get to the underlying tissue. The bone is replaced when the procedure is done. If it is not replaced, the operation is called a *craniectomy*. That procedure is used in many different circumstances, such as for treating a tumor or infection.

However, good ol'-fashion trepanation still has its supporters. One in particular is Bart Hughes, who believes that trepanning can elevate one to a higher state of consciousness. According to Hughes, once man started to walk upright, the brain lost blood because the heart had to frantically pump it throughout the body in a struggle against gravity. Thus, the brain had to shut down certain areas that were not critically needed to assure proper blood flow to vital regions.

Increased blood flow to the brain can elevate a person's consciousness, Hughes reasoned, and he advocated ventilating the skull as a means of making it easier for the heart to send blood to the brain. (Standing on one's head also accomplishes this, but that's just a temporary measure.) Some of his followers have actually performed trepanation on themselves. For better or gross, a few have even filmed the process. In 2001, two men from Utah pled guilty to practicing medicine without a license after they had bored holes into a woman's skull to treat her chronic fatigue and depression. There's no word as to whether the procedure actually worked, or if she's just wearing a lot of hats nowadays.

Everywhere a Yawn

"Contagious yawning," as it is commonly known, is one of the strangest quirks of the human body.

✳ ✳ ✳ ✳

Why Do People Yawn, Anyway?

YOU MAY THINK we yawn because we're tired or bored, or because oxygen levels in our lungs are low (that's the traditional medical explanation, after all). But did you know that babies yawn in utero? (They pick up the habit as early as eleven weeks after conception.) Fetuses don't take in oxygen through their lungs, and there's no way they are tired or bored—they sleep all day, and they certainly haven't viewed enough television to have problems with attention span.

And Why Do You Yawn When You See Me Yawn?

Scientists don't fully understand why we yawn. Does involuntarily opening one's mouth wide serve any useful or healthful purpose? It's something of a mystery. We do know, however, that 55 percent of people will yawn within five minutes of seeing someone else do it. It's a phenomenon called "contagious yawning." Sometimes just hearing, thinking, or reading about a yawn is enough to make you unconsciously follow suit. (Did it work?) Again, scientists don't know exactly why, though they have paid it enough mind to conjure a few theories.

Some researchers hypothesize that contagious yawning is more common among the empathetic crowd. In other words, those of us who demonstrate a greater ability to understand and share other people's feelings are more likely to emulate their yawns. Makes sense.

Humans aren't the only creatures that yawn. Foxes, sea lions, hippos, dogs, and cats are among the animals that do it. Recent studies have even demonstrated that some animals, like dogs and chimpanzees, may suffer from contagious yawning.

The High Line, Naturally

An abandoned elevated railroad track that once delivered cattle to the city's meatpacking district is now one of the most extraordinary public parks in America.

✳ ✳ ✳ ✳

Why Do People Yawn, Anyway?

W HERE ELSE BUT New York will you find native grasses, wildflowers, butterflies, trees, and a fountain 30 feet in the air? Not on top of a building, you understand, but on top of a former railroad bed.

This is the High Line, a one-of-a-kind public park that opened in June 2009 and was immediately embraced by New Yorkers. Its popularity continues to grow, as visitors stroll its lushly landscaped concrete paths and lounge on its benches, all the while relishing some of the city's most striking green space and best views. *New York Times* architecture critic Nicolai Ouroussoff called the High Line "one of the most thoughtful, sensitively designed public spaces built in New York in years."

The first phase of the three-phase park runs along the former CSX train tracks, from Gansevoort Street on the city's far west side up to 20th Street. A second section, which will extend the park to 30th Street, is scheduled to open in the autumn of

2010. A final section, which would take the park farther north to 34th Street, is under discussion

Recycling the Railroad

The High Line has been on the public agenda since 1999, when two friends who lived in the area, writer Joshua David and painter Robert Hammond, began lobbying for fresh use of tracks that hadn't seen activity since 1980. Although some neighborhood property owners hoped to see the old rail line razed, David and Hammond and their group, Friends of the High Line, prevailed after countless public meetings and careful coordination among city, state, and federal officials, as well as widespread grassroots support from the public.

More than 720 interdisciplinary teams from around the world submitted plans to "recycle" the High Line. The winning idea came from Diller, Scofidio & Renfro and James Corner Field Operations. The firms' mantra: "Keep it Simple, Keep it Wild, Keep it Slow, and Keep it Quiet."

The unusual plantings—more than 100 native plants perk up the first half-mile section alone—were carefully chosen to reflect the park's beginnings. Railroad tracks peek out from flowerbeds and grasses. Gardens are deliberately a little wild and even scraggly, a nod to the isolated, deserted feel of the tracks after years of abandonment. The trees, flowers, and shrubs have a natural, unforced feel. Green spaces and flower plantings are punctuated by steel rails, massive metal support beams, and views of the Hudson River.

This being New York, unexpected fun popped up soon after the High Line's opening, when an enterprising young woman whose apartment faces directly onto the park realized that the fire escape where she had been hanging her laundry to dry also offered an excellent performance venue. The Renegade Cabaret was born, to the delight of appreciative crowds that gather along the High Line.